CHICAGO PUBLIC LIBRARY
D1232010

MAN AND HIS GOVERNMEN

An Empirical Theory of Politics

→ refer to his group article

key concepts – in notes at end?

1 – power (defined as resources)

2 – ideology (see chpt 4–5) social or political idea system

relating to source of [illegible] + to more or less coherent group

e.g. interest group → yield a challenge social order or [illegible] of [illegible] —

e.g. definition of power, or power components (resources) May still

be a code, not a propositional statement, but symbol or metaphorical statement.

MAN AND HIS GOVERNMENT

An Empirical Theory of Politics

CARL JOACHIM FRIEDRICH

McGRAW-HILL BOOK COMPANY, INC.

New York
San Francisco
Toronto
London

3456789 BP 9876

MAN AND HIS GOVERNMENT

Library of Congress Catalog Card Number 63-15892

To all my students

And gladly wolde he lerne, and gladly teche.
CHAUCER

preface

When to the sessions of sweet silent thought
I summon up remembrance of things past . . .

I BELIEVE THAT I ought to offer an apology for the temerity of this book. To review and summarize the political experience of mankind in order to see whether it does not yield some fairly general conclusions about what contributes to political order and the good life and what detracts from these universal goals is as much needed a task as it is a foolhardy one to undertake. Yet, somehow I felt that it ought to be attempted once more and by one who had spent a lifetime with the materials of politics, not only in theory, but in practice, not only in one country, but in many, not only pragmatically, but philosophically. The materials are multiplying, the efforts at building and at rebuilding political orders are world-wide, the dissatisfaction with the results achieved is fairly widespread. Yet I would be the first to admit, even to insist, that this work is neither the first nor the last which seeks to deal with the political experience of mankind in general terms. From the *Politics* of Aristotle to the works of contemporaries, the questions dealt with in the following pages have occupied the best minds, because after all is said and done the fate of man hinges upon his ability to weave the relations with his fellows into an enduring fabric of ordered community in which rulers and ruled are united in the pursuit of common goals.

My debts are so many that it would be unfair to single out particular persons for acknowledgment as one can do at the end of a more circumscribed research. As much as possible I have tried to indicate such indebtedness by inclusion of at least one significant work of such friends and coworkers in the bibliography. But there are those who do not write scholarly studies from whom I have nonetheless learned more than I can say, the practitioners of the art of government whom it has been my privilege to know and work with over the years. There are also the many generations of students who have contributed in discussion and argument to the clarification of issues and who have helped to eliminate errors of all kinds. To them I have decided to dedicate this book, because it is truly theirs as much as mine. Quite a few have achieved position and honor over the years, and probably are better than any book one could ever write.

Some parts of chapters have appeared in the form of articles and chapters, but since in each case such publication was made conditional upon the prior claim of this publication, it would seem vain display to recite these various items; they are readily found in the bibliography. It has seemed best to separate my own writings from the rest of this list of books used and cited. There is involved here an appearance of author's vanity which must be weighed against the honest recognition of one's earlier work. Since many of the questions dealt with in this book have received more elaborate treatment in other of my writings, the empirical slant of my outlook requires reference to these bits and pieces for documentation purposes. They are listed according to date, and reference is made to them in the notes by such dates. The same method is employed with all other footnote material; name and date readily enable the reader to look up the full reference in the bibliography. The inconvenience occasioned by such checking is overbalanced by the reduction in footnote material.

It remains to thank those who have materially assisted me in the course of the years that this book was in the making. Friends who read all or parts of the manuscript and who gave searching and helpful criticisms included Karl Deutsch, Paul Kekskemeti, James H. Meisel, Talcott Parsons, Richard Rosecrance, Judith N. Sklar and others who may prefer to remain unnamed. The Twentieth Century Fund, upon the recommendation of its distinguished director, August Heckscher, made a major grant. Harvard University, besides providing a sabbatical leave, awarded me the Ford Research Professorship for two terms which the Ford Foundation initiated. I also owe a debt of gratitude to a number of publications and gatherings of scholars wherein I was first given the opportunity to present some of the problems, ideas and materials; wherever possible, acknowledgment has been made in the notes and in the bibliography to which they refer. In these notes and bibliography the persons who more directly assisted me have a large share and deserve a great deal of credit. Miss Roberta Hill, ably assisted by Mrs. Irmgard Zeitler and

Miss Anegrete Martens, put all her editorial talent, acquired in the editing of *Public Policy* and *Nomos,* to full and much appreciated use. Research and editorial assistance of greatest value was also rendered by Marion Kilson, Charles D. Ward, and John Power at Harvard, as well as by Johannes Borger and Klausfrieder Bastian at Heidelberg. Their friendly candor provided not only much needed aid in battling with footnotes and inconsistencies, but also cherished encouragement when the spirit flagged. The truest friend in travail throughout remained my dear Lenore, lover of good style, who suffered many an agony as she struggled with successive drafts; I cannot hope to satisfy her standards. Still I would say:

But if the while I think on thee, dear friend,
All losses are restored and sorrows end.

CARL JOACHIM FRIEDRICH

contents

Part II The Dimensions of Power and Justice

Part III The Dimensions of Equality and Freedom

Part IV The Governing Processes and Their Modes of Operation

Part V Ranges and Levels of Government

The Theory of Politics as Human Experience

In knowledge that man only is to be condemned and despised who is not in a state of transition.
Lord Acton, in his INAUGURAL

A man should never be ashamed to own he has been wrong, which is but saying, in other words, that he is wiser than he was yesterday.
Alexander Pope

THEORY, AS DISTINGUISHED from philosophy and opinion, is the more or less systematized body of demonstrable or at least coherently arguable generalizations based upon rigorous analysis of ascertainable facts. As such it is the hard core of most sciences or fields of learning, though some of these fields like history seem to avoid such generalizing or indulge in it only on the fringe of their scholarly endeavors. Politics by contrast has at least since the Greeks, progenitors of Western science, been subjected to such analysis, and the givens of political experience have been drawn upon to support political theory. Although often denounced, because of the controversies surrounding its tenets and because of the abuse to which it is exposed by the practitioners of the art of politics, political theory continues to exert its fascination upon man. And necessarily so; for politics engulfs all human beings and its fateful inescapability has been dramatically reenacted in the twentieth century.

What is theory? Or rather: what kinds of theory are there? Considerable difficulty has been caused by the belief that all generalizations are more or less alike, and that therefore only one kind of theory is possible. Even a cursory review of the corpus of learning shows this view to be mistaken. Theories may be of three rather distinct kinds, namely, morphological, genetic and operational. The great controversy about Copernicus' view was a morphological controversy, that is to say, a debate as to the pattern or configuration of the astral world of which the earth is a part. The Darwinian controversy was concerned with a genetic theory, namely, the origin of species which it asserted to be generated by the struggle for survival which the fittest won. The Newtonian law of gravitation constitutes an operational theory, claiming that bodies fall in a certain way, and constructing an explanation for it.

Political theory contains theoretical generalizations of all three kinds. The age-old controversy over forms of government, as well as more recent discussions of "patterns" and "types," is an instance of morphological theorizing. Theories about the origin of the state, or of parties or of organizations in general, are clearly genetic. Theories about the working of various political entities, such as Michels' alleged "iron law of oligarchy," constitute operational theories. Beside these varieties of theories, all of which contain propositions, i.e., explicit statements about political phenomena, an important part of theoretical work addresses itself to "defining" these phenomena. Such defining often deteriorates into arguments over words, especially in politics, where words have emotional connotations of which the theorist cannot deprive them. Adequate theorizing requires defining, because without clear definitions it is impossible to advance coherently arguable, let alone demonstrable, propositions. But scientific defining must start from the phenomena, rather than from the words. Therefore, it is important to avoid asking what "authority" or something else of this order "really is" or "really means" (asking, in other words, for the essence of it), and to ask instead what the general features, traits or characteristics of a set of phenomena are, describe them in general terms and then attach to them the verbal symbol most nearly suitable among the available words. Sometimes, the coining of a new word is necessary, but generally speaking this is undesirable, and the rule should be to use available words. It is admittedly tempting to substitute for the words in common usage an entirely novel system of signs, and thus instead of speaking of power, authority, and the like, to discourse upon factor *p*, factor *a*, and so forth, as defined. Such attempts, though stimulating as an exercise, are foredoomed to failure, because political theory has itself a function in the political order which it can fulfill only if it succeeds in communicating.

But does one really communicate if he employs words precisely which in common use are employed in a vague and even contradictory way? For example, in the chapters that follow, "authority" is used as meaning or referring to a political phenomenon of very broad scope, but frequently only alluded to in passing or neglected altogether in common speech and political analysis. Can it really be said that in using it in a precise way one is communicating? It seems highly doubtful that one does so to anybody but him who takes the trouble to assimilate by long and arduous study the scientific and theoretical context of the proposed use. But antecedent to such perfect communication is a more limited kind, namely, the challenge which results from propositions made regarding such matters as authority which the ordinary understanding would find both puzzling and perhaps provocative. Such provocation is vital to the theoretical (and scientific) enterprise if the insights which have been gained are to find the attention which they deserve.

It is not a question of discovering or determining what a term "really means," but it is rather a matter of describing a certain phenomenon in as general a form as the available data permit and then searching for that term which in common parlance seems to come closest to serving as a useful sign to denote this phenomenon. Thus, for example, the question is not what "authority" really means, as when we seek to determine it dogmatically by consulting authorities high and low, including dictionaries, but rather whether to employ the term "authority" to describe a recurrent political phenomenon. With Locke, Dewey and many others it might be said that "so the thing be understood, I am indifferent as to the name."[1] But is it really a matter of indifference? Against my former view, I would say: no, it is on the contrary a matter of the highest moment, just how a particular thing or event is named. The reason is that a scientist wants to communicate his findings, and the political scientist perhaps more than any other. He cannot be indifferent to the words he employs simply because they are in common use. Yet he must not allow himself to become enslaved by this common usage; rather must he treat such usage for what it is, namely, a confused, contradictory set of hunches as to political reality. In the light of a more penetrating study of this reality, the political scientist will employ terms as signs explicitly *as*signed to phenomena precisely circumscribed and described. Thus the word *designates* a particular experience.

What is customarily referred to as "definition" of political concepts (as of all other concepts), is therefore really a matter of identifying a phenomenon of primary experience in the political field and then designating or denoting it by the term most suitable in common parlance. That such a procedure of identification and denotation involves a certain amount of arbitrary judgment, is evident. But the range of this arbitrariness should, in my opinion, be held to the absolute minimum required by accuracy and precision. There are, unfortunately, many instances where common parlance employs a particular term for divergent phenomena. One of the most common sources of confusion and error is the result of

[1] Locke, 1688, par. 146; Dewey, 1929, p. 357.

"personification," a linguistic habit by which the term used to denote a quality or mode is also employed for speaking of the person or persons who do or ought to possess this quality or operate in this mode. Thus the word "authority" is employed for designating a particular political institution, such as the TVA, and again the word "justice" for speaking of a judge, such as a justice of the peace. As long as political science is confronted with the legally sanctioned misuse of such terms for official purposes, all it can do is to identify clearly the phenomena it is denoting by the particular terms.

Concept-formation in such an empirical mood raises the question of comparability and/or type (cf. Note 2). If each description of experience were assumed to be unique, no science or theory would be possible.[2] Actually, the dichotomy between solipsistic uniqueness (concreteness) and universalistic abstractness is a false one; every experience contains elements of both. Attention may be directed toward one or the other component, and what is said about it will be greatly influenced by which side is emphasized. In the study of politics, the emphasis on uniqueness and concreteness will generate historical and legal studies, the emphasis on generalization will produce theoretical and "scientific" results.

It is an inevitable consequence of this condition of the political theorist that there will be a multitude of voices. Only the most megalomaniac and self-centered man will believe that he has a chance of coercing his brethren into compliance with *all* his definitions. All he can hope for —and this is already a great deal—is that the genuinely interested will make the effort to understand his definitions and to test his demonstrations in terms of them, rather than in terms of other definitions, which happens lamentably often. The consolation is that political theory is itself a political battlefield and that the lost cause is not necessarily the worst, or lost forever. For the rest, one has to say with Confucius: "I won't teach a man who is not anxious to learn, and will not explain to one who is not trying to make things clear to himself. . . ."[3]

But what about political philosophy? Political philosophy is often seen as essentially the sequence of master expositions of political ideologies, rationalizations as it were of preconceived notions whether of class or other interest. This kind of two-barreled attack is leveled against political philosophy as at once normative and composed of outworn norms; its place is to be taken by non-normative, value-free science. There can be no question that the history of political philosophy is, among other things,

[2] This appears to be the position of Jaffa, a, 1960, p. 271, who after adopting the criterion of complete detachment as the crucial one for "theory" argues that political theory is not possible, in a general and universal sense, because the key questions such men as Aristotle asked, e.g., "What is a *polis?*" were based upon an assumption which "seems to have been a unique experience."

[3] Wisdom, 164 (from *The Analects*, transl. Lin Yutang).

what it is thus alleged to be: highfalutin propaganda; [4] but this undeniable fact does not preclude the possibility that it is also a record of various approximations to the truth, that is to say, of the true and within reason verifiable generalizations concerning established matters of fact. Plato may be wrong about many propositions he sets forth in *The Republic*, the *Statesman* and *The Laws*, but is he wrong in insisting that the question of law and right is one which every political community faces, and that that question inevitably raises the issue of justice which in turn opens up the problems of what is a norm and what is a virtue? [5] Dissatisfaction with the more specific proposals Plato made need not prevent us from recognizing that these propositions are true or that they contain at least partial truths. In arguing the value of such past work on politics by philosophers and others, I would stress the continuous reevaluation that the increase in historical knowledge brings. By this I do not mean in any sense a "great books" approach which treats these labors of the past as something to be handled as a "given" akin to biblical revelation.[6] What I am interested in are the nuggets of insight that can be gathered through the study of government and politics which such earlier works open up, as an antidote to the frog's perspective that a preoccupation with contemporary situations is likely to engender.

But political philosophy, truly speaking, is something else than the history of past political philosophies. It is that branch of philosophy and political science, in my understanding, by which the two are linked; it brings the main knowledge of political science, both facts and generalizations into philosophy, and it brings relevant aspects of philosophy to bear upon this knowledge.

It is immediately evident that a discussion of this relationship is dependent upon understanding among the discussants about philosophy as well as about science. To raise this point is to plunge into the quagmire of highly, indeed hopelessly, controversial issues. For, to start with philosophy, there are so many philosophies, past and present, that any attempt at reaching agreement among even a small group of philosophers is out of the question. But if agreement on the kind of philosophy to adopt seems

[4] This problem is at the heart of a recent and fairly extended controversy over the interpretation of Plato. A group of writers, including Warner Fite, 1934, R. H. S. Crossman, 1937, A. D. Winspear, 1940, and Karl Popper, 1946, vol. I, all attacked Plato's political philosophy as elitist, aristocratic, antidemocratic, authoritarian, even totalitarian. More recently, several writers have come to the rescue of Plato, among them John Wild, 1953, and William C. Greene. I lean toward the first position, though I certainly would reject the proposition that Plato was a totalitarian.

[5] Lasswell, 1951, p. 12, following Dewey and Northrop, speaks of the "problem approach" as the distinctive feature of the policy sciences, including political science. But has any inquiring mind, including the political philosopher, ever denied the guiding importance of "problems"?

[6] Contra, Hacker, a, 1954; but cf. his views in the study of 1961.

unlikely, perhaps there could be a measure of agreement on what philosophy is. Unfortunately philosophers are sharply divided on this issue as well and so are the dictionaries. One says that "philosophy is the study of the truths or principles underlying all knowledge and being (or reality)" and also that it is "the study or science of the principles of a particular branch or subject of knowledge." [7] Another tells us that philosophy is "love of wisdom or knowledge, especially that which deals with ultimate reality, or with the most general causes and principles of things." [8] There are some important divergences here; one speaks of study and science, the other of knowledge and wisdom, but ultimate reality and the principles of such reality are involved in both; philosophy appears to be knowledge of a very general kind.

But what is science? If we turn to the same sources we find that science is "a branch of knowledge or study dealing with a body of facts or truths systematically arranged and showing the operation of general laws," or more generally, "knowledge, as of facts or principles, gained by systematic study," "a branch or body of organized knowledge." I believe that these latter definitions, while general enough, omit two very important aspects of all sciences, namely, (1) the agreement on method, and (2) the training of the human beings engaged in scientific work. It would be more appropriate to define a science as "a body of ordered knowledge, known to and progressively enlarged by the specialists in that field of knowledge through the use of methods which they as a group have come to accept as workable ways for arriving at that particular kind of knowledge." It should be noted, however, that from time to time a new method may be discovered; the process of its adoption resembles that of the acknowledgment of new facts and generalizations. Still, it is this agreement upon the use of particular methods which distinguishes the scientist-scholar from the layman—and the charlatan—and which renders scientific statements capable of being effectively argued with other scholars. The methods, the ways of arriving at the result, allow all members of the fellowship of this particular science to retrace the steps which led to the statement, to reexamine the reported facts and to test the generalizations based upon them. It is this process which gives order and coherence to the progress of science and scholarship, indeed makes it possible. It is the *new* evidence, or the *new* generalization, which occupies the fellowship of scholars in the particular field, receives detailed criticism and either wins out or is discarded. A scholar who challenges a well-established fact or a generally accepted theory (generalization) will accompany his proposition by evidence which fulfills the standards of accuracy and relevancy established in that field of learning. This means, among other things,

[7] *The American College Dictionary*, 1947.

[8] *The Concise Oxford Dictionary of Current English*, 1929.

familiarity with the existing literature and knowledge of possible counter arguments. These propositions hold true for all scientific work. They show that the agreement on methods of work is as symptomatic for a "science" as the "body of facts or truths" or of "principles"—that this agreement on methods is at the very core of what is meant when the definitions speak of a body of "organized" knowledge; it is organized, because it is given logical coherence to a degree as a result of the consistency of the methods employed in the gathering of the particular knowledge of that science. It is clear from these observations, or ought to be, that the different sciences are also distinguished from each other by their methods, and that any suggestion that the method of one *should* be employed by another is suspect, until extensively tested and until shown to have produced significant results. While experiment may be the method in one, documentation in another, case analysis in a third, the results as assessed by the fellowship of the workers in the field remain the ultimate test.[9]

All this is probably familiar enough, but there is a need to establish a firm basis of common understanding of "science" in general, before entering upon a discussion of the relationship between political philosophy and political science which is, of course, part of the more general problem of the relationship between philosophy and science. Indeed, something more needs to be said by way of clarification, as far as political science is concerned, about the degree of generalization possible and the importance of it in scientific work. The striking successes which modern physics and chemistry have achieved with quantitative methods have led many people to feel, and philosophers to say, that these methods are "better" and "more scientific" and that propositions based upon them, called "laws," are the real test of "scientific" work. Actually, the value of these methods and the striking results achieved with them are due to the very nature of the subject matter of these fields. These particular propositions which one might call "descriptive formulas" are on a high level of generalization. But it is an error to think that the level of generalization is the acid test of "scientificness." Astronomy, for example, operates on a much lower level of generalization than physics; much of its most striking work is in fact concerned with particular description of such things as the corona of the sun. Yet, there is no good philosophical ground for preferring physics to astronomy on this score. It may be replied, however, that both are operating with precise quantitative data. We must reject that argument and repeat that not only accuracy, but also relevancy and adequacy of the results, are valid tests of scientificness. Human anatomy is no less a science than chemistry. The progress toward a more scientific history in

[9] Brecht, 1959, offers the most recent exploration of this matter; but Meynaud, 1959, and Duverger, 1959, also deserve attention.

the last few generations is almost totally unrelated to problems of quantity. History, more relevant to the concerns of the political scientist, was through the critique of sources and the critical use of other types of evidence made "more scientific" than it had been. In short, neither the degree of generalization nor the degree of quantification is in itself an "absolute" criterion of scientific progress, but must be evaluated in relation to the material in hand and to be assessed. Aristotle put it very nicely: "It is the mark of an educated man to look for precision in each class of things just so far as the nature of the subject matter admits." [10] This holds not only as between science and various kinds of practical skills, but also as between the sciences themselves. To put it more pointedly, every scientific statement, no matter what its degree of generality, is a hypothetical description of what are believed to be observed phenomena; the more recurrent the phenomena, the more general the description can be. But how often a thing happens does not determine how relevant it is; for in the center of all efforts at knowing stands man, and the degree of relevance is determined by the extent to which the observed phenomena are related to man in the universal chain of being.[11]

We do not have to go as far as Immanuel Kant's metaphysic of the "thing-in-itself" in order to appreciate that we are never really describing merely facts, but observations of these presumed facts. A brief statement concerning the shortcomings of Kant's position may be in order here. Kant's statement suffers from the positing of an entity behind and beyond and wholly separate from what we observe, so that the "thing-in-itself" is presumed to stay forever wholly outside our knowledge.[12] Hegel's bitter critique that this implies the denial of all rational knowledge of reality is justified, but he goes to the opposite extreme.[13] It would seem more in keeping with scientific progress and its metaphysical implications to assume that the human understanding is progressively appropriating the real world and the things in it—for how else could one explain successful engineering action based upon such scientific knowledge—and at the same time recognizing that this process is never complete, and that there are

[10] *Nicomachean Ethics*, I. The passage continues, significantly: "It is evidently equally foolish to accept probable reasoning from a mathematician as to demand from a rhetorician demonstrable proofs." Cf. for this also Perelman and Olbrechts-Tyteca, 1958, *passim.*

[11] Lovejoy, 1936, pp. 186ff.

[12] See for the "Ding an sich" *Prolegomena*, par. 26, and elsewhere (in Friedrich, 1949, p. 80). Kant was, by his position, led to the famous overstatement that "the intellect does not derive its [nature's] laws from nature, but prescribes them to nature" (*ibid.*, p. 91, par. 37).

[13] *Werke* (ed. Lasson) vol. III, *Logik*, p. 28: ". . . Nichtigkeit des Gespensts des *Dings-an-sich*, dieses abstrakten von allem Inhalt abgeschiedenen Schattens. . . ." Cf. also, for Hegel's own conception of the *Ding-an-sich*, the same work, vol. II, pp. 106ff., where the Ding-an-sich is defined as "wesentlich-unmittelbar" and as "wesentliche Identität der Existenz."

always aspects, phases—in short, parts—of things studied which lie outside man's knowledge *at that point*, which may be appropriated later. There are formulations in Kant which in fact support this view. Political science has every reason to be grateful to Kant, following Locke, for having established that human experience is conditioned by what human minds are like in their operations, and that even the most abstract and general law is conditioned by the "forms" of thought which the human being brings to all description of observations. In short, we are, as just claimed, never describing *merely* facts, but observations of these presumed facts.

In the field of history, broadly speaking, these "facts" are "events" which are believed to have occurred and which in their occurrence have been experienced by human beings, partly through observation, partly through participation, partly through surmise.[14] Sympathetic understanding (*Verstehen* in Max Weber's sense) does the rest. The uniqueness of all historical events as they occur in their specific constellation once and never again, means of course that validation of the experience through repetition is excluded. The reports of the event as it occurred are the only record of what occurred and must therefore be the focus of all scientific inquiry. This means that in the large area of historico-political facts with which political science is concerned we are dealing with reports about events, not with events themselves, directly. I do not wish to have these remarks understood in any radically nominalist sense, however. I believe, myself, that a "correspondence" with underlying reality must be supposed. The evaluation of reports must therefore be in the center of our interest, and our "methods" will be shaped by such evaluation. To illustrate, a hundred reports about a hundred interviews with a hundred escapees from the Soviet Union are inherently neither more nor less "scientific" (i.e., relevant) than one report about one speech of Stalin. It all depends upon what happens to be the subject under discussion. If it is the role of "ideology" in the Soviet Union, the latter may be far more weighty and significant as evidence for the proposition that ideology continued to be a significant factor.[15]

When we speak of verification, we mean that the description, of whatever degree of generalization, and whether quantitative or qualitative, is capable of being tested by whoever possesses the requisite training according to the methods appropriate for the field of experience involved. It would therefore be more precise to speak of corroboration, perhaps.[16] Such corroboration presupposes that the descriptions must correspond to

[14] Social science methodology, especially in anthropology and sociology, has developed techniques of combining the first two in the role of the "participant observer"; such methods constitute a rational elaboration of what has always been a major source of reports upon which historical knowledge is based.

[15] For the entire preceding discussion see Friedrich, 1961, pp. 17ff. Also Collingwood, 1946.

[16] Popper, 1959, chap. X.

the phenomena covered by them, whether general or particular, and therefore if new discoveries of hitherto unobserved facts (reports) are made, the description or descriptive generalization must be accordingly revised. This general rule has very serious implications for such sciences as political science, in which new facts constantly present themselves as political practices and institutions and the thought corresponding to them evolve. Thus, the emergence of totalitarian dictatorships in our time—congeries of facts unprecedented in the history of political systems[17]—presents the political scientist with numerous novel problems, but so did the emergence of modern constitutionalism. Not only the evolution in the actual world of politics, but also the rapid accumulation of politically significant data in such fields as prehistory, history, ethnology, anthropology and psychology confronts the political scientist with new issues that imperiously demand adequate correlation and systematization. The more immediate concern with contemporary government, particularly American and European government, has limited the work of political science, more especially political theory, and kept it from exploring these issues, leaving political science with any number of propositions that probably will turn out to be outworn and untenable when properly tested by the available "facts."

Some of the preceding remarks presumably have, by their evident philosophical implications, already served to illustrate the connection between political theory and philosophy. But it is necessary to elaborate this connection and to show its vital significance for the science of politics. To recall the dictionary definitions quoted above, philosophy appears to be concerned with ultimate reality and its principles, and therefore also with the principles of a particular branch of reality. It would be possible to develop this proposition further by showing how the science of politics, as expounded by Aristotle, is related to and depends upon Aristotle's general philosophy. But such an exercise would not carry much weight with those who would claim that, while this was very true for the time of Aristotle, just as in physics so in political science we have now come to detach ourselves from such teleological views, and that a non-normative and nonphilosophical, strictly "positive" science of politics is both feasible and useful.[18] I am not going to argue the problem in terms of the proposition that positivism itself is a "philosophy." For all positivists would pre-

[17] The unprecedented nature of totalitarian dictatorship is variously delineated in Friedrich (ed.), 1954, Arendt, 1951, and more fully developed in Friedrich and Brzezinski, 1956. For a more recent discussion cf. Bracher, Sauer and Schultz, 1960.

[18] Such a demand has been voiced by a number of writers and was the subject of a committee exploration of the APSA in the twenties; for example, G. E. G. Catlin, 1927 and the writings of Charles E. Merriam, are earlier attempts. Most recently, the work of Lasswell and Kaplan, cited above, has advanced this position. In a more sophisticated form, the position is also central to Brecht, 1959, and to much that is said and written in the "behavioral" branch of political science.

sumably readily admit that if that is all that is meant by philosophy, some kind of philosophy is involved in political science. Rather do I propose to show how and why philosophy in a wider sense, and more especially through its political branch, is relevant to and cannot be bracketed out of political science, except for limited and specified purposes. In other words, I propose to block the retreat often adopted by antiphilosophical writers who say that "in any set of definitions some terms must be left undefined on pain of circularity. The chain of definitions must have a starting point. . . ."[19] For while this observation is true enough, it does not absolve us from concern with these basic terms. It will be found that definitions or characterizations of political science usually include the word "power," and sometimes include the words "justice" or "value," as well as "action," "person," "sentiment," "symbol" and "group," or related terms. Thus some writers define political science as a "policy science" which "studies influence and power as instruments of the integration of values realized by and embodied in interpersonal relations."[20] These words, or some of them, if left undefined, presumably possess referents resulting from the experience of some groups of human beings (college professors, for example, or Americans, or English-speaking persons, or English-speaking American college professors). The crux of the argument involves the potential change in these referents, resulting from changes in word usage that are consequent upon philosophical argument and discussion, that is to say, changes in the view of being or reality, and in the principles and truths regarding it, which are defined as the province of philosophy. Philosophers who thus "shape our thought" are actually themselves responding to widely felt experiences that may be associated with political, economic, artistic or technical change and evolution.[21]

At this point it might be argued by some that this is a question of ideology—a matter which will be discussed more fully below (Chapter 4). Ideology, intrinsically a political phenomenon, even if not as sharply defined as is done there, provides no valid ground for objecting to the relevance of political philosophy to political science, but rather proves it. For political ideologies are ideas in action, political action. Whether and to what extent the ideas contained in an ideology are "true" is an important question and attempts to answer it are a never ending quest. Such answers are of considerable urgency not only to those who accept a particular ideology, but also to those who reject it. It may well be a fact that Plato's ideas were related to the ideology of the aristocrats at Athens. If so, it would not thereby be proved that they are in error, in whole or

[19] Lasswell and Kaplan, 1950, p. 3, fn. 1.

[20] *Ibid*., p. xii.

[21] On another occasion, Friedrich, a2, 1958, I proceeded to document this proposition by relating recent writings of three philosophers to political science, pointing out the implications of their conclusions. Cf. also Catlin, 1957, Brecht, 1959 and Mannheim, 1953, part III, pp. 97ff.; similarly Strauss, 1959, pp. 25–27.

in part. The fact that any set of ideas may become part of an ideology must be considered inherent in their very nature. Modern positivist ideas are no different from other ideas in this respect, nor do they become a myth on this account, nor do they therefore "structurally resemble lies," as Mannheim insisted concerning all ideology.[22] From this it follows that the ideological potential which is generally admitted, does not detract from, but rather heightens the significance of political philosophy for political science (in the sense defined above).

More broadly speaking, the ideological potential of any political proposition, whether philosophical or scientific, makes more important the question: Is it true? In political matters, this question tends to be taken pragmatically or operationally, that is, it tends to be identified with the question: Is it useful? But the standard of truth in the sense of ultimate validity cannot be avoided if the ideological potential is to be clearly differentiated. Ideology considers ideas in terms of their usefulness; science tries to get beyond that in terms of the ascertainable correspondence of statement with fact, of report *A* with report *B*, and so forth, in infinite approximation to a past event which has disappeared in the vortex of time. The degree of correspondence is an arguable proposition, carrying conviction in accordance with methodological maxims. Thus truth is a matter of degree, too.

The search for more truth is going on forever. What may be true at one time, ceases to be true as new insights develop. These changes profoundly affect politics, power, justice, order—they all depend upon what is believed to be true. Philosophically, one can understand authority as the marginal configuration of truth, since beyond each truth there is still another truth, a new horizon, which renders it partial. Hence philosophy, in spite of all its questioning of authority, always at a certain point, the point of farthest reach, must accept that something is not yet analyzed, that is to say, on the basis of "authority." Even for the philosopher (as indeed for the scientist) there is a point at which the meaning of authority is power—the power of truth that is "beyond understanding." At this point authority may be said to be a configuration of truth which is accepted in reverence and faith, though not yet rationally comprehended, though the act of acceptance itself is a kind of rational comprehension, namely, the comprehension of the inherent and ineluctable need of authority itself.[23]

[22] Mannheim, 1936, p. 238. See below, Chap. 4, for detailed analysis. Cf. also Young (ed.), 1958, pp. 185ff.

[23] Jaspers, 1947, pp. 769ff., develops the relation between truth and authority at considerable length; he shows authority to be a configuration of truth; its "inner dialectic" he sees as springing from the tension between the truth that is known and the truth that is in the process of being discovered. For a critique of his view of authority see below, Chap. 12.

This need of the truth-seeker to recognize the finiteness of all found truth, as contrasted with the infinity of all truth to be found, does not oblige him to consider the problem of truth as resolvable only in terms of mere relativity, as is suggested by the notion of ideology as a designation for all philosophy and more particularly political philosophy. Even if one argues, *Sum, ergo cogito*, rather than *Cogito, ergo sum*, there are statements to be made about the workings of politics (e.g., Athenian democracy or democracy in general) that are more true than others. The standard of true or false, involved in all scientific work, links in the last analysis, through its relationship to what are authoritative statements, political science with political philosophy, as indeed it does all sciences with all philosophy. This issue cannot be avoided by talking about a pragmatic or operational test, that is to say, about whether something worked or not. The reasons are not far to seek; for on the one hand such a pragmatic or operational test is in turn subject to the question of true or false, and on the other hand since politics deals with very complex situations involving many contingencies we cannot know whether something will work because it has worked in the past. Actually, the resolution of questions in political theory (as in political practice) calls for the marshaling of the available evidence in all its complexity and range, including more particularly the broad insights of philosophy.

Thus, to conclude, political science and political philosophy are intimately tied, the one cannot be usefully pursued without the other, and political science in this respect is not at all different from other sciences which likewise are linked to philosophy. We have argued this proposition only generally here, but the proof of it lies in all that follows. No discussion of the basic issues of politics, power, authority, law, and the rest is possible without referring to philosophical premises. When one considers the controversies over political philosophy in relation to these issues, he discovers that the argument against the role of philosophy in political science resembles the argument against theory in political (and other) science. In fact, we have a recurrent pattern in which he who knows something particular argues against him who knows both more and less by knowing something about a larger class of things. The practitioner of politics, the politician, holds the scientist in low esteem, questioning his work as mere "theory," by which he means something unsubstantial and essentially false. The specialist in some particular phase of descriptive political science doubts the value of "theory," calling it "generalities" which he considers misleading and essentially false. The theorist who cherishes the notion of a general systematic political science in turn objects to the political philosopher as a man concerned with "ideological" questions, with value judgments which he considers subjective and essentially false. They are all, however, talking in terms of truth, and the question "What is truth?" which they presumably must be able to answer in order to vindicate their claims—practitioner, specialist, theorist and philosopher alike—is the most fundamental and philosophical question there is.

This question can never be answered, except in relation to human experience, in any field. In politics, the theoretical inquiry ought therefore to begin by asking: What kind of experience is political experience? To answer this question an understanding is needed about the "meaning of meaning." From what has been said about truth, it follows that meaning in the scientific theoretical sense can never be simply a verbal question. We are primarily concerned with reality, and only incidentally and secondarily with the words used to designate the reality inquired into. Obviously these are fighting words which require careful elaboration.[24] The reality we are concerned with is the range of human experience in politics.

All scientific understanding and knowledge rests upon experience of some sort. The sensationalists, often called empiricists, were in error when they undertook to reduce all human experience to the experience of the senses. Feeling and willing, as well as creative and inventive innovation, are part of human experience, and so is the intellectual and spiritual life of man. In the sciences concerned with the realms of nature, sensory experience is the primary guide to true knowledge when combined with the resources of the mind; the latter are as important as the former, and thinking is experienced as much as seeing or hearing.[25] The realm of experience which constitutes politics is not primarily sensory experience. Then what is it?

It would be much easier to arrive at philosophical clarity if the several kinds of experience [26] could be seen as a logical and coherent unity. This is not in fact possible, and all efforts to see them so—and they constitute a considerable part of the history of philosophy—have led to the denial of one or another part of experience. Both idealists and materialists have sought to escape from the uncertainties of human existence, to interpret away the ever renewed experience of the unexpected, of the perplexing and the chaotic. Dewey, in a brilliant review of these ever renewed efforts at substituting the stable for the unstable, the lasting for the changing, being for becoming, called it *the* philosophic fallacy which "supplies the formula of the technique by which thinkers have relegated the uncertain and unfinished to an invidious state of unreal being, while they have systematically exalted the assured and complete to the rank of true Being." [27]

[24] Gellner, 1959, developed the contrast as a critique of the school of logical positivism, from a sociological viewpoint, but his treatment is not entirely satisfactory. Cf. for the classical statement Ogden and Richards, 1923, 1938.

[25] This view has recently been carefully elaborated by a leading natural scientist, Michael Polanyi, whose *Personal Knowledge*, published in 1958, is a landmark. Cf. Friedrich, a, 1962.

[26] Michael Oakeshott, 1933; E. Husserl, 1938.

[27] Dewey, 1929, 1958, p. 52.; next quotation from p. 65.

Again: "One of the most striking phases of the history of philosophic thought is the recurrent grouping together of unity, permanence (or 'the eternal'), completeness and rational thought, while upon another side full multiplicity, change and the temporal, the partial, defective, sense and desire." In contrast to such views—and they are widespread indeed—he pointed out that a broad empirical philosophy perceives that thinking is a continuous process of temporal reorganization within one and the same world of experienced things, not a jump from the latter world into one of objects constituted once for all by thought."[28]

Nor is this all. Thinking is itself one of the several modes of experiencing himself and the world which man undergoes continually. There is nothing to indicate that this mode should be placed above all other modes and made their master and judge. But neither should it be rejected as unworthy of respect, as is done by irrationalists. Thought, logic and reason are one, but only one primary experience, by which the situation of man as a person is defined. How is it to be related to the other modes of experience? And what are these other modes? There seem to be essentially three: (1) sensory perception, or observing the world, (2) choosing among alternative courses of action, or willing, and (3) making something new, or procreating, inventing and discovering. If these primary modes of experience are combined with the experience of thinking, they are discovered to imply *logical* principles which are *logically* in conflict or contradiction with each other. Thus the experience of observing, of having a succession of sense impressions, leads to the principle of causation, a logical hypothesis linking the several observations and combining them into a chain of experience. Hume analyzed the hypothetical nature of the law of causation; Kant in turn showed how important this law is for all orderly thought dealing with sense impressions. Without positing the category of cause, Kant thought, it is impossible to think about the experience of the senses. This proposition holds also for derivative fields of experience and thought, such as history which, as was said, presents itself to the person who wants to think about it as a series of reports about events which allegedly happened but which can never be observed again by the senses. If the hypothesis of causation is generalized, that is, if all things and events are explained in terms of antecedent things and events,[29] one arrives at the philosophical position of determinism. A deterministic world is a world in which external causation reigns supreme.[30] In its political implication, such a view resembles certain religious positions; its fatalism paradoxically enough begets a radical activism on the part of

[28] *Ibid.*, p. 68.

[29] In a sense, "every existence is an event," as Dewey wrote (*op. cit.*, p. 71), but there is some use in distinguishing things and events, especially in the dimension of politics.

[30] MacIver, 1942.

those who see themselves as chosen instruments of some predominant cause, as the believers in early Islam, in Calvinism, and in Marxism do.

The experience of choosing between alternative courses of action, of making a decision in a situation possessing contingent aspects, surely is as primordial to the human condition as that of observing the world around and about; when it is thought about, it yields the hypothesis of freedom. It is impossible to engage in the act of willing if one does not presuppose that he may act either one way or the other. The hypothetical nature of such freedom of choice was formulated most sharply by Hobbes, but Kant was able to qualify this conclusion and show that the hypothesis of freedom is necessary for an acting person—necessary in a logical sense, as causation is necessary for an observer; the respective experiences presuppose the principle in terms of which the mind understands them and carries on from them. The hypothesis of freedom, too, may be generalized, though it is more likely to remain restricted to human beings (and of course divine beings, if such are included in the respective world view). To the extent to which it is generalized it leads to a philosophy of indeterminism. An indeterministic world is a world of orthopraxis[31] in which free men, persons, decide what to do in situations they are placed in. In its political implications, such a view too has found religious expression, and many of the great religions, including Christianity, have struggled to make room for it, in order to provide a ground for attributing responsibility to human beings in their social and political actions. Stoicism, humanism and liberalism are united in placing such an assumption in the center of their world view, their *Weltanschauung*, and deriving from it a powerful impetus to reforming activity.

Existing monistic philosophical systems may therefore be divided into two classes. There are those which reject the hypothesis of freedom, or at least reduce it in scope to some sort of human self-deception; they are deterministic and are built either upon the primary experience of sense impressions and observation, or, when the work of historicists, upon reports believed to rest upon such observations. Then there are those which, if they do not reject the hypothetical law of causation, greatly restrict its range of application to a distinct and separate "realm of nature" and interpret it as a "phenomenal illusion"; these systems are voluntaristic and built upon the primary experience of choosing and willing.

But thought may reject either of these horns of the dilemma of an inherently contradictory logic of the patterns of experience which define man's situation. For there is still another possibility which consists in abandoning monism in an attempt to hypostatize two sharply separated worlds, the world of norms and the world of events. This was done by

[31] I trust that it is permissible to use this term in analogy to the orthogenesis of the biologists referred to below.

Kant and quite a few others who constructed dualistic systems which are then in need of some kind of link to bring them together again. All these attempts are unconvincing if experience is made the test. As empirical philosophy, they are afflicted with a measure of philosophical inadequacy; for evidently, one of the primary experiences of observing, willing and thinking is being argued away in the effort to achieve coherence. This is true even prior to considering the fourth primary experience of making something new, which is universally human through the act of procreation, but which takes numerous other forms of innovation in the various fields of production, invention and discovery. The political significance of such innovation is discussed below at greater length (Chapter 21). Here it needs only to be remarked that such innovation is even more evidently at variance with the presuppositions of a deterministic universe and creation has therefore served to reinforce the cogency of the objections to a neglect of freedom as implied in primary human experience.[32]

From what has been said, it follows that the whole of human experience cannot be made logically consistent, and man finds himself confronted with and placed in a situation which is plurally experienced as consisting of some components which are causally determined, others which are freely chosen as alternatives to rejected possibilities, still others which are freely invented as alterations and innovations of the situation, and all of which are reflected in thought according to the ways of logic. A radical philosophy of experience must accept and live with this plurality of givens, not arguing or interpreting away any of them as of a lesser order of truth. Such an empirical philosophy thus appears to be a general view of the world and of man's existence which starts from all that is given to man in primary experience, rather than selecting one or another of these primary givens as preeminent. And since these primary experiences lead to logical implications which clash with each other, the world and man's existence are primordially problematic. The arguments which such contradictions entail are endemic in human experience, they are "built-in," and in this sense a dialectic is built-in likewise. Problems are the first order of being, and not merely derived from operational and related notions as in much of pragmatism.[33]

"The world is a scene of risk. . . . Plague, famine, failure of crops, disease, death, defeat in battle, are always just around the corner, and so are abundance, strength, victory, festival and song." A philosophy of

[32] Cf. Oppenheim, 1961; Adler, 1961; and below, Chap. 20, for recent views.

[33] Dewey, 1929, esp. pp. 99ff., 122f., and 223ff., seems to argue in such operational terms. But in works published in 1925 and 1929 the problematic is given simple existential status; he stresses moreover that cultural phenomena emphasize the perilous and precarious features of existence. I should like to add birth and the union of the sexes. The operational view has since been developed by several thinkers; see Anatol Rapoport, 1954.

experience may therefore be called a philosophy of the problem—the term "problem" taken in the very concrete sense in which the word *problēma* originally meant in Greek something which, like a roadblock, is thrown across our path. The ever-recurring question is how all human experience in its plural significance may be made fruitful for the progressive understanding of a particular range of experience and its problems. Pluralism is the hallmark of our philosophy of experience, and the kinship with Aristotle springs from his tendency toward pluralism. It has particular cognitive value in the sphere of politics.

In such a problematic and pluralistic view, the endeavor to evolve a systematic theory of politics and government appears paradoxical. A system seems to call for stability, order and timelessness. Nothing political ever is stable, ordered or timeless in an absolute sense. A government, a political party, a constitution or a law can achieve only relative stability, relative order and a relatively long duration in time. Therefore, the degree of stability, order and duration in time are themselves problems of politics. The systematic is problematic, and a system has meaning only as it supplies a framework for the solving of these and related problems.[34] That this is a crucial and difficult task in science, is generally recognized.[35] In the political sphere, problems often impose themselves. This is from the scientific viewpoint troublesome, but cannot be avoided. It is true of what follows. Asking the right questions concerning these patent problems may nonetheless be the acid test of true understanding and eventual results.

The following pages are cast into the framework of a systematic treatise. The reason for such careful interrelating of all the aspects of politics and government, past and present, arises from the need of the human mind to see things as ordered and therefore as a unity, rather than as chaos. But when Kierkegaard cried out, "Put me in a system and you negate me. I am not a mathematical symbol. I *am!*" he stated a basic truth which is as true of political man as it is of man in general. Since political life is constantly changing, new, emergent potentialities color the past as they shape the present. But since there is not only chaos, but also order, since the affirmation is as real as the negation, the systematic approach has its place. However, the system should be conceived as open, rather than closed, as dynamic, rather than static; neither system nor order should be made into fetishes. This danger of ossifying insight into academic pedantries can perhaps best be avoided if thought remains oriented toward *problems*. That is to say, the systematic approach should serve the problematic one. If reality, political reality, is seen as value-filled, not value-free, then political analysis needs to be value-oriented. And this not only in the sense of recognizing that human beings cherish values and act

[34] Cf. regarding "system" Note 1.

[35] Merton, 1959, p. 1f.; E. B. Wilson, Jr., 1952, chap. 1.

accordingly, but also in the sense that the writer on politics engages in a political act, and that his foremost concern is bound to be to contribute to an understanding of right action. "What shall I do?" "What must we do?" These are the key problems of all politics. Political analysis shapes the values as it proceeds in the study of their workings (Chapter 2).

In accordance with this outlook it is incumbent upon me to state the problems which more specifically concern us as we review the totality of the political experience of man. They are essentially three. First, why is it that everywhere on earth men are at present more dissatisfied with government than they apparently were only a short two generations ago? Is it a drift into misgovernment, or excessive demands made upon the rulers, or an unmanageable situation, or all three of them combined? The second problem is consequent upon the first: Can anything short of world government remedy the present breakdown of parochial government? If not, is there any possible way of achieving world government, if one considers past human experience? The third problem is supplementary to the second, but vital to it, and it is: How can government be effectively organized in those lands and by those peoples who have lost their "ancient ways" under colonial rule, yet have achieved or are on the way to achieving autonomy? All three problems may be stated as part of one key problem which has been the key problem ever since men began to study and analyze government systematically: how to be governed well. We are no longer primarily interested in the question of an "ideal" or "perfect" political order, which fascinated the Greeks, just as the question of an "ideal" or "perfect" human body fascinated them. What we want to know is what makes a government adequate to its tasks, so that the rulers secure what the ruled require. And we are ready to admit that this question cannot be answered without taking time and place into account. But is there not perhaps a general pattern of which the particular forms of rule are but specific applications? If so, it would greatly facilitate the answer to our second and third problem, and it is my belief that this is so. Such a belief justifies the systematic approach: to look for the persistent core in the ever changing pattern of government.

This is a viewpoint which lies beyond liberalism and conservatism, as well as communism and fascism. For the efforts of transcending the perversions and the atavism of the totalitarians by a "return" to outworn ideologies are foredoomed to failure. Neoliberalism and neoconservatism have their real merits and affinities. But the time for such culture-bound ideologies is past. Mankind is moving into a panhuman phase in which all human experience will have to be examined and brought to bear upon universal problems of government and politics. For while they have their cultural and local dimension, they may contain a general core common to all mankind.

In our search for these universals the problem of semantics, of the "meaning of meaning," is basically changed.[36] To interpret words essentially as designations of modes of experience, and therefore to search for the primary experiences which constitute the political sphere, is the central task of the pages which follow. This approach is in line with what was pointed out some time ago as the essential procedure of another theorist, Mises, in dealing with the controversial subject of probability. It was said that he does not pretend "either to say what the term probability usually means or, still less, what it ought to mean. He takes a large class of phenomena with which everyone would admit that probability has to do and proceeds to create a concept that in fact enables us to think effectively about some of them." [37]

To give a brief preview, the theory is developed in the following way. In discussing first (Part I) the political *person* and his sphere of action we hope to lay a foundation by offering a view of man in the political perspective, fully realizing that this perspective is only one of those in which man can be viewed. It would, from a philosophical viewpoint, perhaps be better to offer a rounded view of man in all his different preoccupations—art, science, religion, economics, and so forth—but this does not seem feasible, nor is it necessary for a political theory from our experiential viewpoint. It is enough to acknowledge that politics is *one* of the primary fields of experience and that the experiences which constitute this side of man's nature are necessarily part of the life of all but marginal human beings. This foundation rests upon the recognition of the *political person* as the embodiment of man's activity in this field. But such a person can be understood only in terms of his functions, purposes and values (Chapter 2). Their discussion shows that institutions, decisions and policies are interdependent and not alternatives, as is at times asserted (Chapter 3). This leads to the confrontation of interests and ideas, and the function of the latter, particularly in the form of ideologies, is the topic of Chapter 4. Because of the rivalry of ideas and interests, political myths are generated and the future projected in terms of utopian order notions;

[36] Ogden and Richards, 1938. We agree with the fundamental tenet of this work, that many of the problems which have occupied the attention of philosophers and logicians are pseudo-problems, because the underlying reality—that is, the "referent"—was neglected. This referent is typically and usually some kind of general human experience.

[37] Nowell-Smith, a, 1947, where he discusses Mises. Nowell-Smith adds some further comments. "The fact that his use of the term 'probability' corresponds to no previous use and the fact that the technique he elaborates does not help at all in many cases where we normally talk about probability detract in no way from the value of his concept. He does not provide a theory about "what probability really is," but a technique for formulating and solving specific problems: and the only valid way of 'refuting it . . .' would be to show that, in fact, it sheds no light on any situation in which we have to think or act." It is essentially the problem of the White Knight.

symbols are evolved for both, as much as for basic communication, and are made part of the political environment (Chapter 5). Myth and utopia raise the question of valid belief and of the convictions based upon such belief; religion and ritual thus form the focus of Chapter 6. On the basis of the foregoing, it becomes possible to delineate a theory of (political) organization and relate it to the twin problems of rational conduct and political style (Chapter 7) and from such a theory to proceed to a comprehensive theory of the political community (Chapter 8). While many other issues are treated incidentally, if briefly, the foregoing appear to be the essential steps in circumscribing the sphere of action of the political person.

Upon this foundation, the basically problematical position of man unfolds as manifest in three spheres: power, justice and freedom. The several chapters of Parts II and III devoted to these explorations describe the decisive features of the situation in which man finds himself in politics; their varied combinations define some of the many different constellations this situation may exhibit. Within the sphere of power and justice (Part II) power and leadership (Chapter 9), rule and rulership (Chapter 10) and influence and anticipated reaction (Chapter 11) are scrutinized. They are then juxtaposed to political authority (Chapter 12), legitimacy (Chapter 13), justice (Chapter 14) and law (Chapter 15). Within the sphere of equality and freedom (Part III), political equality (Chapter 16) appears in its relation with the political elite (Chapter 18); the conflict is of course mediated through representation and responsibility (Chapter 17). With respect to each of these phenomena, the central experience which constitutes its core is identified, and then propositions of a very general nature are tentatively formulated to adumbrate their working. The same kind of analysis is then undertaken for the sphere of order and freedom. First the interaction of order and disorder as the setting for freedom undergoes analysis (Chapter 19), and then the three dimensions of freedom are distinguished and explored (Chapters 20 and 21); freedom of independence, of participation and of innovation are shown all to be vital to politics.

There follows in Parts IV and V a broad study of the governing processes in and through the concrete political order. Chapter 22 shows that the founding process is the most basic, though often neglected; but defending and expanding the political community is almost equally so (Chapter 23). The basic operational processes are settling disputes, making rules and taking measures (Chapters 24 to 26); within the context of the last the problem of bureaucracy, raised in the discussion of the elite, is studied further, and the fiscal basis of government is discussed. The broad range of the process of negotiating a political bargain is next considered in its internal and external dimension (Chapter 27). The processes of succession (Chapter 28) involving the use of party as the "backlog" supply of political leadership are shown to be crucial to all government, on the level of rulership.

Part V explores the ranges and levels of government. Local community, tribe and region are basic, and therefore their analysis precedes (Chapter 29) that of state and nation (Chapter 30); in treating of the latter, sovereignty is assigned its limited historical place. The next two chapters address themselves to the experience which has been had in efforts to transcend the local and national community, especially in seeking to establish a "world order": empire and federation. Empire, the imperial enterprise, is described and analyzed as the simpler and more primitive endeavor at universal order through coercion (Chapter 31), while federation (Chapter 32) appears as the more complex and sophisticated method for accomplishing the same result by consensual agreement. Both are processes crystallizing into structures of transnational and potentially universal scope.

By way of a conclusion which is really a panoramic view of prospective developments, three final chapters discuss the process of political change as manifest in tradition and education, in resistance and revolution and in the model of a future political order, both parochial and universal. Political tradition and the education by which it is transmitted along with other elements of the cultural heritage are shown to be the basic processes between which political phenomena oscillate (Chapter 33). By contrast, resistance and revolution constitute the points of discontinuity and breakdown (Chapter 34). The political experience of mankind points toward theoretical and practical efforts at transcending the present crisis; it suggests a model of minimal requirements of good government. The prospects are, in the light of experience, not especially encouraging; but solutions are not excluded by past experience either (Chapter 35).

Throughout, the polarity of persons and processes is stressed. Institutions are and must be seen as crystallizations of processes, functions as projections of persons. In many cases, political problems become unsolvable if this relation between persons, processes, functions and institutions is lost sight of. Excessive emphasis upon one or another of these components of all political situations is a distortion of experience. *Politica est res dura*—it is a hard thing, and calls for the most hardheaded analysis. But analysis takes time, and time is limited. At the start of any political theory one should put the warning that situations change and that right action in politics depends more than perhaps in any other human sphere on the right time. The Greeks had a word for it: *kairos.* It is that fleeting moment in the history of human affairs when the opportunity knocks. These are the decisive constellations which must be appreciated in all their complexity and uniqueness if we are to avoid the arrogance of the theorist who believes in patent solutions or final answers. He can help by discovering and analyzing the recurrent situations, and by identifying their universal features. But he must content himself with such understanding of genesis, operation and design. In the Inaugural from which the quotation on the title page of this chapter is taken, Lord Acton added a sentence from John Hunter, the seventeenth-century political theorist and constitutionalist, which might well be recalled here: "Never ask me what I have said, or what I have written, but if you will ask me what my present opinions are, I will tell you." For no matter how hard we try, political theory is not certain and final; it deals with reality, the most fateful reality which confronts man, namely, himself in politics, where man is at his best and at his worst. That is why the political theorist is always in transition, more so than any other theorist. The reality with which he deals is the most kaleidoscopic part of man's experience.

note **1**

Some Thoughts on System Analysis

THE REMARKS WHICH FOLLOW are obviously not intended to offer more than a few general observations on my understanding of "system" and "systematic." In my view, the concept "system" refers to a complex of experiences which are related in a distinctive and seemingly necessary way to each other. System analysis has received striking and novel impulses, especially in biology, from the new field of inquiry known as cybernetics.[1] But no attempt will be made to deal with this aspect of the matter, especially since it seeks to interpret organic processes mechanically.

But what kind of experiences are involved in system perception? Is it manifest in the things, as when one speaks of a political or legal system, meaning that the system is embodied in the very institutions and processes which analysis discovers in the descriptive material placed at its disposal by research? Or is it merely in the mind of the analyst? a superimposed order devised by the inquiring mind to provide clarity and understanding? Our position is that the system is "real," that it is found in the political (as well as other live) data shaping the experiences into ordered wholes. At the same time, the system does not exhaust the reality, but is continu-

[1] Wiener, 1950; Ashby, 1956, to mention only two works in the growing literature.

ally challenged by emergent phenomena which are alien to the system and tend to destroy it or at any rate to replace it by another, and that again either gradually or cataclysmically. The assertion that political systems are real does not mean, of course, that they are necessarily either understood or even known. Nor does it mean that a system that could be thought of is necessarily actualized. Since systems are constantly undergoing transformations, the inquiring mind tends to be behind times. Burke once remarked that political theory limped behind political practice by about fifty years. There is wisdom in this observation, but it is one-sided. The situation of revolutionary change is characterized by a reversal of the sequence; theory anticipates practice, and the system which it envisages is slow in coming into being as practice follows the challenge of theory. The same holds for any other change in which invention and deliberate innovation (Chapter 21) play a decisive role.

The foregoing remarks call for a more precise understanding of what a system in general is, or rather what the term denotes in the way of observed, experienced reality. This is the more important as a number of writers have spoken of the "political system" or the "social system," making system the central focus of their analysis of political or social phenomena, *without* indicating, let alone making theoretically clear, what is to be understood by a "system." [2] This is the more surprising, since system analysis has received increasing attention from biologists and other scientists, and their results can be usefully employed by political theory.[3] It is recognized that systems may be composed of inanimate matter, e.g., a solar system, organic matter (the body system), or of thought elements, e.g., a philosophic system. General system theory aspires to covering them all. For in all these fields constellations of parts may be observed which follow a very general pattern. If the world is seen as composed of integrated wholes which conceivably form a hierarchy, then the world might be said to be a system. If such a system is seen as a game of chance, then the uncertain features, the probabilistic aspects, appear prominent. The real world is both, perhaps.

When several parts that are distinct and different from each other compose a whole, bearing a defined functional relation to each other which establishes a mutual dependence of these parts upon each other so that the destruction of one entails the destruction of the whole, then such a constellation shall be called a system. In exploring this proposition further, the several components might usefully be inspected. It might be helpful if the organic system of a body is used for illustration. The bodily system is first of all composed of certain distinctive parts, such as brain

[2] Easton, 1953; Parsons, 1951, to mention only two prominent instances. Cf. below, Chap. 2, for further critique.

[3] Bertalanffy, a, 1951. Cf. also the other contributions to this report.

and nervous tissue, bones, muscles, skin and the several organs such as heart, liver, stomach, and so forth. There are also other parts, such as eyes, ears, hands and feet. The second component asserts that these parts bear a functional relation to each other; this is likewise immediately apparent. But some of the parts could function without the others; the parts are not all equally dependent upon each other. This observation leads to the third component, which claims that some parts are mutually dependent upon each other in such a way that the destruction of one of them brings about the destruction of the entire system. Interaction there is between all the parts, but some parts appear vital, others incidental—and there are some in an intermediary position, such as the skin, of which much may be lost, but beyond a certain limit, its loss engenders the collapse of the system. The same holds true of the nervous tissues, and even of the brain, not all of which is vital. To make the application to politics of this comparison and of the notions associated with it, the parliamentary system might be used as an example. It is composed of various parts, of which the parliament and the executive establishment are vital in the sense that the system cannot exist without them; there are other parts, such as courts, a press and parties, which bear a defined functional relation to each other and to the vital parts, but which could possibly be dispensed with. Or it might be that, for example, the press, like the skin, could be dispensed with in part but not in its entirety. We are confronted with the existence of constitutive as contrasted with supplementary parts. Such supplementary parts may have very significant roles to play, and the well-being of the system may well depend upon them, even though the survival of it does not.

There are any number of political systems, and it is a crucial task of political theory based on empirical research to determine what they are, what are their constitutive parts, and how many of them can be found (and possibly constructed). That is the reason the problem of the forms of government has been and has remained an important, indeed a central, topic of political theory; it has not advanced as have knowledge and understanding of the political behavior of individuals and groups in recent years. One wonders whether improved research techniques, developed in cooperation with other social sciences, might not prove productive in exploring political system problems.[4]

[4] A different and I believe antiquated view of a system is given by Almond in his introduction to Almond and Coleman, 1959, pp. 7–8. It is there defined in terms of the "properties" of certain "interactions" (the latter remaining undefined). These properties are said to be (1) comprehensiveness, (2) interdependence, (3) existence of boundaries. These properties are a restatement, actually, of the conventional definition of the "state" as given by Vinogradoff, Jellinek and others. There is a similar tendency to be observed in those "systematic" efforts which make "legitimate physical compulsion" the key criterion of what is political—a view which is critically examined below, Chaps. 9–13, in terms of power, authority and legitimacy.

In drawing the organic analogy, as system theory suggests, familiar theoretical ground has been entered which has been hotly contested for many centuries. Analogies drawn between the body politic and the human body are as old as Herodotus and the times he describes, if not older.[5] There can be little question that these organic analogies have been grossly abused for ideological and propagandistic purposes. But it is doubtful that we can say they have *no* value, even though it is true that such an analogy as usually stated "has no longer, in either its pseudo-biologic or its metaphysical form, any significant place in political theory." [6] The fact that the organismic analogies have been abused and misstated does not prove that they do not contain a kernel of scientific value; astronomy developed from astrology, and chemistry from alchemy. Unless one is prepared to abandon the notion of a "system," governmental and political, he is faced with transforming a nostrum into a valid generalization based upon established matter of fact. This is done through adequate system theory which does not draw simple analogies, such as "the head is the king" or "the Soveraignty is an Artificial Soul, as giving life and motion to the whole body." [7] Incidentally, organic analogies are by no means the exclusive preserve of conservatives and authoritarians. Such an analogy is put to effective use by Sir John Fortescue in praising a constitutional as contrasted with an autocratic order. He calls attention to the central role of the heart as "the first that lives having within it blood which it distributes among all of the other members, whereby they are quickened and do live: semblably in a body politique, the intent of the people is the first lively thing, having within it blood . . . which it deals forth and imparts as well to the head as to all the members of the same body whereby the body is nourished and maintained." [8] He goes on to argue that the laws are like sinews, and so forth. Outmoded as are the specifics in these organic analogies, they do rightly insist upon the systematic aspect of a political order. Adequate modern system theory would seek to identify the functions and processes and their effective interrelations, and to determine the degree of their constitutive importance in the several systems.

[5] Coker, 1910.
[6] Coker, 1934, p. 26, fn.
[7] Hobbes, 1651, p. 1.
[8] Sir John Fortescue, *De Laudibus Legum Angliae*, chap. 13.

note 2

Types and Models

MORPHOLOGICAL THEORY is the story of types and models. Generally speaking, types are discovered or recognized, while models are constructed or built. Typology is an important part of political theory, as is model-logy. The recognition of what is typical of a class of things or events underlies all concept formation. Typology is therefore part of any inquiry into the relation of experience and the conceptualization of it. An issue in typology is an issue about the structure of the reality concerned; as such it is closely related to order and ordering.

In recent years, the discussion about typology has been complicated by the notion of a so-called "ideal type." The term was presumably coined by Max Weber,[1] though others have suggested that a "type" is "an ideal configuration of distinguishable, but not always separable features." [2] Weber's proper notions are rather obscure and controversial. What Weber had in mind it is now impossible to say, because of the contradictory explanations he himself has given. It would appear, though, that he recognized both generalizing and individualizing ideal types, that is to say, both

[1] Max Weber, 1923, pp. 9–10, and 1922, pp. 190ff. Cf. also Parsons, 1937, pp. 601ff., and Schelting, 1922, pp. 329ff. Cf. also Gerth and Mills, 1946, pp. 323f.

[2] Morris Cohen, 1931, pp. 364ff. The tendency to stress the a priori character of an "ideal" type is often found in political writers at present; e.g., Rosecrance, a, 1961. It is at variance with Weber's notions.

an ideal type of "bureaucracy" and one of *the* Renaissance or *the* Protestant ethic. He speaks of them as "constructed," which suggests that they are, properly speaking, models rather than types. Such constructions are to make it possible to "locate" the historical phenomenon, "to see if, in particular traits or in their total character, the phenomena approximate one of our constructions: to determine the degree of approximation . . . to the theoretically constructed type." In this sense, these ideal types are "merely a technical aid." But they mean more, because of the logical and teleological consistency which Weber calls "rationality" and which he thought has had a hold on man's mind. What this would seem to mean is that the construction of an ideal type seeks to distill an "inner" rationality which the observer of a given reality imputes to the reality—a viewpoint which is philosophically rooted in a belief in an underlying rational order, in spite of protestations to the contrary.[3] In this connection Weber introduces the notion of "meaning" (*Sinn*) and claims that by seeking adequate meaning (*Sinnadaequanz*) we can arrive at type concepts which are unequivocal (*eindeutig*).[4] He admits that sociology also uses the "average" type. Such average type he believes not to require any methodological comment, because in case of doubt it is always the ideal type which sociology is looking for. He also suggests that in terms of content, the ideal type is a construction which constitutes a "utopia." Such an ideal type is gained "by emphasizing in thought" (*gedankliche Steigerung*) certain elements of reality. Its relation to empirical reality, to the facts of life, consists in helping us to understand this reality. The ideal-typical concept is meant to educate the judgment; it is not a hypothesis, but is meant to orient the forming of hypotheses. "It is not a description of reality, but wants to provide unequivocal means for expressing such description."[5] It is the "idea" of various existing realities. Thus the notion of a "town economy" (*Stadtwirtschaft*) is not an average of all observed town economies, but an ideal type.[6] But we

[3] The above passages are found in Gerth and Mills, 1946, pp. 323–324.

[4] Referring to such terms as "bureaucratic" and "feudal," Weber states: "Damit mit diesen Worten etwas *Eindeutiges* gemeint sei, muss die Soziologie ihrerseits 'reine' ('Ideal'–)Typen von Gebilden jener Arten entwerfen, welche je in sich die konsequente Einheit möglichst vollständiger *Sinn*adaequanz zeigen . . ." 1925, p. 10. He adds that such types do not appear in reality any more than do the "reactions" in a physical experiment under laboratory conditions. There seems a curious confusion here about the concept of reality; for surely the laboratory is part of reality, which is why it can be used to "test" propositions, whereas Weber's constructions cannot be similarly "tested."

[5] M. Weber, 1922, p. 190.

[6] Again, Weber describes the process of construction in terms suggesting an intuitionist procedure: "Er wird gewonnen durch einseitige *Steigerung eines* oder *einiger* Gesichtspunkte und durch Zusammenschluss einer Fülle von diffus und diskret, hier mehr, dort weniger, stellenweise garnicht, vorhandenen *Einzel*erscheinungen, die sich jenen einseitig herausgehobenen Gesichtspunkten fügen, zu

are not told what apart from inner consistency determines the selection of the particular aspects which are being emphasized, or whether the criteria employed for this purpose are themselves conditioned empirically or in some other a priori fashion. Weber's position is or appears to be a sort of astigmatic idealism in which the farther vista of the transcendent origin of the general ideas which serve as a basis for the judgment as to what is important and hence worthy of emphasis remains hidden and uncertain.

Such an intuitionist basis is undesirable from a scientific standpoint, because there appears to be no way of settling any disagreement by reference to scientifically ascertainable matter of fact or documentation. All the problems of the "meaning of meaning" present themselves.[7] To the extent that the construction of ideal types is of the generalizing kind, it should be replaced by model construction which is justified by its operational value in elucidating complex factor analysis (as Weber himself recognized). Apart from such model construction, there may be a place for searching for the average type, a problem to which we shall return presently. When it comes to the individualizing ideal type, I fail to see how it differs from all historical concept-formation. A student of the Renaissance will naturally seek to determine what are the significant features, and he may in addition to that undertake to describe their interrelation and, where possible, their consistency. Life is, however, not always consistent, and certain historical phenomena, notably styles, do not exhibit a logical consistency, but rather various forms of polarity.[8] Mental phenomena, such as the "Protestant ethic," are more likely to be "meaningful" in this logically consistent sense than other things and events.

In view of all these bewildering complexities, another leading scholar has suggested that we ought to distinguish three "levels" of type analysis. These three levels are (1) the strictly conceptual type which is the concept (*Begriff*) of logic, (2) the average type or "morphological" concept, and (3) the ideal type. A concept in logic is proper for describing a group of phenomena when every element of the definition is present in every one of the phenomena. An average type is seen as a general configuration or pattern (*Gestalt*) of which some elements may be lacking in any particular phenomena belonging to the group which the type describes. An ideal type, finally, would describe an entity which is characterized in such a way as to be never present in any reality, but which is used to assess the reality in terms of the idealization which

---

einem in sich einheitlichen *Gedanken*bilde. In seiner begrifflichen Reinheit ist dieses Gedankenbild nirgends in der Wirklichkeit empirisch vorfindbar, es ist eine *Utopie* . . ." 1922, p. 191. The radical idealism and nominalism of the procedure thus is explicit and evident.

[7] Ogden and Richards, 1923, 1938.

[8] Friedrich, 1952, and a, 1955, illustrates these points in the case of the baroque.

the concept presents.[9] It is evident that the ideal type as here characterized is a species of norm. Again it remains obscure, however, wherefrom the criteria are derived which constitute the normative elements. Both authors speak of the process in a rather vague and indefinite fashion. It seems impossible to specify in empirical terms what is the basis of "idealizing" some elements in the total configuration. It is claimed that all samples of a certain group of phenomena belonging to a group or species can be arranged in order, beginning with those fulfilling "minimum" conditions and progressing to samples representing the group "purely." Empirically the series will stop at a certain point when reaching what is described as the highest degree of typicality. It may then be "completed," like the projection of a curve, it seems, by using the imagination to produce the "ideal type." But what are the grounds for this kind of projection? By what criteria are we to determine whether a feature is "pure" or not? It would seem that we would have to know the ideal type in order to answer these questions which obviously call for a clear-cut *petitio principii.*

In contrast to the ideal, the average type is of great value to an empirical political theory. The classical method for discovering the typical in a class of things or events is to compare them to discover what is alike and what not and then to construct, on the basis of actual results which may be observed or documented, either the conceptual or the average type or both. Leaving aside concept formation as a *locus classicus* of conventional logic, the average type exhibits a congeries of qualities which, while recurrent in a certain class of phenomena, do not constitute by themselves an individual entity, but characterize any number of them as they occur in reality. The typical American or Frenchman is thus a human being who, while resembling in many qualities other human beings, is characterized by a few traits which are found in greater frequency among Americans or Frenchmen than among others. A typical American is gregarious, a typical Frenchman polite, so it is claimed.[10] A typical parliament, in the sense of an average parliament, consists of a substantial number of persons, popularly elected, and occupied with making rules for those who elected them. Such an average parliament also engages in much oratory, develops a camaraderie among its members and is jealous of its prerogatives . . . and so forth and so on. Virtually all the phenomena with which political science is concerned yield average types, if broad-gauged comparative studies undertake to demonstrate the common characteristics in the various phenomena of politics.[11]

[9] Rüstow, a, 1953.

[10] Whether such national types can be scientifically demonstrated to exist, may be an open question; they are certainly believed to do so. Hence the dubious category of national "character."

[11] How close this operation is to concept-formation can be seen from John Stuart Mill's discussion of concept-formation on the basis of comparison, in his *Logic,* bk. IV, chap. II. Cf. also C. Sigwart, *Logik* (5th ed.), pp. 1873ff.

It is, however, incumbent upon us to recognize still another type which is important in political studies. It is suggested by the expression, often heard about persons, that a particular action is "typical." Here the typical is that which is symptomatic. It refers to that aspect or quality in a group of phenomena which makes the individual or group distinctive or indeed unique. Actually, in talking about a typical representative of a certain nationality, people often have in mind this symptomatic type rather than any average. Thus what is significant is often a trait in exaggeration so that it is easy to recognize the species by the symptom which the representative exhibits. It seems to me that this empirically recognizable symptomatic type has played a certain role in making the notion of an ideal type popular. Nevertheless, this type is empirically grounded, and the recognition of the trait or traits is not a matter of uncontrolled intuition or emphasis in thought, but an observable peculiarity which may in fact be as complex and hard to define as a congeries of bodily characteristics. The symptomatic type is more valuable in the description and analysis of persons than of institutions and the like. It cannot be said, however, that it is of no use in regard to the latter. Indeed, in certain kinds of model construction, the symptomatic type may be the prime source for the determination of the qualities or elements to be selected for the model. The danger is that of "caricature." A caricature exaggerates one or more traits for the purposes of characterization and easy recognition. It is perhaps not without significance here that the interpreters of Max Weber have rendered his term "emphasis in thought" as "exaggeration." [12] An ideal type would then be a kind of caricature, distorting the given facts by intuitionist fancy. The symptomatic type, on the other hand, is an individual entity in a species or group which exhibits to a marked degree a trait or trait complex which uniquely characterizes the particular species or group. To give an institutional example: if it were considered that what uniquely distinguished parties from other kinds of social groups were their preoccupation with the securing of governmental posts for their leaders, a party which exhibited this trait to a marked degree and more so than others would be considered typical.

But generally speaking, and in light of the analyses which follow, it is fair to say that the average type is of much greater importance in the analysis of political (and generally social) institutions and processes than the symptomatic type. It is secured by comparison of as many entities of a particular sort as possible, and by recognition of what they have in common. These entities may be other politically relevant givens, besides institutions and processes, e.g., systems, situations and persons. Thus a typical administrator will exhibit certain traits. Empirical research may disclose (as indeed it did) that there are ten or more such traits,

[12] Parsons, 1937, p. 60.

but that any one administrator is apt to possess at most six of these traits, some of them being in fact contradictory. Obviously, it would be impossible to describe a typical administrator in general without doing violence to the empirical givens. It will be necessary to subdivide the class "administrator" into several kinds, each of which will possess an average type—a person who possesses six qualities in the requisite degree.

Typology has been especially important in the history of political science when it comes to systems. The question of how many types may be distinguished remains an open one. The question is more fully discussed below (Chapter 10). Here it may just be noted that any one or two criteria, such as "number of rulers" or "rule according to *nomos* or not," are likely to be inadequate. This inadequacy is illustrated by the rise of totalitarianism. Although it is the rule of one (presumably) and not according to *nomos,* totalitarian dictatorship cannot be adequately characterized by these two traits, simply because it shares these traits with absolute monarchy, despotism and tyranny—historical types from which it is politically important to distinguish totalitarian dictatorship, even though it might be convenient to denounce it in these terms.

The discovery of an average type can be, and often is, the basis of the construction of a model. Such construction may take the form of either adding or subtracting traits, as well as that of abstracting from special features of the concrete trait. The latter is a form of subtracting. Such models might be called empirical. Models may also be constructed by free fancy, like games; but this kind of model-construction has played only a limited role in political thought. Such models have been called utopias (Chapter 5) and have served to highlight the dissatisfactions felt with actual governments. They may be "negative" models in that they exhibit some of the traits most objected to in exaggeration. At that point they became caricatures, if empirically based. Perhaps the most celebrated model of this type is offered in Huxley's *Brave New World.* Its empirical base is only thinly disguised. Model-construction has a distinctive role not only in political theory but in political practice, as will be apparent in the sequel.

In any case, it ought to be evident from what has been said that morphological theory is an important part of political theory, unduly neglected by those who recognize only operations as a suitable field of theoretical inquiry. Indeed, since all political operations occur within "systems" (Note 1), a failure to comprehend the configurations within which they occur—that is to say, a failure to understand the problematical nature of all such configurations—is apt to lead to an overestimation of the significance of particular operations characteristic of particular or even unique configurations, e.g., the tendency of much behavioral work in the past to identify the operations of American or English-speaking political man with those of political mankind.

part

I

The Political Person and the Political Act

chapter

1

Man, Common and Uncommon: The Political Person

Personality is what a man really is.
W. Stern

ARISTOTLE'S *Politics* OPENS with a discussion of community, and asserts that the *polis* is the highest community, since it strives for the highest, the noblest goal or purpose. Ever since then, the discussion of politics has been concerned with collectives as the primary given of political life and inquiry. The state, meant as the *polis* in a more general sense, has been the focal point, and power has been seen as the state's most characteristic ingredient. Individualism and its political doctrine, liberalism, have rejected the implicit philosophy and insisted that the individual human being, the person, comes first, and out of him the community and the state must be constructed. Hobbes was the first major political philosopher who prefaced his discussion of the state by a long disquisition on man, but he has had many followers.[1] Since the scientific and historical record gives no evidence of man outside a community—even some of the primates live in communities [2]—this appears to be an untenable position. We can no more "define" man without political "community" than we can define political community without man. All

[1] Lasswell and Kaplan, 1950; pp. 3ff.; Catlin, 1927, pp. 141ff.

[2] Köhler, 1927, pp. 266ff.; Carpenter, 1934 and 1941; Yerkes, 1935; Zuckermann, 1932 and 1933.

the available evidence supports the view usually attributed to Aristotle that man is a "political being" in the sense of a communal being which can only be understood within the context of relations with other similar beings.[3] At this point it might be well to state at once that we are not, in keeping with a great tradition, concerned here with distinguishing man from the animals, for two reasons: first, because we do not know enough about animals, and second, because man has many qualities in common with the animals. The delineation of a configuration is not necessarily a matter of delimiting it in relation to other configurations.[4]

Discussions of politics in terms of human nature must start from the basic given of all political experience: community. It contains a paradox which has been unfolding over the centuries in the dialectic of political thought. The term "dialectic" is used here and throughout in the original Greek meaning derived from *dialegesthai*, i.e., to discourse or to discuss, and *not* in the Hegelian or Marxist sense of an inherent quality of history or society, except in so far as history and society are infused with intellectual activity. Dialectics is embodied in the words, not in the things with which politics deals. Dialectical materialism is, therefore, a contradiction in terms.[5] The dialectic of political thought has struggled with the paradox that "living in community" appears to be a universal trait of human nature, while at the same time these communities exhibit the greatest variety and, hence, seem to preclude the possibility of other "common" traits found wherever man is "in politics."

The environmentalist argument—environment taken to mean the social as well as physical setting within which human beings live and die—holds that the political and social environment is so effective in determining the behavior of men that "it is hopeless to attempt the construction of an adequate science of politics on the basis of alleged permanent factors in human nature." [6] This argument does not necessarily deny that there are common traits, such as the noted trait of "living in political communities," but it does deny that the traits which can be shown to be universal suffice to "explain the enormous variations in political conduct. . . ." [7] No reasonable argument in support of basic common traits would maintain, however, that these traits are suitable

[3] The term "animal" traditionally used for translating *dzōon* contains a gloss, *dzōon* signifying an animate being. So does "political" in our sense, since Aristotle wished to stress the relation to the *polis*, thus injecting a teleological judgment. What he says really "means": Man is an animate being who is intended to live in a *polis*.

[4] Koffka, 1935.

[5] Popper, 1945, vol. II, chap. 5; 1957; A. G. Meyer, 1954, chap. 3.

[6] Lasswell and Kaplan, 1950, p. 5.

[7] *Ibid.*

for explaining "the enormous variations"; rather, it *would* insist that it can explain the striking recurrences which provide the basis for the variations. If stated thus, the "human nature" argument would seem to have the better of it. For how could there be "variations" without something that is being "varied."

There has in recent years been a striking revival of the notion of such a basic "human nature," suggested by the inherent logic of the human condition, as well as by the primordial experience of the interdependence of man and the community. Philosophically, it has produced a new "anthropology." [8] This anthropology is variously supported by empirical ethnological research, although the prevalent mood of ethnological anthropologists has been relativistic until recently.[9] Additionally, legal thought has seen a revival of "natural law" which, starting around the beginning of the century, has been gaining momentum since the rise of totalitarianism.[10] Finally, modern psychological research, in spite of its rich variety of outlook and interpretation, has tended to reestablish man as the substratum of psychic manifestations.[11] All these revivals and rediscoveries are, of course, partly a response to the situation, the *political* situation, in which man finds himself today. The coming "world civilization," heralded by the ever closer contact and interaction of men from the most diverse backgrounds, beckons men to search for the common ground which unites them. Panhumanism offers itself as the view based on what men have in common. The very idea of a universal bill of rights, as embodied in the UN Declaration, is based upon it.[12]

But do these various views which recognize mankind as united through what men have in common offer a foundation for political theory? The classical natural law doctrine, as initiated by Plato and Aristotle, if not by the Sophists, and developed by the Stoics, stressed "reason" as the common ground, and derived from this reason certain elementary rules of communal conduct. They are embodied in the famous triad of the Roman law: *Juste vivere, neminem laedere, suum cuique tribuere*. As stated, these propositions are norms of conduct which could hardly be called descriptive of the normal behavior of man. Up to a

[8] Scheler, 1923; Alfred Weber, 1953, esp. chap. 1; Jaspers, 1947, pp. 212ff., and 1949, pp. 306ff.; Arendt, 1958, esp. pp. 22f.; Gehlen, 1940; Wild, 1953, chaps. 4, 7 and 8; Northrop, 1959, chaps. 7–9.

[9] Kluckhohn, 1949, p. 2 ("What common ground is there?"), and throughout; Eiseley, 1946 (Modern Library ed.), esp. pp. 79–126; Chardin, 1959; M. Mead, 1949, chaps. 3–7, and throughout.

[10] Friedrich, 1958, especially chap. 19; Haines, 1930, *passim;* d'Entrèves, 1951; Erik Wolf, 1955; Fuller, 1940; Rommen, 1947; Welzel, 1951; contra, Kelsen, 1957. Cf. also *Annales de Philosophie Politique*, vol. III, 1959, "Le Droit Naturel."

[11] Teilhard de Chardin, 1955, 1959; Allport, 1960, esp. part I.

[12] Friedrich, 1942, chap. 10; Hocking, 1959, chap. 4, and 1956, pp. 182ff. For the last aspect see Holcombe, 1948.

point, to be sure, man, communal man, lives justly, hurts no one and gives to everyone his due. Certainly, there have always been people, particular men, who did act like that. But men, at some time or another, and not infrequently, violate all these prescriptions, so that they will not do as descriptions of man's behavior.

The history of political thought is strewn with alternative suggestions of a more or less speculative type. Plato made *eros* the universal motif, Hobbes thought men predominantly strive for power, Hume saw their behavior moulded by custom and utility, both rooted in "passion," Rousseau insisted that "sympathy" and other emotions were at the center of political conduct. If one considers these various views and their implications for politics, it becomes clear that the fault they all share is the attempt to reduce human nature to *one* dominant principle, and to try to interpret political community in terms of this common ground. Any such attempt is foredoomed to failure because no inherent hierarchy can be established among several such universal traits. Besides the universal trait of living in communities which has been stressed at the outset, four traits seem to have been generally recognized: pliability and adaptability, having and sharing of purposes, experiencing oneself as self, and communicating with each other through language. All these traits are in a sense comprised in the old idea of reason; none of them can be conceived without implying the notion of reasoning of some sort. But unfortunately a great many rather dogmatic and untenable arguments have been advanced under this heading in terms of various forms of rationalist metaphysics. Reason has even been personified—it was the goddess of the French Revolution—but has in any case been treated as if it designated some kind of substantive content or other, such as the classical natural law doctrine just mentioned. The problem is further complicated by the controversy over reasoning in terms of values (or ends) as contrasted with that in terms of means [13]—a distinction which is tenable only when used heuristically. Human nature's second most universal trait, presenting a further paradox, is its range of pliability in response to diverse situations. The common human nature is not an actuality, but a potentiality. The various traits which have been isolated and given preeminence [14] are all there, to be kaleidoscopically combined into endless variations. Pliability and the resultant adaptability mean that man is forever inventing new ways of coping with novel situations—seeming dead alleys that provide the challenge for a new departure. This capacity to combine varying

[13] Max Weber's dichotomy of *Wertrationalität* v. *Zweckrationalität*, 1922 (English, in part, 1954), and 1925, pp. 16ff. Cf. also Parsons, 1937, pp. 642ff., and the brief comment on the means versus ends dichotomy in Parsons and Shils, 1951, p. 413. Cf. also the interesting note on the rational and reasonable, Aron, 1962.

[14] Parsons, 1951, pp. 32–33, speaks of plasticity and sensitivity as "biological properties" or "characteristics."

"traits" of his "nature" as man confronts different situations is exemplified in much of the human experience that is analyzed in later chapters.

Situations and responses to situations are, therefore, vital elements of political analysis at all times and under all conditions. A man is situated, he occupies a situation, when concrete aspects of his environment, and more particularly his political environment, are meaningfully related to his behavior, the actions he wants to take, the thoughts he tries to think, the emotions he inclines to feel. It is not enough to speak of the acts [15] in specifying a situation. For the meaningful relationship involves thoughts and feelings just as much, and sometimes more so, than actions. The political situation of the United States in the world probably is more meaningfully related to the thoughts and feelings of Americans than to their actions! Similarly a response to a situation may be a thought or feeling rather than an act, and it is misleading to neglect such responses in political analysis. It is the range and variety of thought and feeling that constitute the pliability of man, communal man. As every response to a situation brings about a new situation differentiated from the preceding one by what the response has added: $S(1) + R = S(2)$, the infinite complexity of all political relations is traceable to this primordial fact of human nature.[16]

The third primordial trait of man *qua* man is the range of his purposiveness. It is being stressed in differentiating Homo sapiens from his nearest relatives in the animal kingdom, the primates. These, to be sure, have purposes, but they are exceedingly short-range and limited in scope. The range of man's purposiveness, especially the capacity to pursue a purpose over long periods of time, even exceeding his own life span, is closely linked to memory. Memory is the ability to recall past events of every variety, from eating to dreams, and more especially thoughts. Memory "feeds back" these past events and through such feedbacks persistency in purpose is achieved. Man can no more be "without purpose" than he can be without responses to environment, or without community. This "being with purpose" is the foundation of reasoning. One does not need to adopt Hobbes's cynical idea that reason is reckoning in order to perceive this close tie of purposiveness with the rational faculty of man which served as the basis for most "natural law."

The particular purposes are very varied, of course. They include satisfying the basic physical and material needs which man's physique imposes, more particularly, food, clothing, housing. Even these elementary requirements have proliferated into a bewildering variety of individual and group preferences, partly determined by climate, partly by

[15] Lasswell and Kaplan, 1950, pp. 4–5.
[16] Hampshire, 1959, chap. 1.

ors too numerous to mention. We find the same cultural tion in the field of sex and love.[17] It is, therefore, hardly surprising tnat the political sphere should exhibit a comparable richness of diversity in purpose and consequent practice. If kinds of apes can be as different in temperament and predisposition as chimpanzees and orangutans,[18] the corresponding diversities among human groupings need occasion no surprise. It is, therefore, not possible to arrive at an empirical proposition which describes man in terms of a single purpose,[19] be it power, order, freedom, or any other. Nor are we really helped by such "realistic" remarks as Goethe's celebrated *Der Hunger und die Liebe erhalten das Weltgetriebe.* Not unity of purpose, but variety, variability (in keeping with man's adaptability) and multiplicity of purpose are the common traits of man. He is, in a very basic sense, a plural being.

This built-in plurality of purpose has in recent years been elaborated in sociological studies of the "roles," and it has been rightly remarked and empirically demonstrated that every man has a number of such roles to fulfill.[20] It is evident that the role a man plays makes his function effective, and both role and function are meaningful in terms of purpose. Behavioral analysis in terms of role and function is, therefore, clearly in the last analysis teleological. Because of the primordial purposiveness of man we cannot dispense with the teleological view in the sciences of man.[21] Nor is there any basic ground for juxtaposing the organic and the purposive, as has so often been done; because the purposive *is* part of the human *organon,* and the two are necessarily part of any analysis of political phenomena.[22] The desire to be rid of purpose in scientific inquiry was understandable at a time when natural science sought to free itself of speculative, superimposed fetters, derived from revelation and devoid of empirical grounds. Even in the study of man such notions as were, for example, embodied in natural law impeded the objective inquiry into to-be-observed matters of fact. That is to say, not only value as an object of inquiry, but also value discovered through scientific inquiry,

[17] M. Mead, 1949, pp. 51–160, gives a good general survey.

[18] Hooton, 1940, pp. 3–51.

[19] We speak of "purpose" rather than "goals," because the latter suggests something completely "outside and beyond" the person, whereas "purpose" suggests the positing of the end. Contra, Parsons, 1951, *passim.* In certain contexts (see below, Chap. 2) "objective" is to be preferred to "purpose."

[20] On the role and its importance within the social setting see Parsons, 1951; "what an actor does in his relations with others in the context of its functional significance for the social system" (p. 25) he calls a person's role.

[21] Emmet, 1958, pp. 103ff.

[22] W. Y. Elliott's suggestion of a "co-organic" nature, while preoccupied with the false antithesis of organic and purposive, is fundamentally sound in seeking to transcend the dichotomy. But it seems to me that the word "function" in conjunction with "purpose" provides an adequate tool for political analysis. Cf. 1928, chap. 12.

and value, therefore, believed in by and presumably motivating the scientist.[23] But when empirical inquiry itself discloses the ever-presence of purpose, it is contrary to scientific truth to continue to insist that the study of man, and more especially political inquiry, can be carried forward without continued reference to purpose. And this means not only past purpose, but present and future purpose. A value-free political science is therefore a contradiction in terms; for if it is value-free, it is no longer science. (For an elaboration see Chapter 2.)

At this point the basic human experience illuminating this purposiveness must be faced. This basic experience is that of *self*.[24] Such self-experience is the fourth basic trait humans have in common. The self is that something in man which is believed to persist as he grows up, matures, ages and passes away. It is, by each self, felt to be self-identical in spite of all the evolution and transformation that it may experience. The self may also be described as an "aggregate of memory feedbacks." Thus each man experiences, properly speaking, only this one self which is *himself*, but he imputes a similar experience to other men, and thereby posits the uniformity which unites him with other men into mankind. But it is only the selfness which he imputes, not the particularity of his own self. This particularity he experiences on the contrary as distinct, unique, and never before or after to be repeated. It may be a figment of his imagination, but he feels it so. It is the self here-and-now in all its rich freedom of potentiality, the "I," the only one and his properties. This self needs other selves, the "you's," because they are like him, and because he cannot experience himself as different, except in community with others, who experience him as the "other," the "you." And since the others are different, community requires adaptation, and it presupposes common purposes (Chapter 8). Such common purposes of a community of "selves" can never be completely common, precisely because the selves are separate and apart. The core of the community of purposes is, at the same time, the fact that only such community allows human beings to become "selves." [25]

The coming together of human beings into communities and the experience of self in confronting the "other" is inconceivable without communication. The elaboration of communication is *language*. In any elaborate sense, community means, therefore, language. The ability to

[23] It may be objected here that it is not the study but the promotion of values that is rejected by those who want political science to be value-free. But our reply is that you cannot separate the two, that the study necessarily promotes a value, or the opposite if it is shown to be a disvalue.

[24] G. H. Mead, 1934; Allport, 1960, chaps. 1 and 2.

[25] Rosenstock-Huessy, 1956, *passim*. The prophetic form in which R.-H. likes to clothe his thoughts ought not to be allowed to stand in the way of recognizing the depth of his insight.

communicate by words is the fifth basic trait of man, closely linked with the other four.

We say basic trait, because no community of men is known which did not, does not possess "the gift of speech and a well ordered language." [26] Language, *logos*, has, therefore, at times been made *the* distinctive trait of man. It *is one* of them. It provides symbols (Chapter 5) which serve the function of effective communication between groups of human beings. The symbolism may embody terms of reference to things in the broadest sense of data experienced as external to the speaker and listener; it may also embody terms of reference to feelings, thoughts and other goings-on which are internal to the speaker and have to be transposed through empathy, sympathy or analogy to similar goings-on in the listener. All language is listening as well as speaking; the ear is almost as much the organ of language as are the tongue and the larynx,[27] though the latter are customarily and understandably stressed by the linguist.

Language is embedded in culture, as culture is embedded in language. The two form "Siamese twins"; they cannot live apart from each other. This important aspect of language has been at times overstated, when it has been alleged that a given language is capable of handling *all* references and meanings that a given culture is capable of. It seems on the contrary striking that no language possesses this capability; that all languages fall short of the richness and variety of human experience; the constant striving of all languages is directed toward finding more adequate expressions, and the role of poetry in all community life, and more especially in politics, is rooted in this fact.

Language, therefore, also limits community. It has been said that "as our scientific experience grows we must learn to fight the implications of language." [28] But not only scientific experience grows; political, legal and social experience grow also, and much political conflict results from linguistic shortcomings—the tyranny of words, in an expressive phrase.[29] These difficulties are in part rooted in the interpenetration of language and experience which has caused men from the primitives to the moderns

[26] Sapir, in his article on language in the *ESS*, 1933; Vossler, 1925, chaps. 1 and 3.

[27] Vossler, 1925, chap. 2; Rosenstock-Huessy, 1956, pp. 140ff.

[28] Sapir, 1933, p. 157. This truth has especially serious implications for a political science worthy of its name; such a science stands in constant danger of being engulfed by the ideas and ideologies of the political communities to which the seeker of this kind of scientific truth belongs. But it is not a matter of excluding the values, but of making them explicit, even more, making them the focal point of his inquiry—a special kind of objectivity which understands its own subjectivity and transcends it. Cf. below, Chap. 2.

[29] Chase, *The Tyranny of Words,* a popularized presentation of some of the findings of modern semantics; for this field cf. the classic by Ogden and Richards, 1923.

to mistake words for things and to seek for the "essence" of reality in the words used to designate this reality as experienced. Language "does not as a matter of actual behavior stand apart from or run parallel to direct experience, but completely interpenetrates with it." And, therefore, "for the normal person every experience, real or potential, is saturated with verbalism." [30] Because of this fact, linguistic symbols can come to serve as substitutes for the reality to which they once referred and which no longer exists.

Language provides the means for communicating not only in space but in time. It binds the present with its past and its future. Human culture with its vast storehouses of past experience would be impossible if these stores of knowledge and experience could not be transmitted from generation to generation. More especially, political institutions are the outgrowth of communicated experience, experience that has been discussed and argued about and finally verbalized in distinctive form. In fact, "time" emerges through language, because it enables political persons to communicate not only with each other, but with the past and the future.[31] The relation of language to nationality and race has been a major weapon in the armory of modern politics. Nationalism has posited a necessary and close relationship. The careful refutation of these notions by anthropologists and linguists has not been able to dislodge the passion which these contentions arouse. The reason is political; the link to nationality and race may be wholly specious; all available evidence shows that it is. But what is not specious is that a common language or its equivalent in common sayings and habits of speaking is one of the decisive bonds of political, as of all other, communities, as the fifth basic trait of political man. Such determined efforts as that to "Americanize" immigrants through the teaching of English, similarly to Russify the Finns, to "Italianize" the Tyrolese or to cement the new nations of Ireland and Israel through the revival of ancient "tongues" are sometimes successful and sometimes not. Such efforts are based upon a political insight, or perhaps instinct, which often overestimates this *one* element in community. Similarly, the growing linguistic diversity of India, as its many-cultured subgroups seek to escape from the predominance of one of them which speaks Hindi, constitutes both a serious danger to the political cohesion

[30] Sapir, *loc cit.*

[31] Burke's famous phrases expounding "prescription" and "presumption," in a speech on the constitution, May 7, 1782, *Works*, chap. 7, pp. 91–104, really aim at this point, though the specific role of language is not mentioned but implied. In terms of our analysis, Burke was the captive of the language of the past, as embodied in the institutions which he knew. Therefore, he could assert that "the species is wise, and . . . as a species, it almost always acts right." These thoughts embody Burke's historicized version of Rousseau's general will.

of India and a sign of political vitality which may well be resolved in effective federalism [32] (Chapter 33).

Besides community, the other three basic traits of plasticity, purposiveness and selfhood, are dynamically related to language. There can be neither purpose nor selfhood without it. For language also bears a most distinctive relation to individuality. Each person expresses himself in the style of his speaking perhaps more directly than in any other way. That is why politicians must be "speakers." Their mode of communicating themselves to their fellow men generates emotions, thoughts and other expressions of selfhood which bind them into a community that is thus continuously reborn through speaking and listening. The mutuality of genuine community is here vividly seen: both leader and led listen as well as speak, and in doing the one also implicitly do the other (Chapter 9). That all adapting to new situations involves linguistic innovation we have already hinted above. It is not necessary to elaborate upon this theme here, since it will be recurrent throughout our analysis.[33]

We pause to tie up what has so far been said. Man is a being living in communities, pliable and infinitely adaptable, having and sharing purposes which specify his communal function, experiencing himself as a self and communicating with himself and others by a language (vocal signs). In some ways all this was "meant" by Aristotle when he called man a political being—for the *polis* allowed for all these manifestations of manhood. But in the course of time, the word "political" having been both broadened and narrowed,[34] this set of "meanings" has become obscured and needs explicit restatement. When, under what aspects or conditions, may we call such a man a person? "Persona" originally refers to the mask worn in proceedings before a court or in the theatre. It was therefore meant to hide all the self but that role which he was to play in the proceedings. As we said before, each self plays many roles, and thus would be many persons. But in modern thought, the concept of the person has just the opposite meaning. It designates what we might call the totality of the roles an individual is called upon to play. In spite of the multiplicity of purposes, roles and functions, whether memories or potentialities, there is an over-all unity which binds all of them together into a person. The organized combination of individual traits which he displays in fulfilling his varied roles, is called a person's

[32] Cf. S. S. Harrison, 1957; Deutsch, 1953.

[33] Reference should be made also to Jespersen, 1922, 1949; Shenton, Sapir and Jesperson, 1931; Vendryes, 1921; Vossler, 1925; Weinreich, 1953; Wiener, 1950, chaps. 4 and 5; Woolner, 1938.

[34] Broadened by being applied to all kinds of orders, not just the *polis;* narrowed by being applied only to that part of the order which has to do with its ordering (Chap. 9 and following below).

personality.[35] This unity is *experienced* by the individual, though he cannot prove it, and it is this experience which makes the self a person.[36] And only when the community is composed of such persons does it become a *political* community in the strict sense, because only such persons can order their relations, by communicating with each other concerning their purposes, by adapting themselves to each other, and thus by elaborating roles and functions in the order to be. At this point, we pass from the personal to the public sphere, so to speak. For the ordering of their relations makes such persons exhibit themselves to each other. They thus become a "public."

Yet, in ordering their relations, and elaborating the roles and functions, politically, they produce a differentiation which has given rise to a great many doctrines which sought to establish or maintain the idea of a preordained group qualified by superior ability to govern or rule the rest (Chapters 10 and 20), various grounds for their superiority being alleged, such as divine selection, exceptional intellectual ability, wealth and the descent by "blood" from such superior beings. As against such notions, modern thought has favored the notion of a general capacity for participation of all in government. This notion is the heart of the American tradition of the common man.[37] He is not the average man, but the communal man, that is to say, everyman in his communal participation. Since such communal participation varies greatly, the image of the common man contains a normative component. This component might be highlighted by a statement such as that Abraham Lincoln was the common man incarnate. Incidentally, the writings and speeches of Lincoln show clearly the religious origin of the notion: the people, the common men speaking through their majority, are able, so the doctrine holds, to guide even the most eminent statesman, because they are

[35] W. Stern, 1923 (2nd ed.); Allport, 1937, chap. 2, esp. p. 48: "personality is—what a man really is." This brief definition Allport elaborates as follows: "P. is the dynamic organization within the individual of those psycho-physical systems that determine his unique adjustments to his environment." He presents this definition as a synthesis of contemporary psychological usage. The further elucidation of the terms of this definition, based upon a general survey of the various definitions, philosophical, legal and social-scientist, shows it to be close to the simpler one offered in the text. More particularly the "psycho-physical systems" are later shown to be "traits." Note also the diagrammatic summary of definitions on p. 49.

[36] Scheler, a, 1961, p. 243, "*die unmittelbare miterlebte Einheit des Erlebens,—nicht ein nur gedachtes Ding hinter und ausser dem unmittelbar Erlebten,*" romanticizes this central insight, by speaking of "erleben" instead of "erfahren" and makes it thereby purely subjective. It is precisely the fact that the self becomes through the experience of its unity a "thing behind and outside the immediate experience" which establishes it as a "person."

[37] Friedrich, 1942, *passim;* what follows is the core of that book, not in ideological but in ontological perspective.

said to be the voice of God.[38] The true meaning of such notions is not that everyone is equally good at governing, or even at criticizing the government, but that it is *unpredictable* who among the people might be either good at it or interested enough to participate effectively.

It is obvious that there are two distinct levels to which this proposition might apply, one the level of actual government *operation*, the other the level of popular *control* of the government. Just as the Judaeo-Christian religious faith maintained that the humblest might be religiously elect, the ones most gifted in the charismatic sense of I Corinthians 13, so the democratic faith, taken in its broadest meaning and *including* the totalitarian perversions of it, maintains that the humblest person might be not only most gifted and dedicated to controlling the government, but also to participating in it. But while the religious faith is wholly transcendent and dependent upon revelation, the democratic faith can and ought to be subjected to scientific empirical testing, as well as to reasoning exploration.

Such rational exploration discloses that the notion of unpredictability is related to the five basic traits which constitute man as man. This holds true just as much for the participation *in*, as for the controlling *of*, government. The persons whom we have seen characterized in their potential common manhood by communal living, infinite adaptability, shared purposiveness, selfhood and lingual communication, are certainly displaying the greatest variations in all these basic traits. But it is common experience that even among individual members of one family the extent to which human potentiality is actualized in these several respects is unpredictably divergent. None of the factors which in the past have been argued as the basis for a "natural" elite has ever sufficed to make it even probable that propensities in these five basic traits are in actuality distributed in a model way to favor the chosen group.

Four propositions are particularly relevant to any empirical scientific test of the asserted chance distribution of the basic traits. These need to be implemented, of course, further by tests concerning those more specific traits or characteristics which constitute the ability to participate effectively in rule or government. We shall, therefore, now restrict the argument to the general traits which are called for in the controlling of the government, that is to say, the "role of the citizen," as contrasted with that of the "ruler." But before these empirical tests can be discussed, it is necessary to free the discussion of a set of rationalist assumptions which were very generally made in the age when the "belief in the common man" arose. For it is these rationalist assumptions which are usually the

[38] Cf. the recent study by W. J. Wolf, 1959, esp. p. 150: "In the Puritan interpretation the people became aware that they were instruments of Providence. This was slowly transmuted into a reliance upon the people as the corporate bearer of God's wisdom." There are, of course, medieval precedents for this, developed by the church in its struggles with secular powers. Cf. Gierke, 1939, pp. 143ff.

butt against which are directed the doubts which have challenged the asserted chance distribution of the capacity to control the government.

The assumptions are three, but they are interrelated and all rest upon an overestimation of the role of reason in the communal life of most men. This excessive, rationalist faith in reason was voiced by many, but by none perhaps with greater verve than Thomas Paine, who wrote: "Certain I am that when opinions are free, either in matters of government or religion, truth will finally and powerfully prevail."[39] Put briefly, what this means, as far as government is concerned, is this: give a man the facts and plenty of time, and in the end he will see the rational, the reasonable way to act, and having seen the way, he will follow it.

This general proposition may be broken down into three distinct propositions. First, a man, when confronted with a problem, especially a communal problem, will make every effort to learn all the facts he can. Second, in light of these facts, he will eventually arrive at a sensible, rational conclusion as to how to deal with the problem, using the knowledge of experts, when needed. And third, man possesses or at least will always eventually acquire the steadfastness, the strength of character, as it is called, to carry out the conclusion, i.e., to act rationally as well as to think rationally. Common experience contradicts each of these propositions; most men neither seek the facts nor draw rational conclusions from what facts they know, nor do they always follow the conclusions they have been led to draw. This common experience is further reinforced by the findings of modern psychology and social science. The work of Freud[40] and Pareto,[41] to mention only two famous examples, contains the evidence in support of a rejection of such rationalist assumptions. The anti-liberal movements which have fed upon the findings of these and other scientific explorations have usually drawn two erroneous inferences which are also very widespread in scientific writings in this field. First, they have argued that because men are not as rational as the old ideology assumed, they are wholly irrational (irrationalist fallacy). Second, they have maintained that the few who act in accordance with the rationalist premises (Communists, fascists, autonomous men, and so forth) are predestined to govern (elitist fallacy). We shall later consider these fallacies in their context (Chapters 2, 8 and 20). For our purposes at the moment, it is sufficient to drop the rationalist premises, and return to the four propositions about the chance distribution of a capacity to participate in controlling the government.

The first of these propositions may be stated as follows: the political judgments of all men are fallible. This is due to the fact that political

[39] Paine, 1794, p. 286.

[40] Freud, 1940, 1949; see also Lasswell, 1930.

[41] Pareto, 1935, vol. I, and *passim.*

judgments deal with the contingent which is only in part, if at all, foreseeable.[42] Good judgment as to whether a certain proposed course of action will work turns not only upon its technical features, which are subject to expert appraisal, but also upon an understanding of the people whom it affects and their preferences (value judgments). Such understanding is rarely found to any greater extent among those who possess technical expertise than among the average; often their very expertise interferes with their balanced appraisal of this factor or set of factors. Assuming that in any given population the distribution of the probability of errors of judgments is random, only a system which provides for the effective participation of all will enable those with potentially high scores of good judgment to come to the fore. Errors of judgment result from a great variety of factors, depending upon the extent of experience in many different fields—a corollary to our first proposition. As a consequence, different persons will score high in different fields of political activity and at different times.[43]

The second proposition specifies the collective aspects of the problem by stating that it is not the political judgment of the individual, but of a large group of persons that is sought in organizing the control of the government. Attempts made to argue for the adequate, let alone superior, judgment of every particular man, like those of the early enthusiasts for democracy, have failed; the position is obviously untenable. The proposition which is tenable essentially amounts to asserting that in any population the collective judgment of a majority is more likely to be "right" in the sense of allowing for the various contingencies involved than the political judgment of any one individual, no matter how superior. This proposition is a probability judgment and may occasionally prove wrong. It has traditionally been highly offensive to intellectuals, whose spleen was succinctly voiced by Goethe when he said: "Majority is nonsense, intelligence is only in the few." The opposite view was stated (and overstated) by Lincoln: "Remember, Dick, to keep close to the people—they are always right and will mislead no one." They are not *always right*, but the probability is good that they are. The reason for this proposition's correctness is to be found in the dependence of what is "right" in politics upon the value preferences prevalent in a given group or community. A majority is more apt to be "right," because any course of action is, to the extent that value preferences are involved in it, affected by what the majority prefers. It might hence be objected that the proposition is tautological. But this is not so, because the value preferences, while important, are not the only determinants of rightness. The more technical or external to the community they are, like those involved in

[42] Aristotle, *Rhetoric*, III. 17.
[43] Bruner, 1944.

foreign policy and military affairs, the less likely it is to be true. As a consequence, it is possible to say that the more important these value preferences are for a decision, the greater is the probability for the second proposition. There is another reason for the truth of this proposition, which leads to the third proposition.

The third proposition concerns the content of the judgments involved in politics. These judgments do not deal with matters of exceptional or rare value, more especially not with matters of taste. A failure to bear this in mind has been at the bottom of a great deal of misdirected criticism of the common man, and of democracy.[44] Actually, the judgments of politics are largely concerned with common needs and communal value preferences, as embodied in policies. Policies usually are proposals for changing *existing practice*. Existing practice is part of the experience of most members of the group or community, the community presumably being a going concern. The judgment required of men in politics is usually the answer to a question of the following kind: "Is this policy recommended by the experts good or bad, right or wrong? that is, does it or does it not run counter to our values as embodied in beliefs, customs and habits?" The question frequently asks for a comparative evaluation, in a form somewhat like this: "Seeing that the proposed policy or course of action $p(n)$ required to deal with the need, N runs counter to our values, V, is the loss L involved in damaging them worth the gain in regard to N?" This can actually be put into a simple formula: If N is equal to or greater than V minus L, then $p(n)$ will be adopted. The difficulty with the formula is that N, V and L are often qualitatively so different that no quantitative specification is possible. This is, of course, precisely the reason why "anybody's judgment is as good as the next man's," and the argument as to $p(n)$ can be settled only by the various members of the community who "sense" N, V and L. But it is not always so, and an approximation to quantification can be attempted. For example, suppose the proposed policy is that of leveling a sales tax; here the need for additional taxation may be quantifiable as well as V, the value, that is the custom of paying only the price of goods, and the loss (L) of paying a certain percentage. Even in such an instance, the range of contingency is considerable, and hence the probability of the "right judgment" being a chance distribution is very great. Hence the third proposition that political judgments are common judgments about common needs supports the general premise about chance distribution of the capacity to participate in controlling the government.

The fourth and last proposition concerns the role of character in the forming of political judgments. Character, according to the dictionary is

[44] Lippincott, 1938, who discusses the cases of Carlyle, Ruskin, Matthew Arnold, among others. For America, cf. Parrington, II, 1927–1930, pp. 75ff., 451ff.

"moral vigor or firmness." A man of character, that is, knows or at least senses his values, and is steadfast in adhering to them. He is a man who is consistent in his actions, who follows a persistent course. Whatever the values may be, one can recognize the man of character by his self-consistency. This consistency matters greatly in political judgments. Hence the proposition that character is important in moulding political judgment. Character is a personality trait which is found in all classes and conditions of men; its distribution is chance, and there are no clusters of men of character in any particular group of experts or in any elite, whether of intellect, wealth or prowess. Indeed, as far as intellect is concerned, it has often been observed that intellect endangers the character. The cause is not far to seek. Any deviation from or breach of belief, custom or habit, that is, any violation of value preferences, is more readily "rationalized" by a "clever" man than by a simple one. The recurrent lack of political influence by the intellectuals is closely related to their ability thus to rationalize failure, to uphold the values they believe in, whether they be prevalent or deviant.[45] This *need* not be the case, however; Socrates' celebrated argument in favor of consistency shows that even a man of great intellect may be a man of character. But the very fact that his behavior has been celebrated proves how exceptional it is for an intellectual to insist that he must maintain his values no matter what the consequences.[46] Be that as it may, it is certainly true that character, being important for political judgment and exhibiting a chance distribution, also supports the general proposition.

The four propositions when taken together constitute a clear-cut empirical basis for the so-called "belief in the common man," even though the rationalist premises upon which it was originally based are largely discarded. What matters from a scientific viewpoint, however, is that they support the proposition that the ability to participate in the controlling of the government is "unpredictable." The same holds true, as will be shown later (Chapter 10) regarding the ability to participate in the government itself. Much in the preceding analysis depends, however, upon the empirical grounds for speaking of function, purpose and value, and to these interrelated questions we must next turn.

[45] For a striking argument along this line, see Benda, 1927; also Milosz, 1957.

[46] Chroust, 1957, esp. chaps. 7 and 8, develops a cognate point. There is an obvious link to what Riesman, 1950, has called the "inner-directed man," whom he then has, I believe mistakenly, sought to find in one particular period of American history.

chapter

2

Function, Purpose and Value

Inert refusal cannot save
From work, by mere negation;
Nor can perfection be attained
By bald renunciation.

. . .

While he who can—his senses curbed—
With active powers proceed
To work without attachment, may
Be termed a man indeed.

BHAGAVAD-GITA, Canto III
(transl. Arthur W. Ryder)

NO POLITICAL ANALYSIS has ever been undertaken without touching values. Efforts have at times been made to work out a "value-free" approach in the name of science, objectivity, and similar objectives. From a logical viewpoint, such propositions are self-contradictory, since they make their standard, be it science, objectivity, or what have you, the *highest* value to which all other values must be subordinated, usually without offering, of course, any proof or evidence for such a contention. Indeed, in many instances it is not even a contention, but treated as a "matter-of-course," that is to say, as self-evident.[1] The basic datum of politics, on the other hand, is the fact that men value their life, as delineated in the preceding discussion of man, their communal life as contrasted with their mere physical existence, above all else. It *is* the highest good in the objective sense of empirical *being*, and the precondition of all other experience, political or otherwise.[2]

Value has been discussed from so many different viewpoints that its

[1] The most recent and very thoughtful effort at such a value-free approach is Brecht, 1959, who bases his argument for value-relativism upon what he considers the requirements of science. Cf. esp. pp. 117ff., 135ff., 261ff. Contra, and in support of our view, Krutch, 1959, chap. 10.

[2] But see further discussion of *Summum bonum* below, p. 611.

meaning is often obscured by built-in contradictions. Value is a configuration in the data confronting man, and more particularly political man. This configuration is experienced by the beholder as an objective datum, and elicits in him the approval of the datum in question, crystallizing in the judgment: This *A* ought to be. The three dimensions of the situation involving "ought to be" should be kept clearly distinct: the datum in the object world "containing" or "constituting" the value, the desire or will or similar response elicited in the beholder of the datum, and the judgment expressed by him in light of both. We shall deal with each of these dimensions in turn, the second consisting in a brief consideration of function and purpose (including interest). By way of introduction, a common confusion about "ought to be" needs to be removed which arises as a result of two kinds of value judgments. There are two primary modes of such "ought to be" judgments. These may be expressed by the phrase *A has* value or *possesses* value, or by the phrase *A' is* a value. When social scientists speak of, for example, the value system of a particular society, such as the Navaho, they often fail to state whether they mean one or the other or both. Frequently they mean still something else: namely, the value *judgments* of the Navahos, whether in the first or second form. The judgment that *A* has value usually means that *A* is related to some *B*, that it may be useful in securing *B*, helpful in maintaining *B*, and so forth; it might be called instrumental value. The judgment that *A' is* a value usually means that *A'* is a quality which when found in objects induces men to prefer such objects, other things being equal. We may call this value concept "inherent value." [3]

It is important to recognize that these two kinds of value are not mutually exclusive: that is to say, the two terms are not dichotomic. Any *A* having a value, such as a price, and thus being instrumental in securing money, may also exhibit the quality *A'* which is its inherent value. Economists have had occasion to be concerned with this contrast between inherent and instrumental value, calling the latter "market value" or "exchange value." [4] Thus the Venus of Milo might have a value of 1 million dollars because it *is* very beautiful. In all such cases, the two values are related, but they are not identical and ought not to be confused.

Political phenomena, like economic phenomena, exhibit both inherent and instrumental values. Thus a plan for greater Boston may be sound, that is, feasible and based on true facts, which would be its inherent value; but it may also fetch a prize of $5,000 or not, mould the thought of legislators or not, stir public opinion or not, and these would be instrumental values of such a plan. The relationship and possible conflict between in-

[3] Other terms, such as "objective" and "material," though at times employed, are apt to cause confusion because of the valuational tinge attaching to these words.

[4] For a recent review, see O. H. Taylor, 1960, pp. 101ff., 188ff., 264ff., 325ff., 344ff., 450ff. Cf. also Myrdal, 1929, 1953, chaps. 2, 4, and 6.

herent and instrumental values is at the very heart of all political phenomena, and such phenomena cannot be "known" without taking these values into account. It does not suffice, however, to consider only the instrumental values; the inherent values are at least as central to the task of political inquiry. Preoccupation with the instrumental values leads to value-relativism, while overconcern with inherent values induces value-dogmatism (or value-absolutism). The science of government, as here developed, seeks to avoid either of these pitfalls, and to elucidate inherent value, while exploring instrumental value, realizing that the exploration of instrumental value may change the understanding of inherent value.

Both inherent and instrumental value *are there*. They are not subjective artifacts, imputed to the entities which are said to be valuable or have value by subjects who apprehend them as devoid of such value. The experiencing of value is as much a primary experience as observation of facts devoid of value.[5] Values are, in other words, facts, given as much as any other facts. The self, experiencing such values, experiences them as outside itself and inherent *in*, instrumental *for*, objective givens. The dichotomy of facts versus values, which restricted the term "fact" to certain kinds of facts, more particularly to the facts of physical nature, has become obsolete as a result of the discoveries of modern, post-Newtonian physics. Nothing whatever *is there* in any other sense than the sense of being experienced as being there. The old argument about the ghost that is "experienced" but is not there rests on a fallacy; for, the statement that whatever *is there*, is there in the sense of being experienced as being there, does not permit the statement that all that is being experienced as being there, *is there*. Experience may deceive, and often does. This patent observation applies to all kinds of experience and, therefore, does not provide a basis for contrasting value experience with other kinds of experience. That something may be believed to be valuable when it is not parallels the fact that something may be believed to be straight when it is not, such as the well-known optical illusion of a broken stick seen in a glass of water.

The object-like existence of values, facing the value-experiencing self as a datum to be experienced, ought not to be claimed as the ground for asserting that values are absolute, never changing, eternal, as Plato did.[6] For everything that man experiences as existing he experiences as chang-

[5] R. S. Hartman, a, 1958. According to Hartman's classification, the approach here employed would be classified as "cognitivist": but I am not sure whether "naturalist" or "non-naturalist"—in any case, "empiricist." My view is close to Recaséns Siches, 1948, but influenced by N. Hartmann.

[6] This emphasis on the never changing, eternal aspects of values (ideas) by Plato stands in curious contrast to his argument for the immortality of the soul, which is said to be immortal because it is constantly changing. *Phaedrus*, p. 245.

ing. "Unchanging," "everlasting" and "absolute" are terms which are not given in any experience had by man. They are logical negations of the actual experiences of changing, passing, dependent actuality. They are also "statistical projections" of the experience of data which change very little, last a long time, or are comparatively independent. Values change, like all else, but in changing they continue to become objectified. Furthermore, in the historical perspective, values acquire a specious sort of changeless, everlasting, independent quality, as do all things that have been and, therefore, can no longer change, because they have passed away.

The foregoing reflections show why values are not "ideal" in the sense of being opposed to "real." This ideal quality has more particularly been asserted regarding inherent values.[7] Values, it has been said, are never "realized." But this statement refers to something else than the alleged "ideal" nature of value. Value is a particular dimension of being: namely, the dimension of "ought to be." This "ought to be" may or may not be actualized; in ethical and legal norms it very often is not actualized. But this absence of actuality is not inherent in the value or norm. The beauty of Rembrandt's *Night Watch* is fully actual, it *is there*. When it is said that it constitutes value, such a statement "means" *inter alia* that it "ought to be there." The norm "Thou shalt not kill" implies that "life is valuable," that "life ought to be there." It remains just as much a value if no one is killed and the norm is, therefore, fully actualized, as if many are killed.

Because values are real, because they *are there*, facing the self, every self, value experience is universal. Some values may be experienced only by some persons, but the basic values are experienced by most persons. The parallels are other basic givens, such as colors, forms and sounds. The basic colors, forms and sounds—red, white and green, line, triangle and quadrangle, or the scale—are called basic precisely because they are nearly universally experienced. They are that, in spite of color-blind men and other deviants. Correspondingly, the occasional occurrence of value-blind persons need not disturb us unduly. The fact that they cannot experience even the basic values should be taken to confirm, rather than put into jeopardy, the objective existence of values. The test of the genuineness of experience is that such experience *may not occur*.

Before this analysis can be pushed forward, and to a kind of conclusion, function and purpose will have to be further explored. We saw that multiple purpose is a basic aspect or trait of man. To such plural purposiveness corresponds a plurality of functions, related to man's roles in the community. This plurality of functions, roles and purposes (or objectives) is organized in the self which experiences *it*self as it confronts *other* selves. But just as the traits have to be organized to constitute a

[7] N. Hartmann, 1926, esp. pp. 135–140.

self with a personality, so the selves have to be organized to constitute a community. Such organization can be achieved only through organizing the functions, and this can be done only by considering the purpose-related roles of the persons-in-the-community. But since a community is not a self,[8] it may be more unequivocal to speak of the objectives to which the roles of such persons are related. Their interrelated functioning constitutes the community by realizing its objectives.

Functions in any "system" are bound to be interrelated. They are, therefore, not only functions in themselves, performing certain assigned tasks, but they are also functions of each other, in that special sense which mathematics has developed. Indeed, the formula for any system must be written in such a way that each part which is constitutive can be considered as function of each and every other part. This is what the functioning of a system presupposes (see Introduction). At this point, we shall *assume* that the same can be said of political community (Chapter 8 for greater detail). Were it not the case, the political community presumably would not be a system, but a conglomeration. Among these vital functions, the most widely recognized is that of "governing." Governing, however, is too general a term to admit of role-specification; it needs to be broken down into (1) rule-making, (2) dispute-settling, (3) measure-taking. No politically organized community known to modern science or history lacks these three roles or functions (Chapters 23 to 25). They may properly be called the governing functions. It is not necessary that they be united in one hand; indeed, such concentration is rare, except in some of the smallest communities. However, each of these functions will be exercised by one or more determinate persons who, whatever else they might be, play the role which the function implies: they are legislator, judge or administrator. In the more advanced stages of development of a political order, each of these roles will be sufficiently demanding to reduce or eliminate the possibility of the person occupying it playing many other roles, though nonpolitical "leisure-time" roles such as that of a father may still be feasible.

If functions are thus seen as consisting of the activities of persons playing roles in the community, it will become clear why such a system is mistakenly viewed as a mechanical one. This mechanical view is implied in what goes under the name of "equilibrium analysis." Its most persuasive exponent was Pareto. Pareto defined equilibrium as a state which, when artificially disturbed, would "tend" to return to its preceding condition. In spite of many elaborations of this definition, Pareto's has remained the mainstay of all such analyses, and naturally so, since it rests upon the classical model of mechanics; Pareto had derived it from

[8] Cf. MacIver, 1947, for a good review of the opposite views held in the past, and cf. below, Chap. 8.

his earlier engineering studies.[9] It has been skillfully adapted to the problems of biology, which also deals with "systems" composed of parts which have functions, but they are functions unrelated to conscious purpose or objective. They "serve" a purpose, rather than "adopting" one. Our argument is not in favor of an organic, as contrasted with a mechanic, model, but we urge the inevitability of including purpose (conscious objective) in the concept of function itself. The role of the judge in any community, to use a concrete case, is as such constitutive of the system, as we said. But any and all decisions of a judge in dealing with behavior submitted to him for evaluation and adjudication are informed by conscious purpose (including the purposes provided for him by existing laws). He "decides" what "maintains" the system, and whether a particular deviant behavior should be treated by punishing it in a certain way, for example, by imprisonment or death. What constitutes "desirable change" is a question such a judge cannot help answering in deciding what is "undesirable change." Significantly, the more comprehensive the challenge, the more uncertain the result. The reason is not far to seek. Since the functions are being exercised by persons, and not by inanimate "organs," any challenge will be met by a response involving deliberate "policy" (Chapter 3). Changes that occur in political systems will be fashioned by persons with distinct personal notions of what constitutes justice, order, freedom and whatever other values may be more specifically involved in a given situation. Such terms as "boundary-maintaining" systems[10] do not help at all; even in the concrete case of actual threats to "boundaries" the human persons in control of the situation will evolve policy in line with the total complex of interrelated values to which they are attached, as can be seen in India today, or could be seen in Germany twenty years ago.[11] As a consequence, the equilibrium concept would

[9] Pareto, 1935, par. 2067: "The real state, be it static or dynamic, of the system is determined by its conditions. Let us imagine that some modification in its form is induced artificially. . . . At once a reaction will take place, tending to restore the changing form to its original state as modified by normal change." Our critical view of the dubious analogies involved in applying such a mechanical model to a political community is shared by Emmet, 1958, pp. 72ff. Parsons, on the other hand, in keeping with his notions of "mechanism," employs the equilibrium concept, which he defines as "empirically observed pattern-constancies of a boundary-maintaining system" (1951, p. 483). See above, Introd., pp. 21ff., on "system analysis."

[10] Parsons, *loc. cit.*

[11] Professor Emmet very acutely observes: "I doubt whether it is possible to describe the adjustments which take place as though they were simply due to social institutions working as if they were automatic mechanisms, without supplementing this analysis in functional terms with a study of how some effort of conscious policy making guided by notions of desirable change may give a new direction to social life; in other words, recognizing that some of the things which are happening will need to be described in terms not of function but of purpose." (1958, p. 75.) Our statement above shows that we go further, since function and purpose cannot, in a political order, be differentiated, but are "Siamese twins."

have to be given so broad and vague a connotation as to serve no useful analytical purpose at all. Its place is taken in political analysis by the concept of order (see Chapter 19). Order itself cannot be specified except in relation to purpose (objective), and purpose acquires meaning only in relation to values. Once more, the close link of value, purpose and function is seen from this vantage point. But before I return to value, one other issue requires treatment.

While there is the greatest variety of communal purposes, and while the infinite pliability of man has proliferated an imposing number of distinct cultural patterns, there can nonetheless be observed and empirically ascertained certain recurrent purposes or objectives. Many years ago, I worked out, by comparative analysis, what these purposes or objectives are for the great states of the West.[12] I found four such recurrent objectives: (1) security and territorial expansion, (2) the reduction of external friction, (3) prosperity, and (4) the reduction of internal friction. This finding, built on a large amount of previous historical research, has never been significantly challenged.[13] I am not particularly concerned with the precise words employed in this analysis. Nor does this seem to be the place for elaborating it. Suffice it here to make a few elucidating comments. The first and second objectives are to some extent interdependent, since a reduction of external friction contributes to security, and heightened security makes the reducing of external friction less urgent. To give a patent example, a country, like the United States in the nineteenth century, provided with the opportunity for steady territorial expansion without encountering serious external friction in connection with it, can indulge in a policy of isolation, a policy, that is to say, which pays relatively little attention to the reduction of external friction. It might be objected here that territorial expansion is not a primary objective of modern government. It certainly is not admitted to be that. But a realistic appraisal of the actual conduct of government will disclose that no matter how elaborately disguised by ideological devices, security cannot be separated from the question of who controls the adjoining territory. Hence, we find both the United States and the Soviet Union contending for territorial entities such as Korea, Berlin and Cuba in ideological terms, where formerly it was a matter of conquest. "The empires of the future are the empires of the mind," the old imperialist Churchill said on a memorable occasion in 1944, and events since then have certainly borne him out.

The third and fourth objectives are similarly linked to each other.

[12] These may, on a more abstract level, be reduced to two: (1) reduction of obstacles, and (2) increased means (cf. Deutsch); but it seems doubtful that, stated thus, they are very useful from an operational viewpoint.

[13] Snyder, Bruck and Sabin, 1954, p. 50, claim that no analysis of "objectives" has been made—then "define" objective as "essentially an 'image' of a 'future state of affairs'—a 'set of conditions' to be fulfilled or a 'set of specifications. . . .'" But this is much too rationalist and subjectivist a position.

For prosperity (economic well-being) is endangered by internal friction, while, at the same time, such friction is reduced by increasing prosperity, and vice versa. At present, this link is sharply brought into focus by strikes, especially in vital areas, such as transportation, utilities and basic metals production. Since the entire economy is immediately affected by a work stoppage in these key industries, such friction palpably jeopardizes prosperity. Government has, therefore, frequently been mobilized to reduce the frictions in the name of prosperity, and to increase prosperity in order to reduce the frictions. Attempts to gainsay this role of government only lead to confusion; their initiators fail to grasp the intrinsic purpose of the political community.

There are, however, two further questions which may be raised concerning these "basic objectives" of political community. One is the question of the relative importance or urgency of these objectives: Is there a hierarchy or order of rank which would, in empirically valid terms, require us to rank them? And second, are these all the empirically ascertainable primary purposes or are there others? To take the latter question first (since the first would be affected by the second answer), it should be noted that recurrently other objectives have been urged by political philosophers and supported by sizable movements of men in political communities. I am not now speaking of such basic values as justice, freedom, and so on, which need to be distinguished from purposes as previously pointed out. But in modern states, the objective of politically organizing a nation has been a purpose fairly universally observed. It is, however, a purpose which appears at a particular point in history and which cannot be discerned over long periods when political communities pursued the other four purposes. It cannot be considered "basic," and it may pass away again. (See Chapter 30.) But behind this "historical" objective of organizing a nation, there is hidden a broader purpose which anthropologists have found practically universal and of which the modern nation is but an instance; it is what may be called organizing a culture, following the work of leading anthropologists.[14] Such a culture is not to be seen as something that just "happens," like natural selection, but as something the organization and preservation of which is seen as the pur-

[14] The complexity of the concept is highlighted by Kroeber and Kluckhohn, 1952, where a critical review of a great many concepts and definitions leads to a view "now formulated by most social scientists approximately as follows: Culture consists of patterns, explicit and implicit, of and for behavior acquired and transmitted by symbols, constituting the distinctive achievement of human groups, including their embodiments in artifacts; the essential core of culture consists of traditional (i.e., historically derived and selected) ideas and especially their attached values; culture systems may, on the one hand, be considered as products of action, on the other as conditioning elements of further action" (p. 181). Cf. also Tylor, 1871, p. 1: Wissler, 1923, pp. 1–2: "entire sweep of individual activities is the basic phenomenon. . . ."; Benedict, 1934, *passim*.

pose of all, but more especially of the governing members of a political society. If culture is defined as in essence built around ideas and their attached values,[15] the proposition that the ordering of a political community in terms of its culture is one of the primary purposes of government amounts to saying that the actions of the political community are moulded by its value judgments. This is a general proposition which transcends purpose and will be considered below when value judgments are treated. Here, it suffices to conclude that organizing a culture is not a distinctive purpose of the political community.

The other question as to a preordained ranking of the basic objectives has been a main argument among political philosophers. More particularly, security and prosperity have been argued as the predominant ones from the viewpoint of analogies to individual psychology (e.g., Hobbes) or from other considerations. Where culture has been included among the basic objectives, it has been urged as the predominant purpose (Plato, Aristotle and their followers). For the good life is, when empirically inspected, seen to be the life of a particular kind of community at a certain time, such as the Greek *polis.* Actually, culture has not been a purpose of the political order as such, as we just showed. But even if it were, it would not outrank security or prosperity, nor even the reduction of internal and external friction in historically observed communities, except at certain high points of cultural development. The pliability of man invites continuous adaptations, where security or prosperity suggest them.

The foregoing question has alas been linked repeatedly in the history of politics with the problem of a hierarchy of values, of the "highest good" —the *summum bonum* which leads back to Plato and Aristotle. This discussion has usually been carried on in terms of a "good" beyond the built-in precondition stated at the outset. While for Plato the idea, or, *eidos,* of the Good is the highest good, Aristotle considers it to be happiness. The Christian tradition has generally followed Aristotle, certainly since Thomas Aquinas, but giving happiness a transcendental projection in the notion of a paradise where persons live in eternal communion with God. Since the Renaissance, many secular values have been suggested as man's *summum bonum.* Machiavelli thought of the state, as a work of art, as man's highest achievement, and thus valued it most highly.[16] Hobbes, the archindividualist, insisted that self-preservation was the highest good, the "self" meaning the actual physical corpus; [17] his notion was adapted and transformed by Locke when he broadened the self to include man's nonphysical aspects, including various values—thereby making the

[15] Kroeber and Kluckhohn, *loc. cit.*

[16] Friedrich, 1957, chap. 1, and the literature cited there.

[17] Hobbes explicitly rejected the notion of a "highest good," but implicitly argued it as the "first law of nature." Cf. *Leviathan,* chap. XI.

argument self-contradictory and, to a degree, tautological. There have been many conflicting notions concerning the highest good put forward in recent work. Brecht, after reviewing them,[18] concludes, in keeping with his value relativism, that each of the claimants advances more or less impressive arguments, but that none has been able to "prove" scientifically that his particular value is *the* value, and hence, that if there is a highest value, we cannot hope to establish it in an empirical fashion by evidence which would be transmissible. We hope to show below why this argument is itself inconclusive, but will only remark here that empirical evidence goes to show that different persons value different *A*'s most highly, and that even the same person values different *A*'s most highly at different times. The evidence forces us to the conclusion that no rank, no hierarchy of values exists as a universal preference of politically organized man. He refuses to "make up his mind." He prefers to "muddle through" on the basis of plural objectives the claims of which are being adjusted as the situation requires it. Historical communities have been known to jeopardize security for prosperity, or vice versa; they have endangered security for lack of diplomacy (reduction of external friction), and they have wrecked prosperity by the failure to reduce internal friction. But the reverse occurrences may likewise be observed, and anyone familiar with the historical fate of political communities will readily be able to supply instances of all of these "conflicts of purpose." The political rationalist, in the mode of Machiavelli, may deplore such "lightheartedness"; if he is prepared to face the facts, he will have to acknowledge man's evident willingness to live by plural purposes and to take the consequences, though often in the hope of being able to have his cake and eat it too.

Since this is so, the question of value *judgments*, as contrasted with the ontological problem of what is a value, comes into focus. We saw above that a value is either instrumental and inherent, that is to say, *A* having value is good *for* something else having value, or *A'* is preferable to other alternatives. The judgments on the part of determinate persons that these facts exist must be distinguished from the facts themselves, as always should be done, unless we are to withdraw into a world of general make-believe.[19] We say quite deliberately: facts. For as has been shown, it is necessary to face at the outset of a discussion of value judgments once again the premise that values are some kind of facts, just as real and just as stubborn as any other "little fact," in William James's phrase. They are facts in the sense of being experienced as being there. In other words, the values exist, whether there is someone to recognize them or not. The statue of the Venus of Milo does not lose its beauty, and, hence, its in-

[18] Brecht, 1959, chap. 8.

[19] This seems to be Oakeshott's inclination (1959), who interprets all facts as "images," and all language as symbolic of these images.

herent value, because only barbarian hordes, unaware of its quality, are surging through the temple where it has been adored. An act of moral goodness is good independently of any persons present to appreciate it. But even if the proposition is accepted, as far as inherent value is concerned, what about instrumental value? What about a house in a deserted town—does it still have instrumental value? Our answer is in the affirmative, because if the value of a house is considered to lie in its being good for being lived in, this factual relation of *A* (house) to *B* (living quarters) continues to persist, though temporarily (or for long periods) not actualized. There is, however, a kind of instrumental value which perishes, and that is "exchange value"; nor is this to be wondered at. Exchange value is the quality of *A* being good for securing *N* units of money. Obviously, if money has disappeared, or if no one is willing to pay any money for the object *A*, it has "no" value. Actually, this observation need not be restricted to exchange value in terms of money. For it is generally true, and indeed nothing more than the logical consequence of *A* being good for *B*, that the disappearance or devaluation of *B* will affect the value of *A*. *A* is a function of *B*, in the mathematical sense. Economists have at times generalized from this patent fact, and asserted that all values are relative; but it is only certain instrumental values that are relative—relating, that is, to the value of the thing to which they are by definition related.

At this point, the relation between values and interests should be explored. If value is seen as "any object of any interest" (R. B. Perry), there should be little need for specifying both "values" and "interests" when speaking of persons, groups and communities, unless the view is adopted which insists upon the reality of values. Interest then becomes the subjective dimension which is suggested by the original Latin *interesse* (to be between, to take part in, to be involved in something). Interest is that which links the person, group or community with the value. Ordinary speech does not clearly differentiate. The value "justice" that men are interested in, often is also described as an "interest"; the same holds true of "food." In actual fact there might exist objects which embody values, and there exist persons who take an interest in such objects because of that value. Values being "objects-of-interest" (Perry), any object may be said to have a potential dimension of value, just as it has a potential dimension of being perceived by the senses, or another of affecting other objects. It is carrying this analysis too far to claim that value is "that special character of an object which consists in the fact that interest is taken in it." This position psychologizes both value and interest.[20] As a consequence it makes value dependent upon the valuer; as we have pointed out, the beauty of the Venus of Milo is not dependent upon

[20] For an interesting comment see Stevenson, 1944, pp. 268–271. Perry's statement is found 1926, p. 124; what follows is discussed on pp. 125–126 and *passim*.

someone who is around to observe and appreciate it, nor is the holiness of Buddha's life, either. The valuer's role is to discover the value, not to create or constitute it. It is different with interest. Interest arises when a valuer develops a disposition to act toward an object possessing a value dimension. It may be merely to see a work of art again, or it may be possession or creation, whether imitative or novel, but interest involves a person, group or community in the value of an object. Hence interest produces purpose and thereupon establishes function.

There has been a very general inclination among social scientists, backed by the formidable authority of men like Kant, to draw not only a sharp but an absolute distinction between "value judgments" and existential judgments. Indeed, whole systems, such as Kelsen's "pure" theory of law, have been erected upon the proposition that these two types of judgments are so different that they constitute different "realms" and hence that you cannot argue from an existential to a value judgment.[21] Yet all political life is shaped and moulded by precisely such arguments. Because democracy does not work, it is claimed to be no good and worthy of being demolished; or, reversely, because democracy is the political order of the free, and freedom is a priceless value, democracy will work if only we work hard enough, and so on. Persons who argue thus may be mistaken, either as to "facts" or as to "values" or both, but there can be no question that they argue from one to the other, and quite coherently so.

The reason is not far to seek. "This table is good" is understood to be a value judgment. "This table is wooden" is taken to be an existential judgment. The auxiliary verb "is" appears in both propositions and gives them their common form; yet it has been customary to insist that these are different kinds of statements, and in a certain limited sense they are, but this difference is reiterated rather than elucidated by the broad terms "value judgment" and "existential judgment." They refer to different kinds of facts or existent givens. One asserts that the table has an inherent value, the other that it is made of a kind of wood. In the Aristotelian schema of *aitiai* (causes), the first judgment refers to a final *aitia* (which means a frame of reference, rather than a cause), the second to a material *aitia*.[22]

There are two more such judgments, according to Aristotle, that

[21] Kelsen, 1945, introd., pp. 40ff., 110ff., 375ff. The very title claimed for his theory by Kelsen should have served as a warning; for few words are so clearly valuational as "pure." Who wishes to be impure? Kelsen is patently involved in self-contradiction here; for he argues from what he states to be the "facts" concerning his theory to its value; namely, "purity." Cf. Ebbinghaus, a, 1961, for a recent discussion.

[22] For the Aristotelian doctrine of *aitiai* in relation to his political philosophy, cf. McKeon, a, 1941. For *aitia* as ground of pleading, cf. also Friedrich, 1958, chap. 3.

concerning the maker of a thing (efficient cause), and that concerning the form or shape of a thing (formal frame of reference). There may be good reasons for distinguishing each of these kinds of judgments, but it is more than doubtful that because data may be discussed in these several ways, within these several frames of reference, they (or any of them) should be erected into mutually exclusive worlds of being. They are aspects of one world, not integral parts of discrete worlds. In some ways, the distinction would be clearer if we did not label the two kinds of judgments in which we were here especially interested "value" and "existential" judgments; for value judgments are existential judgments: they state that a value exists. Nor can we speak of the contrast in terms of factual judgments; for values are facts, as has been pointed out. Existential judgments may be valuational or nonvaluational, the latter falling into a variety of subgroups. Yet, if it is clearly understood that the term "existential judgments" refers to nonvaluational judgments, it might be feasible to proceed in these terms with the discussion of the relationship between judgments concerning the existence of values and other judgments concerning nonvaluational existence.

In light of what has been said so far, it can now be stated as a primary proposition that value judgments and existential judgments are interrelated, and that they can be converted one into the other. For example, any proposition in the form "X possesses the value *Y*," if analyzed, would show a connection with one or more existential judgments. "Monogamy is good" may thus be connected with such existential propositions as "When monogamy is practiced, children receive much attention from their parents," "Children require attention from their parents for their development," and so forth. This is true whether the value alleged is moral, esthetic or otherwise. But more specifically, as we stated at the outset in defining "value," "Monogamy is good" means "Monogamy is preferred to polygamy." If such actual preference is investigated, it will show the complex of values, consequences of a utilitarian sort and the like which lead men to such preferences. Such an analysis leads on to inferences, to the effect that it should be preferred, had better be so preferred, and so forth. From this it follows that any science of politics is necessarily value-oriented. The concern of such studies is to determine why men do, as well as why they ought to, prefer certain situations, institutions and processes to others. Far from being "value-free" the study of politics is concerned with values in the light of all the facts. It asks how democracy or totalitarian dictatorship works, because it hopes to be able to provide grounds for preferring one to the other. This is just as true of the minutiae of politics as it is of the macrocosm of institutional orders. It seeks to refine, restate or change the values, because political experience has brought to light new data which need to be evaluated. A man like Max Weber, who prided himself upon his value-free social science, was, in fact, preoccupied with two values (as far as his work had a bearing upon political science), the value of a free, parliamentary democracy, and the value of an effective public service. Besides that he was an ardent nationalist. He was also occupied with the corresponding disvalues, as well as the disvalue of the kind of order Marxism was advocating. Most of his work can be understood only if it is seen in the perspective of these value preoccupations. Similarly, Pareto was preoccupied with the value of a competitive free market economy and the kind of liberal political order corresponding to it, as comes to light in certain footnotes. This patent fact does not, of course, prove that they were right or wrong. They may have just been contradicting themselves. Even so, the *actuality* of their work derived from the value orientation which made such work meaningful to their contemporaries.

In recent years, the value orientation of political and social inquiry has been receiving increasing recognition. Thus Myrdal, in his remarkable study of the American Negro's position in contemporary America, insists that it is as important to ask, "What *should* the position of the Negro be?" as to inquire what it is. These two questions he considered intimately linked to each other; they should both guide scientific inquiry. Any number of other works in the several social sciences could be similarly referred to. Suffice it to mention that Lynd, in a dramatic reversal of an earlier position, asked, Knowledge for what? [23] and decided that the social sciences should deal with values, but should make them explicit. We go further and demand that they not only be made explicit, but that political and other social studies should be focused on values. It is the hidden value search that must be brought to light, and the refinement, reevaluation and transformation of values that must be understood as the central task of political science, as well as other social sciences.

If it is said that values cannot be proved in the form of transmissible knowledge, the answer is that values can be proved in a larger measure than is commonly realized. They can be made probable, and this is all that most scientific work is today understood to be able to do. The kind of judgment to which political science can lead is that, considering all we know about the functioning of politics, it is highly probable that institution or process *A* is preferable to institution or process *B, C,* or any other known to us, given the particular situation with which we are confronted in the particular instance. Now, it will often be claimed that this is not a value judgment in the "higher" sense, but merely an expedient one, that it does not refer to the "good, the beautiful and the true," which are the essence of value judgments. We hope to have shown that value, when seen in the perspective of the human person who is to perceive the value, is essentially "preferability," in so far as the inherent values are concerned.

[23] Lynd, 1939, esp. chap. 5. Cf. also Easton, 1953, pp. 223ff.

The instrumental values, on the other hand, are reducible to inherent values if their value is to be demonstrated. The fuller implementation of this view will have to await the exploration of the values-in-operation which Part II will give below.

Here it remains to deal with one other matter, and that is the fact that values as the primary objective of political science are not, thereby, robbing it of "objectivity." [24] It is amazing, in view of the constant reference to objectivity, how rarely the term is defined or explained. Objectivity appears as primarily a personal quality of the researcher which makes him exclusively concerned with the "object" of his research; he does not allow himself to be swayed by his personal prejudices, or by the influence of others in pursuing his work. It is obvious that "values," being "objects," are themselves in need of such objectivity on the part of him who inquires into them. When writers like Max Weber discourse on this issue, they usually state that they are indeed in favor of the objective study of values, but that this is something different from letting your own value judgments be a part of the research. I am leaving aside the question of just how this is to be envisaged, that is to say, which would be those values on which the researcher would have no value position himself, unless the matter in hand were remote in time and place; even here the task of selection would intrude into the value judgments.[25] There is the much more crucial issue of *value concern,* which calls for a kind of objectivity which the school of value-free researchers completely overlooks. In so far as values are indicative of communal preferences, the researcher who refuses to be concerned is wasting his time, because he is not elucidating that which needs elucidating. That this is true even of the natural scientist has recently been argued with persuasive power by a number of scientists.[26]

The full implications of this line of reasoning are obliging us to recognize that the so-called "value-free" position is, in fact, a position based upon the valuational judgment that the community's values are irrelevant to the role of the researcher. Far from being "objective," such a position is subjective to the degree of a scientific solipsism for which the symbol of the ivory tower is appropriate. We are as political scientists cast in the roles of guardians, whether we like it or not. Our endeavors are bound to affect the community's values, and the more dedicated and fruitful

[24] Objectivity, according to Diamat, is, of course, only a bourgeois virtue, and should be shunned by advanced social science. The complications arising from this position have been dealt with in an illuminating fashion by Barrington Moore, 1958.

[25] An interesting case in point is the heated argument about social organization in prehistoric times, more especially matriarchy; for a more recent example, one might turn to the current anti-Whig history-writing in England, including the argument about the gentry, for which cf. Hexter, a, 1959; Shklar, a, 1959.

[26] Polanyi, 1958, esp. chap. II, p. 6, par. 2.

they are the more they will do so. We cannot close our eyes to such responsibility. If we prove that a certain line of conduct is sure to lead to disaster, we cannot expect the community to sit idly by. Hence, to lift the values into the focus of our inquiries, to be continually at work in reconsidering them in the light of the consequences which efforts at their realization will have, to balance them against each other and their consequences: this is the core of the task of all the social sciences. This is not to say that the work of causal exploration may not at times take one very far afield into data which seem remote from the central value concern; but even then the work will gain in poignancy and actuality if the values to which such work applies are kept clearly in mind. For then problems will be focused—as, indeed, the preceding reflections are the basis of the problem approach which we favor.

It remains to say a word about the peculiar intellectual operation which applies to inherent values. Ethical value judgments relate to the question: What must I do? But there are others to which this kind of practical question is quite irrelevant. Inherent values, to put it briefly, are calling for interpretation, rather than demonstration, and hence value judgments are explanatory in a different way from existential judgments. If I am to comment on the beauty of a great painting, I can point to a variety of aspects such as the harmony of the colors, the balance of the lines, and so on. If I wish to explain the freedom or the order of a political community, I can point to various comparable arrangements and patterns of behavior. Somehow, there will always be a residue that defies effective communication, that calls for a sharing of the value judgment by him to whom the interpretation is addressed. Hence, the saying, *De gustibus non est disputandum:* one must not dispute about value judgments. Yet, the answer is obvious enough. What do people dispute about, if not about value judgments? It is not worthwhile to dispute about "facts" nor about demonstrable theorems. Why is it both common and highly desirable to dispute about values? Because a value being what it is, it can become more distinct only by an effort at interpretation. At the end, there is not agreement, but understanding. *A* knows what *B* means when he refers to justice or freedom, or any other values upon which political community is built in its specific manifestations.

The sharp differentiations among values, value responses and value judgments, although of great importance, will not be rigidly maintained in what follows. When in later chapters it is evident from the context that value responses and judgments rather than values themselves are meant, especially in the recurrent formula of "values, interests and beliefs" of the political community, the term "value" will often be employed, even though value judgments or responses are meant. It is important to bear in mind, however, that these "subjective" dimensions of value correspond to an objective one in terms of which they function. Thus, the political community rests upon objectively existing values, as shown above, although for purposes of observation and analysis the judgments and responses of the community's members are usually of primary evidential value.

chapter

3

The Interdependence of Institution, Decision and Policy

Chaos umpire sits,
And by decision more embroils the fray
By which he reigns: next him high arbiter
Chance governs all.
Milton, PARADISE LOST

DECISION, POLICY AND INSTITUTION have been the most hotly contested terms of recent political science. Behaviorists have attacked institutionalists, saying that what really mattered were decisions and how they were made; institutionalists have retorted that you could not analyze or understand decision-making without knowing the institutional setting. It is a false either/or. It arose because of the excessive formalism of the institutional approach, and therefore the insistence upon decision may be considered a healthy reaction. Another such reaction is stress upon policy, which in fact constitutes a revival of a view prevalent in the seventeenth century before it was superseded by the "institutional," that is to say, "legalist," approach. This was the approach of the liberal age which emphasized the role of law. The Machiavellians and mercantilists and other absolutists had stressed "policy." In line with their thought it has again been asserted that only policy really matters, and that political science is the science of policy-making above everything else. But in recent years, other social sciences have been proclaimed "policy sciences," because their data have, indubitably, a bearing on public policy.[1] From the

[1] Lerner and Lasswell (eds.), 1951, esp. chap. 1. See also Friedrich, a, 1953; Elsbree, a, 1950.

standpoint of a political theory that stresses persons as the starting point of political analysis, decision-making would seem the primary political act, until it is remembered that such persons are communal beings. For this being-in-community means that the person is related to the institutions which characterize the community or communities of which he is a part. Thus the institution is the primary given within which the decision- and policy-making processes occur. Some of these institutions are themselves the result of political decisions, or appear so, until a more detailed analysis discloses that the original decisions have been modified by subsequent practice to such an extent that the original decision provides merely the starting point for a realistic analysis. Of course, much of this practice will in turn be compounded of decisions of a lesser sort. But it would be a mistake to assume that this is necessarily so, especially in less law-oriented societies than our own.

A political institution is any stably organized syndrome of political acts or actions having a function and/or purpose in the political system, or to put it another way, a relatively stable collection of roles.[2] Such political institutions are more particularly meant to define the power relationships prevailing in the community. Through them the values, as embodied in function and purpose, are "realized." No political community is imaginable without political institutions. Of these the most comprehensive is the government, but other political institutions are the parties, as well as a variety of other entities. Even devices characteristic of a particular constitutional order, such as the pocket veto in the United States, or certain administrative or legislative activities, such as judicial review of administrative acts or the closure, may properly be called political institutions; for all of them are stably organized syndromes of political acts, having a function and purpose in the system.

Political institutions often exhibit an inertia of their own which results in their surviving from one political system into another. Institutions like the French *Conseil d'État* or the German system of municipal administration are cases in point. But such survivals are the exception, rather than the rule. Typically, institutions are system-related and pass away with the political system to which they belong. At times, institutions are seemingly carried over from one system to another, but actually change their nature,

[2] Parsons, 1951, p. 39, defines a political institution similarly, but to say that it is a "complex of institutionalized role integrates" implies a *petitio principii.* Lasswell and Kaplan, 1950, state that an institution is a "pattern composed of culture traits specialized to the shaping and distribution of a particular value" where a culture trait is an "act characteristic of a group." Thus an institution would be a pattern of acts, where "pattern" means a "stably organized syndrome," we suppose, though "pattern" is nowhere defined in that treatise. Our discussion of function and purpose (above, Chap. 2) makes clear how closely the rest of the definition, stressing value-shaping, approximates our own.

because their function and purpose are altered. Thus the party in the totalitarian dictatorship is a different institution from that in a constitutional democracy,[3] the monarchy a different institution under absolutism from what it is under constitutionalism. Some of these transformations are the result of deliberate decision, others just "happen"; that is to say, specific situational decisions cumulatively result in the transformation.[4] The reason for the contrast just described can be understood only in terms of function and purpose. If the function and purpose are carried from one system to another, as is the case with the *Conseil d'État,* the institution is able to persist.

In institutions, as in persons, we face the problem of self-identity. Admittedly, all institutions, like all persons, are subject to continuous change. Some of these changes are "inherent," such as the maturing process which institutions, like men, "naturally" undergo. Other changes are occasioned by outside factors. Numerous examples can be given for such changes in response to outside influence. The American Senate changed as American democracy became more pronounced, and was eventually explicitly altered. The British Parliament changed as the increasing complexity of industrial society promoted the role of executive leadership. Such institutional changes are among the most interesting and important phenomena political science research is devoted to. Because inquiry consumes time, the understanding of institutions in any given society, even if highly literate, is always somewhat behind; Burke thought "fifty years." The fact of continuous change being universally recognized, it remains to determine when such changes are of a magnitude to allow us to speak of a "different" institution. This judgment can be made only in light of both the functioning and the purpose of a given institution. If the purpose is a new and different one, and the institution functions in ways sharply at variance with earlier practice, then the case is clear. It is a matter of investigating the acts which can be observed, and exploring their function in the system as well as their (declared or undeclared) purpose. Frequently, the question is hard to answer, as all these are qualitative factors which may be judged differently by different investigators. Interesting recent instances of these difficulties may be seen in Continental European patry history. Presumably the Social Democratic Party of the Federal Republic is the continuation of the Social Democratic Party of the empire and the Weimar Republic; it is the same institution, though by no means identical. On the other hand, the Christian Democratic Party of the same country is not the continuation of any such earlier party; it is a novel

[3] This point is rightly emphasized by Loewenstein, 1957, p. 11. Loewenstein stresses the ideology as the cause of such transformation; other than ideological factors may be at work.

[4] For an interesting recent instance of the intermingling of both, see Neunreither, a, 1959, describing the changes in the German Federal Council.

institution. The fact that both parties are undergoing a functional change, as the politics of the Federal Republic approaches a two-party system, will not alter this judgment. But what if the Social Democratic Party abandons the key purposes of socialism? Is it still the same institution, or would it be more correct to say that it too had become a new institution, more nearly adapted to the changed functioning of the German government? Similar difficulties present themselves in the comparison of governmental institutions. When is judicial review of legislative acts to be considered a political institution comparable to parliaments, parties and the like? Are the arrangements in the Fifth French Republic, in the Federal Republic and in Italy to be considered the same institution as that which prevails in the United States? [5] Institutional analysis of this kind is neither simple nor obvious, but requires scientific acumen of a high order. This patent fact becomes especially crucial in the deciding upon a new constitution. The decision-makers in such complex processes are often devoid of even an elementary grasp of the issues involved. But this is not the place to pursue the problem further. (See Chapter 15.) The record of many a constitutional convention will amply bear it out. It should, however, be noted, that any constitution-making, especially in the so-called new nations emerging from colonial rule and an antiquated political system perpetuated by such rule, should be inspired by a healthy skepticism as to the possibility of transferring institutions from one cultural and social context to another; the likelihood is that such institutions will function very differently and not necessarily well.

The foregoing propositions concerning institutions have brought us squarely up against the problem of decision-making. To many, as we said, this is the crux of politics; but of course, decision-making is not only, or even primarily, a political activity. Like institutions, decisions are a ubiquitous aspect of human life, and the political theory and scientific analysis of decision-making must build upon general psychological and philosophical knowledge. Decision has become a central concern of the philosophers of the existentialist school, who interpret it as the crux of existence. "Man first of all exists, encounters himself, emerges in the world . . . what is usually called my will is probably a manifestation of a prior and more spontaneous decision. . . . When we say that man chooses himself, we do mean that every one of us chooses himself; but by that we also mean that in choosing himself he chooses all men." [6] This inexorable necessity of having to decide, every moment of his life, is man's freedom and responsibility (Chapters 17, 19 to 21). This viewpoint has been echoed, often without clear recognition of its philosophical roots, by writers in politics and law. One of the most radical wrote at one

[5] Dietze, 1960; Barnet, a, 1959; von Mehren, a, 1954; McWhinney, a, 1957.
[6] Jean-Paul Sartre, 1946, pp. 21ff.

point: "Sovereign is he who decides upon the state of emergency." [7] Such a decisionist outlook is characteristically inclined to interpret the decision as more or less arbitrary, and not derived from reasons, principles or norms. It is "free" in the sense of being not merely autonomous, but "without law." It springs primordially from the human being who exists and who cannot go on existing without choosing, deciding, acting. Even a human being who prefers contemplation in the most radical sense, chooses to contemplate—his is indeed one of the most extreme and difficult decisions to make. Decision-making here is always choosing between alternative courses of action. It leads therefore into what has been called "theory of action" and more especially "social action." [8]

It is easy to overestimate the importance of *deciding* upon courses of action, especially in highly rationalized political orders, when actually even in such orders many actions are repetitive or adaptive without any decision being involved. Another way of putting it is to say that much behavior and conduct is not freely chosen, but socially conditioned. Human activity could be compared to a stream from which the decisions stick out like rocks, but this analogy does not do justice to the constant interweaving of socially conditioned and freely decided action. The determinist holds, of course, that even the freely chosen action is socially conditioned,[9] and in a certain sense it is: the decision-maker orients himself in terms of existing opinions, values, beliefs, as well as other givens of his social environment. But he eventually chooses between possible alternatives, by a complex process of weighing commitments and priorities which easily gives the illusion of an intuition *ex nihilo*. Much decisionist literature insists that the decisional element in a decision proceeds from the "nothing" (*néant*, *Nichts*).[10] Nothing could be further from the truth; a man not only chooses from available alternatives, but invents new ones. He chooses the action which his preferences suggest as likely.

If human life, then, contains a never-ending chain of decisions, it is not surprising that politics, too, should appear in this perspective as a realm of decision, above all. The empirical question then is, however: How are political decisions arrived at? It is obvious that no simple and universally

[7] Schmitt, 1922, p. 9. Cf. for him and the whole problem Krockow, 1958, pp. 60ff.: Schneider, 1957.

[8] Parsons has been particularly concerned with it. See esp. his work of 1937, where he critically reviewed the work of Pareto, Max Weber and Durkheim from this viewpoint, and that of 1951 where he, in collaboration with several other social scientists of different fields (though not including political science), worked "toward a theory of social action."

[9] E.g., Bernal, 1949; cf. also Cranston, 1953, contra, but elaborating the argument.

[10] Sartre, 1946; Jaspers, 1948, p. 450; Heidegger, 1927, p. 287; Schmitt, 1922, p. 31. The emphasis on "nothingness" is, presumably, an expression of the breakdown of liberal institutions in France and Germany since the thirties.

valid answer can be given to this question at the outset.[11] Manifestly, a parliamentary decision to adopt a certain law is arrived at in a different way from a ministerial decision to implement a statute by certain measures; again, a judicial decision about whether such implementation was in keeping with the statutory provisions is arrived at in a still different manner. Mature legal systems have, as a matter of fact, developed elaborate rules for the making of all these decisions; while an element of freedom, of decisional preference, remains, many steps are prescribed by rigid norms, embodied in civil, criminal, administrative and parliamentary procedure, and so on. There may well be common elements in all these decisions, but before we can answer that question, it is necessary to consider the several broad general types in order to determine whether a general common core can be derived from them. (See also Chapters 24 to 26, below.)

However, very important insights may also be gained by a detailed study of a particular decision, carrying the documentary research as far as the available data will allow. This type of decision study will, of course, be limited by the institutional and cultural settings within which the decision occurs, but this may not seriously infringe its value as a pedagogic tool or, if carefully specified, even its value for scientific work. The most ambitious and revealing attempt in this direction has been made in the field of American Federal public administration,[12] but there are significant approaches in foreign policy and other fields.[13] It has proved, however, extremely difficult to generalize from such data, and the need for a conceptual framework is brought out by such detailed case studies.

Broadly speaking, three types of political decisions may be distinguished, as they exhibit differentiated patterns of going about the task of

[11] Interesting attempts in this direction are Lasswell, a, 1955; and Snyder, Bruck and Sapin, 1954. The latter define as follows: "Decision-making is a process which results in the selection from a socially defined, limited number of problematical alternative projects [of?] one project intended to bring about the particular future state of affairs envisaged by the decision-makers" (p. 57). The authors then proceed to give a number of answers, because they recognize that a political decision is "organizationally defined," i.e., conditioned by the institutional context. For this aspect, cf. Herbert Simon, 1947, 1957, pp. 12ff., and chap. 10. The above definition is *too* rationalist and teleological and omits the vital aspect that a *problem* must exist before the challenge for a decision can arise. Decisions are often made without any "envisaged future state," clear or otherwise. Lasswell, a, 1955, *loc. cit.* pp. 382–3, gives a long list of twenty questions to be answered, only the last of which is the institutional context; he starts with the problem situation which "precipitated" the decision.

[12] Harold Stein (ed.), 1952.

[13] Furniss, 1959, e.g., for an interesting study, seeking to relate decision-making to institutional setting. Older studies on foreign policy usually contain some "cases" on foreign policy decisions, as do diplomatic histories, especially the more detailed ones. They lack any conceptual framework, however.

"reaching" the decision. First, there is the decision of a single individual deciding a matter wholly within his range of competency. This kind of decision-making may be further subdivided into decisions with and without advice. Such individual decisions are particularly characteristic for (1) the administrator and (2) the citizen. Most citizens are apt to decide without much advice for whom to vote in an election, or what alternative to select in a referendum, whether to write to their representative protesting a position he has taken or urging him to take one, whether to subscribe to one newspaper or another, whether to go to an election meeting or to read a book about the candidates. These are just random samples of many individual political decisions. To them correspond decisions of the administrator, such as which subordinate to criticize, what reply to make to a complaint, how to phrase a memorandum to his boss, and so forth. All these several decisions may also be made with advice, but whether to seek such advice is part of the individual's decision-making, though it may be imposed by custom, office rule or even constitutional provision. This is the case of the advice-and-consent rule of the United States constitution. Even here, the *decision* on *whether* and *what* to propose is often made without prior advice, and whether to seek advice on what to propose is the decision of the individual office-holder.

The second kind of decision is arrived at by a group's joint action, either unanimously or by some kind of majority (usually prescribed), after the group members have consulted with each other more or less extensively. Courts, commissions, legislative committees and numerous other bodies acting without public participation employ this kind of procedure and at times allow the dissenters to explain their view as well as to offer reasons for their own position. This kind of decision, which may be called *group decision*, carries greater authority (Chapter 12) and is usually employed for matters of some moment. Hence we find in judicial systems that the higher courts hearing weighty cases or cases on appeal make group decisions, while the lower courts act through individual judges.

A third type is the decision epitomized by a legislative body's adoption of a law. Here elaborate argument and discussion, much of it in public, precedes the decision-making by a vote which itself is often a matter of public record. Town meetings and party conclaves, such as America's conventions, are other instances of this type of decision-making. Decisions arrived at by such a procedure are apt to be highly authoritative and of considerable durability; the very process forbids ready reversal of such decisions.[14] This type of decision-making is particularly suited to the making of laws and long-range policy for which wide public

[14] The durability of decisions is, however, also a function of the system; consequently individual decisions may stick in one system, while even laws may prove unstable in another. (K. Deutsch.)

support must be secured. It may properly be called a *public decision*, and is typically made in accordance with elaborate rules of procedure, such as Jefferson's or Roberts' *Rules of Order*, which *may* be employed also in group decisions but can then be easily violated. Each modern parliament has, as a matter of fact, its own rules of procedure, and the success of these bodies is closely linked to such rules. The evolution of such rules is, or should be, concomitant with the institutional position of the parliamentary body.[15] The process of decision-making may, however, be transferred to other groups or even individuals, and often is. The reason is precisely the publicity atending the "formal" process which may make it difficult or impossible to arrive at a decision. Hence party caucuses and even more secluded occasions, such as the proverbial smoke-filled hotel rooms, may become the locus of effective decision-making.[16]

Individual decisions, whether private or official, group decisions and public decisions, while thus fairly sharply differentiated in procedure and scope of application, have certain features in common which constitute the core of decision-making. They all are decisions about what *action* to take in face of a *problem* confronting the decision-maker. Unless there were a problem, no decision would be needed. The political problem, literally the thing thrown in your path and blocking the road (*problēma*), may be institutionally defined, or it may present itself because of changes in the environment—in either case, it imposes itself as something that cannot be escaped. Even the refusal to find a solution is a decision, as the alternative of nonaction is as real as any of the available action alternatives.

Decisions are decisions between *alternatives*. These alternatives may not be very clearly defined, though often they are, but in any case there cannot be decision (or choice) except between alternatives. It is of course not necessary that there be only two such alternatives, though this is sometimes alleged; but there can be no question that such decisions are among the most vexing, indeed terrible ones. Hamlet's cry, "To be, or not to be—" is only the most basic of these decisions. They may be called *dichotomic*. In politics, the decision between peace or war illustrates the dichotomic decision in its most formidable and bitter inescapability. Often decisions are put into dichotomic form when actually several alternatives are available. Even peace-or-war may be a decision of that kind, and political man has reason to be ever alert against the oratorical tendency to make a problem appear in the form of an either-or decision. "Give me liberty or give me death!" is a famous example of this type of rhetoric. In this area of the verbal representation of concrete political problems,

[15] A fascinating case study of this sort of evolution is the history of British parliamentary procedure, for which cf. Redlich, 1908; cf. also Friedrich, 1950, pp. 301ff. and 325ff.

[16] It is shown below, Chap. 11, what and why "influence hides."

the possibilities of mistaking a complex reality providing numerous alternatives for a simple either/or are very great. The problem of any roadblock can be stated as: Either we remove it or we die. But there may actually be various possible detours, as well as possible alternative directions of travel. There is a great deal of romanticism in the oratory of existentialism as it discourses upon man being "thrown" into a certain position and having to "choose" between "being" and "nonbeing." The anxiety which such romantic choices generate is best illustrated, of course, by the unique position of the lover who must either win his beloved or perish. There is good ground for his despair if he cannot win her, but there is also ground for the skeptic's sardonic comment that he will sooner or later find another person to love. Whatever one's view in the field of personal relations, the political sphere is characterized by its prosaic issues, calling for temperate and sober judgment. Most political decisions are not either-or questions, and even where the decision has been seemingly made dichotomic, as in elections where only two candidates are presented, there is the third alternative of not voting for either but abiding by the decision of the other members of the electorate. Not only in group and public decisions, where a fairly extended search for as many alternatives as possible is made, but even in individual decisions, especially official ones, an important aspect of decision-making is the search for possible alternatives. Until the alternatives are clearly defined, the decision will be inadequate.

And yet, any vote has to be taken upon an either-or question. Elaborate rules, such as those about putting and seconding a motion, seek to insure this distillation of an effective dichotomy. Yet, the dichotomy is often merely apparent, hiding a substantial number of alternatives. The "ayes" and "nays" in many votes may group these alternatives, but they do not eliminate them. If a faculty group is finally confronted with a motion to propose a certain candidate for a permanency, the "*nays*" may include not only persons who do not favor the particular candidate, but others who favor a number of other candidates, though they are quite willing to accept this one if none of their special preferences are available (in other words prove not to be "real" alternatives). The same possibility is even more frequently the case where alternative policies are involved. For a fuller analysis of this most crucial set of alternate decisions, the policy concept first needs further exploration. Tentatively we may sum up what has been said regarding political decisions by defining such a decision as the choice of one of several alternative courses of action (or inaction) suggested by a problem situation.[17]

[17] It will be seen that this definition differs in several important respects from the one cited above, fn. 11, p. 75, where analysis is seen as handicapped throughout by a subjectivist bias which is preoccupied with the actor's view of the situation.

"Policy" is one of the magic words of the contemporary world, as it was in the sixteenth and seventeenth centuries. It meant then, though not precisely, what it means now, namely, a proposed course of action of a person, group or government within a given environment providing obstacles and opportunities which the policy was proposed to utilize and overcome in an effort to reach a goal or realize an objective or a purpose. Again, as in the case of decisions generally, there are group as well as individual policies, although it is unusual to speak of the proposed course of action of an individual as "policy." It is much more usual to do so in the case of groups, such as business enterprises, trade unions or parties. Finally, there is, most important of all, public policy: a proposed course of action (as just described) of the government or one of its subdivisions.[18] We are here, of course, primarily concerned with public policy, but other group policies deserve serious attention. It is essential for the policy concept that there be a goal, objective or purpose. Indeed it is the purposefulness of the proposed action which makes it necessary to consider contingencies, such as obstacles and conceivable opposition, as well as possible support to be secured from friends and favorable circumstances. Policy is not any chance course of action proposed by a heedless or reckless person, but a deliberate effort to assess the pros and cons of alternative courses and a decision in favor of the one seen as most likely to bring success. Hence the notion of policy carries with it the belief that it is very important to *know* as many of the conditions as might affect the proposed action. In public policy this is obviously calling for a thorough knowledge not only of the technical and social conditions, but also of the institutional setting within which a given policy is to occur. No one in his right mind would consider it good policy, or even policy at all, to propose that the United States President do things which the Constitution does not permit him to do, or to suggest legislation to the Congress for which the procedural or party conditions provide no prospect of success.[19] Similarly, no policy would even be considered which asked that what is generally known to be impossible be accomplished. In point of fact, however, courses of action are often proposed and decided upon as public policy, simply because it is not *known* that the proposed course is running counter to natural conditions or human factors. Often such conditions are actually known to some people, but these people are not brought into the consultation over the policy, not

[18] The "course of action" concept is interestingly analyzed in Snyder, Bruck and Sapin, 1954, pp. 44ff. Chester Barnard's list of misuses of the term "policy," a, 1940, does not dispose of the term; the one given here is, of course, not included in his list. Cf. also Friedrich, a, 1953, p. 271.

[19] Though it may be argued that cases like NRA, AAA and the Japanese Evacuation Act of 1942 suggest the contrary, they constitute cases of doubtful, rather than evident lack of constitutionality.

are they listened to when they are. Economists often find that their expert counsel is disregarded, and policies are adopted which cannot and do not work. Recently, more recondite fields of knowledge have been brought into the argument, such as anthropology and social psychology.[20] But the basic issue is always the same: how to secure adequate knowledge of all the facts and conditions bearing upon a particular proposed course of action.

Public policy is obviously the work of many persons arguing various aspects of the problem and trying to formulate a course of action which meets all relevant objections of the "experts." But these objections often become entangled with the value judgments in such a way that the actual knowledge involved in such an expert opinion is obscured. Thus, an expert might claim that a proposed sales tax would have dire economic consequences which are objectionable only in terms of the model of an economy which he happens to approve. Then another expert will make the diametrically opposite statement, and the genuine contribution which both of them could make to the controversy is lost. Evidently, in such an instance the first and primary question is who pays the sales tax, as compared to who pays, for example, the real estate tax which it would replace. It would be absurd to enter into the complex tangle of the arguments and counterarguments of such a controversy, except to hint at the fact that the real problem, namely, what are the obstacles to the realization of the objective of the proposed course of action, is thereby obscured.

It is now possible to state more explicitly the problem of the "hidden" alternatives. In many instances of public policy, the apparent decision is a dichotomic one: it is the decision as to whether to go on as is, or to introduce the proposed change. Actually, the proposed change is probably by no means the only possible one, but there are others which deserve to be fully explored. If, to use our previous example, the problem is how to stop the continuous rise of real estate taxes, it might among other measures be worth considering whether an additional amount of income tax should be levied. Income taxes are known to be less objectionable from the standpoint of social justice—primarily a value judgment—but they also have the advantage of relative ease of collection, especially if merely a percentage increase of established tax rates is adopted. The

[20] This is the main argument of Lerner and Lasswell, 1951, esp. pp. 3ff. "If the rationality of the policy process is to be improved, we must single out the intelligence function for special study" (p. 4). Curiously enough, Lasswell, a political scientist teaching at a law school, does not include the primary "policy sciences," namely, political science, law and economics in this exploration of the "policy sciences," though probably nine-tenths of all the obstacles to public policy the disregard of which contributes to its failure are properly comprised within these subjects. See Friedrich, a, 1953

question of relative cost is a matter of fact which can be explored and calculated.

The problem of hidden alternatives is particularly intriguing in the field of foreign policy and international affairs. "Foreign aid" has become a major policy issue not only in the United States, but in most advanced industrial countries. Many differences of opinion are, of course, traceable to divergent value judgments and correspondingly different objectives or goals. Peace, trade, and the containment of totalitarianism have all played their role and continue to do so, apart from straight concern for a moral order. But these objectives apart (and the value judgments involved all have their "appeal" in the different countries), there are very definite problems of *knowledge* involved which have so far received only intermittent attention.

The primary policy issue in the narrow political sense is whether to aid people in accordance with their conduct in the "cold war"—the world-wide conflict between the Soviet bloc and the West. It is possible to see this issue either in terms of "reward" or in terms of "inducement." Both are, of course, by their advocates claimed to be *the* realistic policy. A third alternative, admittedly "idealistic" but claimed to be most realistic in the long run, insists that the aid should be given largely in terms of need and without any regard to other reward or inducement. There are, evidently, other side issues too numerous to mention, such as whether to give priority to industrial or agricultural development, whether to make loans or outright gifts, and so forth.[21] These issues are capable, however, of a degree of technical treatment by economists, agronomists and engineers, whereas the issue of whether to make reward, inducement or need the basis of policy is a strictly political matter, contingent upon the particular advocate's general outlook and viewpoint, as well as on his estimate of the particular situation. For surely one's position may also vary with regard to different countries, or one may incline to compromise between all three to some extent.[22]

The foregoing general discussion of decision and policy has, I hope, pointed the way to a more adequate appreciation of the interdependence of institutions with decisions and policies. Political science has every

[21] Cf. *Public Policy*, vol. IX, 1959, especially the articles by Galbraith, pp. 73–83; David Bell, pp. 84–106; Rudolph and Rudolph, pp. 149–178; and Barbara Ward Jackson, pp. 341–352. Cf. also the recent collective work edited by Braibanti and Spengler, 1961, esp. the papers by Spengler, pp. 1–56; Braibanti, pp. 139–180; and John Montgomery, pp. 243–275. Cf. also for a sharp attack, Banfield, a, 1962.

[22] A popular novel has recently highlighted these issues, but while the authors, Burdick and Lederer, bring forward some interesting "data" as to the malfunctioning of men and institutions engaged in this field, the book is quite unclear as to objectives and obstacles—the two crucial questions in regard to any policy.

reason to be concerned with decisions and policies, but it has equally good reason for being concerned with the institutional setting within which such public decisions and policies occur.[23] And since institutions continually change as a result of decisions continually made in the pursuit of policies recurrently adopted, this complex should be seen as a configuration of interdependent variables, rather than as alternatives for political science research.

[23] An interesting case study is Furniss, 1954. Cf. also Snyder, Bruck and Sapin, 1954.

chapter

4

The Function of Ideas and Ideologies in Politics

The empires of the future are
the empires of the mind.
Churchill

THE NEWER EMPHASIS upon decision, and even more that upon policy, tends almost as much as the older upon institutions to obscure the role of invention, innovation and creativity in the life of man. And yet, if one considers "the immense journey" from the hazy origins of human beings in the *personal* sense, he cannot but be impressed with the enormous range of such creativity.[1] Perhaps it would be better to speak only of inventiveness and the readiness to discover and to innovate; yet even at the most elementary creative level, the propagation of the species, the term "creation" is more appropriate and ought therefore probably to be retained as an over-all concept in spite of its romantic flavor.[2]

In any case, the capacity to discover and to innovate is one of the distinctive features of man. It has very important consequences for politics,

[1] Hence Chardin, 1959, speaks recurrently (for example, 223–225) of invention as crucial to the phenomenon of man. Cf. also Eiseley, 1946 and later—a fascinating set of sketches concerning man's early beginnings.

[2] The vitalist philosophers, especially Nietzsche and Bergson, have contributed their share to the confusion. It seems doubtful, though, whether they are properly called "romantics." Cf. Viereck, 1941, pp. 182ff.; G. A. Morgan, Jr., 1941, pp. 227ff.; Kaufmann, 1950, pp. 113ff. and *passim;* also Shklar, 1957, pp. 51ff., pp. 104ff.

some of which will be explored at a later stage (see Chapter 21). This capacity to innovate is related to and springs from the five basic features of man. It is more especially dependent for its effectiveness upon the pliability and adaptability of man. For without man's infinite adaptability to new and changing environmental conditions the capacity to invent would not have developed, as inventions would remain unused. The readiness to respond to the challenge of the new is a "passive" form of this creativity shared by most men. Their communal life and the having and sharing of purposes are, of course, also primary conditions of invention. The relation of creativity to the experience of the self and to language is less obvious, but nonetheless real. The self is the Archimedean point from which man could proceed to lift the world off its hinges, and language is the concomitant of discovery and invention from the beginning.[3] Language, the vehicle for communicating about external objects by vocal signs, leads straight into the problem of ideas.

Ideas are the means of discovery, invention and innovation. A man, say, confronted with the task of dragging a heavy load *discovers* that it moves more easily when rolled along on some round stick, probably a chance tree trunk or a round stone, *invents* the wheel and by this *innovation* sets a vast chain of consequences in motion which transform human existence. He has the "idea" of a wheel. The wheel did not exist before he made it; man forms an image of it in his mind, and then finds out by trial and error, through experimental operation, that it "works." Idea in this "popular" connotation is an "intuition," an *Einfall*—something that "falls into someone" like a "flash of insight," as the saying goes. Sherwood Anderson in his *Winesburg, Ohio* has drawn an unforgettable picture of a "man of ideas," forever going about seeing problems where others see a familiar setting, and getting inspired about ways of dealing with these problems:

> Men watched him with eyes in which lurked amusement tempered by alarm. . . . Although the seizures that came upon him were harmless enough, they could not be laughed away. They were overwhelming. Astride an idea, Joe was overmastering. His personality became gigantic.

This concept of an idea is rather different from that of Plato and Hegel, who conceive of the idea as something transcendent, whether an unchanging entity (Plato), or a working force in history (Hegel). From both must be distinguished "ideals"; for they are normative propositions intended to shape man's conduct. As is well known, the term "idealism" is bedeviled by its alluding to any one or all of these "meanings," though in common parlance an idealist is a person who will be motivated in his

[3] Cf. Chardin, 1959, pp. 164ff. and 254ff.; it is heartening to find one's reflections on this important point confirmed by so great an authority on early man.

actions to a greater degree than most others by the ideals he cherishes. This form of action-related political science would seem to be the necessary consequence of the value concern which we have shown to be the logical concomitant of a full grasp of role, function and purpose in politics (Chapter 2). This reflection is reinforced by the fact that the pursuit of truth, implied in all scientific work, is itself an "idealist" enterprise. It is rather touching to observe ardent scientific idealists urging the scientific invalidity of all ideals.

But the idealism which arises from value concern needs to be distinguished from the belief that ideas are the ultimate reality, even though there is an obvious connection. This connection is particularly striking in the figure of Plato, for the simple reason that among the ideas which possess ultimate reality he places the key virtues, presided over by the idea of the good. For obviously such ideas are readily converted into ideals in the sense just discussed, and the two forms of idealism are thus united. But the inclusion of the virtues is not necessarily the consequence of the (metaphysical) conviction that ideas are the ultimate reality. If these ideas are seen exclusively or predominantly in relation to the existential realm, representing the archetypes of other beings and "things" in the most general sense, then such an idea-ism might on the contrary mean a withdrawal from action of any sort and the eventual search for a "nirvana." [4] The sharpest and most precise rejection of this sort of "idealism" was offered by Kant in his *Critique of Pure Reason.* In rejecting it, he offered the following proposition: "The empirically determined mere consciousness of my own existence proves the existence of external objects." [5] This proposition is stated in explicit antithesis to Berkeley and Descartes, both of them representing the idealism which constitutes "a mighty objection" to a basic truth Kant had just formulated, to wit: "If we do not start with experiences or do not proceed according to the laws of the empirical connection of phenomena, we shall in vain pretend to divine or to explore the existence of any thing whatsoever." [6] He rejects the idealist proposition, because inner experience is possible only because of external experience which provides the notion of persistence in time. "The determination of my existence in time is possible only because of the existence of accidental things which I observe outside myself." For, so Kant comments, "the consciousness of myself in the idea of the I is not at all an intuition [*Anschauung*], but a merely intellectual idea of the self-activity of a thinking subject." [7] This does not mean, of course, that external objects

[4] Northrop, 1946, perhaps overdrew this contrast as he confronted the "aesthetic" Eastern with the "theoretic" Western position, but his work is illuminating in this respect. Note especially chaps. 3, 9, 12 and 13.

[5] Kant, 1787, p. 200. My own translation.

[6] *Ibid.*, p. 199. My own translation.

[7] *Ibid.*, p. 203.

necessarily exist when we imagine them; but such imaginings can only be the result of former external observations or combinations of them. Arguing thus, Kant overstates a good point; for surely man manages to imagine things which have never existed, and which he truly invents. With this remark, we are back at our first form of ideas which are created by men in response to challenges which man seeks to transcend by solving the problem presented.

The rejecting of philosophical idealism need not prevent us from recognizing (1) the enormous role of ideas in the sense of innovating inventions, any more than (2) the role of ideals in giving reality to normative propositions and values. For to govern is to invent. The political institutions which mark man's slow evolution from the primitive community of distant times [8] to the vast structures of the modern state and indeed the emergent world community have been *invented* by men, distinct *persons*, who had *new ideas* of how to deal with the problems they faced. Our difficulty in political theory arises in part from the fact that most of the political inventions, like other basic inventions, were made in times and under circumstances that preclude scientific study and analysis of the process. In a recent work of monumental learning, Alexander Rüstow has persuasively argued that the process of superimposition (*Überlagerung*) made possible by certain technical inventions which gave the particular groupings superior fighting power was the basis for achieving large-scale political organization.[9] In the sequel he describes some of the evil results of this superimposition, including sadism and masochism, theocracy (hierocracy) and the "feudalization" of "education" or even of the "self." During the isolation of the last ice age, those men who had learned to herd horses and other animals attacked and overwhelmed the settled farmers and established themselves as rulers. This process was recurrent. For long periods the layers may stay separate and apart; the resulting dualism of social structure Rüstow would call "medievalism" or "feudalism." This typical "feudal" social structure is characterized by rigid division into a layer of conquerors who have successfully superimposed themselves, and a broader layer of the conquered who have come to accept their masters. Why does a higher culture result from such "superimposition," such conquest? Because such conquest makes possible the effective organization of large numbers of human beings over large areas. The need for an elaborate division of labor results in what he calls the "law of the culture pyramid," [10] according to which there is a relation between the breadth of the

[8] They are still probably preserved in certain tribes with arrested development. Cf. Thomas, 1959.

[9] A. Rüstow, 1950, pp. 40ff. Hunters subjected planters; cowherds, planters; cowherds, peasants (pp. 55–66). The decisive weapons were the chariot and the horse, pp. 66ff. See also below, Chap. 10, and Friedrich, 1955.

[10] Cf. for this also Coste, 1899, pp. 154–156.

base and the height which the culture can achieve. The missing link in this argument is constituted by ideas and inventions in the politico-governmental field itself which appear crucial to the entire process. Consequently, such notions, while highly stimulating, remain largely speculative. We just do not know whether these inventions were actually the work of such conquerors, whether they discovered the necessary ingredients of large-scale organization, whether they were, in other words, the "idea men," or whether these inventions were made by others and then merely assimilated by them and adapted to their use. Another recent effort of imaginative speculation on these political inventions was undertaken by Wittfogel, who reconstructed the building of Oriental despotism in terms of the tasks of handling scarce water resources and therefore suggested the term "hydraulic" state of political order for these enterprises.[11] It was, according to this construction, the *idea* of how to utilize water for irrigation that was the decisive factor.

The truth is that we know very little about how these inventions were made and how the innovations consequent upon them were brought into being. But from what we are now able to observe close at hand in emergent structures it is allowable to infer that the more noteworthy institutional wholes were not invented in their entirety in "one fell swoop." Rather, they do constitute accretions of many small inventions, made over a considerable period of time, as men moved in a novel direction in politics. The infinitely complex operations of modern bureaucracy which can now be described by an abstract model were worked out step by step over centuries.[12] For example, records and files have become so much a matter of course today that we tend to forget that a great deal of ingenuity and determined effort went into their development; the same may be said of such decisive matters as differentiation of functions and qualification for office. A good many of these "inventions" were rediscoveries of matters long before worked out by the great administrators of Rome and the ancient East. The important point is that "ideas" moulded the political practice—a process which continues unabated.[13]

The most dramatic innovations in recent times have occurred in the working out of totalitarian dictatorship. It is a common mistake to think that this form of government was formed at once upon the Bolshevik revolution of 1917. Nothing could be further from the truth. The Russian revolutionaries thought of the dictatorship in conventional terms, and saw it as a transitional arrangement which would soon pass, in accordance with Marx's analysis and prediction. But the problems by which they found

[11] Wittfogel, 1957, pp. 11ff., 23ff., 50ff., and *passim;* he critically developed a well-known article by Karl Marx.

[12] T. R. Tout, 1920–1933, for many illustrations; cf. also for other countries, Friedrich, 1950, pp. 601–602, and chap. 2.

[13] Lasswell, a, 1955, gives some interesting recent instances.

themselves beset forced them into large-scale innovations which culminated in a full-fledged totalitarian dictatorship within a decade of the revolutionary outbreak.

We shall deal below with some of the more technical inventions made within the context of the democratic order (Chapter 21). Here it is important to point out that such inventive ideas are linked to operative ideas (ideals) in the form of ideologies. The concept of ideology has been of great importance in recent scientific analysis and political oratory. Like propaganda, it denotes for many "the other fellow's ideas which are wrong." Karl Mannheim, a number of years ago in a pathfinding study, insisted that particular ideologies "structurally resemble lies." [14] "The term denotes that we are sceptical of the ideas and representations advanced by our opponent; they are regarded as more or less conscious disguises of the real nature of the situation, the true recognition of which would not be in accord with his interest." [15] This sort of psychologizing approach to ideology is highly misleading. It stemmed from Mannheim's earlier preoccupation with the Marxist position which sees all ideas as "superstructure" of the economic condition of man. Fundamentally, his analysis was concerned with "proving" that the Marxist position was likewise "ideological" in this sense. In the political perspective, it is not of primary importance whether ideology contains misrepresentations or not. Take, for example, the statement from the Declaration of Independence that "all men are created equal." This statement, when considered in purely observational perspective, is undoubtedly incorrect. Antidemocrats have never wearied of dwelling on this aspect of the matter. The Declaration also asserts a considerable number of "facts" to prove the "absolute Tyranny" of the British King. Some of these "facts" are quite fanciful, others are quite true, e.g. the proposition that "prudence will dictate that Governments long established should not be changed for light and transient causes. . . ." Of all these statements, some true, some false, the first alleging the equality of men is most distinctly ideological, not because it is either true or false, but because it receives its significance from the

[14] Mannheim, 1953, p. 238 and elsewhere. The entire phrase refers to particular ideologies, which he distinguishes from "total ideologies" discussed below; it reads: ". . . all those utterances the 'falsity' of which is due to an intentional or unintentional, conscious, semi-conscious, or unconscious, deluding of one's self or of others, taking place on a psychological level and structurally resembling lies. . . . We speak of this conception of ideology as *particular* because it always refers only to specific assertions which may be regarded as concealments, falsifications or lies without attacking the integrity of the *total mental structure* of the asserting subject." (Italics in the original.) This book contains Mannheim's original work of 1929, as well as an article of 1931 and an introductory chapter intended to introduce the subject to Englishmen and written after he had come to England. The work is meant to make ideology the key to the "sociology of knowledge."

[15] *Ibid.*, p. 49.

implication it carries: hereditary privileges are bad and should be abolished, and a society without such privileges is good and should be established. In short, men should be treated *as if* they had been created equal, and public policy should be framed in accordance with this projection.

Ideologies are action-related systems of ideas. They typically contain a program and a strategy for its realization, and their essential function is to unite organizations which are built around them.[16] It is confusing and fails to provide the opportunity for political analysis, to call any system of ideas an ideology, such as the philosophy of Aristotle or the theology of the Old Testament. Such systems of ideas *may* provide the *basis* for an ideology, but only after being related to action in a specific sense and for a specific situation. Ideologies are sets of ideas related to the existing political and social order and intended either to change it or to defend it. They came into use in connection with modern party activity. Napoleon Bonaparte is credited with inventing the term, which he coined to belabor a group of opponents who insisted upon what would be called the revolutionary ideology. The ideas an ideology contains are as such action-related and may or may not be very true and appropriate; what makes them "ideology" is their function in the body politic. The ideology is a set of ideas which unites a party or other group for effective participation in political life. Such a functional political concept of idealogy is particularly useful in assessing its role in totalitarian dictatorship.

In contrast to such a functional concept of ideology, the term has been broadened to cover any "general system of beliefs held in common by the members of a collectivity. . . ."[17] Such a definition would make an ideology a characteristic feature of any politically organized community, serving the purpose of integrating the community. It resembles Mannheim's notion of a total ideology as "the characteristics and composition of the total structure of the mind of this epoch or of this group,"[18] but omits the latter's historical dimension. There is no sense in arguing about word usage, but since the terms "belief system" and "value system"

[16] Leites, 1953, p. 24 and elsewhere, calls this kind of ideology an "operational code," but it is more than that, namely, a system, more or less, of ideas relating to action. Clyde Kluckhohn, in Parsons and Shils, 1951, p. 432, speaks of ideology as a "system of ideas," but does not develop the implications. It is striking, indeed, that this ambitious attempt at formulating a general "theory of action" makes no other analysis of ideology, and hardly refers to ideas at all. All earlier analysis in terms of ideas is swallowed up by an analysis in terms of "values," yet these are treated as subjective givens, rather than as the objects which are subjectively reflected in "ideas." This is in keeping with the mechanical view of system criticized in the Introduction.

[17] Parsons, 1951, p. 349; similarly, Spiro, 1959, p. 180.

[18] Mannheim, 1953, pp. 49–50, 111; Lasswell and Kaplan, 1959, pars. 3.1., 6.1. and 6.3., politicize this notion, calling an ideology a "political myth" and defining it further as a "pattern of basic political symbols."

are common coinage for these phenomena, which they refer to, there is no sense in also calling them ideology; we need a term to designate a reasonably coherent body of ideas concerning practical means of how to change, reform (or maintain) a political order, and "ideology" offers itself conventionally as the best word for these specific phenomena. Such a body of ideas is typically based upon more or less elaborate criticism of what is wrong with the existing or antecedent order, including the criticism of the critics.

Such a political ideology may be partial or total, depending upon the range of the criticism involved. If it entails a total rejection of the existing order, and ideas about a total reconstruction, the ideology may properly be called total. Such total transformation is utopian, and where adopted as the program of a political movement or party it calls for the employment of violence. Total ideologies characteristically also encompass the positive acceptance of war as an instrument of politics, be this class war or war between other groups such as races or nations.[19]

In the light of this analysis, it is a mistake to speak of phenomena like nationalism as ideologies. Nationalism is primarily a sentiment or a body of feelings associated with the sense of self-identity of particular nations. It is typically devoid of any specific notions concerning the political or social order as such, except to insist that the order should be in keeping with "national traditions." This term is usually so vague as to have no specific institutional or behavioral content, until converted into a specific ideology. This understanding is important for a grasp of the role of ideology in newly emergent political orders, in many of which nationalism is a very powerful force. Something more than nationalism—for example, socialism—is needed. In contrast to the rival ideologies of democratic liberalism, democratic socialism and communism, nationalism has little or nothing to propose beyond the insistence upon national independence in politics, economics and culture. Such independence, to be sure, is likely to cause political change, but only where nationalism provides the framework for wholly new political orders, as in certain African states compounded of an assortment of tribes along quite arbitrary lines, does nationalism acquire genuine ideological content. It may, however, become associated with any of the rival ideologies and is in fact so associated.[20]

Ideologies are highly dynamic entities. Although some of the values, opinions and beliefs in specific ideologies may persist over long periods of

[19] Popper, 1945, p. 28. For a further elaboration of the problem of totalitarian ideology, compare Friedrich and Brzezinski, 1956, chap. 7. It may be objected that Gandhi and Tolstoy, for example, expounded total ideologies and yet rejected violence, but the nonviolence is itself a utopian element, and in actual political practice violence ensued.

[20] A somewhat different view is taken by Bowie, 1959, and his associates; note esp. pp. 50ff.

time, they are, as action-related systems of ideas, subject to constant change as the action is either attempted and succeeds, fails, or is diverted into new channels; or, if no opportunity for such trial and error is offered, they may be revised in the light of criticism or a changing social situation. The recent discussions in all socialist parties concerning the idea of nationalization is a striking instance of this constant flux in ideological content. The ideologies of totalitarian movements and states have similarly undergone rapid change. Such changes always raise the problem of perversion and corruption. At which point is a change tantamount to the abandonment of an ideology? No general answer can be given to this question, except in terms of the organization the ideas of which the ideology expresses: as long as the organization continues, the presumption has to be in favor of the continuity of the ideology. Corruption and perversion are fighting terms, employed by the opponent both within and without the organization.[21]

It has recently been suggested that ideologies are passing away, and will soon disappear from the political life of man.[22] If this prediction is meant to cover partial ideologies, it is as unlikely as the proposition that parties with specific ideas and programs of political and social change will pass away. Ideology is vitally related to the political process, because without ideas there can be no political action. The argument for a disappearance of ideologies is actually an ardent plea for abandoning the fanatical adherence to ideologies. Its humanist author suggests that experience has shown the limits of all ideologies and the evil consequences of a fanatical adherence. The evidence for such a contention is overwhelming, but will the small voice of reason prevail against the roar of masses aroused to political passion?

It seems, on the contrary, that ideologies will increase in importance, because the function which ideology fulfills in the political order is becoming more important. In all the countries now emerging from feudal bondage and colonial rule the establishment of a viable political order depends upon the invention of ideas which are meaningfully related to the problems their new situation has created. The "nationalist" movements which have accompanied these developments have usually crystallized into "parties" with distinct ideologies which are meant to provide the general ideas for mastering the task of community-building. The situation here really calls for integration, and the ideology plays a crucial role in bringing it about.[23] A striking illustration is provided by the development in

[21] For illustrations cf. Friedrich and Brzezinski, 1956, chap. 9.

[22] Aron, 1955, pp. 315ff. Contra, Jeanne Hersch, 1956.

[23] Parsons, 1951, pp. 517–519, relates ideology to integration in the processes of social change, which makes greater sense than his suggestion (pp. 349–350), criticized earlier, that any system of beliefs held by a community is an ideology, i.e., a system of ideas oriented toward the evaluative integration of the collectivity.

Puerto Rico. Neither nationalism nor Americanism, let alone the existing belief system, provided any effective mode for reintegrating a rapidly disintegrating cultural community. But the ideology of the Popular Democratic Party, led by Luis Muñoz Marín, embodied in the slogan *Pan, Tierra, Libertad* and spelled out into a detailed set of ideas as to how to deal with the situation actually confronted by the "desperate isle," the "stricken land," [24] soon served to integrate the desperate and starving masses of Puerto Rico. It has since become an operative ideology of fairly general significance for underdeveloped countries.[25] At the very center of it is the leaders' conviction that only inventive ingenuity and innovation can hope to master the situation.

Ideology focuses attention upon the interrelation between language and politics. When Churchill exclaimed that "the empires of the future are the empires of the mind," [26] he not only bade good-bye to old-fashioned imperialism, but he also implied that the capacity to capture men's minds by ideologies would be decisive. This capacity turns upon the ability to put into words, effective words, what needs to be done. Franklin Delano Roosevelt was an ideologist of high caliber. He succeeded again and again in finding the right expression for indicating the preferred course of action.[27] Ideology makes explicit and comprehensible the ideas which underlie proposed political and social change. It is therefore not in opposition to science, as Marx originally proposed, but builds upon such elements in science as are suitable for the task in hand. The potency of the several rival ideologies by which contemporary societies are rent is derived from this juncture with scientific insights. Their rivalry results partly from divergent value preferences to which these scientific insights are linked, and partly from different emphases in utilizing such insights. It is, therefore, from the scientific side that the rivalry of ideologies can be attenuated.[28]

Ideologies, as action-related systems of ideas, are exposed to an inherent danger. This is the danger that the projected action is palpably unrealizable. When that occurs, the ideology turns into utopia. It is par-

[24] Rexford Tugwell, 1947, who employed this term as the title for his challenging book.

[25] Friedrich, 1959, for further detail.

[26] In his speech upon receiving the honorary doctoral degree at Harvard, Sept. 6, 1943, published in *The Ceremonies in Honor of the Right Honorable Winston Spencer Churchill*, 1943, p. 15.

[27] Besson, 1955. On p. 190, this author rightly defines ideology as "a design for the future in the area of governmental and social life" (*auf das Gebiet des staatlichgesellschaftlichen Lebens bezogener Zukunftsentwurf*), referring in turn to Spranger, a, 1954.

[28] A similar view has recently been outlined by Aron, 1962, chaps. 17 and 18.

ticularly likely to happen when the ideas embodied in the ideology express not realities, but myths. The range of issues involved in this dimension of politics is so great that it seems better to devote a separate chapter to myth and utopia. At the end of that inquiry, it will also become possible to deal with political symbols, as they are crucial for myths, utopias and ideologies, and provide the expressive link between them.

chapter

5

The Political Myth, Its Symbols and Utopian Order

The heroic myth,
being a common possession of all,
knit the entire [*Greek*] *people together.*
Carl Burckhardt

SOME TIME AGO, a leading political scientist argued that the American Constitution was the country's social "myth," having defined a myth as "the presentation of the ultimate speculations of metaphysics, including cosmology, in a coherent system of symbols. . . ."[1] He saw myths as methods of cultural instruction, to convey esoteric thought to the vulgar. There can be no doubt that such educational results are an important by-product of myths, but they are not the core of their political function. The rationalist age saw them essentially as "untruths" that could not stand the glare of science's searchlights. We have become less arrogant in our intellectual pretensions, and are more ready to recognize that myths may have a significant, maybe even a vital, function in the political order. They provide an underpinning, as will be shown, to the ideas prevalent in a political community. Men's finite minds need the myth for the purpose of mastering their situation; if everything had to be worked out in rational terms, nothing would ever get done, least of all in politics.[2]

[1] Elliott, a, 1938, p. 210. Elliott had earlier drawn attention to the importance of "myths" in political analysis. Cf. 1928, chap. IV.

[2] Voegelin, 1956, p. 83. "Today it is no longer permissible to regard the myth as having no other purpose in the history of mankind than to provide a stepping

Writers like Pareto had great sport in applying the rationalist yardstick to the myth. As a prime example of nonlogical conduct, it occupies a considerable place in his general analysis of society. He recognized its essential function and examined many historical instances.[3] Several general propositions which Pareto developed, are, therefore, worth brief mention. For one thing, he recognized that myths have a historical basis, or else are imitations of myths which do have it.[4] For that reason he would consider the myth a "deformed" reflection of something real. But when is a reflection "deformed," since surely it cannot be identical with the real it reflects? Some myths, he says, are to be taken as "historical facts plus a fictional appendage," [5] and indeed the first kind of myth develops out of the second by a gradual weakening of the "factual" content. Statements of this kind reflect the viewpoint which led Pareto to set forth and believe in a "value-free" social or political analysis. This leads to the notion that the selective process involved in myth-building is arbitrarily value-oriented, and can be substituted for by another in which the historical "facts" are related without reference to the values cherished by him who tells the tale. He consequently arrives at the naïve and erroneous proposition that "myths and the like are made up of experiences wrongly interpreted and fallacious inferences from the real facts." [6] By what standard are we to say that the experiences are "wrongly" interpreted or that the inferences are "fallacious"? Obviously, by the standard of verifiability and consequent communicability. We have discussed earlier (Chapter 2) the complex relation between facts and value. Instead, if we follow Pareto's discussion, we find that it trails off into a long disquisition about animism and totemism, but we never learn, except in terms of some gratuitous "detached observer" how the myth might have been "rightly" interpreted or the "correct" inferences drawn. Pareto fails to elucidate the function of the myth in such terms, although he is clearly enough aware of the fact that it had a variety of functions, as his analysis of specific myths shows: his critique of the allegorical interpretation [7] reinforces this conclusion. Thus we are left with the important insight into the functional value of myths, but instead of an analysis of this key point, we hear in great detail that the human beings who shaped the myths in response to their concrete situation

---

stone for more rational forms of symbolization . . . the myth has a life and virtue of its own." In writing thus, Voegelin follows a general trend, most broadly developed in its philosophical implications by Cassirer, 1925. Cf. also Bachofen, pp. 195ff., 491ff., 560ff., and *passim*.

[3] Pareto, 1935, pp. 221f., 461ff., and *passim*.

[4] *Ibid*., par. 347, and again in par. 681.

[5] *Ibid*., par. 350.

[6] *Ibid*., par. 692.

[7] *Ibid*., pars. 764–797.

used standards of selection different from those of a professor of sociology in nineteenth-century Switzerland—not exactly a startling point that calls for pages and pages of illustration.

There are many kinds of myths: theogonic, showing how gods came into being; cosmogonic, describing the origin of the world; cosmological, portraying the world's working; and anthropological, dealing with man's origin and development. Beside these, there are soteriological myths, about man's salvation, and eschatological ones, projecting the end of man and world and even of the gods. All these myths have their political bearing, but there is a more specifically political myth, and that is the founder myth, that is to say, the myth or myths dealing with the foundation and origin of a particular political order or a number of them. Myth at this point bears a close resemblance to legend and has a kinship to ancestor-worship. Typically, the origin is personalized in a hero who possessed superhuman qualities which enabled him to accomplish the feat. Likewise, the Founding Fathers at Philadelphia, though recurrently "debunked" by irreverent iconoclasts as ordinary mortals, are seen by the community at large as men of superhuman wisdom and courage, and it is their deeds which correspond to the work of Theseus in founding Athens. For the Constitution is a document capable of rational analysis and interpretation, not a myth; rather, the poetic tale of how it came into being is a myth, and a myth of vital importance for the American political order.

The foundation myth shaped the image of the *polis* from the outset. Carl Burckhardt has given a vivid picture of how these myths sprang up almost as soon as a new *polis* was founded. But the foundation myth is transcended in the great common myths of all the Hellenes, especially as they were embodied in the epic poetry. "The heroic myth knit the entire people together, being a common possession of all."[8] The foundation myth manifested itself in the worship of the founder. As Fustel has written: "The founder was the man who accomplished the religious act without which a city could not exist. He established the hearth where the sacred fire was to burn. . . ."[9] Theseus, Romulus and Aeneas are only three of the best-known among the dozens of mythical founders whose acts of violence, forcing villages into forming a *polis* (*synoikismos*), were thus gilded in after ages.

It is a serious question whether a political community can achieve political order without developing a foundation myth (and the same may be said, probably, of religious communities, that is to say, churches). For the actual process is not likely to be in accord with the value judgments and beliefs of the community, but instead will exhibit the cold rationality

[8] Burckhardt, 1898, 1930, pp. 62ff. See also chap. 22.

[9] Fustel de Coulanges, 1889, p. 188. Fustel's views are, of course, dated; but in putting the matter as he does, he expresses the myth.

of reason of state. So offensive an event is not likely to provide that basic unity which the working political community calls for. This is a very serious problem for the now emergent political orders. Everywhere we can observe the springing up of political myths, including the worship of the founder. It is a striking feature of the Soviet Union, where the figures of Marx and Lenin have achieved the halo of idealists of the purest water, in spite, or perhaps as part, of their presumed purity of cold realism. A similar halo has developed around the figure of Kemal Ataturk. How many of the more recent leaders will become part of a viable myth is hard to predict; where the community becomes effective, it is bound to happen.

Obviously, such myth-making is carried forward by various persons: followers, poets and simple folk. In an age of rational discourse and historical analysis, the devices are more subtle and the tales more elusive. But eventually, they are woven into a pattern of convincing make-believe which provides a reasonably secure foundation—or the community perishes. More abstract documents, such as Magna Charta or the Bill of Rights, may become important elements in reinforcing such myth-making, even though in themselves they are subject to rational analysis. This is in part due to the failure of people to read such documents with critical detachment, but rather to recite them in ritualistic sonority, typically selecting only those passages which lend themselves to such recital.

The absence of a founder myth in the case of political orders imposed from without is extremely serious, even when genuine assent is secured. The colonial regimes which are now disintegrating with such rapidity testify to this danger, even though many other factors are at work. The "nationalism" which is springing up everywhere is itself to a large extent a "myth" of potent impact. It has been erroneously described as an "ideology," as we pointed out above (Chapter 4), presumably because its potentialities as probably the most powerful myth were not duly taken into account. It could, of course, be argued that, while a myth to the believer and follower of a nationalist movement, nationalism is an ideology to the historian of such a movement, provided it becomes the organizing force for political action taken on behalf of such a nation. But, typically, a nationalist movement merely asserts that a nation whose existence is taken for granted in the national myth should be independent (free). What specifically is wrong in the existing society other than its lack of independence typically divides the adherents of such a movement into rival camps of divergent ideological content. Thus the Indian independence movement consisted of a motley assortment of conservatives, liberals, Socialists, Communists and believers in Hinduism such as Gandhi himself. As soon as independence was achieved, these ideological orientations came to the fore and provided the ideological focus of political parties and movements. The ideology of these parties contrasted with the Indian national myth which unites all Indians against outsiders, though sometimes the ideology provides a modification of the myth. This is not a question of either/or, but rather a recognition of the diverse function of ideas in the political field, a myth providing grounds for an ideology, and an ideology often procreating a myth.[10] Perhaps the most profound of all these national myths is that of Israel; it unites men of the most diverse backgrounds in the common sense of being one nation since times immemorial.[11]

Not only its strength makes the national myth so dangerous but also its vagueness. It often derives its most powerful support from an accompanying antimyth, be it tyranny, colonial oppression or capitalist exploitation. It all began with the tyranny of King George III, but the actual image of colonial oppression now operative in the minds of men is no less mythological. The most striking myth of modern times is, however, that of capitalist exploitation. All three of these myths serve, like the monsters of old, to provide the setting within and against which the founding of the new political order has to be achieved. In advanced societies, such as the Italian and German ones, the myth of the impending seizure of power by the Communists had to be conjured up to provide the antagonist against whom the founder hero had to succeed.

The often lamented weakness of German and Japanese, if not of Italian, democracy, cannot be separated from this question of how to surround the founding of a political order with a convincing myth. This is difficult to do within the shadow of foreign bayonets. However, the bitter enmity toward the defunct regime did, at least in the Italian and German case, provide a powerful antimyth, reinforced by the resistance record of at least some of the founders. This conflict is a facet of the personality image of Adenauer which has considerable political potency, as it had in that of Theodor Heuss, the Federal Republic's first president. Typically, the rulers of the East German occupation zone have worked with the same antimyth, and have sought to reinforce their position by the myth of a communist victory over Fascism. No one knows how far the myth carries or how many believe it; about its existence there can be very little doubt.

Some of the instances just mentioned illustrate the extraordinary rapidity with which myths grow up. They grow faster than the proverbial ivy which covers college buildings with tradition in the brief span of five or six years. There can be very little doubt that myths are often willfully created by men who insist on perpetuating the one-sided view of things which guided them during the action which led to victory in the struggle of founding the new order. They are enormously aided in this drive by the employment of symbols which connote to the devoted follower the drama of the birth of a group or a nation. Flags are often the visible expression of some decisive act, but there are many other symbols of com-

[10] Cf. Shklar, 1957, pp. 206ff., and *passim*.
[11] Halperin, 1961, chaps. 1 and 4, and the literature cited.

parable significance. Symbolic acts, such as the coronation of kings or dedication of monuments, serve to convey the myth without detailed specification. There is more symbolism in contemporary life than is generally recognized, and the political order is richly ornamented with symbols of every kind.

It is highly doubtful that a political order could endure without effective symbols—not only symbols for its myth, but also for its ideology and the values and beliefs upon which such ideology rests. In the next chapter, the symbolism of beliefs will be explored in conjunction with religion. Here we must deal at somewhat greater length with the symbols of government, and more especially the founding of a political order. Take the following statement: "However you reduce the functions of your government to their utmost simplicity, yet symbolism remains. . . . You abolish the etiquette of a royal court, but at official receptions you ceremonially shake the hand of the Governor of your state. Just as the feudal doctrine of a subordination of classes, reaching up to the ultimate overlord, requires its symbolism; so does the doctrine of human equality require its symbolism."[12] Here presumably the symbolism consists of "doctrines," i.e., ideatic embodiments of value preferences. But it would seem doubtful that the handshake referred to is symbolic in any precise sense. There has been a considerable danger of depriving symbols of their distinctive role in the political order by thinking that "almost all human conduct is symbolic."[13] Like the notion that all believed-in ideas are "myths," this theory signifies a corrosion of the true symbols of any political order. Symbols are signs for meanings transcending the empirical content; symbols therefore refer to something else, usually by simplifying a complex and absent person or thing.[14] The coat of arms of a landowner, the flag of a country, the signature of a writer—these are typical symbols of considerable political relevance.

Symbols have been classified in a variety of ways, depending upon the standpoint of the particular writer.[15] In political analysis, the typology

[12] Whitehead, 1927, p. 62.

[13] Arnold, 1935, p. 17. This stimulating little book is characterized by a very loose use of the term, so that practically everything a government does becomes a "symbol of government."

[14] S. Langer, 1942, *passim.*

[15] One of the more significant definitions of symbols was given by Sapir in the *ESS,* 1934. He himself, being preoccupied with linguistic phenomena, proposed to divide them into "referential" and "condensation" symbols, the former being such language "agreed upon as economical devices for purposes of references," and the latter "allowing for the ready release of emotional tension." Sapir himself later suggests that the two are frequently intermingled. I would go farther and question the taxonomic soundness, because *all* symbols are necessary "references" and the question of the degree of emotion attaching to them is evidently a matter of the referents. A very broad conception of symbolism is set forth by Whitehead, 1927, pp. 7ff.

of symbols is suggested by the uses to which they are put. Leaving aside the religious sphere for the moment, we observe these main symbol referents: institutions, persons (including groups), values, ideologies and myths. There is no need to say much more about the first three; that Harvard University is symbolized by its shield VERITAS, that a man is symbolized by his initials, that love is symbolized by the color red—these are phenomena familiar to all. These examples show at the same time that symbolization is closely related to representation (Chapter 15). The symbol, by referring to *A*, represents it, makes it (or him) present for the particular purpose in hand. The symbol, therefore, enjoys a protection comparable to the value of the thing or person represented.

All linguistic expression is symbolic representation. So is all mathematics. But when the entities referred to arouse no emotion, neither do the symbols which refer to them. The opposite is the case with political symbols. Political symbols, even in their linguistic attire, are value-related, and, therefore, are apt to arouse tension and strife. The familiar opinion that "there is no need to argue about words" is contradicted by political experience. If A customarily calls the institutional complex he most highly values "democracy," and B proceeds to call an institutional complex he disvalues and rejects "democracy," how can A avoid arguing about words? The symbolic role of the concatenation of the letters A, D, C, C, E, M, O, R, Y when suitably organized plays so powerful a role as a key symbol in the political order of which he is a member, that he feels compelled to reject as a misuse or abuse the employment which B wants to make of it. But B may have his own value-related reasons for insisting upon this use of the symbol "democracy." In that case the argument may continue for a long time, for symbol conflicts have a way of persisting as long as the values symbolized continue to hold their emotional appeal.[16]

The example just mentioned carries the discussion forward into the realm of ideology. For such terms as "democracy" derive their significance from the ideological implications they carry. As we stated the case, this need not be so. Democracy in both contexts may refer simply to the actually existing political order *as it is*. But it is likely to do more. Democratic ideology is likely to intrude itself; either it is that of the constitutional democracy which is embodied in the ideas of liberal and democratic thinkers or it is proletarian democracy as envisaged by Marx, Engels and Lenin. Such ideological conflict becomes embittered if meta-rational symbols (not words, but things) are brought forward. The recent bitter quarrel over what flag or flags are to be hoisted at the Olympic games, when Germans are to be honored as victors and participants, is symptomatic. Policy considerations are, of course, a factor, but the depth of emotions aroused by the conflict is explainable only by reference to the rival ideologies which the two symbols might represent.

[16] For further concrete material, see Friedrich and Brzezinski, 1956, chap. 10.

The fact that ideologies are directed toward the future, and concerned with a content capable of being rationally disputed about makes them less suitable subjects for symbolization than myths. Indeed, the myth becomes embodied in the persons incorporating the myth. "The Founding Fathers offered the convenient Pantheon in which divergent views of orthodoxy might be reconciled,"[17] but this function is far outweighed by the role they play as personifying the founding myth as such. They absorbed and transcended the discovery myth of Columbus and the covenanting myth of the Pilgrim Fathers, but only the three myths in combination provide the American community with the integrating beliefs of the "almost chosen people."[18]

In our time, such myth-making has been consciously manipulated in the case of the Fascists' "March on Rome." But Mussolini's Italy never made "a go of it," as it did with many other symbols. When this manipulative stage is reached, myth and ideology tend to become intertwined, even confused. Hammer and sickle, swastika and fasces are symbols both of myth and ideology. Each in its way suggests both origin and destiny, past and future. In any case, they are well known to many who have no clear-cut ideas with regard to either. Each of these symbols hints at the foundation myth: hammer and sickle at the revolutionary proletarian worker, swastika at the Nordic race, fasces at the "grandeur that was Rome." But at the same time, each symbol also provides a concrete image of the ideological projection. Thus hammer and sickle suggest a social order dominated by the proletariat. The fasces, themselves a symbol of the Roman lictor's *potestas,* also suggest the new order of discipline and obedience which the Fascist ideology demanded. Finally, the swastika, symbol of many and diverse uses in the heathen past, also symbolized the Nazi's ideological challenge of the Christian social order and its true cross, and stood for the new order of racial dominance and world conquest. The symbolic merging of myth and ideology, of origin and destiny, is highly characteristic of these totalitarian systems. It is probably significant that the Communist symbol is constructed, is invented, in light of the ideology, and then invested with a tie to the myth of origin, in keeping with this ideology. It corresponds to the highly conscious and rationalist pattern of the social thinking of the Soviet Union. The swastika, by contrast, suggested little more than heathenism, having no particular connection with either German history or the thought that went into the Nazi movement. That it was a "hooked" cross, and that it antedated the Christian era, were its primary assets, it would seem. That the harsh and sober way of life of the pristine Roman Republic which conquered the world should have appealed to the founders of Fascism is clear enough. But why the symbol of the policeman rather than other nobler symbols should have been

[17] Elliott, a, 1938, p. 220.
[18] W. J. Wolf, 1959, pp. 96f., 117ff., 149ff.

selected, is a question which probably leads again into the metaideological sphere: the glorying in violence and in personal coercion which was the stamp of Italian Fascism.

If values, ideologies and myths, no less than persons and institutions, call forth the rich variety of symbolic representations we have briefly alluded to—and what has been said is fairly familiar—the question arises of what *political* function is being served by this constant proliferation of symbols and myths. The answer which can here only be stated ex cathedra is that such symbolization powerfully assists in governing, by reinforcing authority, where power and influence might not suffice or be as efficacious (Chapter 12). For symbols suggest, and the myth they refer to personifies, the reasons why a particular political order "makes sense." They build an emotional underpinning, and thereby provide a shortcut, for effective cooperation and subordination. Hence, every political order will be very deeply concerned about the integrity of its symbols, and will seek to prevent, or to revenge, their defiling. On the other hand, and for the same reason, deviant and more particularly disloyal groups and persons will make every effort to belittle such symbols. Similarly, revolutionary movements will make symbol perversion one of their primary objectives; for if the symbols of the existing order can be made ridiculous or repellent, the values they stand for will be disintegrating; reversely, if the values disintegrate, the symbols begin to appear ridiculous.

The world of political symbols has always included antisymbols, that is to say, symbols of the enemy, his values and myths. But only in advanced literary societies, where ideological factors play a major role, does the antisymbol become of primary importance. Thus the "Bolshevik" is a wild and violent, black-bearded revolutionary of low morals in the symbolic armory of American rhetoric. Similarly, the totalitarian movements have developed fairly detailed negative symbols. They embody a stereotyped [19] image of the enemy. For the Nazis it was the fat, rich Jew or the Jewish revolutionary; for the Fascists it was first the Communist subversive, later the degenerate, corrupt and weak bourgeois; for the Soviets it is the warmongering, atom-bomb–throwing American Wallstreeter; for the Chinese Communists and many a colonial revolutionary it is the Yankee imperialist and the Western exploiter. These negative images accentuate by contrast the positive value of the regime. They are powerful symbols, displayed on the wallboard, in motion pictures and the press with relentless repetition.[20]

A number of writers have tended to stress symbols, rather than

[19] The psychological category of "stereotype" is the equivalent of these personified symbols, when looked at from the standpoint of the analysis of the individual consciousness. Popularized by Lippmann, 1922, it has been studied in its impact upon politics in a number of contexts.

[20] Boorstin, 1960, has recently discussed an interesting case, the American image of Europe, in this perspective.

myths, in their general analysis of politics and society,[21] often by so broadening the concept as to identify it with all political phenomena. Myths may, in fact, be interpreted as symbols within the context of so broad an interpretation. For they are images of origin and growth.

It has been observed that "even the most elementary orientation of action on animal levels involves signs which are at least the beginning of symbolization." [22] Without signs, there could be no orientation, no selection among alternatives. Symbolization, in this broad linguistic sense, is really identical with thought. The statements made about it sound more original than they are; for example, that symbolization is the necessary condition for the emergence of culture appears obvious. Symbols, and more especially political symbols, are of real interest only where they are functionally related to the political order, and this is primarily so, as we have shown, in the case of symbols relating to ideology and the foundation myth, although symbols in the personal, institutional and valuational sphere do play their role in various contexts. There is one important dimension of the ideology myth which requires further exploration, and that is the role of utopian thought.

It has been asserted that "the ideology is the political myth functioning to preserve the social structure; the utopia to supplant it." [23] Nothing could be farther from political reality and from our analysis of it than that statement. An ideology is, as we saw in the previous chapter, concerned with the criticism and reform of a particular political situation. Here ideology is defined as a myth, when in fact it is an action-related system of ideas as to possible change. This latter meaning is attributed to "utopias." [24] Utopias, however, are actually a particular kind of myth. Originally, utopia, or no-place, was meant to be a playful rearrangement of items in the social scene to produce an image that was admittedly wholly imaginary but was believed to be able to serve as a matrix for assessing the existing political order. I am not here concerned with the question of what Thomas More meant *Utopia* to be,[25] but with what it came to mean. There can be no question that utopias were intended as

[21] E.g., Charles Merriam, 1934, pp. 105f.; Lasswell and Kaplan, 1951, pp. 10ff., 103ff. In the latter discussion, Lasswell and Kaplan defined political symbols as "symbols that function to a considerable extent in power practices," which leaves open the question itself; symbol, in the earlier passage was left undefined, but it was stated that it was "whatever has meaning or significance in any sense." As indicated above, so broad a signification robs it of analytical value.

[22] Parsons, 1951, p. 10.

[23] Lasswell and Kaplan, 1950, p. 123.

[24] Lasswell and Kaplan, in making these suggestions, claim to follow Mannheim, 1936, *passim,* but I believe mistakenly. Mannheim sees utopia as imbedded in ideology, as it has been at times, especially in socialist thought.

[25] This question has been the subject of extensive controversy among historians of ideas; cf. Hexter, 1952, pp. 11ff., and *passim.* For an interesting survey of utopias, cf. Lewis Mumford, 1922; also Berneri, 1950, pp. 52ff.

criticism of the existing society, but in terms sufficiently poetic and beyond practical realization as to constitute no revolutionary proposal for action. In this perspective, it is clear that utopias resemble, but at the same time exhibit a sharp contrast to, ideologies: they contain systems of ideas that are critical, but not necessarily action-related, and they are at the same time like myths in presenting these ideas in the form of concrete, and preferably personified, images. An interesting question is presented by Plato's *Republic*, usually spoken of as the archetype of utopia, since he unquestionably inspired all later utopias. Actually, Plato's *Republic* (and to a lesser extent the *Laws*) does not fit these categories very well, because Plato thought of his republic of guardians as realizable,[26] though not very likely to be realized, and he embodied his ideas in concrete and personalized, mythlike images. It seems to me that Plato's thought should be considered a quasi-utopian ideology, cast in the form of a soteriological myth.

Utopias, such as that of Thomas More and Campanella, as well as the socialist utopias of the first half of the nineteenth century (including the utopia sketched in the *Communist Manifesto*, 1848), all described a perfectionist model of a political social order, by way of contrast to the existing state of affairs. In a sense all these utopias were secularized versions of paradise. But just as there was a hell to correspond to paradise, so it would seem possible to project the negative features of the existing society and compose a utopian order characterized by a maximum of such faults. Such negative utopias have become the fashion in the twentieth century. Perhaps the best-known is Huxley's *Brave New World*, but Orwell's *1984* and others similarly undertake to portray a world to come which would clearly be hell by selecting the hellish features of contemporary society for emphasis, and indeed exaggeration. These negative utopias, like the positive ones of another climate of thought and feeling, are intensely political in purpose and impact. While the positive utopias fed upon man's optimism and hope for progress toward a better world, the negative utopias express an increasing pessimism and the "farewell to progress" which animates enlarging conservative circles.

But whether utopias are positive or negative, they represent, in a functional political sense, a species of myth, not foundation or growth images, but eschatological myth-making. Yet they are not genuinely eschatological, because they contain the element of conscious make-believe. Any image of a future society spoken of as utopian, is by that very term given a surrealist dimension which, by removing it from action-related ideas, suggests by inversion that this certainly will not be the end, even though it can be thought of as a "possible-impossible" end.

It is questionable whether utopias have any very explicit relationship

[26] Plato, *Republic*, V. pp. 499–502; VII. p. 541.

to political doctrine, though such a relationship may exist. It is a common occurrence that political opponents will call each other's ideologies "utopian." What they mean to suggest by such an epithet—and the most famous instance is Marx's dubbing all socialists before him "utopian"—is that the particular ideology contains elements which are unrealistic, so that the doctrines and ideas contained in it become unrelated to action. We can see at this point the intimate interrelationship between ideas, ideologies, myths and utopias. Ideologies, to be effective, are apt to contain elements which transcend demonstrable possibilities of action, because of the very nature of ideas; such elements will be embodied in myths and projected in the form of utopias. The only possible conclusion is that all ideologies contain utopian elements, and that all utopias contain ideological elements, and that the tie is provided by the continuous oscillation of ideas and myths. If there were a possibility of knowing the truth of things to come, as well as things that have passed away, an ideology free of utopian ingredients and a utopia unrelated to ideological preferences might possibly be built. Man's finite mind being what it is, and the task of political order continuing to confront it, the interweaving of the two by means of ideas and myths is bound to continue. It is none other than Pareto, who, in spite of his deep skepticism concerning man's capacity for rational (logico-experimental) conduct wrote: "One may predict that there will continue to be absolute T's (ideals) and imaginary T's (ideals) represented as real; for barring some change in the ties we see functioning about us at present, society will never be able to subsist without them." [27] The absolute T's are the utopias we have been examining with a view to clarifying their function in the body politic. They provide the impetus for the forward thrust, as well as the link with the established bonds of any political order.

[27] Pareto, 1935, par. 1307.

chapter 6

Religion and Ritual

Ah Sze, you love the lamb,
but I love the ritual.
Confucius

MYTH, IDEOLOGY AND UTOPIA, they all contain beliefs which are beyond proof. Ideologies more particularly have been spoken of as "secular religions" or as "political religions." [1] Such a distortion of religion in purely psychological terms suggests itself in a time of weakening religious ties; it was philosophically adumbrated by no less a man than William James.[2] James observed at the end of his study that "originality cannot be expected in a field like this, where all the attitudes and tempers that are possible have been exhibited in literature long ago," and yet we have since seen not only the emergence of the pseudo-religions of totalitarianism, but also the religious philosophizing that goes under the heading of existentialism, derived from Kierkegaard, but exemplified in Marcel and Jaspers, if not in Heidegger and Sartre. James described himself as a supernaturalist, though not attached to the "refined supernaturalism" of the philosophers who divide the world of the ideal

[1] Voegelin, 1938.

[2] William James, 1902, where the entire argument is built on religious "sentiment" as the core of religious *experience*. It is significant that the positivists, more especially Pareto, did not wish to admit the religious experience to be experience at all; his discussion of the subject is given under the heading "Theories Transcending Experience" (1935, pars. 368ff.).

from the world of the actual in the tradition of Kant. "Notwithstanding my own inability to accept either popular Christianity or scholastic theism, I suppose that my belief that in communion with the Ideal new force comes into the world, and new departures are made here below, subjects me to being classed among the supernaturalists of the piecemeal or crasser type." [3] Passages such as these have a curiously dated ring. And yet, the issue which James is considering, namely, the function of religion in the life of the individual, and hence of the group, is more vital today than when he wrote. The challenge to organized religion provided by totalitarian dictatorship has vitalized the issue of religion and politics. It is impossible to deal with the political community and its order in a realistic manner without exploring the role of religion. But this exploration is made extraordinarily difficult not only by the vast amount of ancient learning that surrounds the subject of religion, but also by the range and intensity of the controversy surrounding it. Not only is Christianity divided into a number of rival churches with sharply conflicting dogmas concerning the relation of church and state, but it is confronted by the vast array of competing religious faiths and organizations which are traditional in the different parts of the globe. Evidently no view of religion and its organization in churches which is dogmatically derived from the Christian tradition would be suitable for general political analysis.

What is it that all these different religions have in common? Is there a core that can be identified, or do we have to start from the premise that religion is a "collective name" for a group of phenomena that have no common core? Such a premise is hard to accept from a logical viewpoint, because it implies that the one word "religion" has a number of different meanings. Pareto, in his mocking, nineteenth-century positivist treatment of religion, tries to distinguish two kinds, religion alpha and religion beta, the first characterized as "the sum of scruples that interfere with the free exercise of human faculties," while the second is "a belief in higher beings with whom it is possible to establish relations." [4] Alpha and beta are not present, however, in all phenomena called religions, and so the analysis breaks down again. It is obvious that these are not two *kinds* of religion, but two *views* of religion which itself remains obscure.[5] Pareto may, in this respect, serve as typical of the kind of agnostic *Religionskritik* which undertakes to "prove" that religion is not "scientific"—surely not a very significant observation. However, it brings into focus a point which *is*

[3] James, 1902, p. 511.

[4] Pareto, 1935, I, pp. 238–239.

[5] Pareto's own analysis rambles off into a long and rather banal discourse on natural law as a presumed manifestation of religion; his effort is directed at demonstrating that human thoughts have a basis in sentiment (residues, he calls them) and lack logical coherence as a result (derivations), two rather self-evident points, it would seem.

crucial, namely, that, like science, religion is oriented toward truth, but that it is a different kind of truth from scientific truth. The conventional formula for designating its truth is to call it "revealed." The truth of science is "demonstrated" by certain types of evidence, such as documents, experiments and ratiocination, whereas the truth of religion is not. The famous formula of *Credo quia absurdum*, I believe *because* it is absurd, might be called the archetype of the religious position regarding truth. If we proceed from this basis of revelation, and ask next who it is that reveals such truths, we naturally answer: God. This sacred word refers, however, to a very great variety of possible beings, and often beings in the plural at that. This is not the place to elaborate upon the question of divine beings; suffice it to state that very large numbers of human beings have acknowledged their belief that such beings exist and that they have "revealed" truths which could not otherwise be demonstrated. This is what might be called the dogmatic side of religion.

There is, however, another side which does not refer to truth, but rather to right action. That the two are linked, we have stated earlier (Chapter 2); such linking is the peculiar province of religious conduct or behavior. Right action may be based either upon considerations of expediency, or upon example. Some of the founders of great religions, such as Confucius, have primarily set an example. Confucius did not claim to have received the truth from a divine being, as did Moses and many others; he inspired his followers by his conduct. In a striking discussion with one of his disciples, Confucius said: "There are three things about the superior man that I have not been able to attain. The true man has no worries; the wise man has no perplexities; and the brave man has no fears." Tsekung then said, "But, Master, you are exactly describing yourself." This and related themes recur throughout the writings of Confucius: "The things that trouble or concern me are the following: lest I should neglect to improve my character, lest I should neglect my studies, and lest I should fail to move forward when I see the right course, or fail to correct myself when I see my mistake." To this we might add the story according to which Tsekung wanted to do away with the ceremony of sacrificing the lamb in winter. Thereupon Confucius said, "Ah Sze, you love the lamb, but I love the ritual." [6] It is the ritual, embedded in historical tradition, that constitutes the other dimension of religion. Ritual consists of the rites or ceremonies, conduct symbolically related to beliefs. While religions the world over show the greatest variation in the relative emphasis placed upon ritual, there is no religion which does not contain some ritual as well as dogma.[7] Such ritual constitutes as deep a need for

[6] Lin Yutang, 1938, pp. 162, 163, 168.

[7] It is due to James's psychologizing approach that he thought he could "ignore the institutional branch" of religion and confine himself to "personal religion pure

man as does the belief in a divine being, and can replace it to a large extent. Walter Pater, in *Marius the Epicurean* has beautifully portrayed the central importance of religious ritual, as have many other writers, especially those dealing with the Orient. Confucius and men like him disprove the proposition that "founders of every church owed their power originally to the fact of their direct personal communion with the divine." We cannot cite Christ, Buddha and Mahamet, Luther and Calvin in support of this proposition; for all of them were representatives of predominantly dogmatic religions. The polytheistic religion of the Greeks, as "founded" by Homer and Hesiod, did not owe its ability of founding the Greek cults to the poets' capacity to communicate with the divine, but to their "poetic" capacity to portray the gods' doings; thereby they set exemplars of right conduct, later much disapproved of by Plato as "immoral." It was Socrates who insisted upon the idea of a divine voice, his *daimonion*, in the discussions over right conduct.[8]

These two aspects of man's religion, the ritualistic and the dogmatic, A. D. Nock, in an important study some years ago, linked to the role of prophecy. What he called "the two opposing poles of man's spiritual history" he described as follows: "One is the system of religious observances of a small social unit with elementary needs and interests and no important contacts with other cultures. . . . The other is the religion of a prophetic movement in the first ardor of the founder. . . ."[9] Most of religion actually lies between the two poles, and it is important to realize that the first may broaden into the formalized ritual of a vast empire, such as China, while the latter may contract into the slender following of a dissident sectarian.

Seen in the perspective of politics where religion is part of a community's belief system, the dogmatic and the ritualistic emphases are merged as both beget conviction. The great Gibbon once wrote: "The various modes of worship, which prevailed in the Roman world, were all considered by the people as equally true, by the philosopher as equally false; and by the magistrate as equally useful."[10] This usefulness of religion results from the strengthening of convictions concerning human

---

and simple" (*op. cit.*, p. 30). It is the Protestant Christian whose religious premises speak here. Hocking, 1940, pp. 69ff., stresses the ritualistic ingredient in Oriental religions, and the consequent possibility of "plural belonging."

[8] Socrates was undoubtedly not the first, but his name will forever be linked to this innovation. See Gigon, 1947; A. E. Taylor, 1933. On Greek religion, see Jaeger, 1947; Nilsson, 1950; Guthrie, 1950, which contains in chap. 2 an interesting review of the literature.

[9] Nock, 1933, pp. 4–5. Nock too speaks of Greek religion as "following tradition," and characterizes it by the statement that "a city honoured certain deities to whom it looked for the satisfaction of its needs" (p. 17).

[10] *Decline and Fall*, chap. 2.

conduct. Ethical behavior is motivated by such convictions; indeed it is difficult to imagine it without them, since in common understanding such behavior is characterized by the tension between what a human would like to do and what his inner voice tells him he ought to do. When a "virtue ethic" is seen as "fulfilling" the law of a "command ethic," it points to this convictional core.

Both the dogmatic and the ritualistic aspects of religion crystallize into organization. This organization may be, but need not be, a church. A large number of religions have depended for their organizational needs upon the political community. Thus the Greek *polis* no less than the great Oriental empires, such as China, or Egypt, built its political organization upon religious foundations, by intimately associating statecraft and priestcraft. In the Greek *polis*, as well as in Rome, religious acts accompanied the daily life of the citizen. In Athens, "the new-born child was received into the family by being carried around the hearth. A little later, it was entered in the Phratria, a kind of religious community, and a sacrifice was offered; such a sacrifice was also offered, when a boy's hair was cut off, i.e., he entered adolescence, or when a girl was married. Youths and maidens participated in processions, choirs and festivities. When a youth had reached manhood, he usually was given some kind of religious task; for the priestly offices were numerous and distributed among the citizens; also secular officials, such as generals, had to offer certain sacrifices. Greek religion was inseparably tied to the society and its parts." [11] This was the setting within which the Greek person lived and moved. The individual was a link in a chain, and the most terrible penalty was to be banished from the city, because it meant that a person lost his religious bonds. Ritual in such a setting is the very condition of life and being.[12] In such a setting, ritual is central to religion and impinges upon the political community at many points. It is therefore natural that the maintenance of ritual should be looked upon as crucial for the survival of the political community itself, reinforced as it is by the notion that the gods are displeased if the ritual observances are neglected, and are likely to visit their wrath not merely upon the offending individual, but upon the community which harbors him. From the standpoint of the political analyst, this ritual aspect is, therefore, the more important side of religion. As it is manifest in observable conduct, it lends itself to behavioral analysis.[13]

[11] Nilsson, 1950, p. 18.

[12] Cf. also Jaeger, 1947, where this "political religion" is contrasted with the "natural religion" of the philosophers, both being contrasted with the mythical religion of the poets—a differentiation made by Varro, *Antiquitates rerum humanarum et divinarum.* Varro was a contemporary of Cicero. Cf. J. Burckhardt, 1898.

[13] This position is also taken by Alfred Bertholet, in *ESS*, who considered this the "objective" side of religion. "On the objective side religion involves the

The most important aspect of ritual, from a political standpoint, is that which invests the ruler with sacred observances, placing him in a special relationship with the divine being. It is very common for kings to be looked upon as descended from the gods, and titles such as "the son of heaven" are very frequent in the history of government. Frazer was preoccupied with these issues, and no one can read his exhaustive study *The Golden Bough* without being struck by the ritualistic features of early government. Eighteenth-century rationalism, in its struggle against a tottering and antiquated absolutism, inclined to treat these phenomena as clever tricks. Writers such as Rousseau argued that lawgivers had pretended to have consulted the gods in order to provide their work with divine sanction.[14] In a famous passage, Rousseau undertakes to contrast the "religion of man" and the "religion of the citizen." The former is purely internal: "sans temples, sans autels, sans rites, bornée au culte purement intérieur du Dieu suprême et aux devoirs éternels de la morale" —it is the pure and simple religion of the New Testament, the "vrai théisme, et ce qu'on peut appeler le droit divin naturel." The other, which is written for each separate country, provides the proper gods, patrons, and protectors. "Elle a ses dogmes, ses rites, son culte extérieur préscrit par les lois." This kind of religion he says is that of the "premiers peuples." And then there is a third, "plus bizarre, qui donnant aux hommes deux législations, deux chefs, deux patries, les soumet à des devoirs contradictoires. . . ." This, which he sees in Tibet, in Japan and in the Roman Catholic Church, Rousseau would call the religion of the priest. All three types of religion have, according to him, serious defects, the third so obviously so that it would be a waste of time to argue the case. For whatever disrupts the social unity is worthless. This sort of judgment is shared to this day by many Protestants in America and elsewhere, who dislike what they call the "divided loyalty." He likes the civic religion, as far as its political effects are concerned, but dislikes it because it is based upon error and deceit and is given to vain ceremonial; it also leads to arrogance and aggression, and thereby endangers the state. The religion of man is saintly, sublime and true and makes men recognize each other as brothers, but this kind of religion is bad, because it has no particular relation to the political order, and hence does not help to legitimize the laws, thus loosen-

---

recurring performance of certain human activities and thus belongs to the realm of external phenomena; on the subjective side it is part of the hidden experience of the psychic life." Leaving aside the objective-subjective distinction with all its complications, it is undeniable that religious ritual is concrete in the sense of being observable, even though its meaning can be *understood* only if these ritual observances are seen as symbols of the belief in the divine beings to which they refer; in this sense the belief *is* primary.

[14] Rousseau, *Contrat Social*, bk. 4, chap. 8.

ing the political bond. Finally, instead of attaching the citizens' hearts to their state, it alienates them from politics as from all earthly things. So this religion, too, will not do, from his viewpoint. To cope with the situation, he would have the sovereign institute a civil religion, as a sort of code of sociability, and banish from the state whoever refuses to accept this civil religion; one of its crucial articles would require tolerance in matters of religious dogma, beyond the tenets of this civil religion. He describes this religion in terms of its dogmas, which he says should be pronounced with precision. "The existence of a divinity, powerful, intelligent, beneficent, foresighted, and providing a life to come, the happiness of the just, the punishment of evildoers, the sanctity of the social contract and of the laws, these are the positive dogmas." It is obvious, in retrospect, that such a *dogmatic* religion would neither be compatible with the dogmatic content of other religions nor would it have any particular political significance. It is interesting however that we find in the schools of contemporary France something on this order in the so-called *Leçon Morale.* This is to teach the children to practice "the principal individual and social virtues (temperance, sincerity, modesty, kindness, courage, tolerance), to inspire in them the love of work, the taste for cooperation, the spirit of teamwork, the respect for one's word of honor, the understanding of other people, the love of one's native soil, the obligations toward one's family and toward France." [15] Such ethical instruction has its value, no doubt, but it is not the civil religion of Rousseau's proposal. Rousseau saw the problem, but he failed to resolve it in political terms. Due to his Christian background, he overestimated the dogmatic aspect, and neglected the ritual and ceremonial aspect. This, as we said, is primarily a question of sanctifying the ruler, which leads to the problem of legitimacy (Chapter 13).

The kind of religion which Rousseau calls the priestly religion and which presupposes a separate organization for religious purposes, both ritual and dogmatic, is a distinguishing feature of Western politics, though it is found in a number of other societies. The ancient Hebrews developed it to some limited extent, and religious organization has served to ensure the survival of the Jews after the destruction of their political order in 70 A.D. But the Jews are, of course, not the only minority which has fallen back upon religious institutions to protect itself in a politically hostile environment. Indeed, the development of the early Christian church was due precisely to its being in that position, and the experience of its founders, more especially of St. Paul, would account for this development at least in part. But the Roman jurists, even after the emperors had adopted the Christian religion, would not admit the autonomous

[15] *Le Livre des Instituteurs,* 1948 (19th ed.), p. 161, as quoted in Wylie, 1957, p. 65.

corporate status of the church, but would see it like all other corporations essentially as a creature of the Roman state.[16] It was only in the period of political disruption and feudal reconstruction that the church emerged as a separate organizational entity. The process is one of the most fully explored in the history of Western institutions, as is the eventually disruptive effect of the secular activities in which the church became necessarily embroiled. All the great political theorists from Thomas Aquinas to Rousseau and Hegel were concerned with the issue, taking and defending the several possible positions, and usually arguing it with considerable passion. Thomas Aquinas defended the independent corporate status of the church, Marsilius of Padua insisted that priests must be restricted to strictly spiritual care, Machiavelli would have the state resume the religious functions of antiquity, Althusius, like Calvin, saw the government as a servant of the religious community, Hobbes made the church an appendage of the state and its ruler, Locke saw religion as a matter of the individual conscience, and Rousseau's views have just been stated at some length. It is clear from even so sloganized a survey that the Western preoccupation was with dogmatic problems on the one hand, with the organization aspect on the other. Yet, behind these controversies there always stood the crucial question: How is the ruler to be sanctified and thus legitimized in the use of force for maintaining the political order? This question is not only at the heart of the great medieval struggles over investiture and oaths of allegiance, but it is also the real core of the doctrine of the divine right of kings, later attenuated to a doctrine of "ruling by divine grace." [17]

It would lead too far afield to enter into the doctrinal positions expounded in connection with these views; suffice it to point out that the recurrent problem was how to detach the divine sanction from any specific ecclesiastical ritual or ceremonial, such as the crowning of the medieval emperors by the popes. The coronation ceremony is, however, to this day surrounded with religious symbolism which in the case of Britain and certain other kingdoms is reinforced by the notion that the ruler is the head of the church. Even in strictly secular republics, such as the United States and France, oaths of office are considered essential

[16] The vast legal and political consequences of the development of the idea of a separate church establishment were traced in masterly fashion by Otto von Gierke in his monumental *Das Deutsche Genossenschaftsrecht*, a work which is however marred by the romantic preoccupation with a presumed "Germanic" origin of the notion of corporate personality which is at variance with a great deal of evidence about numerous other societies and cultures.

[17] In the history of political thought, a considerable amount of confusion has resulted from not observing this distinction, and yet the *Gottesgnadentum* is something much more nearly compatible with constitutionalism, if not with democracy, than the divine *right* of kings. It is one thing to rule by divine right, another to do so by divine grace.

to the legitimate exercise of governmental functions. In many older political orders, the ruler is surrounded by the mysterious penumbra of a majesty approaching the divine, even if he is not deified or believed to have descended from the gods. He shares to some extent the numinous quality of the "hidden secret." This majesty, this awe-inspiring sanctity of the ruler is, in constitutional orders, imputed to the constitution, and at times to its interpreters. Hence, ritualistic observances surround this "inner sanctum" of the order. Attacks upon it are experienced by the community at large as outrage, as sacrilege, as *lèse-majesté*.

These forms of religious sanctioning of political leadership need to be clearly distinguished from religious leadership as such. A great deal of confusion has been occasioned by Max Weber's unfortunate coining of the term "charismatic leadership." Under this heading, Weber includes Moses and Christ and other founders of religion, as well as inspirational leaders and demagogues of strictly secular persuasion. Weber himself describes the charisma in psychological terms (see below, Chapter 9). The term appears in the New Testament in a strictly religious sense [18] as a "gift" which springs from God's grace. It played an important role in the organization of early Christian communities, which was seen as charismatic, rather than legal. These charismatic gifts call each man to his particular service, which constitutes an office.[19] Priestly ordination institutionalizes such charisma, and yet there remains the notion of the "free" charisma which comes directly from God, and may turn up anywhere in the religious community; laymen as well as ordained priests are capable of the kinds of leadership and service which such charisma bestows.

The genuine meaning of charisma, then, is rooted in the belief in a divine being and order, whereas the leadership of a Hitler or a Lenin is based upon the inspirational appeal of a dynamic or even fanatical personality. But there is a further significant difference, as far as the prophetic form of charismatic leadership is concerned. The founders of religions, and even their "renovators," like St. Francis and Luther, are characteristically inspired by intense religious experiences, encounters with a divine being more especially. Such an experience typically demands of the charismatic leader that he go forth and communicate to others the message he has received and which is to save mankind (soteriological myth). Such a charismatic leader may be called "spontaneous." Because of this intensely personal form of experience the typical spontaneous charismatic leader is not interested in organization; in fact he is characteristically hostile to organization. "My kingdom is not of this world" and similar sayings are symptomatic of this leadership. There is a striking *political* or rather *antipolitical* reason for this position: the religious ex-

[18] Romans 20:3–8 and I Corinthians 12–14.
[19] Sohm, 1892, I, pp. 26ff., and II, pp. 235ff.

perience is one not of power, but its opposite: the complete surrender of the "I" to the divine being. Spontaneous charismatic leadership owes its overwhelming impact upon those with whom it comes into contact precisely to this sense of being an instrument of transcendent powers.

But the spontaneous impact of the prophet passes with his death and personal disappearance. At this point, the institutionalization of the new charisma sets in. A priesthood derived from the original prime mover takes over and organizes a church or at least a continuous following. In primitive religion, the priest had been the agent of *mana*, an impersonal, supernatural force. The revelations of the founder in the more rational religions (Christianity, Judaism, Buddhism, Mohammedanism, Hinduism, etc.) now become the sacred possession entrusted to his immediate followers who in turn hand it on by some process of ritualistically sanctioned "endowment" (in contrast to the hereditary endowment of a priesthood with innate "powers") often involving long training both of character and mind. Because the priesthood is a holy estate, many taboos are found to be characteristic of it—the celibacy rule of the Christian priesthood (and many monkish orders) being a characteristic example; it is found in many other priesthoods. It is generally the idea of contamination which is at work in such taboos.

Any ritual involving a cult, rites and ceremonies, is bound to bring into being a priesthood which possesses the special qualifications and more particular knowledge which the administering of such rites call for. In more advanced ecclesiastical organizations, such priests may be expected to have a detailed understanding of the symbolic significance of the very rites which they administer; ritual and dogma thus are intimately linked in the activities of such institutionalized charismatic leadership. But it is inevitable that organizational and, hence, political problems arise in the course of the growth of such priesthoods. As the organization is elaborated, either in churches or as part of the government, the conflicts and other concomitants of power appear. At this point, the most perplexing issues of religion present themselves. A church or religious organization can obviously survive only if it meets the requirements inherent in the manipulation of power upon which organization depends, while at the same time keeping the religious faith intact. The organizational requirements are likely to conflict with the ideal ethical projections of religion, and the history of all churches is replete with the clashes between the two positions, both equally able to appeal to the religion for ultimate justification.[20] It was at the heart of the challenge of St. Francis and many another religious "reformer." Priests are notorious for their keen appreciation of the requirements of power.

[20] This drama has been especially vividly portrayed in Bernanos' *The Diary of a Country Priest*, 1937, but it is a recurrent theme in both history and novel.

The extent to which religion should be recognized as a part of the political order has been and remains a subject of fierce controversy. It has jeopardized the efforts at constitution-making in such countries as Israel and Pakistan, not to mention Italy and Germany in the recent past. In both of the former, priests and other religious groups dedicated to orthodox forms of their respective religions have waged vigorous and at least partly successful fights for the inclusion of such orthodoxy in the basic law. Thus, the draft constitution of Israel contained a provision making the "basic principles of Jewish law" a part of the constitutional order; similarly, the fundamental provisions of the Koran were to be a part of Pakistan's constitution.[21] The problem posed by these controversies is a very serious one for all the emergent nations; for the history of government amply demonstrates that without adequate roots in religious tradition, both dogmatic and ritual, laws and more especially basic laws have little strength. It is the consequence of their value-relatedness which moulds community and political order.

In the history of political order, the interaction between religion and law has been continuous and profoundly significant. Practically every legal system if traced to its origin is found to have emerged from tribal customs sanctioned and hallowed by religion. Western legal tradition has emerged from the archaic forms familiar from such sources as the book of Leviticus of the Old Testament, and the beginnings of Roman Law as codified in the Twelve Tables. At the same time, the tribal political order helped to mould the religious notions which prevailed. Even though one avoids the shallow positivism which "explained" basic religious views by relating them to features in the political order, he can recognize the manner in which specific forms of law and government have helped to shape religious views. The notion of God as a judge and lawgiver may serve as a familiar illustration.

The frequent resemblance of notions about the political and the cosmic order have recurrently led to rather farfetched theories,[22] but there can be little question that a constant interaction occurs. God seen as a ruler of the universe is surely analogous to the king as ruler of the city, and it has been suggested that the relative importance of male and female gods is directly related to the patriarchal as contrasted with the matriarchal order; such analogies show, however, that the spread of certain religious beliefs, more especially the belief in particular gods, is intimately linked to the political fortunes of the communities professing the particular faith and practicing the cult which flows from it. However, as

[21] Friedrich, a, 1949; Dunner, 1950, esp. chap. 8; Binder, 1961, chaps. 4–7, and 11.

[22] Voegelin, 1956, pp. 21–22: "The symbolization of political order through analogy with cosmic order . . . the political organization grew from independent city-states to empires . . . and parallel with its growth evolved the conception of empire as an analogue of the cosmos and its order."

the history not only of Christianity but of many other religions, such as Buddhism, shows, religions often spread without any such political support or even under very adverse conditions of persecution. The great leaders of the Christian church who were, surely, not unaware of the value of effective political association, did not rest until they had won the emperors of the Roman order over to their faith.

The interrelation between religion and politics is only a special aspect of the general cultural setting of religion which from an observer's viewpoint suggests that religion is somehow "caused" by a variety of other cultural phenomena. To the nonreligious rationalist, such an "explanation" is eminently reasonable and suggested by the "sociology of religion."[23] It is, in such a view, simply a psychological phenomenon, an illusion "caused" by these "factors." Such a position is no longer possible. Religion, like mythology which precedes it and is intertwined with it, is a primordial experience of man. Whether "God exists" or not, is beyond scientific discourse; but since all existence is inferred from human experience, and since the human experience which we call religious certainly occurs, it is as reasonable to assert the existence of God as to assert the existence of the cosmos or of the political order.[24] The full appreciation of this argument is a helpful premise to all empirical understanding of politics, because of the extent to which values and all that depends upon them, more especially community, are rooted in religion. The fact that there have been many religions is not scientific evidence *against*, but rather *for*, the fundamental tenets of religion: that there exists a divine being, and that right conduct is conduct moulded by the preferences of such a being.

These statements raise once more the problem of ritual as right conduct. A. N. Whitehead interpreted ritual very broadly as "the habitual performance of definite actions which have no direct relevance to the preservation of the physical organisms of the actors."[25] He wished to

[23] A number of very important works belong to this category; from among them one might select Simmel, 1912; Max Weber, 1922–1923 (3 vols.); Malinowski, a, 1925; Pareto, 1935; Emile Durkheim, 1912.

[24] Bernoulli, 1933, put this well when he wrote that religion "is not an autonomous activity of man or a unilateral manifestation of the human spirit, but involves a process of vital and reciprocal interplay" between man and the divine being. Cf. also Cassirer, vol. II, 1925, part 3, chap. 2, pp. 216ff. Brecht, 1959, pp. 456ff., has devoted some very carefully reasoned pages to showing that "total abstinence from mention of the divine alternative in scientific discussions is not justified. Both alternatives, namely that God exists and that he does not, should be given equal weight scientifically, since neither is capable of scientific proof and neither can even be awarded a higher degree of scientific likelihood" (p. 479). In our view, this sort of statement does not take adequate account of the experiential basis of religion, and overrates the nonempirical aspects of "scientific proof."

[25] Whitehead, 1926, p. 20. The further quotes are from pp. 25 and 31.

link ritual to emotion, and thought that both religion and play have their origin in ritual. The myth then "not only explains but reinforces the hidden purpose of the ritual which is emotion." This statement carries a deep insight too far. Emotion is indeed the concomitant of the ritual, but not its purpose or end, nor has religion its origin in ritual any more than ritual has its origin in religion. Religion is *always*, as previously pointed out, in part ritual, and Whitehead himself recognized it when he considered rational religion to be a "religion whose *beliefs and rituals* have been reorganized with the aim of making it the central element in a coherent ordering of life. . . ."[26] Such a reordering affects both thought and conduct; they are both rationalized in terms of consistency and purpose. The habitual performance of definite actions is right when it fits into this order, and the order thereby acquires a sanctity which is deeply felt by all those belonging to it.

When Rudolf Otto developed his famous thesis about the "numen" as the central phenomenon of religious experience,[27] he psychologized the experience, but the "holy" is nonetheless a crucial feature of the phenomenon of religion. If we understand it as not merely something felt, but also as something inherent in the "around-us" which inspires this feeling, a further key to the understanding of ritual is provided. For ritual performances, from the most ordinary to the most exalted, symbolize the "unknown" which is known to be there beyond what is known. The vast array of "taboos" which the anthropologists have studied with such assiduous care[28] all arise from this knowledge of the unknown. In the case of the savage, it is implicitly believed by him that certain unknown forces shape the course of nature and must be assuaged. But even today in the advanced context of the highly rationalized, if not overrationalized, society of our time, the feeling of the "unknown" is pronounced, is indeed on the increase, as manifest in such aberrations as the wide popular interest in astrology.[29] The astrological "advice" printed by many perfectly rational newspapers in response to popular demand very usually contains such "negative precepts," that is to say, taboos. But if this diversion of modern mass man is merely a perversion of religion, religion to this day has maintained many ritualistic taboos, and the secularized application of it in politics is likewise full of it. The violation of such taboos is often at the heart of political defeats at the ballot box.

[26] Italics mine.

[27] Otto, 1927, p. 7, and *passim*.

[28] Frazer, 1959, pp. 17ff. "Sympathetic magic is not merely composed of positive precepts; it comprises a very large number of negative precepts, that is, prohibitions . . . the negative precepts are taboos. . . ."

[29] Jünger, 1959, pp. 75ff., has said some very interesting things about this trend, but he fails to see clearly the function of astrology as a substitute for religion, as contemporary man responds to the heightening knowledge of the "unknown."

Among the religious rituals (and taboos) of greatest consequence for politics has been ancestor worship. While reduced to a minimum in contemporary society, and not ever an important ingredient of Christian ritual (though the many tablets and stones in Christian cathedrals testify to a residual survival of such ancestor worship), ancestor worship has moulded such diverse societies as Imperial China, Hindu India and classical Greece. In each instance, ancestor worship, whatever its doctrinal basis, served to strengthen tradition and thereby to tighten the bonds of cultural community. It seems highly doubtful whether any political order can long endure without a firm ritual of ancestor worship. It is, however, primarily of importance in the ruling group. In a hereditary monarchy, the ancestor worship may be restricted to the ruling house, in an aristocracy to the great ruling families, but in a democracy reverence for the ancestors will be fairly widespread. It is very impressive to observe how rituals (and taboos) supporting ancestor worship have compromised with the predominantly rationalist spirit of American society by "jumping over" the immediate, and possibly living, ancestor to those further removed in time. Organizations such as the Daughters of the American Revolution are symptomatic of a reverence which strikes the foreign visitor as curious. There are, of course, other factors involved, more especially nationalism. It must be remembered, however, that nationalism is itself a type of secular religion in which the "nation" has become the divine being at whose altar the sacrifices of the faithful are willingly laid down. Much ritualistic conduct is associated with this religion of nationalism which often exhibits traits of the most primitive types of religion, as contrasted with the lofty faiths of the great "rational religions."

A final word needs to be said about the relation of religion to social change. There can be little doubt that religion has often been a potent force in promoting social progress. Art, science and ethics, no less than politics, have benefited from the deep dedication which religion inspires in men united by a common belief in what is divine and what is right conduct. It must, however, be remembered that religion also has often proved to be a great obstacle to advancement. Both its progressive and its conservative effects are deeply linked to its very essence. Both dogma and ritual have been at once embodiments of established wisdom and ingrained habitual conduct, and seedbeds of new ideas and novel departures in action. The reason is not far to seek. For since both dogma and ritual are concerned with and expressive of the "knowledge of the unknown," the potentiality of innovation is matched by the fear of it. In the basic tradition of the Old Testament this dialectic of religion is made fully manifest. As prophet and priest battle with each other, the prophet speaking of the new that God has revealed to him, the priest questioning his message in light of the old that was revealed before, they symbolize the dual direction of religious impact upon society and more particularly the political order.

chapter

7

Rational Conduct, Organization and Political Style

A natural style astonishes and delights us; we expected an author and we find a man.
Pascal

THE DILEMMA OF RELIGION which arises from the clash between conviction and ritual and which the dogmatic tenets seek to mediate is mainly engendered by the problems of organization. This dilemma is not limited to the religious sphere. In education, learning, the professions, and wherever objective norms and values are pursued, such norms and values may come into conflict with the requirements of the organization which provides the framework of cooperation for those engaged in the particular activity. Even political parties find themselves continually in difficulties, as party principles clash with party practice. It is evident that a theoretical analysis of organization is crucial for political understanding.

Organization theory has been discussed considerably in recent years.[1] There has been much emphasis on it, especially in studies of administration and of "social action." The predominant tendency, in keeping with Western cultural givens, has been to emphasize the "rational" component, and to see organization in terms of some sort of "means-end" design.

[1] Barnard, 1938; H. Simon, 1947, 1957: Selznick, a, 1948; Parsons and Shils, 1952, to mention only a few.

There can be little doubt that such designs play a central role in organization patterning, but the analysis of the preceding chapters does not permit our making it the central feature of organization theory, either in terms of genesis or maintenance, let alone disintegration.

Organization theory calls for comprehensive treatment, from a cultural as well as an economic and political standpoint. Value, purpose and function, institution, decision and policy, ideas, ideologies, political myths, symbols and even utopias are all involved in such a comprehensive theory of organization and the relation it bears to political rationality and style. To organize human beings means to discover, make explicit and maintain their common (including complementary) values and purposes; to persuade or coerce them to work together in the pursuit of these values and purposes by fulfilling definite functions, as members, contributors, officers, and so forth; to stabilize these functions by suitable institutionalization, so that decisions, more especially policy decisions, may be continually made and executed; and finally to embody the means of persuasion, i.e., the ideas, in a suitable myth, ideology or even utopia relating the organization's values and purposes to the larger group, nation or culture within which it operates. This process is readily recognized in modern literate societies, and anyone who has undertaken to organize several groups will have little difficulty in identifying the several operations involved. It is clear that in the process of consolidating any organization the formation of myths, symbols and utopias will be taking place. Even small organizations will at least require a name as an identification symbol, will quickly develop a foundation myth in which a certain person or persons are "credited" with more or less than they have actually done, and will project a more or less utopian set of goals which serve as lodestars but are generally acknowledged as unattainable in the foreseeable future.

Up to this point there would not appear to be any particular difficulty with a theory of organization. It flows quite readily from the previously established basis as a combination of the several factors involved. There is, however, a real question as to whether organization theory would be justified in seeing organization so definitely as the result of rational, deliberate action the purpose of which is the bringing into existence of an organization. As we saw when considering religion, organization seems to "grow" out of certain kinds of situations. Human beings responding to the situation are building organizations without intending to do so. Often they even build organizations, although they do not wish to do so, because the requirements of the situation "force their hand." And even when an organization is intended, it frequently seems to acquire an impetus of its own and to "grow" beyond what its founders "had in mind." These processes are not infrequently precipitated by rival organizations which consider themselves threatened by the new unit or which actually spring up because the organizing of one set of values and purposes calls forth the organizing of competing and conflicting values and purposes. The requirements of an organization fighting for survival may be markedly different from those needs it had responded to at the outset.

This problem of conduct required by the tasks essential for the survival of an organization has played a great role in the history of political theory in terms of "reason of state." Reason of state was and remains a doctrine of both normative and descriptive content. Descriptively it states that the "rulers" who are responsible for a state will violate, when the state's survival requires it, the commands of God and man in order to ensure its success; normatively, the doctrine claims that rulers *ought* to do so. We are evidently here confronted with a special case of a conflict of values and an alleged resolution in favor of organization values, either in fact or in norm, or both. The "organization man" of recent popular fame is an individual who is inclined to stretch the term "survival" to include virtually all situations in which the organization's well-being is involved, resolving almost any conflict of values in its favor.[2] Broadly speaking, this is the issue of politics and morals.

It used to be considered axiomatic that human beings had, by the law of nature, the right to defend themselves to the utmost of their power.[3] But how far may a man go in violating ethics and morals in defending himself? Christian and other theology is full of more detailed and often highly controversial doctrines attempting to answer that question. Notions of passive submission have competed with calls for tyrannicide and various degrees of resistance[4] and rebellion. The answers are to a considerable extent determined by the degree to which the defense of the faith is involved in the situation. Doctrines, such as St. Augustine's of the just war, are also part of this range of issues. One might in a sense even speak of the clash of reason of church and reason of state, as the rivalry between these two organizations has precipitated some of the most vigorous arguments about organizations and their survival. But only when there is a clash between the commands of an ethic of high normativity (and the convictions it engenders) and the requirements of organizations whose welfare and survival are at stake does the issue arise of which "reason of state" is the most striking example. Reason of state is merely a particular form of the general proposition that actions suited to the end and purpose of securing an organization's well-being and survival will and ought to be taken by persons who have functions to fulfill in connection with such

[2] Whyte, 1956. Riesman's "other-directed" person is a flabby variation of this type; Riesman probably overestimates his ubiquity in contemporary America, as contrasted with other times. Most human beings, a good part of the time, are "other-directed," but few at any time are always "other-directed." Riesman, 1950.

[3] Cf. for what follows, Friedrich, 1957, pp. 3ff., and the literature cited there.

[4] Lewis and Jaszi, 1957; Pfister and Hildmann (eds.), 1956. See also Chap. 34.

an organization. Much modern organization theory comes down to asserting that men in organizations will act like that (and ought to do so). Such a view is said to be "realistic." [5]

Actually, such a theory is highly unrealistic; for human beings do not always or even usually act in this way. There is the tale of a Jainist king who because of the Jainas' taboo about water refused to allow his army to fight during the rainy season, and as a result lost his crown and his life. Numerous similar instances can be given from history in all ages; Machiavelli compiled some in an effort to persuade his reader that rulers *ought* to disregard any and all values which conflicted with the radically rationalized course of action required by the political situation in which a ruler might find himself.[6] Where rulers did not do so, the question which a realistic political theory needs to ask is: Why did they not act in accordance with this particular rationality? The answer is not a simple one, because the actual historical reasons were very numerous. The Jaina king would have said the gods forbade the killing of animate beings, that many such beings lived in water and water should, therefore, be treated with reverence, which would be impossible if an army fought in the rainy season. To an observer not believing what the Jaina king believed this reason seems simply superstition and hence folly. But if the political order actually was believed to be rooted in the values emanating from the king's belief, then its destruction under the particular circumstances could not be avoided, because a violation of taboos would conceivably also have destroyed it, but from within rather than from without. There are in any order and hence in any organization which structures such an order actions which cannot be taken, because the values and purposes of the organization itself are at stake. In the world-wide rivalry of Communist totalitarianism and democratic constitutionalism, this law of politics can be seen at work. Recurrently, states in either camp are found to be prevented from taking apparently rational actions and adopting corresponding policies because of taboos imposed by their respective beliefs and convictions. Thus, the United States did not refuse to turn over to the

[5] "Realism" has been particularly stressed in relation to international organization and relations, emphasizing (1) objective laws of human nature, (2) interest in terms of power, (3) transformation only through "workmanlike manipulation," (4) moral principles applicable only in terms of concrete circumstances, (5) moral aspirations of a particular nation not universally valid. Cf. Morgenthau, 1948, 1954, pp. 3ff. A more radical statement was offered by the same author in 1951, speaking of the "moral dignity of the national interest," and proclaiming that the U.S. is "groping toward a reason of state of its own" (p. 39).

[6] Machiavelli, *The Discourses*, e.g., bk. I, chaps. XXX–XXXIII, LI; bk. III, chaps. II–V, XIX–XXII; *The Prince*, chaps. XV–XIX. Strauss, 1958, has argued that Machiavelli was wicked in propounding such a norm; he might likewise have argued that Machiavelli was in error from an experiential viewpoint. For men who did not accept his norm had their *reasons* for doing so.

Soviet Union parts of Germany she had conquered, although it was clearly against her national interest, because her foreign policy is based upon a belief in observing contractual obligations; the same belief was at work in persuading the United States to evacuate Korea in the face of a situation clearly threatening war. Similarly, the United States failed and fails to impose conditions of a political and economic sort in connection with foreign aid, even when such conditions appear vital to the success of the aid program, because of her belief in "nonintervention" and in "independence." But the Soviet Union is found to be similarly handicapped by her belief system. Her policy in Germany has been motivated throughout by her mistaken belief that the Communist rulers of East Germany "represent" the masses of the German people; she makes mistake after mistake, because of her conviction that time is on her side and that the Communist parties are bound to increase in size and influence, when manifestly the opposite is the case. These familiar instances of contemporary politics are merely inserted here for the purpose of showing that the general problem of how far conduct can be rationalized purely in terms of specific organization objectives is rooted in the very nature of organizations.

We find Thucydides struggling with this problem. In a celebrated discussion between the Athenians and the Melians the Athenians announce what amounts to a doctrine of reason of state in no uncertain terms. "Might makes right, and by the necessity of their nature, [men] always rule, when they have the power." Justice exists only among equals and "the powerful exact what they can, while the weak yield what they must." [7] The Athenians had argued the same line in an earlier discussion with the Spartans. In these reported discussions, it remains obscure how Thucydides himself judged the issue. Yet, there is a clear indication that Thucydides thought this bald doctrine of the Athenians one of the causes of their later difficulties. What he seems to suggest is that the treachery which they encountered later was the just desert of such cynics. But he does not, of course, by arguing thus, abandon his basic preoccupation with reason of state, as has sometimes been suggested. He merely puts forward the very sensible proposition that a certain amount of pretense, of hypocritical acknowledgment of the values which most members of the community acknowledge, is part of that "rationality" of means which the doctrine calls for when it enjoins the utmost in exertions on behalf of a given community. Indeed, a moral justification of such hypocrisy may well be argued in some such terms as its value in ensuring the survival of a cherished community organization.

The issue is still relatively easy when put in terms of patriotism, of the maintenance of an empire, or of a political order which is not itself

[7] *The Peloponnesian War*, bk. V, chap. 29.

seen as the essential condition for normative conduct or for the maintenance of a system of values. For an empire is not a moral being in the sense in which the Christian church is. Here the issue of how to conduct the organization rationally in terms of survival presents itself in all its dramatic urgency. This problem of the clash of rationalities was most clearly appreciated by the Jesuits, and Pascal's bitter attacks upon the Jesuits are not very penetrating. If it is assumed that organization is not necessary, naturally anyone in charge of the organization will readily subordinate the requirements of its survival to considerations of moral value. But if the organization itself is believed to be essential for the survival of these values, if it is firmly believed that there will not be any Christianity without a Christian church, or no good life without an Athenian *polis* or without the survival of a particular nation in the modern world, then the consequence will necessarily be that all means necessary for the survival of this organization are "rational." "Reason of organization" is the necessary consequence of the potential conflict between the existential needs of an organization and the values and purposes for which it exists. The error of the doctrine lies in assuming that it is known and knowable what these necessities are. Could the Jaina king know that his army would be defeated and his kingdom lost? Could the Athenians know that if they did not exterminate the Melians, a similar consequence would follow? The highly contingent nature of complex political and social causation makes it impossible to have such knowledge, and to demonstrate it with sufficient cogency to "justify" the violation of the value judgments involved.[8] Conversely, ethics must be concerned with what to accept as adequate proof, and what kind of risk to prefer in the face of uncertain evidence.

In the heyday of "reason of state" thinking, this overconfidence about knowing what the truly rational conduct was produced the doctrine of the *arcana imperii,* or secrets of empire, governance and rule. It embodied a conviction that such knowledge was *difficult* to achieve and hidden from most men. But there were men—kings and their counselors—who did know these secrets, and who therefore were able to know and foresee the probably right and rational course of action. Many experts on diverse policy matters still strongly incline toward such a view (Chapter 3). Oblivious to the usual divergence of opinion among themselves, they urge their respective "rationalities" upon policy-makers as certain, when they are actually merely indicative of probable courses of expedient action. The organization man has not only a right but a responsibility

[8] Thomas Aquinas, *Summa Theologica,* II.I.q.196.art.6 (end of *Respondeo*), and Johannes Althusius, *Politica,* chap. XXI, pp. 6–16, 25, and 59ff. are two religious men concerned with law and politics who recognized clearly the ethical implications of necessity. Cf. also Friedrich, 1957, introd. and chap. III.

(Chapter 17) to take the nontechnical values of the organization into account in making his decision.

Rationality thus involves the broad range of contingency in all matters concerning the future course of events, including the value judgments of all those persons who in the future may influence this course. This is not a matter of calculation so much, as of sentiment. The successful organization calls for leadership which is thoroughly representative of what the persons composing the organization feel and are convinced of as right conduct (Chapter 15). This is the realistic reason that it is a mistake to believe that rational decisions can be calculated on machines. The brilliant results which have been achieved in pushing forward this type of analysis do not justify the extravagant claims advanced on their behalf,[9] but they also need not be rejected because of these unjustified claims. If it is alleged that the central concern of administrative theory is with the boundary between the rational and the nonrational aspects of human social behavior,[10] the answer is that no such boundary exists, because of the interdependence of fact and value judgments. Administrative theory is a part of political theory, and its main concern is generalized propositions based on established matter of fact about the management of organizations, these facts including all that can be known about the value judgments, ideas, ideologies, and so forth, which the organizing of human groups implies and calls for.

Returning now to the descriptive definition of organization as the process of organizing, we are in the light of the foregoing able to reject certain positions which have played a significant role in recent years. Chester I. Barnard more than twenty years ago made a theory of organization the basis of his interesting analysis of the functions of an executive —a subject on which he was certainly qualified to speak on the basis of his practical experience as well as his theoretical mastery of the political and administrative generalizations available. After stressing that all persons belong to many different organizations, he urged that an (formal) organization should be understood not as a "group of persons," but rather as a system of consciously coordinated activities or forces of two or more

[9] See H. Simon, 1947, 1957, chaps. XXIV–XXVII. This author claims that he does "not regard the description of human rationality . . . as hypothetical, but as having been verified in its main features." The difficulty is philosophical. Simon does by no means deny that "every decision involves elements of two kinds . . . 'factual' and 'value' elements respectively." He asserts it, p. 45. But he adopts the "positivist" theory as to the nature of scientific propositions, citing Morris, Carnap and Ayer, among others, in support of the statement that "factual propositions are statements about the observable world and the way in which it operates." For the problems such a simplist proposition presents, see above, Chap. 2. The above proposition is rejected by Oakeshott, 1962.

[10] H. Simon, *op. cit.*, chap. XXIV.

persons [11] who are "cooperating." A system is taken to be "a whole because each part is related to every other part in a significant way"—a view which has been rejected earlier. But even if this is accepted, organizations do not consist merely of activities, but of persons who in their very being are personally involved beyond anything that could reasonably be called an "activity." [12] It is also unfortunate to introduce the qualification that such activities are "consciously" coordinated. As the later discussion shows, this term is to suggest that the coordination is deliberate. It has already been pointed out that while this deliberate effort is characteristic of many organizations, it is by no means so of all, nor of many phases of organization that become ritual, or occur in response to external stimulus.[13] In spite of his formalistic "definition," Barnard rightly states that an organization is more than its parts, but it is not only more, but also less. It is seen to be less once it is recognized that the parts are persons, even though persons only in their existential relationship to the values and purposes of the particular organization in which they are more or less involved.

The theory which Barnard builds for the formal organization as defined has to be implemented by a concept and theory of informal organization. The distinction between formal and informal organization has its theoretical uses, though it is not nearly as novel as is often believed, having played a vital role in politics and law in the interpretation of such key phenomena as the cabinet system of parliamentary government and parties. But in Barnard's theory it is unduly extended and generalized, in order to remedy the defects which his theory of formal organization involves.

This theory is defective for another very important reason. It is a genetic theory, seeking to explain how organizations come into being. He notes three necessary and sufficient conditions: communication, willingness to serve and common purpose. There can be little doubt that these are necessary conditions of organization; indeed they are all given in the descriptive definition we offered above, besides others which Barnard does not initially mention. But these conditions are not sufficient for explaining the genesis of organization. There are literally hundreds of common purposes which persons able to communicate with each other are willing to serve, but which they cannot serve, because no organization

[11] Barnard, 1938, pp. 73ff. Barnard here and throughout employs the term "cooperation" in an undefined and indistinct sense.

[12] The overemphasis on activity in this connection parallels that on decision-making; cf. above, Chap. 3.

[13] Lasswell and Kaplan define an organization even more inadequately as a "pattern of solidarity and cooperation" (1950, p. 31). Such a definition says both too little and too much.

exists. Probably as a consequence of his depersonalized concept of organization, Barnard completely overlooks the role of the founder, the promoter who initiates, builds an organization.[14] The founding role is decisive and must be included in any genetic theory of organization. The founder it is who perceives the potential organization, whether because of a vivid sense of the purpose he believes to have in common with his associates, because of his skill in organizing or because of his capacity to communicate. All these and other factors enter into the equation describing the successful founder. Bertrand de Jouvenel has probably been most explicit in insisting upon the role of the founder or promoter in organization, although the issue has been of importance in economics for a long time,[15] in recognition of the role of the entrepreneur. De Jouvenel, himself an economist, does not develop his thought as part of a theory of organization, however, but rather within the context of leadership and the problem of group formation.[16] "Let us begin at the beginning," he writes; "there is in fact no such thing as spontaneous convergence of wishes which have arisen simultaneously in the breasts of all. What we see in fact is, not participants coming together, but one or several promoters making incessant approaches to potential participants with a view to *bringing them together*. The process of formation gets into gear through the initiative of a single man, who sows among others the seed of his purpose. Some of them, in whom it rises, turn into a small group of apostles for the scheme, and these form the nucleus that preaches and recruits." [17] De Jouvenel is right in insisting that the mistake of much theory of association and organization (associations are one kind of organization) is "to overlook the role of the founder—the *auctor*—in the formation of the group."

The role of the organizer, or founder, is institutionalized in the leadership roles of the men who carry on, the administrators or, as de Jouvenel calls them, the "stabilizers." This is the "executive" of Barnard's pioneering analysis. The integration does not continue automatically, nor

[14] Are we naughty in suggesting that in overlooking it, Barnard showed himself the faithful servant of existing organizations—American Telephone, the Rockefeller Foundation, the Christian church, and so forth?

[15] Schumpeter, 1934; Marshall, 1925.

[16] B. de Jouvenel, 1957, chaps. III and IV, on leadership and group. It should be noted that Barnard explicitly rejects the group as a working concept, considering it vague and intangible (1938, pp. 68f.). Correspondingly, Barnard works with a different concept of authority; he considers it "the character of a communication [order] in a formal organization, by virtue of which it is accepted by a contributor to or 'member' of the organization as governing the action he contributes . . ." (p. 163). For de Jouvenel, authority is "the faculty of gaining another man's assent" or (and he thinks it comes to the same) "the efficient cause of voluntary associations." See below, Chap. 12.

[17] B. de Jouvenel, 1957, p. 28.

is it automatically achieved through values, ideologies or other impersonal entities.[18] For values, precisely because they are objective entities and not merely subjective attitudes or beliefs, need the founder and the leader in order to become a working factor in the mind of the participants in an organization. Once more it is demonstrated by these phenomena that organization must be seen not only as a structure, but as a process.[19]

At this point, the style of an organization comes into view. For the personal characteristics of the founder and his associates are likely to shape the conduct of the organization, whether it be political, economic, religious, or other, for a considerable time. This is generally recognized in business organizations; it is equally true of others. The personal style of the founder of a monkish order, to mention a striking illustration, was usually embodied in very specific and detailed rules of personal conduct. But in due course, the personal style of the founder is likely to recede in contrast with the style of the mass of members, unless protected by strict rules.

But what is style, and more especially political style? In Schiller's *Wallenstein*, one of the minor camp followers of the great general is heard to say: "And how he coughs and how he spits, that has at last been copied. . . ."[20] An entire army, organized by this great military entrepreneur, adopted his style of behavior, or tried to. In the strictly literary field, style includes diction, expression, rhetorical figures, an author's prevailing mode of thinking, and any peculiar words that might signify the writer's personality. No one could confuse a passage from Carlyle with one from Milton, nor either with Macaulay. What is true of verbal behavior is equally true of other ways of self-expression. Style is a decisive aspect of painting, music and all the other arts. It is not surprising that it should also be a factor in politics. Wherever a person with a self moves, the movement will show distinctive traits revealing his personality.[21]

[18] As is implied by Parsons, 1951, pp. 349ff., and many others.

[19] Parsons, 1960, pp. 16ff., chaps. 1 and 2, treats them primarily as structures. For him, orientation toward the attainment of a specific goal is primary in the concept of organization; his discussion shows that he wishes to restrict the notion of organization to "deliberately chosen" purposes. The "founding" stages are referred to merely in passing, in conjunction with "entrepreneurship" (p. 27).

[20] *Wie er sich räuspert, wie er spuckt,*
hat man ihm glücklich abgeguckt. . . . *Wallenstein's Lager.*

[21] Allport and Vernon, 1933, pp. 4f., 173ff., undertake a careful evaluation of this proposition with the aid of empirical psychology. Allport, 1937, pp. 489ff., states that "style represents the most complex and most complete form of expressive behavior." "It involves the very highest levels of integration." ". . . style . . . the external aspect of [the structural] consistency [of personality]." "Style is a characteristic not only of verbal expression, but of any articulate complex-level of activity as well." ". . . There are occupational styles that cling to the performance of any individual in the course of his daily work." See, contra, Spiro, 1959, part III. He interprets style too narrowly "as types of arguments" (p. 178).

Because of the need for coordination and cooperation, including coordination of expectations, certain elements of common style are factors contributing to the cohesiveness of organization. Since style is expressive of personality, value preferences will be embodied in stylistic modes of conduct. These stylistic peculiarities may be primary obstacles to effective organization, as has been discovered in intercultural efforts at organizational cooperation. Not only between countries, but within them, such conflicts may be very marked. As the needs for effective cooperation between men from Alabama and New England have multiplied, their regionally determined personal style of conduct has had to be transcended by a style now common to an increasing number of business organizations in the United States.

Political style, more specifically, is closely related to the preferred modes of political conduct. It has been remarked how different are the styles of, say, the State Department and the Department of Agriculture. In the founding stage, the personality of the first chief may mould such organizations for a considerable period. Perhaps the most important single issue of organization style is that of cooperation versus hierarchy (direction). It is one of the shortcomings of Barnard's organization theory that he broadens the concept of cooperation to cover all situations in which people "work together," including the chain gang and its foreman.[22] If this is done, a new word is needed for designating the kind of situation in which people work together voluntarily and for their mutual benefit. We prefer to stick to the actual meaning of the word, and not say that all organizations are "systems of cooperation," but rather that they are all arrangements for working together, but that the style may be "cooperative" or "directive." In the cooperative organization the contributions of the participants are elicited and voluntarily made; in the directive organization they are ordered and enforced. It is evident that both styles of conducting an organization are "workable" and effective in the sense that they are able to produce results. But the "authoritarian" personality, so-called, (Chapter 12) will be more likely to succeed with the directive type of organization, the nonauthoritarian with the cooperative. Both kinds of leadership have their distinctive style of operation, and it is likely to pervade the organization from to top bottom. It is, however, rare that an organization is purely of one type or the other; they shade into each other, and so do the styles which prevail in them. This fact does not deprive the distinction of significance, however; a person of a certain personality structure (alternating between submissive and domineering) will fit better into an organization in which the style is predominantly of

[22] 1938, chap. VII and *passim*. Selznick, Parsons, and others have adopted his terminology. Selznick claims that the indivisibility of control and consent makes it necessary to view formal organizations as systems of cooperation. This we question.

the corresponding type. It is for this reason justifiable to consider some persons better adapted to serve in certain kinds of organization, for example, armies, than others. Similar reflections apply to such complex organizations as modern states. Thus the "style" of the American administrative services is strikingly different from that of European countries, which in turn markedly differ from each other. These differences are, of course, subtly related to what is commonly referred to as national character, but this category is not very satisfactory, as the cases of Switzerland and Bavaria demonstrate.

Political style varies not only from country to country, but also from age to age, and it is strikingly revealed in the record of the conduct of official business. Style is, as a matter of fact, an important principle of historical interpretation, and of periodization. How styles come into being is highly controversial, but it would seem that political life has much to do with it. It provides the setting within which basic changes of experience occur and take shape.[23] This has been noted by Shapiro, who observes that discussions of style are affected by the political (he says social) divisions: empires, dynasties, cities, classes, churches, and so on. "In many problems [of style] the importance of economic, political and ideological conditions for the creation of a group style . . . is generally admitted." He notes the relation of Greek art and the *polis*, of Counter Reformation and absolute monarchy to baroque art, and so on.[24] But such explanations are superficial, because they do not penetrate the emergence of these organizations themselves.

Here we are face to face with the genuine problem of style as a concept for interpreting political and social reality. Although it appears at first sight as rendering all forms of expression relative to culture, to period, to organization, etc., it can become important as a principle of order only if it serves to develop a norm or standard. Only if there are norms does it become possible to speak of good and bad, of sound and unsound employment of a particular style. Style is, therefore, not (or ought not to be) an escape from norms and values, but a means of making them explicit. Thus the notion of adequacy is crucial; an adequate application of a particular style is an application in accordance with the norms it embodies. This notion, for scientific purposes, calls for rational treatment; no emotional, intuitive or subjective "feeling" will do. Thus the style of an organization, and indeed any political style, is the visible manifestation of its core values, beliefs and purposes. Consequently, the task

[23] For a development of this issue cf. Friedrich, a2, 1955, pp. 145ff. Shapiro, a, 1953, p. 287, has defined style as "the constant form—and some times the constant elements, qualities and expression—in the art of an individual or a group," but at the same time has recognized that the term may be "applied to the whole activity of an individual or society. . . ." Style is thus the "visible sign" of the unity of a culture.

[24] Friedrich, 1952, where the baroque style is discussed at length.

of stylistic analysis is that of uncovering and understanding the basic norm as the rationalized basic *experience* which characterizes an epoch, a group or an organization.[25] Certain basic experiences are recurrent, and, hence, shape the style of organizations again and again. Thus the vision of a new order and the concomitant desire for the destruction of the existing one are such basic experiences which have moulded revolutionary organizations under the most diverse conditions. Again, the need for observing the niceties of sacred ritual and for thoughtful interpretation of revealed truth has shaped the conduct of religious organizations, and the contrast in the style of these two types of organizations may be observed in diverse times and places.

If style serves to highlight the imponderables of conduct appropriate to specific organization types, it does by no means exhaust the impact of the founder and leader upon the organization. It is necessary now to return to the theory of organization in more specific and detailed terms. We saw that the founder and leader (executive) in organizing human beings for the attaining of objectives or purposes must discover, make explicit and maintain their common values; must persuade or coerce the participants [26] into working together by fulfilling definite functions; must stabilize these functions by institutionalizing them, so that decisions may be continually made and executed; and finally must embody the means of persuasion or the ideas motivating his action in suitable ideology relating the organization's values and purposes to the larger group within which the organization is to operate.[27] An organization, in the broadest sense, is any combination of human beings which exhibits the aforementioned four characteristics. Such a combination may properly be called an "organization," whatever the specific purposes or ends may be. An organization is a functioning whole, but it is not necessarily cooperative, as we have seen. It is possible to advance several very general propositions regarding organizations. In the next chapter, when dealing with communi-

[25] In applying this conclusion to a particular historical period, namely, the baroque, I wrote: "What was the decisive experience? What was the basic experience from which such an emotion sprang? . . . I am inclined to assert that for the baroque the decisive experience was that of man's power (and of his impotence. . . ." Friedrich, a2, 1955, p. 150.

[26] Barnard, 1938, pp. 68ff., stresses the fact that an organization consists of others than its "members" in the usual sense of that word, and hence suggests "contributors." But both terms, and several others, such as "customers" (clientele) are needed, and the several terms may be generalized as "participants," as mentioned before. H. Simon, 1947, 1957, p. 16, employs the term "participants" too.

[27] Recent writings on organization theory have not elucidated these processes, but have rather concentrated on the administrative aspects of internal structure; cf. Barnard, 1938; H. Simon, 1947, *passim*. This kind of discussion overlaps and to some extent merges with the generalizations concerning bureaucracy; see below Chaps. 18 and 26. Cf. also Parsons, 1960, pp. 27ff.

ties, we shall show that communities may be either organized or unorganized. Here, the corollary proposition needs to be noted in passing (though it cannot be elaborated prior to the discussion of community) that organizations can be or become communities, and often serve to develop a community of some sort.

Organizations are moulded in their structure and modes of working together by the purpose as well as by the organizational environment. Thus, for example, single-purpose organizations permit and encourage a hierarchical structure and a directive mode of work. Such single purposes are notably profit and victory, that is, the defeat of the enemy. Hence we find military and business organizations usually exhibiting firm subordination and "unity of command."[28] In multiple-purpose organizations, and in organizations with "transcendent" purposes, more especially churches, both "unity of command" and hierarchical subordination are difficult to achieve and to maintain, because of the potentialities of "conflicts of principle." The structure in such organizations often is nonhierarchical, providing for consultation and criticism, and the mode is cooperative. But both these propensities are frequently counteracted by another factor moulding structure and the mode of working, namely, the size of the organization. For the larger an organization, the greater the propensity toward hierarchical structure and the directive mode of working. Even multipurpose organizations, such as churches and governments, will exhibit the latter type of structure and mode as they grow in size. The only known method for counteracting this propensity successfully is the periodic review of organization behavior by a large part of the participants in the organization, and notably, in conjunction with it, a federalizing of the organization, that is, a breaking up into autonomous units (Chapter 32). The most familiar illustration is, of course, Western democracy, but how powerful is the trend toward the directive mode is shown by the propensity of political parties, vital for organizing of effective participation, to evolve a strongly hierarchical and directive pattern.[29]

A third generalization concerning structure and working mode of organizations is contained in the proposition that organizations will adopt hierarchical structure and directive mode of working in response to external challenge. Hence, the more competitive the situation, or the more uncertain the chance of survival, the more hierarchical the organization. Directive patterns and rigid subordination to these directives will be pro-

[28] H. Simon's objections to the insistence on "unity of command" in administrative organization by Gulick, a, 1937, pp. 9ff., and others is quite justified, but the reasons do not become clear. Cf. H. Simon, 1947, 1957, pp. 22ff.

[29] This propensity was the theme of Robert Michels' well-known study of political parties, first published in 1911. But what Michels proclaimed as the "*iron law of oligarchy*" actually can be stated only in terms of probability, and is subject to a variety of potential countervailing forces. Cf. Michels, 1915.

nounced where the organization is faced with continual struggle for survival.[30] Political parties in modern democracies are faced with a highly competitive situation, and their propensity toward subordination and unity of command could be explained by that factor alone; it is reinforced by the large size of these organizations in mass democracies, and the "single" purpose of victory.

Functions in an organization will, of course, be related to objective and purpose. Such purposes are of seemingly infinite variety, and whatever reasoning discloses as suitable means toward their attainment can become the basis of organized function. Such functions in turn will determine structure to a large extent. Once again, the three divergences—single or multiple purpose, size of organization and degree of danger—will mould functional development. But these matters lead too far afield here, and will be treated later in conjunction with bureaucracy (Chapters 20 and 25). For here we are face to face with stabilized functions.[31]

Myth and ideology as broadly communicable versions of the ideas embodied in the organization are as vital to the functioning of an organization as the differentiation of functions and their stabilization. The relative importance of myth as contrasted with ideology depends upon the degree of "rationalization" of a particular culture. In previous chapters, both myth and ideology have been discussed, and their bearing upon organization and community noted in various contexts. More especially, the foundation myth was specified as persisting even among highly rationalized human beings. Such a myth usually is designed to aid the growth of a sense of commitment and involvement on the part of the participants. The ideology, on the other hand, while similarly committing the participants, projects their organization purpose outward by relating it to the environment. It does so by suggesting the contribution the organization is going to make, either through "re-forming" the environment or by maintaining it and preventing unwanted changes.[32] This ideological ingredient of live organizations may be specifically directed toward the political order, as in parties and interest groups, or it may have a more recondite significance, as in churches, universities and business enterprises. But the thought concerning such organizations, piously cultivated by its participants, will always cluster around basic values of communal and

[30] Lenin's discussion of why the revolutionary Bolsheviks could not be "democratically" organized and conducted, in *What Is to Be Done?* 1903, presents a striking instance of the recognition of this "law."

[31] H. Simon's discussion of "administrative behavior" is to a large extent a restatement of the same issues discussed earlier under the heading of bureaucracy; thus "morale" is discussed under "organizational loyalties," and so on. Cf. Friedrich, 1937, chap. II, and the literature cited there.

[32] For a fuller understanding of this phrase, see Chap. 4 above; there ideologies are shown to be action-related.

cultural relevance, such as "faith," "truth" and "service," and the emblems and other symbolic signs bear eloquent testimony to this fact. That is the reason why symbols of all kinds are quite important to organizations —shorthand expressions of their mythical or ideological links with the larger whole within which their organization lives and works.

These questions call for fuller exploration of the political community; for it provides the key to organizational environment. This is true even though the political community is a politically *organized* community and therefore exhibits organization as one of its facets. To treat organization and community as either identical or contradictory is to misunderstand perhaps the most important condition of the political order and of the government which is its organization. This is the human element in both. In the words of Pascal: "When we see a natural style, we are astonished and delighted; for we expected to see an author, and we find a man." The penetrating insight of this remark applies not only to literature, but to all human creations, including organization. A modern catchword speaks of the organization man; he is the perversion of the creative author of whom Pascal speaks and who moulds the organization in his image and creates its style.

chapter

8

The Dimensions of Political Community

Every community
is aiming at some good.
Aristotle

AT VARIOUS STAGES in the preceding analysis, community has been introduced as the necessary setting of man as a political person and of his realm of action. This is hardly surprising, when one recognizes the political person as a "being living in communities." Value, function, institution, decision and interest, as well as ideas, myths and beliefs, are the intrinsic aspects of the political person, as we have seen. Indeed, it is these several aspects of the political person which constitute the dimensions of community. We have spoken of a community of values, interests and beliefs, and at the final point in the analysis of organization theory the issue of community arose with renewed urgency.

Community is "real" in the same sense in which persons, values, interests and beliefs are real. It is not compatible with our approach to politics to interpret it in a psychological sense, though a community has, of course, a psychic dimension of the greatest importance. Even less is it admissible to treat it merely as a "concept" which is used in political and legal arguments but the referent of which is vague and varied.[1] A com-

[1] This is advocated by John Ladd, a, 1959, with considerable persuasiveness. His argument rests upon a sharp distinction between theoretical and practical concepts which cannot be admitted for political science; cf. above, Introduction. Actually, Ladd himself implies it by giving "two essential features" of community, namely,

munity is, we may suggest hypothetically, composed of persons who are united by one or more of the following aspects of their personality: values —including purposes, interests, ideas and ideologies—myths, utopias and their symbols, and finally, religion and its rituals. Characteristically, a political community is a group of persons united by having some part of all of these aspects in common; the absence of one or more of them has been believed to constitute an element of weakness—a dubious position, as we shall see. Certainly, specific communities comprised within the political community, such as families, churches, professions, are characterized by the predominance of one or another of these aspects. It has been customary to refer to these latter communities as "imperfect" in contrasting them with the "perfect" community that is political, and which is frequently referred to as the "state." This terminology we shall try to avoid. It is not the characteristic of the political community that it is more perfect—whatever that may mean—but that it is more comprehensive. But this very comprehensiveness detracts from the intensity of commitment on the part of many persons composing the community. Only the politically minded will ordinarily exhibit that intensity of concern for the political community which others reserve for their family, their church or other groupings.[2]

The persons belonging to a community are usually referred to as its members; because of the many dimensions of community, and the numerous subdivisions of these dimensions, e.g., in the professions, most persons belong to and are hence considered members of a number of communities. Such plurality of membership is, however, typically restricted within the various classes of communities, so that a person "belongs" to one family, one church, one profession and—one political community. The reason is obvious. Since each community is united by a specific configuration of values, interests and beliefs which its members share, commitment to one such configuration excludes commitment to another. It is however questionable whether in view of the peculiar nature of political community this generalization can properly be extended to political communities. In federal unions the persons characteristically belong to two political communities, the component unit and the all-inclusive one, for example, in the United States to the Union and to one of the states. If such federal unions are included in a broader political community, as is the case in the British Commonwealth and in the European Community that is now emerging, many persons actually belong to three *political* communities,

---

that it provides the "background" for formal organization and that it has "organic character." Both these features are indeed part of the reality of community, as the text will show.

[2] The recent work of Catlin, 1962, chap. 7, rather stresses distinctions we should prefer to minimize, therein following MacIver; it came out too late to be utilized here.

for example, Canadians in the first, Germans in the second of these groupings. In any case, most persons are members of many communities, and the potential conflict of loyalties resulting from such plural belonging constitutes one of the key problems of politics.

Communities, and more especially political communities, may be structured or unstructured. Typically, the larger and the more permanent they are, the more structured they will be. In the discussions of institution (Chapter 3) and organization (Chapter 7) some of the key features of this process of structuring which produces institutions have been examined. When a community becomes structured, an organization comes into existence; the obverse may also happen, namely, that an organization is brought into being which in turn produces a community, or so it seems. For the truth of the matter is that no organization can come into being without the previous existence of a community (of values, interests or beliefs) for which organization provides effective institutionalization. What has led to the contrary impression is the preoccupation with the activities of the persons deciding upon organizing a group, as well as the fact that an organization resting upon a common unity provided by one value, interest or belief may in turn lead to the emergence of other common values, interests or beliefs. This process of gradual extension of a community is, however, not limited to organized communities, but is to be observed wherever communities exist. The most familiar example is that of a successful marriage which, starting upon the limited unity of mutual attraction, eventually grows into a community of far-reaching inclusiveness. Such a community remains unorganized, and hence unstructured or largely so, because of its small size. It is nonetheless one of the most "perfect" in the sense of becoming fully developed. The belief widely held among men that such a marriage is "holy" or constitutes a "sacrament" is thus amply justified by actual experience, if these words are taken to express a sense of great value and firm belief.

In view of what has so far been said, it is hardly surprising that community has been a central concept of political and legal philosophy since its beginning.[3] Aristotle opens the discussion of politics with a characterization of community (*koinonia*) as "aiming at some good"—elaborated as a group of persons having some values, interests and beliefs in common. Among the many such communities the highest is the *polis*, he thought, and it is above them all (*kuriotáte*) because it embraces them all. Not only secular customs, interests and beliefs are comprised and institutionalized in the *polis*, but the religious faith and ritual as well. In modern terms the *polis* is both church and state; in fact it is neither, but the

[3] The following historical sketch is a condensed version of the author's contribution to *Nomos II*, entitled "Community" and published in 1959 under his editorship.

political community which provides the basis for both these institutional complexes. The differentiation of these institutional complexes became necessary when the political community grew in size and included many different peoples and their religions; the history of the Roman Empire demonstrates the process which occurred also throughout the Orient. Aristotle's political analysis is of great value precisely because it treats of the undifferentiated political community, even though this fact is a source of much confusion.[4] And because he does, he stresses the importance of limiting the size of the community. "If there are too many [citizens], it is not a *polis,* but an *ethnos* [nation]." To a modern mind which thinks of the nation as the political community above all others this argument sounds strange indeed; the reason is that modern man has come to take the differentiation of the institutional complexes of state (government) and church for granted. The nation can be a political community precisely because it has a common interest and belief in its government; it can leave the strictly religious beliefs to separate communities institutionalized in different churches. Some of the most difficult problems in the new nations have arisen from the fact that this kind of separation of political and religious values and beliefs has not been consummated. Various Arab countries, Pakistan and even China, provide contrasting illustrations for this difficulty which exposes them to the danger of a breakdown in which the communist or other totalitarian ideology promises a way out precisely because it secularizes life completely, transforms the party program into a substitute religion, and thus undertakes to reintegrate the community.

The Greek concern with the right size of the political community is in part inspired by the recognition that neither individual persons nor groups can exist for long without some life of their own.[5] A community seen as common unity presupposes persons who exist by themselves, who have certain things in common which bind them together, but who have also other things not in common which give them a separate and distinct individuality. The failure to appreciate this existential given vitiates most communist and much socialist thought, though socialism at its best has always recognized it. Aristotle's criticism of Plato's "ideal" *polis* turns largely upon this issue; for he insists that it calls for too much unity. The butt of the argument is, of course, Plato's plan for a having in common a "community" of wives and children, as well as of property, that is, of

[4] The paradox consists in the fact that Aristotle's term for all that pertains to the undifferentiated community (*tá politiká*) has become the term for distinguishing the political from other dimensions.

[5] The importance of these long-neglected problems of size for the evaluation of community has been stressed by A. Rüstow, 1950, I, pp. 263ff.; they deserve much further exploration in order to avoid a romantically impractical approach such as vitiated the interesting analysis of Dewey, 1927.

having in common what constitutes the crux of personal life, namely, a family and a sphere of work of one's own, which is the primordial meaning of property. Leaving aside some of the questions of interpretation, the objection appears valid, even if Plato's argument applies only to the guardians. For they as the outstanding members of the community ought to have the most rounded personalities. Their community ought not to be a total unity, but unity in diversity. Some matters should be shared, while others are not. A harmonious working and living together of distinct but complementary persons forms a genuine community. It is not true that a community is more fully a community the more things those composing it have in common.

Does this conclusion contradict what was said above, namely, that a political community is united by having purposes, interests and beliefs, including religion and its rituals, in common, and that the absence of one or more of them constitutes an element of weakness? Only in this sense that it qualifies the statement to mean that a comprehensive community, that is to say, a political community, has some part of each of these elements in common, but by no means all of them. There is a point at which weakness results from excessive unity. The well-known "passion for unanimity" which animates totalitarian dictatorships is a case in point,[6] whereas the practice of toleration and the recognition of an ineluctable freedom of conscience by contrast avoids this danger. It would be interesting to trace the evolution of the concept of community through its transformations in Stoic, Christian and early modern thought. Cicero, St. Augustine, St. Thomas Aquinas and the natural-law schools are landmarks in this evolution of the notion of community. As the community became differentiated from state (government) and church, its concept was adapted to the changing political reality. The emergence of the modern nations eventually provided a new point of departure which is marked by the names of Rousseau, Burke and Hegel.

While these writers did not actually "rediscover" the community, as has been claimed,[7] they gave it a new content by identifying the political community with the nation. In turning against the cosmopolitanism of the Enlightenment, Rousseau rejected the view of Diderot and others that mankind constitutes a community, on the ground that a community must have common possessions, such as a common language and a common tradition. Rousseau, not always but at times, carried this notion to the point where he insisted that all a person's ideas are shaped by the political community in which he lives, that this community is constitutive of a person's personality and that man is inconceivable without such communal bonds. Furthermore, a community, he thought, possesses a personality of its

[6] Friedrich and Brzezinski, 1956, chap. 13.

[7] Sabine, 1950, pp. 575ff. Rousseau, 1762, book III, chap. 13.

own, and hence social groups must be seen in analogy to organisms in which the parts are nothing apart from the whole. He coined the term "general will" to express these notions. This "will" is a personification of the common good, and is based upon a powerful emotional and spiritual bond, a "sense of communal belonging," as it were.[8] The most obvious community of this kind has in recent times been the nation (Chapter 30). Thus the very *ethnos* which Aristotle has rejected as too large for genuine community is for Rousseau the political community par excellence, in spite of his liking for the small community on the one hand, and his Europeanism on the other. These preferences were echoes of personal experiences but they were transcended in the Jacobin version of Rousseau's doctrine. Here the nation with its language, culture and law emerges as the "sacred community." These notions were further extended in the thought of Burke and Hegel as well as the Romantics. They are implicit in Burke's concept of the prescriptive constitution, embodying the nation's traditions. The community of the nation now appears as "a partnership, not only between the living but between those who are living, those who are dead, and those who are yet to be born." [9] Many other familiar phrases of Burke could be adduced to show that he conceived the nation to be the result of organic growth and that it represents the highest and the most important community.

Hegel elaborated upon these notions by making the nations the successive executors of ideas expressing the will or purpose of the "world spirit." No world community corresponds to this world spirit, curiously enough. Hegel's cosmopolitanism is purely transcendent and metaphysical, but Marx in "turning Hegel downside up again" insisted upon the existence of the world community, and proclaimed the world revolution as the necessary step toward an eventual world order for this community. It comprises the universal class in which all the class structures of the past are submerged and transcended. Hegel stopped short of such a universal community. Reluctant though he was to make any predictions about the future, his comments on America and Russia clearly suggest that he was inclined to see the future in terms of new nations embodying new ideas which the world spirit provided for them when the time came.[10] Hegel furthermore insisted that the nation's values must be preserved and developed by the "state" and that only such a political organization is capable of expressing the community's common concerns.

Even this very brief sketch shows that there has been fairly general

[8] That there is a strong rationalist residue in Rousseau's concept of the general will has been persuasively argued by Robert Derathé, 1948. Cf. also B. de Jouvenel, 1957, pp. 105ff., on the notion of the "public good," and Friedrich, 1948, chap. 6, on the complexities of the "general will."

[9] Burke, 1790–1839, vol. III, pp. 52f. and 120.

[10] Cf. Friedrich, 1954, pp. li ff.; Kojève, 1947, *passim;* Löwith, 1941, pp. 44ff.

agreement on the central place which community occupies in the political life of man, both conceptually and actually, even though this has not meant general agreement on what constitutes it. The skeptic may insist that what this means is that under the guise of a common term very different referents have been hidden, so that at least theoretically speaking there is no agreement on the role of community in political thought and action. A more detailed examination would disclose, however, that in spite of contrasting emphases there is a common core. This common core is circumscribed by three great debates on the nature of community. First, there is the debate over whether the community, other values apart, is primarily a community of law or of love. Second, there is the debate over whether the community is organic or purposive. And third, there is the argument over whether the community exists, is existentially there, or whether it is willed. The three issues are closely linked with each other, as one follows from the other. In fully developed theories, there is likely to be either a preference for seeing the community as based on love, organic and existential, *or* based on law, purposive and willed, though other intermediary positions are also found. It is our contention that these alternatives are ideatic and misleading. Actual communities are never either one or the other of these six possibilities, but are always to some extent all of these. The purpose of political analysis is to explore the extent to which they are one and to which they are the other and to devise methods for determining an answer to these questions. There may eventually be strictly quantitative criteria for all six constituents, but in the meantime a fuller exploration of these relationships is both possible and necessary.[11]

In the famous argument of Augustine against Cicero, cast in Christian notions of community and centered on Augustine's criticism of Cicero's pagan notions of people, *respublica*, and *civitas*,[12] it becomes clear to the detached reader that Augustine is right in stressing love, even though his objection to Cicero is beside the point; for the fact that Cicero did not share Augustine's religious beliefs, more especially his belief in the one and only God, did not prevent him from seeing that religion is a very important element in community and that the reverence for divine beings cannot be dissociated from the idea of natural law.[13]

In indicating what we consider to be the dimensions of community, we included both law and love, or, to put it more abstractly and scien-

[11] Elliott, 1928, part IV, insisted upon this duality with regard to the second of these issues, and coined the term "co-organic" in order to indicate the dual aspect. This was an important step in the right direction. See also his reevaluation, a, 1959.

[12] St. Augustine, *City of God*, II. chap. 21; XIX. chap. 17. pars. 20–24.

[13] *De Legibus*, I. 6, and I. 31–32. Cf. also Krüger, 1888, p. 40; and the discussion in Friedrich, 1958, chap. IV. It might be noted in passing that *diligere* has also the meaning of "valuing." Further comment below in Chap. 14.

tifically, both common interests and common values. Law is in this sense a formal expression of what common interests imply and call for. Cicero himself had hinted at this by linking the agreement on law with the community of interests, but this *communio utilitatis* deserves to be seen in the widest connotation of utility, such as it was given by the utilitarian school.[14]

The interlocking of values, interests and beliefs serves to resolve the second debate which argues between the organic and the purposive. It is in the first place necessary to see the organic needs of the persons associated in community not only in physical, but also in psychic relations. Nowhere is the primordial ruthlessness of organic necessity more evident than in the efforts of two human beings who are in love with each other to surmount all obstacles which stand in their way—a theme which has provided a substantial part of the poetry of man, in song and tale. The organic need of persons for each other, in family, village and nation, and at last in mankind, is invariably expressed in purposes which they share, in purposes which complement each other, and in purposes which supplement each other. The interaction of need and purpose is not necessarily initiated by need any more than by purpose. Organic relations are expressed in purposes, and purposes which unite men lead them on to organic relations. In the political community, the fact of *connubium* has always been an outstanding criterion. The complexity of Europe's politics is well illustrated by the fact that royalty of different nations intermarried regularly, aristocracy and big business occasionally, artisans and peasants hardly ever. Was Europe then a political community? Yes and no; it was a political community in its ruling groups, but not a very close one. The extent of communal relations was severely limited. At the present time, the establishment of predominantly purposive units, such as the Coal and Steel and the Economic Community, is extending the fact of *connubium*—one of a number of indices showing that organic factors are beginning to implement the purposive ones. From the outset, of course, the organic need of common security against the threat of totalitarian submersion by the U.S.S.R. has been operative.

What has been said in the preceding two paragraphs leads on to the corresponding answer in regard to the third alternative, which is concerned with whether communities are existential or willed. All actual communities are necessarily both. There must *exist* a community of values, interests and beliefs before any willing can occur for the realization of these values, interests and beliefs. But unless such willing does occur, the values, interests and beliefs may disintegrate and the community may be dissolved. This is the reason, as noted before, that the impression could

[14] Jeremy Bentham, 1843, vol. I, esp. chaps. I–V; John Stuart Mill, 1863; Plamenatz, 1949.

gain currency that the willing of that which is necessary for the realization of common values, interests or beliefs is the prime originating factor in community-building, i.e., that the promoter of a community is its actual creator. Much more will be said about these matters below (Chapters 9 and 22), but here it must suffice to call attention to the fact that the political process is carried forward by persons who continually express their existential given in a great variety of activities that build community as they presuppose it.

The tensions implicit in this dichotomy of existence and willing constitute the "dialectic" of community, which also finds expression in the duality of love and law, of the organic need and the conscious purpose that communal living entails. Within the context a stipulative definition of community must take account of this dialectic. Our hypothetical "definition" of a community as a togetherness of persons who are united by having in common some of their values, interests, ideas (including ideologies), myths, utopias and their symbols, as well as religion and its rituals, needs to be qualified accordingly. The uniting, in other words, will be partly by emotional attachment and partly by subjection to common rules, responding partly to organic need and partly to conscious purpose, expressing what already exists or what is explicitly willed. Interestingly enough, this rather complex stipulative definition is not very far from current lexical definitions of community—as it should be, following our canon (above, Introduction).

It remains to see what tentative propositions concerning political community may be advanced at this stage of our analysis. The proposition that a community disintegrates when the values, interests and beliefs which unite it disintegrate is logically a tautology. For since a community has been described as a group of persons who have values and interests as well as beliefs in common, the disintegration of the latter patently entails the disintegration of the former. Hence the term *anomie*, while a shorthand way of speaking of such disintegration, does not explain anything in particular.[15] On the contrary, it carries with it the danger that the continuous change in such values, interests and beliefs which characterizes any live community is mistaken as a sign of disintegration, and even as a suggestion for halting such changes by unnecessarily unifying the community. As such it can in turn serve as a partisan political symbol for conservative preoccupation with the maintenance of particular values, interests and beliefs (Chapter 2). More careful consideration of the problem suggests that further breakdown of the

[15] Cf. S. de Grazia, 1948, who undertook to deal at greater length with the phenomenon which was so designated at an earlier point by Durkheim, 1893, bk. III, chap. 1, par. 3.

components of these processes, and if possible quantification, is needed before the analysis is likely to yield useful scientific insights.

Aristotle at one point makes the statement that since the existence of *nomos* (law, custom) means order, the prevalence of good *nomos* (*eunomia*) means good order (*eutaxis*). Without stopping to examine this kind of analogical argument in greater detail (and there are some real problems hidden here), one might say that absence of *nomos* (*anomie*) means absence of order. But when precisely are we justified in speaking of the absence of *nomos*, of common values, interests and beliefs? For since a community does not presuppose any particular number or combination of such values, interests and beliefs, that is, of such constituents of *nomos*, we would have to try to establish some formula indicating a minimum point—a point which in the oratory of our time has been hinted at by the term "civil war situation." It will be recalled that this term has served as a ground for asserting the need for reintegration, if need be by violence, through such totalitarian movements as the remaining residue of values, interests and beliefs suggest. What this means is that particular values, interests and beliefs are made absolute in the expectation that a new community will result, as the Hitlerian term *Volksgemeinschaft* amply suggests. These developments clearly indicate the danger which an approach to politics through communitarian concepts entails.

If, then, the formula for community is

$$c = p^n(xv + yi + zb) \quad \text{where } p = \text{persons}, \; v = \text{values}, \; i = \text{interests}, \; b = \text{beliefs}$$

the problem would be to determine at what values of x, y and z the value of c would approach zero, obviously an extremely difficult task. But the matter is further complicated by the fact that it is not merely a matter of the v's, i's and b's disintegrating and disappearing, but also a matter of their possible polarization. That is to say, the community may be threatened not so much by *a-nomie*, but by *dis-nomie*—a state of affairs wherein some substantial number of the persons who are members of the community are attached to a given value a, while a substantial number of others insist upon the disvalue of a and cherish its opposite. Thus, the disintegration of the belief in private property has been accompanied by a belief in common property, and the two value attachments have served to put their respective believers into a posture of gladiators fighting for supremacy.

This type of development could be described as the establishment of an *anticommunity*. For all the characteristic features of community formation are found in the deviant group, and since they are territorially intermingled, the political aspirations of the new community are bound to be directed against the disintegrating community in the midst of which this kind of community is developing. It is for that reason very important that any dissent which becomes organized remain within the established community. Leaders often fail to realize the urgency of this task before it is too late. Keeping the channels of communication open and providing for a measure of continued participation are rather crucial for such a strategy. This argument shows why outlawry of dissenting groups often accomplishes nothing but driving the dissenters into the forming of an anticommunity, which eventually replaces the community from which they have been excluded. The Christians in the Roman Empire, the Puritans in England and the bourgeois in France are familiar illustrations.

What further complicates the political analysis as well as any program of political action is that a certain amount of such antagonism is part and parcel of any healthy community. The "peace of the graveyard" which some protagonists of communitarian views seem to cherish is not even desired in a communist totalitarian community, much less so in a progressive democratic one. A pluralism of interests, values and beliefs is not only a fact, but a desideratum of its politics. The need for dissent is as great as the need for common ground.[16] Indeed it may be and has been argued that only agreement on the "rules of the game," that is to say, on the procedures for reaching compromise and decision, are needed. Others have maintained that an "agreement on fundamentals" is of decisive importance (Chapter 2). Neither proposition may be universally true, but each may in turn depend upon both environmental factors and the prevalent values, interests and beliefs. That is to say, the acceptance of some values, interests and beliefs (such as the cherishing of the value of discussion, the interest in economic progress and the belief in the dignity of man) on the part of a substantial majority of the members of a given community may make an agreement on the "rules of the game" sufficient for the maintenance of a viable political community. Whereas if there is no such majority, agreement not only on rules but on certain fundamentals may be necessary if the community is to be maintained. What has been said should make it clear, in any case, that the formula concerning the interrelationship of a disintegration of values, interests and beliefs and the maintenance of community raises rather than answers problems.

Any political community, like any organization (Chapter 7), develops over time (1) myths, especially a foundation myth, (2) symbols, especially integration symbols, and (3) utopias, especially perfection

[16] Cf. Friedrich, 1942, chap. 5. Dahl, 1956, chaps. III and IV, developed some stimulating formulas for this type of situation. See also the further analysis below in Chap. 11, where the need for dissent is analyzed.

utopias. This proposition, from which no exception is known within past human political experience, is nonetheless often neglected. Many writers, especially in the rationalist period, have treated myths, symbols and utopias as if they were avoidable "illusions" or "errors" which a more enlightened community could escape from by rational communication. But the experience of the very organizations built by persons inspired by such misconceptions proves the persistence of these propositions; the Jacobin Clubs, no less than academies of science and reform organizations of various hues of rationalist progressivism, exhibit the same propensity toward myth, symbol and utopia.[17] And it is the communal aspect of human togetherness which accounts for these propensities; for they provide the emotional bonds by tying past, present and future into a coherent whole which appeals to the emotions (Chapter 5).

The foundation myth typically provides both a simplification and personification of complex and impersonal forces. Thus the recurrent myth of the heroic founder of the Greek *polis*, as well as of Rome, personifies in simple and personal terms the trials and agonies of domestic strife, the decision to seek a new location and the settlement on an alien and hostile shore. Popular notions of the founding of the Italian and the German states in the last century are not very different, any more than the familiar myths about the Pilgrim Fathers and the sages of Philadelphia. Such a rationalist challenge as Beard's insistence on the economic interests,[18] even if it were true, could not hope to survive the insistent communal pressure for an effective myth, as Beard himself came to realize.

Symbols, such as flags, songs and coats-of-arms similarly provide the senses with a readily seen or heard representation of the community (Chapter 16). The complex values, interests and beliefs embodied in the existent community as it lives and evolves from day to day and from year to year can be only emotionally comprehended and affirmed by most persons, if such values can thus be "looked at" and honored. Such conflicts as those over the saluting of the flag by children in a democracy's public schools can readily be understood if this persistent need of a community's symbolization is recognized: those who refuse wish to demonstrate their rejection of the community as the "highest" community, as all testimony of, for example, Jehovah's Witnesses shows, while those

[17] Nelson, a, 1959, notes the pervasive influence of perfection utopias, but himself calls for another one at the conclusion of his analysis, when he writes: "Humanity has no chance to endure if society will not learn in this hour to become humane, . . ." that is to say, "if our cosmos is to have a future, it must learn to do without its two most persistent *illusions*, apocalyptic cosmism and redemptive futurism." (Italics mine.) I should say that the prospect of survival is dim if that is a necessary condition, and on Nelson's own evidence of the persistence of this sort of illusion.

[18] Beard, 1913, *passim;* cf. Chap. 22 below.

who seek to enforce the ritual obeisance are determined that the community's existence be fully recognized. That the latter in doing so come into conflict with a basic value of the community, namely, the toleration of religious diversity, constitutes the tragedy of such situations, from which only a highly authoritative tribunal can extricate the community by providing some species of "reinterpretation" of the word signs, representing the values involved.

Utopias, finally, provide the hope that the values and beliefs cherished by the community will eventually be realized, in the face of their manifest failure at the particular moment. For whatever the particular values and beliefs, and indeed interests, cherished by a specific community, the actual behavior of actual persons who are members of the community will fall short, often far short, of their ideal projection or image. This is inevitable not only because actual behavior is moulded by personal, as well as communal, interests, but because the several values, beliefs and interests do not ever form a consistent and coherent whole but clash with each other at numerous points. Only completely rational beings would be capable of even formulating or evolving a coherent "system" (hence the objections to speaking of these syndromes of actual values, interests and beliefs as "systems." All political communities therefore live by utopian projections, democracies just as much as totalitarian dictatorships, monarchies as much as republics, but the degree of dependence varies greatly. When actual conditions seem especially unpromising for the realization of prevailing values and beliefs, the utopia may become transcendent, in the form of some kind of notion of a paradise hereafter. Evidently, this sort of utopia presupposes a belief in the immortality of man, body or soul, and hence the communal pressure for the evolution of such a belief becomes very strong in certain situations.

A second major proposition relates to location in space. The political community, in contrast to many other communities, has typically a territorial dimension. It lives and evolves within a defined territorial boundary. Typically, that is, when it is "fully developed" through organizational implementation. Prior to such organizational implementation through a government (or "state," as some prefer to say), a political community may manage to persist without a clearly defined territorial boundary. Good examples are the Jews, the Irish and the Germans, and many of the now emergent nations; it is symptomatic for the underdeveloped state of the communal existence that there can be observed a strong political "pull" within such a community toward effective organization, often over very long periods of time. A leading sociologist has tried to make this territorial aspect of community the very content of the concept. He would not "treat community as a type of concrete social unit, but as an analytical category," namely, "that aspect of the structure of social systems which is referable to the territorial location of persons." [19] It is evident that since we are treating the community as an actual and real social unity, such an approach is not compatible with ours. Nonetheless, it contains a very suggestive approach, from our point of view, to the territorial aspect of community. It seems more appropriate, however, to speak of this as the locational or spatial aspect; for the fact that the home or residence of the family community is *located* somewhere gives it a location, rather than a territory—the latter term being more suitable for the description of the political community proper whose government has "jurisdiction within a defined boundary." In any case, political communities, whether undeveloped or underdeveloped, *exist* in the political sense; they exhibit the dimensions we have suggested as characteristic, and they provide therefore opportunities for the exercise of power, leadership, influence, and the rest of the typically political manifestations of communal human behavior. Other communities, for example, churches, and professional groups, do not necessarily or even usually possess this territorial aspect; their members are frequently scattered over wide areas and characteristically interlarded, as any "map" of the distribution of church membership in larger countries will disclose.

A third major proposition concerning community states that a community becomes structured in organization as it grows in size. Size may refer to the number of persons belonging to the community, or it may refer to the spatial scattering of membership, or both. This proposition is of primary importance in the sphere of political subdivisions, such as parties and "juntas," clubs and interest groups. The recurrent desire to avoid organizational stratification and hence bureaucratization, expressing itself, for example, in the insistence that a certain party is not a party, but a movement (de Gaulle), is unrealistic and a kind of political romanticism. The same may be said of recurrent attempts, especially in politically underdeveloped countries, to avoid parties altogether and to seek for a substitute in small "neighborhood" units and the like. For important as is the local community with its close bonds of neighborhood and kinship (Chapter 29), it is no substitute for, but a complement of, the role of parties and interest and professional groups in the large-scale political community of today. The need for organization in large-scale communities is paramount, and results from the tasks of communication where decisions have to be arrived at involving the community's values, interests and beliefs and their adaptation to a changing environment through decision and policy (Chapter 3). In newly emergent nations this task of effective political organization may be of the greatest urgency, and yet be extremely difficult. Numerous crisis situations have arisen because of the heedless adoption of types of political organization, such

[19] Parsons, a, 1959, p. 152.

as parliamentary democracy and totalitarian dictatorship, which presuppose political conditions and habitual modes of behavior not to be found in these communities. The discovery and possible invention of suitable organization patterns is not necessarily a matter of imitating or even of adapting preexisting forms (Chapter 21).

A fourth proposition, closely related to the preceding one, is that organized (institutionalized) political communities are *better adapted* to reaching decisions and developing policies than unorganized communities. This proposition follows directly from the theory of organization presented in the preceding chapter. Organizing means ordering the relations between human beings and their behavior in such a way that they become capable of acting together; decision-making and policy-formulating are primary features of such acting together. Stress must here be laid upon the fact that while such communities are better adapted to do this, unorganized or partially organized ones are not entirely incapable of arriving at such "decisions," as some schools of thought on government and law incline to assume. Multiple experience may well lead to adaptive behavior, even where organization is lacking or quite imperfect. This can be seen in conditions where leadership rests upon a genuine charismatic basis, or where the pressure is great enough to beget parallel decisions in all or most members of a community, as when resistance to a conquering or occupying power is called for. In the emergent nations, such processes can often be observed; however, organization will occur as soon as the opportunity offers. What has been called rather clumsily the "routinization of charisma" is likewise a process of transforming an unorganized community. It is an error, suggested by both Pareto and Max Weber, to assume that these organization processes are necessarily "rationalizing" processes.[20] Indeed, due to the exigencies of organization, these processes may be less rational than the original community. Thus, the community which binds the founder of a religion or political movement through the charisma which links leader and led is typically more rational in the sense that discussion and conviction provide proof and hence real authority, than the myths and symbols which the organization afterwards develops for the maintenance of effective authority (Chapter 12).

Every one of the foregoing propositions may be capable of quantitative specification. Such quantitative specification calls for the exploration of a last feature of community which is of primary importance, and that is communication. We have so far implied without specification that community presupposes the capacity of members to communicate with each

[20] There is a significant difference, though, because in Weber the sense is qualified and approaches that of efficiency in organization. Cf. Parsons, 1937, for a clear exposition of both.

other. This implication must now be subjected to further exploration.[21] It has previously been noted that increasing sophistication concerning language (Chapter 2), as well as the findings of modern psychology, reinforced by such intuitive insights as are found in Dostoievsky, Kafka and Faulkner, among others, have raised serious doubts as to the degree of effective communication even on the most intimate level of personal community. "When do human beings really communicate?" is a question which few will feel ready to answer dogmatically at the present time. These perplexities refer, however, to the individual and his realm of feeling and understanding. For the formation of community it is characteristic that human beings succeed in communicating enough of each other's world to be able to act jointly for the attainment of seemingly common values, interests and ends believed in. This fact is obvious enough on the strictly material plane. Physical referents, such as bridges and roads, provide obvious focal points for communal activity. This common experience is then extended to more complex human referents, such as schools (education) and police (security). It may well be that a detailed inquiry would disclose that not two persons of a community of several hundred persons "mean" the same referent when they decide by majority vote to build a new school to improve "education." Still, they argued and eventually concluded the argument by adopting a policy.

Communication includes, in any case, not only linguistic communication, that is to say, communication by means of word symbols, but the employment of many other symbols as well. They range all the way from the fleeting expression of mood on a human face to the dollar offered in exchange for goods.[22] It is obvious that communication then is a necessary, though by no means a sufficient, condition of community; there can be no community without communication on a considerable and stabilized scale. This indisputable fact has given rise to the notion that the degree of community may be measured by the quantity of communication.[23] In a rough way, such a premise seems reasonable enough. As the community among French, Germans and Italians has been increasing during the last decade, communications also have been increasing very rapidly. These increases can readily be measured statistically: it can be ascertained how many people travel from country to country, how many do business with

[21] Deutsch, 1953, esp. chap. 4; also the same (ed.), 1957, esp. pp. 36ff.

[22] If all such symbols are included in the meaning of "language," as Parsons suggests at one point of his analysis (1959, p. 173), then his statement that a minimum requirement of community is a "common language" (*ibid.*, p. 169) is acceptable. But from the context it is doubtful that this is his meaning; for the statement is preceded by the proposition that "communication always implies a common culture," which is patently erroneous. Not only the increasing world community belies it, but such phenomena as communicating by signs in a foreign land, or by certain gestures with a dog.

[23] Deutsch (ed.), 1957, chap. III; cf. also Deutsch, 1953, chaps. VI and VII.

each other, how many monetary units are being exchanged, how many letters and telegrams are being sent, and so forth. These are all indices of communication, and if increase in population and other extraneous factors such as the general level of business activity are taken into account, they might be combined into a general "index of community." There may, however, be considerable pitfalls in such an approach. This might be illustrated by one or two nonpolitical instances. Is the extent of familial community, say, that between two marriage partners, to be measured by the number of words exchanged between them? Is the depth of a religious community to be ascertained by a similar index? To ask these questions is to answer them in the negative. Reflection upon such instances discloses that the index only works where "other things are equal," that is to say, where the same kind of persons are involved in the same kind of community. It may therefore prove reasonably useful in a situation where a political community is evolving within a relatively short period of time so that the constituent elements in the situation remain relatively similar. But great caution is indicated, while it must be remembered that in situations of that kind the index is not really needed, as there are other less costly ways of ascertaining the "facts."

Communications can be manipulated for political as well as other purposes. It is not possible to differentiate concretely a distinct category of communications which might be called "information," "orientation," or whatever, and of which it could be said that it does not imply the attempt to influence behavior.[24] Since any item of information which is "relevant," that is to say, enables a person to perceive something he did not perceive before, affects his behavior—as when I am told that there is a "biting dog" at a certain house I am planning to visit—it is not very likely to be communicated unless the person who communicates it wishes to affect the behavior of the person he "informs." In any case, there is no way of ascertaining whether he does or not, in many situations, and the alleged specific difference is therefore beyond observation. If, then, all communication is directive to a greater or lesser extent, the only question of importance is the direction toward which it points. Communications may be either community-oriented or not. This alternative is not a question of the intention of those involved in the situation, though such intention may often enter in, but is an existential question of fact. If the communication is of a sort to contribute to the realization of common values, interests and/or beliefs, it is communal communication; otherwise, not.

These observations have an important field of application in the sphere of propaganda and its analysis. Propaganda is communication di-

[24] Parsons, 1959, pp. 168–69, following Bales, 1951, as well as others, has made such a distinction; it is an "idealizing" category which defies realistic analysis.

rected toward getting definitely known persons to do certain things or to abstain from doing them. Propaganda is action-oriented. It is therefore typically paid for by the organization which is likely to benefit by the action. Propaganda is typically carried on *within* a community by subgroups, either to secure action by the community (if organized) or by various members of the community. Much effective propaganda is done by information, and the relative degree of truth of the content of the communication is not what determines its propagandistic function.[25] Propaganda may therefore be communal communication or not. This depends upon whether it contributes to the realization of common values, interests and/or beliefs.

It is apparent that no modern community of any size could possibly subsist without a continuing flow of propaganda, any more than without effective communication. This conclusion has often been overlooked by the more naïve rationalists who conceive of education and information as means of "pure" communication. They hence are much occupied with propaganda analysis, believing that a communication is revealed as worthless or at least as dubious if shown to have been propaganda. The political question, however, is not *whether* communications are propaganda or not, but by whom they are issued and what purposes they are intended to serve. If communications emanate from acknowledged leaders speaking with authority on matters of common concern, they are indeed propaganda, but they are building and integrating the community and hence politically of positive value, as far as the members of that particular community are concerned. Much pointless political romanticism can be avoided if these elementary insights following from the role of communications in community are borne in mind. Content analysis of such communications is of considerable importance, because such content analysis provides clues as to the decisive questions of value, interest and belief.

These considerations bring the analysis to the point where the interaction of values, structures and processes in the political community becomes paramount. To this analysis Part II is devoted. But before we turn to power, justice and freedom as the crux of this analysis, it may be appropriate to mention the rapid spread of the concept of community in the political parlance of the present day. Not only the notion of a world community, but the heated discussions over the metropolitan community and the establishment of the Coal and Steel Community, the European Economic Community and finally the community which calls itself French under the Fifth Republic bear witness to this popularity of the term. Why

[25] In keeping with our methodological position, which insists upon stipulative definitions, it would be more accurate to reverse the above sentences, and to say that "action-oriented communication shall be called propaganda," etc. Cf. for this complex, Friedrich, 1950, chap. 24, and the literature given there.

should this be so? The preceding analysis suggests the answer. In all these instances the situation is characterized by the presence of a substantial measure of common unity, manifest in a sharing of values, interests and beliefs, which lacks or is insufficiently provided with effective organization. The great metropolitan communities, for example, though united in the common experience of an ever wider extension of the distance between home and work and the consequent problems of transportation and communication, present in most countries an unbelievable patchwork of ancient political structures, cities, towns and related units of every variety. Time and again very pressing problems of concrete action remain unsolved for many years because the metropolitan community remains unorganized and hence incapable of effective action. It is an astounding fact that until very recently no living person could say how the metropolis of New York with its fifteen million inhabitants was governed, because literally hundreds of units of government form an undecipherable labyrinth in which the inhabitants as well as their ill-advised "rulers" grope their uncertain way. Here was community without government, a political community without organization.[26] The situation in Europe and in the world is not markedly different. The task of how to structure government for such emergent communities, unprecedented in their scope, cannot be effectively tackled without an analysis of all the political experience which man has had to date. And even this experience serves only as the jumping-off point for discovery and invention on an unprecedented scale.

[26] See below, Chap. 29; Wood, 1961, at last gave a general analysis; so did Sayre and Kaufmann, 1959.

part II

The Dimensions of Power and Justice

part

II

The Dimensions of Power and Justice

chapter

9

Power and Leadership

Power is precarious.
Herodotus

A leader is best
when men barely know he is there,
not so good when men obey and acclaim him,
worst, when they despise him. . . .
Lao-tzu

POWER IS A CENTRAL CONCERN of political science. It is a phenomenon which is universally recognized, but difficult to understand. Like all data of the real world it defies rigorous definition.[1] Most famous among the attempts at definition is Hobbes's; he states that "power is the present means to secure some future apparent good." [2] Such a definition is both too broad and too narrow. Too broad because it makes it impossible to distinguish power from wealth; for what is wealth but a present means to secure some future apparent good? Hobbes's reply to such an objection would have been, of course, that wealth is a "form" of power. He says as much in the discussion that follows his definition. Whatever may be the argument here on broad philosophical grounds, it

[1] Power has been the subject of a great deal of inquiry and controversy in recent years. Among full-length treatments of *political* power, see Catlin, 1927 and 1930; Merriam, 1934; Russell, 1938; Lasswell, 1936 and 1948; Brady, 1943; B. de Jouvenel, 1948; Hunter, 1953. Besides these a good many articles, as well as significant treatments in books primarily concerned with other matters, especially in the international field, have added significant basic insight and helpful detail. No attempt will be made here to evaluate all this writing; a careful digest is given by Franz Neumann, a, 1950.

[2] Hobbes, *Leviathan*, 1641, chap. 10.

is operationally important today to draw this distinction in order to differentiate political from economic concerns and thus politics from economics. Actually so broad a definition as Hobbes's really identifies power with the totality of resources available to a man—the means by which he can realize his values or purposes. If power is thus defined, what does it mean to say that "life is but a ceaseless search for power after power unto death"—the famous claim of Hobbes recited to this day? It simply says that men seek that which they desire, which is little short of tautological.

But Hobbes's definition is not only too broad, it is also too narrow. For it talks of power as if it were a thing, something to have and to hold, and maybe to sit upon like a bag of gold. Power at times possesses this quality but at other times not at all, and it is important to see it in its dual nature, because only this Janus-faced quality gives to power the perplexing dynamic quality which men feel but find it difficult to account for. Hobbes actually goes beyond this conception as he develops his argument. But the Hobbesian legacy has been troubling political theory in a variety of contexts. Curiously enough the theorizing of a good many constitutionalists, notably Harrington, Montesquieu and *The Federalist* (Hamilton), has been afflicted with this view of power as a possession. Indeed, much theorizing on the separation of powers reads as if the political power in a community were some kind of cake which it is the task of a constitution suitably to distribute among naughty children all of whom want more of it than they ought to have. Even Locke falls into this error when writing of power in the Second Treatise, although he develops a very different view in a broader philosophical context.

Power is not primarily a thing, a possession, but rather a relation, as Locke insists in *An Essay Concerning Human Understanding*,[3] where he states that "powers are relations, not agents." Indeed power is primarily a relation.

If power is looked at in the dimension of time, it becomes clear that its relational quality is the more evident the longer the time span involved. For it is in the rise and the decline of political power, whether of individuals or of larger groups, that the relational quality, the fact that power is always power *over* other men, becomes evident. In a certain sense, therefore, it is possible to say that the stress upon its quality as a thing, a possession to have and to hold, is the result of an illusion. But such a statement is not wholly justified. Due to the institutionalization of power relationships presently to be discussed (see next chapter) the power attached to a certain office *is* a thing, a possession to have and to hold. To

[3] Bk. II, chap. 21. It is curious and has been noted especially that Locke in his *Essays on Civil Government* (bk. II, p. 4) builds the argument upon Hobbes's concept, though the other notion implicit in his general philosophy also plays its part.

be sure, the office may be lost as a result of the way the power is used, but while the office is held the power is in the hands of him who holds it.

Therefore it is appropriate to say that power is *to some extent* a possession (p^1), and *to some extent* a relation (p^2). It is the ratio of the two ingredients which political science must continuously be concerned with. The difference between political phenomena in which the ratio of p^1 to p^2 is greater than one and those in which the ratio of p^1 to p^2 is smaller than one is familiar to the study of politics. The first is typically a stabilized office, such as is occupied by a hereditary monarch, or an official of a firmly established republic. The second ratio, $p^1/p^2 < 1$ is seen in such phenomena as the leader of a party, or even more pronouncedly in that of the initiator of a movement or the organizer of an enterprise—in short, a founder. The process of political foundation always requires as the initial act that one actor, L, persuade another, A (and in turn B, C, and so forth), to work with him in realizing an objective; in most cases this means that A and B must add many others to join with them in pursuit of this objective. All these actors, A + B + C, . . . , are in the typical case united by their willingness to *follow* L, because of the relation existing between them and him, which is one of voluntary subjection to his leadership.[4]

Power, it would seem, is that relation among men which *manifests* itself in the behavior of following. Following means typically that the A's, B's and C's do what L wants. To put this basic observation another way, one might say that when the behavior of a certain group of men conforms to the wishes of one or several of them, the relation between them shall be called the power of L over A,B,C. . . . It is evident that such power is not only characteristic of the kind of relation we just sketched, but is likewise found in stable offices where it is "possessed" by him who holds the office.[5]

The ubiquity of the latter phenomena has given rise to a serious error which would restrict power to those situations in which a man finds obedience for his *commands*. It is true that often the explicit command of one (L) and the resulting behavior of others (A,B,C, . . .) *are* the manifestation of a power relationship based upon obedience, but this basis is only one of the possible forms which such a relationship may exhibit. In

[4] The founding processes have in recent years been most effectively emphasized by Bertrand de Jouvenel, whose two main works contain many apt illustrations.

[5] Similar definitions have been offered by a number of writers in recent years. However, Easton, 1953, p. 144, and Lasswell and Kaplan, 1950, pp. 74ff., do not. The former says that "power is present to the extent to which one person controls by sanction the decisions and actions of another." Even so, the latter, after also stressing "sanctions," state that power is "a relationship in which one person or group is able to determine the actions of another in the direction of the former's own ends," which is broader and comes closer to our view. Cf. also Goldhamer and Shils, a, 1939; H. Simon, a, 1953; and March, a, 1955; as well as Dahl, a, 1957.

situations of dynamic and highly fluid leadership especially, L does not *command*, but he *suggests* or *persuades;* he may also be followed by others as they *anticipate* his wishes or reactions. The last named form of power is influence (Chapter 11). But there are also the "matched" or "balanced" power situations in which negotiation and compromise are the manifest signs of the power involved.

Certain writers have complicated the analysis of power by the introduction of the concept of control, using it for purposes of "defining" power. At times a simple tautology is involved, when power and control are actually treated as synonyms. In other cases the emphasis on control unduly narrows the scope of power.[6] "Control" seems to us best suited for designating a particular form of power, namely, that form in which formal techniques of ordering and supervising are employed. Thus the demand for parliamentary "control" of foreign affairs usually implies that a parliament is to be involved in foreign policy decisions and/or negotiations by formal action, such as participation of a committee on foreign affairs. Control of expenditures by, say, a special officer such as the Comptroller General of the United States likewise is meant to specify that this officer has formal functions in connection with the validation of specific items of expenditure in detail. Control is, therefore, always based upon power—it is a form of power; but much power is not effectuated as control, but in other forms.

The instances just cited show further that control is, in a sense, power once removed. When one person or group exercises power and another person merely makes sure that the power was exercised according to some fixed standard or for some definite purpose—a situation which is very common in politics and government—"control" is the proper designation. A board of directors typically controls the executives of a corporation, but a superior does not merely control his subordinates, he directs them, he wields authority and general influence—all modes of power which are distinct from the mode just discussed which we may properly designate as control. In scientific work, to control an experiment means to provide a standard of comparison for checking the inferences; it is our contention that a similar operation occurs in politics which therefore might be correspondingly called control.[7]

Unless it is clearly understood that behavior may conform, because of

[6] Lasswell and Kaplan, 1950, seem to use it as a synonym of "power," while Banfield, 1961, p. 309, identifies control with direction; Oppenheim, 1961, chaps. 2–3, similarly suggests "causes to act" as the meaning, distinguishing further between "having" and "exercising" control.

[7] *The American College Dictionary,* while allowing the possible identification of control with power, defines it more precisely and restrictively as meaning "to exercise restraint" as well as "to hold in check" or "to curb." This seems to justify the use of the word for the phenomenon described.

a variety of signs indicating the preference of him who holds the power, and not merely because of commands, the phenomenon of influence remains obscure. Influence is a kind of power, and not only may but usually does profoundly affect the institutionalized exercise of power. It will be more fully explored below. At this stage in our analysis it is perhaps sufficient to call influence a "hidden" kind of power, provided it is understood that this hiding can be more or less thorough. This quantitative difference in the degree of secretiveness is not directly related to the extent of the influence; very great influence may be very secret. It tends, however, to become known in the course of time. The conditions for such secrecy are varied and not very well understood at the present time. In any case, influence is rarely, if ever, exercised in the form of commands; persuasion, suggestion and even insinuation are its characteristic forms. In many power situations, the hard core of power, exercised through formal commands, is surrounded by a larger sphere of influence.[8]

Having given a brief indication of the nature of power as a relation of men manifest in conforming behavior, we may now raise the question: What is the source of power? On what basis or foundation does it rest? But before we can undertake to answer these questions, something further is required by way of an elucidation of the nature of the power relationship. If we consider the dynamic situation which gives rise to a power relationship in its broadest sense, we find that virtually anything that human beings value can become the basis of a power relationship. It can do this in one of two ways: either through the necessity for several human beings to get together and form a group, in order to secure it, or through several of them possessing and, therefore, being able to provide something which others would like to have. Thus protection against violence is desired by most men, but during most of human history only lim-

[8] Lasswell and Kaplan, 1950, p. 74, speak of power as "a deference value with which political science is especially concerned; it can be described in terms of its domain, scope, weight and coerciveness. Forms of power can be distinguished according to the value upon which power is based. . . ." They undertake to formulate basic propositions concerning power which serve as postulates to be developed and subjected to empirical investigation. One such proposition is the following: "Two forms of power are interdependent; a certain amount of several forms of power is a necessary condition for a great amount of any form." Lasswell and Kaplan do not verify this or the other propositions they state in a strict empirical sense; they merely offer illustrations. In order to confirm or elaborate them (empirical verification being a contradiction in terms) it would be necessary to discover among the varied power situations one where a particular form was predominant. Even if such a situation cannot be found, it would be impossible to prove that it had not occurred without the other forms accompanying it. A conclusive demonstration of impossibility requires other than empirical data. See regarding the problem of political impossibility what is said below in Chap. 21.

ited groups have been capable of providing it. This fact has been the ground on which political power and more particularly government has been rationalized, justified and theoretically explained, especially in the so-called "contractual" theories which were in great vogue in the past.[9]

The extreme case is, of course, that of conquest often cited in controverting the contractual theories; such arguments overlook this fact that the conqueror can provide protection (including safety against his own followers) and the submission occurs as a *quid pro quo* for such protection. This power situation in which the person having power *possesses* it, that is, finds other human beings willing to act in accordance with his wishes, may be represented by a diagram as follows:

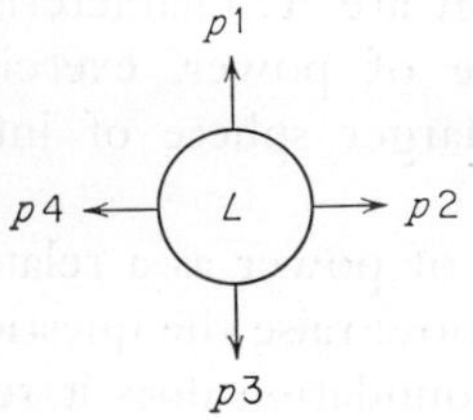

p1

p4 ← L → p2

p3

where p^1, p^2, p^3, p^4 = powers possessed by L
L = leader possessing power

Here power seems like a material substance and might therefore be called "substantive" or "coercive" power. But there is always the possibility that some persons might reject the value upon which it is based, and then it either ceases to exist or must be built upon another value. Epictetus' discussion about the tyrant is in point here. The tyrant says, "I am the mightiest of all men." "Well, and what can you give me? Can you enable me to get what I will to get? . . ." "But I can behead you." "Well said. I forgot, of course, one ought to pay you worship as if you were a fever or a cholera. . . . For when a tyrant says to a man, 'I will chain your leg,' he that values his leg says, 'Nay, have mercy,' but he that values his will says, 'If it seems more profitable to you, chain it.' "[10]

If the value or purpose requires the cooperation of a number of human beings, then the power of one or several among them will rest upon his or their capacity to provide the leadership for securing the desired good. They "lead" the way, so to speak, and those who follow recognize their capacity to do so. This kind of power may be represented by the following diagram:

L • ——— P ——— • A,B

where A,B = persons involved in power relationship
L = leader

[9] D'Addio, 1954.
[10] Epictetus, *Discourses* (ed. Oates, 1940), pp. 258, 8.

What really happens is that *L organizes* the cooperation. Such power may therefore be called consensual, cooperative, or relational power.[11] The expressions "coercive" and "consensual" or "cooperative" power are misleading if taken as designating exclusive and separate phenomena. As previously pointed out, they are aspects of all power situations. In many actual power situations, however, either the coercive or the consensual aspect predominates to such an extent that it is permissible for purposes of concrete analysis to neglect the minor aspect and thus simply to speak of coercive or consensual power. Thus, concretely, the power of an absolute monarch may be said to be coercive, that of a leader of a democratic party consensual. But it is not permissible to contrast the power of a totalitarian dictator and a democratic chief executive in these terms, because both exercise power which is to a considerable extent coercive and to a considerable extent consensual, though the ratios may be different.

In order to understand the full implications of these statements we must return now to the question about the sources of power—a question which may also be called that about the origin of power. The terms "coercive" and "consensual" indicate that the source of these two aspects is to be seen in what happens to the followers whose conduct conforms to the wishes of the power-holder. The first rests upon the coercion or constraint resulting from the fact that L possesses something that A,B,C . . . want to secure, and which L uses to coerce or constrain them to conform to his wishes. We say constrain as well as coerce because the term "coercion" carries too large an implication of violence. But if it is clearly understood that coercion also covers the kind of mere constraint which may be the result of an attachment or of mental or psychic deficiencies of the followers, coercion may serve to designate any situation in which the conduct of A,B,C . . . conforms to the wishes of L, because he makes them conform out of their *fear* of not securing what he can either give or withhold. These aspects are predominant in the thought of Hobbes and the numerous writers who have stressed the coercive aspect of the power situation.

The second or consensual aspect of power originates in the consent of A,B,C . . . to cooperate with L in securing a good which they all desire. Now it may be said that those coerced also "consent" [12] and that even the

[11] In my *Constitutional Government and Politics*, 1937, and *Constitutional Government and Democracy*, 1941 and later, I spoke only of substantive and relational power; but these terms lack precision because cooperative or consensual power and coercive power have in common that they are both aspects of the power relationship. As pointed out above, neither of them occurs in pure form; it is a question of their ratio in any concrete power situation.

[12] Hobbes's discussion of "liberty" (*op. cit.*, bk. II, p. 21), anticipates all later attempts of this sort. See below, Chaps. 20 and 21.

prisoner is "free" in his chains. Such sophistry gainsays one of the basic human experiences. The difference between being coerced and cooperating lies in this: that in the case of coercion, once the means of coercion are taken away, the human being acts differently (leaving aside here the metaphysical problem of the freedom of the will) from the way he did while they were at hand. To understand the difference is not really hard. Many examples could be used. We cite one: the political situation surrounding a plebiscite held either under the supervision of one of the parties or of "neutral" forces. Here it becomes manifest what really matters. If he who holds the power can determine what those following are going to want, the situation is of the coercive type; if the followers determine it for themselves, and join the leader in the pursuit of their independently chosen objectives, we may speak of a consensual situation.

Power, then, may be exercised either through coercion or consent.[13] However, as already mentioned, it is important to realize that coercion and consent are not mutually exclusive: they are each operative on their own. A large amount of political thought and analysis rests upon the idea that either coercion can be defined as nonconsent or consent as noncoercion. But coercion has a force of its own, as has consent, and in most power situations both are operative in varying degrees and combinations. Therefore the most general formula for power is power (*p*) equals coercion (*cc*) plus consent (*cs*), where the instances in which either *cc* or *cs* approaches zero may be considered marginal. Consent and coercion are both real forces, generating power.

Both consent and coercion involve obviously psychological data. The different psychological schools have given surprisingly little concentrated attention to these phenomena, however. Thus, for example, in the index to the writings of Sigmund Freud, neither term appears.[14] But for the purpose of the present analysis, the psychological ambience may be taken in the crude form which common experience provides. Most important from a political standpoint, because of the implications for the understanding of power, is the fact that both coercion and consent refer to several different processes. There is not just one way to be coerced or one way to consent. What are these different modes of coercion and consent?

An inspection of the political scene discloses three primary forms of coercion: physical, economic and psychic. In the political sphere, physical coercion, usually referred to as brute force, occurs either by military or by police action. Its means are physical violence, especially killing, and imprisonment and the punishments associated with it. We do not need to

[13] B. Moore, Jr., 1958, pp. 1ff.

[14] Freud (ed. Brill), 1938. Psychologists have not generally employed the terms "coercion" and "consent." Dissonance theory and work on opinion and attitude change relate to the issue. Cf. Kelman, a, 1961; Festinger and Aronson, a, 1960.

lose much time over it, even though its role in the history of human government has been enormous. The vast scale which physical violence has once more assumed in our time has obliterated the liberal anarchic dreams of a world without such physical coercion. (See Chapters 23 and 34.)

Economic coercion takes primarily the form of withholding the means of securing a livelihood. It is at the heart of the phenomena which preoccupied Karl Marx and his school when he talked about control over the means of production. Since that time it has become the main weapon in the arsenal of totalitarian dictatorship. For once the government controls all means of production there is no escape for the man who engenders the government's displeasure. He can be virtually starved to death. In that sense, Marx's views on government, tersely expressed in the dictum that "the state is the executive committee of the ruling class," have become an accurate description of the kind of government the Communists have built.[15] Never before had the means of economic coercion been so vast as under a system which makes the central direction and management of the entire economy one of its key features. Nonetheless, there was a measure of truth in Marx's emphasis on the importance of economic coercion which the control of the means of production implies. Such coercion may be crude and consist in the threat of losing one's livelihood, when one is unwilling to support the politics of those who own land and factory. Such crude coercion, while now rare in advanced industrial societies which have developed a democratic political order, was the usual practice not so very long ago in Britain and the United States, no less than in France and Russia. It still survives in certain types of discrimination, especially as practiced against racial minorities. But the economic coercion may be more devious and take the form of controlling news and other communications via the advertising in newspapers and on the radio.[16]

Economic coercion also is at work in many corrupt practices. The possession of economic resources readily engenders this kind of coercive power. Not only the buying of votes and actual monetary rewards, but all the more indirect forms, such as gifts, or influencing the judgment of those who exercise governmental functions, are instrumentalities in this sphere of politics. Here again it is a question of degree of corruption, and quantitative studies might well shed further light on the conditions under which corruption grows. That corruption is endemic in all government is practically certain. That there are striking differences in the extent of corruption between governments which are formally similar, such as Great Britain, Switzerland and the United States, all functioning constitutional democracies, is equally patent. It is possible that a law could be

[15] The ideological and psychological implications have been brilliantly portrayed in Djilas, 1957.

[16] Friedrich and Sayre, 1940; Llewellyn White, 1947; Siepman, 1946; Friedrich and Sternberg, a, 1943.

stated which would say that the degree of corruption varies inversely to the degree that power is consensual, but care would have to be taken not to mistake apparent consensual power for actual power of this kind. For it would appear that precisely in those situations where the semblance of consent is replacing the reality, as happened in many American cities in the course of the nineteenth century, corruption is rife. The power which is believed to be consensual having to a considerable extent become coercive, it lends itself to the more extreme forms of corruption, especially when the economic interests at stake are high. Tammany Hall is a sort of example for this situation. There is a tendency on the part of critics of democracy to assert that developments of the kind just indicated are typical for democracy. If that were true, our tentative law would not really hold. Historical studies show how erroneous such assertions are; in Prussia no less than in England or imperial Rome corruption was ubiquitous.[17] The real difference is that in free societies corruption is often uncovered and brought to public notice, whereas in autocratic government it remains largely hidden. The vast corruption of a totalitarian dictatorship is evident in the secret documents of the Fascist and National Socialist regimes. Reports from the Soviet Union suggest similar conditions.[18] This is particularly noteworthy because these totalitarian movements achieved power partly on the claim that they would make an end of the corruption which characterized the preceding regimes, which in the case of tsarist Russia and China was actually notorious. It is also interesting that such corruption should have come so soon after the triumph of the revolutionary forces, since the history of the French Revolution reveals a similar situation.

Besides physical and economic coercion, psychic coercion plays a major role in the genesis of power. The so-called "compelling" and "authoritarian" personality [19] is the primary example of such psychic coercion. To a considerable extent the phenomena which Max Weber discussed under the heading of charisma and charismatic leadership belong in this category of psychic coercion. But of even greater importance in contemporary mass societies is the role of propaganda; for propaganda is psychic coercion to a large extent. Typically, the propagandist seeks to use the communication channels at his disposal to make people do things which they *might* not, and presumably *would* not, do if not thus exposed to slanted information.

Even a casual inspection of the propagandist and his purposes yields a definite distinction between several communication processes, namely, propaganda, education and information. Since all propaganda presupposes

[17] Dorn, a, 1931, 1932; Namier, 1929; Furber, 1931.

[18] Fainsod, 1958. Soviet publications provide ample proof in their own articles against corrupt practices.

[19] Adorno, 1950.

a propagandist, it may be useful to approach the problem of what is propaganda in terms of the activities of such a person. He may be described as one who hands out information in order to gain advantages for himself or the group for which he is acting, the latter type being, of course, vastly more important than the man who engages in propaganda for himself. These advantages may be of many kinds, but in modern politics two objectives predominate: to persuade people to join an organization, or to persuade them to support an organization financially. "To contribute his vote or his dough," would be a shorthand way of putting it. This from a political viewpoint is the hard core of the work of the propagandist, while around it cluster the more general activities which are concerned with attitudes, propensities, and states of mind.[20]

The coercive potential of all such propaganda activities can be reduced by making propaganda competitive, by throwing the doors wide open to everyone, so that every attempt at propaganda can be met by counterpropaganda. Contrariwise, autocratic governments, and more especially totalitarian ones, will strive to establish a complete monopoly of control over the mass communication media.[21] There is, of course, in free societies a certain undeniable advantage accruing to people with great financial resources. By hiring propagandists, they can transform the means of economic coercion into those of psychic coercion. But counteracting those forces, there are the enthusiasm, devotion, and the superior knowledge possessed by the underprivileged and their spokesmen, and they may count for more than the economic resources of the financially mighty. This has often been overlooked by critics of democratic society. Observing the undeniable impact of financial support given by vested interests to propaganda campaigns favorable to their side, such critics have exaggerated the extent of this coercive power. But once it is clearly understood that competition mitigates the impact, it is evident—especially in light of the proposition demonstrated above—that all power is partly coercive and partly consensual, and that the realistic question is that of the balance of these two factors—that "the cure of propaganda is more propaganda."

At the same time, it is apparent that the phenomenon of psychic coercion and the power generated by it raise some of the most difficult questions of politics and power. For it is at this point that the distinction between coercive and consensual power becomes most elusive. In many concrete situations it is extremely difficult to establish by empirical data whether power is exercised through consent or constraint. Hence all the elaborate controversies about whether the United States or the Soviet

[20] Doob, 1948; Lasswell, 1939; cf. also Friedrich, 1950, chap. 24, and Lasswell, Casey and Smith, 1935, 1946, for extensive bibliographies.

[21] Friedrich and Brzezinski, 1956, chap. 11.

Union is more democratic. Each power stresses about the other the coercive features, and insists for itself upon the consensual features. Such an argument has less interest to one who has grasped the relatedness of these two aspects of all power. It raises the question, though, about the consensual sphere of power.

What are the sources of censensual power, or rather, the sources of power in which the consensual aspect predominates? It is evident that all three sources just discussed with respect to the coercive aspect may also generate power which is largely based on consent; they can generate consent, too. The entire field of operations involving negotiation and compromise provides occasions for the exercise of power in which constraint and consent are intermingled; here power does not manifest itself in commands, but in proposals, counterproposals and the rest of the instrumentarium of negotiation and diplomacy. Power is matched by countervailing power, and a balance is struck between them for concrete occasions.[22]

But there are other ways of looking at the consensus which results from these processes. If one considers the values or purposes by which consent may be engendered, there would seem to be as many processes as there are such values, and any attempt at analyzing the consensual sphere of power from this point of view would parallel a theory of values.[23] But it is also possible, and from the political standpoint it would be more appropriate, to seek a differentiation in terms of types of leadership, specified so as to disclose the behavioral characteristics of both leader and led.

In short, the question of how consent is generated leads into the general problem of political leadership. Leadership like power has been an age-long concern of political theory. Yet it continues to be the occasion for serious theoretical controversy. With some of this controversy we have to be concerned. It involves both the typology and the operation of leadership. Leaders are power-holders, but they are also power-spenders and power-makers. It does not suffice to note that leaders are the "most active power-holders," nor is it necessarily true; underlings are frequently more "active" than their superiors.[24]

The most widely accepted typology specified in terms of the basis of consent is Max Weber's trichotomy, implied in his typology of rule, of which a critical analysis is given in the next chapter. In terms of the

[22] Friedrich, 1938, *passim;* Morgenthau, 1948; Schelling, 1960. Cf. below, Chaps. 11 and 27.

[23] See above, Chap. 2, and Scheler, 1916; N. Hartmann, 1926; Perry, 1926. Parsons, 1951, p. 100, suggests this link without elaborating it.

[24] Lasswell and Kaplan, 1950, pp. 152ff., lay stress on "activity." Their further assertion that leadership is "a function of prestige" is derived from this erroneous emphasis on the "holding" of power; it is equally and perhaps more correct to say that prestige is a function of leadership, as it accrues to the power-*maker*.

specification of the traits of leaders it is unfortunate, because it argues grounds of legitimacy (see below, Chapter 13) rather than behavioral traits. The latter are more readily specifiable in terms of social roles and the success achieved in fulfilling them.[25]

There appear to be three primary roles of leadership, namely, initiating, maintaining and protecting leadership, to which correspond characteristic behaviors of the followership: imitating, obeying and acclaiming. On this highest level of abstraction we may describe these types of leadership and followership as follows.

The initiator or innovator, who may be conqueror, entrepreneur or lawgiver, to mention only the most generally recognized forms of initiating leadership, strikes out along novel lines of political action which "inspire" those following him into imitating his action, associating themselves with him. Crossing into unfamiliar, and presumably hostile, territory is the most elementary form, perhaps, of such leadership, described in legend and song. These leaders are the founders whom political writers like Machiavelli have praised to the point of placing them beyond "good and evil." Abstractly considered, such statements are poetical exaggerations of the undeniable fact that initiating leadership transcends the established systems of values as it proposes to conquer or invent new values.

Maintaining leadership upholds the established order of things. The conservator reinforces old lines of political action which are familiar to all those following him. They obey his commands, and thereby associate themselves with the existing government and its traditional ways of "getting things done." This kind of leadership is more specifically "authoritative," in that the reasons for what it asks from the following are based upon the generally recognized beliefs, values and interests of the community (Chapter 12). Plato and Aristotle were preoccupied with this type of leadership because of their concern with stabilizing a particular type of political order, the *polis*, which they took for granted as preferable to all others, and as capable of being protected against all comers.

Protecting leadership provides security for the following, more particularly security against bodily destruction, but also security for a particular way of life, a culture and its values, beliefs and interests. Protecting leadership elicits acclaim from the following, who willingly grant, as a result of their delight at being protected, whatever is required to have the leader continue those activities which provide the desired security. Acclaim is a very passive type of behavior on the part of a following. Hobbes focused attention upon this form of leadership and followership. The poignancy of his analysis results from the universal importance of protection and security, the inadequacy from the fact that men wish not only to

[25] For a comprehensive theory of social roles see Parsons, 1951, pp. 236ff. We do not follow his systematization, however.

be protected (more especially against violent death) but also to conserve the established order and, if possible, to conquer new worlds.

All forms of leadership elicit consent and consensus and hence provide a foundation for consensual power. The much argued charismatic leadership may appear in all three basic forms. The term was first proposed by Max Weber to designate the kind of leadership epitomized by men like Moses, Buddha, Mahomet, and the like, who possessed a transcendent "call," a belief shared by their following in a divine being who had called them to their founding enterprise. Weber generalized this phenomenon in two ways, first by also applying it to inspirational leadership not associated with the belief in a transcendent divinity, and secondly by speaking of a "routinized" charisma, that is to say, a charisma which has become "institutionalized" in a church or other organization.[26] These two extensions rather confuse the analysis; routine and charisma are contradictory terms, if the initial specification of the term "charisma" is taken at all seriously. Weber was led into these confusions by his preoccupation with rule, rather than leadership—not having clearly differentiated the two—and they have continued to plague analysis in the field.[27] The notion that a divine being has "called" the leader may provide consent for initiator, conservator and protector alike; it is a special form of legitimacy as analyzed below (Chapter 13). But as the behavior of initiator, conservator and protector is differentiated, as is the behavior of their following, leadership legitimized by charisma partakes of the differentiation, and no common traits can be ascertained for it. St. Francis, an initiator, Pope John XXII, a conservator, and Emperor Louis the Bavarian, a protector, to note three striking illustrations, though all were invested with charisma, did not exhibit common traits of leadership. At the present time, charismatic leadership is of minor importance simply because the faith in a transcendent being is not sufficiently strong or general to provide an adequate basis for legitimizing leadership, whether it is of the initiating, the preserving or the protecting kind.

The grounding of charismatic leadership and power in a faith in God or gods makes them important categories with broad applications in the history of leadership, rulership and government, especially in early times. Charismatic leadership exhibits two primary forms, (1) that wherein the faith and the charisma which it provides are novel and serve to found and establish either a new religion or a new version of an old religion (typical instances are Buddha, Jesus, Mahomet, as well as St. Francis, Luther and Calvin), and (2) that wherein the faith and charisma are old and tradition-

[26] M. Weber, 1925, part III, chap. 9.

[27] Cf. the treatment of totalitarian leadership by Franz Neumann, 1941 (vol. II, 1944), as an outstanding example. My attempt to correct this misunderstanding in *Totalitarian Dictatorship and Autocracy*, 1956, has unfortunately led to further misunderstandings. Cf. Friedrich, a, 1961.

alized and hence serve to buttress an established religion and its ecclesiastical organization. Some of Weber's cases of "routinized" charisma belong in this category. Such charisma and the power and leadership derived from it may and often do have political and governmental ramifications, especially and commonly in the second form. They have usually been treated under the heading of "divine" or "religious" leadership and power; the only reason for substituting the term "charismatic" is that it is less weighed down with value implications.

It remains to make some general observations applying to both forms. Charismatic leadership is clearly affected by the doctrines of the particular religion from which it springs, and more especially by the conception of the deity with which it is associated. The notion of charisma developed by Christianity and sketched above attributes only to Jesus, its founder, explicit personal divinity, but treats all other *charismata* as flowing into individual believers by the grace of God. But whatever the particular doctrines believed in by those who accept a given religion, their behavior is molded into conformity with the preferences of those who possess charisma.

Thus in many primitive religions the king, who often is also high priest, is accepted as long as the signs of divine favor or power remain in accord with the belief that he is divine or enjoys divine favor. The specific features of such a relationship of ruler and ruled were a major concern of Sir James G. Frazer, who in the first part of his celebrated *The Golden Bough*[28] describes in considerable detail the "magic" of such kings. Although his views about the role of the king in primitive society require considerable modification,[29] these modifications do not affect the basic relationship and the charismatic quality of such leadership. Indeed, the more recently recognized fact that "he serves as the typification of the community rather than as its superior benefactor" fits much better into the analysis of power we have offered above.

As Frazer notes, "the notion of a man-god, or of a human being endowed with divine or supernatural powers, belongs essentially to that earlier period of religious history in which gods and men are still viewed as beings of much the same order,"[30] and hence the god can be understood as being "incarnate" in the magician, priest or ruler. This notion of "incarnation" or "inspiration," that is, of a process by which a "spirit," something divine, has entered into some man, giving him divine power, is very widespread; Frazer even calls it "world wide," citing many examples from different cultures. If this can happen temporarily, it may also happen to certain men permanently and thus make them into divine

[28] Frazer (ed. Gaster), 1959.

[29] *Ibid.*, pp. 125ff.; the next quotation *ibid.*

[30] *Ibid.*, p. 61.

beings. Whether the functions then remain purely spiritual or sacred, as in a priesthood,[31] or also encompass the worldly is a secondary though important question.[32] Presumably related to such "primitive" notions was the "deification" of rulers characteristic of many imperial systems, notably Egypt, China, Mexico and Peru. But, as Frazer notes, "in the House of Commons under Elizabeth it was openly asserted 'that absolute princes, such as the sovereigns of England, were a species of divinity.' "[33] The entire tradition of the "divine right of kings" is rooted in this approach.[34]

Whenever such charismatic power is imputed to the ruler, it serves as a cloak for absolutist pretensions. These pretensions are usually directed against a priesthood which seeks to restrict the ruler's arbitrary power and subject it to some kind of rule, often embodied in a code as in the Old Testament, and directly or indirectly traced to the divine being. This struggle reappears in such figures as James I, although in a secularized form—Sir Edward Coke pleading the cause of the common law and its learned interpreters against the king's "natural reason." [35] But for James himself it was not merely a matter of natural reason; he was deeply convinced of his "divine right" and the consequent sanctification of his behavior in all matters of state.

Since inspiration is a significant aspect of charismatic power and leadership as here delineated, the temptation is great, especially from a psychological viewpoint, to lump all those kinds of power and leadership together which rest upon any kind of inspiration. That is precisely the temptation to which Weber succumbed. He succumbed to it partly because of his fallacious belief that political (and sociological) inquiry and conceptualization should be unrelated to value judgments (*wertfrei*). His lumping together of the founders of religions and of demagogues, even pirate chiefs, he explicitly justifies by reference to this value-free sociology.[36] Our reasons for maintaining the diametrically opposed view have been developed above in Chapter 2. Charismatic leadership has its psychological dimension of inspiring confidence in common with many other kinds of leadership, but it is distinguished from them by its close tie to religion. Historically, this has led to the vast struggles discussed by

[31] Krige and Krige, 1943, who show the "rain queen" of the Lovedu as purely spiritual.

[32] Cf. on African kingship, Busia, 1951; Gluckman, 1940; and Richards (ed.) 1960, who respectively describe the Ashanti, Zulu and Bantu as linking the two.

[33] Frazer, *op. cit.*, p. 69.

[34] Figgis, 1896, 1914.

[35] R. Pound, 1921, p. 61.

[36] M. Weber, 1925, pp. 140, 754, 758, and elsewhere. On p. 753 we read: "Thus the concept of 'charisma' is here used completely value-free." Secularists like Weber did not even notice that an identification of heterogeneous values itself implies a value judgment.

Weber under the heading of "state and hierocracy," and more usually under that of "state and church," familiar to all scholars from medieval European history, but actually recurrent phenomena throughout the history of human culture. Looked at in the political (power) perspective, it means that it depends upon the prevalence of a religious faith and that it deteriorates with such faith unless it is transformed into different kinds of power, military, economic, and so forth.

As we noted earlier, this faith may be novel or old and traditional. In the latter case, charismatic power becomes institutionalized, organized and in the sequence bureaucratized in the manner characteristic for all power and all bureaucracy.[37] The phenomena here to be observed have been brilliantly analyzed by Weber under the headings of *Veralltäglichung* (making it an everyday affair) and of *Versachlichung*, as already noted, although by his confounding them with comparable processes in other cases of inspiration he misses some of the important aspects of the religious sphere. Instead of the personal inspiration of the founder of a religion, one finds the impersonal inspiration of the religious teachings of the founder, associated to be sure with the continued *personal* paradigms of the founder himself, as embodied in the doctrine of the organization. This impersonal inspiration is still inspiration in the true sense, and various rituals will be devoted to keeping the inspiration alive. Secular movements have recurrently attempted to copy the processes; from Rousseau and the Jacobins to Marx-Lenin and the Bolsheviks[38] such pseudo-charismatic procedures have provided a pale replica of the genuine charisma of religious faith. The fact of this happening is perplexing; it suggests that charisma, whether genuine or spurious, does not provide an adequate basic typology of leadership, but only of power. Power may indeed be differentiated and distinguished according to the particular *source* from which it springs. Leadership, on the other hand, if it is not simply to be identified and confused with power, needs to be differentiated according to the function it serves. The basic typology of leadership, political leadership, is a function of the political order.[39]

The several forms of coercive and consensual power decline in ways corresponding to their rise. Coercive economic power, for example, disintegrates as the economic resources upon which it rests disintegrate. That seems obvious enough, but the situation is complicated by the fact that the possessors of wealth may deflect increasing amounts of their declining wealth to political purposes, that is to say, toward transforming their

[37] Friedrich, a, 1961. For bureaucracy see also below, Chaps. 18 and 26.

[38] Brinton, 1930, draws a good portrait of the Jacobins' pseudo-religious cults; cf. also Voegelin, 1938.

[39] In the perspective of her own concern with function, Dorothy Emmet, 1958, chap. 8, dealing with charismatic power, comes to conclusions which serve to support the critical evaluation of Weber given in my article.

wealth into power. Such a procedure is evidently self-defeating, as it is apt to hasten the disintegration of the economic resources. A similar phenomenon may be observed in the psychic sphere, for example, in the process of aging. Here what was once effective inspirational leadership may fall back more and more upon psychic coercion, even though such psychic coercion may in turn lead to the distintegration of the inspiration which at one time provided the source of power. Another important factor may be involved: the change in values and purposes upon which consensus is based. We shall have more to say upon this when discussing authority. At this point in our analysis the following law (general hypothesis) suggests itself: the growth and decline of power are cumulative. The growth is cumulative up to the point of full employment of the resources of the power-seeker (coercive power) and of full realization of the common values and purposes of the power-followers (consensual power); beyond this point it starts to disintegrate. The decline of power is cumulative up to the point of complete exhaustion of the resources of the power-holders (coercive power) and of the disappearance of common values and purposes of the power-followers (consensual power).[40] This law is hinted at in the saying that nothing succeeds like success, to which might be added that nothing fails like failure.

At this point, the objection may be raised that unless potential resources are excluded, the proposition becomes meaningless. But while there can be no doubt that the possibility of an increase in the resources of a power-holder complicates the analysis, it would seem impossible to exclude potential resources. Nor does such inclusion of potential resources destroy the value of the proposition, because the potential of such resources is not unlimited. For although unquestionably a leader, as he gathers and organizes a following, secures potential chances of coercion (more especially when seizing power, that is, when forcibly acquiring the coercive resources of the "state"), opposition also develops. Power is usually acquired under competitive conditions, and the competitors check the cumulative growth beyond a certain point. Thus on the upgrade mounting opposition checks the acquisition of resources, while on the downgrade it hastens their decomposition.

The existence of potential resources is probably the primary factor in producing the cumulative effects in both the rise and decline of power. The range of potential resources expands as power increases and is being organized and institutionalized. But just as an avalanche or a hurricane, no matter how vast and powerful, eventually comes to a standstill, so the accumulation of power may be arrested as in the case of the natural

[40] Since this law involves quantitative ratios, its empirical confirmation by quantitative methods seems indicated. But the construction of the necessary indices as a first step presents very serious difficulties.

phenomena just mentioned by an appearance of external obstructions unrelated to the power accumulation itself, such as geographic or demographic factors. More usually the accumulation of power is limited by phenomena directly related to its own growth and themselves part of the total power configuration. On one hand, there are the breakdowns that occur from excessive size of organization, involving all sorts of inefficiencies and corruptions. On the other hand, there are the counterforces which spring up as those adversely affected by the growing power seek to organize "countervailing" power; [41] internal resistance and the operation of the balance of power in interstate relations are well-known and outstanding instances of this propensity of power to beget a counteracting power and thereby to check itself, so to speak.

In this connection the problem of the hierarchical structuring of power deserves brief comment. The proposition has been advanced that "power groups develop into hierarchies." [42] It appears true that this is usually the case, provided the size of the group and the range of power, as well as its duration, are sufficiently great. This tendency toward hierarchical structuring is intimately related to the process by which power becomes rule (see the next chapter).

A final and, in a sense, concluding discussion of power as a value is in order. In analyzing political power as manifest in conformity of conduct, we have related it to the values prevalent in a community. But such power is itself a value, indeed one of the most cherished values. Hobbes's celebrated dictum that the life of man is but a restless desire for power after power unto death [43] overstates this point, but inasmuch as many other values, though not by any means all, can be secured through power, it calls attention to the crucial role of power in value-pursuit. There have been times, such as the baroque age and our own, in which the preoccupation with power has been pronounced. In such periods, the political aspect of life becomes predominant. Such preoccupation with political power has recurrently been disturbing to those cherishing other values as primary, especially the religious and the esthetic values. The dislike for power has never been more forcefully expressed than in Lord Acton's famous dictum that "all power corrupts, and absolute power

[41] Galbraith's well-known book by this title, 1952, described one very specific instance of the operation of such countervailing power.

[42] Lasswell and Kaplan, 1950, p. 205. For detail see below, Chap. 18. This proposition rests upon the definition of a hierarchy as "a structure of power relationships of varying amounts of power" (*ibid.*, p. 204). This definition appears to lack precision. A hierarchy involves a ranking of the power-manipulators, as well as a structuring of their relations.

[43] Hobbes, 1651, chap. 11. ". . . a general inclination of all mankind, a perpetual and restless desire of power after power, that ceaseth only in Death. . . ." Cf. also Friedrich, 1952, pp. 27–30. See above, p. 160, for a critique of this statement in Hobbes. The excessive breadth of his concept of "power" renders the statement tautological.

corrupts absolutely."[44] But it is not entirely clear in the context what is to be understood by "corruption." Presumably, the moral judgment and conscience are corrupted by power. But "without power, justice is unavailing."[45] The two are linked as basic determinants of the value pyramid. If inspired by a desire for justice, power ennobles as it heightens the sense of responsibility (Chapter 14). Is it fair to say as Acton does that "great men are almost always bad men, even when they exercise influence and not authority: still more when you superadd the tendency or certainty of corruption by authority"? Authority here stands for power, and the requirements of power are seen as in inexorable conflict with the moral code. "The inflexible integrity of the moral code is, to me, the secret of the authority, the dignity, the utility of history."[46] But while this conflict is ever threatening, the moral code itself calls for self-exertion on behalf of what is right, and therefore calls for power. The problem of the conflict of the requirements of power with the requirements of other values, especially justice, is only a special, though very important, case of the general problem of the conflict of values which their plurality engenders (Chapter 2). If power is understood as conformity of conduct, it is self-evident that when such conduct conforms to and can be shown to be good, the power which brings it about does not corrupt the power-followers and may not corrupt the power-holder. A more general proposition is in fact indicated than the one Lord Acton formulated. Power, when taken as a value, will at times conflict with other values. When such conflicts occur, power is necessarily endangered, no matter how they are resolved; for it is either weakened directly by the neglect of its proper requirements, or indirectly by the perversion or sacrifice of other values which the community cherishes and by the consequent weakening of authority (Chapter 12). Because of this interaction of power and other values, sometimes called the dialectic of power,[47]

[44] The statement is found not in one of his major writings but in a letter in which he criticizes another scholar for "the canon that we are to judge Pope and King unlike other men, with a favorable presumption that they did no wrong." He feels that in view of the crimes committed by persons in high places, "historic responsibility" should implement "legal responsibility." He adds: "I would hang them . . . for reasons of quite obvious justice; still more, still higher, for the sake of historical science." Acton, 1948, p. 364.

[45] Pascal, *Pensées,* p. 298. The French word is *puissance,* which may also be translated as "might." It is at times forgotten that Pascal adds immediately: "power without justice is tyrannical."

[46] Acton, 1948, p. 365. Acton continues: "If we may debase the currency for the sake of genius, or success, or rank, or reputation, we may debase it for the sake of man's influence, of his religion, of his party, of the good cause which prospers by his credit and suffers by his disgrace."

[47] Friedrich, 1957. Cf. the interesting article on power as value in the jural perspective by McWhinney, 1960.

consensual power is to be preferred. Here lies the deepest reason for the greater vitality of constitutional democracy.

It remains to point out that the different forms of power are readily transformed from one into the other. Not only in the coercive sphere can we observe a constant flux, physical coercion being transformed into economic and it in turn into psychic coercion, but the same holds true for the consensual sphere. Here, too, the several forms of leadership, while distinguishable at any particular moment, tend to merge one into the other, as we have had occasion to note in passing. This possibility of transforming the different forms of power into each other suggests the conclusion that there is a common core in all power phenomena. This assumption we started with, and it seems to be confirmed by the reflections upon power which our starting point led into. All the different forms revolve around the basic issue of how to secure coordination of action among many persons for common purposes. This is the problem of organization. But thus far we have dealt with this phenomenon of coordinated action in the emergent state, so to speak. We have been concerned with the situation in which human beings become disposed to act or to conduct themselves, to act in accordance with the wishes of one or several among them. We have thus the power situation, and we have said that those whose preferences are being followed have power. But there are significant differences to be observed if such a power situation becomes stabilized. Such stabilized power becomes to a certain extent structured and "organized." The specific phenomena to be observed here are those of rule. To the issues which rule and rulership present we now turn.

chapter

10

Rule and Rulership

El gobierno no es un fin en si mismo,
sino un medio para la apropriada organización
de una communidad politica.

Luis Muñoz Marín
in his Gubernatorial
Message of January 19, 1960

RULE IS INSTITUTIONALIZED political power. From the law about the cumulative growth and decline of political power can be derived the proposition that power tends to become stabilized, that is to say, that power tends to be transformed into rule. Rule is characterized by the fact that the conformity of conduct which power produces becomes habitual. Therefore rule typically produces the kind of coercive power which can be treated as a possession. Rule as a kind of power is subject to the propositions concerning power in general, but it exhibits specific traits which cannot be observed when power of the nonstabilized sort is being considered.[1]

The stabilization and eventual institutionalization of power is closely related to the phenomena of authority and legitimacy to be discussed below. They play a vital role in these processes. At the moment, we

[1] "Rule" is the English equivalent of the German *Herrschaft*, which occupies such an important place in Max Weber's political thought. Unfortunately, it has been obscured by erroneous translations of the term which amount to a gloss and lack clarity. Thus Talcott Parsons in his translation of certain sections of *Wirtschaft und Gesellschaft* translates *Herrschaft* as "imperative control." "Rule" is the general term, as are the derivatives "ruler" for the corresponding German *Herrscher*, and "to rule" for *herrschen*.

shall assume that power has become stabilized, that is to say that the followers A,B,C . . . conform habitually to the preferences, expressed or implied, of the leader, L. The leader is on the way to becoming a ruler.

In order to become rule, the leader's stabilized power has to be institutionalized, that is to say structured. What does it mean that power becomes structured? It has lately become fashionable to use this term "structure" in a rather vague way, and to speak of the power structure of the community imprecisely for the purpose of designating those informal and fluctuating power relations which are unstructured. Characteristically, such works fail to give any indication as to what structure means.[2] Structure means, generally speaking, that there is a stable and ordered relation of parts, such as characterizes a building, from which the term is derived. It has been meaningfully applied to many other entities, e.g., an organic body or a poem. Structure is closely related to system. It always presupposes that there are identifiable parts, and that they are arranged in some kind of design or pattern. Thus it is the static aspect of a system, its "skeleton." The structuring of power presupposes its separation into parts. Before power can become structured, it must be stable. The stabilization of power precedes that erecting of a structure which produces institutionalization.

An institution has been generally described as a habitual human relationship;[3] it is a key concept not only in political science, but in sociology, law and other social sciences. In modern economics, the so-called "institutionalists" are a school stressing the patterning of economic relationships in such entities as market, enterprise, contract, and the like. A political institution is a similarly stabilized pattern of power in which the conformities of conduct have become regularized, have become a "configuration." This regularization of the conforming conduct (c) has great advantages from the standpoint of conserving energy. Relatively firm expectations can be built upon such stabilized patterns of power (p), and the consequent strategies of power-handlers gain a measure of predictability. A ruler (R) and his subjects form a configuration or design (c') which lends itself to effective manipulation. Hence the formula

$$c(A,B,C,\ldots)^{t} \cong L(p) \text{ becomes } c'(A,B,C,\ldots)^{t} \cong R(p)$$

with t (time) relatively small in the first formula, while it is relatively large in the second, so that as t increases L changes into R. In primitive societies the only political institution may be the kingship combined with

[2] Floyd Hunter, 1953.

[3] Parsons, 1951, pp. 39ff., and *passim.* He there defines an institution as a "complex of institutionalized role integrates"—a definition involving a *petitio principii.*

that of high priest.[4] That is to say, the only parts of the structure may be the ruler and his subjects. Yet we find a highly stable kind of relationship, exhibiting detailed design, and hence properly described as rule.

We speak of the institutionalized pattern of rule as government. The rulers or governors may constitute a vast and complicated design, as in modern constitutional regimes, or they may be monocratically arranged in one simple hierarchy, as in autocratic regimes, including totalitarian dictatorship. The appeal of such regimes to the simple mind lies in their manifest order; the consequent infringement of both justice and freedom appears less important than the optically impressive unity. But whether the design is complicated or simple, the structure of such a government forms a pattern which is composed of the several institutions identifiable as parts of the whole. Government may therefore in its most general sense be defined as an institutionalized pattern of stabilized power, or rule.

Rule (*Herrschaft*) has been classified in a variety of ways. Such classification raises the problem of typologies of political order.[5] Perhaps most famous are the typologies of the ancients, which were based on two criteria: the number of rulers and an over-all ethical evaluation of the quality of their rule; subjection to the prevailing law or custom (*nomos*) in Plato, or the rulers' concern with the common good, happiness, in Aristotle. Proceeding on this basis, common speech and philosophical discourse distinguished the rule of one, a few or the many. Herodotus, in reporting a discussion among Darius and his conquering gang about what form of government to adopt, has it proceed in these terms, and although unhistorical, it is indicative of common Greek views on the subject.[6] Philosophers subdivided the three forms into good and bad types, Plato classifying them according to whether they are *nomos*-observing (*ennomon*) or *nomos*-neglecting (*paranomon*). These are the "lower" forms, which must be chosen if and when a philosopher-king who possesses true knowledge is not available: "the nearest approach which these lower forms of government can ever make to the true government of the one scientific ruler is to do nothing contrary to their written and traditional customs [*patria ethe*] of [i.e., as embodied in] their established laws." [7] In the discussion which follows, this dichotomy is developed into the sixfold typology of monarchy, tyranny, aristocracy, oligarchy and the two kinds of democracy (not separately named), the distinction of "ruling with law or without law" being the key. Aristotle in terms of

[4] Frazer (ed. Gaster), 1959; Hocart, 1929; Evans-Pritchard, 1951; Fortes and Evans-Pritchard, 1940.

[5] For a discussion of the problem of type, and more especially the notion of an "ideal" type, see above, Introd., Note 2.

[6] *Histories,* bk. III, chaps. 80–83.

[7] *Statesman,* p. 301 (Jowett's translation corrected).

his teleological outlook introduced as the evaluative principle the question as to whether a government serves the common good (*sympheron:* useful, expedient) in seeking to maximize the happiness of those who are being ruled, and distinguished between a democracy, which does not, and a timocracy, which does.[8] Both Plato and Aristotle add a seventh form which embodies, according to Plato, the idea of a well-ordered *polis* and which is ruled by either one (in *Statesman*) or several (in *The Republic*) who possess true knowledge and philosophical insight. According to Aristotle, it is a "mixed" or blended constitutional order, and one is tempted to interpret it as constitutional democracy, were it not for the fact that under modern constitutionalism the *nomos* or basic law is freely chosen.[9]

Aristotle introduced yet another principle of typology, realistically derived from actual Greek political life, and that is the class analysis in terms of the rich and the poor. He asserts that "the real difference between democracy and oligarchy is poverty and wealth."[10] This in turn leads him to the conclusion that the best rule for most states is that of the middle class, avoiding both extremes. This judgment rests upon "neither assuming a standard of *arete* [virtue] that is above ordinary persons, nor an exceptional education" and hence proposes "a form of government which states in general can attain."[11] He therefore argues that the best political community (*koinonia*) is composed of people that are neither rich nor poor, but rather in the middle (*mesoi*); limited, but sufficient, property in the possession of many will provide the basis for a stable constitutional government (polity) which is best.

This typology, limited though it was to the order of the *polis*, has continued to dominate men's political thinking to this day; other typologies have been suggested in addition. The most common of these at present is the dichotomy of democracy and dictatorship, exemplified by the constitutional regimes of the West as against the totalitarian regimes of the East. A dichotomic classification, while impressive on account of its simplicity, is suspect from a realistic viewpoint, because nature tends to be pluralistic, rather than monistic or dualistic. The latter types are apt to be mental constructs rather than empirically derived types.[12] They may be reinforced, as they are in our time, by a concrete

[8] The Aristotelian discussion is not entirely clear, since timocracy is also called "polity" (*politeia*), which is the generic term and used for designating the model as well.

Nicomachean Ethics, 1160, a-b; *Politics,* 1279, a-b; 1289, a.

[9] *Politics,* 1323ff.

[10] *Ibid.,* 1279b–1280a; 1290, a-b.

[11] *Ibid.,* 1295a.

[12] An interesting classification cast in terms of autocracy and constitutional democracy is given by Loewenstein, 1957, chaps. III and IV.

polemical situation; Greece in the period of the Peloponnesian War was similarly divided into "democracies" (Athens) and "aristocracies," or "oligarchies" (Sparta). The Aristotelian classification was no doubt an attempt to transcend this polemical dichotomy. There is a good deal of precedent for the present dichotomy in past European thought and experience. English writers, such as Fortescue and Sir Thomas Smith, were fond of contrasting the British constitutional order with the continental royal kingdoms such as France.[13] A similar tendency appears in Machiavelli who, as a partisan of the Florentine Republic contrasted princely and republican rule. This dichotomy is central to both his major works and links them in providing a common political outlook.[14] This tradition became in Montesquieu's brilliant analysis the basis of a distinction between despotic and nondespotic (monarchical or republican) regimes which moulded the thought on types of rulership for the entire liberal era.

As against all these dichotomies, as well as the Greek tradition, modern writers have, during the last century, developed still other typologies based upon a variety of criteria. Most important perhaps is the typology suggested by Marx and Engels, following Lorenz von Stein.[15] In their thought (as well as that of many followers) the classification of types of rules is based upon economic class divisions. The class controlling the means of production is seen as the governing class, and hence systems of rule are described as feudal, bourgeois, capitalist and communist. But in spite of the historical reminiscences suggested by what the Marxists have to say on feudalism, the Marxist position is in fact basically built on the dichotomy of the capitalist and socialist systems of rule, and this outlook is reflected in Soviet political oratory to this day.[16]

Marxist insistence upon the importance of the ruling class was transformed by two Italian theorists, Gaetano Mosca and Vilfredo Pareto. Mosca gave to the ruling class a noneconomic connotation and built upon it a monistic typology according to which all political regimes are fundamentally alike in being oligarchic, providing for the effective exercise of stabilized power by a relatively small group of persons, the ruling class. Similarly, Pareto argued that all political systems are systems of rule by an elite of those best qualified to rule; his concept of the elite is analyzed in greater detail below.[17] These attempts, which have been followed in more recent writings of a number of others both in America

[13] Fortescue, 1476; T. Smith, 1583; Harrington, 1656.

[14] Strauss, 1958; Chabod, 1958.

[15] Marx, 1847, pp. 92–93; 1859, pp. 9ff.; Engels, 1892, pp. 170ff.; 1884, 1948, pp. 224ff.; von Stein, 1849, 1921, vol. I, pp. 49ff.

[16] Tucker, 1960.

[17] Mosca, 1939; Pareto, 1935—cf. Chap. 18, below.

and in Europe,[18] would seem, in light of our general analysis, characterized by the view that institutionalized power is less important than the more fluid forms of power that defy stabilization and institutionalization. This fascination with "hidden" power is never as such analyzed. There may be times when informal power is "more powerful" than institutionalized power, but it may well be doubted that this is always true. The argument would have to be faced in terms of a manageable quantitative index of power which we are far from having developed. In any case, these analyses fail to provide a typology of rule in the sense of institutionalized power relationships.

Another widespread tendency in typologizing political order stresses the major objective or end of the political order. While more common in Continental Europe, it has lately been making headway in English-speaking countries and is manifest in the term "welfare state." It is not really a very helpful category, since the common "welfare" (Aristotle's *sympheron*) has always been the alleged end of government.[19] All these typologies tend to be dichotomic and to serve the purpose of either extolling the virtues or denouncing the shortcomings of a particular political order, such as the welfare state, and to contrast it with all other states not characterized by the particular priority. As such, they serve as tools for propaganda rather than for scientific analysis. It is doubtful that in view of the generality of human purposes involved in the construction of political order this sort of typology has more than ephemeral value.

In this connection, mention might be made of the extended recent controversies over the type of rule suitable for political parties and interest groups, especially trade unions. As these groupings have in the course of time become increasingly recognized as centrally important for the operation of democratic government, it is only natural that a demand should have been put forward for their "democratization." This tendency has been reinforced by the rise of totalitarian movements which are apt to develop strongly autocratic internal organization.

Ever since Lenin sounded the call for such radical autocracy, and since Ostrogorsky and Michels offered their commentaries,[20] this issue

[18] E.g. Mills, 1956; and the contributors to R. Treves (ed.), 1961.

[19] One wonders whether the popularity of these terms in Germany may not be due to their leaving open the question of just what is the relation between the end and the political order which it is presumably indicating. Thus the *Rechtsstaat* may also be a political order subject to law, i.e., a constitutional order, rather than one which primarily directs its efforts toward maintaining law and order. These terms are usually difficult to translate.

[20] Lenin, 1902; Ostrogorsky, 1902; Michels, 1911. Macmahon, in a penetrating essay on Ostrogorsky in the *ESS*, noted the "vast naiveté" underlying his outlook; in a sense the same can be said of Michels, though his tongue is perhaps more in cheek. See below, Chaps. 18 and 26, for further treatment.

has continued to agitate both scientific and popular opinion. Very frequently, the opponents of such autocracy, or "Boss Rule," have been naïve followers of Rousseau who believe that you can institute direct democracy—a rather improbable scheme even where the organization is small enough and the situation in which it is placed sufficiently placid. Actually, organizations, directed by not only convinced but experienced democratic elements, such as the British Labor Party, have undergone a slow evolution toward a complex pattern of constitutional democracy in which the characteristic elements of this type of political order (see below) are found. It is generally to be observed that the exercise of rulership in any organization is likely to resemble one or another of the types to be observed in governmental organization. There is no need for developing a separate typology, as far as the available evidence goes.

Still another typology was suggested by Max Weber. It seeks to make the type of legitimacy and leadership the basic criterion, and thus suggests three types, the traditional, the rational-legal and the charismatic type of rule. The rule of a leader whose authority (legitimacy) is based upon tradition, as in a hereditary monarchy, is one basic type. Another results when the leader's authority (legitimacy) is consequent upon a legal order which has been effectively rationalized. The third, and in many ways most distinctive, type is that of a leader whose authority rests upon charisma or a sense of being called, either by divine or other transcendent powers (Chapter 9). A searching critique of Weber's typology involves obviously an analysis of his notion of authority, identified as it is with legitimacy, which will be given below (Chapters 12 and 13). The matter is further complicated by Weber's pretense that his typology is value-free, when it is patent to any reader with a different value viewpoint from his that the rational-legal type is in Weber's view much to be preferred.[21] At the same time, it lumps together the leadership types of Moses and Mussolini, which exposes it to the comment that "a man who cannot distinguish between great statesmen, mediocrities, and insane impostors may be a good bibliographer; he cannot say anything relevant about politics and political theory."[22] This particular typology confuses the phenomena of power and leadership with those of rule and rulership, in our terms, just as it confuses authority and legitimacy (Chapters 12 and 13). It also assumes that any system of government is *necessarily* legitimate. Any system of government, any political order, may be either legitimate or not, depending on whether it is believed to be rightful rule in the view of those who live under it. Such beliefs may be based upon a number of grounds, including those which Weber chose

[21] Similarly Strauss, 1959, p. 21, who observes that the "very expression 'routinization of charisma' betrays a Protestant or liberal preference. . . ."

[22] *Ibid.* See also below, Chap. 18.

to stress. But how a government is conducted, how the rulers behave, is the crucial principle for purposes of determining its type; not what those subject to it believe, important as that factor is.

One of the primary objections to the typologies just outlined is that they do not provide us with guidance when we are faced by the problems of the emergent political orders of former colonial dependencies. For they fail to take into account the general social structure and the level of industrial and economic and social development. There is, nonetheless, a widespread suspicion entertained today that the complex structure of a constitutional democracy may not be suited to the conditions of these territories and peoples. What is not as generally appreciated is that the fairly complex structure of totalitarian dictatorship may be no more suited to them. It has for a long time been recognized that so-called "primitive" peoples possess political orders suitable to their stage of development. Recent comparative studies of feudalism have reinforced the older notion that a feudal order arises out of a condition of anarchy consequent upon the distintegration of a highly developed system of rule.[23] We know that the absolute monarchies were closely linked to the process of territorial integration and consolidation of the modern nation state—and be it said in passing that these monarchies were not simply "the rule of one," as the typology of the ancients would suggest, but compounded of several key factors, among which "legitimate blood descent" and not effective rule was a crucial quality of the monarch, and hence a feature of his rule. And we suspect a link between a highly developed industrial technology with stabilized organization and "democracy," on the one hand, and between the need for initiating and carrying forward such industrialization and "dictatorship" on the other.

All this suggests that what is called for at present is a typology in which the criteria of societal development are suitably recognized. This is only natural; for typologies are not arbitrarily constructed classifications, since a particular type appears in response to a concrete political situation and the problems it poses. Our sketch of past typologies shows this clearly enough. From Aristotle to Pareto and Weber the political need involved in stressing certain types of rule is evident. Whether it be the need of transcending the internecine warfare of the Greek *poleis* or the class struggle, the buttressing of one national or party outlook or the other, the criteria of classification are suggested by the purposes and values involved in the analysis.[24]

The dichotomic typologies, linked to the notion of constitutional

[23] Coulborn (ed.), 1956, esp. pp. 364ff.

[24] It is the more striking that Merriam, 1945, chap. V, in discussing "types of rule" bases his analysis entirely on the ancient Platonic typology, reduced, however, to monarchy, aristocracy, and democracy old and new, that is to say, deprived of their normative distinction between *nomos*-observing and *nomos*-neglecting types.

government, which have played such a large role in the political thought of the West, were foreshadowed in the Greek division and distinction between *nomos*-observing and *nomos*-neglecting rule. But as already remarked, the *nomos*, or basic law, became, in the West, a constitution, not made by a single and divinely inspired legislator, a Lycurgus or a Solon, but worked out in debate by the representatives of the people and adopted by them as a fundamental charter. Thus the dichotomy of rule is linked to the dual nature of power. For where such procedures are adopted, consensual power is given the broadest possible scope, while the failure to do so was seen as autocracy and hence as basically government not by consent, but by coercion. Since the two aspects of power are usually found in combination with each other, since all power is only partly consensual and partly coercive, such a dichotomy, while not entirely without foundation, ought to be understood as a shorthand expression. Types of rule, like power, cannot really be *either* consensual *or* coercive, but all types of rule are partly consensual and partly coercive, and it is a question of the degree of both, and of their ratio to each other. Since consent may also be the consequence of long habituation, and to some extent always is, it is quite possible, and has often happened, that a more autocratic rule may be more consensual than a constitutional rule which a majority has adopted against the wishes and preferences of a substantial minority or minorities. In the underprivileged countries which are in the process of evolving a new political order this situation may often be observed. The old order, though marked by a traditional autocratic rule, was more generally consented to (though usually without enthusiasm) than are the new "constitutional" arrangements evolved by a revolutionary group which at times does not command a majority following. The dichotomic typology in terms of constitutionalism versus absolutism was related to the developmental requirements of Western civilization in the past few centuries. It provides no adequate basis for a typology of universal application. Similarly the Greek typology, especially in its normative aspect, was the outgrowth of the problems faced by the Greek, and especially the Athenian, *polis* in the fifth century, and provides no meaningful basis for a comprehensive assessment of types of rule. Such an assessment needs to be related to significant features of the social structure and prevailing values and beliefs. The latter aspect enables us to recapture the universal significance embodied in the Greek notion of *nomos*, not as a simple alternative between a rule which is related to values and beliefs and one that is not, but as a yardstick by which to assess the relative degree of such relatedness. On the basis of these reflections, one might tentatively suggest the following typology:

1. Anarchy–fragmented rule
2. Tribal rule of the king-priest type

3. Despotic monarchy (rule over extended territories)
4. Oligarchy by the nobility, either by birth or cooption
5. Oligarchy by the wealthy
6. Oligarchy by priesthood–theocracy
7. Direct democratic rule
8. Tyranny
9. Bureaucratic rule under a hereditary monarch
10. Parliamentary-cabinet rule (government by elected representatives)
    a. Aristocratic—nobility and wealth predominating
11. Democratic—all classes included
12. Presidential-congressional rule (government by an elected president and an elected assembly)
13. Military dictatorship (including pretorian rule)
14. Totalitarian dictatorship

Each of these types has, of course, variations and there are transitional kinds of rule, but most actual governments can be subsumed under these thirteen types. It should also be noted that under the last five types, the bureaucracy is apt to play a large role if the government's sway extends over any considerable number of people and/or amounts of territory (large-scale rule). It will be seen that these types do not arrange themselves into any kind of neat scheme. They do, however, follow a rough developmental pattern from one to fourteen, as far as the order of their appearance is concerned. This pattern should not, however, be taken to imply any evaluation, as might be presumed by those who still think in terms of simple unilinear progress in time. The value of any particular government corresponding to one of these types is from a pragmatic viewpoint the consequence of the degree of its "working"; from an ideological viewpoint it may result from the purposes to which the particular government is addressing itself, from the national or class group which predominates, from the religion it professes, from the degree of general consent it enjoys, and various other considerations.

From the standpoint of the more narrowly political analysis of power situations, the degree of general consent is evidently very significant for the analysis of rule. Such consent may be structured in a variety of ways. It will not do simply to count the heads, as perhaps expressed in a referendum, though such a test is entitled to serious consideration. The consent may be of the "diffuse" kind, but if we take into account not only the number of persons, but the degree of intensity with which they consent and indeed support the government, we come to realize that consent may be patterned by being concentrated at certain points in the populace. There will always be variations in degree of intensity. But the variations may become so great that the consent of some is so limited as to approach zero, while the consent of others will be so intense as to outstrip all other values and engender a striking readiness for sacrifice. These possibilities do not alter the fact that the rule will be the firmer and better, the more general and intense the consent is.

There would appear here the need for some effective quantification. If all human energies present in a certain populace are of the magnitude E, and those energies needed for nonpolitical purposes be x, the amount available for consenting to the political order will be $E-x$. The energy of each individual in the populace being e^n, likewise his energy available for support of the system of rule would be e^n-x^n. Of any determinate number of individuals it can be said that a minority of them may expend so large a part of their energy on supporting the government that the sum of this energy exceeds the sum of energy expended by a majority which might be available for another type of activity. This situation does in fact prevail in the totalitarian dictatorships of our time, where the members of the ruling party give such energetic support as to provide the necessary minimum of consent. For according to our proposition about the dual nature of power (above, pp. 160–161) purely coercive power cannot last.

Consent, then, is a matter of both degree and distribution among the populace. It can be related to the value of a particular rule only in terms of its "working," as we said. That is to say, to the extent that consent facilitates ruling—and it always does to some extent—the working or not-working of a particular government may turn upon the measure of consent it can elicit. This may indeed be a decisive consideration. In the one-party systems which have been springing up in certain under-privileged countries—Mexico, Bolivia, United Arab Republic, etc.—the party obviously has the function of organizing consent to the transformation which an effective modernization and industrialization entails.[25] It may, in such places, be unwise to try to develop a two-party, let alone a multiparty system. Lord Balfour's famous dictum that the British "were so fundamentally at one" that they "could safely afford to bicker" has application here, but in the obverse sense. For in the absence of such fundamental unity, it may be necessary to postpone the bickering and utilize the mass party for the purpose of effective integration. Turkey provides an interesting example of the danger of forcing a two-party system in a situation which is not as yet ready for this type of patterning of consent. For the unity which Kemal Ataturk had so strikingly brought about upon the basis of the consent of his one-party following has dangerously disintegrated since that time and was evidently not sufficient for the kind of distribution of consent which the two-party system presupposes.[26]

[25] Blanksten, as well as D. Rustow in Almond and Coleman, 1959, pp. 455ff. and 369ff. S. H. Rudolph, a, 1961, is very interesting on India. Cf. below, Chap. 28.

[26] Karpat, 1959, though giving the background for such a hypothesis, does not explicitly make the point. See also D. Rustow, a, 1959; Lerner and Robinson, a, 1960.

Presumably, it should be possible on the basis of detailed comparative study to arrive at a general evaluation which would tell us both which of these types of political order is absolutely best and which is best for various situations to be specified. The types we have delineated are average types,[27] but their large number seems to call for further classification. One of the principles of evaluation is associated with the contrast between consent and coercion and the related issue of how many of those comprised in the political order participate in it. Just as Aristotle, transforming Plato, asked concerning the conventional numerical classification whether the rule of one, a few or the many was directed toward the common good or not, so one could ask whether each of the fourteen types was autocratic or heterocratic.[28] Related to the Aristotelian norm would be one which might ask whether a rule was legitimate or not (Chapter 13). But while such reclassifications are both possible and in certain contexts scientifically valuable, they are not directly related to the structure of these types.

Instead, it might be asked whether these types embody recurrent orders of the body politic or whether they more or less fit a historical sequence. Involved in this mode of inquiry is also the ancient question of whether such sequences occur in cycles are not. Even a brief inspection of the list of types will disclose that these several alternatives are not mutually exclusive. For certainly these types of rule recur in various contexts. They also fit into a broad historical sequence which to a certain extent is cyclical. Impressed with this evolutionary aspect, the liberal age was inclined to assume that the sequence embodied demonstrable progress, in the sense that the type which came later in time also was more advanced and hence "better." The emergence of totalitarian dictatorship has shaken such easy assumptions, except among the totalitarians themselves. But how could the appearance of totalitarian systems have done this, if there had not been value premises hidden in the ready assumption of progress? Weber's preference for the rational-legal order has been mentioned, but similar comment can be made about other writers. Such comment does not, however, carry the implication that a new search is in order for a typology which neglects value judgments, but rather that an effort needs to be made to make explicit the values implicit in each of these types of rule. For these values are part of the configuration, the *Gestalt*, of each of these types as it provides the formal and informal organization for a particular community with its values, interests and beliefs. This makes it possible to select the type which is

[27] See above, Introd., Note 2.

[28] *Auto*cratic rule is a rule in which the ruler himself (*autos*) is able to determine what matters, whether to take care of it and how; *hetero*cratic, a rule in which the ruler or rulers are subject to another's (*heteros*) determination, as the American Congress and President are subject to those who made and those who can amend the Constitution.

suitable for a particular community, both in terms of the values extrinsic to the political order, such as those embodied in its religious and ethical beliefs, and in terms of the values intrinsic to the political order, such as its viability and functional adequacy in terms of the required tasks. For if a community wants economic development, which requires central planning, and a particular type of rule does not provide it, this type is not likely to give satisfaction, although it may be acceptable on other grounds. At this point the problem of the hierarchy and conflict of values introduces itself (Chapters 2 and 6, above). It must be faced. With these cautionary remarks in mind, we can attempt to indicate a bit more fully what the common features of the several types are, and how they are related to each other.

We put anarchy first, because it would seem to be a type of rule which is found among primitives, and which recurs from time to time. To those accustomed to organized and institutionalized rule, anarchy has become a term of distinctly pejorative connotations, especially since a group of fanatical enthusiasts for this condition undertook to hurl bombs at assorted rulers of autocratic states.[29] Anarchy, properly speaking, is however a condition of politics, not where every member of a group rules himself, but where small groups do, in a pattern of spontaneous cooperation. Such societies have been described by anthropologists as "segmented," "decentralized" or "stateless," but their key feature is that they have no *arche*, that is, no pattern of government or institutionalized rule, and that each group, such as family or clan, is on its own. Durkheim called this situation one of "direct power" (*pouvoir immédiat*). Anthropologists have spoken of "uncentralized societies" in which "authority" is vested in persons possessing either (1) a status associated with segmentary lineage, or (2) chiefship in a village, or (3) a status associated with age, or (4) a position on a village council.[30] Thus we read: "When there is no centralized political authority for the whole society, external relations of local groups are often conceived in lineage terms. The roles in which internal political authority is vested may also be attached to lineages, but they can be attached to other structures. These may be age classes, ritual congregations, village councils and associations, secret societies and other selective associations. All these may be found in conjunction with lineage structures." Perhaps the most extreme case of such "open" society is that of the Comanches (United States Plains Indians), which suggested the term "anarchy" as the most appropriate, in spite of its disvalue associations. No Comanche tribe is a political unit in any strict sense. The significant unit for purposes of action that might be called political is the "band," ranging in size from one family to several

[29] Gueli, a, 1958.

[30] Middleton and Tait, 1958, extending Fortes and Evans-Pritchard, 1940. The quotation is found on p. 6.

hundred. The individual is linked to the band by free attachment. The basic principle appears to be a sharp separation of civil and military affairs. We learn that "in a society as simple and as homogeneous as was that of the Comanches there is little need for the development of governmental institutions. Add to this the extreme individualism of the Comanches, and a situation exists in which neither social needs nor ideology work to stimulate the development of government. Consequently, Comanche government was at a minimum, legal precepts were rudimentary, and the enforcement of . . . law remained the responsibility of individuals rather than officials." [31] This sort of arrangement is symptomatic for the nonrule type of rule; the inhabitants of the Marquesas Islands of Polynesia exhibit a similar complete decentralization of leadership; each tribe is conceived of as a family with a chief whose office is patrilineally inherited. "The chief," Linton wrote, "was looked upon as the director of group activities, and in some places at least, as the owner of the tribal lands. His power was . . . not absolute however, and in case of oppression his followers might desert him and pass into the service of another chief." [32] We have given these somewhat more detailed indications in order to indicate the complexities of this "type"; in some ways it continues as a mode of local government in many more advanced societies.[33]

Tribal rule of the king-priest type is found in many primitive societies. Anthropology has been preoccupied with this kind of rule, whereas political science has neglected it.[34] It occurs in many different forms, but the power of the ruler in such a system appears to be closely related to his magical functions pertaining to crops, fertility and success in war. There can be little doubt that the capacity for military leadership is also crucial in many such societies. At least one writer has made the difference between such warrior societies and others the basis for a comprehensive philosophy of history.[35] This type of rule is familiar to Western thought

[31] Hoebel and Wallace, 1952, p. 209. Similar situations are found among the Nambicuara of Brazil; cf. Levi-Strauss, 1948; and the Siriono (Bolivia), cf. Holmberg, 1950.

[32] Linton, 1925, p. 268. In the shorter summary of 1939, Linton describes the chief's position in more detail on pp. 159–160. Other uncentralized systems of rule are found among the Ojibwas, for which cf. Jenness, 1935; and Landes, 1937.

[33] Both the romanticism of the Russian "mir" and of the Indian village are associated with such traditions; cf. S. H. Rudolph, 1961; also Oscar Lewis, 1958.

[34] Merriam, *op. cit.*, p. 183, complains that "the anthropologists revel in analyses of 'headship' of innumerable types and colors." Maybe so; but the neglect political scientists have shown for these findings now handicaps their usefulness in constructing a political order for the new nations.

[35] A. Rüstow, 1950, who suggests that the warrior tribal rulers by their conquest and subjection of more pacific groups initiated the civilizing process which depended upon the creation of larger units; at the same time this *Überlagerung*, or superimposition, generated all the evils of coercive power from which mankind is suffering to this day. Cf. Friedrich, a 3, 1955.

through much of the Old Testament, as well as early Greek, Roman and Germanic bodies politic. As it expands, it is likely to be differentiated into societies in which the religious aspect predominates and which therefore show a propensity to develop a theocratic pattern. (Since this is a rule of priests, it should really as Max Weber suggested be called "hierocratic" —the term "theocracy" being a euphemism attesting the persuasive skill of priests.) But whether theocracy should be considered a distinctive type seems doubtful, in spite of Calvin's Geneva; for just as in ancient Israel, the civil rulers in Geneva remained, and the broadly exercised influence of the priests parallels the influence of other classes and groups in other societies which do not thereby become distinctive types of rule.

When tribal rule of the king-priest type is extended over large territories, comprising many tribes and nations, as happened particularly in the ancient Orient, the institutionalization of rule is significantly implemented by the appearance of a bureaucracy.[36] Such a bureaucracy may and often does combine priestly and administrative functions. In Egypt, China and other monarchies of this type we find such bureaucracies based upon an official doctrine the mastery of which constitutes the primary requirement for selection. (For detail see Chapter 31, below.)

The tribal rule of the king-priest type often develops into oligarchic rule by the nobility. This is particularly apt to occur where the capacity to wage successful war has been crucial in patterning the system of rule; for when the situation becomes stabilized, the king is not able to maintain himself against his "brothers-in-arms." In larger domains, this development is less likely to take place, though in feudal Europe and more particularly in England it became fairly general. Feudalism seems to provide a favorable setting for such an evolution, as the history of medieval Japan suggests, especially if an island situation minimizes foreign dangers to national security. Probably the state of the art of war, and more particularly the balance of aggressive and defensive weapons, is a factor of major importance.

Oligarchic rule by the nobility at arms is at times transformed into an oligarchic rule of the wealthy, as happened in Greece and Rome, and in many medieval cities of Europe, of which the most notable and durable example is Venice. Such rule is likely to be less coercive than that of a military nobility, because the acquisition of wealth is apt to be possible for men of exceptional ability coming up from below. At the same time, it is precisely for that reason less likely to endure; the gradual broadening of the ruling class eventually leads to democratization. We possess detailed accounts of many of these developments, such as Aristotle's history of the constitution of Athens and the accounts of Roman history and medieval cities. The rule in both these forms of oligarchy is still

[36] Eisenstadt, a, 1958. See below, Chap. 18.

predominantly based on coercive power, though the consensual factor is often considerable.

Democratic rule in the strict sense (as compared to modern constitutional democracy) is relatively rare; brief periods of Greek and medieval European town history provide outstanding illustrations, as do a substantial number of primitive societies. It is in its nature possible only within the narrow confines of a single community, for the people have to gather to exercise the rule. A heedless majority, swayed by oratory, may engage in the most senseless and oppressive acts against individuals and minorities. It testifies to the limitations of such rule that it should in practice lead to tyranny, while in theory it precipitates such reactions as the philosophically reasoned conservatism of Plato's call for a return to either the rule of a king-priest or of a priestly oligarchy. Yet Pericles' Funeral Oration, as reported by Thucydides, suggests that under favorable conditions such radical self-rule of a people may provide the setting for the highest achievements. Many primitive peoples [37] have lived effectively for long times under this sort of rule.

Direct democracy also is found in smaller groups, especially when motivated by strong democratic sentiments. Workers' councils and trade unions have often attempted to operate by direct democratic rule. The notion that "what concerns all should be decided by all" has proved a powerful slogan in such groups. But usually such primitive democracy has soon been superseded by a "bureaucracy," or an inner clique of operators. "If, therefore, democracy means that everything which concerns all should be decided by all, and that each citizen should enjoy an equal and identical share in government, trade union history indicates clearly the inevitable result, . . ." Sidney and Beatrice Webb have written, and they have added that "government by such contrivances as rotation in office, the mass meeting, the referendum and initiative, or the delegate restricted by his imperative mandate, leads straight either to inefficiency and disintegration, or to the uncontrolled dominance of a personal dictator or an expert bureaucracy." [38] Therefore, they thought, direct democracy ought not to be attempted, but rather "modern" representative democracy, modeled on the parliamentary system.

Tyranny, to which democracy has recurrently given rise when it proved incapable of handling the task of government, is almost universally condemned as oppressive, unstable and ineffectual. It is the rule of a single individual for his own good, as he sees it; it may, therefore, include a serious effort at promoting the public interest if the tyrant sees his own good that way.[39] But tyranny usually vindicated Lord Acton's famous

[37] Murdock, 1959, chap. 6.
[38] Sidney and Beatrice Webb, 1897, 1902, pp. 26ff. The quote is on p. 36.
[39] Werner Bergengrün, 1949.

dictum that "absolute power corrupts absolutely" (see above, Chapter 9, for a discussion). Tyranny is typically based on the most radical deployment of bare coercive power, and more particularly its physical variant, violence. It appeared in the Italian cities of the Renaissance. Tyranny has also been recognized in the form of an abuse of monarchical power. The middle ages, devoted as they were to monarchy, distinguished this sort of tyranny as one by exercise (*quoad exercitium*) from tyranny without title. It does not seem scientifically admissible to follow this usage; particular acts in contravention of the established beliefs of the community, while certainly a serious problem, do not alter the nature of a regime or rule. Tyranny seems to belong to periods of waning or extinguished faith when "chaos is king"—the kind of condition which the Greeks called *anomie*.[40]

A hereditary monarchy supported by a developed bureaucracy is a distinctive kind of rule, going under the name of absolutism. Such a rule is not, however, characterized by indifference to the established beliefs of the community, but rather built upon it. The habit of obedience upon which it rests is grounded in the claim that the ruler is "the representative of God on Earth," the symbol of the divine order. He rules by "divine right" or (later) "divine grace," often providing his subjects with an opportunity to be heard in "estates' assemblies" and by petition. Its instrumentality of rule is the bureaucracy executing the law. While coercive power certainly plays a vital part, consensual power is an important factor as well. The Roman Empire was its exemplar.

The functioning of the four (or five) remaining types of rule will be discussed at greater length in later chapters and will therefore not be especially characterized here. They all combine coercive with consensual power in various ways, and they all employ a large-scale bureaucracy, including a professionally directed army and police force. They are, in short, modern states, that is to say "states" in the distinctive sense (Chapter 30). Each of the fourteen could, more fully, be discussed in terms of how it comes into existence, that is, how it is founded, what persons constitute its rulers, and what ends it is supposed to serve as well as actually is serving. All these matters will be more fully discussed later, when in Part IV we come to consider the concrete political order. At this point in the analysis, it remains to consider the question of evaluation and to determine whether there is, or indeed can be, a "best" political order, a best form of rule.

We have spoken already of the dichotomy of autocracy and heterocracy. This alternative is characteristic of other evaluative classifications which are cast in terms of *either/or*, and attach value to the "either" and disvalue to the "or." Thus it is clear that the confrontation of autocratic (at times spoken of as authoritarian) and heterocratic (often spoken of

[40] Durkheim, 1893; S. de Grazia, 1948.

more specifically as democratic) regimes is meant to devalue all those types of rule which can be categorized as autocratic—an enterprise which is aided by the common pejorative sense of the words autocratic and authoritarian.

A similar and related dichotomy we have already mentioned is that between constitutional and nonconstitutional regimes. Here the crucial value is that of a constitution, more or less broadly defined, and thus any system of rule which is subject to a constitution is said to be good, any without it bad. This value judgment may in fact be so powerful an ingredient of prevailing ideological moods that even palpably nonconstitutional regimes, such as the Soviet Union and its satellites in Europe, will "adopt" a constitutional code, although the rulers have no intention of allowing themselves to be subjected to its provisions.[41]

A third and divergent mode of dichotomic evaluation is cast in terms of social class analysis, and asserts that a classless political order is good, while one in which the rulers act for and represent a ruling class is bad. However, since it is not alleged that any such classless political orders can be found in the past, this particular attempt at classification is blatantly ideological and unconcerned with empirical analysis as such. Therefore, we find in this scheme a derivative evaluative classification in terms of historical development. It holds a political order relatively good which corresponds to the phase of history in which it occurs.

As against such dichotomic evaluations in terms of a single distinct factor presumably permeating the entire political order and making it either good or bad, the question remains: Is there conceivably a political order which can be said to be best, either among the fourteen types which have historically appeared or to be devised in the hope of transcending them? There can be little doubt that many of the founders of new orders in the emerging nations are looking for precisely this kind of model order. On the basis of the analysis given here, such a model order could be envisaged only if the values dominant in the community were such as to support it. In other words, a universally applicable model would presuppose a universally acknowledged set of basic values. That such a set of values does not now prevail, is apparent. Hence the quest is usually put in terms of an adaptation to prevailing values and beliefs in particular communities. But even when seen in this perspective, such a model political order would conceivably serve the purpose of a lodestar if an evolution of the values in the direction which it requires could be envisaged and perhaps promoted.

In this connection, it is important to realize that Plato and Aristotle,

[41] A closely related, though not an identical, evaluation is involved in the German term *Rechtsstaat*, that is to say, government according to law; it is then a question of whether any particular political order can be qualified as *Rechtsstaat*, regardless of what its pattern of rulership is. This category obviously served a paramount political purpose, in attributing value to a nonconstitutional monarchical regime.

who epitomized the Greek search for such an order, used the term "political" in a restrictive sense which implied a first dichotomic preference. For from among the political orders in the above classification they selected with naïve cultural idiosyncrasy the Greek *polis* with a sacred *nomos* as the only true political order, deeming all others, and more especially Oriental despotism, to be bad. They then superimposed upon this first dichotomic evaluation a second one strictly within this charmed circle of the *polis,* and asked what would be an "ideal" or a "model" *polis* (the first Plato's, the second Aristotle's question, I believe). In other words, they had no intention of even considering as possibly good the kind of political orders found elsewhere throughout the world. Hence it is not surprising that their particular solutions to the problem of which political order might be best does not apply to the modern world.

It is not possible to undertake to answer this question about the best political order at the present stage in the analysis. Only after the entire gamut of political experience has been reviewed and analyzed will it become possible, in the last chapter, to adumbrate an answer to this crucial, indeed decisive, question. For the empirical approach which is being used precludes a consideration of that which *is* best without being able to discuss it in terms of what *works* best.

At this point, it can only be said in conclusion that rule, seen as institutionalized political power, has been organized in a considerable variety of ways. It can further be said that a broad survey of these ways suggests fourteen different patterns of rulership, appearing in different context and at different times. There seems to be clear evidence that these patterns appear in historical sequence, but that this sequence is repeatedly broken, and repeated within the context of the distinct "great" cultures or civilizations, and that this advance and retreat exhibits some regularities that suggest a typical cycle, but not uniformly so. Various modes of basic evaluation in terms of an either/or, dividing types of rulership into good and bad forms, were noted, and the ground for constructing a "best" form was broadly sketched. But whether such a universally valid form can actually be designed was left undetermined until the very end of the analysis.

chapter

11

Influence and the Rule of Anticipated Reactions

Those who know, do not talk,
Those who talk, do not know.
Lao-Tzu

INFLUENCE IS A KIND of power, indirect and unstructured. We have seen that power manifests itself by the behavior of a person or of a group when it conforms to the preferences, whether expressed or implied, of another person or group. The phenomena of influence indicate, as previously noted, why power should not be held to be a matter of commands. We have urged that the term "power" should be used to designate that relationship between persons in which the behavior of a certain group of men conforms to the wishes of one or several of them. Such a relation is one in which ruler and ruled are bound together for the securing of values and objectives (they may be identical, complementary or mutual—see discussion above, partly by consent and partly by constraint (coercion). Power from this viewpoint may also be seen as the ability to decide what shall be done in a certain situation, but it is a mistake to overemphasize decision, as the phenomena of influence show. A great deal of power-wielding involves no conscious making of decisions at all. We shall nevertheless use mostly decision-making situations to demonstrate our propositions regarding influence, for the simple pragmatic reason that they are easier to document. It should be kept in mind, however, that influence often works most effectively by creating a certain ambience for decisions through its effect on attitudes, beliefs and values unrelated to immediate decisions.

Influence is largely power not expressed as command, although it is not sound to assert the reverse, that is, that all power not expressed as command is influence. For, the preferences to which the behavior or conduct of those subject to power conforms may be expressed in other forms, such as praising or condemning a certain kind of behavior, or simply adopting it in order to have it serve as exemplary and worthy of emulation. If these qualifying situations are borne in mind, one may characterize influence by saying that it usually exists when the behavior of B is molded by and conforms to the preferences of A, but without the issuance of a command.

Influence is of vast scope and frequently serves to adjust an institutionalized structure of power, a system of rule, to the actualities of the power situation. When new forces arise, not provided for by the formal structure or pattern, they will undertake to influence those holding the formal power. Such influence may be exercised by psychic, economic or even physical means of actual or potential coercion. The concubine of a prince, the butler of a great lord, the father confessor of a politician, the secretary of a senator, these and many others may be wielding influence over particular persons. Individuals and groups may also be influencing large numbers of persons, whether organized or not: in every legislative assembly some men are more "influential" than others, pressure groups influence governments and their subdivisions in a democratic setting, a parliament or its committee may influence the men in charge of foreign policy, and so forth and so on. In all these situations, the conduct of the influenced is being altered by those who exercise the influence, and this is done in a variety of ways, as we just said. Psychic means are perhaps the most all-pervasive means of influencing persons who are susceptible of being influenced. The fascination emanating from a powerful personality, or the persuasive seductiveness of a person of superior intelligence, the charm of a lovable man or woman—these are some of the psychic means of influencing the conduct of others. The psychic is, however, almost entirely limited to individuals, since groups of persons do not have a psyche except in those rare instances where, moved by a common inspiration, they feel and act in unison. The most characteristic means of group influence is the economic one. Not only the so-called pressure groups, but particular enterprises acting through the media of advertising and similar influences are to be noted here. This must not be taken to be the only means, though; when a parliamentary committee influences its country's foreign office, no economic means are employed; it is rather the residual political power that is here at work. Physical means are strikingly illustrated by the relations between states; often the policy of a lesser power is continually influenced by the preferences of a more powerful neighbor whose military power it has reason to fear, or to appreciate because it provides its own protection. Such moves as partial mobilization, concentration of troops at the border, or the appearance of naval vessels off the coast are manifestations of the underlying relationship. But physical means of influence are not restricted to this sort of situation. I remember once talking to the manager of a sugar plantation in Puerto Rico who explained that he was not introducing machinery for cutting sugar cane, because the desperately poor, yet violent, hidalgos would no doubt murder him if he did. As he spoke one sensed the fear which influenced him to continue an unsound practice against his business judgment. This sort of case is probably not as unusual as may at first appear. Yet, the more usual and important form is the threat of revolutionary violence and related phenomena (Chapter 34). In these situations the residual capacity of most humans to resort at times to violence serves as an important corrective to the possible abuse of power.[1]

By whatever means it is exercised, influence is an all-pervasive factor in power relations. As the original Latin verb *influere*, to flow in, suggests, it rests upon the capacity of human beings to imagine and thus to anticipate the reactions of those who are affected by their actions. Influence flows into the human relation whenever the influencer's *re*action might spell disadvantage and even disaster for the actor, who foresees the effect the action might have and alters it more or less in accordance with this foresight. We said at an earlier point that situations of direct and structured power are surrounded by influence like the magnetic field that surrounds the magnet. It is therefore characteristic of influence that it often counteracts the explicit command relationship. The mutuality of the power relationship is frequently safeguarded by the presence of a measure of influence. It has often been noted that even the most ruthless tyrant is recurrently persuaded to alter his conduct by the thought of the reaction of "the people" or some other group to what he proposes to do. He too anticipates the reaction, that is, is influenced and, therefore, ready to yield, albeit reluctantly.

The situations in which influence plays a role are difficult to diagnose precisely because of the elusive quality which influence possesses. Political theory has consequently paid relatively little attention to influence, though recognizing its role in a variety of contexts such as the "informal government" and the "informal organization." [2] For extended documentation one has to turn to history and the work of historians, who are forever laying bare new strands of influence as the more intimate thoughts of men in action are revealed by private papers, secret documents, and the like. Thus while it was claimed in public by high officials of the British Foreign Office before the First World War that Parliament had very little

[1] Galbraith, 1952; Banfield, 1961.

[2] Roethlisberger, 1941, stated this point well, though the originality of the findings is not as great as some of the comments would suggest.

if any influence on the conduct of British foreign affairs, a perusal of the documents published later revealed such influence practically on every other page. One finds officials arguing about what would be the reaction of Parliament to various courses of action. Perhaps the most famous, and at the same time the most unfortunate, result of this influence was the failure of Lord Grey fully to communicate to Parliament and public, or even to the German imperial government, his commitments to France and Russia because of the anticipated refusal of Parliament to accept such a policy.[3] Another very far-reaching influence of this kind is seen in the relation of Congress to the Supreme Court of the United States, where the constitutionality of proposed legislation is involved; here, too, the reaction is being anticipated most of the time.[4]

These and many other similar instances show that much influence serves to prevent, rather than occasion, action. It is negative rather than positive in its impact upon the person or persons influenced. This is not generally true, however, and cannot therefore be made the basis of a proposition about influence as such. It is nonetheless worth exploring whether the distinction between positive and negative influence is not important in the analysis of influence.

It would seem that the distinction is not important when "negative" influence merely means that one decision or action is preferred to another, as in all those cases where, when one course is rejected, another is automatically resolved upon: so-called dichotomic alternatives, such as peace or war. Even here one must be careful not to overlook possible intermediate states such as that of truce. But the distinction *is* important in cases where the rejection of a certain course of action means that no action is taken. Of course, from a strictly logical viewpoint even such a decision is one which can be described as positive, that is, positively in favor of the status quo. The existing state of affairs has, however, an important peculiarity: it is known to a larger extent than any contingent future can be. This is the reason why influence tends to work in the negative. It is easier to assess and therefore to know the preference of any person or group with regard to the existing state of affairs, than it is to know his preference for any possible future and hence contingent one. Many common sayings, such as "let sleeping dogs lie," attest to this insight. The Germans have a saying, derived from their authoritarian past, which counsels any man to stay away from his prince unless called into his presence, the thought there being that the prince as power-holder is likely to prefer the existing state unless he indicates otherwise and this reaction may therefore usually be anticipated.[5]

[3] Friedrich, 1938.

[4] Cf. the rich material and acute analysis in Truman, 1951.

[5] "Gehe nicht zu Deinem Fuerst, wenn Du nicht gerufen wirst," is countered by the right of petition—one of the earliest rights of a people seeking a share in governmental power.

This issue is linked to the general problem of access which recent analysis has highlighted.[6] It is a primary concern of anyone seeking to influence another. It has been asserted in this connection that the basic factor affecting such access is the position of the spokesman in the social structure, but it would seem that such a generalization is warranted only within the context of modern Euro-American culture.[7]

Hence we may say that influence predominantly works for the existing state of affairs. In this, as in many other respects, influence resembles more formal power. Yet the genesis and growth of revolutionary movements shows, as just mentioned, that power, including the formless power that is influence, can be deployed for the alteration of the existing state of affairs. The conditions under which this happens are closely tied to the problems of coercion and consent and the kinds of situation to which they give rise. (See Chapter 34.)

The interaction of consent and constraint gives us a decisive clue as to the nature of influence. The workings of influence are very elusive, because most influence changes the conduct of people without any outward appearance of change. Though constraint in many situations may play a very considerable role, it is often obscured by manifest consent. Psychoanalytic research has uncovered the deeper layers of quite a few of these situations,[8] but it is rare that political settings will permit this type of inquiry, and the kind of vague and even wild guessing that some psychoanalysts engage in as a substitute is most unsatisfactory from a scientific viewpoint, though it may yield startling and stimulating hypotheses.[9] Be that as it may, political science requires methods which do not have to wait upon such constellations. The influence of public opinion or of a parliament upon the conduct of governmental affairs is devoid of ascertainable manifestations. Why is this so? Our preceding analysis has already provided the answer: because the person or group which is being influenced anticipates the reactions of him or those who exercise the influence. This inclination of all persons exposed to influence to anticipate the reactions of him who has the power to issue commands, bestow benefits or inflict penalties of all sorts, constitutes a general rule of politics. It causes influence to be so often difficult to detect, and even obscures the operation of more explicit kinds of power relations. It is the factor which is at work in surrounding acts through which power is exercised with a penumbra of often unforeseen consequences (see below).

The operational rule of anticipated reactions provides in turn the ground of a technical rule for discovering influence, related to a proba-

[6] Truman, 1951; chap. 11 is entitled "The Dynamics of Access in the Legislative Process." Cf. also pp. 369–391, and 264–270.

[7] Cf. the interesting essay by Carl Schmitt, 1959. The access to the executive in the American political order is discussed by Truman, 1951, pp. 437–478 and 482–497.

[8] Adorno et al., 1950.

[9] Freud, 1930; Lasswell, 1930; Fromm, 1955.

bility rule [10] of great importance in politics: any political context in which we observe one or more instances in which a previous decision or action is reversed is likely to be permeated by the influence of the individual or the group to whom the reversal can be traced in the specific case. This is so because, as a result of the reversal, or even before it, because of its *possible* occurrence, the person or persons under the influence of another will anticipate the reaction of him who exercises the influence. The influence of a leading judge upon his court could be asserted if important reversals could be traced to his known views, such as might be embodied in earlier dissents (Holmes). The influence of certain pressure groups could be similarly demonstrated.[11] Again, the way in which the Senate by its veto power affects judicial nominations could be adduced as evidence for such a rule of anticipated reactions.[12] Finally, the role of public opinion largely corresponds to this pattern as the government seeks to anticipate the reaction of the public.

The rule of anticipated reactions is a probability rule. Like all such rules it does not permit us to exclude the possibility that the phenomena it refers to do occur under different conditions. Complete absence of reversals in a given case does not necessarily indicate absence of influence; on the contrary, it might indicate a very powerful influence. If the fear of a certain person is very great, his reactions might be anticipated at all times by him who fears him. Admittedly this is a marginal case; but it does occur in politics. In such cases there are likely to be other indications of the presence of influence, more particularly explicit indications of preference on the part of the influencer and conforming behavior on the part of the influenced person or persons. The rule of anticipated reactions might therefore be extended by adding: "This is also likely to be the case when the conduct of certain persons is seen recurrently to conform to the known preferences of another person or persons." But even if this condition cannot be observed, it still is not permissible to argue that the context is free of influence. The positive rule must not be converted into a more far-reaching, because exclusive, negative statement.

There also occur quite a few situations in which influence plays a considerable role, yet no reversals occur, because the formal power structure is such that explicit reversals are unlikely. Indeed, the rule of anticipated reactions is most likely to work where a formal but largely dormant power (and command) relationship prevails.

But why should such reversals occur? If influence is at work in mak-

[10] In 1937, pp. 16–18, I first stated this probability rule, calling it the rule of anticipated reactions. As the above discussion makes clear, we really need to distinguish between two such rules, the operational one, which operates fairly universally, and the heuristic one, which applies in certain specific situations.

[11] Childs, 1930. Cf. also references in Friedrich, 1950, pp. 649–650.

[12] K. C. Cole, a, 1934.

ing people conform to the preferences of those who influence them, why is it that at times they do not? The answer to the query is the answer to the corollary query which would inquire why the rule of anticipated reactions should hold. It is not a simple answer, but runs the gamut of possible explanations for deviant conduct. First, there are the possible errors in anticipation, due to oversight, incomplete information, lack of insight, and the like. It is possible to forget about the preference, though it be known; it is also quite possible that he who wishes to anticipate the reaction does not know what the preference of the influencer might be. Politics abounds with such instances, so it does not seem necessary to supply examples here. Whenever such a breakdown in anticipation takes place, the influencer is apt to protest and if necessary to insist that the decision be reversed, the action revoked or revised. Hense the possibility of discovering the otherwise hidden influence on such occasions.

But there are two special cases which deserve some further exploration, namely, reasonable uncertainty and deliberate defiance. It may well happen that a body or individual who is generally under the influence of another wishes to test the other to see whether a reversal will be demanded or whether one can "get away with it." Thus the Congress might decide that in a legislative decision of doubtful constitutionality the bill's adoption might clear the road for formal determination of the question. Or an administrative official might wish to see whether an action protested by a Congressman or member of Parliament would be challenged. In such cases the reaction is indeed being considered, but it is felt that it cannot be adequately foreseen, or if foreseen, cannot be approved and accepted. Even such cases will suggest influence, if, upon the actual occurrence of such conflict, the decision is reversed. Therefore, this type of situation cannot be cited as arguing the limitation of the rule of anticipated reaction, as has occasionally been done.

These examples just given, as well as some earlier instances, bring out an important insight concerning the veto as a political institution. It would seem that the veto is an attempt at institutionalizing influence. It is obvious that when someone is given a right to veto a decision, or even to delay it, his views are likely to *influence* the decision because his reaction is being anticipated. In such a case, we do not need the rule of anticipated reactions, because the veto takes its place. Admittedly, it is an institutional device for "balancing" an institutional structure in which power is divided; the purpose is to interlock the divided powers in such a way that they do not operate as completely separate entities, but coordinate their several decisions. It has proved highly efficacious as a device, but this result would not be possible if people did not anticipate each other's reactions and adjust their conduct to such anticipations. Some of the critical comment on political structures organized by a division of powers noticeably fails to take into account the operation of such influence through anticipated reaction.[13]

It has been argued that deflection or deviation of a policy from a line initially laid down might be used as an index for anticipated reactions, in addition to the reversal of a policy. Such a suggestion seems to make sense, but upon more detailed analysis it will be found that deflection and deviation of policy are terms which denote one or more reversals of some narrow aspect of the policy under consideration. Thus in foreign policy it might happen that the interest of a particular minor power is not originally included in a proposed step, but upon sufficiently vigorous protest from that power the policy is altered enough to permit its covering the instant case.

The rule of anticipated reactions is a relatively crude device. It merely discovers the presence of influence, but it does not provide any means for measuring or even assessing in a general way the scope and intensity of an influence which is known to exist. The subject of "measuring influence" is perhaps one of the most complex and elusive in political science. It may be surmised that, for example, the failure to develop predictive generalizations from the study of interest groups is traceable to this source. Nonetheless, once the presence of influence is established, either by the rule of anticipated reactions or by some other method, the extent of the influence can be investigated in a variety of ways. A careful analysis of the available evidence of existing preferences of the influencer may be matched by a corresponding analysis of the preferences of those subject to his influence. If the two preference patterns clash at various points, the degree of conforming behavior will provide an index of the strength of the influence exerted; for it takes a stronger influence to overcome a deviant preference than an indifferent one, obviously.

Two recent writers[14] define influence in terms of "value position" and "value potential," the latter terms designating the actual or potential share a particular individual or group is able to secure in a given setting (value pattern). They then relate their definition of the "elect" to the amount of influence, while the amount of power is said to determine the "elite." It is on this basis asserted that influence varies with power so that very great power would mean very great influence. The proposition in this unqualified form is not correct, even if their definition of influence be accepted. Actually, as we have indicated above, influence frequently operates as a corrective to direct and institutionalized (structured) power, and influencers often exhibit a tendency to avoid getting into power positions. Lasswell rightly asserts that "to exercise influence, is to affect the

[13] J. Allen Smith, 1930; Laski, 1933.

[14] Lasswell and Kaplan, 1950, p. 60. The accompanying quotations occur on pp. 201, 203 and 83.

policies of others as to weight, scope and domain." However, the analysis is distorted by an attempt to distinguish power and influence not only relatively but absolutely,[15] though treating them as closely related. If, on the contrary, influence is seen as a kind of power, then the propositions concerning power in general apply to it, *ceteris paribus*.[16] But in any case, influence and power are such that whoever wields power, as defined by us, is certain also to wield influence. Formal and informal power cannot be separated and assigned to particular persons, even though one or the other kind of power may predominate in particular situations and be more frequently used by particular persons. There are all kinds of ways of classifying power: by its source, by the degrees of coercion and consent, by its manifest operational signs, such as commands, negotiations, and so forth. Influence cannot be identified with any of these as it occurs in all of them. A command or a negotiation often has an effect far beyond the expressed and intended one, because the persons involved have influenced others, whether they be part of the immediate situation or not. Yet for many situations, it is admissible to describe influence as power not expressed as command. All the many situations in which the subordinates in a hierarchy or the people and other large groups influence the action of their superiors or representatives are clearly of this order. The power of the "poor" in power is typically influence. The great range of political phenomena which constitute resistance are linked to such influence; potential resistance occasions it.

This kind of influence is therefore operative on a considerable scale even in the most powerful dictatorship. There is a "level of tolerance" beyond which even the most ruthless autocrat dare not venture, except at his peril. Much of the present discussion about the "democratization" of totalitarian regimes is due to the operation of such influence. Some argue

[15] This contrasting of power and influence, while central to such discussions as that of the elect and the elite, is not consistently maintained, as when Lasswell and Kaplan write, "power is a type of influence." Such a statement would suggest that influence is the more inclusive term, and thus diametrically opposed to our position, which understands influence as a kind of power; it is formless power as contrasted with formed power—perhaps the terms "unexpress" and "express" power could also help to make the situation clear. Lasswell and Kaplan try to distinguish power as a type of influence which participates in decisions which involve severe sanctions. For a discussion of this aspect of the matter see above, Chap. 9. "Formal power" is, for Lasswell and Kaplan, "authority"—a view which we reject in the next chapter. The interesting study of Banfield, 1961, is theoretically unsatisfactory from our viewpoint, because it assumes power to be a kind of influence; cf. pp. 307ff.

[16] Lasswell and Kaplan, 1950, by contrast, formulate only one proposition concerning influence, and that a tangential one, namely, that the permeability of a group varies inversely with its influence (pp. 62 and 201ff.), which appears to be dubious and not supported by effective argument or data. In this connection, they assert that influence is the particular instrument of the "elect" as distinguished from the "elite." Concerning the difficulties with this distinction see below, Chap. 18.

that the Soviet regime has been "forced" by its people to make concessions regarding living standards and the extent of terroristic secret-police practices, others that they were decided upon by the rulers and hence are due to their enlightenment. The fact probably is that Stalin had exceeded the limit of tolerance; but there is probably also involved a gradual transformation of values and interests shared by rulers and people, such as occurs in all political orders and does not necessarily signalize any significant change in the basic order; for influence is always working for these modifications and adaptations, as has been shown above. What are the general propositions concerning the working of influence which can be demonstrably supported by known facts? The key propositions concerning influence, besides the rule of anticipated reactions, are the following.

First, influence may be based upon any value preference *shared* by the influencer and the influenced. This proposition is merely a special statement of a more general proposition concerning power, given above (p. 159). But it seems worth repeating it here, because this proposition is often obscured by the everyday view of influence. When it is discovered that an industrialist like Goldfine has used his "influence" with a man like Sherman Adams, the presidential right-hand man, to secure special advantages, the general impression is that the value Goldfine is after is something quite different from Adams' preferences. This is, of course, true. But these divergent values are not the *basis* of the influence. This might be a variety of things, such as common friends, common interests, common ideas, and so forth. Without such a common set of values, influence cannot be effectively wielded, except in those cases where deception occurs and the person or group that is being influenced is led to believe that there is such a shared value when in actuality it does not exist. Much propaganda is built on this type of deceptive influence.

The second proposition can be stated thus: influence increases when the security (and the sense of it) decreases. This is especially so when the security involves the shared value upon which the influence is based. This proposition is a corollary of the first proposition. For even when the shared value itself is not immediately involved in the situation threatening the security of the influenced person or group, such a security threat brings a heightened feeling of the need for help, and this feeling is at the bottom of much influence anyhow. The feeling may have a very crass material basis: a candidate for elective office may need the ready cash which certain persons can provide; their influence will be correspondingly great. And because of the working of anticipated reactions such influence does not depend upon the person exercising it desiring to do so. It may be very real even when such an influencer protests that he "has no influence." One cannot go by the opinion which such an individual or group may have (one of the more severe limitations of interview evidence, by the way), but only by what the actual behavior of the persons involved in the situation reveals. It is evident that the second proposition carries quantitative implications. The formula for it,

If $s(t^1) < s(t^2)$ then $i(t^1) > i(t^2)$ where s = security
and i = influence
If $s(t^1) > s(t^2)$ then $i(t^1) < i(t^2)$ t = points in time

cannot readily be made the basis of accurate calculations, however, in most contexts, because we lack indices for security. What is more important, there do not yet exist any indications of the rate of increase of influence relative to the rate of decrease of security; these items are apt to differ for different types of situation.

Third, it may be stated as a definite proposition that influence (formless power) decreases when the relation of the influencer to the influenced is made public. The proposition results from the significant role which secrecy plays in the wielding of influence of every kind. To be sure, not all influence is entirely secret. It is often known to exist in a general way, but much influence derives its efficacy from being hidden. Hence the constant effort to render ineffectual the role of influencers who are being disapproved of, by focusing publicity upon them. Such laws as the one providing for the registration of foreign agents, or the reporting of pressure groups, or for the disclosure of contributions to party funds, are all designed to reduce, if not to obliterate, influence by making its possible existence public.[17] I once wrote that all power hides. It was a nice epigram, but it is not true. For a great deal of power cannot hide. Embodied in governmental institutions and organized as institutional rule, it is of necessity in the public's view. Coercive power, by its very procedures, even if not institutionalized, cannot hide. It is therefore necessary to restrict the saying to that formless power which is influence. Influence hides, or tries to do so. And it does so because it seeks to remain or to become as large as possible, as all power does; this it cannot do if made public. Ask any propagandist where he gets his money and you will see him squirm, because he realizes the dangers inherent in such a disclosure of the source of his funds, and hence of the direction of the influence he wields.

There is, however, one way of escaping the consequences of disclosure to an extent, and that is to transform influence, which is formless power, into formed (or formal) power. This leads to our fourth proposi-

[17] Price, a, 1955; Overacker, 1932, and articles in the *APSR*.

tion, namely, that influence seeks to become formal power when its operations become public. The transformation of influence into structured, if not yet institutionalized, power (rule), is a process which can be observed continually, and there are some striking illustrations, such as the evolution of royal advisory bodies in such kingdoms as England and France. As soon as the relations between such a body and the king become widely recognized in public, it is superseded by yet another informal body which can render effective advice (influence the king).[18] But in many other situations, the formalization of power will be attempted by the influencer when his influence becomes stabilized and hence generally known. It is, however, not always possible to bring about such a transformation, because the person or group influenced may not be willing to subject itself to formal power relations involving commands. Then the previous rule (our third proposition) applies and the influence declines.

In addition to these generalized propositions, it remains to say some more about the so-called "forms" of influence alluded to at the outset. In discussing power, we identified three kinds of coercion and hence of coercive power: physical, economic and psychic.[19] To speak of forms of influence, when influence is typically formless power, seems not very sensible. There are, however, different kinds of influence which one might specify as material, personal and intellectual influence. Material influence occurs in all those situations where material values are the basis of the influence, as in a family in contemporary America where the breadwinner may yet maintain a great influence though stripped of formal power and authority. In the political sphere, material influence is a major factor in the work of pressure groups, even when no "corruption" is involved.[20] This type of influence is nonetheless in popular view and parlance identified with corruption and bribery. This identification is unsound. There are many types of material influence, that is to say, influence based on material considerations which are not at all corrupt, such as the influence of the taxpayer upon the tax-spender, the influence of the consumer upon the producer and the influence of the donor upon the beneficiary. Oftentimes the influence of the contributor to the party finances is in the same

[18] Friedrich, 1937, pp. 257ff.

[19] Above, pp. 166–70, Chap. 9. Lasswell and Kaplan, 1950, p. 84, define form of influence as "a kind of influence relationship specified as to base value and scope." They add that "a form of power is a form of influence in which the effect on policy is enforced . . . by relatively severe sanctions." In a comprehensive table they list sixty-four "forms of influence and power" which resemble in rangy scope the long list of "powers" given by Hobbes (chap. X, p. 161). It does not seem very satisfactory to list such items as "love," "rape," and "credit" as "forms of influence and power." We prefer to use the term "form" more abstractly. Yet, in essence we agree with their specifications, yet not as "forms," but as "kinds."

[20] Key (4th ed.), 1958, pp. 158ff.

class. Corruption occurs when such influence is employed for illegitimate purposes which are alien to or remote from the material interest involved. Material influence obviously then plays a vital role in politics; it provides the bridge between the economy and the political order, and is the special realm of that "countervailing power" which has recently been stressed in an important analysis.[21]

The personal kind of influence is based upon feelings or emotions. Inspiration is the key factor in this sphere, and such phenomena as inspirational (charismatic) leadership are its manifestations. There are as many types of this kind of influence, however, as there are feelings or emotions, and no useful purpose would be served by listing them here. Any emotion by which A is bound to B will make A anticipate the reactions of B and hence be influenced by him, hatred as well as love, resentment as well as devotion, distrust as well as loyalty, and so forth. Many of these influences are very fleeting, others deep-rooted and lasting. It is this sphere of personal influence which renders the whole subject of influence so elusive and which defies scientific analysis in many important areas. It is highly significant, and politically relevant, that many emotional bonds are mutual, so that A not only influences B, but is influenced by B. Everyone is familiar with the phenomenon in the realm of personal experience, especially in the different types of love relation; wife, daughter, mother, friend, they all not only are influenced but exercise influence, often profound influence of a politically important kind, if the loved one is the power-holder. In a sense, the cooperative pattern of political order is built upon such mutual emotions, binding leader and led, and thereby subjecting the leader to the influence of the led in all kinds of ways.[22]

Finally, there is the kind of influence based upon superior knowledge or ability. This intellectual kind of influence often turns the official hierarchy upside down, as ministers influence kings, subordinates their superiors in public administration, or eggheads the hardheaded politicians (nutheads?). This kind of influence, while as ubiquitous as the other kinds, might also be differentiated from the influence of the wise counselor. The former could be subdivided into as many types as there are forms of knowledge, and thus we would have technical influence, legal influence, and so on. Not much is gained by this sort of classification, however. What is really needed is more precise and detailed studies about the three kinds of influence and about whether they exhibit special traits which could be made the basis of specific generalizations going beyond the four

[21] Galbraith, 1952, esp. chaps. III, IX, X.

[22] The possibility of such mutuality of influence is related to what has been called "horizontal" as contrasted with vertical influence, in Katz and Lazarsfeld, 1955, pp. 221ff. They have developed some interesting though limited evidence for the operation of such horizontal influence and have shown it to be pervasive.

general propositions we have made and which seem to apply to all kinds of influence.[23]

Although the study of influence is shot through with psychological issues, the political theorist cannot leave the subject to the psychologist because of its close relation to all political situations, to all power relations. There are many such situations where political analysis is both possible and necessary, because of the tie-in with other dimensions of political analysis and theory. The whole field of public opinion and propaganda is of this order. The interactions between rulers and ruled are indeed incomprehensible without adequate attention to the operation of influence. Why do people behave the way their rulers want them to when the rulers have no effective means of coercion and the people are reluctant to obey? What is the range of tolerance for both rulers and ruled? Why and under what conditions do the rulers anticipate the reactions of the people who are subject to them? Both Americans and Soviet people subscribed heavily to governmental loans during the last war; so did Germans. In the American case influence was used in the form of elaborate propaganda campaigns to "sell" the loans.[24] While a system of enforced savings might have been used, it was considered preferable to employ influence for accomplishing the desired goal. In the Soviet Union, probably, and in Hitler's Germany certainly, the coercive power of the government was brought to bear upon the situation. As the German case allows us to document, it would be a mistake to consider both situations as primarily the result of influence because no commands were issued; not merely the appearances, but the context, must be taken into account. Similar or parallel considerations apply to the position of Soviet writers and artists at the present time. To what extent do they conform because they really believe, to what extent because they are influenced and to what extent because they yield to coercion of whatever kind? Though speculative opinions abound and daring conclusions are derived from such speculative assumptions, the theoretical understanding of influence as a kind of power alerts the political scientist to the perilous uncertainty of most of the assertions heard in regard to this context. The Soviet writer may be rather uncertain as to the danger threatening him if he engages in a certain utterance. He knows that he can deviate somewhat, and to a certain degree must, if he is to be "original." (See Chapter 21 for further development of the problems of invention and innovation.) But in calculating this degree, he is obliged to anticipate reactions, especially when no explicit rules exist. On the other hand, there is also the counterpull of the

[23] Sociologists have been studying influence; cf. Katz and Lazarsfeld, 1955; besides their general analysis, note esp. chap. XII; cf. also Merton, a, 1949; Bennis et al., a, 1958; Kipnis, a, 1958; Freeman and Showel, a, 1951; March, a, 1956; Raven and French, a, 1958; Torrance, a, 1959; Warner, 1949.

[24] Friedrich, 1942, p. 200 and note; Odegard and Barth, a, 1941.

"love of adventure," linked as it is to what Freud called the "death wish." This counterpull argues against formulating any such proposition as entirely rational conduct in terms that survival and personal advantage might suggest. To make the point more specific, it might be said that "the greater the perceived degree of certainty that coercive sanctions be applied, the greater the likelihood that influence will produce conforming conduct, even if no command is involved."[25] Such a proposition has nonetheless a certain degree of probability in its favor, since the counterpull is itself a deviant kind of behavior.

A final point to be developed to round out both a review of the kinds of influence and to supplement our five propositions (all of them involved in this point) concerns the operation of influence in balanced power situations of all sorts. For these, as we have seen in Chapter 9, negotiation is the typical instrument of effectuating decisions and accomplishing other kinds of actions which the political situation might require. In such situations, influence is apt to play a rather considerable role. Not only between governments but also within governments and between governments and smaller groups, negotiation and the attendant compromise occupy a very considerable part of the working time of power-handlers. Treaties and contracts have to be concluded, as well as other decisions arrived at. These operations might be illustrated by the need of interdepartmental agreement in large-scale organizations, such as modern government. The concurrence of several subunits may be required. Thus the determination of a specific issue of foreign policy in the United States usually concerns several departments, Defense, Treasury, Commerce, as well as State; other units such as USIS and ICA may also have to "concur" in the determination. In arriving at it, the negotiators will usually feel that they must also try to anticipate the reaction of the formally authorized decision-makers, namely, the Congress and the President. In such a situation, each component element disposes of a certain amount of power which is "independent," or rather, separate from the rest. This power is obviously not one of command or coercion, but it is not merely influence either. The primary source of power of each power unit is lodged in the function which it is charged with: it is one of the rulers. But a secondary source may be typically influence, such as the persuasiveness of its negotiator, the better access to President or Congress, the support of public opinion or of particular groups among the public. All the component units are aware of the power resources

[25] This proposition, though stated differently, was suggested by a seminar paper of Donald Blackmer in 1960 which helped to clarify several issues on influence. He urged that influence and command be juxtaposed as a basic dichotomy of power—a theoretical position that contradicts the line taken in the text above. Swayze, 1962, offers an assessment in terms of the successive phases of Soviet development. Cf. above, Chap. 6, for a general appraisal.

of each, both the structured and institutionalized elements and to some extent at least the measure of influence. Usually, though not always, the several parties will prefer not to carry the issue to the formal superiors, for various obvious reasons. If all of them are sufficiently interested in reaching a determination, all the different kinds of influence will be mobilized by each of the units to secure the outcome which each prefers. The successful negotiator is one who knows how to marshal not only rational persuasion and conceivably the threat of potential breakdown, but also bluffing, he knows how to hint at reactions not only of President and Congress, but also of public opinion. The more convincingly he can make the case for his unit in terms of ultimate success, the greater will be the influence he will wield.[26]

Such a case as this shows once again that influence cannot be separated from other forms of power in a total power situation. Not only the units which are weak in other kinds of power resources, but also the stronger ones, will often prefer persuasion and influence to full utilization of coercive power. There are a number of reasons for preferring consensual agreement to a show of "force." Not only in international but in internal, not only in intergroup but in intragroup power contests, influence serves to veil the stark "realities." The so-called "realist" often turns out to be the man who fails to appreciate the subtler realities of influence in the total balance of power.

The hint at bluffing and other kinds of deception and self-deception calls for a concluding comment on the "influence" of nonexisting entities. For it is a mistake to think that only actually existing persons may exercise an influence. It is precisely the tendency of men to anticipate reactions of those believed to have power over them which makes it possible for nonexistent entities to wield a powerful influence, simply because of a mistaken belief on the part of those who shape their behavior in accordance with what is believed to be the preference of such a nonexistent entity. Some of the most striking phenomena of public opinion belong in this sphere. A telling instance occurred at the time of the agitation over the Townsend Plan. A majority of Congress was so deeply concerned over what they believed to be public opinion on the issue that a real danger of its adopting a measure in keeping with this "plan" existed, until a Gallup Poll was able to show that among those polled there was no such preference.[27] Even more illusionist are many of the references to "world public opinion." For it is very doubtful whether anything of the kind exists. To be sure, the reference often is to much more concrete entities which the arguer for political reasons does not

[26] Morley, 1874, 1921; Lasswell, a, 1931; Lasswell and Kaplan, 1950, p. 100; Schelling, 1960; Stevens, a, 1958. For further detail see below, Chap. 27.

[27] Bruner, 1944, chaps. 8 and 9, esp. at pp. 156ff. This work contains other interesting material.

wish to mention, for example, the opinion of delegates to the United Nations, or of the rulers of certain neutral nations, and so forth. Such cases have fascinated certain imaginative writers into constructing situations in which a country is governed by a nonexistent ruler; the handling of the Japanese government in the Tokugawa period has some features of this sort of world of illusion. Kafka has perhaps been most effective in depicting the influence of nonexistent entities.[28]

Influence then is a kind of power very difficult to describe except in negative terms, such as noncoercive, noncommand, and so forth. No situation moulded by power relations is without it in some measure; its several kinds, notably material, personal and intellectual, all are deployed in different power situations, and more particularly in those where a group of power-handlers is confronted with the need for joint action. In such situations, spoken of as balanced, though incorrectly, the role of influence is paramount. Theory and analysis, quantitative and other, have a rich field for further exploration and testing not only of the propositions here formulated and presented, but conceivably of additional ones, and for more precise versions of those here offered.

[28] Kafka, 1926, transl. 1930; also 1937 (transl.).

chapter

12 Political Authority and Reasoning

He who believes upon authority, entertains the opinion, simply because it is entertained by a person who appears to him likely to think correctly on the subject.
George C. Lewis, 1849

EVER SINCE THE EIGHTEENTH-CENTURY REVOLT against the established authorities in church and state, there has been a marked tendency among freedom-loving individuals to view authority with a jaundiced eye, if not to denounce it. When Charles S. Peirce wrote a generation ago that "when the method of authority prevailed, the truth meant little more than the Catholic faith," [1] he was echoing this sentiment. Rationalists have maintained that the implication here is that "the method of authority" is some kind of unreasonable superstition which must be superseded by the clear voice of reason. The Jacobins who erected altars to the Goddess of Reason did not realize how authoritative was their outlook. Much depended upon their authority for their particular reasoning to prevail.

In reaction against the rationalist challenge, conservatives since Bonald and de Maistre have made a fetish of authority beyond all reason. The pointed phrases in which de Maistre denounced the rationalism of the Enlightenment and the revolution center upon this issue. Because reasoning, *raisonnement*, could lead to the dissolution of all social order, to anarchy and terror, men ought to and were in fact ready to submit

[1] Peirce, 1923, p. 55.

themselves to authority without asking the "reasons why."[2] (Similar views are frequently expressed in contemporary American conservatism.) The stress in all these writings is on a tradition which at that time still appeared in a decidedly authoritative form. Very commonly a particular tradition is thus identified with all tradition, but events since de Maistre's time have demonstrated what history had already shown to be the case in a variety of contexts, namely, that political tradition may be of many hues, revolutionary and progressive as well as reactionary and conservative (Chapter 33).

Such views in turn stimulated men to restate the revolutionary rationalism in new and more historical terms. Saint Simon and, following him, Comte, believed that there were "organic" and "critical" ages to which, in the case of Comte at least, types of mental attitude corresponded: the authoritative versus the critical. In either case, they both identified reason with analysis, and analysis with scientific inquiry. The hopefulness and indeed almost chiliastic expectations which both thinkers cherished in envisaging an increasingly rational organization of society and more especially production (industrialism and science) made them exaggerate the conflict of reason and authority as much as the revolutionaries and counterrevolutionaries before them.[3]

Such excessive rationalism, which identifies "reason" with "scientific proof," overlooks the fact that, where such "proof" can be offered—and it usually cannot in politics—authority is not involved. It furthermore overlooks the fact that such "proof" is not the only kind of reason, but a very special and rather limited kind; consequently it concludes that reason and authority are antithetical. All that is really antithetical is this kind of reasoning and the reasoning of those whose authority such rationalism questions. People who argue thus typically wish to substitute another kind of reasoning for the reasoning they attack. In the eighteenth century it was a matter of substituting another authority for the authority of church and monarchy. This is not intended as a value judgment, as a judgment as to whether the revolution was good or bad, but it *is* intended as a judgment as to a shift in *reasoning upon values* which the transition from traditional to philosophic or scientific authority demanded. Because of this shift, a new kind of reasoning seemed "worthy of acceptance" not to all, but to some, Frenchmen. It is only recently that this aspect of

[2] De Maistre, 1845, pp. 135ff.

[3] In view of the vast and diffuse nature of the writings of Saint Simon, Bouglé's selections, 1925, are useful. For Auguste Comte, see his *Cours*, 1830–1842, where his notion of a rationally and scientifically based political reorganization of society is developed. Such a reorganization is founded upon the historically argued conviction that the evolution of mankind followed a predetermined course through three stages: the theological, the metaphysical and the scientific (positive). See Lévy-Bruhl, 1900, for Comte; and Manuel, 1956, for Saint Simon.

reasoning has once more been fully recognized. Against the restricted "Cartesian" notion of reasoning as only that of logical proof, the Aristotelian tradition of rhetoric has been appealed to in a "new rhetoric." To the restricted notion of evidence there must be opposed a broader concept of reasoning which is directed in a thoroughly rational way to securing or increasing the assent of the mind to propositions which are set forth in more or less elaborate arguments.[4]

In this perspective, it may well be asked whether reasoning and authority are really antithetical, that is, whether authority has no basis in reason. We shall hope to show that authority and reason are closely linked, indeed that authority rests upon the ability to issue communications which are capable of reasoned elaboration.[5] Or rather, that this ability is a crucial aspect of power and rule for which the multihued term "authority" might well be appropriated. For this ability is a vital factor in rendering power consensual, as will be shown presently.

In common usage, authority is often confused with power; the word "authority" is taken to be a synonym of the word "power." In more learned discourse, authority has been defined as a particular kind of power, such as "formal power" or "rightful power." It has been spoken of in relation to persons, as well as to other entities such as law or a dictionary. The problem of what makes people "accept" authority by obeying commands or believing a message, has given rise to a variety of interpretations of authority. Authority has been juxtaposed not only to reason but to freedom or force. It has been praised and condemned in all these contexts, and as a result the word has been incorporated in a pejorative adjective, "authoritarian"; regimes and personalities have been condemned by being called "authoritarian." [6] In most of these discussions, on both the popular and the learned level, it has been assumed that authority is a peculiar something that can be possessed, gained and lost. Against such views it has been argued that there is only power based upon constraint (coercion) and that authority is merely a make-believe, based upon religious faith at best, upon deliberate deception at other times.

Before proceeding with the analysis, it may be illuminating to cast a glance at the Roman antecedents from which the word "authority" is derived. *Auctoritas* is, according to Mommsen, not readily definable in its original meaning. It has predominantly the sense related to the verb

[4] See for this view the important study published by Perelman and Olbrechts-Tyteca in 1958.

[5] Friedrich, a2, 1958, pp. 28ff., and the literature cited there. This volume contains a variety of approaches to the phenomenon and the concept of authority. Cf. also Sternberger, 1959; Kessel, a, 1959.

[6] Adorno et al., 1950, *passim.*

from which it is derived: *augere*, to augment.[7] *Auctoritas* thus supplements a mere act of the will by adding reasons to it. Such augmentation and confirmation are the results of deliberation by the "old ones." The *auctoritas patrum* is, for that reason, more than advice, yet less than a command. It is advice which cannot be properly disregarded, such as the expert gives to the layman, or the leader in a parliament to his followers. This augmentation or implementation and confirmation had in ancient Rome, as elsewhere, religious overtones. While it was not intended to set limits to the free decision of the community, it was intended to prevent a violation of what was sacred in the established order of things. It was believed that because such violations were a crime (*nefas, Unrecht*) against the divine order, they might jeopardize divine favor. Thus, the preservation of good auspices probably was the basic idea underlying the *auctoritas patrum* vested in the Senate. It was a matter of adding wisdom to will, reason to preference, a knowledge of values shared and traditions hallowed, to whatever the people wanted to do. Later on, *auctoritas* became a more general concept, involving something of what our modern word "author" suggests.[8]

But why bother with these ancient verbal connotations? Because they bring out the role of reasoning and thereby help to get clearly into focus what is probably the central fact to which a great many of the situations refer in which the word "authority" is employed. When there are good reasons for doing or believing something, such action or thought acquires a quality which is otherwise lacking, it becomes "authoritative." This connotation has been overlooked by that rather numerous group of writers and philosophers who thought they could build law upon power alone, and more especially that kind of power which is expressed in explicit commands. The power of him who willed something was, they thought, what gave someone's decision authority. Hobbes, as well as Rousseau and many others, thought that the sovereign will was the source of all law.[9] Much Anglo-American legal tradition has, by contrast, retained the older notion, originally Stoic, that reason is of decisive importance in providing law with the necessary authority.[10] It is this view which assigns to the judge such a central position; he, as a man learned in the law, is seen as lending the statutory "decisions" of an elected

[7] This derivation has been questioned; cf. Heinze, a, 1925.

[8] Mommsen, 1888, III, pp. 1033ff., and Guthrie, 1950, pp. 183ff. Cf. also Heinze, a, 1925. Mommsen's notions are here elaborated and corrected.

[9] Hobbes, 1651, chap. X; Rousseau, 1761, bk. II. For Hobbes the key to authority is "the right of doing any act," right and power being practically synonymous, as in Spinoza's frightful dictum that "the big fish devour the little fish by natural right." Spinoza, 1670, chap. XVI.

[10] Coke, 12 *Reports*, 65; Friedrich, 1958, chap. 10.

legislature an additional quality, by relating them to the basic principles of the law and thus making them authoritative. The problem of the law and what makes it authoritative is only a special, though very important, instance of the much more general problem of power situations in which the preference of him who exercises the power may or may not be capable of support by reasons which are valid for him who conforms in his behavior to such a preference. But before proceeding with the analysis, it may be well to look at the matter from still another standpoint.

In his forthright little study on political verbiage, T. D. Weldon makes an effort at clearing away some of the thick underbrush that has grown up around the word "authority." He remarks that until recent times no clear distinction has been drawn between power and authority, and that it is "too simple to identify 'authority' with 'force' rightly or justly applied." He then differentiates four kinds of authority, ranging from pure force to unquestioning confidence, and on that basis asserts that "force exercised or capable of being exercised with the general approval of those concerned is what is normally meant by 'authority.'" Thus, if the followers want wickedness, they will obey a wicked authority.[11] And yet, at the start of his analysis, Weldon had pointed out that authority somehow is related to the fact that he who possesses it could produce reasons, if challenged. Such was the case of the Roman Senate, such is the case of the judge. To say, as Weldon does, that "the proper use of force is always authoritative" is quite inadmissible–indeed no advance over the position he himself had criticized–unless this statement is made into something closely approximating our position by giving to the adjective "proper," qualifying the noun "force," the meaning of "reasonable" in the sense of possessing adequate reasons for him to whom force (coercion) is applied. Be it added that Weldon himself seems to recognize as much; for he tells us that when people begin to ask the question "Why should I obey X?" X is on the way to losing his authority.

This last observation deserves further exploration. For when such a question is raised, a number of answers may be given. One answer would be in terms of hierarchy and status: because X is, for example, your elder, your parent. Another might be in terms of religious belief: God has commanded you to do so. A third would be in terms of interest and advantage: because X may make you his heir and successor. A fourth would be in terms of personal emotions and loyalty: because he loves you and you are devoted to him. A fifth would be in terms of law and the consequences of disobeying it, because article so and so of the code requires you to do it. Such a recital, even if incomplete, suggests some of the lines of reasoning upon authority. At the same time, it shows the link between authority and power; for if the person who is being addressed

[11] Weldon, 1953, pp. 50–56. Cf. also Nowell-Smith, 1949.

acts in accordance with the command at issue, then X has power over him. It incidentally shows us once again how many facets power has: an established hierarchy, a religious belief, a utilitarian advantage, love and loyalty, accepted law—they all may be sources of consensual power (Chapter 9). But the answer to the question "Why do men obey?" does not carry us far into an understanding of authority. The reason is that the elementary reasoning which these answers give does not make sufficiently explicit much of the augmentation, the enlargement of reasoning. The implied escape into the psychological concomitants of the particular datum of political life called obedience suggests that a crucial component of its ontological sphere has not yet been laid bare.[12]

We have, thus far, spoken of authority in terms of obedience because Weldon put the problem in that perspective. It is very commonly done, and this is understandable enough, because of the close link between authority and power. In action-related situations, where the conduct of B as a consequence of the communication of A (or even his anticipated reaction) conforms to A's preference, whether express or implied, authority, as an enlargement and reinforcement of power, is manifest in patterns of obedience. But there is another phase of authority, political and other, which can best be understood if one considers the situation of the teacher, the scholar or even of the dictionary. Some very interesting special problems are presented by the authority of nonpersonal entities of which the politically most relevant are laws and constitutions. It might be argued that one could bracket these entities and their authority, because such authority may be traced back to the human "author" who brought them into existence. But the difficulty here is that it is often debatable who *was* the maker of the law or other entity (not formally, but in fact). In the case of the American Constitution, for example, one might well ask whether the Fathers at Philadelphia, or the long line of judges who sat on the Supreme Court and other high courts, or even the congressmen and President were the "author"; it may even be said that the Constitution as it exists today is the creation of the entire American people. To be sure, in the case of a dictionary, it might be different, yet typically the makers are little known to the user, and hence its authority cannot be said to be traceable to them. The authority of impersonal entities is comprehensible only in terms of the rational component of authority which is more readily analyzed in the case of authoritative communications of personal agents.

Leaving aside then for the moment the authority of such impersonal entities and before considering the strictly political field, it may be well to

[12] Max Weber, 1925, pp. 16–20 and *passim* equates authority with legitimacy, and thereby misses, the confusion apart, the key aspect of authority, namely, its relation to reason—a recurrent feature of psychological and nominalist misinterpretations of phenomena. See for an extreme case, Jerome Bruner et al., 1956.

analyze more fully the situation of the teacher, the scholar, the doctor or the lawyer. In their cases authority appears to be related to the fact that the person wielding authority possesses superior knowledge or insight. Frequently, for instance among scholars accepting each other's authority, the authority of X obviously rests upon the fact that he could give extended reasons for the opinions he expounds.[13] It is not necessary, however, that these reasons are conclusively demonstrable in order for such reasoning to be authoritative. Indeed only where they are not thus demonstrable is authority in the strict sense involved. Knowledge is transmissible, even though its ultimate grounds may remain obscure.[14] What matters is the additional reasoning, the *more* of reasons that can be given for the communication of him who has authority. If a doctor says, "You must rest for three weeks," the patient accepting his authority will ordinarily obey. He does it because he knows that if he asked, and time and other circumstances permitted, the doctor could give him elaborate reasons derived from his competence as a medical knower and practitioner. The real question which is being asked by him who wishes to test authority is not "Why should I obey?" but "Why should I agree?" It is the capacity for reasoning or more precisely for reasoned elaboration of a communication that matters. This capacity *is*, it exists, whether recognized by anybody or not. The authoritative quality of impersonal entities is now more readily comprehended. In the case of laws, it is presumed that careful consideration of alternative courses of action has taken place. Plato, who was deeply concerned with authority as against power, therefore quite appropriately proposed in the *Laws* that each law should be prefaced by a preamble—a kind of introductory argument in which the reasons for it are set forth.[15] But whether they are set forth or not, these reasons exist, and they are what gives the law authority. If one wished, one could call authority which is based upon explicit reasons rational authority, as has been done in the past, but such a usage carries the danger that all other authority would be considered as nonrational, which would be wrong. In order to avoid the possible objection on verbal grounds that "authority" has not been used precisely, because what was asked was beyond reason, it is necessary to stress that we are talking about reasoning, about the ability to argue effectively and at greater length, to elaborate, in other words, in a way that makes sense.

But it is said this is all very well for the authority of such technicians as doctors and lawyers, and even more of scholars, but political authority is different. The authority of him who wields power, it is claimed, must

[13] Friedrich, a (ed. Young), 1958.
[14] Brecht, 1959, re transmissible knowledge; at pp. 115ff. and 561 fn.
[15] Plato, *Laws*.

be seen in a context of "blind" obedience to commands issued by the power-holder, and the blinder the obedience, the more authoritative the power-holder. We have already shown (Chapter 9) why this view of power is too limited, and why power is handled rather than held. This error has aided the confusing of power and rule with authority. To be sure, in popular parlance the two are often equated, as mentioned before, but what we are proposing here is in fact that there are power situations which are differentiated from others by the fact that the wielder of power has the capacity to elaborate what he prefers by reasoning which would make sense to those who follow him, if time and other circumstances permitted. Such reasoning very usually involves the values and beliefs, as well as the interests, of the group within which the power is exercised. The power-handler shares with his followers all or part of such values and beliefs, and therefore could, and at times will, explain to his following the reasons he acted in a certain way and more especially why he preferred them to act likewise. What we are proposing is that this capacity for elaboration in power situations should be called political authority. If that proposal is rejected by anyone, he will have to suggest another word for designating this vital political phenomenon. A somewhat similar approach was taken by de Jouvenel when he argued that authority is "the ability of a man to get his own proposals accepted."[16] But this way of putting the matter confuses again authority with power; for that ability may result from brute force. We must ask what enables a man to get his proposals accepted, or, to use another of de Jouvenel's formulas, "to gain another man's assent." When that ability to gain assent is rooted in the capacity for reasoned elaboration, authority is at work.

If it is agreed that power can be implemented and enlarged by the capacity for reasoned elaboration, and that this capacity be called "political authority," then it follows that political authority does not designate any kind of power or rule, but a quality of the power-handler or ruler. When I speak of authority—let it be understood hereafter that we are from now on speaking of political authority—I wish to say that the communications a power-handler offers in connection with the exercise of his power exhibit a very particular kind of relationship to reason and reasoning. They are capable of reasoned elaboration, that is, there exists the potentiality of such reasoned elaboration, but they are not usually so elaborated, and they are certainly not demonstrated through

[16] B. de Jouvenel, 1957, pp. 28–31; also, a, 1958, pp. 160f. In the latter article, he argued that authority is "the efficient imperative." An imperative is a *kind* of communication, rather than a *quality* of communications, and yet it would appear from the context that de Jouvenel really means the latter, and that he also includes the notion that it is therefore a quality of persons who are able to issue such communications.

scientific discourse. A communication that is "proven" scientifically requires no authority for its acceptance.

In light of what has just been said, it becomes possible to sharpen the focus on authority as a *quality* of communications, rather than of persons.[17] When we speak of the authority of a person, we are using a shorthand expression to indicate that he possesses the capacity to issue authoritative communications, that is, communications capable of reasoned elaboration. And furthermore, when we say X possesses authority, we thereby propose to suggest that the communications which X addresses to A,B,C . . . are based upon reasoning that has meaning not only to X but also to A,B,C . . . in the sense of being based upon knowledge which they possess, or opinions, beliefs and values which they share with X. This statement is meant in an ontological sense, however, and not in a psychological one. I am not here concerned, to stress it again, with the problem of persuasion; it is not a matter of X's ability to "influence" the thinking and acting of others, though such influence is often involved in such situations. What matters is that this capacity to issue communications which may be elaborated by reasoning is there, that it exists, and that as a consequence a community of opinions, values and beliefs, as well as of interests and needs, is manifested in such communications.

Because of this community, of which authority is a manifest sign, the power wielded with authority is likely to be consensual power. In line with the aforesaid striving of power-wielders to transform their coercive power into consensual power (or to keep consensual power consensual as it acquires coercive potentiality) there is a parallel propensity for power-wielders to acquire authority. The reasoned elaboration may be provided by themselves or it may be left to associates, the priests and propagandists "who surround the throne." Or it may be merely hinted at by such claims as the divine right of kings or the historical laws of dialectical materialism. In fact, the belief in authority is usually helped by such general claims which are difficult or impossible to put to the test. Rousseau, in a famous passage of the concluding chapter of the *Contrat Social*, suggests as much when he assigns in Machiavellian fashion this task to what he calls "civil religion." Such an instrumental devaluation of religion is not sound. The true religion does, however, provide the basis for reasoned elaboration and hence for authority, as much as does a false religion invented and developed for this purpose.

As far as the opinions, beliefs and values involved in such reasoned elaboration, that is, in such augmentation, are concerned, they may be one or many, readily identifiable or highly speculative and abstract. One value, such as truth or justice or health, may predominate, or there may

[17] This position is also taken by Barnard, 1938, pp. 136ff.

be an infinitely complex array of values, such as are represented by a culture or a way of life.[18] What matters is that some propositions, whether judgments or commands or decisions or policies, can be elaborated by suitable reasoning in terms of these values, opinions and beliefs, while others cannot be so elaborated. The capacity of men to speak in meaningful terms, to say the things which may be reasonably elaborated, varies enormously. And among the most important phenomena of political life are those connected with the waning of this capacity due to transformations in the values and beliefs of a community. The process of aging leadership in consensual power situations is usually associated with the disintegration of authority. The actions of the "old one" are no longer understood, because they make no sense in terms of the altered values and beliefs; his capacity for reasoned elaboration is declining and finally is gone. This often carries with it a decline of power, though just as often the power continues, but it gradually becomes more coercive, less consensual.

In this connection it is necessary to insist once more that such "reasoning" is not necessarily, nor even usually, employed in fact,[19] though it may be hinted at or suggested by symbols and myths. The role of symbols (Chapter 5) is to be found in this representation of values and beliefs which carries the implication that reasoned elaboration could be given by the power-handler. Crucial is the "potentiality" of such reasoned elaboration. In other words, not the psychological concomitant of a belief in the capacity of the authority for such reasoned elaboration is decisive, but the actual presence of this capacity. If this is clearly understood, the possibility of "false" authority becomes comprehensible, whereas it remains obscure as long as the psychological concomitants of authority are said to constitute its nature. For situations often arise, wherein the capacity for reasoned elaboration was believed to exist, when it did not. Such errors are a common occurrence in political relations among men. The error may be the result of developmental divergence, as sketched just above, or it may spring from a deliberate "faking" of authority, a pretended capacity for reasoned elaboration which when put to the test is "shown up." The extraordinary rapidity with which authority disintegrates under such conditions has often mystified political analysis. It is not really difficult to understand, once it is realized that what appears as a disintegration of authority is really merely the unveiling of an accomplished fact which occurred over a considerable period, or in the case of faked authority, the unveiling of the fact of the nonexistence of the capacity for reasoned elaboration.

[18] See Brecht, 1959, chap. 8, for a review of diverse "highest" values that have been argued in recent years.

[19] This aspect is also stressed by H. Simon, 1947, p. 1.

Genuine authority is present when a power-handler actually possesses the capacity for reasoned elaboration; the respect, esteem, or other psychological concomitants, while undoubtedly present too, are corollary phenomena. Power, wealth, and a host of other data of politics likewise occasion these psychological reactions.

While authority must be clearly distinguished from power, as we said, it is evident from all that has been said so far that the capacity to communicate authoritatively, that is, to be able to enlarge upon what is being communicated in terms meaningful to those who are being addressed, has a vital relationship to the phenomena of power. Indeed, there can be no question but that this capacity always gives some additional power to him who possesses authority; hence authority is one of the sources of power, mostly of the consensual type. It is especially likely to give influence beyond the particular office or other source of power, as it increases the propensity to anticipate the reactions of him who possesses it (Chapter 11). This explains the undoubted fact, occasion of much political comment and analysis,[20] that much power may continue without much authority, and conversely that much authority may be held without much power. Many tyrants have exercised vast power with little authority, while men of conviction living under their rule had great authority without much power. If the precise concept of authority which has here been developed is used and authority is seen as essentially a possible quality of the communications of a power-handler, such a divergence is readily comprehensible.

The foregoing analysis also helps in understanding better the peculiarly fluid quality of authority, and of any power based upon it. Since opinions, values and beliefs, as well as interests and needs, are continually changing in response to changes in the environment and to creative innovation, whether of a political, aesthetic, technical or religious nature, it is quite possible, indeed it is a recurrent experience, that a person may lose his power based on authority not because the commands he gives or the opinions he utters are less "authoritative" in the sense that they may not be elaborated by reasoning, but because such reasoning is related to opinions, values and beliefs that have lost their validity in that particular community. It is therefore necessary to sharpen further the definition of authority as the capacity for reasoned elaboration by adding: in terms of the opinions, values, beliefs, interests and needs of the community within which the authority operates. We shall say, therefore, communal reasoned elaboration. When one says that, in a certain situation, a man has "lost his authority," this is really a shorthand expression: he has lost power because his authority, or rather the

[20] Lasswell and Kaplan, 1950, pp. 133ff., having defined authority as "formal power," cannot cope with this phenomenon in terms of authority.

authority of his communications, is disintegrating, that is to say, the community is changing, and his capacity for *communal* reasoning is therefore declining. This is what *anomie* refers to.[21]

This tie of authority to the values and beliefs of the community was once succinctly stated by Burke when he wrote: "The sense of the whole people, most gracious sovereign, never ought to be contemned by wise and beneficent rulers; whatever may be the abstract claims or even rights of the supreme power. We have been too early instructed and too long habituated to believe, that the only firm seat of all authority is in the minds, affections and interests of the people, to change our opinions on the theoretic reasonings of speculative men. . . ."[22] There is implied here, of course, the recurrent misunderstanding that authority *is* in the minds, etc., when as a matter of fact authority *results from* what is in the minds of the community.

Before indicating what this means in terms of justice, one other perplexing situation may be clarified with the aid of the foregoing analysis, and that is the role of authority in totalitarian societies. If authority is interpreted as some kind of power, whether "formal," or "legal," or "rightful," the role of authority in totalitarian systems remains obscure. Some say with reference to a totalitarian regime, if they identify themselves with it and its rulers, that the authority of the ruler is very great. Others, identifying themselves with the subject elements of the population who are coerced into obedience by psychic, economic and physical power, insist that there is no authority, or very little, in such a totalitarian society. The analysis of authority as the capacity for communal reasoned elaboration makes it possible to resolve this difficulty. In contrast to constitutional regimes where authority is diffuse and pluralistic, since authoritative communications issue from many centers of authority, such as churches, schools, trade unions, parties, all kinds of associations, as well as the government, authority in totalitarian societies is strikingly centralized and intensified at the center of the totalitarian movement. Thus the authority of a Lenin, a Stalin or a Hitler when confronting his followers is very great, while his authority in confronting the rest of the society is weak, and vanishes altogether in the oppositional groups. Probably, though this calls for further detailed investigation, the authority of a dictatorial leader in his movement is greater than that enjoyed by a democratic leader, even among his party following, while it is decidedly weaker among the remainder of the people. To put this another way, political authority is both enlarged and reduced: enlarged when one considers the followers, reduced when one considers the rest of the people. At present it does not seem possible to quantify further and thereby to

[21] Durkheim, 1893; S. de Grazia, 1948.
[22] In his "Address to the King," *Works,* vol. V, p. 135.

compare the two situations in their entirety. Authority is not being centralized, but it is being concentrated at the center of such a totalitarian society. The explanation, in terms of our analysis, is obvious. The decisions and preferences of a Stalin or a Hitler, cast in terms of the regime's ideology, that is, the values and beliefs embodied in the movement's creed, could as a rule be elaborated by extensive reasoning based upon this ideology.[23] It cannot, by the same token, be elaborated for the rest of the people who do not accept the ideology. Here may lie an explanation, incidentally, for the frantic search for unanimity which characterizes these regimes.[24]

But what about the communal aspect of totalitarian authority? The answer may be put in three different ways. Either one could say that such societies are still composed of the entire national community, and hence argue that authority is weak, or one could insist, as the totalitarians do, that the totalitarian movement is a representative elite (Chapter 20) and constitutes the community, and then argue that authority is very great; or one could maintain that such societies are compounded of two separate and distinct communities, in one of which authority is very great and power consensual, in the other authority quite weak and power coercive. I lean toward the third alternative. In any case, this situation is only an extreme case of a recurrent phenomenon, namely, that a larger community comprises a plurality of smaller subcommunities. It is obvious that in such subcommunities authority will often be possessed by persons who do not command it in the larger one; for example, the authority of the Pope among American Catholics, as contrasted with the lack of it among Protestants.

These observations lead to the problem of justice. A fuller analysis will be given later (Chapter 14). Here it remains to point out that justice in the political sense is the epitome of all that is in conformity with the communal values, opinions and beliefs, and more particularly therefore with what can be authoritatively stated as satisfying the demand for equality.[25]

The bald statement that political authority is just provides a shorthand expression for the fact that authority in so far as it is the capacity of reasoning upon values provides the bridge between power and justice. In that perspective it would be possible to assert the proposition that authority justifies power, provides power with an explicit argument for

[23] The speeches and writings of men like Stalin and Khrushchev bear this out. Cf., e.g., Werner, 1940.

[24] Friedrich and Brzezinski, 1956, chap. 8.

[25] Compare Perelman, 1945, who suggests that the formal, as distinguished from the concrete, conception of justice means that "the same treatment should be accorded to beings of the same category" (chap. II). This is Aristotle's notion, clearly, linking justice and equality.

the relations to values prevalent in a given community.[26] This proposition raises the problem of legitimacy, political legitimacy, and permits the deepening of the answers to the question "Why should I obey?" that is to say, the problem of political obligation. To this set of issues the next chapter is devoted.

Catholic preoccupation with a specific revealed source of reasoning has in turn led Karl Jaspers to construct a radical antithesis between authority based upon reason and "Catholicity." [27] Only if authority is "recognized as illumined by philosophy, authority is not lost," for "in philosophizing I grasp authority as the limiting configuration (*Grenzgestalt*) of truth. . . . " Jaspers' notion that authority when "grasped" by reason and thus mastered by it is different and superior to authority which is transcendent and absolute underestimates on the one hand the amount of reasoning involved in Catholic authority, and overestimates the power of reason in mastering authority on the other. Authority can neither be equated with reason and truth, nor made antithetical to them. There is some ground for seeing authority in antithesis to reason when the latter is identified with the rigid rationality of demonstrable truth. But truth has a wider connotation and embraces many kinds of existential situations; this Jaspers rightly stresses. Truth also is one of the key values to which authority in many contexts is vitally linked. It is the predominance of this value in the life of scholars, and the extent of their consequent sharing of it, which allows them to accept each other's authority where they would not accept that of a journalist or preacher. Theology, by contrast, involves reasoned elaboration of a transcendental system of beliefs (or revealed truths). Ecclesiastical authority rests upon it. Actually, the great *Summa Theologica* of Thomas Aquinas is one of the most far-ranging efforts at reasoned elaboration ever attempted by the mind of man. Its mastery therefore lends authority among those who accept its theological premises.

But, we are told by thoughtful critics, most of the people who accept authority, whether of church or state, have no idea of these elaborate reasonings, would not understand them and do not care to learn about them. This may well be true, as it is when one consults a doctor or engineer, but it should be stressed once again that it is the *potentiality* of such reasoned elaboration that matters. Much institutionalized authority is maintained without the persons involved being able to elaborate. Authority and power in such situations are intertwined. These institutionalized situations have occasioned much of the confusion between authority and power. For there is always a considerable number of people

[26] Friedrich, a1, 1958, pp. 47–48.

[27] Jaspers, 1947, esp. pp. 767ff. See also Rommen, 1945, pp. 417ff.; Hauser, 1949; see below, Chap. 14, for an elaboration.

around who are obeying, believing or conforming because they submit to power in its various forms, including physical violence, but who talk about it as obeying authority. Far be it from me to insist that all obedience or other kinds of conformity are the result of authority—such a view can be taken only by him who confuses authority and power. What I insist upon is that the potentiality of reasoned elaboration of communications, that is, the potentiality of supporting communications by valuational and instrumental reasoning, provides a strong ground, provides a potent ground, for maintaining conformity in matters of action, opinion and belief where a community exists. It seems to me that this potentiality of reasoned elaboration is the differentiating characteristic of what men have had in mind when they have spoken of authority as contrasted with power—just as the Romans did when contrasting the *auctoritas patrum* with the *potestas magistratum* and the *libertas populi*.[28] It is related to truth as much as to any other value about which men can and do reason. It is a result of the fact that man, endowed with reason, is yet a finite being whose reason is likewise finite and enclosed within definite limits. An excessive belief in human reason is apt to lead to extravagant claims on behalf of authority. Yet, the reach of authority is forever confined to the reach of reasoning. There can be no absolute, no total, authority, because there is not open to man any absolute truth or total reason. The belief in such absolute truth is associated with a claim to absolute authority.[29]

The relation between truth and authority as here analyzed helps to understand better what is meant by "false" authority. It is that illusion which recurs in political situations when men issue communications as authoritative which are believed to permit reasoned elaboration when actually they do not. That is why the psychological interpretation of authority leads astray. For, as we have said before, people may well believe that a certain communication could be effectively elaborated and therefore worthy of acceptance when no such possibility does in fact exist. The falseness of such authority is revealed the moment the pretended potentiality has to be actualized. It may actually happen through the failure of an action as much as through lack of elaboration. There is nothing subtle or surprising in all this: "genuine" and "false" are terms which customarily refer to the possibility that an appearance may be deceptive.

In a remarkable study on the influence of authority in matters of opinion, a nineteenth-century liberal of the utilitarian persuasion con-

[28] Cicero, *De Republica,* II. 33. "Nisi aequabilis haec in civitate compensatio sit et juris et officii et muneris, ut et potestatis satis in magistratibus et auctoritatis in principum consilio et libertatis in populo sit, non posse hunc incommutabilem rei publicae conservari statum."

[29] Cf. on truth and justice, below, Chap. 14.

cluded that "in the present state of the civilized world, the progress of society will depend in part upon legislative improvements, and upon those measures which a government can command or influence; but it will depend still more upon the substitution of competent for incompetent guides of public opinion; upon the continued extension of their influence; and upon the consequent organization of a sound authority in all the departments of theory and practice." [30] In a striking sentence, this same writer lends support to the position here developed: "He who believes upon authority, entertains the opinion, simply because it is entertained by a person who appears to him likely to think correctly on the subject," and he accordingly defines the principle of authority as that of "adopting the belief of others, on a matter of opinion, without reference to the particular grounds on which that belief may rest." Cast into the less hopeful mood of our skeptical age, one might say instead that the maintenance of a measure of civilized existence depends upon the continued operation of authority in the sense sketched here.

But it still is true that only when what is commanded and asserted can be thus reasoned upon and defended is authority secure. To return to Burke once more, he adds with commendable poignancy to the comments quoted above: "Much power is tolerated and passes unquestioned where much is yielded to opinion. All is disputed where everything is enforced." The distinction between power and authority is clearly perceived here. The minds, the affections, the interests of the people, wisdom and equity—these are the true ingredients of the political phenomenon we called the capacity for communally reasoned elaboration and proposed to call authority. It is one of the basic phenomena of all political communities, large and small. Without it, the political community cannot endure.

[30] G. C. Lewis, 1849, pp. 6–7.

chapter

13

Legitimacy and Political Obligation

L'homme est né libre, et partout
il est dans les fers. . . .
Qu'est-ce qui peut le rendre légitime?
Je crois pouvoir résoudre cette question.
ROUSSEAU, LE CONTRAT SOCIAL

IF JUSTICE IS A QUALITY peculiarly related to and closely associated with authority, legitimacy may be said to stand in a similar relation to rule. Rule, that is to say, stabilized and institutionalized power, may either be exercised in accordance with what, to put it simply, is right, or it may be exercised regardless of right. We have seen (Chapter 10) that the distinction between "good" and "bad" governments Plato developed in constructing his typology of the different kinds of rule was built on whether such rule observed the *nomos*, the basic communal norms, or neglected it. If the ruler observed the *nomos*, he called him "just," and if he did not, "unjust." The meaning of both the term "good" and the term "just" is essentially "related to the *nomos*," that is to say, to the values and beliefs cherished by the *polis* community over which the rule was exercised. But Plato was not satisfied with the implied relativism. The question "What makes a rule just?" was in fact the central problem of Plato's political philosophizing. This question led him into metaphysics, and more especially into his doctrine of ideas, as he sought to reconstruct a rational basis for *nomos*, or right, to replace the traditional basis which had disintegrated. Our own conception of justice is that of value-relatedness in an objective, existential sense (see next chapter). It may be said, in a sense, to stand halfway between Plato's transcendental metaphysics and the subjectivism of the Sophists. In so far as there can be no community without shared values, and in so far as there is a central, universal core to such values (Chapter 2), we agree with Plato that it is of crucial importance for the political order that rulership be exercised in relation to such values. In so far as these values vary beyond the core and must be appreciated before they can play a role in politics, we reject his ideational metaphysics as not relevant to politics and misleading because of its absurd consequence of asserting that philosophers either are or should be rulers. Kant rightly argued that they should not be.[1]

But there is another side to rule, which may be described as its legitimacy. It is possible for a ruler to appear entitled to his rulership, that is to say, to be believed by those subject to his rule to have a right to it. The same can be said of a system of rule. This phenomenon is not identical with the general problem of consensus. It is a very particular form of consensus, which revolves around the question of the right or title to rule. Such right or title to rule has been founded upon a variety of beliefs, grounded in religious and metaphysical notions of a great range. The magical belief in "descent from the gods," manifest in supernatural powers of the ruler, is very widespread; from the primitive tribal kings and priests described in numerous anthropological studies[2] to the "son of heaven" in Chinese and Japanese imperial rule we find this foundation of a title to rule. The belief in blood descent which assimilates rule to the right of property has been a widespread ground for claiming title to rule and its acceptance. The notion that the ruler resembles, as a *symbolon*, God on earth, has been related to both these notions as an important ground of legitimacy. The mere fact of the rule having been exercised in a certain way for a long time, or from time immemorial, in other words, the prevalent custom and tradition, has provided another basis for such title. Finally, the fact that those who are being ruled have expressed a preference for a person through voting for him in an election has more recently been the preferred mode of establishing a right or title to rule. In analogy to this procedure, a system of rule (constitution) has been considered rightful, when accepted in a referendum or at least by elected representatives in a constituent assembly (convention). That rulers are carrying out a mission assigned to them by the laws of history or biology has lately also been claimed, but the factual record is too incomplete to be sure that this claim is really grounded in a sufficiently widely held belief to qualify as a title to rule; the rulers making such claims have themselves conceded the uncertainty by holding manipulated elections and referenda to reinforce their claim.

[1] Kant, 1795.

[2] Kroeber, 1948, chap. 9; Hoebel, a1, 1958; Frazer, 1959, part I.

There can be no doubt that it is an important question of fact whether a given rulership is believed to be based on a good title by most men subject to it or not. We propose to call this the question of legitimacy; but as usual, it is not the word that matters, but the understanding of the factual situation. Once that is clear, it becomes possible to formulate certain general propositions concerning legitimacy.

The question of legitimacy must not be confused with that of legality, though under certain circumstances the distinction is not easy to draw.[3] The legality of a rule is the result of its being in accordance with the positive law; it may therefore be the same as legitimacy when the prevalent belief is positivist and merely asks that title to rule be in accordance with the law in order for it to be considered legitimate. Here it might be said that legalism is itself an ideology justifying rule. A special form of this type of legitimacy would be the belief that merely a certain measure of "rule of law" legitimizes a government, as some lawyers might hold. Yet there have been many situations in which perfect legality of a given rule did not provide legitimacy, for example, the rule of Louis XVI in France in 1789. The ground of belief having shifted, the rightfulness of the rule, the belief in it among those subject to it, had disappeared. Conversely, in all those situations where a ruler abuses his power, breaking the law, the question of his legitimacy in doing so is distinct from that of legality. It may be perfectly legitimate, if believed to be in accordance with some generally held belief.

Legitimacy has been a favored hunting ground of political and partisan propaganda. This is perfectly natural; for it is often uncertain whether the rule is being exercised in accordance with prevalent belief or not. The term, as a matter of fact, became current in connection with the great controversies leading to and away from the French Revolution. Rousseau started the debate in the famous opening sentences of his *Contrat Social*, where, after asking why man, being born free, is everywhere in chains, he asserts that while he cannot explain that fact, he can set forth what makes it legitimate.[4] He then develops his idea of "democratic" legitimacy grounded in acceptance of general rules or laws, ideally by the general will, but actually by majority vote. His notion of a voluntaristic legitimation called forth a radical reaction in terms of traditionalist views. Burke proclaimed immemorial custom the basis of the prescriptive right

[3] Carl Schmitt, 1928. Kelsen, 1942, p. 117, contra, identifies the two. Legal norms, he says, "remain valid as long as they have not been invalidated in the way which the legal order itself determines. This is the principle of legitimacy." Kelsen relates legitimacy to the basic norm, the crucial concept of his theory. His position is correct, as we suggest above, as long as there prevails a general positivist belief.

[4] Rousseau, 1761: "L'homme est né libre, et partout il est dans les fers. . . . Qu'est-ce qui peut le rendre légitime? Je crois pouvoir résoudre cette question." Cf. also Derathé, 1948; and Hendel, 1934; Cassirer, 1954.

of the constitution,[5] de Maistre argued divine right in terms of alleged Catholic doctrine,[6] and many others followed with arguments all of which amounted to saying that rule, unless legitimate, was bad and then, insistently, that some particular belief was the true ground of legitimacy, and hence the only ground on which title to rule, legitimate rule, could be claimed. Actually, the "will of the people" won out in the long run, and by the middle of the twentieth century the prevalent legitimacy is thus democratic legitimacy. A curious echo of the revolutionary controversies was provided in this century by Ferrero, who argued that legitimacy was crucial to the exercise of power. In a rather confused argument he sets forth four kinds of legitimacy, namely, (1) legitimacy based on election, (2) democratic legitimacy, (3) legitimacy based on inheritance, and (4) aristocratic-monarchic legitimacy. These are really two sorts of legitimacy, as the first two and the last two are obviously and admittedly linked. It is obvious that (1) and (3) are "bases," whereas the other two are terms designating the handling of power (rule). But as we have already indicated by our recital of various grounds on which title to rule has been based, such a simple dichotomy does not suffice.[7]

Another attempt to simplify and systematize the numerous grounds upon which claims to legitimacy, that is, titles to rule, may be based was made by Max Weber. Essentially, Weber after confusing, if not identifying, legitimacy with authority (Chapter 12), suggests that three such grounds be distinguished, namely (1) traditional, (2) rational-legal, and (3) charismatic. We have in another connection (above Chapter 9) critically analyzed and restricted his notion of charisma and charismatic power. He himself tries to cope with the difficulties resulting from the fact that legitimacy essentially refers to stabilized and institutionalized powers by developing the notion of a "routinized" charisma. This kind of charisma when you come right down to it is noncharismatic in Weber's sense, and a very confused notion at all events.[8] But the objections are not

[5] Burke, "Speech on Representation," May 7, 1782: "Prescription is the most solid of all titles. . . . It is accompanied by another ground of authority . . . presumption. It is a presumption in favor of any settled scheme of government against any untried scheme that a nation has long existed and flourished under it. It is a better presumption even of the *choice* of a nation—far better than . . . actual election. Because a nation . . . is an idea of continuity. . . . And this is a choice not of one day or one set of people, not a tumultuary and giddy choice; it is a deliberate election of ages and of generations; it is a constitution made by what is ten thousand times better than choice; it is made by the peculiar circumstances, occasions, tempers, dispositions, and moral, civil, and social habitudes of the people, which disclosed themselves only in a long period of time. . . ." *Works,* vol. V, p. 405.

[6] De Maistre, 1843, p. 255; also pp. 168ff. "Le principe très vrai que la souveraineté vienne de Dieu."

[7] Ferrero, 1942, chap. IV.

[8] Friedrich, a, 1961.

only to the charismatic ground of legitimacy, as a rather unhelpful way of referring to the various types of religious legitimacy, but also to the "rational-legal." It might be argued, and has been, that this position (Weber's) is not untenable if it is recognized for what it is, namely, another ideology. But those holding the position would scarcely allow this line of argument, for their proud claim is to be scientific. Yet in some ways the objection here is more basic still, because of the decisive importance of clearly distinguishing between legitimacy and legality, and the equally decisive importance of not restricting the term "rational" in such a way that it excludes reasoning in other than positivistic and relativistic terms of what Hobbes so revealingly called "reckoning" (for Hobbes is the archfather of all such views). Only the category "traditional" as a ground of legitimacy in Weber's classification is sound.[9]

If one reviews the various grounds recited above, it would seem that a more acceptable classification of types of legitimacy would be (1) religious, admitting of a number of subtypes, (2) juristic (philosophical), (3) traditional, and (4) procedural and pragmatic, based on performance. The religious subtypes would presumably relate to the several religions and their distinctive notions about rule and rulership, such as the Christian, the Confucian, the Mohammedan, and so forth; the juristic or philosophical subtypes would refer to the several conceptions of forms of government and would therefore parallel the types of rule (Chapter 10); the traditional ones would do the same, but not in terms of a belief based upon philosophical reasoning, but upon custom. In fact, in any strict sense, the traditional forms of legitimacy are not really distinct, but implement the religious and philosophical ones. Procedural are the notions relating the elections of various kinds, more especially the democratic legitimacy of a majority vote. Finally the pragmatic types are as numerous as possible performance-preferences, such as success in war, prosperity, as well as order and peace. Quite frequently, legitimacy based on performance also implements the religious and philosophical types; thus a son of heaven in ancient China lost his legitimacy if disasters befell (as do many primitive rulers), because such disasters were interpreted as indicating divine disfavor. Democratic legitimacy in modern states is similarly subject to performance tests, especially in the economic realm, and the legitimacy based upon a majority's preference in an election may be broadened or narrowed by performance.

All these grounds are "rational" in the sense that legitimacy as here defined implies reasoning upon the title to rule, simply because the belief of those who are being ruled is capable of being stated as a reason for

[9] Max Weber, 1922, vol. I, pp. 6 and 7, and vol. III, pp. 9 and 10, esp. at pp. 762ff. For an interesting recent example, cf. Binder, 1962, which is based on Weber's categories.

accepting a system of rule. Once this is identified as the core of legitimacy, it becomes quite clear what is the relation of legitimacy to authority. For authority as the capacity for reasoned elaboration is capable of creating legitimacy whenever it provides good "reasons" for the title to rule.

From what has so far been said, it is clear that legitimacy can be achieved only when there exists a prevalent belief as to what provides a rightful title to rule. If the community is basically divided on this matter, then no legitimacy is possible. This is at times connected with what the Greeks called *anomie*, that is to say a state of mind in the community when no *nomos*, no prevalent notions concerning what is right, exist any longer.[10] But while often observed, and more especially in the Athenian *polis* of Plato's day, this connection does not always exist. It is possible for a community to be basically divided on much of what constitutes right, yet to have a prevalent belief as to what constitutes a good title to rule, as was the case in the period of the religious wars in Europe, when blood descent and symbolic representation of God on earth were generally accepted as good titles to monarchical rule.[11] It is also possible for a community to be basically agreed on most of what constitutes right, yet to be split on its belief as to what constitutes legitimate rule, as happened in France recently and prior to de Gaulle's assumption of power; de Gaulle's opting for democratic constitutionalism reestablished the legitimacy of this type of rule because of the authority which de Gaulle could bring to it.[12] From these situations it follows that a division in the political community on what constitutes legitimacy must be distinguished from general *anomie*, even though it has a relation to it.

Furthermore, it is very important to draw a clear distinction between the absence of any cherished standards and value judgments (*anomie*) and the presence of clearly defined divergences in such standards and judgments. The "agreement on fundamentals" as a necessary prerequisite of political order has haunted political theory since the days of Plato and Aristotle. Whatever was right for the Greek *polis*, the situation of the great modern states with their millions of people is radically different. Dissent is vital to the maintenance of intellectual and cultural, as well as political, vitality. Far from presupposing an "agreement on fundamentals," as writers from Burke to Laski have argued, constitutional democracy has achieved political order in diversity and has managed to organize decision-making in spite of *dis*agreement on fundamentals. The argument has, of course, a semantic aspect since much depends upon what is understood by "fundamentals." Commonly such fundamentals would certainly comprise religion, culture and views on the economy and its organization. On all

[10] Durkheim, 1893; de Grazia, 1948. See above, Chap. 12.
[11] Löwenstein, 1952, pp. 175ff.
[12] Friedrich, a, 1959, and Wahl, a, 1959.

these fundamentals, the greatest diversity has characterized such polities as Great Britain and the Dominions, the United States and Switzerland. Fundamentals may generally be taken to be basic beliefs or convictions which provide the starting point for all discussion on actions to be taken, propositions that cannot be further analyzed and hence provide a foundation. The question as to what constitutes a fundamental cannot in a strict sense be answered, except autocratically. In a free society there will be disagreement on what constitutes a fundamental. It is worth recalling that *concordia*, concord, was the battle cry of the factions which fought the religious wars of sixteenth- and seventeenth-century Europe; for they too were convinced that agreement on fundamentals was essential to political order, and they considered it obvious that religion was the most important such fundamental.

The issue of legitimacy shows, however, that there ought indeed to be a *measure* of agreement on one fundamental, and that is the kind of rule that is right and the sort of ruler who is entitled to rule. In a democracy, this question will be settled in a constitution (written or unwritten), and an acceptance of the "rules of the game" laid down in the constitution will be the one basic agreement required. As this constitution typically embodies basic human freedoms, including more particularly the freedom of self-expression, the basic agreement may also paradoxically be called the agreement to disagree.[13]

Kant believed that an autocracy was able to grant greater freedom of conviction and self-expression than a constitutional monarchy. He was echoing Frederick II of Prussia's well-known quip that in his kingdom "everyone can go to heaven according to his own liking." [14] Kant thought that Frederick's policy was advancing enlightenment, because it showed that the freedom of public discussion of religious convictions "need not cause the slightest worry regarding public security and the unity of the commonwealth." The power of such a despot was so great that he could blandly say, "Argue as much as you want and about whatever you want, but obey." The ruler of a free country, Kant thought, could not be so tolerant. "A great degree of civic freedom seems to be advantageous for the freedom of the spirit of the people and yet it establishes impassable limits. A lesser degree of such civic freedom provides additional space in which the spirit of the people can develop to its full capacity." [15] Kant was thinking of the restrictions put upon Catholics and Non-Conformists in the England of his day and completely failed to anticipate the breadth

[13] Friedrich, 1942, chap. V, for further detail on the application of this principle to democracy; cf. also Bay, 1958, for a striking discussion of the relation of this issue to that of freedom. Cf. also below, Chaps. 20 and 21.

[14] Kant, in his essay *Was ist Aufklärung?* of which a translation is found in Friedrich, 1949, pp. 132ff.

[15] *Ibid.*, p. 139.

of freedom to be achieved soon afterwards in the American Constitution, and in the sequel in England and elsewhere. Conversely, the totalitarians of our time have shown an obsessive concern with agreement on fundamentals, and for a clear-cut ideological reason. Since their claim to legitimacy is based upon a secular ideology, more especially in the Communist case upon the interpretation of history embodied in dialectical materialism, it has proved very difficult for them to provide even the minimum of freedom in matters of religion and other basic convictions, in spite of their vast and virtually unassailable power.

If legitimacy can be achieved only when there exists a prevalent communal belief as to rightful rule, it follows that there may be political conditions under which legitimacy is not possible. Such conditions are usually felt to be undesirable, for the good reason that it is helpful for a government to be legitimate. We are face to face with a primary proposition regarding legitimacy, namely, that legitimate rule is more effective rule, other things being equal, than nonlegitimate rule. This proposition is really a corollary to a proposition about consensual power (see above, pp. 164ff.). For the reason for this proposition is that legitimacy enhances consensus and consent, and consent facilitates rule. There are possibilities for quantification here, both in respect to the degree of intensity of belief and the extent of its acceptance. Thus, when rule is based on elections, such rule will be more effective (other things being equal) if 80 per cent of a given political community hold a belief that elections are a ground of legitimate rule than if 60 per cent hold it, and less so than if 95 per cent hold it. The factor of intensity complicates the situation, because we lack proper indices for it; but it is probably correct to say that a greater intensity of belief on the part of 60 per cent may make it the equivalent of 70, even 75, per cent of a less intense belief, but that no degree of intensity could make a belief held by say 25 per cent strong enough to satisfy the requirements of legitimacy. Since such beliefs are relatively simple propositions, they may be ascertained and made the basis of reasonably definite statements concerning whether a given rule is legitimate or not.

The fact that legitimate rule is apt to be more effective rule has the consequence that rulers seek to remain or to become legitimate. This second proposition is important for an understanding of certain kinds of political activity, for example, the totalitarian "passion for unanimity"[16] and their retention of democratic voting procedures under conditions which make these procedures a sham. There are two ways in which rulers may attempt to make their rule legitimate. One is to assimilate their conduct to the prevalent belief, that is to say, take some action which would legitimize their position. Thus Napoleon Bonaparte, not content with an

[16] Friedrich and Brzezinski, 1956, chap. 8.

attempt at democratic legitimacy through referendum votes, "crowned" himself Emperor and afterwards married the daughter of the Emperor of Austria in an effort to adapt himself to prevalent notions of monarchic legitimacy (both being juristic types). Not content with these efforts, he sought a measure of religious legitimacy through a concordat with the Holy See.[17] The other method is to try to change the view concerning the title to rule which prevails in the community. The large-scale efforts at indoctrination along certain lines of ideology characteristic of totalitarian regimes involve such an attempt, for example, to convince people that, in accordance with the notions of dialectical materialism and the view of history it implies, the rulers are "executing" the laws of history and therefore are "entitled to rule." Metternich's harsh measures in prosecuting the rather feeble and timid manifestations of a liberal and democratic outlook cannot be understood in terms merely of his position as an effective servant of the legitimate monarch who was the Emperor of Austria, because these liberals and democrats were not in a position to challenge his rule. But they can be understood as attempts at broadening the extent to which monarchical legitimacy was accepted by the people.[18] History is replete with parallel examples, the most famous perhaps being the French King Henry IV's adoption of the Catholic faith in order to legitimize his rule over a country which had a majority believing that only a Catholic could rightfully hold title to the monarchy. His cynical exclamation upon entering Paris in 1594 that "Paris is worth a mass," showed profound insight into the conditions of effective rule. The development in the Soviet Union is interesting from this point of view, because it shows the possibility of a bifurcation in grounds of legitimacy; for while the legitimacy based on belief in dialectical materialism continues to provide that kind of "convictional" ground among members of the Communist Party, recent pronouncements of the rulers of Soviet Russia have increasingly referred to democratic legitimacy by speaking of "what the Soviet people like," and they have stressed plebiscitary "elections."

The first proposition must be implemented by a third which directly follows from it, and that is the following: legitimate rule maximizes political obligation. This proposition presupposes an understanding of what "political obligation" means. We wish to use this much abused term to designate the conviction on the part of the ruled that they should *obey* the rulers, that is, to conduct themselves in accordance with the rules made by those who do the ruling.[19] Maximizing such a conviction means the ruled feel "obliged" or "bound" to render obedience. We have earlier

[17] Lefebvre, 1935, vol. II, iii, pp. 2–4; vol. V, i, pp. 3–4; Geyl, 1949, p. 84 and *passim*.

[18] Kissinger, 1957.

[19] Green, 1879, 1927, esp. pp. 29–48; Kelsen, 1945, chap. 10, for traditional formulations.

explored (Chapter 12) five answers to the question "Why should I obey?" as related to paternal power. Each one of the answers, in terms of religion, status, interest, emotion or law, may with equal cogency be applied to a political ruler. But religion and status (tradition) work essentially through the title to rule in affecting men's conduct, and it can thus be seen that at least two (and maybe all) the answers to that question "Why should I obey?" are given once legitimacy is secured. And since, as we have seen, legitimacy, too, is a matter of degree, this rule can be stated in more nearly quantitative terms: the degree of effective obedience to a given rule is directly proportional to the degree of legitimacy which such rule possesses. The degree of political obligation, that is, the conviction that such obedience is due, is of course also proportional to the degree of legitimacy. Degree of legitimacy is taken here to mean the number of persons in a community who consider the title of the ruler good. If this number approaches 100 per cent, the degree of effective obedience will also approach 100 per cent, provided there are no interfering factors. With interfering factors, it will approach whatever is the percentage these factors will permit. The question of obedience involves, for example, the efficacy of punishment, which divides the various schools of criminal law, to mention only one major factor. This problem would take us too far afield here; we shall return to it in the chapter on responsibility (Chapter 17).

Here it seems necessary to explore further the problems of legitimacy in relation to traditional notions of justice, and more particularly to the Aristotelian doctrine which links justice to equality and interprets it as expressing various notions of equality. Legitimate government has been claimed to be "just" government. If, as in Hobbes and his positivist followers, the legitimate is equated with the legal, and the legal with the just, the proposition is nothing but a tautology. If more is meant by "just," then such a proposition may easily be an overstatement. We are anticipating a bit what constitutes a just political act—a question which will be dealt with more fully in the next chapter. In the present context and in light of the preliminary notion of justice as the epitome of all that is in conformity with communal values, convictions and beliefs, it remains to see whether justice in the Aristotelian sense bears a particular relation to legitimacy. The Aristotelian doctrine means that the acts of the political community, no less than those of individuals as citizens, are executed, when just, in such a way that wherever a *quid pro quo* is involved, as it is in rewards, punishments, offices and assignments, equals are treated equally. This was Aristotle's celebrated argument about distributive justice.[20]

[20] Aristotle, *Nichomachean Ethics,* V. esp. 1131a ff. He noted that arguments about what is equal are "the very source of all the quarrelling and wrangling in the world." The quotation in the text *ibid.*

In the political perspective, distributive justice is the important dimension. Distributive justice "is concerned with the distribution of honor, wealth, and such other goods as may be shared by members of the community." Its peculiar field is public law, and hence it is especially relevant to legitimacy. What distinguishes the radical democrat from the more or less aristocratic or plutocratic man is that he bases his political decisions, and hence more especially his decision as to who is entitled to rule, upon the notion that each man is equal to every other man in the ability to decide correctly who should rule him. He does *not* assert that all men are equally capable of ruling. In fact, he argues that the differences between men in this respect are so great that their selection cannot be left to such accidental forces as heredity or such extraneous capacities as the ability to acquire wealth.

Nonetheless, it is possible to say that Aristotle undertook to show that justice is peculiarly related to the value embodied in the idea of equality. This value assumption in favor of equality is translogical (Chapter 2), as it would be quite possible to argue that it would be better, perhaps in the sense of being more amusing, more stimulating, more in keeping with what nature decreed—*variatio delectat*—if equals were treated unequally as they are by fortune, if not by providence. But such subtleties have not appealed to most men; they have preferred equality. As Aristotle pointed out, however, such an assertion as that justice calls for equal treatment of equals raises more questions than it answers. For who is to be considered equal to whom? Leaving aside comparative evaluation as the core of judgments on what is just (Chapter 14), as well as the search for equality (Chapter 16), it should be noted here that in the process of legitimizing democratic rule, each adult person is made equal with every other such person by the deceptive device of giving him one vote in general elections. While such a device is far from accomplishing the pretended political equalization, it constitutes an important first step. How much so, has for some years been highlighted by the various devices utilized to withhold the vote from the Negroes in some states of the United States. But it is not the individual by himself, but the individual as a member of a group discriminated against, whom the vote would provide with great equality. This situation demonstrates how equality is subject to quantitative comparison in terms of more or less.

In short, we can say following Aristotle that the decisive distinction is that between numerical and proportional equality. Numerical equality equates each man as a unit with each other man. It is what we now ordinarily understand by equality and what we mean when we say that all citizens are equal before the law. Proportional equality gives to each man that which he is entitled to according to his ability, his achievements, his character, and so on. On closer examination, it is readily seen that the distinction between numerical and proportional equality and justice is not well stated in this form. It would be more nearly true to say that all justice is more or less proportional, and that numerical equality can be applied only in certain situations where all men can be treated as equal, as is the case in many provisions of the penal law. For even the most ardent egalitarian will not argue numerical justice in a field such as taxation. Jurisprudence has escaped from the paradoxical implications of numerical equality in this field by the device of "classification." When a tax law differentiates between the rich man and the poor, and levies higher taxes on the rich, it makes them unequal before the law. But, so the answer goes, the law "applies" to them equally; it is the law itself that has classified them according to wealth and income.[21] From what has been said, we may derive the proposition that the more nearly alike men are believed to be in a given situation, the more nearly numerical is their equality and the justice based upon it.

Now it is clear that in any kind of government, legitimacy always involves some kind of proportional equality, because the title to an office, high or low, will always be based upon reasons related to qualities which differentiate between men. If we look over the various grounds given above (p. 235), we find that they all relate legitimacy to differentiating characteristics. Even the most radical democrat in arguing for popular election of all office-holders does not plead for a random choice, but for picking him who seems best to the electorate. There is, however, one method of selection which appears to be based on a marginal notion of absolute and undifferentiated equality, and that is the choice by lot. It has therefore often been alleged that choice by lot is "democratic."[22] It should, however, be spoken of as anarchic, rather than democratic; admittedly it is egalitarian. Thus a person chosen by lot is beyond the pale of the argument about legitimacy, so to speak. The office is legitimate, but the person occupying it owes it to the breakdown of all notions concerning what would be a just title to an office.

But once the assessment as to which men are capable of ruling is placed in the discretion of a popular majority, it is evident that whatever happen to be the preoccupations of the people will determine the choice. The representativeness of different contenders will become a decisive factor (Chapter 17). So will the political situation in which the community finds itself. It has rather cynically been remarked in recent years that the ruler who improves the standard of living will be considered legitimate. More especially the achievement of "full employment" or something closely approximating it is often featured in contemporary industrialized communities. Only recently a leading American politician, in pleading for

[21] We omit here Aristotle's complex argument about arithmetic and geometric proportionality; see for this Kelsen, 1957, pp. 110–136.

[22] E.g., Werner Jaeger, 1943, vol. II.

the legitimacy of federalism, cited the capacity of his state to cope effectively with unemployment and proudly cited figures in support of his claim.[23] The capacity to "deliver" in terms of economic welfare certainly always has been an important source of legitimacy: the king as rainmaker (Chapter 10) is a well-known illustration, as is the Chinese belief that the "Son of Heaven" proves his legitimacy by his ability to provide for his people.

But other considerations, rivaling economic welfare, have frequently intruded themselves. Among these the most important is unquestionably "security," both in military and political (diplomatic) terms. Hobbes was the theorist who most radically affirmed the proposition that a ruler who fails to provide security loses his right to rule. "The obligation of Subjects to the Soveraign, is understood to last as long, and no longer, than the power lasteth, by which he is able to protect them." [24] Political obligation toward ruler and government depends upon effective performance by ruler and government in realizing the community's goals. This general observation is by no means restricted to government. In any association the leadership will have to prove its right to lead in similar fashion. This patent fact opens up the possibility of corruption of the political order, and this possibility has recurrently served as a ground for the criticism and even the rejection of popular government. The famous instance of Rome's corruption by *panem et circenses*, by the offer of free food and free shows, is only one of numerous cases where the corruption of the people's discretionary judgment concerning legitimacy has perverted the political order. What the critics of such situations have often overlooked is the incontrovertible observation that every political order has its specific mode of being perverted, which is tied, of course, to its peculiar system of rule and the mode of legitimizing it. For since legitimate rule is rule which is exercised by him who is believed to have a title to rule, it may be perverted by corrupting the believers.

In the twentieth century the above general propositions are qualified by the role of ideologies in determining the general outlook on the "right to rule." Broadly speaking, people are inclined in a nontraditional and nonreligious age to look toward ideologies for determining what is right and what is wrong (Chapter 4). Therefore, the ideology acquires a predominant power to legitimize rule. In democratic societies, this power is limited and provides additional scope for the party leader when he achieves office. Such legitimacy as his success at the polls gives him with

[23] Rockefeller, 1962, chap. 2.

[24] Hobbes, 1651, chap. XXI. He argues this proposition on the premise that "the right men have by nature to protect themselves, when none else protect them, can by no Covenant be relinquished." Such a normative argument may readily be stated in existential terms as the propensity of men to defend themselves. "The end of obedience is protection" is an existential universal proposition.

his following helps him to get over the setbacks and failures of his stewardship. His following explains away many of these failures in terms of the particular ideology. In totalitarian dictatorships, the official ideology upon which the ruling party is built provides the most effective ground for legitimacy.[25] This ineffable impact of the ideology through its legitimizing function probably explains the role of the party in the struggle over succession (Chapter 28).

A distinctive pattern of legitimacy, not to be confused with the typical totalitarian ideology, is that provided by modern nationalism. More especially in the newly emerging political orders, but already in the national unification and liberation movements in Europe (Italy, Germany, Poland and the Austrian succession states), the most potent source of legitimacy was effectiveness in forwarding the freedom of the emergent nation. Political figures as divergent as Bismarck and Cavour, Masaryk and Pilsudski, Bolivar, and the host of their equals in contemporary Asia and Africa all derive the legitimacy of their rule from their effectiveness in liberating and uniting the group that finds itself as a nation in the nascent political order. It is frequently impossible to determine whether the leader legitimizes the nation, or the nation the leader. The right to rule emerges in the interaction between the two, often in the course of violent sanguinary conflict, for example, in Algeria.[26]

All these forms of legitimizing rule in terms of popular preferences, whether broadly defined by ideologies or narrowly by such goals as prosperity, security or national freedom, are characteristic of an egalitarian outlook on legitimacy. This outlook is preoccupied not with what intrinsic capacity men have to govern, but with what performance they are able to offer. The "capacity" is relegated to the "lower" echelons of administrative personnel who are expected to demonstrate "merit" through elaborate examinations based upon long training and/or experience. At this point, the kinship between the democratic and bureaucratic outlook is patently demonstrated. Their joint emphasis contrasts sharply with the aristocratic view, as well as with its assorted "elitist" revivals in contemporary writings on politics (Chapter 18).

By contrast, the aristocratic notion of legitimacy is based on the belief that the capacity to rule is hereditary, and on the disbelief in the capacity of most men to make a sensible choice between different candidates for public office. The same disbelief animates the plutocratic idea of legitimacy, but it argues positively that the acquisition and possession of wealth makes for sound rule. We omit here reference to other types of legitimacy and content ourselves with these three kinds of juristic-phil-

[25] Friedrich and Brzezinski, 1956, chaps. 3 and 7. Cf. also Brzezinski, 1962, chap. 3, pp. 65ff.

[26] Tillion, 1958, esp. chap. 3.

osophical legitimacy in order to show how the idea of justice intrudes itself into the arguments about legitimacy. It is a special sort of distributive justice, if you will, to assign offices according to merit, variously defined. Though rulership is a burden as well as a prize, let alone a reward, notions about merit are at work in determining the ground upon which legitimacy is based in a particular community.

But is this all that can be said? Does the problem have to be left in this strictly relative frame of reference? Is there no reason for preferring one kind of legitimacy to another on generally valid grounds? The answer to this question turns upon an aspect of justice which has only recently received a certain amount of attention, and that is the relation of justice to truth. It will be explored in the next chapter. As with authority, arguments concerning legitimacy cannot be stated without facing the question as to whether the propositions upon which such statements rests are true or not. What is true is admittedly an open question; but the avoidance of claims to absolute truth does not prevent one from recognizing that some statements are more true than others, as far as we know. This possibility affects all statements concerning legitimacy. They too are matters of degree. One kind of government, one kind of ruler, is more legitimate than another, and this demonstrable fact profoundly affects the authority and power he is able to wield. This means, however, in its application to legitimacy, that the findings of political science, as well as of other social sciences, are crucially relevant to a final proposition concerning legitimacy. We have used the term to denote whether a given rulership is believed to be based on a good title by most of those subject to it. As scientific knowledge spreads, certain grounds appear to an increasing number of persons no longer right, because the assertions associated with the particular ground are no longer believable; they appear untrue. Quite a few of the types of legitimacy which have played a great role in the past have ceased to do so because scientific knowledge does not permit, for example, the belief in the importance of "blood." Therefore we can say that legitimacy, being a special case of distributive justice, is affected by the progress of scientific knowledge as it affects the beliefs that can be entertained in any modern community. The weakness of monarchy today is a striking instance of the truth of this proposition. But we must hasten to add that the ideological abuse of scientific knowledge, as it has occurred in modern totalitarian movements, demonstrates the dangers inherent in this relation among science, truth, justice and legitimacy. For on such ideological abuses of economic and biological knowledge has been erected the positive claim to legitimacy of communist and fascist rulers. Negatively, these rulers have challenged the claim to legitimacy by democratic rulers, pointing to perversions of the vote by class-motivated capitalists, and in the process undermining the legitimacy of any political order but their own.

chapter
14
Justice: The Just Political Act

Twice is he armed that has his quarrel just.
Shakespeare

And four times he who gets his fist in fust.
Josh Billings

WHAT IS JUSTICE? One of the perennial questions of political and legal philosophy, it has produced many a normative or stipulative reply. In the pages which follow, an attempt is made to answer a more specific question: What aspect of political situations do men usually refer to when they say that the acts involved in it are just? Before taking up this question, we shall briefly indicate which questions about justice we do not propose to take up, and why. After having delineated the answer to our proper question, we hope to show the further light which it throws upon the problems of authority and legitimacy. Finally, we shall deal with the reasoning component and the link of the just to the true.

The famous triad *Honeste vivere, neminem laedere, suum cuique tribuere* (to live honorably, to injure no man, to render to every man his due) is not only the broad formula of natural law upon which the *Corpus Juris Civilis* is supposed to rest, but also the ground upon which philosophers, notably Leibnitz and Kant, have built their theories of justice.[1]

[1] Each correlates one phrase of the triad with a particular kind of justice, Kant by distinguishing a *lex justi, lex juridica* and *lex justitiae*, of which the last more specifically deals with justice. Justice is interpreted by Kant as commanding: "Enter into a state in which for everyone what is his own may be secured toward everyone else!" *Metaphysik der Sitten*, in *Werke* (ed. Cassirer), vol. VII, p. 38.

These propositions have been treated as intuitively known and universally accepted; their formulation is so general that it is as difficult to dispute such a claim as to prove it. In this connection its "eternal" validity has time and again been asserted. Burke, although at other times he wrote of the dubious and uncertain nature of justice, at one time asserted that "there is one thing, and one thing only, which defies all mutation; that which existed before the world, and will survive the fabric of the world itself; I mean justice; that justice, which, emanating from the Divinity, has a place in the breast of every one of us . . . and which will stand, after this globe is burnt to ashes, our advocate or accuser before the great judge . . ." [2] Here the religious basis of such a view is made laudably explicit; Burke treats it as based upon transcendent convictions. Jurists, whether accepting or rejecting them, have tended to the view that it is difficult to specify definite legal norms as derived from these propositions. These are much discussed problems, but we shall not try to deal with them.[3]

This approach undoubtedly expresses an elemental view of justice in general.[4] But we shall here not be concerned with justice, but with the function of justice in the political community. What particular act or complex of acts and/or events, recurrent in all politics, what concrete political experience, is meant when people speak of justice and injustice? This is the empirical question to which the following analysis is addressed.

[2] *Works*, vol. VIII, 1839, p. 572.

[3] A valuable recent treatment of the legal aspects, stressing the importance of "mine" and "thine" and the assumption of "title" in legal justice, is found in Davitt, 1959, esp. chap. III. Cf. also the interesting discussion in K. N. Llewellyn, 1960, esp. at pp. 59f. and 268ff., which links a "felt duty to justice" with what he calls "situation sense." He states that "there is indeed at work, and consciously, a recognition of and a will to avoid some possible results as being *un*just, or, more closely, unfair." Both authors offer many references to cases.

[4] An interesting discussion of this traditional concept is found in the brief but brilliant study by Perelman, 1945. He expounds the notion that formal or abstract justice is "un principe d'action selon lequel les êtres d'une même catégorie essentielle doivent être traités de la même façon" (p. 27), and then proceeds to show that if one considers the several possibilities of what might be understood to be the basis of classification (equal merit, equal work, etc.) one finds that to the abstract and formal notion of justice there correspond "concrete" notions which are based upon *value* judgments held in particular groups and communities within which justice is discussed and made the basis of decisions. It will be seen that in the political perspective only these concrete notions of justice are relevant and that, therefore, the above definition needs to be modified by adding "according to the value preferences prevailing in a given community." Cf. also the interesting summaries on "national" conceptions by Eugenio Garin, Luis Recaséns Siches, Gregory Vlastos, Ch. Perelman and W. G. Becker, in *Revue Internationale de Philosophie*, Nr. 41, 1957, with an introduction by Richard McKeon on "The Meanings of Justice among Traditions of Thought," pp. 253–257.

It is not pretended that this question is the only one which might be raised with regard to justice, but that it is one possible one, and an important one at that.[5]

We do not propose to deal, either, with the issues David Hume raised when he discussed justice in utilitarian terms. His views have recently had a rebirth in the writings of certain language philosophers;[6] like his, they seem to be premised upon the proposition (unproved) that "all virtuous actions derive their merit only from virtuous motives,"[7] and that, therefore, just actions can be just only as a result of "artifice" or conventions. "It [this convention] is only a general sense of common interest," related to the notion of mutuality which makes a man behave toward his neighbor as he wishes the neighbor to behave toward him, more especially regarding property. Hume's ingenuous argument is necessitated by his dubious assumption—a secularized version of Christian ethics. For while there can be no question that motivations play their role in ethics, and hence particular acts may be considered just because "utility pleases," as Hume put it, the justice of acts and rules is a less subjective datum. The justness of a judge's decision does not depend upon whether he was motivated by Hume's general sentiments, *or* rather, because, being very ambitious, he saw it as a chance to secure advancement, *or* again, because, being of a particular religious persuasion, he entertained certain prejudices. The quality of justness in his decision depends upon its possessing a certain objective relation to the setting in which it occurs; this concept will presently be more explicitly specified. At least, that is the political theorist's view of it, as he observes political behavior and seeks to generalize upon it. Justice expresses a political relation of persons and things and as such has a function in political situations.

Of the three constituents of the triad, the Roman law singled out the third for special emphasis; indeed, the *Corpus Juris* begins with identifying this triad with justice after explicating the *suum* as meaning *jus*.[8] But it discusses it as a quality of human beings, or rather of their will, and adds the specification that it must be a constant and perpetual will. In

[5] Perelman, in his work cited above, develops an interesting distinction between a just act and a just rule, the latter being said to be just when it is not arbitrary, in the sense of being in keeping with a system of norms from which it derives. This distinction, whatever its value for other purposes, is not germane to our question, since, politically speaking, rule-making is a particular kind of political act; arbitrary acts, as well as rules, are unjust.

[6] Notably Mabbott and Rawls; cf. Mabbott, a, 1953; Rawls, a, 1956, pp. 3ff. Cf. also Nowell-Smith, 1954, pp. 263ff. and 271ff., and the shrewd comment by Gregory Vlastos in the piece cited in fn. 4.

[7] Hume, *Treatise*, 3.2.1.

[8] *Justitia est constans et perpetua voluntas jus suum cuique tribuens;* see *Institutions* I.1.1. The broader formula, used above, is found *ibid.*, I.1.3.

short, it refers to justice as a subjective quality.[9] Again, we are not here concerned with such "excellence," that is, with justice as a "virtue," as a commendable trait of human beings.[10] It is well known that the great philosophers of classical antiquity, especially Plato and Aristotle, were very much preoccupied with this aspect of the matter, and their core question was: Who is a just man? In terms of the present analysis, it is not difficult to answer this question once our primary question has been resolved; for the just man is the man who behaves justly, that is, who takes just action, who acts justly. Whether such behavior is in turn the result of a certain character, a disposition of the "soul," as Plato was inclined to argue,[11] is a question for the psychologist and perhaps the metaphysician; for it seeks to *explain why* people act justly, rather than to describe what it is that they do when they are said to be so acting. It will be shown that there may also be strictly political explanations for a man's acting justly, but these explanations may be said to be extrinsic, as contrasted with the intrinsic explanations of psychology and metaphysics (as well as religion).

Since the ancients, it has been recognized that justice is closely related to goodness. Plato, in drawing his famous and questionable analogy between the individual human being and the political community, asserted that a just political community was one in which a lasting order prevailed. In such an order the wise ruled, the "spirited" or energetic carried out the rulers' orders and defended the community, while the moderate attended to the various economic and related chores. The Good in the fullest sense was thus realized. Justice served goodness by ordering human relations in a stable hierarchy. This is not the place in which once more to restate Plato's doctrine of ideas which provides the rational (philosophical) underpinning for such an elitist structure. The Platonic position is cited because it contains a specific *political* doctrine of justice as the ideally right ordering of the political community. Even he who shares neither Plato's political outlook nor his metaphysical convictions, can recognize that implicit is the proposition that justice has something to do with whether actions of men in communities are in conformity with the values and beliefs shared by the members or not. But if justice were merely to be defined in terms of such conformity with communal values and beliefs,

[9] God, in the Jewish and Christian theology, also possesses this quality to a supreme degree, but it manifests itself only as "distributive" justice; cf. Thomas Aquinas, *Summa Theologica*, I.q.21.art. 1.

[10] See for a classical treatment of justice as a virtue N. Hartmann, 1925, who in his ethics of values contrasts justice as a *Tugendwert* with the situation value (*Sachverhaltswert*) of law (chap. 44, esp. at pp. 384ff.).

[11] *The Republic*, 434a and 441b and c; 443c: "The just man acts to order his own inner life . . . and is at peace with himself."

it would become indistinguishable from goodness. A distinctive trait of the particular kind of goodness of actions which is justice must be identified (and has been identified, of course).[12] It is implicit in the Aristotelian doctrine which relates justice to equality.

We are now at the point where the basic position may be stated explicitly; for this doctrine relating justice to equality may be put more broadly by stressing the comparison involved in equality judgments. An action may be said to be just, and hence likewise a rule, a judgment or a decision, when it involves a comparative evaluation of the persons affected by the action, and when that comparison accords with the values and beliefs of the political community. This is the point of Aristotle's *isotes*, which is politically relevant and which can be summed up in the statement that equals should be treated equally. For the alleged equality can become a standard only when it is concretely stated what are the values and beliefs relevant to a determination of equality.[13] The recurrent political situation which can be observed wherever human beings live in political communities is that actions are praised when they appear to be based upon a comparative evaluation of the several persons affected that is in keeping with the prevailing values and beliefs; and that other actions are condemned when they do not appear so based.

Such a tie-in with prevalent values seems to be at variance with the notion of impartiality which is customarily associated with "justice." The proverbial "blindness" of justice refers to this aspect of just acts and just rules; they are said not to differentiate between persons. Actually, as we have just seen, such differentiation is typically part of a just act. It is just *because* it differentiates. Aristotle's distinction between proportional and numerical equality was meant to cope with that difficulty, and we can similarly say with Orwell's big brother pig that "we are all equal, but some are more equal than others." The role of impartiality is analogous: only an impartiality moulded and determined by the value preferences of the political community is considered truly impartial. To put it paradoxically, only a partiality to the prevalent values will appear truly impartial. To let

[12] Perelman, in his contribution to the symposium cited in fn. 4, proposes to make the justice of the person distinctively higher than that of the act and the rule, namely, the *rejection of inhumanity*, thus adding another *summum bonum* standard of justice, linked to those expounded by del Vecchio, 1951 (5th ed.) and 1955 (Engl. ed.), Recaséns Siches (fn. 4) and the late Radbruch (fn. 13). He sums up his view thus "L'acte juste est correction, rejet de l'inégalité. La règle juste est raison, rejet de l'arbitraire. L'homme juste est conscience, rejet de l'inhumanité. L'idéal de justice . . . combine tous ces points de vue. . . ." *Ibid.*, p. 359.

[13] Perelman, 1945, pp. 15ff., identifies six formulas; Brecht, 1959, pp. 30ff., briefly describes fifteen in terms of highest values as "absolute standards of justice"; Radbruch, 1932, pp. 12ff., 58ff., 70ff., points out the partisan nature of these several "figures" of justice. Cf. also Brecht's acute comments, pp. 357ff., and Kelsen, 1957.

women and children use the fire exit first appears "just"; the guard seeing to it appears impartial in insisting upon such partiality.[14] Such partiality appears just because it conforms to the values and beliefs prevalent in a given community. What the requirement of not being partial asks of the just act is that it not deviate from what the prevalent values and beliefs call for in comparative evaluation of persons and their situations, by yielding to particular interests. Is it then a matter of disinterestedness rather than impartiality? No. For the same objections can be raised to disinterestedness. All that really can be derived from the general principle of comparative evaluation is the absence of arbitrariness. For such arbitrariness is clearly incompatible with adherence to prevalent beliefs in making the evaluation.[15] It has therefore always played a role in discussions on justice.

Related to this avoidance of the arbitrary is that of the impossible. The structure of the relation is somewhat different, however. An act that attempts the impossible when taken by a person by himself may be considered stupid rather than unjust, or even noble under certain conditions. It becomes unjust if it consists in a demand, order or other norm requiring of those to whom it applies that they do the impossible. *Ultra posse nemo obligatur* is an ancient rule expressive of such inherent injustice. Again, we can say that it derives directly from the very nature of comparative evaluation in terms of prevalent values and beliefs. The difficulty with this derivative principle stems from the uncertainties surrounding what is "impossible," especially in the political sphere.[16] Patent impossibility is rarely involved in these situations, so that what seems unjust to one may seem quite just to another. It is existentially unjust only when the impossibility can be supported by reasoned elaboration in terms of the prevalent values and beliefs.

The avoidance of the arbitrary and the impossible reinforces the comparative evaluation that is just when it is adequate. Discrimination and classification do not appear as "deviations" from a presupposed general equality, but as reasonable differentiations against which the proponent of equality has to argue. In modern philosophy, the problem has often been reversed, because of the value claim of equality, especially in America. It then becomes the task of political theorizing to "explain" such "deviations." One might attempt to "explain" all such value-determined deviations from an absolute numerical equality of treatment by interpreting them as based on three grounds: (1) agreement, (2) special contribu-

[14] Such "dialectics" of impartiality seems inadequately recognized in G. Vlastos' paper cited in fn. 4 above.

[15] This point is made by Brecht, 1958, pp. 296ff., in what he terms the second, third and fourth postulates of justice. The absence of arbitrariness is also made a key criterion of just acts by Perelman, 1945, pp. 67ff.

[16] Helmut Schoeck, 1959, *passim*. Cf. Friedrich, a, 1958.

tion and (3) special need.[17] There can be no question that all three of these grounds involve particular and communally determined value judgments, providing qualifications of one sort or another. It does not seem very satisfactory, however, from a political standpoint, first to erect an unreal standard—absolute numerical equality—as the norm, and then to treat all real situations involving justice as deviations from it. Actually, the three grounds identified here possess relevance even within our more general conceptual framework; for there may, from time to time, be deviations from the communally determined comparative evaluation of persons and situations. These are indeed based upon one of the three grounds. But it is evident that each provides only a limited leeway; because agreements (contracts) become invalid if they deviate too markedly,[18] special contributions will themselves be evaluated in terms of prevalent values and beliefs, and the same holds true of special needs. Thus the above-mentioned just action at a fire exit might be justly altered if an old man in a wheel chair appeared (special need) or a fireman wanted to pass (special contribution). The prevalent values cannot be avoided in determining what is just.

Before we enter upon a fuller exploration of the links between justice and other basic political phenomena, it seems desirable to reinforce the preceding analysis by considering injustice as a disvalue related to disvalues and disbeliefs. It is a remarkable fact that men's feelings are more sharply aroused by an act of injustice than by one of justice.[19] Whatever may be the psychological reasons for this fact and they are many—the ontological or existential ground upon which it rests is the threat to the beliefs and values cherished by a person and the consequent anxiety induced in him. An unjust act causes a man anguish, because it not only challenges a particular belief and value, but, because of the interrelation of such beliefs and values, it challenges the community as a system of shared values and beliefs. Conflicts over justice are embittered by explicitly experienced injustice. One claims that it is unjust to take his property, another that it is unjust that his children should not be properly educated; one argues the injustice of having to continue a marriage without love, another that it is unjust to leave children without a home. Such arguments can, with difficulty, be fitted into the generalizations in terms of justice; it is more evident that they involve comparisons. In any case, they show

[17] Vlastos, in his contribution to the symposium on justice (fn. 4) in which he deals with the views of the English-speaking philosophers, suggests the triad as a summary of their varied approaches; cf. esp. p. 343, ". . . most important component of justice . . . the equal claim all men can rightly make on the community simply because they are men. . . ."

[18] Note the provisions in various legal orders to the effect that a contract which violates good mores is void, for example.

[19] Cf. Cahn, 1949.

that justice relates actions to the entire value and belief system by insisting that they be based upon valid comparisons of the persons involved and their several competing value claims.[20]

Such value claims and their comparisons are, both on account of the *number* of values and beliefs and the degree of intensity with which they are felt, not absolutes, but they possess degrees of strength. Hence all analyses of just political acts proceed not in terms of a radical dichotomy of *either* just *or* unjust, but rather in terms of *more* or *less* just. It is the degree of relatedness to values which determines the relative justice of an act, and hence also of a person as political actor. Such degrees of justness may be, though they usually will not be, quantifiable. An important field of more detailed inquiry lies ahead here. Due to the in-built contradictions of value aggregates found in actual political communities, recurrent attempts have been made to relate justice to the "inner convictions" of individual persons, the "disposition of the soul" that was mentioned at the outset; but by so doing, we remove the just from the political perspective. The most just act is the act which is compatible with the largest number of values and beliefs, allowance being made also for their intensity. Thus it might be claimed that it would be more just to let the man in the wheel chair pass, and less just (and in that sense, unjust) to allow some of the women and children nearest the exit to precede him. As a result, controversies about justice may frequently be reduced in sharpness and bitterness by seeing them as alternative ways of effectuating a distinctive part of the value aggregate of the community.

The requirement of "prevalence" of the values and beliefs involved in the comparison raises the question of when such prevalence does in fact exist. That question calls for an exploration of authority and legitimacy. Justice, in the political perspective, is therefore inseparable from both authority and legitimacy. Conformity with values and beliefs prevailing in a political community raises issues which are beyond unequivocal demonstration; assertions concerning it will therefore turn upon the two questions: Does the person who asserts such conformity speak with authority? and Does he legitimately occupy the position or office which enables him to speak? Conversely, the authority of an actor, a rule-maker or a ruler will contribute to the acts and rules being just. Authority is associated with communications having the potentiality for reasoned elaboration, and the bearer of such authority presumably possesses the capacity to actualize this potentiality. One of the most important kinds of reasoned elaboration is that which elaborates in terms of the common values and beliefs shared by a political community. Since the comparative evaluation of persons affected by a given action, such as a rule or a decision to be made, turns upon values, obviously it is held to be just when the judgment upon

[20] Friedrich, 1958, p. 199. Cahn, 1949, pp. 124ff.

which the evaluation is based accords with the value judgments of those who consider it just; unjust, when the opposite. The bald statement that political authority *is* just power, or *ought to be*, provides a shorthand expression for the fact that authority provides the bridge, that is, the link, between power and justice. Actually, a given person may possess the capacity for reasoned elaboration in terms of one set of values, for example, Christian, and not in terms of another, Masai. Therefore, Nterenke can say to his English lawyer friend: "You might have presented the case with more knowledge of what a Masai feels. Our language is very different. Our life is also completely different. A translation into English words is not enough. Our traditions, our feeling also must be translated. . . . Your law is not our law. . . . To us cattle are just as important as people. That is an absolute fact." [21]

The linking of authority with justice has been traditional in Catholic political thought. It is built, however, upon the notion that only a particular kind of reasoning, namely, that which is in accordance with Christian theology, provides authority of a genuine kind. It involved a dramatic reevaluation of the concept of justice, as found in Cicero, and derived from Plato and Aristotle. This reevaluation is explicitly set forth by St. Augustine in those passages in which he disputes Cicero's conception of a republic as founded on justice.[22] Recalling that justice means to give to everyone what is his (due), he states that since in the Roman Republic "demons" were worshipped, rather than the true God, it is evident that God did not receive what was due him. Therefore, unless one were to refuse the name of republic to Rome, which seems inconvenient, it is better to reject the Ciceronian definition [23] and to substitute another. The great bishop suggests that we might "say that a people is a gathering of reasonable beings bound together by common agreement as to the objects of their affection, and that a republic is composed of such a people." [24] We have only to observe what a people cherish in order to discover its character and the kind of political order which suits it. In modern words a political community rests upon common values and beliefs. But there exists a true *civitas,* the city of God, in which justice in the full sense is realized, and its representative on this earth, the church, is the nearest

[21] Richard Llewellyn, 1961, pp. 25–28. This entire moving account is concerned with a trial that was "just" according to British and Christian standards, but "unjust" according to Masai values. Therefore the court had no authority, in spite of its power, except for the British.

[22] *Civitas Dei,* XI and XIX. Chaps. 21–24, referring to Cicero, *De Republica,* I.25. Figgis, 1921, chap. III, and R. W. and A. J. Carlyle, *Medieval Political Theory,* vol. I, 1903, pp. 510ff.

[23] *Op. cit.,* XIX chap. 21. 1926, esp. pp. 186ff.

[24] *Ibid.,* chap. 24. The famous statement "Remota justitia quid sunt regna nisi magna latrocinia" must be interpreted accordingly.

approximation to it, whereas *regna* and *respublicae*, kingdoms and republics, are serving to maintain peace and order. The church makes use of this peace, while the heavenly city "calls citizens out of all nations, and gathers together a society of pilgrims of all languages, not scrupling about diversities of manners, laws and institutions whereby earthly peace is secured and maintained."[25] But within this *civitas* authority is hierarchical, and that means justice is determined accordingly, in part directly by the priesthood, in part indirectly by secular powers. The overarching requirement of doctrinal authority calls for an evaluation of the activities of the latter by the former. This conclusion was not stated by St. Augustine; it was, however, implicit in his outlook and was, reinforced by Platonic notions, evolved in the course of the Middle Ages.

This view becomes generally valid if it is recognized that different beliefs may produce different authorities, and that it is the function of authority to ensure that comparative evaluations of situations and persons are made by those possessing the capacity for reasoned evaluation, such as judges, teachers and, more recently, experts and specialists. The appearance of the latter has caused some very serious difficulties, as a number of trials and retrials have made evident. For if, in criminal law, it is thought that an illness, and more especially a mental illness, constitutes a valid difference and may justify nonapplication of the law, then the determination of whether a given individual belongs to this special category or class of persons becomes of vital importance. The authority of a psychiatrist is obviously tied in with his professional training and standing; even if a court or jury, let alone the general public, can follow his views only in part, they will be accepted as authoritative because of his capacity for reasoned elaboration of the comparative evaluation he has offered.[26]

Does such a position oblige us to accept value-relativism and hence a relativistic conception of justice?[27] By no means. For the values themselves are not beyond reasoning and reasoned elaboration, as is evident in the case of the medical expert. Actually, the argument about values is going on all over the world. While the starting points may be as far apart as the Christian and the Masai, the search for justice will lead to an elaboration if the human beings cherishing these values are thrown into community. Indeed, it is the essence of politics, in a way, to argue about justice, that is to say, to argue about who may be compared with whom for what treatment. Modern parties are organizations fighting over, or

[25] *Ibid.*, chap. 17. In the sequel, St. Augustine stresses that the church "preserves and adopts" these secular systems of rule. McIlwain's divergent interpretation, in 1932, pp. 154ff., is unconvincing. Cf. also Horn, 1934, vol. I, pp. 32f.

[26] S. de Grazia, 1952; Szasz, 1959.

[27] As is Kelsen's belief, 1957, pp. 22ff. It rests upon the false notion that values and facts are radically apart (p. 20).

arguing over, justice.[28] Justice is not static, but highly dynamic, since it seeks to relate the evolving values of the community to what is done on its behalf, whether in rule-making, settling disputes, or any other activity. Even in those ages when men thought that the only task was to find, to discover, the rules, they were actually fighting over them, as we can readily see in studying legal controversies in the European "Middle Ages," so called. Justice is never given; it is always a task to be achieved. Its incomplete realization does not result from the complexity of the criteria, but from their fluidity.[29] In fact, fluidity is not the right word either; for it is the steady evolution and devolution of values which causes the difficulty. Since this evolution occurs in time, and the evaluation also takes time, the standpoint of the original evaluator and the subsequent one who claims that the original one was "unjust" may differ by the value differential that has occurred in the intervening period. "Perfect justice" could be achieved only in the completely stable community, as Plato fully realized. And since he did not wish to give up seeking perfect justice, he had to seek to make the political community perfectly stable. In the process, freedom had to be surrendered for most of the community's members, with the result that the values involved in the comparisons which rendered actions just turned into disvalues.[30]

The Platonic blind alley brings us back to the problem of legitimacy in its relation to justice. It has often been said that legitimate government is "just" government. This proposition, when stated in such bland form, is an overstatement if viewed in light of our conception of justice. (It can, of course, be meant simply as a definition of justice, in which case it would mean that a just ruler is a legitimate one, a just man a man who is legitimately doing whatever he is doing.) But it contains a kernel of truth. For if justice relates communal values and beliefs to actions by providing comparisons between persons and their situations and thus enabling the actor to treat "equals" equally, then the extent of the success in doing so

[28] Radbruch, 1932, chap. 8, pp. 58ff.

[29] Perelman, 1945, pp. 44ff., argues that the employment of two or more characteristics is necessary in making a comparison and establishing a class. And he seeks to relate this issue to the problem of equity which would mediate justice; but equity is not opposed to justice, but mitigates the law. The difficulty is not that, and equity is not "une tendance à ne pas traiter de façon trop inégale les êtres faisant partie d'une même catégorie essentielle." His illustration of workers who are to be rewarded both according to their work and to their needs shows it; this is not a situation calling for equity, but for two interrelated pay scales, establishing the rate of pay by plotting the rates of work on one coordinate and the rates of need on the other. The point where they intersect will give the "just" rate of pay. (More complicated multiple factors present only minor mathematical difficulties.)

[30] For the proposition implied in the foregoing, which derives from the fact that values call for a valuer, that is to say, a free man who can choose between different possible positions, cf. Chaps. 2 and 20.

will help to convince those affected by the action that the ruler or other actor is a rightful ruler or actor.[31] In view of the very specific meaning which equality has acquired in modern political parlance, it is better to speak here not of equality, but of adequacy. When Aristotle, in his famous analysis of justice in terms of the mean (*mesótes*), undertook to show that justice is related to equality, he really had in mind the arguments of the various parties in the Greek city states over what was adequate treatment in terms of believed-in values. The suggestion that proportional equality must be admitted as an alternative to numerical equality was a skillful attempt at devaluing the argument in favor of equality in the modern sense of eliminating inequalities unsupported by the prevalent value judgments of the community. Proportional equality is inequality for which an argument, a reasoned elaboration, can be provided.[32]

It is the value system in its positive content which typically establishes the adequacy of the comparison upon which the inequality of treatment is based. If a man is punished justly, the comparison is not only or even primarily with other men likewise punished, though this is an important factor in the judgment. It is also usually a matter of making "the punishment fit the crime." The "fittingness" calls for comparison of the man before and after. Today, whipping a man publicly for stealing would seem unjust, even if it were done generally and to all thieves. It did not seem unjust to a community which valued property more and human life and dignity less.

This argument, insisting on adequacy and comparability of evaluations involved in decisions and actions, is peculiarly relevant in considering the relation between legitimacy and justice. All legitimacy being, as we said, a believed-in right to act, or more especially to rule, presupposes inequality (or, proportional equality). It calls for a judgment which says this person possesses the unusual qualities required for ruling us. If he does not, his rule is illegitimate. Such a judgment may be based upon several very different kinds of values: descent, merit and capacity, and election (confidence of those ruled), the last being perhaps the most important. They can, as is well known, occur in combination: only a man of certain descent (American born) and capacity (literate) who has been duly elected may thus be a legitimate ruler. Such a brief hint serves to bring out that legitimacy is a result of a communal judgment similar to that which the actor who acts justly engages in: a comparative evaluation

[31] See Chap. 13 for the proposition that legitimate rule is rightful rule, and that legitimacy is the term which describes quite generally the kind of situation in which the actor is believed by those affected (or most of them) to have a right to act, though not necessarily to act as he does.

[32] For an interesting, if one-sided, critique of Aristotle, see Kelsen, 1957, pp. 110–136; cf. also Salomon, 1937, an interesting study which is however concerned with *Recht* rather than *Gerechtigkeit*.

of a particular sort and thrust. Thus we conclude that legitimate government is not "just" government, but it is government based upon just action of those who establish and maintain it.

At this point in our analysis, it becomes important to consider further a position which Aristotle first developed when he distinguished between distributive (*dianemētikon*) and amending or corrective (*diorthōtikon*) justice. The distributive justice "is concerned with the distribution of honor, wealth and such other goods as may be shared by members of the community," more especially, therefore, power and rule.[33] The peculiar field of such distributive justice is, therefore, public office. What distinguishes the democrat from the more or less aristocratic or plutocratic partisan is that he bases his political decisions, and more especially his decision as to who is entitled to rule, upon the conviction that each man is equal to every other man in the ability to decide correctly who should rule him. He does not, except when he carries these views to their radical extreme, assert that all men are equally capable of ruling. In fact, he argues that the difference between men in this respect is so great that the selection of rulers cannot be left to such accidents as heredity or the acquisition of wealth involves.

The aristocratic notion of legitimacy is based upon the belief that the capacity to rule is hereditary, and on the disbelief in the capacity of most men to make a sensible choice between different candidates for public office. The same disbelief animates the plutocratic idea of legitimacy, but it argues positively that the acquisition and possession of wealth provide the basis for sound rulership. Omitting other types of legitimacy, we might say in sum that these three familiar types of legitimacy show how the idea of justice, of comparative evaluation for differential treatment, intrudes itself into the argument about legitimacy. It is a special sort of distributive justice, and though rulership is a burden, as well as a prize, or perhaps a reward, comparative evaluation is at work in determining the ground for legitimate rule.

Thus an interaction is apparent between legitimacy and justice: a just act is required to produce the legitimate ruler, while the legitimacy of the ruler helps render his actions just by providing them with the legitimacy which bare or brute power does not possess. This important double link between legitimacy and justice and the parallel link between authority and justice is at the present time manifested in the emergence of the new nations. The demand for an independent government or political order is based upon the interrelationship between justice, authority and legitimacy. The colonial power lacked authority and legitimacy to an increasing extent as the

[33]*Nichomachean Ethics*, 1130b ff. *Diorthōtikon* is often incorrectly rendered as "commutative"—a term used by Thomas Aquinas. In the view here favored rule is "stabilized and institutionalized power." Cf. Chap. 10.

values embodied in and expressed by its decisions and actions which were not those of the subject peoples were subjected to critical evaluation by them. Lacking such legitimacy and authority, they are deemed "unjust." The argument turns upon the fact that a new community is emerging whose value judgments are different from those of the former rulers. But it might here be interjected that such rule was always unjust. To support that argument, recourse is usually had to the particular concrete position of democratic legitimacy and the inherent belief in the equality of all men. It is patent that the men who set up colonial empires did not entertain such a belief, even though they may have professed the Christian faith. For this faith is far from unequivocal on the matter of rule, and the equality which it insists upon is that in the face of divinity; for "we are all miserable sinners." There exists another line of reasoning leading to the conclusion that such rule is always unjust. This argument depends upon a nonrelativistic conception of justice that requires further exploration now in another direction.

Since all justice presupposes comparison and evaluation, it is intimately linked to reasoning, as our demonstration of its link with authority has already indicated. The ancient symbolism of justice, blindfolded and cold, is indicative of this rational component of justice. It is most apparent in the work of courts. The judge is supposed to have good reasons for his decision. These reasons are intended to relate the decision to previous decisions and the rules involved in them. Hence his work can be stated in terms of syllogisms. Yet, basically, his work is not different from that of others who share in the government of the community. They, too, have to engage in extensive ratiocination. The life of the law certainly is shot through with logic, though equally surely it is not to be equated with logic. Judge Holmes's celebrated dictum may seem to deny this, but he would have been the first to recognize that it was a false dichotomy; for the life of law is reasoning upon experience.[34]

The tie between justice and reasoning suggests another tie, equally important and not always sufficiently emphasized, and that is the tie between justice and truth. An act, a decision, can be said to be just only if it is based upon objectively true thought, upon correct information.[35] To put this proposition in reverse may make its cogency more evident. When-

[34] Perelman, 1945, stresses the logical aspect, and in our view exaggerates it. He develops what he calls an "imperative syllogism" and claims that it exhausts the problem of the application of formal justice. But he rightly also insists upon "la parenté existant entre la justice et les exigences de notre raison" (pp. 56ff.). But must one carry this point to the extreme of alleging that "la justice formelle se ramène donc simplement à l'application d'une règle?" Such a proposition demonstrates once again the dubiousness of the category of "formal justice." Cf. above, fn. 4.

[35] Arnold Brecht, 1959, chap. XI, pp. 404ff., has rightly emphasized truth as among the "postulates" of justice. It is, however, an ancient notion; St. Augustine wrote (in *Against Lying*): "What is against truth cannot be just."

ever it can be shown that an act, whether of rule-making, settling of disputes, or any other, was based upon untrue information, whether because of lies or misunderstandings, the resulting act will seem unjust if the untrue assumptions were crucial for arriving at the decision to act in that way. That the facts be not untrue is a necessary premise of the comparative evaluation; it would not "hold" if the facts were not so. In terms of our earlier analysis, the comparison is falsified and thus a discrimination is applied which would not be found if the falsehood had been absent (or the reverse, of course).[36] Because this requirement of truth is so very apparent, "the necessity of stating it explicitly and inquiring into it is often overlooked." [37] In fact, the proposition linking justice with truth raises for justice the entire range of problems which truth conjures up. Obviously they cannot be here explored.[38] But two points need brief discussion. One is that truth is always an "open question." Truth is not given us, except as a task to be pursued. Because of its dependence upon truth, justice is likewise an "open question." It likewise can never be certain in any absolute sense. That is one reason that justice calls for tempering by mercy. It is not merely the element of discrimination which it contains but the uncertainty surrounding any "facts." The role of truth accounts for the importance of authority in rendering acts just; through reasoned elaboration authority can fill the gaps in the knowledge of truth. A comparable role is played by legitimacy, when the "right to decide" accomplishes what reason could not.

The other point is that truth is, in the political realm, often "impolitic." The famous "secrets of rule," the *arcana imperii* upon which the sixteenth and seventeenth centuries built their arguments in favor of "reason of state," often suggest that important information remains undisclosed. Chesterton, in *The Man Who Knew Too Much*, told a number of stories, in each of which the rendering of justice was made extremely difficult or impossible because of some secret of empire that could not be revealed. The administration of criminal justice is full of such situations, and criminal law has developed definite rules for dealing with a variety of them. Here is one of the points at which the divergence of law and justice is patent; law requires that it be made public,[39] and one reason why clemency is at times indicated is that the rule of law which is public does not

[36] In the case of justice as a quality of persons (which we excluded from this analysis) the above means that the actor must believe that the thoughts upon which his actions are based are true.

[37] Brecht, *op. cit.*, p. 414, emphasizes this point and adds that the proposition that "all men actually postulate truth in justice" is "nothing better than an 'inductive' generalization from observed fact." We think it *is* something better; for it inheres in the comparative evaluation upon which justice is based.

[38] For a recent comprehensive discussion see Jaspers, 1947, esp. part III, pp. 453ff.

[39] This aspect of law has been stressed from Cicero and Thomas Aquinas to Kant; even in the totalitarian regimes it is recognized.

meet the concrete situation which contains undisclosed aspects which have to be kept secret.

Circumstances such as these have at times misled thinkers into maintaining that truth is not a necessary condition of justice. What they recite are such cases as make a jury (and possibly the judge) deny that a certain fact existed, because the defectiveness of the legal rule would produce an "unjust" result. Actually, such cases prove, on the contrary, the paramount importance of the link to truth. Those seeking a just decision in such an instance are actually questioning the rule, not the circumstances of the situation. It is what has been called "situation sense," which means a sense for the situation as it actually exists,[40] that provides the truthful guide to the just decision, as against the truth-distorting implication of the defective rule. How justice is linked to truth in such cases may well be hidden from the casual onlooker or even the interested outsider. This is the circumstance which relates this phenomenon to the "secrets of rule."

The rational aspect of justice, derivative from the comparative evaluation of persons and situations upon which justice is built, has often been made the basis of arguing against anything like the "feeling for justice," or *Rechtsgefühl.*[41] While it is true that such arguments have often taken the form of circular reasoning when they presupposed the justice to which the feeling is related, it is nonetheless important to take account of the fact that some such feeling universally exists among men. We have already referred to the anxiety which is part of a sense of justice and have suggested that it is linked to the felt threat to the entire system of values which justice ties to particular acts by providing the appropriate comparative evaluation of persons and situations. In that sense one could perhaps speak of an *Unrechtsgefühl,* or sense of injustice. This threat to the values of a community involves as we said the political order of the community as such. Obviously, then, the rational component of justice and the feeling associated with it are not opposed to each other, but themselves part of the total syndrome of justice. A feeling that an injustice has been done is a feeling that the reasoned elaboration of the political order has been put in jeopardy, that something counterrational has occurred. If untruth becomes legitimate and authoritative, the foundations of authority and legitimacy are shaken and threatened with destruction. This set of reflections is the obverse of those upon which David Hume would found his society, a sense of the value of the communal bond.[42]

[40] Cf. K. N. Llewellyn as cited above, fn. 3.

[41] Krabbe, 1906; cf. also, 1919, 1922, esp. pp. 47f. This view has recently been stated in the theological perspective by Brunner, 1950, pp. 4ff., when he asserts that "in jedem Menschen lebt ein Gefühl von Recht und Unrecht. . . . Es ist ein wie immer unklares Wissen um eine Ordnung, um etwas, was sich gehört, das sein soll, eine Ordnung, die nicht verletzt werden darf."

[42] David Hume, 1739, 3.2.2.

It is, therefore, in a sense true that "the just is the straight, the unbendable, is that which is oriented toward the same point."[43] But only within the limits of allowable comparisons. Beyond it, this very "straightness," when it violates the sense of justice, is rather characteristic of the law in its conflict with justice than of justice itself. It is undoubtedly the function of justice to serve as a standard for evaluating the law. In the word jus-tice, the *jus*, that is, *droit*, right, *dikē*, etc., is embodied, and such words as *dikaiosyne* and *Ge-recht-igkeit* carry the aboriginal implication of ancient right (believed-in values) as against positively established law (statute). Justice, in the legal perspective, can be understood only if it is taken to be the "right" solution, be it act or rule, toward which the law is oriented as an approximation.[44] Such an approximate realization is a dynamic process which takes place in time; it is dominated by forces struggling with each other for their effectualization within the general framework of the political order, as we have seen. But the underlying assumption of all such processes is the notion that political acts *ought to be* just in the sense in which we have described justice. Justice in this sense introduces the dynamic element into the legal order and continues to transform it in accordance with the emerging groups and the values which they cherish and insist upon.[45]

This dynamizing function of "justice" in the legal sphere, its specific political function, may be made more explicit by a further reflection upon the Aristotelian notion of justice as equality. If one starts from the premise that men ought to be equal to each other, that they should, for example, be "equal before the law," the question of equality becomes political; for it now becomes important who determines the relevant comparisons by which such equality is assessed, and more specifically who makes the just law. Such answers as were given by Rousseau in his doctrine of the general will evade the real issue. The development of modern politics in the West has given a fairly unequivocal, conventional answer: it is the majority of the people who decide about laws and their application to persons as classified into categories of equals.

Such a reference of the problem of justice to a majority decision does not solve it, but transposes it to another level of discourse. This level is the politics of a constitutional democracy. Only if it can be asserted that

[43] Brunner, 1950, p. 27. "Die Gerechtigkeit ist das Gerade, das Unbeugsame, auf den gleichen Punkt Ausgerichtete."

[44] For the following cf. Friedrich, 1958, pp. 191ff. The dubiousness of Perelman's concept of "abstract" or "formal" justice may once more be seen in his assertion that there cannot be any conflict between formal justice and law; such conflicts can occur only between "concrete" justice and law, because in concrete justice the "values" are specified on the basis of which a law may be judged "unjust." Cf. 1945, pp. 39–40.

[45] Justice as a standard of law is greatly stressed by W. G. Becker in his contribution to the collective study mentioned above, fn. 4.

in every free community there exists a sufficient number of conscientious and responsible persons who seek to find not only compromises between conflicting interests but a higher "synthesis" transcending the particular interests (and an accommodation of divergent values, beliefs and convictions) can the problem of justice be solved in the sense that a continuing concretization of the general task of successfully comparing persons in terms of believed-in values can be achieved.[46] That this is not always merely a matter of finding the diagonal in a parallelogram of forces between rival interests should be patent, though certain schools of thought in both jurisprudence and political theory have argued the opposite. Theirs was a useful corrective to the overstress laid on values transcending the interests of separate elements in the political community, the so-called "public interest" or "common good." [47] But it exaggerated. For while quite a few laws are nothing more than such compromises of particular interests (and as such, just), there are others which embody common interests and which usually involve passionate arguments concerning justice. For example, the laws regulating military service, or generally the governmental service, can scarcely be said to be compromises between rival interests. What holds for laws, holds equally for judicial decisions and other acts, of course. In all such cases, the common concern in the well-functioning of the political order is taken to be a first step toward the achievement of justice. Plato and Aristotle were right in stressing this aspect of the matter. Where they went astray was in believing that all or even most laws and other political acts belonged in this category, and in not recognizing that much of it is a matter of particular interests and their adjustment to each other. Nor was Plato right in thinking that just decisions on general rules were a task for the wise alone, to be arrived at without consultation with the members of the community at large. Aristotle had a sounder appreciation of this process, and at one point explicitly stated that the many are often better judges than the few,[48] not individually, but collectively. "Not the thoughts of the clever or wise, but the talk of the people create the law. . . . Thus a genuine, necessary right will be called for and implored, until it becomes law." Thus one modern thinker supported the view that "justice must forever be realized anew." This requirement of renovation does not, however, imply a particular authority, such as the people, unless it is realized that the continuous transformation of values and beliefs occurs in the community at large in response to new experience, while the tensions and crises engendered thereby call for a continuous adjustment of particular interests to each

[46] For the problems of the "common man" see Friedrich, 1958, pp. 194ff., as well as Kluckhohn, 1949, chap. IX.

[47] For the "public interest" cf. *Nomos V*, 1962.

[48] *Politics*, 1281b–1282a. Aristotle, in discussing the best form of political order, reverts to the elitism of Plato, however; cf. 1328b–1329b.

other, as well as the redefinition of the common interest or interests. That common interest is first and foremost an interest in the maintenance and well-functioning of the political order itself.

Let me conclude the argument by a rather poignant illustration of general import. A major political act of which the justice has been disputed through the ages is war. The argument over *justum bellum* shows very well how in the common man's view a just war is either a war fought for survival or one fought for an ideal (transcendent value). It is evident that wars may be compared and evaluated in terms of the values of very different and potentially hostile political communities, and consequently may appear just or unjust to either party. If, on the other hand, peace is posited as the paramount value, as was done by Kant, for example, then the notion of a just war appears absurd. The world community might well incline toward such a view, and seems increasingly to do so. But this development is not unrelated to technological developments which appear to render the attainment of the goals formerly sought by war actually unprocurable by that means. By these developments war ceases to remain an arguable just act, except in self-defense, due to the principle which excludes from justice those acts which are based upon a will to achieve the impossible. (See also Chapter 24.)

By way of summary and conclusion, the following might be said. After excluding some of the great traditional issues surrounding the just as a quality of acts, rules and persons, more especially whether justice is a relative or absolute value, or what it is in and by itself, and more specifically still what kind of excellence or virtue it is in persons, we concentrated on that aspect of political situations and acts which is very widely observed and inherent in most of them: the comparative evaluation of persons according to the prevailing values and beliefs of a political community. This, we showed, is the true kernel of Aristotle's doctrine of equality in relation to justice; in its original form it is paradoxical, because it suggests that the essence of equality is inequality.

That some values are prevalent, and that persons will be differentiated according to such values, seems indisputable. Such comparisons can be "in accord" with the prevailing values only if the facts upon which they are based are not untrue, if the relation between facts and values is not arbitrary, and if the norms derived from such comparisons are not asking the impossible. The criteria "not untrue," "not arbitrary," and "not impossible" are, in other words, derivatives of the inherent meaning of the quality of "just" as defined. A political act is just, therefore, if it is based upon a balanced evaluation of the persons it affects, comparing (and classifying) them upon the ground of values prevalent in the political community concerned. We finally showed that such a view of justice as a quality of political acts (including rules) mediates the tension between power and authority, and provides a deeper understanding of the legitimacy of rulers and their acts. By contrast, justice when defined in terms of the highest good, as has been done by philosophers, political and legal, from Plato to the present day, constitutes a specific application of the general principle of comparative evaluation; it resembles in its specificity the selection of some particular religious and national value system. Such normative definition of justice is not excluded by our analysis, but should be seen as the act of personal preference which it is in most instances. Only a reasoned elaboration of such a preference in terms of the demonstrable practical consequences for any given political order constitutes scientific knowledge. That such demonstrations are possible, only the analysis of actual political orders can show; the demonstrated links between justice, authority and legitimacy are an indication of the more fruitful lines of inquiry.

chapter

15

Law and Its Perversion

The law is always too short and too tight for growing humankind. The best you can do is do something and then make up some laws to fit and by the time that law gets on the books you would have done something different.

Robert Penn Warren, ALL THE KING'S MEN

AMONG THE POLITICAL ACTS whose justice is most commonly assumed and most often debated are laws and their aggregate, which is called the law.[1] But laws are not necessarily specific acts, such as commands issued by a legitimate ruler possessing authority; any prevalent rule which is usually enforced by such a ruler may be said to be a law, even when it simply expresses a regularity of behavior or conduct on the part of members of the political community. Since such rules apply to many persons at different times and in different places, each such rule really "contains" a great many commands or norms of conduct which would have to be reiterated over and over again if no general rule were possible. The making of such rules is among the most general and universally recurrent activities in the concrete political order (Chapter 25). Whether they are just or not is a question of fact to be determined by the comparative evaluation which has been analyzed in the preceding chapter.

It is important to realize that apart from the potential conflict be-

[1] The word "law" has no precise equivalent in continental European languages, which follow the Roman dichotomy of *jus* and *lex* and distinguish between *droit* and *loi, Recht* and *Gesetz, diritto* and *legge*. Cf. Friedrich, 1958, pp. 200ff. for further comment and literature.

tween the norms involved in such comparative evaluation and the rule as it is enforced, there exists a further inherent normative tension which results from looking upon law as tied to the activity of a *legitimate* ruler possessing authority. A norm, especially if embodied in a command enforced by an illegitimate ruler, might be considered not to be law by those questioning his right to rule. The same tension arises when the ruler behind a law does not possess authority. If the terms "authority" and "legitimacy" are taken in the precise meaning that has been developed above, such a view possesses a presumption in its favor, although since both authority and legitimacy can be false or "fake," laws may also be said to be false or "fake." Now a "fake" law, the logician might assert, is nonetheless a law of some sort, and to this we would assent. Hitler's laws were some kind of law, but they were not the kind of law that existed in Germany before his dictatorship or since. The distinction is vital. It will be more fully developed below. But first some related questions must be dealt with.

The philosophy of law has for many centuries been argued in terms of the problem: Is law a rule of reason or an act of will? Thomas Aquinas is perhaps the most renowned exponent of law as a rule of reason; he defines law as *quaedam rationis ordinatio ad bonum commune, ab eo qui curam communitatis habet promulgata* (an order of reason for the common good made public by him who has charge of the community).[2] This definition is in sharp and explicit contrast to the Roman law dictum that the preference of the ruler is what has the force of law (*quod placet principi legis habet vigorem*), a strictly voluntaristic interpretation of the law. Thomas Aquinas notes that this dictum must be understood as being subject to a higher reason. He goes as far as Cicero in denying the quality of law to any command which is in contravention to such higher reason as embodied in the natural law. Such a proposition is excessively normative. It also raises the vital operational issue as to who is to decide whether any given rule is contradicting the natural law or not. The difficulties inherent in this issue have filled the pages of many key works in political theory since that time. Bodin, Althusius, Hobbes, Spinoza, Rousseau, Kant, and many others have struggled with the inherent problems. We recall this controversy in the hope of transcending it by the behavioral approach suggested by our initial statement, employing the term "law" to designate a plainly specified type of political situation. If that situation as specified is analyzed with reference to the great debate over reason and will, it will be apparent that law is compounded of both will and reason. When we propound this proposition, it is not meant to be a verbal escape such as is offered by Rousseau and Kant, who simply eliminate the diffi-

[2] Thomas Aquinas, *Summa Theologica,* II.I.q.90.art.4. Cf. also Friedrich, 1958, pp. 42ff., for detailed comment and literature.

culty, or try to, by the concept of a rational will. We would say, on the other hand, that the making of the law is an action, freely willed by certain persons, namely, legitimate rulers who possess authority. The element of reason is built into this approach through the requirement of authority, which is the capacity for reasoned elaboration. Without that authority, the command presented as a law is existentially defective and correspondingly reduced in its ability to oblige. We have already seen how political obligation is tied to authority through legitimacy. But since authority is the capacity for reasoned elaboration and such reasoned elaboration will be undertaken in terms of the prevailing values, interests and beliefs of the community in which the authority exists, it is plain that the degree to which reason is a factor and plays a role in law will vary considerably in different communities. Hence it is not surprising that historically societies have vacillated between the two notions.

A related question, often confused with that of law's rationality, is the following: Is law what people actually do, in other words, is law a generalization based upon what is the prevalent behavior of various persons and authorities in a community, especially of courts, or is law a norm that says what men ought to do? The "Realists" in American jurisprudence have in recent years insisted upon the former notion,[3] but it has been expounded in various forms in the past, for example, by Hume who thought law was essentially what is useful, supported by custom and habit.[4] The difficulty inherent in this position results from the fact that if law is prevalent custom, it is difficult to comprehend the imperative "ought" aspect which a command involves. For if people do it, why tell them that they ought to? Now it may be argued that the command is addressed to the deviant members of the community, as in much criminal law, and that is certainly true. On the other hand, experience would suggest that many more members of the community would exhibit deviant conduct if the law did not exist. People stop at red lights because the law says so; to claim that the law says so because people stop is a manifest misstatement of the political situation that the word "law" refers to. However, there is some reason for insisting on the custom-embodying, habitual aspect of the law, and a strictly normative interpretation which only sees the *ought* in the law is likewise misleading. This is so because law can be nullified; if few, or none, obey it, it ceases to *exist*. We often find that what is alleged to be "the" law does not in fact "exist," because it is not enforced, because few or no attempts are made to employ coercive or even persuasive means to regulate behavior in accordance with the alleged norms. In some American states, fornication is a "crime," but the law is nulli-

[3] K. N. Llewellyn, 1930; Thurman Arnold, 1935, chap. II; Jerome Frank, 1930. Cf. the review of Frank in Cohen, 1933, pp. 357ff., and Friedrich, a, 1935, commenting on K. N. Llewellyn, 1933.

[4] Hume, 1789, bk. II, pp. 241ff.

fied with impunity by most of those who wish to fornicate. At this point, mention might also be made of "laws" which, because they are contrary to the nature of the situation, human or otherwise, cannot be enforced. If a legislature tries to make rules about private conduct not readily subject to public supervision, it is likely to fail. As was aptly remarked by the late Gaetano Salvemini, "Not even Mussolini can put a secret policeman behind each marriage bed." Some such argument might be applied to the case of laws on fornication, as it might generally to attempts to regulate private conduct. So the strictly normative view of law, as contrasted with the empirical one, is likewise untenable. It would seem that when law is employed as a term designating the enforceable rule, enforced by a legitimate ruler possessing authority, these difficulties are avoided. For evidently such rules will be expressing the values, interests and beliefs of the community, and hence will be rooted in custom and habit as exhibited in the behavior of the members of such a community.[5]

Another crucial issue is concerned with what has been called the hierarchical structure of law. Put in the form of a question, this issue may be stated as follows: Are all legal norms equally valid, or is there an order of priority, so that if two norms conflict, one has precedence over the other? It is pretty generally agreed among jurists that the answer to this question must be in favor of the second alternative, whether they recognize a natural law or not. Any natural law doctrine, such as Cicero's or Aquinas', is, of course, committed to the hierarchical view of law by subordinating all other law to such natural law. But even if this view is rejected—and its rejection usually means a refusal to put the legal order within the broader framework of "nature and nature's God"—there still remains the possibility of recognizing a hierarchical ordering of law. Thus constitutional law is subordinated to the "generally recognized rules of international law," ordinary legislation to constitutional law, state legislation to federal legislation, general administrative ordinances to legislation, to mention only the more important "levels" of the hierarchy of legal norms that have been acknowledged in various communities. Such an ordering usually means that the rules of the "lower" level are invalid if they contradict those of the "higher level," though in the federal sphere particularly there may be "jurisdictional" delimitation, meaning that a rule made within the assigned jurisdiction of the state or other component unit is valid per se, with various kinds of arrangements made for deciding whether this is the case or not.

What needs to concern us particularly in a general political theory of law is the notion of a "constitutional" law. It means that there exists

[5] The position here taken bears a relation, of course, to the view expounded earlier that facts and norms, factual behavior and normative preferences, are linked in fact and in logic; see above, Introd. and Chap. 2. G. Jellinek, 1900, 1929, pp. 337ff. Also Cohen, 1932, pp. 248ff.

law, in the sense of rules enforced by the legitimate ruler possessing authority, which "constitute" the framework of government. Aristotle's concept of the *politeia* has often been taken to mean this sort of thing, and has hence been translated as "constitution." Likewise people have spoken of the constitution of every kind of political regime. But *politeia* does not mean what we have just called the law of the constitution, but simply political order; not every community has a constitution in the sense above indicated. It is a particular kind of political order in which the political order itself, the framework of government, to employ a traditional American term, is subjected to explicit rules having the status of a special law. The Greek *poleis* developed such law, and so did the Roman Republic. But it has had its greatest flowering in the West, both medieval and modern, while it is absent in many other political societies. We are not here concerned with the historical question of why and how it arose,[6] but with what it connotes. The legitimate rulers need not be the people, as the modern democratic outlook might suggest, nor even the elected representatives of the people. Such constitutional law may be made by a monarch, or it may be the joint product of many generations, acting through "the King in parliament." It may even be attempted by a dictator (Cromwell). The decisive question is whether it organizes an "institutionalized system of effective restraining rules for governmental action." That is to say, the exercise of governmental functions is itself defined by rules enforced by the legitimate rulers. The built-in dialectic appears in the paradox that such a rule consists of giving a command and then treating it as binding upon oneself. It can occur only when the reasoning of which the legitimate rulers would have to be capable can refer to certain beliefs which make such subjection of the government to law "reasonable." There are a number of possibilities here. In the modern world, two such beliefs have been of central importance. One is the belief in the dignity of man, that is to say, the belief that every human being has certain "fundamental rights," among which there are the maintenance of life, the enjoyment of liberty and the pursuit of happiness, to paraphrase the Declaration of Independence. On the other hand, there is the belief in the corruptibility of all men when entrusted with power and the consequent need to check and control them continually if abuse is to be avoided.[7] The latter belief leads to the notion that power should be divided and carefully circumscribed; the former serves to establish an inviolable sphere within which each man *qua* human being is "autonomous."[8] The religious basis of both these views is well known. Only the notion of an inviolable sphere,

[6] McIlwain, 1940; Friedrich, 1950; Spiro, 1959.

[7] This belief is not necessarily carried as far as it was (presumably) by Lord Acton when he said that "all power corrupts, and absolute power corrupts absolutely." See the comments above, Chap. 9, pp. 178ff.

[8] Friedrich, 1950, chaps. 7–13.

however, is rooted in Christian beliefs, whereas that of restricting power was shared by Greeks and Romans. By itself, it provided a much feebler basis, manifestly, than when reinforced by the personalist notion of the dignity of man. At present, the latter is spreading without the religious basis upon which it rests; it is not surprising that it seems to lack vitality under these conditions. One hates to think how few Indians, for example, have any idea that their constitution provides basic rights, let alone what such rights are or how they could be defended when violated by the government. Even in a Christian context, as in Puerto Rico, it was recently discovered that only 7 per cent of the populace had any notion as to their rights.[9] Similar findings have been made for Italy and Germany.

A constitution presumably embodies a system of power relationships which has been effectively institutionalized. No informal "countervailing power" or other amorphous influence, no matter how effective when at work, satisfies the descriptive concept of the political situation which the term "constitution" is meant to denote. For a constitution is essentially law, and law states enforced rules. This does not mean, of course, that a constitution is a static, never changing given. On the contrary, a constitution is a living system.[10] But just as in a living, organic system, such as the human body, various organs develop and decay, yet the basic structure or pattern remains the same with each of the organs having its proper function, so also in a constitutional system the basic institutional pattern remains even though the different component parts may undergo significant alterations. For it is the characteristic of a system that it perishes when one of its essential component parts is destroyed. The United States may retain some kind of constitutional government without, say, the Congress or the federal division of powers, but it would not be the constitutional system now prevailing. This view is uncontested even by many who do not work with the precise concept of a constitution here insisted upon. It raises, however, some difficult questions which the judiciary of the United States illustrates. The Supreme Court now appears to be an essential part of the system, and indeed the Constitution provides for some kind of Supreme Court, though not the particular one which now exists. As everyone knows, the Court underwent a rapid evolution after it had been organized by legislation. This evolution was highlighted by the successful claim to interpret the Constitution, even to the point of holding laws adopted by the Congress and accepted by the President to be unconstitutional. Would an elimination of this part of the Court's jurisdiction, by constitutional amendment, alter the constitutional system so profoundly that we would have to speak of a new Constitution? The prob-

[9] Comité del Gobernador, 1959, pp. 5ff.

[10] Sternberger, 1956, pp. 23f. The idea of the constitution as "living" fits into the broader concept of the "living law" which Hall has expounded; cf. Hall, 1958 *passim*, and many other works there referred to.

lem is arguable. What makes it difficult to explore this "counterfactual conditional" in any depth is that the American public is to date so thoroughly convinced that this *would* revolutionize their constitutional system that such an amendment is virtually out of the question. But the recent moves in Congress in connection with the segregation decisions "to curb the Supreme Court" suggest that such an attitude may not remain unchanged. As long as it does, it may be soundest to side with the majority view.[11]

The problem of the living constitution may be seen also in the events which led France from the Fourth into the Fifth Republic. It seems now generally agreed that in spite of the smooth transition which was effected as a consequence of the moderation exhibited by both the National Assembly and General de Gaulle, a distinctly new constitutional order was created.[12] There remain a president, a senate, a national assembly, and so forth, but all these institutions have changed their relations so profoundly that it would be misleading to interpret the order as identical with the preceding one. *Treize Mai* 1958 was the beginning of a revolutionary transformation.

These two illustrations, and others which might readily be adduced, suggest that the question of whether a constitution continues to live or not is a matter of judgment concerning the extent of the transformations which have occurred. Such judgment may often be extremely difficult. When, at what particular point in time, did the Roman constitutional order cease to exist? It is the prevailing view that it did so at the accession of Augustus. We incline to agree because, according to our concept of law and constitutional law, the accession of Augustus *is* the decisive point, because the former legitimate rulers possessing authority had ceased to possess that authority and indeed toward the end they had lost the very legitimacy which alone entitled them to enforce the rules for the ordering of the government. When Augustus stepped forward, he possessed authority and he soon acquired legitimacy as a ruler who governed without only the empty trappings of a vanished constitutional order. The dictum of the *Corpus Juris* which was cited at the outset was a correct statement after this time; from the rule of Augustus on, what pleased the prince *had* the force of law.[13] In spite of the difficulties involved, we state it as a proposition that a constitutional system ceases to exist when one of the parts crucial to its operation ceases to function. This proposition is in a sense obvious since a system has been defined as a syndrome of parts, every one of which is vital to its operation. It merely explicates what is

[11] Congress, 1958, pp. 357–369, important testimony by Griswold, Pound and Brian.

[12] Friedrich, a, 1959; Kirchheimer, a, 1958; M. Harrison, a, 1959; Goguel, a, 1959; Wahl, a, 1959; Hoffmann, a, 1959; Prelot (2nd ed.), 1960.

[13] Syme, 1939, esp. pp. 322ff.

implied in the proposition that a constitution is a system—a proposition which is often taken for granted but which really needs explicit statement. As such, it is part of the general legal system for which it provides the foundation; hence the expression "basic law." In the hierarchy of legal norms it ranks foremost. Nonetheless, it is subject to the same processes of gradual transformation through custom and practice. From this fact may be derived another important proposition concerning a constitution. It is that the longer a constitution has existed, the more numerous will be the deviations from what was contained in the original document, seen as an ordered whole of rules enforced by a legitimate ruler possessing authority. These deviations may be embodied in "formal" amendments, that is to say, commands formulated by those whom the constitution itself entrusts with the function of amending the constitutional law. Or, more usually, the deviations may occur as the result of implementing legislation such as that of organizing the Supreme Court, or laying down statutory rules for parties, and so forth. Or, also usual enough, the deviations may consist in practices adopted by those who are entrusted with a particular function, as such practices become a rule of custom. Such practices may then be violated by a particular office-holder, which violation in turn may lead to their being formalized. A striking instance of this is the practice which grew up in the United States of a president not serving more than two terms, which in turn was violated by F. D. Roosevelt, and was therefore afterward embodied in a specific rule limiting the presidential tenure to two terms. In recent German constitutional development a number of comparable situations have altered the position of the chancellor, the federal council and the president, to mention only the more striking instances. Again, the way in which De Gaulle has broadened the "meaning" of Article 16 of the Constitution of the Fifth Republic is a startling instance of constitutional change through practice.[14]

In a country with a constitutional order which is not embodied in an explicit ordered whole of rules designated as "the" constitution, such as England, the situation is nonetheless quite similar. For the government, if ordered in accordance with the criteria of a constitutional order as defined, will function on the basis of a number of rules, such as the Act of the Settlement, the act regulating and restricting the House of Lords, and so on, as well as the kind of customary practices just described. Since only England today really represents this type of constitutional order, it would be a mistake to erect it into a separate category when its fundamental working is so nearly like that of other constitutional systems.[15]

The most famous instance of a transformation of the British system

[14] Macridis, a, 1962. A rather formalistic view of constitutional interpretation occurs in Forsthoff, 1961.

[15] Jennings, 1940, chap. 1; Morrison, 1954, chaps. 5 and 9; Greaves, 1938, chaps. 1 and 3.

of constitutionalism occurred in the eighteenth century when, after the accession of the kings of Hanover to the British throne, Walpole and his friends managed to develop a practice of actually ruling the country with the support of an effective majority in the Parliament, which they secured by all means at their disposal, including straight money payments for services rendered. At the end of this development, the British constitutional order had been basically transformed, with parliamentary majorities supplanting the King as the effective rulers of the country.[16] Leaving aside all detailed refinements, it is a process which illustrates the difficulties of determining the answer to the question: When is a customary practice an implementation of the existing system and when does it imply the transformation into a different system? This problem is part of a broader issue confronting the student of all law, more especially constitutional law, and that is the problem of perversion.[17] When Hitler claimed that the firing of the German parliament building in March, 1933 was the work of the Communists in order to scare enough of the electorate into voting for him and to give himself an excuse for barring the Communists from participation in the election, he perverted, even if he did not break the Constitution. When Walpole built his "system" of parliamentary corruption, he perverted the established order in Britain. It is well to confront these two situations, because one of them is viewed in a favorable light on account of later developments, and the other in an unfavorable light on account of what it brought on. Such a confrontation serves to show that the perversion and corruption of a constitutional order is in itself neither good nor bad. It all depends upon the authority of those who undertake it.

The perversion of rules through misinterpretation or corruption is a general problem, not limited to the political field. It is, however, very frequently motivated by a change in political ideology or by the alterations in values and beliefs associated with the evolution of the political order. Corruption, though usually seen as simply the result of man's desire for unearned gain, is a much more general political phenomenon which has not received the attention it deserves. Its political function has been overlooked by political theory (Chapter 9). Leaving aside here the problem of the disintegration of political orders manifest in widespread corruption, it remains to deal with perversion of rules through misinterpretation, whether intentional or not. Such perversion needs to be seen, when considered politically, in confrontation with the breach of rules, whether by tort or crime. This is so not because many breaches are the result of misinterpretation or malinterpretation, but because both perversion and breach of a rule constitute a challenge to its intended univer-

[16] Namier, 1929, esp. chaps. I and IV.
[17] Von Hippel, 1955. See for formalistic perversion, Spiro, 1959, pp. 181ff.

sality; they constitute "exceptions," and all exceptions weaken a rule. To this reflection should be added the further one that when the exceptions multiply, when the exception *becomes* the rule, the rule ceases to "exist" in a politically concrete sense. A law, a legal rule, may be destroyed by disobedience as much as by misinterpretation; both forms of violation are apt to pervert the rule in due course.

In light of our analysis of the just political act it is, however, questionable whether the reinterpretation, or even the violation, of existing rules can justifiably be called a "perversion" if that word is understood as indicating a disvalue in terms of the political order. It would rather seem that the comparative evaluation of rules, especially by judges but also by administrators, is an important part of their function. Their acts, politically considered, are worthy of respect, and hence authoritative, only if they are just. Indeed, the recurrent commitment of unjust acts will, as we have seen, undermine their legitimacy as well as their authority. In a highly developed political order, it is important, however, that any major change in the rules be made by the particular rule-making authority which the system provides. Since this is a matter of uncertain judgment, there has always been an inclination to try to escape from the difficulty by pleading for clearness and precision in the law. Aristotle noted that "it is best that laws should be so constructed as to leave as little as possible to the decision of those who judge." [18] And Voltaire, in the spirit of rationalism which inspired the great codifications, exclaimed: "Let all the laws be clear, uniform and precise: to interpret laws is almost always to corrupt them." [19] Not only then, but at other times, the idea of unifying law into one great body or corpus has appealed to those who wished to escape from the uncertainties of the law. From Justinian to the present day, codification has been related to this desire to escape fom the perversion of law which seems to be the result of interpretation by judges and administrators. A code, whether of an entire body of law prevailing in a particular community, or of a subdivision such as commercial law, may appear in three distinguishable forms. It may be, first, the notion that the existing law is to be brought together and "digested," clarified and systematized, but not altered in any important respect. A second form of code seeks to rationalize a body of law by relating it to a broad and universally valid philosophical outlook, as the natural-law codes of the eighteenth century tried to do. A third form thinks of codification as lawgiving in the sense

[18] Aristotle, *Rhetoric,* I.13. Aristotle here also gives various suggestions as to the perversion of the law when perversion suits the case; for example, "If the meaning of the law is equivocal, we must turn it about, and see in which way it is to be interpreted so as to suit the application of justice or expediency. . . ." I.15.10.

[19] Voltaire, in the *Philosophical Dictionary,* 1764, art. "law." He carried this notion one step farther when he wrote: "Voulez-vous avoir des bonnes lois? Brûlez les vôtres, et faites-en des nouvelles."

of willed preference for a new and better world. Each of these three forms is, however, inspired by the notion that a code helps in systematizing the law and thereby keeps it from "perversion." Both Justinian and Napoleon, to mention two famous codifiers, entertained the vain hope that their codes would reduce interpretation to a minimum. Not long after the code was finished, Napoleon commented a bit ruefully: "The Code had hardly appeared when it was followed almost immediately, and as a supplement, by commentaries, explanations, developments, interpretations, and what not. . . . I was in the habit of saying to the *Conseil d'État:* Gentlemen, we have swept out the stable of Augeas; for Heaven's sake, let us not clutter it anew." [20] Such exaggerated hopes highlight the importance of seeking precision and clarity in the making of rules (laws) to the extent that the prevailing state of beliefs and values makes it possible to do so. From the political viewpoint there is to be observed a certain oscillation between statement, elaboration, reinterpretation and eventual restatement of the law. The history of law is full of these oscillations and of the comments of various jurists on the subject of the multiplication of the law—the "glorious uncertainty of the law." A politician might well say, with Ulysses Grant, that "I know no method to secure the repeal of bad or obnoxious laws so effective as their stringent execution." Such counsel of *après nous le déluge* or *fiat justitia, pereat mundus* brings out the fact that a law may be perverted by its very application. Against such perversion, the philosophically minded have pleaded through the centuries, from Plato and Cicero to our own times, that laws bind only when they are in accordance with right reason.[21] This doctrine, revolutionary in its implications, can itself become the source of law's most general perversion. For how is the citizen to know what is right reason?

The question which is raised by such claims is put more cautiously by those who would make the law's criterion the question of consent. "Just law," it might be claimed, "is a system of reasonable rules which are grounded in the common experience of man, which seek to realize justice, which are created with the participation of all the members of the legal community on the basis of a constitution and which rest upon the continuous common effort of these members." [22] Or, to put it more flatly, as Richard Hooker did: "Laws they are not which public approbation hath not made so." [23] But in putting it thus, all depends upon what

[20] Friedrich, a, 1956, p. 16. I have given further literature on the general problem there; cf. also the article by Pound (in the same volume) who discusses in a comparative perspective the problem of codifying Anglo-American law.

[21] Cicero, *De Legibus;* Thomas Aquinas, II.II.q.12.art.2; Hooker, 1594 bk. I, chap. 89; Leo XIII, *Rerum Novarum,* 1891.

[22] Friedrich, 1958, p. 229.

[23] Hooker, 1594, bk. I, chap. 10, p. 8. For the general problems of consent and consensus see above, Chaps. 9 and 10.

is meant by approbation. If such approbation is believed given by custom or former enactment, as Hooker thought, if in other words some kind of generic consent will do, only a very general criterion is provided and all depends upon who is legitimately entitled to interpret this general consent. As my previously quoted statement suggests, few men of democratic convictions would be willing to let it go at that; they would insist that a constitutional order is needed to organize this "approbation" by providing for effective participation of the members of the community and their representatives. Such an order offers a presumption in favor of existing law being just, though it also offers ways and means for challenging such law in terms of justice and for seeking the alteration of rules through interpretation in courts and through amendment in legislatures.

To link the preceding general propositions with our starting points about law, it can now be seen that rules based on commands made by illegitimate rulers, or by legitimate rulers without authority, are perversions of the legal order. The perversion of a legal order may thus proceed with the aid of "law" which is defective because of the ruler whose command it embodies. We can perceive at this point the core of real insight which the doctrine of the "normative power of the factual" embodies. Not every factual operation has normative power; merely the fact that rulers do certain things or take certain actions does not give them normative quality. But if the rulers are legitimate and if they possess authority (both legitimacy and authority taken in the precise empirical sense which we have suggested), then their taking certain actions recurrently, though without a constitutional or other legal right to do so, may in course of time transform these patterns of behavior into norms which will eventually be embodied in formal law. The pocket veto of the American President is an interesting instance in point here. The mere fact that a number of Presidents who were legitimate rulers with real authority pocketed legislation and thereby prevented it from being formally completed did in time provide them with a right to do so under American constitutional law. It would be foolish, however, to assume that this and many other similar examples would really convince those who insist upon the radical separation of fact and norm. They would either argue that the right had existed right along and was merely made manifest, or suggest that what provided the particular norm with its normative quality was not the continuing practice, but rather the value judgments of those concerned. Common political experience tends, however, to argue the other way, and to explain the emergence of values from the recurrent practices—a general proposition of which the situation here described is but a special instance.[24]

The problem of such perversion of the law leads logically to the

[24] Cf. Chap. 2 above, as well as Polin (2nd ed.), 1952; and for the contrary view, Brecht, 1959.

further problem of the breach of law. Perversion is, in a broad sense, a breach of the law, but it needs to be distinguished from a deviation from the norm which is *open* in the sense that it breaks a law which is approved both by the rulers and the ruled's prevailing view of what is right. Such breaches may be distinguished as "formal" breaches of the law, as contrasted with the "informal" breach which perversion constitutes. But the line cannot be drawn sharply, and there exists a large area of twilight. Former thinkers have been content, in the manner of positivism, to interpret a breach of law simply as the violation of a specific legal command, more especially a statutory provision. If one thinks of law as essentially a matter of command, and particularly as the command of a sovereign will, then the phenomenon of the breach of law is indeed essentially a contravention of such a command. It is different if law is seen as subject to and oriented toward the standard of justice. For if justice must be continually created anew by a creative process which seeks to realize what is right in the law, if therefore, to speak figuratively, justice is understood as a lodestar rather than as a goal to be achieved, the breach of law becomes problematical. An enactment, even a constitutional enactment such as the Eighteenth Amendment, may lead to violations of such positive law on a large scale, and a breach of law in the sense of right may not be involved. For it is the very question of whether such a provision, such an enactment, is right which is at issue. This sort of nullification of law is a much more common occurrence than is customarily admitted, particularly in the field of personal relations (and in politics). Hence the saying that rules are "honored in the breach"; that is to say, what is right is being recognized in the violation of such provisions of the positive law.

The same sort of conventional disregard can be observed in "political" fields, such as electoral laws, party finance, and the like; as in the case of personal relations, the possibilities of effective enforcement are very limited. In these fields of law, the "unwritten" law and right consist in the recurrent violations of the written law, particularly of the statutory enactment.

Such disregard may at times go on for quite a while, until finally the abuses reach such dimensions that either rule-making or dispute-settling activity will step in to set things "right." There exists a certain range of tolerance for deviations from the norm about which we ought to know more. A judicial settlement or judgment, indicating the limit, may have important corrective value, even though it raises serious enforcement problems.[25]

Neither the deviations nor the corrective actions are necessarily

[25] These observations apply to both the desegregation and reapportionment decisions of the U.S. Supreme Court of recent years. In the latter case, the decision conjures up the threat of suits by voter groups which may, by dint of anticipated reaction, restrain the legislature from the more extreme abuses.

perversions, though usually proclaimed to be by political oratory. Only when the rather vaguely defined limit of tolerance is reached, when something approaching the negation of the rule in question is consummated, is the law being perverted.

One can appreciate this plurality of the sources of law and the breaches of law which result from it without accepting the radical view of philosophical anarchism as presented by Godwin, Kropotkin, and in a modified way by Thoreau. Godwin took the view that all law is unjust *qua* law, that injustice is the consequence of political institutions,[26] except in so far as it merely declares the "decrees of reason." Largely the law is a matter of "capricious" rules. The "rules of justice" are better taught by life than by "catechisms and codes." Moreover, "every case is a rule to itself." Hence there must either be constantly new laws or the sense of the law must continually be "refined" and "twisted," that is, perverted. "The consequence of the infinitude of law is its uncertainty." Such uncertainty defeats the very purpose of law, namely, to have rules which the citizen can depend upon. "Law was originally devised that ordinary men might know what they had to depend upon, and there is not at this day a lawyer existing in Britain presumptuous and vainglorious enough to pretend that he has mastered the code." Hence to Godwin, law seems a labyrinth and a mass of contradictions. From these and other reflections, Godwin concluded "that law is an institution of the most pernicious tendency." [27]

Views such as these were put even more radically by Kropotkin and Proudhon. The former put it in terms of a contrast between customs that are beneficial to society and hence need no law to be followed, and laws which are "of advantage to a ruling minority." This theme we find in Bakunin and Marx and many other revolutionaries. "All law has for its object to confirm and exalt into a system the exploitation of the workers by a ruling class." [28] Proudhon added: "I will have no laws."

Henry David Thoreau, while not denying the value of law as such, insisted on the measuring rod of justice and "right" as suggested by the individual conscience. "It is not desirable to cultivate a respect for the law so much as for the right," he wrote when pleading for civil disobedience.[29] As is well known, Thoreau's position was developed in response to the specific injustice of slavery. His argument was cast in terms of an extreme case of injustice, and he insisted that the just man could

[26] William Godwin, 1793, ed. 1926, chaps. IV, V, VII, and *passim*. The editor rightly remarks that he had innumerable predecessors in this view, notably Swift and Mandeville; Hume and other utilitarians had been inclined to consider that the presumption is against law.

[27] *Ibid.*, bk. VI, chap. VIII.

[28] Bakunin, 1871; cf. also Marx, 1844. For the Proudhon quote see 1851.

[29] Thoreau, 1849.

not accept *so manifestly* unjust a law as that legalizing slavery, that he would have to refuse to pay the taxes in support of such a legal community and that he must resign himself to the fact that "the place for a just man in such a community is the jail." [30] John Brown, as everyone knows, went even further in such radical rejection of the legal community; he tried to force the abolition of slavery by an armed revolt. In spite of the fact that this revolt was roundly condemned at the time and was immediately suppressed, John Brown became a symbolic figure during the Civil War and a kind of popular hero.[31] We can see, in these well-known events, a typical case where positive law and right were in such deep conflict that a breach of law could appear as a defense of what was right; it shows the limits of a legal order, founded upon past enactments.

Besides the breach of law resulting from nonrecognition of the claim to justice of an existing positive legal rule, there exists also the kind of breach of law which violates a rule of law acknowledged as right. This is the particular sphere of the criminal law, though even here a conflict of the kind just discussed is at times involved. According to older views, the guilt of the person to be punished is to be found in the disturbance of the legal order. The criminal must answer for the fact that he disturbed the public order, whether he realized it or not (ignorance is no defense). But in order to protect the accused against arbitrary punishment, the principle was developed—and this principle was by no means an innovation of liberalism—that a penalty could be inflicted only on the basis of a law which was "on the books" at the time the presumed crime was committed (*Nulla poena sine lege*). Admirable as this principle appears under ordinary conditions of a stable political order resting upon a reasonably firm foundation of values, convictions and beliefs, it fails under extraordinary conditions where the comparative evaluation of the just act is rejected by a substantial group of citizens. The problem presented itself at the Nürnberg Trials, when the National Socialist leaders were to be tried whose acts appeared unjust to most men, both inside Germany and out. The problem has reappeared at the Eichmann trial.[32] It is capable of resolution in terms of the view here developed, which encompasses the notion of the reasoning basis of the just in terms of prevailing values and beliefs.

[30] *Ibid.*

[31] For a philosophically unique portrait see Stephen Vincent Benét, 1928.

[32] Rogat, 1961, for a balanced appraisal of the legal problems presented by the Eichmann trial. Cf. also Arendt, 1963. On the Nürnberg Trials, the numerous writings often fail to develop this crucial point, because the defenders of the National Socialist perpetrators of the various actions stressed such matters as "lack of jurisdiction" while their accusers appealed to the "conscience of mankind" without clarifying the legal bearing of it. Cf. T. Taylor, 1949, for the official version.

In the light of these general principles there has been much discussion about the nature of punishment and penalty. Great schools of criminal law have sprung from these controversies. Originally the penalty was seen as atonement; it took the place of revenge and was measured out in accordance with the desire to reestablish the balance between the members of the legal community which had been disturbed by the crime. An eye for an eye, and a tooth for a tooth—this formula of the Old Testament, which resembles the formulas in many another primitive law, expresses such an outlook very well. In contrast to such primitive notions, which still play a role even in the legal thought of the most civilized societies, several theories have been developed which discuss the penalty in regard either to its cause or to its effect. The expounders of the contractual theory have seen the consent, whether tacit or expressed, of the criminal as the ground (cause) of the penalty. Those who have favored a theory of retaliation have grounded the meaning of a penalty in the conception of a transcendent justice—the sort of justice that Aristotle described as "corrective." The latter view can be stated in terms of a rule of law, as was done by Kant, who went so far as to justify even the death penalty as rightful retribution to be demanded by the reason of each member of the legal community. Besides this theory of retaliation, that of intimidation has played a considerable role. According to this theory, penalty must be explained by considering that not only the criminal but also others who might otherwise be tempted to commit a particular kind of criminal act should be deterred from it by the fear of the penalty to be expected. The psychological assumptions upon which this theory rests are dubious, to say the least; it has often been observed, of both criminals and others, especially children, that the penalty, or perhaps the danger represented by it, provides a temptation to commit the act which it is designed to prevent. For the majority of men this may be untrue, however, since the average person is certainly deterred from many minor infractions of the law by his fear of the penalty.

Alongside these older theories, the notion has gradually gained ground that the person committing a breach of law is abnormal, is a sick person. Sociological and psychological studies have suggested that the criminal act is not an isolated phenomenon but must be seen as part of the human situation and therefore must be understood as grounded in the person's physiological and psychological nature as well as in his social setting. This view of crime leads to the conclusion that the penalty is a means of improving or reforming the person involved in the criminal act. By such means one must try to influence him. Alongside such notions the "technical" thought of protecting the community may play a role. Yet these two approaches are diametrically opposed to each other, when their philosophical foundation is considered. The contrast becomes evident when we take into account the criminal law of totalitarian societies, which continue to operate with concepts of law and right when actually their approach is dominated by regard for the requirements of maintaining their system in power. Here we find that the pretense of "reeducating" the man who has been arrested by the police, by which phrase is meant that he is to be made into an adherent of the system, serves as the basis for applying to the alleged perpetrator of a crime techniques designed to destroy his psychic self. It is important to avoid this danger, while yet attempting to serve the community's interests: its security and the man's improvement.[33] Recently an attempt has been made to deduce the penalty as a necessary consequence from the coercive nature of law and thus to see it as direct coercion. "A penalty is simply a substitute for the failure to enforce obedience." [34] But law, understood as right order, is not adequately interpreted if only its coercive character is stressed. As we have seen, law, as the aggregate of rules in a political community, constitutes a complex effort at regulating the relations between members of the community in terms of their varied values, interests and beliefs. Common, complementary and contradictory values, interests and beliefs are accommodated by the vast number of rules which seek to discover the common features in cases which are admittedly unique in their human fullness and complexity. The comparative evaluation by which it is determined whether a political act, be it rule-making or rule-applying, is just, or rather whether it is more just than available alternatives, constitutes a presumption in favor of its legality.

It may be said, therefore, that each of the theories about the true nature of punishment and of the breach of law has clarified some *one* aspect of the matter, but that only when taken together in their entirety do they give a realistic picture of these phenomena. A formal breach of law occurs in the fully developed legal community when a group or an individual cannot or does not wish to recognize the authority of the legal proposition he violates, that is, when by his act he rejects the value judgments involved in the law he challenges. The penalty is frequently accepted quite consciously by those who commit such a breach (consent theory), is felt by the majority who accept the value judgment as a just retribution for the breach (retaliation theory), but causes others who may also question the controversial value judgment to avoid the penalty by obeying the law (intimidation theory), makes those who have already been punished once obey the law the next time (reform theory), and finally induces the administrators to strengthen their enforcement machinery (security theory). Evidently, the several aspects of the breach

[33] For a discussion which fails to do so, though it raises this important issue squarely, cf. Radbruch, 1932 (3rd ed.), pp. 164ff.

[34] W. Burckhardt, 1927, pp. 283ff. The quote is from pp. 288–289; a similar position is taken by Kelsen, 1945, pp. 50ff. Accordingly, Kelsen recognizes only retribution and prevention as purposes of criminal law.

of law and its penalty are elucidated by the several theories, but only their combination enables one to understand the entire situation.

In conclusion, it may be said that the breach of law as an attack upon the legal order usually results from the lack of authority of the law and of those who administer it, the officials and judges; this lack of authority also affects the effectiveness of the penalty adversely. If penalties are no longer understood and considered justified, they appear to be arbitrary acts, and even their deterrent effect, if it subsists at all, is greatly limited. Order, which every legal system seeks to realize, ought therefore not to be placed in opposition to justice as if it were a rival value, let alone be placed above it. For justice and order are, as our further analysis of order will show, dependent upon each other. They cannot be realized in a legal community except jointly. The lawmaker mediates between the two as best he can, as does custom in its more or less stable rules and modes of conduct. It has been claimed by no less an authority than Justice Holmes that "while there is still doubt, while opposite convictions still keep a battlefront against each other, the time for law has not come." This claim is not true. If it were, the time for law would never come; for there is always doubt and there are usually opposite convictions. Indeed, where convictions are unanimous no need for law arises. Law, as we have shown, expresses partial and in democratic communities usually majoritarian consensus. Disobedience, nullification, evasion and "conscientious objection" are part of the life of the law. They endanger it and they may pervert it, but they do not in themselves constitute the perversion of the law but rather the paradox of its existence.

part

III

The Dimensions of Equality and Freedom

part

III

The Dimensions of Equality and Freedom

chapter

16

Political Equality and Its Uses

I am just as good as you are,
and a damned sight better.
AMERICAN SAYING

THE REPLY OF BIG BROTHER PIG to the horse protesting the absence of equality in Orwell's *Animal Farm* has become justly famous: "We are all equal, but some are more equal than others." The absurdity of this remark hides a profound truth beneath its paradoxical expression "more equal." It is a fact that equality does not permit comparison; hence the comparative is absurd; even the language revolts at it. It knows "good" and "better," "long" and "longer," "big" and "bigger," but there is no equaller (though this wisdom of the language is less evident in English, where many adjectives for other reasons have no comparative, but readily form it: "beautiful" has "more beautiful"). And yet, we recognize the possibility of more or less equality. "There is greater equality for the Negro in the United States today than fifty years ago," we say. Plainly this way of speaking is an imprecise simplification of the statement: "The position of the Negro more nearly approaches equality. . . ." And this more precise way of putting the matter discloses yet another facet of equality: it is apparent that equality is a limit which might be approximated, but which is not "realized." So not only on Animal Farm, but in all political societies "some are more equal than others."

It has already been mentioned in the discussion of justice that

Aristotle's linking of justice to equality represented a basic insight (Chapter 14). We saw there that the arguments about equality always involve one's view of man and what is to be considered important in evaluating him. The idea of equality, the value assumption in favor of equality, is beyond discursive proof with reference to many or all possible evaluations of man. If one says, "Men are born free and equal," and implies that they ought to be so born, and that having been so born, they ought to remain so, one asserts, but does not prove, the desirability, the value, of equality. Aristotle saw that men generally incline toward assuming such a value, that they incline to insist that they ought to be treated equally because they believe themselves to be equal. He also observed and analyzed with care a variety of inequalities between men which should be the ground for treating them with discrimination. He linked the existence of such inequalities to partisan arguments about who is entitled to rule, some saying that the noble-born are, others that the well-to-do are, still others that the well-educated and those of superior intelligence are entitled to rule. This run of arguments is the core of the issue of legitimacy, as we have seen. But apart from this issue of who is *entitled* to rule, what does equality mean?

Following our procedure of arguing from experience and conduct that can be experienced and hence empirically known, it would be sensible to start from the recurrent situation that some men are treated differently from other men in the political order to which they all belong. Thus some men are taxed very much more heavily than other men; the difference may be that between paying no income tax at all and paying over 90 per cent of your income in taxes. It would seem that they are treated "unequally." But then a consideration is offered which would read something like this: "The obligation to pay taxes is related to the ability to pay taxes. If two men are different (unequal) in that one earns only the minimum needed for bare survival, while the other earns a thousand times this amount, then it is just, in the sense of treating them equally, to exempt the income which is needed for bare survival from all taxation, and thereafter to tax men in accordance with, that is, proportionally to, their income." It is not necessary to pursue this argument further into the complexities of modern tax legislation to perceive that equality of treatment is here related to a quality of person, and it is plain that sharp differences of opinion might arise as to the relevance of such qualities. Yet, if the prevailing view in a given political community as to the quality involved in various kinds of situations and of conduct is the basis of the differentiation, that situation is distinct from one in which the differentiation is unrelated to the prevailing view. We propose to use the term "general equality" for designating the status of persons in a political community in which the first of these conditions exists. But more specifically, we propose to employ the term "legal equality" for the purpose of designating the status of persons in a political community in which men are equal before the law in the sense that any differentiation of treatment is based upon some legally explicit differentiation in quality, that is to say, that men are by the law itself divided into classes of persons having characteristics specified by the law. In a democracy, where the laws are adopted by a procedure providing for popular participation in legislation, such classification is likely to correspond to the "prevailing" views as to what qualities are relevant to what kinds of differentiation, so that general equality is safeguarded by legal equality.

Such a bland statement must not be taken to gainsay the possibility, even the probability, of sharp differences of opinion. A "prevailing" view, democratically speaking, is a majority view. The problem may be further complicated by a federal system and the regional differentiation consequent upon it. The equal protection clause of the Fourteenth Amendment, though certainly making the Negro more equal than he had been before, fell short of making him equal to non-Negroes, either in his own view or that of many others.[1] Besides, democratic communities, even though rendering homage to the general principle of equality, by proclaiming such propositions as that "equality before the law is the essence of democracy," often not only accept but glorify inequality.[2]

It may therefore be thought by some that equality is one of those vague, general notions which have no relation to any specific and detailed item in the world of politics. This is, of course, far from true. Actually, notions of equality and inequality intrude themselves continually into the political decisions that have to be taken. One of the most striking instances of recent years is a German law bearing the cumbersome title of Law for the Equalization of Burdens.[3] This statute undertook to deal with the consequences of the Hitler war in which some people had lost everything because of bombings, reparations and other acts of violence, while others had preserved most of their possessions. In fact there was the greatest variety of "burdens" which people had had to bear, and these burdens were completely unrelated of course to any "virtue" of the individuals concerned; the most devoted resistance fighter found himself penniless, while the most ruthless Nazi might be completely "unburdened." The conception of this legislation was, therefore, to "equalize" these material damages, that is to say, distribute them more equitably; e.g., children of parents helplessly "cooped up" in the Soviet Zone were to be provided

[1] Warsoff, 1938, *passim;* Fraenkel, 1944, chap. XXI; Berger, 1952, chap. IV on New York law; Myrdal, 1944, *passim.*

[2] Tawney, 1931, chaps. II and III.

[3] *Lastenausgleichsgesetz,* 1952. The best commentary on the *Lastenausgleichsgesetz* of 1950 is by Harmening, 1953, and later. For its history, see Hielscher, 1948; Neuhoff, a, 1958, and the tenth anniversary report of the bank handling the transactions required under the law, 1960.

for out of what became one vast repository of residual national wealth. The central provisions were relatively simple: to put a mortgage on all existing property, which was to be paid off in the course of years with interest, and to use the proceeds for reimbursing those who had lost in excess in a variety of ways. The underlying idea that there should be some "equality" in the sacrifices imposed by an unwanted war was obvious enough. But it was discovered very soon that the idea of "equality" involved in such a proposition was far from clear. Who was to be considered equal to whom? More specifically: Did "equalizing" mean that people should be reimbursed in *proportion* to the losses, so that the rich man who had lost a million would get half of that million back, while the poor man who had lost ten thousand (his house) would also get half of it back? In this view the material property was the decisive consideration. Or should each German get back what he had lost up to a certain sum, say twenty-five thousand, so that the little people might get a much larger share of their loss back, while the rich would get much less in proportion? Here the decisive consideration was the human being involved. The parallel question presented itself, of course, for the burdens to be imposed: Should they be made relative to ability to pay or should they be uniformly imposed? It is plain that ideas of social justice would be crucial in finding an answer; in fact the instance of this law is only a special case of a recurrent problem in tax legislation. Beyond the problem of what is just in the sense of being in consonance with the equality and inequality of treatment involved, there lurks of course the problem of "economic consequences" in all such legislation. When we hear today that certain kinds of taxes "spur initiative," or "encourage saving," or whatever other such general policy aspect might be brought forward, the argument really implies that what may seem just and equal, when considered in relation to the individuals concerned, should in fact be regarded as affecting the common good, and if so regarded, should be decided differently and may be in a sense diametrically opposed to the previous reasoning. To put this argument another way, one might say that the *others* who were not at first part of the situation are brought into it, and that in order to treat them "justly," that is to say equally, or (to put the matter negatively) to avoid inflicting upon *others* undeserved burdens such as might result from an ill-functioning economy, one is justified in treating the original contestants "unequally." "Equality for all" could be the slogan for such a policy.

But what about political equality? Such political equality would presumably mean that in the field of political activities a similar state of affairs prevails as in legal equality. There are differences between men, both in terms of qualities and preferences. When in a given community all men are given an undifferentiated *opportunity* to participate in politics and to exert themselves with a view to acquiring power, such a community shall be said to provide for political equality.[4] Why should one speak of an equality of opportunity rather than of a particular quality? Because it is precisely the absence of any particular quality, or rather the failure to recognize the presence of any such quality, that leads to political equality. As long as there exists a prevalent belief that some quality or combination of qualities is required or at least desirable for an effective participation in politics, there is no reason to provide for an equality of opportunity; it could not be successfully exploited by all those lacking the qualities required, anyhow. This kind of argument is best seen in its full force in those situations where a political community professes to a belief in political equality, but in fact does not practice it. Thus in ancient Greece, even the ardent democrats were so fully persuaded that only a Greek could effectively participate in the life of the *polis* (and often even persuaded that only an Athenian could participate in the life of the *polis* that was Athens) that the notion of "slaves by nature" was commonly accepted[5] by them as readily as by any aristocrat. Likewise many Americans have since the beginning of their political order been ready to insist that black and red men could not effectively participate in a free society, and yet they would confidently speak of America as the "land of the free" (as the Greeks had done before them), although political equality was not actually realized because equality of opportunity did not (and does not) exist.

But does full equality of opportunity to acquire power ever exist? Let us exclude the differences in vitality, intelligence, capacity to inspire, and other such inborn qualities which certainly differentiate between men. For the equality of opportunity reasonably means that all men should be equally able to exert their natural gifts to secure such power as might be available. Even then, in all known societies characterized by the provision of political equality in a general way, there will be inequalities resulting from education, wealth, connections, and so forth. In our time, the Soviet politicians like to claim that theirs is a political order excelling in political equality because the inequalities of wealth have been eliminated. This elimination of the wealth which is inescapably present in a competitive free market economy[6] admittedly constitutes a real increase in political equality. But this is offset by a decrease resulting equally ineluctably from the entrenched power of the party hierarchy. The Soviet theory has, as a matter of fact, had to admit that equality

[4] Lasswell and Kaplan, 1950, speak of "access to power" and add that "if political equality were defined so as to exclude the existence of the elite, the concept would be vacuous."

[5] Aristotle's reasoning upon this subject, *Politics,* I.5, has always seemed to me one of the most impressive instances of circular argumentation, involving a patent *petitio principii* resulting from preconceived value notions.

[6] Tawney, 1931, pp. 12ff.

is limited. Lenin, claiming Engels as his authority, once stated that "any demand for equality which goes beyond the demand for the abolition of classes is a stupid and absurd prejudice."[7] In view of the "new class" which Djilas has described so effectively, even this claim is untenable because the abolition of classes to which it refers is historically limited to the preceding Tsarist society (Chapter 27).

Nonetheless, both the democratic and totalitarian political systems of our time provide for greater equality of opportunity in the political sphere than did many orders of the past. The reason is that the *dis*belief in the presence of any manifest innate qualities justifying political inequality is very general, and still spreading. But such "greater" equality is a quantitatively defined *comparative* equality of opportunity. This fact challenges the political scientist to spell out the quantitative comparisons involved and to establish definable criteria for determining the degree of approximation to a full realization. The difficulty lies in what might constitute an index of equal opportunity. Voting rights, while important, are only one rather limited aspect of the matter. Opportunity for securing educational advantages, based largely on ability to profit from them, is probably more important. Opportunity to compete for any and all offices on the basis of successful completion of the necessary educational preparation would be a third, and still more vital, one. Participation through all media of communication in the shaping of opinion and policy would be likewise of considerable weight. The mention of these four aspects of the matter shows that the task is not an easy one; it also shows that the task is nonetheless not beyond the realm of feasibility. But even prior to the establishment of such an index of equality certain general propositions can be formulated concerning this aspect of the political order. Before attempting such a formulation two matters should be somewhat further clarified.

Political equality, in the sense of equality of opportunity, rests not only upon the disbelief in the existence of manifest signs of political aptitude, but also upon the belief that in this field, as in certain other fields of human endeavor, success depends upon the degree of "will to power" and the related sense of "being called." On the basic level of general civic participation in community affairs, this sense of being called takes the humble form of a sense of civic duty which distinguishes the "common man" from less interested citizens. He might, as a matter of fact, more appropriately be called the "communal" man.[8] The opportunity to participate is granted to all because one cannot foretell who among them will feel this sense of political obligation and hence will participate; yet such participation is of crucial importance for the working of a democratic

[7] Lenin, 1935, XXIV, p. 293; Djilas, 1957, *passim*.

[8] Friedrich, 1950, *passim*, and more esp. prologue. See also Hicks, 1946.

community. The totalitarians advance a corresponding argument, and the elaborate setup for youth in such organizations as Komsomol [9] is the institutional effort to locate the potential participants once and for all. On the other hand, and by contrast, it is perhaps the greatest flaw in Plato's political analysis that he has Socrates escape into the excuse of a "royal lie" when confronted with the crucial question of how to locate the "men of gold" who are suitable material for the guardian class. The argument in favor of equality of opportunity asserts that this sense of communal dedication and consequent interest in power and potentially in rule can be discovered only by giving all equally the chance to exhibit it, in order to show whether they have it. The argument rests upon a great deal of practical political experience. Princes as well as nobles who inherited the position of power showed time and again a striking lack of interest in as well as ability for the performance of the tasks of politics.

Yet one more reflection is called for. The equality of opportunity for participating in politics is only a special case of the general equality of opportunity for participating in various kinds of professional activities. This equality is a special case of the general equality we have defined above. But it is worth noting that this general equality of opportunity to pursue a particular profession has often existed where political equality was excluded. In this connection, it might be mentioned in passing that the caste system of India, religious in its general foundation, extends the notion of fixed and assigned functions to the whole complex of professional human activities, basing them all on blood descent. It would, however, be an error to assume that this system rejects the idea of equality as such.[10] It is different from other systems in that it assumes that human beings must be classified according to their function in the general scheme of things. In its full flowering, the caste system of India proliferated into hundreds or even thousands of subdivisions only vaguely related to the original system of the four basic castes of priests, warriors, workers and serfs. Religious notions, involving responsibility and the immortality of the soul, provide the general framework for a pattern of over-all equality "in the long run." Once again, some are more equal than others.

With these qualifications in mind, we can proceed to the formulation of some general propositions. We shall restrict these to political equality as being our more immediate concern. The first of these propositions is that political equality maximizes the time and effort which members

[9] Friedrich and Brzezinski, 1956, chap. 4.

[10] Kroeber, in his article on "caste" in the *ESS*, defines it as "an endogamous and hereditary subdivision of an ethnic unit, occupying a position of superior or inferior rank or social esteem in comparison with other such subdivisions." Kroeber rightly insists that "no single factor or set of factors is to be looked for as the universal cause lying at the root of caste."

of the political community will devote to politics. This follows as a corollary from the equal opportunity of all to participate in politics. It is readily confirmed, however, by empirical observations. Such observations have not yet been put into quantitative form, as far as we know, but it can be seen by such indices as the amount of the social product devoted to various political activities, such as parties, elections, newspapers and other forms of communication, and so forth. This wide range of activities has in turn been the ground for some thinkers to reject political equality as leading to the squandering of human resources. What such thinkers usually overlook is that political activity would be wasted only if a definite basis for selecting those suited for it could be offered. No convincing demonstration of the existence of such a syndrome of traits has been made, nor is it likely that it will be made (Chapter 18).

The second general proposition is that political equality is compatible only with democratic legitimacy. This proposition follows logically from what has been said about legitimacy in general; for if there is prevalent in the community a belief that the title to rule and hence the right to rule rests upon special qualities (Chapter 13), evidently political equality cannot exist. Practical experience confirms this logical argument. More specifically, the reasoning of the totalitarians which claims that the Soviets have provided greater equality overlooks the difference between political and other kinds of equality. An ideology which proclaims that only those who understand and accept dialectical materialism, and hence are class-conscious, are entitled to rule makes political equality impossible.

The preceding statement of the proposition is, however, defective in that it treats political equality as an absolute, rather than a relative, matter. We have already shown that actually political equality is a matter of more or less. It is a matter always of whether there is greater political equality in one situation or order than in another. With this in mind, our second proposition might be restated as follows: Political equality is increased by the degree to which democratic legitimacy is embodied in the political order. By stating the proposition in this form we make clear that there can take place a gradual increase in political equality as the notion of democratic legitimacy gains ground. The position of the Negro in the United States amply demonstrates the working of this general principle. As more and more people become convinced that there are no specific qualities which manifest themselves in such signs as white skin color or "Nordic blood descent" that are required as a title to rule, greater political equality will result, as those who lacked the formerly required sign are permitted to participate in political activities. A similar observation can be made at present all over the world; as ancient notions of legitimacy collapse, masses of people often completely devoid of all qualifications for political participation are nonetheless permitted to vote and even to let themselves be elected.

A third proposition concerning political equality that is of primary importance relates it to power. It may be stated thus: Increasing political equality increases the fluidity of power. Power is fluid, we said, when it rapidly changes hands and even in the same hands increases or decreases over short periods. Consensual power is more fluid power, and political equality enhances the amount of power that is consensual, or rather changes the ratio of the consensual to the coercive. It would be interesting to clarify this proposition by quantitative tests or statistical inquiry. Recent work in American politics tends to confirm the proposition in a general way.[11] The same trend may be observed in various European political societies, more especially in Germany, where the fluidity of power has been strikingly increased in the course of this century. No indices of fluidity having been constructed, we have to be content with the rather vague evidence that is at hand. But what Pareto [12] called the circulation of the elite is a phenomenon connected with the fluidity of power, and we consequently also state it as a corollary to this proposition that "increasing political equality produces increasingly rapid circulation of the elite." It is another question whether such greater fluidity is desirable or not, and opinions have differed widely on this score. Generally speaking, it may be said that the basic difference of opinion on this subject is one of the major constituents of a temperamental predisposition toward conservatism or progressivism.

The three propositions which we have formulated suggest the uses to which political equality has been and may be put. The fact that equality has been so much bound up with ideological preoccupations and partisan struggles has obscured the fact that it might be looked at from the viewpoint of its political uses. Some shrewd politicians have, however, always been aware of these uses, the most important of which was the increase in the power of themselves and their parties. Thus Disraeli, although as a presumed conservative opposed to greater fluidity of power, successively increased the English electorate by extending the vote to ever larger numbers of people, convinced that such broadening would help the Tories to defeat the Liberals,[13] as indeed it did. In the longer run, however, it prepared the ground for the rise of the Labor Party and the consequent transference of power to quite different elite groups, such as trade union secretaries. A similar thing happened in Germany under Bismarck. His willingness to grant the general vote to all Germans in Reichstag elections after 1871 was prompted by the expectation that such a broadening would provide him with a firm support. It did at first; but when soon afterwards the Socialists achieved a wide electoral sweep, Bismarck in a panic tried

[11] For example, Key, 1958, *passim;* cf. also Key, 1961, esp. chaps. 2, 3, 8 and 11.

[12] Pareto, 1935, pars. 2026ff. See also below, Chap. 18.

[13] Monypenny and Buckle, vol. IV, 1916, chaps. 4, 14 and 15.

to withdraw the equality which had been granted by outlawing the Socialists.[14]

These are simple, clear cases of increasing political equality. It is, however, quite possible that the situation may be more complicated, because political equality may be increased by granting a small amount of political participation to many, while it is decreased by withdrawing a great amount from the few. In the Roman Empire we observe such a process; the extension of citizenship to more and more non-Romans gave them a greater degree of political equality, while the emasculation of the Senate and other Roman bodies reduced the equality for the relatively few who had formerly fully shared such power. These well-known events are paradigmatic for certain political maneuvers of the totalitarians. In Russia and China vast numbers of persons have been given a tiny bit of opportunity for political participation, and thus political equality has been increased. But the former participants in power have been completely deprived of it and only a very small number substituted for them, namely, the upper cadres of the *Apparat*. Again, it would be difficult to be sure about whether in numerical terms there took place, on balance, an increase or decrease in political equality.

Another very important use of political equality is its educational value. The more people are permitted to participate in politics, and to an increasing extent, the more they will gain a measure of understanding of the issues and realities of political life. The same result will follow from increasing the extent of people's participation. This increase in general political understanding makes it easier to adopt innovations and to effectuate those adaptations which a changing political situation calls for. The advantages of such broader political understanding are especially manifest when the survival of the community is at stake in war. Generally speaking, much better effort and sacrifice can be expected and is offered by the members of a community enjoying a large measure of political equality than by those who do not.[15] Not only in these crisis situations, but in the everyday activities of politics, greater political education makes for greater inventiveness and general commitment.

A third important use of political equality is its discovering of hidden political talent. Since the qualities that make for effective participation in politics are obscure and unfold in the practice of them, only a broad pattern of participation will unearth those with the most decided capacity. This statement is never readily granted by those who are convinced that electoral procedures are likely to produce men of mediocre gifts; the literature of the apologists for monarchy and for the different

[14] Eyck, 1955, pp. 298–306.

[15] This was noted by Machiavelli, *Discourses*, bk. I, chaps. V and LV, and by a good many other writers on political life.

types of aristocracy, especially the intellectual one, is replete with arguments in support of such contentions.[16] But there are two replies to them. In the first place, only a fairly detailed comparison with the quality of personnel employed in the absence of political equality and when it is present would provide convincing proof of such a contention. None has to my knowledge ever been attempted, but a comparison of American Presidents with English or French prime ministers would be illuminating, and tend to make the argument doubtful. Is there any English prime minister to compare with either F. D. Roosevelt or Wilson in this century except Churchill? Is not Abraham Lincoln in the perspective of time a greater statesman than either Disraeli or Bismarck, not to mention the French prime ministers of the Third Republic? The striking number of talented leaders who have appeared in Germany since broad political equality was achieved is another indication.[17] Such achievements ought not to let us forget, however, that to these heights correspond the low points of Fillmore, Harding and Coolidge. There is a risk involved, but is it greater than those experienced with heredity?

The other reply to the argument against the usefulness of political equality as a method for locating political talent is that such political equality need not go all the way to include what was after all only one of the four modes of full political participation (above, page 294). The totalitarian systems of our time have attempted precisely that: to broaden political equality as far as possible, without adopting the electoral methods which are associated with free competition for all political positions. Such an approach reduces political equality without a doubt; whether that reduction is compensated for by more successful identification and selection of political talent must at the present time be considered an unsettled issue. In the less developed countries where the masses of the electorate are often lacking in political experience such a limitation of political equality has a strong appeal, and the efforts of the military in backing a hierarchically organized bureaucracy constitute attempts to accomplish this result without adopting a totalitarian pattern of rule.

In conclusion we can say that general political equality designates the status of persons possessing an equal opportunity to participate in political life, whereas legal equality designates the status of persons in a political community in which men are equal before the law, which may, however, specify classes of effective differentiation. Both are parts of general equality, which can be defined only in relation to prevailing beliefs and value judgments. After showing the difficulties inherent in ever

[16] See for a thoughtful example Bryce's famous chapter on "Why Great Men Are Not Chosen Presidents," 1888, chap. 7.

[17] Max Weber dwelt upon this aspect of political equality, its pragmatic usefulness in providing a *Führerauslese,* in his essays on parliamentary government written in 1917. Weber, 1918, pp. 55–80.

approaching closely to a political order exhibiting the characteristics of genuine political equality, and demonstrating the need for a comparative approach in terms of more or less political equality, we then proceeded to formulate several propositions concerning political equality. Noting the "belief in the common man" as a potential political participant, we developed the propositions (1) that political equality maximizes the time and effort spent on politics, (2) that political equality is compatible only with democratic legitimacy, and (3) that increasing political equality increases the fluidity of power and the consensual component in the power ratio. We pointed out that each of these propositions calls for much further quantitative work. Finally we discussed the uses to which political equality can be put; it can obviously be made to increase the power of particular politicians and parties. Its primary use, however, is the real service it can render to political education. The secondary use is the discovery of political talent. This use is directly related to the first general proposition and has been put into a particularly interesting form in totalitarian dictatorship.

It can be surmised from this brief sketch of the uses of political equality that such equality can be considered a tool of politics without regard to the ideologically based value judgments which are usually adduced in support of it.

chapter

17

Political Representation and Responsibility

The grand discovery of modern times,
the system of representation.
James A. Mill

POLITICAL EQUALITY beyond the village raises the issues of representation and responsibility. For unless those entitled to participate but unable to do so can be represented by others who are responsible to them, the chances of organizing political equality in viable political structures will be limited, indeed. Our modern methods of securing both representation and responsibility through elections—methods which have been proclaimed especially "rational" by those who believed man to be "rational"—have made us forget that through long ages responsible conduct and representative quality had to be achieved by other means, mainly of a religious order. In the sequel such preoccupation with electoral methods has obscured the extent to which other than electoral methods are still employed. The ancient ways are more powerful than is generally realized. Anthropologists and those using their vocabulary have scored easy intellectual triumphs by pointing to these survivals and suggesting that they are all there is to government.[1]

Historically speaking, the responsible conduct of power-handlers has been brought about not only by political, administrative or judicial sanctions, but through religious belief as well. This religious belief at the same

[1] Thurman Arnold, 1935; Thorstein Veblen, 1904.

time provides the basis for representation. The notions of legitimacy we examined in Chapter 13 lead on to representation. Legitimacy as the right to rule, involving as it does the reasoning upon the title to rulership, typically carries the notion that he who represents either God or the people or both is "entitled" to rule. At the same time, such representation is believed to secure "responsible" conduct. When the kings of Israel are being chided by a prophet for misconduct, their representative quality is put into jeopardy. When the dams broke in ancient China, it was taken as a sign that the actual ruler of the empire had ceased to be the "Son of Heaven." [2] Much primitive ritual is concerned with making certain that the representative quality of the ruler is being maintained so that his conduct may be correspondingly "responsible."

What political realities do these two terms in general denote? It would seem that political representation designates all those situations where some rulers (R) who are entitled to rule (be they God, gods or men) are not able to be present and hence not able to exercise the function of ruling and, therefore, another or others are taking their place and thereby "making them present," so to speak.[3] As for responsibility, it refers to situations in which rulers are in the habit of giving an account of their doings to their followers A, B, C. . . . In modern "rational" systems of responsible and representative government, the two notions are linked by the proposition that if R represents A, he is presumed to be responsible to A in the manner just described, that is to say, he is answerable to him for what he does. But this linking of representation and responsibility is not inherent in the two situations which the concepts designate. It is therefore desirable to proceed at first with a separate analysis of representation.

The notion that one person is being made present by another has metaphysical overtones which are perplexing. They are related to the symbolization discussed earlier (Chapter 5). It may be useful at the start to recall what two major political thinkers, Hobbes and Rousseau, who were concerned with representation, had to say about it.

It seems strange that representation should at one time have been an important idea in the arsenal of absolutism. This possibility is made most explicit by Hobbes; his entire conception of state and community rests upon the idea of representation. He wrote: "A Multitude of men, are made *One* Person, when they are by one man, or one Person, Represented. . . . For it is the *Unity* of the Representer, not the *Unity* of the Represented, that maketh the Person *One*. . . . *Unity*, cannot otherwise be understood in Multitude." [4] Hobbes's doctrine of the governmental compact, according to which every man covenants with every other man

[2] Wittfogel, 1957, pp. 95f. For other examples, cf. Frazer, 1959, part III.

[3] Friedrich, 1937, 1950, chap. XIV, and bibliog. Cf. also A. de Grazia, 1951.

[4] Hobbes, 1651, bk. I, chap. XVI. Italics in the original.

to make one man or an assembly of men their representative, is rooted in his conviction that the unity of a comm-unity or state cannot in any other way be achieved, nor understood. And why is that so? Because, Hobbes answers, each individual composing the multitude is a being utterly apart, moving like a particle of matter through space and time. Therefore only the superimposition of one such individual, or a small group, over all others can bring unity and order out of multitude and chaos. This insistence upon unity as the key problem of political order had had, of course, a long history before Hobbes. Especially in the Middle Ages writers like Dante and many others had dwelt upon unity as the key argument in support of monarchy, harking back to the Stoic: one God, one world, one state. The problem of making a multitude a person, one person, is the problem of political action when such action is seen as based on will or choice. If action is seen as a product of reason, the unity of the represented may be discerned in what "reason commands."

It is a commonplace that Rousseau rejected the idea of representation as a sound basis of democratic government, that is to say, government in which the people are entitled to rule on the basis of political equality. This position is linked to his difficult notion of the "general will." But more immediately he argues that as soon as public affairs cease to be the primary occupation of the citizen, the state is bound to perish.[5] In such a situation, whether it is a question of going to the assembly or to war, the citizens prefer to appoint deputies, pursue their private interests and stay at home. Thinking of the disintegration of the Roman Republic, Machiavelli also had argued that from indolence the citizens allow paid mercenaries to tyrannize the fatherland and "representatives" to sell it for profit. Similar considerations of political prudence led Rousseau to assert that the general will can be discovered only by consulting the citizens themselves, and indeed even then is not always found.[6] It is an idea which has persisted and been institutionalized in referendum and initiative. The deputies of the people, if such exist, are on that account for Rousseau not its representatives, but merely have a commission to attend to certain things which the law prescribes. Every law which the people have not approved is null and void; it is no law at all. Rousseau was led into these errors by his giving too much weight to his theory of the general will as the source of all legislation and by his uncritical preoccupation with the political experience of the ancient *polis*. For there can be no question that representation is an ever recurring fact of political life, playing a decisive role in many types of rule.

Both Hobbes and Rousseau assumed that political representation must

[5] Rousseau, *Contrat Social*, bk. III, chap. XV.

[6] *Ibid.*, bk. II, chaps. II–IV; Friedrich, 1948, chap. 6; Derathé, 1950, pp. 344ff., 397ff.

be of the people in its entirety, as a whole. The current notion of representation is different, indeed. It is built upon actual experience of the representation, not only of the whole, but of its component parts. The many specific groups and interests in the community—local, professional, commercial and social, to mention only the more important divisions—all are "represented" in various ways,[7] either formally in a body such as the national economic councils of Germany, France, and others, or informally by so-called pressure groups which are more appropriately called interest groups. Such representatives are, however, distinguished from the elected representatives such as legislatures, parliaments, presidents, and so forth, by being usually provided with a definite mandate to do certain things. This is an important and real difference even though the lines are often blurred and though, generally speaking, much representation involves both aspects.

Before it is possible to proceed with this analysis, the existential aspect of representation must be made explicit. For due to modern electoral procedures in which a particular representative is chosen from among several candidates, the willed, the voluntary aspect of representation is usually in the foreground of attention. Representation is, however, in many situations a fact which transcends all willing, all voluntary selection. If a Frenchman travels in the United States, he will be taken by many people whom he encounters as a representative of his nation, regardless of whether he has been chosen to represent it. He may in fact be a quite unrepresentative man, a saint or a scoundrel, but since he does in fact and simply through his existence, by his being there, make something of the French people *present*, he *represents* them. This fact may be as embarrassing to him as to other Frenchmen. He may make all kinds of efforts to counteract the attitude of those he meets, explaining that he does not represent France and the French people. Nonetheless, his very existence in a non-French environment invests him with a peculiar quality which is that of representation. It is important to bear this aspect in mind in exploring further the problem of the mandate.

Usually, when speaking of a mandate one refers to what might be called an "imperative" mandate, that is to say, a mandate which consists of explicit orders to a representative to do what the "principal" wishes. In private and commercial relations such a representative is called in law an "agent." Early political representatives were such "agents." The representative assemblies of the later Middle Ages were composed of great lords who spoke for themselves and agents who "represented" counties and towns (in England). In continental Europe, the people were often divided into three "estates" which were respectively composed of clergy,

[7] Herring, 1929, *passim*, esp. introd.; Key, 1958, pp. 158ff.; Truman. 1951, chap. III.

nobility and burgesses. These estates roughly corresponded to the British "Lords Spiritual and Temporal" and "the Commons." There were many local variations which need not detain us here; what matters is that the important groups in the community were thus made present. They were at first, in England, called together by the King for the purpose of securing their consent to additional taxes and other levies. Whatever may have been the reasons in various lands, these representatives when gathered together bargained, petitioned and in other ways acted on behalf of the groups they represented. The Lords, speaking in their own name, apart, such representatives were essentially agents of local powers, frequently acting under special instructions. Gradually, the notion developed that when such a body acted together—when, for example, in England the "King in Parliament," after having settled disagreements and reached a compromise, adopted a statute—then such a body represented the whole body politic.[8] This historical development suggests that it might be difficult to draw a hard and fast line between agents with definite instructions or mandates and representatives empowered by a general mandate to attend to the "common good." [9] An elected body may and usually will be composed of men who are both agents speaking for different interests and a representative group concerned with the common good. To paraphrase and contradict a famous statement of Burke, a representative assembly is both: a deliberative assembly from *one* nation with *one* interest, that of the whole, *and* a congress of ambassadors from different and hostile interests.[10]

In light of the general characteristics of the political situation to which it was proposed to apply the term representation, we can now specify the particular kind of representation which has become a central feature of modern government as voluntary (or willed) political representation. Such representation may be described as a process by and through which the political power, and more especially the influence which the entire citizenry or a majority of them might have upon governmental action, is, with their express or implied approval, exercised on their behalf by a smaller number among them with binding effect upon the whole community. The minority or minorities are, in such a situation,

[8] Sir Thomas Smith represents the maturing of this view in *De Republica Anglorum*, 1583. In part II, chap. 1, dealing with Parliament, he wrote: "The most high and absolute power of the realm of England, consisteth in the Parliament. . . . For every Englishman is intended to be there present, either in person or by procuration and attornies, of what preeminence, state, dignity, or quality soever he be, from the Prince (be he King or Queen) to the lowest person of England. And the consent of the Parliament is taken to be every man's consent." Quotation, slightly modernized, from the original English translation.

[9] Continental European, and especially German, writings on representation try to do just that. See, e.g., Leibholz, 1929, chaps. I and VIII.

[10] Burke, *Works*, vol. II, pp. 12ff. Cf. also Friedrich, 1950, pp. 264f.

represented also, but through involuntary representation—an aspect to which we shall presently return. In thus characterizing voluntary political representation, or rather in using the term for designating the process described, we have advisedly spoken more specifically of "influence" (Chapter 11) and not of control or even participation; control is too narrow, and personal participation is precisely what is prevented by the nonpresence which gives rise to re-presentation. Representation organizes indirect participation (Chapter 20). The general expression "governmental action" rather than "legislation" is needed, because an elected executive is comprehended just as much under a "willed" representation as is a legislator; the same holds true for a judge. The most essential part of this process as described is, however, covered by the phrase "with their express approval." This "express approval" has two sides to it. On the one hand it is the generic approval which is embodied in constitutional provisions regarding representation—the particular institutions of a particular constitutional order. But it also refers to the specific approval which the voters in electing a particular person or set of persons to represent them have voiced for their "representative quality." This kind of willed representation is, of course, a key feature of modern parties—their electoral base (Chapter 28).

We have already noted that the modern tendency has been to think of representation only in connection with such voluntary acts. But when human beings represent other human beings existentially, it is usually due to their belonging to the same community of value judgments, beliefs and interests. Elections, when seen in this perspective, are a method for finding persons who possess this representative quality. In a country with divergent cultural backgrounds present in the population, such as the United States, Italians will tend to vote for an Italian, Swedes for a Swede or at least for a Scandinavian, and the Irish will prefer an Irishman. This well-known phenomenon is not necessarily the result of clannishness, but rather due to the inherent nature of the requirements of representation. The nonvoluntary aspect of representation injects itself.

But in the complex industrial society of our time, such representatives also have to perform difficult tasks; for these tasks it is hard to find the best qualified person. That is the reason why in those situations where technical considerations become paramount, election is abandoned in favor of appointment by competent "authority." The American judiciary provides an interesting example of the possible variations. At the lowest level, judges are elected in many states, but no one has yet proposed to have the Supreme Court elected by popular vote. And yet, is not the Supreme Court the representative of the American people, just as much as President and Congress? It is, however, believed to be so important that qualified persons be found to perform its tasks that judges of this (and similar) courts are "found" by President and Congress, in collaboration with professional groups, especially the bar—the brotherhood of law-men. The

Court is not wholly a nonvoluntary representative of the community in matters of law, because the existence of such a Court is willed by the community. But it is only a partially voluntary representative, because apart from this generic approval the Court's members do not owe their position to an act of will of those represented, except indirectly in that they are appointed by the President and with the advice and consent of the Senate, the two together representing the people.

Such partially voluntary representation is found in many kinds of political situation today. The representatives of various nations in international bodies are rarely, if ever, chosen by direct election. Foreign ministers, at least, owe their position to more or less explicit selection by an elected representative, be it a president or a parliament. The many representatives sent into international technical bodies usually are even more remote from any such willed selection; they are permanent officials owing their position to modes of selection based upon qualification for office determined by "rational" and technical considerations. The German Federal Council also offers an instance of this type of representation; although formally the several Länder are represented therein by their minister presidents, they are in fact represented most of the time by permanent officials.[11]

The recognition of the fact that the representative quality of a representative is not necessarily dependent upon his having been elected by those represented, that is to say, the recognition of the fact that not all representation is voluntary, enables one to understand better the generally recognized fact that often elected representatives represent more persons than those who have elected them. With reference to those who did not participate in the election, the representation then is nonvoluntary, either partially or completely so. Members of the armed forces, for example, are often excluded from the electorate, as are persons temporarily absent or handicapped in other ways, such as children, invalids, and the like. They are nonetheless generally regarded as represented by those chosen by their fellow citizens. These examples demonstrate in turn that the electoral process is, properly speaking, a method of finding the representatives, but does not of itself create the representative quality, though under democratic conditions it may help to do so because of democratic legitimacy.

The most important instance of this separation of representation from the electoral process is, however, seen in the universal fact of the minority being represented by those whom the majority has elected. The case is different from the preceding ones in that the minority that is so represented has actually participated in the electoral process, and has therefore shared in "finding" the representative. However, the situation is clarified

[11] Neunreither, 1959, esp. pp. 123ff.

when we say that their approval is generic through their acceptance, through participation and otherwise, of the constitutional mode of finding such representatives. Theirs is a partially voluntary, partially nonvoluntary representation. But what of the more permanent minorities who have no chance of ever electing their own choices, because of convictional, religious, racial or other permanent differentiation? It must be acknowledged that they may be wholly opposed to the system and may even refuse to participate. The answer would be that they are nonetheless represented but by unasked-for representatives who represent them because they exist and occupy the position they do.

Before drawing the implications of these insights in terms of power and authority, a word should be said regarding "proportional representation." From what has been said it should be plain that the advocacy of proportional representation rests upon the notion that only willed, voluntary representation is legitimate in the sense of being right. Considering this argument in terms of what has been said about legitimacy, this means that proportional representation is a corollary of a radical type of democratic legitimacy. It is associated with a notion of arithmetical equality as the only just ground which can be offered for the choice of electors. It is radically individualistic, as well as democratic, and considers only what is right for each citizen, taken individually and separately, and does not ask what might be right for the majority.[12]

As stated before, representation is closely linked with the problem of legitimacy. Let us recall that we designated as legitimate a kind of rule, or ruler, who is believed to be entitled to exercise such rule (Chapter 13). If political representation is seen as the political situation in which those entitled to rule are not able to be present, and therefore others make them "present" and act for them, then much would depend for the title of the representatives upon whether they are "believed" to make present those who are to be represented by them. If they are not so believed, their representative quality will suffer, though due to the existential basis of representation it will not entirely cease. This weird consequence was discovered by those Germans who even though sharply rejecting Hitler as a representative of themselves and the German nation found themselves nonetheless "made present" by him in situations such as the war Hitler started and lost.

In other words, representation may be legitimate or not, depending upon the belief of those who are affected. Those affected are not only those represented, but also those confronted with the representative. This dual source of legitimacy is often overlooked by those who would merely

[12] Friedrich, 1950, chap. XV; Hermens, 1941, sec. I; Donald Ziegler, 1958, chap. 1. The linguistically paradoxical result of the term "proportional representation" is that it does *not* ask for proportional justice, but for numerical justice. (See above, Chap 14.)

acknowledge the belief of the represented as relevant. But the bitter disagreements over the issue of so-called "recognition" actually have their root partly at least in this fact that the "recognition" of a certain regime by outsiders who are not being represented by it at all would "legitimize" it and thereby strengthen it. Whether legitimate or not, representation is a source of power, and may be a source of authority. It is evidently a source of power because he who is present, and thereby enabled to make decisions and take actions on behalf of someone who is absent, derives power from his representative quality. Whether he also derives authority or not depends upon whether he possesses the capacity for reasoned elaboration. An ambassador representing his government derives substantial power from this very fact; that is plain enough. Whether he also gains authority depends upon himself. The marked differentiation in any diplomatic corps, well known to all observers of such a group, is partly a matter of the respective power of the "powers" represented by the different representatives. But subtle, and often marked, differences develop, as the wisdom and other personal qualities related to the capacity for reasoned elaboration are exhibited by one man as compared with all others. Such a man of authority will oftentimes be the representative of a minor power. Due to his authority, his power also extends beyond the power to which he had claim as the representative of the particular government which sent him. A comparable phenomenon is vital for an understanding of the realities of United Nations politics. Certain men have gained a degree of influence far beyond the status of the land they speak for an account of their "authority." They are thereupon often chosen to occupy the position of President of the Assembly, or chairman of one of the committees, thus formalizing their special position, and providing them with additional power.[13]

The links between representation, legitimacy, authority and power provide the basis for a deepened analysis of responsibility. But first let us describe the political situation in which responsible behavior is to be observed.[14] There are recurrent situations in politics when the R (responsible person) who is acting is supposed to render an account of what he has done, to another A, whether Rand A be singular or plural. The modern world has called "responsible" the particular kind of government in which the governor, R, is supposed to render an account to the people, A, either

[13] Loveday, 1956; Abelin, ed., 1958. The election of the third Secretary-General also involved this factor.

[14] Responsibility is a fairly recent term in the vocabulary of political theory, with political responsibility sparking the development. See McKeon, a, 1957, pp. 1ff. This author gives a brief review of the history of the concept and its antecedents. I should like to add that the contributions to *Nomos III* which dealt with responsibility greatly helped me to clarify further my own thoughts on the subject; my own paper therein elaborates the issue of administrative responsibility.

directly, or indirectly to its representatives. This manner of employing the term "responsible" is shorthand for a particular kind of responsibility. For a ruler may be considered responsible to God; and a priesthood may, as in ancient Israel, Egypt, and many other systems, try to enforce the responsibility.[15] A leading anthropologist pointed out, as early as 1926, that "even the chief, whose position is hereditary, based on highly venerable mythological traditions, surrounded with semi-religious awe, enhanced by a princely ceremonial distance, abasement, and stringent taboos, who has a great deal of power, wealth and executive means, has to conform to strict norms and is bound by legal fetters." [16]

One might wish that we knew more about the various modes of enforcing such responsibility; there are hints here and there in the literature which portray facts fitting satisfactorily into the general propositions advanced here. Responsibility may also be conceived in terms of an abstract standard, such as the professional ethics of a particular group, like doctors, and the profession may try to provide the necessary sanctions, even when government officials belong to it.[17] As the scope of the functions of modern government has widened, the difficulty of securing responsible conduct from those representing the public in these activities has greatly increased.[18] Older systems of sanctions for enforcing responsible conduct have weakened and recurrently even broken down. The general outcry about bureaucracy (Chapter 18) is testimony to this development.

Basically, responsibility has two aspects or facets, one personal, the other technical and functional. These two aspects of responsibility and of the responsible conduct which they entail are, broadly speaking, suggested by the proposition that a man may be responsible to another man or he may be responsible *in terms of* a certain standard or purpose. But in either case, the statement that someone is a responsible person means that his conduct *responds* to an outside determinant, or, to put it more correctly, when a person's conduct does respond to an outside determinant, whether personal or functional, such a person may be called responsible. However, since this statement involves the implication that the two facets

[15] There has been a striking lack of interest, it seems, in the problem of responsibility in anthropological writings. Maybe the emphasis on reciprocity in governmental relationships is the reason. Responsibility to the people seems, however, definitely to be an established fact among the Ashanti, Zulu and Lovedu; for the Ashanti, cf. Busia, 1951; for the Zulu, Gluckman, in Fortes and Evans-Pritchard, 1940; for the Lovedu, Krige and Krige, 1943. Some sort of responsibility is also suggested in the writings on the Nambicuara, Ojibwa, Siriono, Trobrianders, Marquesans and Comanches; cf. comments on these above, Chap. 9.

[16] Malinowski, 1926, pp. 46–47.

[17] For example, Garceau, 1941.

[18] Gaus, 1936, chap. 3, esp. pp. 31ff.; Friedrich, 1950, chaps. 19 and literature; Spiro, a, 1953; also 1959, part V.

of responsible conduct can be separated from each other, it needs to be pointed out that they rarely are. Usually a person, P, who is responsible to another person, R, will either have explicit instructions both as to purpose and standard of conduct, as is the case where R is the ruler of P, or P will anticipate R's reactions as to purpose and standard of conduct when R influences P. These basic observations show that the problem of responsible conduct cannot be separated from the relations of power, whether informal, institutionalized or merely consisting of influence.

Two considerations need to be raised in this connection, one with regard to technical standards, and the other with regard to the public interest. A leading political scientist once wrote: "The responsibility of the civil servant to the standards of his profession, in so far as those standards make for the public interest, may be given official recognition. . . . Certainly, in the system of government which is now emerging, one important kind of responsibility will be that which the individual civil servant recognizes as due to the standards and ideals of his profession." [19] These standards are frequently derived from fields of advanced technical knowledge, such as medicine, engineering and the related natural and social sciences. Typically there exists a *communis opinio doctorum*, as the scholastics called it, a fairly generally agreed view as to what is sound. This broad common agreement is at times obscured by the sharp disagreements which arise among persons "in the know" about advanced positions in a given technical field. But most of the time, it is not too difficult for the "insiders" to tell the professional from the charlatan. Responsible conduct on all such occasions is conduct in accordance with these technical standards. It is one of the most familiar instances of conflict in government that the B's possessing a certain technical competence are convinced that a particular conduct is required of them when judged by technical standards, while a different conduct is asked of them by those A's to whom they are personally responsible. The A's may be the public, or they may be the people's representatives, or even the official superiors of such responsible persons, comprised in a bureaucratic hierarchy. According to the old and generally sound rule that the "experts shall be on tap, but not on top," [20] it is held that technical responsibility in such instances must give way to personal responsibility.

This simple political and democratic solution to the problem is, however, often objected to on the ground that the damage resulting from a technically erroneous conduct may be so great, although unknown to the R's who wield power, that the official who is technically competent is really responsible only if he takes a stand which is uncompromising in

[19] Gaus, 1936, p. 40.

[20] For further thought on the "sense of workmanship," see Friedrich, 1942, chap. 6.

terms of his standards for the "right" action or policy. The overruling consideration is said to be the "public interest." Such arguments become particularly sharp and perplexing in fields such as the military, where the very existence, the survival, of the R's may be at stake and depend upon the responsible conduct of the P's. Now the public interest is a broad and many-faceted category which cannot be broken up into technical fields.[21] Not only is there the problem of coordinating the several technical fields with each other, but there is also the more general interest in the maintenance of a particular kind of political order. Typically, medical science may suggest interference in highly private matters, police and tax collectors may correctly consider that a certain kind of conduct on their part will give superior results vital to the survival of the particular order, yet such several lines of conduct may be rejected by the public and its representatives because they violate values which are basic and constitutive of the order itself. There is no ultimate way of determining what *the* public interest is, except by consulting the public. But the manifest dangers of a miscarriage of responsible conduct suggest that safeguards need to be maximized to make sure that the public has had an opportunity to learn of all the different implications of a given line of action or policy.[22]

At this point it becomes quite clear that generally responsible conduct in politics becomes possible only within the context of public policy. It is in public policy that personal and functional responsibility are united and in a sense transcended (Chapter 3). But even under highly effective arrangements for determining public policy by a balancing and merging of the community's value preferences, beliefs and interests with the technical requirements of a given field of endeavor, there will be a range of conduct on the part of public representatives which is at least controversial in terms of responsibility. Policies, like laws, cannot be made sufficiently detailed to fit all situations, and therefore must leave much to the discretion of those who operate and execute them. The extent of such discretion varies and is extended or contracted in some measure at least as a result of technical considerations,[23] but it always involves three notions: (1) that a choice between several existing alternatives can, and indeed must, be made; (2) that a novel solution be found, an invention or an innovation be made (Chapter 21); and (3) that such a choice is not to be made arbitrarily, wantonly or carelessly, but in accordance with the requirements of the situation. This means that ordinarily discretion operates within a framework of rules, implementing them and elaborating them. If we ask what is to exclude arbitrary, wanton or careless choices, the answer will be in terms of responsible conduct. A person of discretion,

[21] Herring, 1936, chaps. I–III; Huntington, 1961, *passim*.

[22] Friedrich, a, 1940; Gaus, 1936, p. 38; Stamp, a, 1937; Robson, 1928, pp. 55ff.; Friedrich, 1957, chap. 1.

[23] Friedrich, a, 1958, pp. 40ff.

that is, a person exercising discretion as it is intended to be exercised, is a person who will conduct himself in accordance with the instructions of the anticipated reactions of a superior or ruler and in line with the technical requirements of the function he is exercising. Such discretion can be conferred because the A's holding power in its various forms and possessing authority are able to find persons who will be ready to act in such a way as to be able to answer for their conduct.[24]

Whoever the particular persons between whom a relationship of responsibility is operative, a number of propositions suggest themselves on the basis of the previous analysis. First, we can say that responsibility transforms coercive into consensual power; indeed this proposition may in a sense seem tautological because of the nature of consensual power (Chapter 9), resting as it does on consent. But this is not truly so, because of the multiplicity of possible sanctions. In any case, it would be more precise to say that the ratio of consent to coercion increases when responsibility increases; and, vice versa, when the ratio of consent to coercion increases, responsibility of the power-handler increases likewise, regardless of to whom he is supposed to be responsible.

The second proposition asserts that the greater the responsibility, the greater the authority, and vice versa. This statement may at first seem puzzling, particularly to those who think of responsibility only within the democratic context. For in this context surely, they would argue, the dependence upon popular approval which the rulers' responsibility involves would seem to reduce their authority. Some would even argue that it entirely disappears. Now it is unquestionably true that greater responsibility of the power-handlers to the people *may* weaken their authority, but it does not do so necessarily. The question is whether their over-all responsibility is greater or less. It will often be found that the responsibility pattern as a whole is weakened, even though popular responsibility is increased. For example, many would argue that the Congress or at least individual Congressmen act less responsibly than the judges of the Supreme Court, meaning thereby that not only what the people are supposed to want, but also other standards, are part of the pattern of responsibility. If this statement is accepted, it would provide a kind of confirmation for the proposition we advanced; for few would question that the authority of the Supreme Court is greater than that of the Congress. A great many other instances could be adduced for this important proposition. It provides some practical hints as to how to heighten the authority of the governors. Nor is this proposition to be wondered at. Responsibility calls for reasoned argument in support of whatever a governor may decide to

[24] *Nomos III* explores some of the many realms of responsibility, including criminal law. In jurisprudence this range of issues has been argued under the heading of "attribution."

do; hence the capacity for reasoned elaboration is needed when power is to be exercised responsibly.

A third proposition has already been implied above when we pointed out that representation may or may not be legitimate. Responsibility increases the chance that voluntary representation will be legitimate. Political representation that is voluntary, that is willed and asked for, necessarily brings with it a belief that those who do such representing are entitled to do it. But even nonvoluntary political representation may have this effect, for example, if the representative is responsible to a divinity whom those subject to the representative ruler believe to be the true God. The same can be said, *ceteris paribus,* about some believed-in standard or norm of conduct.

Fourth, responsibility always increases the influence of those to whom the ruler or governor is responsible. In the case of a divinity this increased influence may actually be exercised by a priesthood speaking on its behalf. If responsibility is defined in terms of a higher norm, the guardians of the norm, such as a professional group, will wield increasing influence, whether for good or ill. The extension of popular responsibility increases the influence of the general public. The last of these statements is almost universally taken to be self-evident, although it is not really so; the arguments which are advanced for and against the extension of popular responsibility are largely couched in terms of assertions about what such greater influence of the people will bring on—to some blessings, to others great damage.

The four propositions which have just been formulated all call for quantitative specification since they assert quantitative comparisons. They apply to representation because of the link between responsibility and representation. Whenever representation involves an actual mandate, making the representative an agent, this is evident; even where the mandate is generic, a responsibility is implied and usually recognized in representation. Is the situation different where the representation is purely existential? Hardly. Whenever an A is made present by a B acting politically on his behalf, B is responsible to A for what he does. Whether such responsibility can actually be enforced is another question. Every type of responsibility has its problems of enforcement. Who would say that because a man is elected and hence a responsible representative, the responsibility will in fact exist? Indeed, one of the curious paradoxes of electoral representation is that the responsibility becomes harder to enforce the larger the majority which elected a governor. This paradox is readily resolved in terms of the analysis we have given above.

chapter

18

The Political Elite and Bureaucracy

The ideally perfect constitution of a public office is that in which the interest of the functionary is entirely coincident with his duty. No mere system will make it so, but still less can it be made so without a system, aptly devised for the purpose.
John Stuart Mill

POLITICAL THOUGHT HAS persistently been inclined to presume that government is a task calling for specially qualified men of exceptional capacity, virtue and intelligence. This inclination is only a specialized version of the view that most human achievements are the creations of great men. Such theories, extolling the deeds of the select few, have exercised a profound influence, and not without reason. In terms of the preceding analysis, it can certainly be said that men differ in power, influence, authority, representative quality, as well as the capacity for freedom in its three dimensions. But the problem of political theory is to determine to what extent such differences can be said to "constitute" an elite which is more than a category in a system of classifying men. It is one of the basic errors in much of the writing on political elites that it argues from the existential judgment that people can be *classified* according to standards of excellence in performance to the existential judgment that an elite exists. But unless such an assortment of persons (a class in the mathematical or statistical sense) also possesses the characteristics of a group with internal cohesion and a consequent capacity for acting jointly, it is hardly justified to speak of them as a political elite. Therefore, a tentative description of the political phenomenon which may properly be called a political, ruling or governing elite may be as follows: it is a group of persons who are distinguished by exceptional performance in politics, who effectively unite (monopolize) the rule of a particular community in their hands, and who possess a sense of group cohesion and a corresponding *esprit de corps,* usually expressed in cooptation; a political elite excels in the ability to secure power and rule.

It may, however, be argued that it would be useful to distinguish a political elite in the statistical sense of those who are "good at politics" from the "ruling" or "governing" elite we have just characterized.[1] We hesitate to accept this suggestion because of the potential confusion as well as the doubtfulness of so designating those who are "good at politics"; for is anyone who is "good at politics" likely to be unrelated to the ruling and governing, if the term "good at politics" is given a specific governmental connotation? It is, of course, true, that in situations of breakdown and revolutionary crisis, a revolutionary leader may be very good at politics, and yet quite unrelated to a "ruling" or "governing" elite of the political order he and his movement seek to overthrow. But he is likely to be the ruler, indeed usually the autocratic governor, of his organization.[2] Our concept of the elite is not restricted to a particular group or level of community formation; it applies to any group whatever. The political elite, seen as ruling and governing, may of course be differentiated according to political community formation: official elites, revolutionary elites, ecclesiastical elites, and so forth.[3]

Perhaps the most striking instance of an elite theory failing to consider the group aspect of political elites (though implying it repeatedly) is that of Vilfredo Pareto and of Gaetano Mosca.[4] Pareto, who systematized and developed Mosca's ideas on this score, sought to give the theory a broader sociological basis. The relationship of the two writers is

[1] This point was first made by Robert Dahl in a discussion of the main thesis of this chapter, on April 13, 1961; cf. for the issue, his study of 1962.

[2] The specific issues of party rule, as seen by Lenin, are discussed below, Chap. 28.

[3] A very interesting general discussion of political elites was organized by the International Sociological Association at their Fourth World Congress in 1959, under the chairmanship of A. P. d'Entrèves; the proceedings were edited and published by Renato Treves, 1961. The main papers were presented by E. Pennati, N. Bobbio, G. E. G. Catlin, W. L. Guttsman, J. La Palombara, G. Lavau, J. H. Meisel, G. Sartori and A. Touraine. Only a partial, general agreement emerged. Bobbio, in concluding remarks, pp. 207–209, identified two main areas of discussion and possible agreement, one that political elites are minorities (agreed), and the other that they must be organized. On the latter point there was disagreement. As we show in the text, it is not a matter of organization but the more general question of group cohesion and self-identification.

[4] Mosca, 1896, 1939; Pareto, 1923, 1935, esp. pars. 2031–2059; Meisel, 1958; Michels (transl. A. de Grazia), 1949.

somewhat controversial.[5] Pareto's elite theory, being of broader scope, rests upon this author's criticism of the rationalist concept of man, as found in nineteenth-century economic and sociological thought. That such criticism overshot the mark was shown earlier (Chapters 1 and 6). Pareto argues from the hardly disputable premise that in any branch of activity, such as a trade, those participating in it can be arranged according to their performance. Pareto does not hesitate to suggest that there exists an "elite" of thieves composed of those who are best in that activity. It is clear that such a concept is purely statistical and refers to persons with particular characteristics, namely, those which make them best in what they are doing. One could also call it functional, in that excellence is for purposes of classification defined in terms of the function the particular individual performs. No attempt is made by Pareto to show that such an "elite" operates as a group. This might not be a fatal objection in the case of such persons as doctors, engineers and scientists, though even here organizations such as academies suggest that for certain purposes effective cooperation among the best may be desirable.

Having defined the elite in a purely statistical way, Pareto proceeds by simply dividing this elite into two classes, a "*governing elite*, comprising individuals who directly or indirectly play some considerable part in government, and a *non*-governing elite, comprising the rest." [6] This distinction is not stated satisfactorily as it stands. It should distinguish political from nonpolitical elites. Pareto's own interest in the circulation of elites should have served to restrict the elite concept to those who play a part in the government, even when that term is not taken too formally. There is, however, a further difficulty in that nonpolitical elites need actually to be further subdivided for purposes of political analysis. These several nonpolitical elites, economic, social, technical and cultural, vary greatly in their relevance for politics among themselves, and in different situations. Thus, to give just one illustration of great moment at the present time, the technical elite which constitutes the core of the military establishment is much more relevant to American politics in the second half of the twentieth century than it was in the first.[7] Along with this

[5] Pareto, 1935, contains an able discussion of the problem by Arthur Livingston on pp. xxxvi ff. However, because of his partiality toward Pareto, this author somewhat exaggerates when he claims: "There is no dialectical or historical connection between Pareto's theory of the elite and Mosca's theory of the ruling class." For Pareto's "governing elite" seems largely identical with Mosca's "political Class" or "ruling Class." Cf. also the stimulating, and in the main convincing, discussion in Meisel, 1958, chap. 8 and pp. 356–360.

[6] Pareto, 1935, par. 2032.

[7] This is the sound kernel in Mills, 1956, chaps. 8 and 9; he overstated his position when including the top military in an American "power elite." The notion of such a power elite is largely "statistical." Yet, Mills rightly emphasized the ascendancy of the military.

ascendancy of the military, cultural elites, especially scientific elites, have assumed decidedly more important roles in American politics in the course of the twentieth century.

The main difficulty with distinguishing between a political and a nonpolitical elite stems, however, from another crucial fact. The problem of elite formation is complicated in two directions in the field of government. To begin with, only a *cooperating* group of the "best" could be said to be "governing"; for government is a complex whole. All that we have shown in earlier parts of this work and will elaborate later as characteristic of the governmental process implies that. Furthermore, arguments involving the importance of an elite, from Plato to contemporary writings,[8] have always tacitly assumed it. Surely, if Plato's guardians were found here and there, indiscriminately dispersed among the rest of the community, they could not accomplish their task. Plato, accordingly, is especially concerned with their forming a close-knit group by the sharing of property, of meals and, as the saying goes, of wives (though presumably wives share the husbands as well). Similarly, the Communist elite of Marx's doctrine is a firmly organized party, and Lenin perfected the master's notions in this respect.[9] Indeed Pareto himself in writing of the "governing elite" seems to envisage them as a cohesive group when he says, for example, "Every people is governed by an *elite*, by a chosen element in the population." [10] The close-knit character of such elite groups does not exclude the possibility of a gradual transformation, of course; every governing elite is subject to such changes. This common observation led Pareto to the formulation of his celebrated "law," based upon his conception of the circulation of classes. "In virtue of class circulation, the governing elite is always in a state of slow and continuous transformation," he wrote.[11] That is to say, new persons join or are admitted to this group, which possesses, evidently, a life of its own. But as so often, this brilliantly speculative author alleges more than the facts which he adduces warrant. Change and transformation there are, certainly. But these changes do not seem to exhibit regularly or even casually a *circular* motion. Rather, they resemble the kind of transformation by which a piece of forest is slowly altered by the gradual substitution of other species; there may be built-in circular regularities, such as the succession of hardwood and softwood trees, but no data are offered by Pareto to suggest it. He merely offers some vague generalities, such as that "velocity in circulation has to be considered not only absolutely, but also in relation to the

[8] Mills, 1956; Meisel, 1958, gives extensive references; cf. also Dahl, a, 1958, *passim*, and Sereno, 1962.

[9] Lenin, 1902, esp. chap. IV, secs. C–E; cf. also Chap. 28 below.

[10] Pareto, 1935, par. 248.

[11] *Ibid*., par. 2056.

supply of and the demand for certain social elements,"[12] or that "the upper stratum of society, the *elite*, nominally contains certain groups of peoples, not always very sharply defined, that are called aristocracies."[13] There follow then some random observations on aristocracies, culminating in the dictum that "history is a graveyard of aristocracies," discussed further below. The reason for Pareto's failure to develop significant insights is due to his not recognizing the cohesive group character of political or governing elites. As such, governing elites are the result of specific constellations of political factors conditioning their development.

If this is true, then obviously the formation of such groups may be subject to specific conditions, and they may be found in some societies but not in others. Both Pareto and Mosca adduce evidence in support of their contention that they are found in all societies, but this evidence is inconclusive in two respects. In the first place, it is drawn from history and therefore would prove only that past societies have always contained elites; a different argument, philosophical and general, in terms of human nature for example, would have to be adduced if their disappearance were to be excluded. No such argument is offered by these authors, though writers like Plato and the theorists in his tradition abound with contentions of this sort. But there is the further difficulty that the historical evidence is quite incomplete and merely serves to show that such elites have existed and actually governed in some societies. That this is true, no one will want to question. In these instances, as Pareto's own evidence tends to suggest, the governing elite is apt to be self appointed and self-renewing, with a great many variations in the methods of cooptation. The crucial fact is, however, that the elite itself sets the standard of excellence by which particular men are to be evaluated. Plato's royal lie is the most famous instance of the hypocrisy involved in all such self-evaluations. Most of the historic elites have not aspired to such spiritual heights as Plato did. More usual standards have been distinguished: blood descent, riches and military valor, to mention only the most usual measuring rods.[14] More recently, Marx and his followers have made "class consciousness" the mark of a governing elite, and in the communist states of our time the ideological commitment of the ruling party has been the "visible" sign of such election.

[12] *Ibid.*, par. 2044.

[13] *Ibid.*, pars. 2051ff. Pareto recognizes, of course, that these reflections are of long standing.

[14] Mannheim, 1936, speaks of blood, riches and accomplishment (*Leistung*), including of course military exploits. This inclusion of accomplishment in general obscures, however, the analysis of the governing or ruling aspect of an elite, but Mannheim not being especially concerned with governing elites is justified in putting it that way.

The difficulty with all such standards for determining who "belongs" to an elite is that there is no readily available yardstick for assessing the performance in the field of government. As we said, it is quite possible to classify persons engaged in technical functions, such as lawyers, doctors, engineers, farmers, cooks, and so forth. There may be considerable difference of opinion, but because of the technical standards involved, a measure of rational agreement can be considered achievable. These purely technical standards can be used because agreement on the value to be achieved can be presupposed. When a doctor is called, health is to be served, when a lawyer, legal rights, and so forth. But can the same be said for "governing" or "ruling"? Plato asserted it in his well-known comparisons of rulers with shepherds, ship captains, doctors, and the like.[15] But he was wrong. The multiplicity of values involved in community living and the consequent difficulty in assessing performance exclude the possibility of treating excellence in government in analogy to excellence in these other activities. Pareto's own evidence in support of the contention that a "governing elite" is the projection of a class which happens to be dominant in society—in close parallel to Marxist views, incidentally—suggests the conclusion that only a fairly cohesive group with common value judgments and interests is likely to agree on the quality of performance of any person engaged in government.

Recently, an attempt has been made to substitute "power" for other kinds of performance criteria in constructing a statistical concept of the elite.[16] To do so was thought "important in the light of the common supposition that to put the concept of elite to the fore in political science is to deny from the outset the possibility of democratic institutions." An elite is then defined as "those with most power in the group." There would be added a "mid-elite" with "less power" and the "mass" with least power. Apart from the objections arising from limiting the term "elite," even when meant politically, to power-wielders, it is evident from the previous analysis that this elite concept is strictly statistical, that is to say, simply classifies persons according to the amount of power they possess. Whether such a statistical classification seems interesting in view of the difficulty of constructing an adequate index of power in quantitative terms will not be discussed here. These authors rightly remark that no more

[15] Plato, *The Republic*, par. 345; *Statesman*, par. 302 A; and *The Laws*, par. 758 A; for key references; there are some interesting variations on the theme in the *Statesman*, *The Laws* and elsewhere, but they do not affect the basic issue.

[16] Lasswell and Kaplan, 1950, pp. 62 and 201ff. It should be borne in mind, however, that these authors do not use the terms "power" and "influence" in the same sense as is done here; for them power is "the participating in making decisions," while "influence" is "value position potential" (pp. 75 and 58). See above, Chaps. 9 and 11, for a more detailed discussion.

than such a statistical class is "contained in such assertions as Pareto's that 'every people is governed by an elite, by a chosen element in the population'; what is said, in effect, is that every people is ruled by—rulers." It seems highly questionable, however, whether in light of this discussion the decision of these authors to retain a statistical concept of the (governing) elite is justified; the paucity of generalizations derived by them from their analysis would suggest abandoning it. It deserves notice that their elite concept is different and distinct from their concept of the ruling class; it is not the class that rules, as in Mosca, but the class "from which the rulers are recruited and in whose interest they exercise power." In other words, their ruling class concept is identical with Marx's concept of the oppressing, exploiting class as expressed in the justly famous phrase of the *Communist Manifesto:* "The modern state power is only a committee which administers (executes) the common business of the bourgeois class," which shows that the exploiting class is also the ruling class. Clearly, such a ruling class, seen as a reservoir from which the rulers or governors, the governing elite, are drawn, is seen as a collective led by those who are conscious of its role and its identity. Indeed, "class consciousness" is, for Marx, the key characteristic of true elite, and hence the communists are the elite of the proletariat, whereas the "elite" which is merely characterized by being a statistical classification of those who have the most power is quite different from a class-conscious leadership which could be, though it need not be, a mere collection of power-wielders. Only such an elite exhibiting group cohesion and a capacity for monopolizing rule possesses the self-identity necessary for political functioning.

The oratory of elitist writers has frequently obscured this insight. In the nineteenth century, several thinkers in reaction against the egalitarian trends of their time developed rather extreme views of this kind, notably Carlyle and Nietzsche. Hero worship and the cult of the superman are exaggerated forms of such elitism; characteristically both Carlyle and Nietzsche were aesthetes, withdrawn from active life. As they contemplated history, they could perceive only the work of great leaders. "Universal history . . . is at bottom the history of the great men who have worked here. They were the leaders of men, these great ones; the modelers, patterners, in a wide sense creators, of whatsoever the general mass of men contrived to do or to attain." [17] Of course, both recognized that such men might be prophets, priests or men of letters, but above all philosophers. Yet, "the commander over men; he to whose will our wills are to be subordinated, and loyally surrender themselves, and find their welfare in doing so, may be reckoned the most important of great men," wrote Carlyle, who added: "He [the hero] is practically the summary for us of

[17] T. Carlyle, 1841, p. 1; cf. also Nietzsche, *Vorrede*, 1883–1885; also 1887, *passim*.

all the various figures of heroism. . . . He is called Rex, Regulator, Roi: our own name is better still: King, König. . . ."[18] From such reflections Carlyle distilled his notion of an aristocracy of talent, a governing elite. "Democracy, which means despair of finding any heroes to govern you, and contented [with] putting up with the want of them [makes it] a dire necessity of Nature's to bring in her Aristocracies, her best, even by forcible methods." He argues, as so many before him and since his time, that "the toiling millions of mankind are in most vital need and [have a] passionate instinctive desire of Guidance." True enough; but his argument gainsays the vital question of how to determine and by what standards to assess the performance of those who offer such guidance, such leadership. That Carlyle should address himself to the captains of industry as the future noblemen, the coming elite, suggests a measure of vision in mid-nineteenth-century England; with Saint-Simon he grasped one key trend of the emerging order. But it was wide of the mark, as far as the "governing" elite was concerned. In this field the pluralism of values and interests rather led to two related developments: on the one hand the democratization of government, which places the evaluation of the performance of the ruler in the hands of the ruled and thereby seeks to insure that the pluralism of values and interests will be reflected in public policies embodying the compromises between rival groups and their values, interests and beliefs, and on the other hand the professionalization of the administrative services which seeks to identify the areas where performance is a matter of objective standards and their skillful application by technically qualified personnel, the bureaucracy. A juncture of these two divergent efforts at institutionalizing the insights which older elitist doctrines had obscured was provided by subordinating the "experts" and "specialists" to the politician-rulers, providing that the latter decided what was to be done (value-oriented decisions), while the former undertook to determine how these decisions were to be carried out or administered "in the public interest."[19]

While the democratic process will be taken up at length later, the problem of the bureaucracy must be further explored within the context of the conception of a political elite. But before we turn to this aspect of the subject under consideration, the role of elites in many past societies and governments calls for some further comment. Pareto's and Mosca's notion of a circulation of elites (or ruling classes) has already been mentioned. It leads logically to a theory of revolution (Chapter 34). At the same time, governing elites have devised a variety of methods for maintaining themselves in power. These methods are practical applications of the "laws" of power (Chapter 9). More particularly, a detailed theory of

[18] T. Carlyle, 1841, p. 196. Cf. also 1843, *passim*.
[19] Schubert, 1960; *Nomos V*, 1961.

political elites would have to be related to the "types of rule" discussed earlier (Chapter 10). If one leaves aside anarchy, which excludes by definition a governing elite, it would seem that of the baker's dozen of types we have identified there are several, namely, despotic monarchy, the three forms of oligarchy, and bureaucratic rule under a hereditary monarch, which are systems with a "governing elite" built into them. In some of the others, a governing elite may be present, especially in a parliamentary-cabinet system of the aristocratic type, in a military dictatorship and in a totalitarian dictatorship, whereas it is excluded in the tribal rule of the king-priest type, and in the three forms of democratic rule. In these latter systems, there may come into being from time to time a kind of crypto-elite, because an exceptional performance on the part of temporary rulers which these systems select from among the entire citizenry may induce a feeling of well-being and apathy leading to nonparticipation on the part of the electorate. However, the "men behind the scenes" who in such situations give the impression of being a "governing elite" can maintain this position only as long as they give satisfaction, that is, as long as their performance, and that of their stooges in the offices, succeeds in realizing the values and interests of a sufficiently large part of the electorate not to make it appear inviting to challenge their rule by invoking the democratic machinery which is available to a dissatisfied majority or even strong minority.[20] The recurrent appearance of such crypto-elites governing local communities in the United States, Britain and Switzerland has led to mistaken generalizations about the power and influence of such groups.[21] They suggest that a certain degree of permanence is as much part of the phenomenon of a true governing elite as the cohesion and the self-appointment of such a group of power-wielders. Otherwise even such temporary and dependent power-wielders as the party leadership in a democratic system or the court favorites become confused with the true phenomenon of a political elite.

At this point, another kind of elite might be mentioned, and that is the "value-shaping elite" in the field of politics. Throughout the range of human society, value-shaping and value-changing is going forward all the time, as has been shown in various fields (Chapter 2 et al.). Much of this

[20] Dahl, a, 1958, rightly states that "to constitute a ruling elite, a controlling group must not be *a pure artefact of democratic rules*" (p. 464).

[21] F. Hunter, 1953; Mills, 1956, makes an equally untenable attempt to apply that kind of analysis to the U.S. as a whole. These tendencies of mistaken political analysis were precipitated by a series of community studies inaugurated by the well-known Middletown analysis of Lynd and his associates, 1929, followed by the Newburyport study. In the latter there is no specific effort made to identify a "governing elite," but merely a "class structure"—the classes being defined in terms of attitudinal tests of "upper" and "lower"—strictly what we called a "statistical" approach to the problem of the elite, and not relevant to the problem of the "governing elite."

value-shaping occurs in connection with the particular activities to which such values apply: art, letters, food, and so forth. Therefore, it stands to reason that the peculiar political values, power, justice, freedom and their derivations, also will be shaped, remoulded and altered by innovations. The human beings participating in this process do not need to operate as a group; like many other elites they can function separately, or even individually. Naturally, this value-shaping elite will extensively overlap with a ruling or governing elite. Thus the impression might result (and often has) that this value-shaping elite *is* a governing elite. Indeed some of the writing in regard to elites in democratic societies has asserted the existence of political elites in democratic societies precisely because of such confusion. But poets and thinkers, even martyrs, may be decidedly part of the value-shaping elite of a particular society without in any meaningful sense participating in the government of their society, by which they may in point of fact be persecuted. These phenomena are of decisive importance when we consider the opinions of those who incline to the view that the value judgments, interests and beliefs of a democratic society under modern conditions of mass communication are manipulated to such an extent that those who shape these value preferences, through ideas, opinions and beliefs, are actually ruling the society by shaping its consensus.[22] The probability is altogether against the coinciding of the value-shaping elite with any governing elite, even in nondemocratic societies. The pluralism of a democratic order is a vivid reminder not only of this dispersion of the value-shaping elite, but also of the absence of any governing elite in a democratic society.

Recently, it has been argued in terms of a concrete test that "the evidence for a ruling elite . . . has not yet been properly examined," especially in the United States.[23] This proposition is based upon the premise that "a ruling elite, then, is a controlling group less than a majority in size . . . it is a minority of individuals whose preferences regularly prevail in cases of differences in preference on key political issues." Such a premise, while related to the definition here used, is not satisfactory if the meaning of power as given earlier (Chapter 9) is borne in mind, for two important reasons: first, that the criterion of its being a minority is inadequate,[24] and second, that it fails to specify the existential quality of

[22] This appears to be the view of Mills, 1956, *passim;* Dahl, a, 1958, reads him similarly, but rejects the view in terms of his insistence upon a test by decisions discussed in the next paragraph below.

[23] Dahl, a, 1958, p. 469. Dahl explicitly states that "we are here concerned with the application of the techniques of modern investigation to American communities."

[24] This is so because in modern electorates, consisting often of millions of people, a minority might consist of many more persons than could conceivably constitute a governing or ruling elite. Defined merely as a minority, it becomes a statistical entity, without group cohesion; Dahl later in his discussion seems to

the group constituting a governing elite, namely, its capacity for power and rule. In spite of these shortcomings, or inadequacies, in the definition as such, the analysis is of great value because it stresses correctly that one valid test for the existence of such a group as a governing elite is the analysis of a series of concrete decisions, and presumably key political decisions. And in a democratic context this would be the best test, if not the only one. Elites, governing or ruling elites, exist in many other contexts, however, as has just been pointed out. Their existence is not beyond proof simply because conflicts over decisions cannot be tested. For example, such political behavior phenomena as deference, prestige and honor—in short, all that Charles Merriam in a striking phrase called "the credenda and miranda of power" [25]—when combined with the observable performance of the key functions of ruling by the kind of close-knit and group-conscious elite that we specified may readily add up to a reasonable "proof" of its existence. It is equally true of these phenomena that they have not been shown to exist in operating democratic societies, nor is it likely that such evidence will be forthcoming, except where a democratic system is in fact disintegrating or has not yet come fully into being, as in nineteenth-century England,[26] or in Weimar Germany.[27]

There is, in the search for some kind of hidden governing elite, a strange fascination which makes the argument asserting its existence one of infinite regress and thus puts it beyond refutation, as has been pointed out. "If the overt leaders of a community do not appear to constitute a ruling elite, then the theory can be saved by arguing that behind the overt leaders there is a set of covert leaders who do. If subsequent evidence shows that this covert group does not make a ruling elite, then the theory can be saved by arguing that behind the first covert group there is another, and so on." [28] Arguments of the sort here criticized have been advanced in various guises and have enjoyed temporary success, appealing as they do to a sense of "mystery revealed" or "suspicion confirmed" which gratifies the disappointed and the dissatisfied. Books about "La République des Camarades," "La République des Professeurs," "The Two Hundred Families," [29] and others are earlier European versions of the contemporary American fashion in this field. Such studies usually fail to make

---

exclude this by saying that an "elite is a well-defined group," but it could be well-defined without possessing the character of a cohesive group capable of operating.

[25] Merriam, 1934, chap. 4.

[26] For this "incomplete" democracy and the consequent survival of a governing elite see, e.g., Dicey, 1905, *passim.*

[27] Cf. for the surviving bureaucratic elite in Germany, Bracher, 1957, *passim.* The background of this bureaucratic elite is elucidated by Rosenberg, 1958.

[28] Dahl, a, 1958, p. 463.

[29] Robert De Jouvenel, 1914; Thibaudet, 1927; Hamon, 1936–1938.

clear what precisely is to be understood by a ruling or governing elite. The argument can be reduced, when the evidence is studied carefully, to a proposition to the effect that there are certain persons in the particular community under scrutiny who have more power than the rest, and who have a certain trait in common, such as belonging to specified families or business and governmental organizations or professions. It goes without saying, evidently, that *some* persons will have more power than others, and that among these persons there will be some who have certain traits in common, especially such traits as riches or intelligence, since these are traits which greatly assist a man in securing and maintaining power.

But only if it can be shown that such a group is a cohesive one with a sense of group identity, and that it has a grip on the governmental power in that community approaching a monopoly, can it be argued that it constitutes a "ruling elite" in the sense in which that term is employed by most of these writers. The *apparatschiki* of the Communist Party in the Soviet Union and other totalitarian systems qualify as an elite in this sense, because they exhibit all the traits that are characteristic of a governing elite, whereas the upper ranks of the American financial community do not, because they are far from possessing a monopoly of governing power, and the conglomerate of corporate, bureaucratic and military leadership does not constitute one either because it lacks group cohesion and consciousness—it is an inchoate statistical entity.

In many past societies, the nobility has constituted a genuine ruling or governing elite; indeed the capacity of men to constitute themselves a group with its distinguishing characteristics has, in the genetic perspective, made them a nobility. Certain writers have claimed that the nobility continues to rule. In so perspicacious a writer as Roberto Michels we find the assertion that "nobility holds itself at the helm [in contemporary society] and does not even dream of disappearing from the stage of history. Though not coinciding with aristocracy, and not constituting more than a part of it, nobility gradually takes hold of it and makes itself its master. . . ." [30] To be sure, this somewhat extravagant proposition (even if restricted to Europe) is qualified by the observation that "nowadays the aristocracy of birth . . . is accompanied by an aristocracy of government clerks, an aristocracy of money, and an aristocracy of knowledge. Put together, these constitute aristocracy in the sense of a ruling class." Since Michels recognizes the steady infiltration of new elements, in the sense of a continuous renewal, these statements are apt to dissolve into vague abstractions about the historical role and significance of the aristocratic orders of the past. Pareto declared that "history is the graveyard of aristocracies," in insisting on the "circulation of elites," which is true enough,

[30] Alfred De Grazia and Roberto Michels, 1949, p. 80. The next quotation is from p. 76. Cf. also Meisel, 1958, pp. 183ff.

but history is also the battlefield on which many striking victories have been won by such aristocracies. Many societies have been moulded by effective governing elites composed of noblemen distinguished by valor, brains and blood descent. The culture of Greece, of the Italian Renaissance and of monarchical Europe was the creation of societies which a governing elite of noblemen ruled. In penning his paean to British noblemen, Harrington was partly inspired by the past glories of Venice, the immortal commonwealth.[31] Much inclined toward the notion of a "natural aristocracy" of wisdom and superior virtue in the elitist tradition of Plato, and arguing the case in similar terms, Harrington persuasively expounded the ideal of the gentleman as the mainstay of a constitutional monarchy. At one point he wrote: "There is something first in the making of a Commonwealth, then in the governing of her, and last of all in the leading of her Armies; which, though there be great Divines, great Lawyers, great men in all professions, seems to be peculiar unto the Genius of a Gentleman."[32] He was, therefore, much concerned with the workings of past aristocracies and thus the role of nobility in government. But he likewise had a sense of deep aversion to a self-regarding nobility; what he calls the "oligarchists," the small cliques dominated by the *libido dominandi* (Harrington's term!), are "of all men least fit for government."[33] Bitterly, he speaks of their pretense of virtue, calling themselves saints, while actually eager "to keep all others out of government." But unless a nobility manages to identify itself with virtue, that is, make good on the claim that its conduct embodies those values and convictions upon which the community rests, it can not legitimize its monopoly of power. Such legitimization has more recently been replaced by asserting the cultural creativity of such groups. Not all comment goes as far as Werner Jaeger, who asserts: "Culture is simply the aristocratic ideal of a nation, increasingly intellectualized." Arguing in terms of heroic valor, he would insist that "the nobility is the prime mover in forming a nation's culture."[34] It would be truer to say with Burke that "nobility is a graceful ornament to the civil order. It is the Corinthian capital of polished society."[35] In a highly cultured society, such as the France of the Roi Soleil and his successors, the nobility played some part in the cultural productivity, and some of its members like Montesquieu were outstanding. There can be little question, however, that as a class the nobility was more concerned with military valor than with culture or even government, and its outstanding members were engaged

[31] Cf. Blitzer, 1960, *passim,* for a fine study of Harrington's political thought.

[32] *Oceana* in *Works* (ed. Toland, 1700), introduction to first part.

[33] See Harrington, *A System of Politics* (in Toland's edition of his *Works*).

[34] Jaeger, 1939, Vol. I, pp. 2–3.

[35] Burke, 1790. The entire discussion of nobility in his *Reflections* is noteworthy for its positive yet restrained appraisal.

in war. The long drawn-out conflict between the nobility of the sword and that of the robe ended in a merger of the two in the generation before the revolution. But this nobility, though certainly a key group in France, had been stripped of political power by Louis XIV, and reacquired only some part of it in the ensuing reigns. So much was this the case that La Bruyère could, toward the end of the seventeenth century, write: "A nobleman, if he lives at home in his province, lives free but without substance; if he lives at court, he is taken care of, but enslaved." [36] The same emasculation of the nobility as far as government was concerned occurred under Frederick II of Prussia, with a similar deflection into military rather than cultural activities. Numerous other historical situations could be cited to show that a nobility can be, but need not be, the governing elite of the society in which it participates, and likewise that it may, but need not, be of major importance in the cultural life and development.[37]

Karl Mannheim highlighted the role of elites as the "culture-creating groups." Like Pareto, he identified the political with other cultural activities, but distinguished "the following types of elites: the political, the organizing, the intellectual, the artistic, the moral and the religious." [38] He then proceeded to contrast the political and organizing elites as integrating elites with others, and linked the development of such elites to the class aspects of society (like Pareto, again, and Marx), but admitted that the concept is difficult to apply in an open society where only performance (achievements) matters. "It is possible," he wrote, "that in such a society the succession of elites would take place much too rapidly. . . ." [39]

Mannheim's argument in favor of the culture-creating role of elites is true enough, if the term is taken in a nongovernmental sense —but if so taken, it becomes rather tautological, since it says that those who are best in various fields of human endeavor create the enduring

[36] Cited by Ford, 1953, chap. VII—a book which ably traces the reemergence of the French nobility to the point where, "if it did not have the strength to suppress the revolution, it had at least recovered enough strength to make the revolution inevitable."

[37] See for a great deal of historical evidence bearing upon these points the study of feudalism in history, edited by Coulborn, 1956. Cf. for an interesting, though somewhat dated appraisal of the role of the nobility in the twentieth century, R. Michels, 1949, chap. 3, "The Elite" (ed. A. de Grazia), previously cited.

[38] Mannheim, 1936, pp. 64ff.

[39] Mannheim, 1936, 1940, pp. 81ff. It should be noted, however, that this distinguished author dropped the emphasis on elites soon thereafter, and in 1943 began to argue in favor of militant democracy. Such a democracy, based upon traditional values and virtues such as brotherly love, mutual help, decency, justice, freedom, respect for persons, and so forth, is then held together by planning—a rather unconvincing substitute for elites, especially governing ones, except if seen as the function of a bureaucratic elite; this view would fail to resolve the issue created by the task of governing a society *without* a governing elite.

works in their respective fields. If, however, by a familiar juggler's trick, the governing elite is included or substituted, then the proposition is questionable. Again, some years ago T. S. Eliot voiced the belief that no society without a governing elite can hope to transmit the culture which it has inherited. Such a governing elite, according to him, "would consist of those whose responsibility was inherited with their affluence and position, and whose forces were constantly increased, and often led, by rising individuals of exceptional talent." [40] Like Ortega y Gasset, Eliot is deeply disturbed by the rising trend toward the oppressive mobocracy which destroyed Athenian freedom in the name of democracy. These fears are by no means groundless, but it is more than doubtful that these dangers can be mastered by a cultural elitism which longs for philosopher kings and ends up by despairing of political order. Bagehot may have been right in nineteenth-century England when he wrote, in discussing the House of Lords, that the order of "nobility is of great use, too, not only in what it creates, but in what it prevents. It prevents the rule of wealth. . . ." [41] Actually, historical orders of nobility have often, even usually, been founded upon wealth—an English proverb alleging that "nobility is nothing but ancient riches." Other sayings call attention to the fact that nobility is somone else's merit, that it concentrates on past rather than present achievement, and so on. Actually, the truth lies in between these pro- and antiaristocratic sentiments. Over long periods of history, nobility has played a highly significant role in providing stability to a governing or ruling elite, by crystallizing civilized codes of conduct, as expressed in the saying *noblesse oblige*. But in modern industrial and managerial society, built on performance in the sober fields of business, science and government, the traditional notion of nobility based upon distinguished blood descent has lost its essential legitimacy. Few if any are inclined to believe that a person is entitled to rule because his ancestors were able to do so. If "the real strength of aristocracy consists in its agrarian roots," [42] as Michels alleged, then that strength is certainly dwindling rapidly, as these agrarian roots are drying up.

The governing elite or ruling class (political class) has, however, been rediscovered in two other groupings very characteristic of the industrial and democratic and mass society, namely, the bureaucracy and the parties. We shall deal with both of them at greater length below (Chapters 26 and 27). Here we merely have to consider whether they

[40] T. S. Eliot, 1949, p. 85, and the entire chap. II; Ortega y Gasset, 1932, chaps. 21 and 22.

[41] Bagehot, 1878, chap. IV. In this connection one might recall Lord John Manners' well-known exclamation: "Let wealth and commerce, laws and learning die, But leave us still our old nobility."

[42] Michels, 1949, p. 74. This author's above-cited contention that the nobility is staying at the helm is certainly obsolete.

can properly be called a governing elite in terms of the clarified concept implicit in assertions to this effect. It is important to observe at the outset that Mosca did not have any conception of the modern mass party and its operation, and that his follower Michels did not make the generalizations which his own data suggested.[43] Michels thought that the political class was divided into three "sectors": the strictly political, the economic and the intellectual. He thought that they overlapped and that to study their interrelations was "the most important and most arduous task before us." Leaving aside the economic and the intellectual "sectors," and concentrating on the political, we find Michels expounding his much-discussed "iron law of oligarchy" by which he generalized the formation of ruling cliques which he had observed in the German Social Democratic party. Although extravagantly praised, this supposed "law" derived its spice from the alleged conflict between the democratic ideology and the not-so-democratic practice of the particular party he had described.[44] It is actually a special instance of the more general proposition concerning power (Chapter 9) and its propensity to be based upon both consent and constraint, namely, that power acquired through consent becomes a possession and thus available for coercion. Such oligarchical tendencies, popularly referred to in the United States as boss rule, also result from the hierarchical aspect of rule as structured and institutionalized power (Chapter 10).

If considered more closely, Michels' argument appears to be the result of confusing two quite distinct political processes, namely, that of organizing consent (the democratic aspect) and that of organizing an operation (the hierarchical aspect). In any case, the existence of smaller groups directing the political mass parties from within, inescapable according to the "recurrent regularities of politics" as manifest not only in the realm of power but in those of influence, authority, legitimacy, and others, does not prove or even make probable the existence of a political or ruling elite except in a statistical sense. At most, we could say that such party leadership constitutes several governing elites, but in doing so we would be gainsaying the crucial monopolistic aspect of a governing elite. Even the proposition that such a party elite monopolizes power for a limited period does not really hold, since the party has to share its power with the bureaucracy and other key groups, such as business and the trade unions.[45]

In one situation, however, the party does indeed provide a "govern-

[43] Meisel, 1958, pp. 177ff.

[44] Michels, 1925 (2nd ed.). In other words, this study amounted to a bit of "debunking." What is correct in the analysis had been stated before Michels by Ostrogorskii, 1902.

[45] For a similar conclusion, cf. Plamenatz, a, 1958.

ing elite," and that is the one-party state.[46] In such a political order—and we have already had occasion above to refer to totalitarian parties in this respect—the party provides a governing elite in the strict sense of a ruling class: its upper echelons are composed of persons possessing a strong sense of group cohesion and *esprit de corps*, they are distinguished by exceptional performance in politics, indeed monopolize the sphere of politics, and thus excel in the ability to secure power and rule. It is, nonetheless, an error to identify such a political order with totalitarianism, which is a particular subspecies of it. Modern multiparty systems have as a rule emerged from a system in which a single party predominated (Chapter 28), and in quite a few states at the present time a single "party" commands so large and permanent a majority that it is said to approach the monopolization of political power. Yet such a party may recognize the desirability of an opposition, it may accept the value of civil liberties, and it may even cherish a measure of divided power in the operation of the government.[47] Under such conditions, the existence of a governing elite is patent. It may be, and often is, a relatively "open" elite, that is to say, an elite quite ready to admit new members on the basis of various convictional and performance tests. Whether such an order is called "democratic" or not depends upon the concept of democracy employed; admittedly the line is at times difficult to draw between such a single-party system and an order of two or more parties which is devoid of a governing elite. For the two kinds of order are often transformed into each other, as can be seen in some of the states in the United States which over extended periods have had one-party systems. In these there has always remained the possibility of the reemergence of a second party, sometimes developing as a party-like division within the single party.[48] Turkey is another interesting special case, where single-party regimes have alternated with attempts at a two-party system; the same is true of a number of Latin American states. Such single party predominance is often accompanied by the existence of several small party-like organizations which engage in criticism of the government but do not expect to participate in it. This situation is different from the typical two- or multiparty system in terms of the time span involved.

Such one-party systems of a constitutional type may be especially suited for situations in which integration or reintegration of the political community is of paramount importance. The situation in France under

[46] Recently it has been suggested that such a state be called a movement state (Tucker, a, 1961); the difficulty with such a term is that it may obscure the vital distinction between totalitarian and nontotalitarian one-party orders, which in fact seems to be the inclination of this author.

[47] Clement Moore, a, 1960.

[48] Key, 1949, chap. 14.

De Gaulle demonstrates the fact that even in old and established constitutional democracies, emergencies may create so disruptive an effect as to call for a single party or movement to overcome it. If the emergency lasts for a sufficient length of time, a single-party dominance may become so firmly rooted as to produce a governing elite directing an open autocratic regime, as appears to be the tendency in a number of emergent nations which have recently won their independence. The reason appears to be the difficulty of maintaining any degree of legitimacy or amount of authority except under conditions of consolidated leadership (Chapters 12 and 13). Such authority and legitimacy are, on the other hand, urgently needed, if the vast tasks of a technological and sociological nature which the rapid transformation of such societies into modern ones poses for the government, whether elite or responsible, are to be mastered. Only then can the bureaucracy function effectively.

Current discussions about a governing or ruling elite usually include all or part of the bureaucracy. Sometimes a government bureaucracy is distinguished from the rest, at other times not. One recent author contrasts the normative notion of a "genuine" bureaucracy, described as "an organized hierarchy of skills and authorities, within which each office and rank is restricted to its specialized tasks," with a "pseudo-bureaucracy" outside government. To such a view, the bureaucrat "or civil servant" is "above all an expert whose knowledge and skill have been attested to by qualifying examination, and later in his career by qualifying experience." Such "normative" use should be avoided.[49] The various ways of describing the governing or ruling elite would invariably include the upper reaches of the bureaucracy, if by bureaucracy is meant the class of persons in a community who perform specific functions of an administrative kind as members of an organization in which such functions are differentiated as well as centrally controlled and supervised (thus forming a hierarchy), being specially qualified for the performance of these functions. Characteristically, such persons exhibit certain specific behavioral traits, more especially objectivity, consistency and discretion.[50]

Bureaucracy thus employed as a term for designating a particular class of persons forming an organized group may be either diversified and pluralistic or unified and centralistic. If it is united and centralistic, it

[49] Mills, 1956, pp. 235ff. Mills' definition is based upon Max Weber's as modified by later discussions; cf. Merton, et al., 1952, esp. the critical evaluation, pp. 27ff. Also Eisenstadt, al, a2, 1958.

[50] Friedrich, 1950, chap. II; Max Weber, 1922, 1925, part I, chaps. 3–5, part III, chap. 6; Lasswell and Kaplan, 1950, p. 205, stress the hierarchical aspect, which they define as "a structure of power relationships of varying amounts of power"—a definition which, while not incorrect, is insufficient, just as is their definition of an elite. Merely the amount of power, even if it were determinable, does not suffice to characterize a hierarchy.

constitutes part of the governing or ruling elite, indeed often constitutes the central core of such an elite, as in ancient China and in the absolute monarchies of modern Europe. In the totalitarian autocracies two rival bureaucracies are operative, those of the party and of the government. Since virtually all members of the upper echelons of the government bureaucracy are also party members, the two bureaucracies together constitute the governing elite.[51] In constitutional democracies, a number of bureaucracies are in competition with each other, notably those of the several parties of the government, including the military (in federal systems these are multiplied), of business organizations and of the trade unions. Churches, universities and other sectors of social life also exhibit an increasing trend toward bureaucratization.[52] The conflicts among these several bureaucracies and the consequent disorder have raised, especially in periods of emergency, the cry for "coordination," if not of "integration." During the two world wars, such coordination was in a measure accomplished in all the major democracies. In normal times the vigorous competition and rivalry among the several bureaucratic *corpora* is not only accepted, but surrounded with a halo of approval; doctrines such as that of free enterprise embody that viewpoint. The diversification and rivalry between the bureaucratic elements is further evidence for the conclusion that no inclusive governing elite exists in the constitutional democracies, though such an elite may well exist in certain organizations which constitute parts of the system as a whole. Indeed, in many of the highly bureaucratized units, such as large-scale business enterprises and certain churches, the bureaucracy is in fact the governing elite. The need for excelling in performance in order to maintain their position within the community at large tends, however, to make these governing elites wide open to new elements, and hence to foster rapid transformation even in these constituent elements.

In conclusion, it might be desirable to repeat the tentative description given at the outset as it has been elucidated in the preceding pages. We said that a ruling or governing elite, in short, a political elite, is a group of persons who are distinguished by exceptional performance in politics, who effectively unite the rule in their hands, and who possess a sense of group cohesion and a corresponding *esprit de corps*. Such political elites are an important and widespread phenomenon, and they characterize the operation of many forms of rule, more especially totalitarian dictatorship. Evidently the persons composing them are not necessarily linked by blood ties, but may enter the elite on the basis of excelling in

[51] Friedrich and Brzezinski, 1956, chap. 16.

[52] This trend has been ridiculed by Parkinson, 1957; it is the subject of many serious studies, for example, the section on the "growth" of bureaucracy in Merton et al., 1952, pp. 60–113, and on the "bureaucrat," pp. 353–396.

a considerable variety of performances. The above discussed "circulation of elites" is a cumbrous way of referring to this phenomenon, which is intrinsic to the very nature of any elite, but more particularly of a governing elite. The notion that a hereditary nobility is a particularly significant and efficacious kind of political elite, entitled to and worthy of special admiration, was found to be a mirage, although the cultural and political contribution of a hereditary nobility may be considerable under favorable circumstances. Other elites than a governing one are, in any case, probably as much or more worthy of admiration, including the scientific elite of our time. Democracy has every reason to foster the development of such nongovernmental elites, and even in the realm of government it has developed, in the administrative bureaucracy, a kind of technical elite in terms of performance. At the same time, a democratic political order is antielitist at its core; instead of relying upon the virtue and other standards of a self-appointed governing elite for securing responsible conduct, it depends upon the willingness of a sufficient part of the citizenship to participate freely in supervising and controlling the temporary rulers and to bring them to account.

chapter

19

Order and the Value of Disorder

Magnus ab integro saeclorum
nascitur ordo.
Virgil

From vulgar bounds
with brave disorder part
And snatch a grace
beyond the reach of art.
Alexander Pope

IN THE HISTORY OF political thought the concept of order, of political order of the community, has received relatively less attention than other concepts, such as justice, power and the state. Yet order has been the presumably self-evident goal of all politics, and in a sense political theory revolves around the problem of how to achieve order. From Plato to Marx, the questions that were asked received answers which suggested a new, a different order. In modern democratic societies, the problem of order, of how to order the relations of the plurality of groups, has come more and more to the forefront and in a sense occupies the center of the stage today.

Order is often assumed to be something perfectly obvious, especially by those who approach it from the point of view of the individual, rather than of the group or community. Thus Simone Weil wrote: "The first of the soul's needs, the one which touches most nearly its eternal destiny, is order; that is to say, a texture of social relationships such that no one is compelled to violate imperative obligations in order to carry out other ones." In this sense, she thinks, "order is the first need of all," yet she also admits that "we cannot even be sure that the idea of an order in which all obligations would be compatible with one another isn't a fiction." [1]

[1] Simone Weil, 1952, pp. 10–12; 1955.

But if we cannot be sure that the kind of state which is here specified as order can even exist, how can it be claimed to be the "first need of all"? Only an order concept which can be specified in such a manner as to become workable has political significance.

The segregation issue offers a striking contemporary example of the recurring conflict over what constitutes order—a conflict which is invariably cast in terms of an argument over what is just. One side insists on justice for the Negro in the full sense of equality (Chapter 14), and it identifies justice with the decisions of the courts, in the tradition of positive law. Their cry is: the legal order must be preserved. The other side insists that if these decisions are enforced, or rather if their enforcement is attempted, disorder will result, that it is more important for order to be maintained than for justice to be done, that in fact the concept of justice espoused by the other side is unjust, and that an unjust decree, even though legal, must be challenged. The curious, and yet highly significant, feature of this particular situation is that the conservatives are against the law, if we designate as "conservatives" those who wish to conserve the status quo. It might be objected that these conservatives are not very explicitly against the law because they challenge the interpretation of the law given by the courts; but considering the position of the courts in the traditional American legal order, it is admissible to say that they are against the law. Politically considered, however, we note that each side in the controversy insists on its own notion of justice and that in this connection the preservation of the *legal order* is juxtaposed to the preservation of the *social order*.[2] Such divergence of views suggests that there exist various understandings of what constitutes order, in a politically relevant sense.

Without reviewing past thought, one might summarize it by saying that there have been four significant ways of characterizing order. First, order is a structured arrangement of parts, and hence political order a structured arrangement of political units. Second, order is a systematic arrangement of parts, the term systematic taken in the sense made precise earlier (Introduction); hence a political order could be an arrangement of political units integrated into a coherent whole so that a systematic unity is achieved. Third, a political order is a community in which peace prevails; law is essential to peace, hence an ordered community is one in which "law and order" are maintained. (Peace is used here in the broad sense meaning not only the absence of physical violence, but the absence of any strife intense enough to threaten such violence.) And fourth, political order is said to exist when there is an absence of nongovern-

[2] It is noteworthy that even today such advanced systematic treatments as Lasswell and Kaplan, 1950, and Parsons, 1951, fail to specify what is to be understood by order, although the latter offers an interesting discussion of what he calls the "motivational problem of order" (pp. 30ff.). Cf. also, Heimann, 1947, pp. 8ff. and 227ff.

mental violence (this concept is similar to, but narrower than, the preceding one).

The difficulty with all these concepts is that they do not relate order to the values, interests and beliefs of the community except indirectly; they do not recognize that the realization of the community's purposes or goals is an essential aspect of a viable order. As a consequence, they fail to reflect the fact that in the actions of various representatives of the different groups of the community, pursuing a plurality of goals, a certain amount of disorder is inescapable and that therefore disorder may be desirable in the political community in order that its goals may be achieved. These definitions insist, either explicitly (third and fourth) or implicitly (first and second), that a complete elimination of strife or violence is desirable, forgetting the profound saying of Heraclitus that "strife is the father of all" (*pólemos patēr pántōn*). This sombre saying [3] was to be sure an exaggeration; for strife is not the father of all, but of some things. But the preoccupation with order tends to overlook even that sphere in which strife—or as we prefer to say, competition—is an important human motivation and cause of achievement, political as well as economic and otherwise. May it therefore not be sufficient to characterize order dynamically as an arrangement whereby the use of force and violence is *reduced* or held at a minimum in the attainment of political ends? This possibility calls for further exploration.

Political order as we said needs to be related to the values, interests and beliefs of the community; for these values, interests and beliefs determine the purposes in pursuit of which the community is ordered, that is, its parts need to be so arranged as to facilitate the realization of these purposes (Chapter 2). The values, interests and beliefs, and hence the purposes, of a given political community are objectively in existence and hence constitute a datum of the specific political situation. Political order is therefore *relative to* the values, interests and beliefs of a given community. This point may also be put in terms of values alone, by saying that order is one value among several basic values, and that it may have to be sacrificed in cases where a conflict occurs between order and justice, or order and security (to mention only two primary value conflicts here). The tendency of some political writers, such as Simone Weil, to make order into the one absolute value in politics, transcending all others, is existentially in error; experience shows time and again that human communities rarely, if ever, prefer order to all other values.[4] The preoccupa-

[3] It is usually rendered as "War is the father of all," but this is surely neither the intention of Heraclitus, nor even called for by the Greek word *polemos*, which has a more general connotation, such as struggle or strife. Heraclitus, it must be remembered, has a penchant for alliteration.

[4] Cf. the discussion on the ranking of values and the *summum bonum* above, Chap. 2.

tion with order which characterizes, for example, the work of Hobbes springs from his admitted fearfulness about his personal physical existence and the consequent importance of avoiding all situations which could threaten it; the fear of violent death is therefore given by Hobbes the status of the dominant "motivation" for man's seeking order at all costs. But he just asserts it; his attempt at "proving" it by his introspective psychology merely proves that such fear was a dominant motive in Hobbes, if indeed it proves anything, since the insights of psychoanalysis have made such introspection highly suspect.[5]

If then political order is relative to the values and beliefs of the community, it follows that what may appear as an utterly chaotic arrangement to the outsider who does not share the values and beliefs of the particular community may in fact constitute order of a high degree to those who share these values. Seemingly anarchic conditions in which there exists no central government or other authority as discussed above (Chapter 10) are possible. The complex societies which some anthropologists have spoken of as "decentralized" exhibit an apparent "disorder" of diffuse groups each with its own authority, yet somehow functioning effectively as a whole. Common human experience confirms the point: the workshop while in use may exhibit a highly dynamic ordering of its parts, the tools, to the workman engaged in building something, while appearing as chaotic disorder to an outsider unconcerned with the task in hand. This observation ought not to be interpreted to mean that order is subjective and *exists* only for the beholder. No, order is an objective datum existing in the constellation which embraces the workroom and the workman in it, while the observer subjectively misjudges it, yet could by more thorough study of the situation come to understand the order which exists.

If what has been said makes sense, "a political order" is a term suited to designate the political situation of a community in which component parts or units are arranged in such a way that the actions required for the attainment of the purposes of the community will be taken. Since not all such actions will ever be taken, and some actions always, it is plain that the order concept is comparative. We can, and indeed we ought, to think of it in terms of less and more order. But because the purposes change, and the transformation required to adapt the ordering of the community to new needs takes time, a certain amount of disorder, resulting from the transition from one to another order, is not only always present, but in fact necessary and desirable. Complete order is achieved only in the "peace of the graveyard"—it means complete immobility and absence of all action. Political action requires mobility and activity,

[5] A reexamination of Hobbes's political thought from a psychoanalytic viewpoint is one of the urgent tasks for the history of political thought.

and therefore a measure of disorder is unavoidable and need not concern us. These insights have relevance for the urgent contemporary issue of war and peace. The real political objection to war is that because of modern weapons development it is no longer a satisfactory tool for effective competition, so that other methods have to be devised. "Coexistence" is an unfortunate slogan, because it conjures up the vision of two self-contained camps having little or no dealings with each other. What is wanted (and from a democratic standpoint even more than from a communist one) is nonviolent competition, competition, that is to say, which shuns the means of physical coercion (though it includes economic and psychological coercion). If such competition can be organized, a real step toward world order will have been achieved.

The amount of disorder increases when new areas of disagreement, new shades of values, interests and beliefs, arise among the members of the community; for in the more ordered community, the sufficiently ordered community, such areas of disagreement are recognized and taken into account in structuring the community. It is from this disagreement on values, clashing with the need for taking communal action, that the conflicts of order and justice arise. The system of values and beliefs in a developed community is normally so complex that what is just for one group may be unjust for others. The relatively ordered community possesses procedures for achieving a compromise between these groups, as far as the specific action is concerned, even though their values and beliefs remain divergent. While such procedures are most highly developed in constitutional democracies of the modern brand, they are not lacking in older political orders. Compromise means, however, that any action directed toward the achievement of a common purpose may entail some injustice for several or even all the groups. This inexorable fact is most dramatically seen in certain extreme situations, as when the home of certain members is forcibly taken and destroyed (even though with due compensation) because a reservoir has to be built, or a conflagration stopped. The compensation which represents the "compromise" will offer the person losing his home the monetary value, but it cannot make it really "right" if the person happens to have the kind of attachment to his home which would keep him from ever selling it for any price.

It may here be asked whether, if disorder is related to value realization in a significant way, it should not be considered part of order. The answer is that this is *possible* (even if dialectical "identification" of opposites is avoided) but that it seems *preferable* to allow "disorder" as a term to stand, even though we recognize that, if the *time* factor is considered, it may be possible to say that what is a "disorder" in time t', may be part of order in t'', on the assumption that t' is smaller than t''. This reflection suggests that the concept of "dynamic order" might be introduced, to contrast with static order, so that a dynamic order would be one in which disturbance factors would be part of the "order," even when the time considered is short,[6] that is, $t \to 0$. But such a concept does not eliminate "disorder." For there would still be disturbances of a greater magnitude to create disorder, dynamic disorder, until such time as the order is reestablished.

In the light of the foregoing we may specify still more explicitly the kind of political situation to which the term "order" may suitably be applied. It is the state of a political community in which its parts, rulers and ruled, are fairly systematically arranged, so as to reduce the use of force (coercion) and provide for the realization of its values and interests in terms of its prevailing beliefs. This way of describing an ordered community provides a synthesis of the main elements of the traditional views: a systematic arrangement of parts and the reduction, though not the complete elimination, of the use of force, adding the important aspect that the ordered arrangement must be related to communal actions which are intended to achieve the values and interests (purposes) of the community's members, in terms corresponding to their beliefs.

Something more needs to be said about the systematic aspects of such an arrangement of parts. In a system the functions of the several parts are defined in such a way that an effective interdependence of mutually supporting operations results (see Introduction). These operational interdependencies are comparatively stable, and hence may be expressed in the form of "rules," or "generalizations." Hence it might also be said that an ordered political situation is one in which the elements correspond to one or more rules. Likewise an ordered political process is one in which the sequence of events corresponds to one or more rules; for the ordered community the same holds. In this very general "correspondence to rules" the link of order to law can be seen; its full appreciation presupposes, however, that law is understood not merely as a system of norms, but also as a system of existential relations (Chapter 15). Further reflection reveals that the rules defining the existence of an order spring from the value preferences and interests (purposes) of the human beings involved in the political situation, the process or the community. "Correspondence to rules" implies "reduction" of force (coercion, violence); it is obviously not necessary to force people to do what they are doing anyhow. There may, however, be the need for coercion at the "fringes" of a situation, a process or a community. At such points, the "normative power of the factual" is in evidence (Chapter 15).

The problem of how to specify political order is not solved by

[6] Such an analysis as this brings out the fact that "order" in politics is related to "equilibrium" in economics, and it is patent that the problems of equilibrium analysis reappear in analogous form. See for this, Samuelson, 1958, *passim*.

elaborating the notion of a hierarchy of "authorities" nor by stressing the need of a highest "authority" or "power," as has recently been reattempted.[7] Such an approach rests upon the preoccupation with decision-making as the crux of order, and is in the last analysis merely a restatement of the Bodinian position. For Bodin's celebrated doctrine of sovereignty (Chapter 30) insists that a well-ordered state (*état bien ordonné*) is one which possesses a sovereign. Political experience offers ample evidence that many well-ordered states do not have such a sovereign, and that other states which do are not always well-ordered—provided the order concept is detached from the hierarchical structuring of rule. If, of course, the presence of such a highest "authority" or "power" is identified with "political order," then no worthwhile proposition concerning the interrelationship can be made, as any statement concerning such interrelationship becomes tautological.

It remains to explore the relation of order to power, rule, influence, authority and legitimacy, and to see whether some general propositions about order can be formulated in light of such relationships. It is evident that both authority and legitimacy are aids in the achievement of order. It follows from the first and third propositions concerning legitimacy (Chapter 13) that (1) legitimate rule is more effective rule and that (2) legitimacy maximizes the political obligation of those subjected to such rule. More effective rule helps to produce the actions called for by the purposes of the community and reduces the use of force (coercion). Similarly, authority helps to create order. For the capacity of reasoned elaboration which is authority renders power consensual (Chapter 12), and consensual power is by definition noncoercive power; hence, coercion is reduced, as required by an order as just described.

Rule we describe as stabilized, that is, "institutionalized," political power (Chapter 10). The process of stabilizing power involves the creation of structure, and structure we characterized as "an ordered relation of parts." At that stage in the analysis, the "ordering" was not further explored, though it was involved in what was said about institutionalization. It is now apparent that rule is ordered power in the sense of linking it to values, interests and beliefs in such a way that action, purposive action, is effectively achieved over a considerable period of time. A political order is therefore also a particular patterning of power in which rule and rulership occupy an integrating position. For integrating means [8] to complete an imperfect thing by the addition of parts, and/or to combine parts into a whole. Thus integration so understood expressly refers to producing more "order" in our sense.

[7] Hans Barth, 1958, esp. chaps. I and VII, and Friedrich, r, 1959. Barth speaks of *Instanzen*, which technically are "courts," or "judges."

[8] According to the *Oxford* and other dictionaries. Cf. also above, Introd.

Influence is indeterminate in relation to order. It may on the one hand help the ordering of a community, process or situation by eliminating tensions and conflicts. The popular French saying "On s'arrangera," meaning that with the help of influence it will be possible to extricate oneself from a difficult situation or conflict, refers to this potential of assisting order. On the other hand, influence may also be marshaled for the disturbing of an existing order, often on grounds that herald a new and emerging order, thereby creating disorder. Much criticism of interest groups exerting special influence is rooted in a feeling that the political order is being disturbed, perverted, even corrupted; all these terms refer to the possibility that disorder is being created, usually on the assumption that the existing order is "right" and any disturbance of it "wrong."

These brief remarks are meant to show that the notion of a political order is closely related to, and fully comprehensible only in terms of, a precise conception of power, rule, influence, authority and legitimacy. It remains to inquire whether some further general propositions concerning order (in addition to the above) are possible at this point. I believe that the following three hypotheses are deserving of attention in considering the building of political orders. First, an order which lacks arrangements for its change will become disorder in time. This proposition follows from the relation between political order and values, interests and beliefs. The life of political communities does not stand still. As stressed earlier in this chapter, there occurs a continuous evolution of such values, interests and beliefs (Chapter 2). This evolutionary change affects power relations, and as we have shown, tends to undermine authority and legitimacy. Authority and legitimacy are vitally related to order, as just pointed out. It follows that arrangements for change by introducing the possibility of small disorders serve to maintain political order, not a particular order, but order as such. The proposition should really be stated in comparative terms, though. The formulation might then be: more order can be preserved by making arrangements for its change, than by preventing it because of the degree of the disorder which such change necessarily involves. This general proposition, which holds for all political communities, however ordered, was for quite a long time overlooked in efforts to build a viable constitutional system. Neither the constitutions of the Cromwellian era in England nor the constitutions of the French Revolution contained arrangements for their change. It is one of the important "inventions" of the makers of the American Constitution to have developed the article on the amendment of the Constitution, though the specific provisions are not perhaps the most felicitous. Nowadays it is fairly generally recognized that a constitution without a method of amendment is incomplete.[9]

[9] Friedrich, 1950, chap. 8, and the literature cited there. Cf. also Chap. 34 below.

A second proposition is to the effect that several political orders may be linked in a higher order comprehending them. This proposition follows from the very nature of a political order (and other orders in the organic world exhibit similar potentialities). The several orders constituting such a higher order are typically the "parts" referred to in the general description of order. It is a consequence of the relation of order to values, interests and beliefs that such a higher order must be based upon the sharing of *some* of the values, interests and beliefs by all the orders that form part of such a system. Thus the union of trade unions or of churches or of professional groups (American Federation of Labor, Federal Council of Churches, American Council of Learned Societies, for example) is built upon a common core of shared values, interests and beliefs. The same may be said of "states" which enter into a federal union (Chapter 32). Such federal unions are subject to the general laws applicable to all orders, as indicated.

A third important proposition may be derived from the preceding ones, namely, that a democratic (constitutional, cooperative) order is more ordered than an autocratic one. Mosca and the antidemocratic theorists of the last two generations who saw and understood power only as an instrument in the hands of a ruling class, or governing elite, look upon order as the integration of a political community by such a ruling class. That kind of approach to the problem of order overlooks the first proposition, and hence cannot account for the need of a measure of disorder. It fails to recognize the function of order in its relation to the values, interests and beliefs of the community. Without purpose, as we saw, there can be only the order of the graveyard, and even this seemingly immobile setting is from time to time disturbed by the need of admitting a new inhabitant. The fresh earth and faded flowers over a new grave are a most unmistakable symbol of the value of disorder, as new purposes (or new instances of an old purpose) come into view. The toleration of a certain amount of such disorder, pregnant with the emergent order of another day, facilitates the task of keeping order related to the values, interests and beliefs of the community. This is not to say that there are no such elements of organized disorder in autocratic systems, notably the totalitarian dictatorships, but in autocratic orders the suppression of open disorder entails deeper disorder. Such hidden elements of disorder, consisting in the maladjustments and tensions often resulting from conflicts between the ruling party and the general public, are greater and far outweigh in seriousness the kind of disorder tolerated in a democratic society. To give just one striking example: when Hitler went to war in 1939, a large majority of the German people was desperate, even though afterwards awestruck by his seeming successes. This situation was in stark contrast to the dedication and all but unanimous enthusiasm with which Americans went to war after Pearl Harbor. The latter spectacle was the more impressive, since they had been vigorously in disagreement beforehand. Many other examples showing the same contrast between democratic and autocratic orders are readily at hand. However, if we are really to confirm our third proposition, we need to develop an index of order—of purpose-related order. This will not be an easy task, and no attempt has been made, to my knowledge.

The problem of the value of disorder also presents itself in the field of public administration. If discretion is delegated in a measure to subordinates, as it must be in any large-scale organization, a certain amount of divergence in behavior—that is to say, disorder—will occur. When such disorder appears, the cry goes up that order ought to be maintained, and a strengthening of centralized direction and even control is advocated. There are both theorists and practitioners who proceed on the assumption that the maximum of such centralized direction and control is desirable. Actually, practical experience, if not theoretical reflection, has shown that since order needs to be related to purpose, and since purpose is inseparable from the functioning of an organization, a certain amount of disorder may be more productive of achievement, may more nearly enable an organization to realize its purpose or goal. These problems present themselves, for example, in the organization of field offices.[10] The matter is inherent in the nature of discretion which delegates "authority." Obviously, the really important question, from the standpoint of administrative management, is not the alternative of order or disorder; but the balance which needs to be struck between an over-all order related to over-all purpose, and differentiated suborders related to differentiated subpurposes.

The observations of the preceding paragraph invite us to resume the discussion of a point of general significance. It must not be supposed that a political order requires agreement on all values, even all basic values in the community. The same holds for interests and beliefs. The proposition has at times been obscured by rather too general statements about "systems of values," and so on, made in anthropological and sociological studies dealing with primitive communities. It has also had a measure of vogue in political theory, where people like to talk about "agreement on fundamentals" as the necessary basis of some kind of society. As mentioned once before, Burke, Bagehot, Balfour and others have expounded various forms of this belief and built upon it some specific appeal for a particular kind of order, such as the English constitution, or the parliamentary system, the party system in Britain and the like. What all these political pleas have in common is the assumption that order presupposes unity of purpose, and stable purpose at that.[11] Actually, demo-

[10] H. Simon, 1947; L. D. White, 1926; Fesler, 1949.

[11] Friedrich, 1942, 1950, chap. 5. Cf. also the interesting confirmation in Bay, 1958, pp. 274ff.; contra, Hula, a, 1939, pp. 284–285.

cratic order is built, not on an agreement on fundamentals, but on the organizing of its dissent. This statement turns of course in part upon the meaning of "fundamentals." But if it is generally conceded that the most universal fundamentals are religion, culture (more especially language), general notions of social justice (and equality), sex and family relations, and food, it is evident without explicit demonstration that such societies as England, France and the United States (to mention only three) have certainly not been in "fundamental agreement" on any of these. There is, however, one fundamental, if we wish to call it that, namely, the political order itself on which agreement (up to a high point) has existed, and it is important to consider this further. This "fundamental" is, in the first place, entirely compatible with the statement made at the beginning of the paragraph that a political order does not require agreement on all basic values, interests and beliefs. It is, in the second place, evident that when restricted to the political order, the positive assertion appears tautological, namely: a political order requires basic agreement on political order in a community. But this statement is not as tautological as it appears. For it attempts to relate the *objective* possibility of a political order to the *subjective* agreement of those subject to it on the basic features of this order. Nobody, as a matter of fact, has to my knowledge ever asserted this as a general proposition; for it would be contradicted by too much human experience. But it is being asserted for some particular political orders, more especially constitutional democracy.[12] Whether the proposition is true, when so restricted and precisely circumscribed, depends upon what is understood by "agreement" on "basic features." For if by that term is meant rational and conscious appreciation of some particular ordering, such as a parliamentary or presidential system, then the proposition is correct only in a most general sense; there have always been wide disagreements on various details of such features. If, however, "basic features" is meant to be a term referring to the effective organizing of dissent through a recognition of individual rights or civil liberties, the function of a system of more than one party, and some scheme of divided powers or at least an independent judiciary, then it is true that the establishing and maintenance of a constitutional order presupposes more or less conscious agreement on these basic features. However, by defining basic features thus, we have once again revealed the limited utility of the statement; it is merely a specific instance of the general rule of legitimacy, namely, that a system of rule functions more effectively if those subject to it believe it to be "rightful" (Chapter 13). For the rest, it is more important to insist upon our negative assertion concerning the plurality and possible contradictoriness of values, interests and beliefs, and the possibility of a political order to organize the dissent to which such plurality necessarily gives rise. There

[12] Notably Burke, Bagehot, Balfour and Laski. Cf. Friedrich, 1942, chap. 5.

is need for such dissent, and not only in democratic societies, because the dissent expresses emergent values and brings them to the attention of the rulers.[13]

The dynamic order to which the organization of dissent gives rise consists of a variety of suborders which may to some extent form a hierarchy but whose relationship in any case is of crucial importance. Our second proposition (above page 343) asserts that several orders can be combined into a higher order comprehending them. The corollary is that an order may also be differentiated into a number of suborders that may be coordinate or subordinate to each other. State and local governments, political parties, unions, professional associations, and many more have been recognized as suborders. The practical problem is largely that of determining to what extent such suborders are to be considered "autonomous" in their respective spheres, and hence not subject to direction from those who rule the more comprehensive order. This problem is in the modern state conventionally solved by denying that suborders have any such "autonomy," but by then proceeding as if they had. No American government would want to tell a church or even a union how to handle its internal affairs, unless their activities impinged upon the interests of others (Mormons, union abuses, and the like). To settle such conflicts and transcend them is the irreducible task of the order within which the suborders are comprehended, and the true, if limited, basis of the hoary claim to sovereignty (Chapter 30). But for a dynamic order of broad scope it is equally important that such conflicts should arise, and that the disorder resulting from them should be understood as expressive of the most important single factor in the life of a political community, namely, the steady growth and the transformation of its values, interests and beliefs.

The second proposition regarding the combination of orders into higher orders has its more far-reaching application in the international sphere. Wherever combinations are attempted, whether they be nearly universal, as was the League of Nations and is the United Nations, or merely regional, the problem of political order presents itself. The more detailed and concrete teachings of political experience will be examined below (Chapters 31 and 32). Here only certain very general observations are called for. The laudable inclination of political scientists concerned with international relations to stress the importance of a theoretical framework[14] might eventually provide the basis for a theory of imperfect

[13] Cf. for all this, the striking empirical evidence developed by Prothro and Grigg, a, 1960, and the comments by Key, 1961, p. 41 and p. 36 fn.

[14] Note especially Hoffmann (ed.), 1960, esp. pp. 4ff. It seems rather doubtful that this dimension of politics can be separated off and provided with an independent body of theory. The several attempts in this direction have produced essentially generalizations about power, influence, and other general topics of political

order. For typically such structures as those mentioned, or indeed the regional structures which have been set up in Europe, Asia and Africa, are all attempts at organizing "emerging" communities in which the values, interests and beliefs are still so widely divergent that even a very loose federal structure presents great operational difficulties. There exists a widespread tendency to speak about world community [15] without any clear indication as to what is meant. The question cannot be answered in terms of a simple either/or. The situation is highly dynamic and transitional. There can be little doubt that there exists today *more* community in the world than in the past, but whether such community has progressed to the point where it will support effective political order seems doubtful. This point would be reached once sufficient common values, interests and beliefs had come into being, so that a substantial part of the world's population felt themselves to be, and conducted themselves in fact as, members of such a community. The data in support of such a contention are inadequate. It has in fact been argued with a considerable show of support that we are all in fact today citizens of an emergent world community, but the exponents of such views usually become rather hortative in asking their readers to believe what they believe and to conduct themselves accordingly.[16] It is not possible to think of a large majority of mankind as "world citizens." There is no use in deceiving oneself about the very grave consequences of the absence of a sufficient measure of both community and order. World government is still far off. World tensions are

---

theory which appear in all significant respects related to general political theory. Certainly the selections offered in the above from Morgenthau, Aron, Thompson, Kaplan, Bernard, Liska and Dunn all exhibit these characteristics; their views are taken up in various parts of the general theory here outlined.

[15] Note, for example, Mangone, 1951; Wright (ed.), 1948. In contrast to the large number of works more or less assuming the existence of such a community, that by Schiffer, 1954, might be mentioned as taking a critical view, and indeed questioning whether there exists any such community. Schiffer builds his argument upon a broad survey of earlier writers, but then overshoots the mark by insisting that only a "world state" would signalize the emergence of a world community. Community, even political community, does not depend upon the existence of a system of rule and institutionalized political order (cf. above, Chap. 8).

[16] Such is the thrust of the interesting study by L. J. Cohen, 1954, who simply defines a community as "a group of people" who "depend upon each other for their means of living." On this basis, he claims that "our world community . . . is a social fact. . . ." But this definition is both too broad and too narrow; there are many communities which do not thus depend upon each other (family, church, and so on), while on the other hand something more is needed than economic interdependence for the existence of political community. Entirely independent trading nations might have mutually complementary needs without political community. See for more detailed evaluation Friedrich, r, 1960.

increasing in many areas. There may be a "promise" but the promise is rather "elusive." [17]

Any world political order will therefore have to be limited to ordering the existing political communities. The value of disorder in such a situation is particularly difficult to recognize, since its disvalue is apparent not only in the threat of war, nuclear war more specifically, but also in the enormous waste of resources for competitive armaments. It is easy to imagine the breakdown of any established political order if it were exposed to similar waste internally, due to the dissolution of community. The situation of France in recent years, as a result of the dissensions over Algeria, may serve as a warning sign.

In analytical terms, the relations between states have the characteristics of mechanical "systems." Indeed, precisely those considerations which oblige one to reject the notion of a mechanical system as a model for analyzing political communities and their orders, and more especially to reject the so-called "equilibrium" analysis, argue in favor of such an approach to the problem of international order/disorder. But not all international situations are "systems." System analysis, properly speaking, breaks down where the input exceeds the capacity of the system; it may be destroyed or it may be the starting point for another and different system.[18]

The "emerging" world order will be dealt with at the end (Chapter 35). Here it remains to add that the international situation provides a rich field for observing influence at work. The continuing negotiations which are the very core of international relations are largely occasions for the display of noncoercive power and the influence associated with it. A theory of international relations which would seek to elucidate the factors of both order and of disorder presumably would start with the process of negotiation as the primary focus of theoretical attention. The older diplomacy [19] in its effort to reduce tensions or at least to minimize them in pursuit of the nations' interests developed an elaborate code, embodying experience with the process of negotiation. This code has been undergoing some striking changes,[20] but in many respects the conduct of international negotiation follows established patterns. To the extent to which this is true, a certain degree of order prevails, assisting the develop-

[17] Harlan Cleveland (ed.), 1961, spoke of the "dialogue of the deaf," picking up a vivid phrase of Father D. Pire; no phrase could serve better to illustrate the point. Among the deaf, community is bound to be imperfect, because of the vital need of communication for all community. Cf. above, Chap. 8.

[18] A most interesting comparative analysis of the historical sequence of such international systems was undertaken by Richard Rosecrance, a, 1962; a more detailed book-length treatment is about to appear.

[19] Cf. Friedrich, 1950, chap. 5, and the literature cited there.

[20] The challenge emanating from the totalitarians is the primary factor in this transformation. Cf. Friedrich and Brzezinski, 1956, pp. 58ff.

ment of political community.[21] But the preference of the professional diplomat for the tried and tested techniques of negotiation is continually challenged in both democracies and dictatorships by interference from factors that are built-in features of these popular regimes. The need for securing the support of the public and its representatives in the one,[22] the concern with ideology and propaganda relating to it in the other [23] have added dimensions to the task of negotiation which have proved extremely bothersome. Oratory and insult, diplomacy by formula and diplomacy by doctrine have introduced complications into the relations between states which have acted as a dissolvent of a good part of the order that once existed. The end of these developments is not in sight.

In conclusion, it might be said that order, political order, can be understood only as highly dynamic—a state of affairs in which the political community's power relations are fairly systematically structured, and as a result the use of force is minimized. Order is a question of procedures, of processes which are more or less recurrent. Reasoning about order, political theory asks the question in terms of more or less order. Complete order and complete disorder are unreal limits between which political situations and constellations oscillate. The existence of a government signalizes a relatively high degree of order. Hence the value of disorder. But the international situation illustrates the opposite danger of too much disorder, in spite of some significant efforts at building structures resembling governments. The significance of generally followed rules of conduct in negotiating differences is likely to be overlooked in comparison with formal structures, but a processual view of politics suggests their continuing importance in maintaining such degree of order as the range of conflicts over values, interests and beliefs will allow.

[21] The intricacies of this field of political behavior have been the happy hunting ground of the history of diplomacy in the classical sense. Over-all analysis has been offered by Nicolson, 1954, systematizing his earlier studies of 1930 and 1933. Nicolson defines diplomacy as the art of negotiation. He deals with it in historical perspective. Cf. below, Chap. 27, for detail.

[22] Among recent detailed studies, one might mention Westerfield, 1955, and Robinson, 1962.

[23] Friedrich and Brzezinski, 1956, chap. 6; and Brzezinski, 1960, chap. 16.

chapter

20

Independence and Participation: Dimensions of Political Freedom

A man's strength, he was saying,
depends on toil to maintain it;
his freedom depends on strength
to protect it; and without free-
dom, what pleasure is secure . . . ?
Mary Renault, THE LAST OF THE WINE

THAT THE VALUE of order has limits, has always been apparent enough to those who value freedom. That freedom in turn depends upon a measure, a degree, of order, has been stressed by all who have argued about freedom under law.[1] But this freedom which is at the heart of such a large portion of political thought and action, while fundamentally one, has a number of dimensions. Many answers have been given to the question What is freedom or liberty? for the two really mean the same, they are true synonyms.

In keeping with our general theoretical position, the problem of political freedom is not to be treated apart from the value judgment which asserts that "men ought to be free." Rather it is concerned with what political situation is being referred to when that kind of statement is made. Since it has for long been recognized that it cannot mean that "all men ought to be free in regard to all actions they might wish to take," since these actions clash and are incompatible, it must mean some-

[1] Isaiah Berlin, 1958, has given a brilliant survey of the falsifications of liberty that can result from this line of argument, under the heading of "positive" liberty. We are here analyzing only "negative" liberty, but in a "positive" sense. Also, Friedrich, 1959.

thing else. Various solutions have been proposed by philosophers, such as Kant's stipulation that each man's freedom must be compatible with every other man's freedom, but such a formula (and others resembling it) does not contain criteria by which to recognize this kind of freedom. Putting aside therefore the valuational aspect of freedom, even though we realize that it is our ultimate concern, our attention may be focused by recalling that political power, like rule and influence, exhibits a dual aspect: it may be a relation and it may be a possession, and is typically both. We also showed that power is generated by constraint (coercion) and consent, and rests typically upon both. These four dimensions of power are vitally related to freedom; for when someone, person or group, has the power to do or not to do something, to act or not to act in a certain way, he is said to be free to do so. Is freedom then a synonym for power? In one sense, yes, and in another, no. For the question of freedom, political freedom, arises in power situations when the power of some participant persons to act as they would prefer is subject to interference by the power of others. This is typically the situation in which power is possessed by some and places resources for coercion at their disposal.[2] Noninterference by another is, therefore, the elemental notion of political freedom. In our own terms, we would say that whenever and to the extent that a political actor appears to act without interference from another, he shall be said *to be free*. As corollary, we would say that whenever an actor feels that he is able so to act, he shall be said *to feel free*. It is evident that one might be free and not feel free, and that one might feel free and not be free. Failure to distinguish these two states clearly is at the core of much confusion in the writings on freedom. It is furthermore evident that no one is likely to be completely free; there will always be some interfering factors. It seems therefore desirable to go a step further and to limit the term "political freedom" to those situations in which an actor is free in an action concerning the political community, that is to say, an action in which the interest of the political community is involved.

How does this hypothetical starting point compare with past theorizing on freedom and liberty? The writings on this subject fill libraries. A group of philosophical researchers recently surveyed a large body of writings on freedom in an effort to discover their common ground. The results of their findings constitute the body of a massive volume. We read there

[2] The very interesting recent study by Oppenheim, 1961, which in some respects resembles mine, is nonetheless basically different in orientation, not only because the author cherishes the illusion (not very firmly, to be sure) that his analysis is (and ought to be) "valuationally neutral" (p. 8; see above, Chap. 2), but also because he builds upon Lasswell and Kaplan, 1950, accepting their views of power, control, influence, and so on, which have been discussed in other parts of this book; cf. esp. Chaps. 9–11.

that "freedom is understood as involving independence of something other than the self." This position was abandoned in favor of "ability to act." [3] Perhaps it would be more correct to say "independence from everything," everything, that is, but the self. For everyone is "independent of something"; everything, by contrast, is certainly involved in the notion of "full freedom." But if stated thus, freedom can never actually exist. In any case, whether stated in terms of something or everything, there can be no question that "independence" is a central aspect of freedom. In elaborating their findings, the makers of the survey just mentioned report that they found three "nuclear" agreements, that is to say, three kinds of freedom, namely, (1) circumstantial, (2) natural, and (3) acquired freedom. The concept of circumstantial freedom stresses that circumstances inhibiting or promoting human action determine the degree of independence and hence of freedom; that of natural freedom, the inborn ability of men as men to originate what they do; that of acquired freedom, the capacity for self-perfection.[4] These three core aspects of freedom, as commonly understood by philosophers, include one, namely, "acquired freedom," which is not properly part of freedom when understood as "independence from something other than self," for this capacity is hindered only by the self. On the other hand, the first, circumstantial freedom, contains two rather distinctive components, when considered politically, in that circumstances inhibiting human action are rather different from circumstances promoting human action. If these are differentiated as meaning either "independence" in the strict sense or "participation," a clearer view is gained, I believe.

But first we must ask whom or what this independence in general refers to. For it may be the independence of the individual from social and communal bonds; it may also be the independence of one group from another. Often these two kinds of freedom do not go together. Those most ardently concerned with the independence of a group—say, a church or a nation—are quite ready to subordinate the members of their group completely to the group's control. These and related facts show that the conception of freedom merely as independence is not enough; it does not indicate sharply enough the distinguishing characteristic of this value. Freedom is also a matter of positive direction.[5] The well-worn distinction

[3] Mortimer Adler, 1954, pp. 520ff., 1958, pp. 609ff., who directed the group's work.

[4] Friedrich in Young (ed.), 1958. To say that Adler's magistral work merely "catalogues" past theories of freedom, as does Oppenheim, 1961, pp. 135–136, seems rather unfair.

[5] Berlin, 1958, argues that group efforts, such as national aspirations, must be understood as a search for status, rather than for freedom, and would thereby distinguish them from freedom, which he would interpret as exclusively meaningful for individuals. I doubt the wisdom of this interpretation.

of "freedom from" and "freedom for" is meant to suggest this positive freedom, but it does not do so very clearly, the reason being that "freedom for" certainly also includes much that is freedom of independence as defined in basic rights.

Any discussion of freedom, if carried on in terms of what "freedom really means," will necessarily get involved in the vast discussion of a philosophical and indeed a metaphysical nature to which the experience of human freedom has given rise. These discussions revolve around the problem of the so-called freedom of the will versus determinism. If we approach this problem from the givens of human experience involved, it is evident that we are confronted by an *aporia*, a paradox which logic cannot resolve. For on the one hand we experience choosing, selecting, preferring, and on the other hand, we experience observing, implying the sequel of cause and effect; having chosen to act in a certain way we discover that this action has certain consequences which follow it. I choose to tell a friend an unpalatable truth, and I find that having done so, I am no longer on good terms with him. Both these basic experiences are projected outward onto other human beings and the world at large; when something happens, I assume that something caused it to happen. If a personal agent is involved, I may assume that he chose to have it happen. Unfortunately, the statements about these two basic experiences are logically incompatible; for if everything that happens has a cause, then no "free" choosing, selecting, preferring—in short, no free willing—is conceivable. These acts themselves must have "causes." A large part of the history of philosophy and theology revolves around these issues, with thinkers either choosing one or the other of the alternative logical possibilities, or transcending the contradiction in a divine being. In the field of political theory, the preference has been for the "libertarian" alternative, though "scientific" schools have clamored for the deterministic one. I myself prefer to stick with the basic experiences themselves and leave the contradiction as it stands.[6]

If that is done, it becomes possible to specify the characteristics of a political situation, as already suggested, and then call it a situation of freedom. When and to the extent that human beings, either individually or collectively, act politically—that is, opine, prefer, decide questions of policy—without the interference of other human beings, they shall be called free.[7] If such action is primarily taken in the perspective of being able to do what one pleases in a private sphere, we shall speak of the freedom of independence; if primarily in the perspective of participating in group action, of freedom of participation. But both these dimensions of

[6] Friedrich, 1958, pp. 4ff.; MacIver, 1942, pp. 56f. Above, Chap. 3.

[7] Similarly, Polanyi, 1951, p. 159, but Polanyi's stress on "command" is too narrow.

freedom are basically characteristic of action and opinion situations in which interference is excluded.[8]

The foregoing statements immediately suggest that freedom and power, while cognate when looked at from the standpoint of the power-holder and -handler, are apt to be, at least in part, in conflict when considered by him over whom power is exercised, under coercive power more, under consensual power less so. But not only the feeling of the persons partaking of the situation suggests this conflict. It is actually a built-in aspect of the situation itself. For any power situation, having been characterized as the kind of situation in which human beings act in accordance with the preference of other human beings, forces us to conclude that those subject to another's power are to that extent not free. In the consensual power relationship, the mutual give-and-take of the power-handler and the power-followers produces a relative freedom for the followers to the extent that the leader is influenced by the preferences of his followers, anticipates their reactions, as it were, in view of the need of maintaining their support. This means that the handler is less free. All men in political society are therefore only relatively free, but the more or less of such freedom is decisive.

In order to enlarge the scope of freedom, seeing that power always limits it for the followers, the modern world has developed the notion of a nonpolitical sphere, that is to say, a sphere wherein the individual citizen remains protected against any interference from the political power-handlers, be they ever so democratically legitimized, as long as he does not demonstrably do specific harm to other individual citizens. No general claim is allowed, such as that the "public good" is harmed by someone sleeping on Sunday instead of going to church or engaging in other worthwhile activities. The burden of proof is on the individual claiming to be harmed.

If the making of choices is a basic human experience, and if making these without interference of another is the experience of political freedom, there is then the possibility of either making a choice with regard to something concerning primarily oneself, such as what church to join, what profession to adopt, what house to buy, or making a choice with regard to public matters concerning many or all, such as what law to make, what person to elect or what foreign policy to pursue. In the first type of situation, freedom is, as we said, a matter of not being personally interfered with by others; in the second, freedom means sharing in the decision-making, which is not being interfered with collectively. These

[8] This distinction is hinted at by Rousseau in his *Contrat Social,* bk. I, chap. VIII; it was further emphasized by Benjamin Constant, 1820, vol. VII, p. 253. Benjamin Constant, however, historicized it in terms of the "ancients" and "moderns." For this he is taken to task by Bobbio, a, 1962, p. 108, who in this article shows Kant to have worked with the two conceptions but to have failed to clarify them.

two spheres of individual activity have been respectively designated as private and public. One could therefore also speak of private and public freedom, in dealing with the freedom of independence and the freedom of participation.[9]

It may be well at this point to elaborate somewhat on the public freedom of participating in decision-making. The Greeks, when talking about freedom, when calling themselves *hoi eleutheroi,* the free, were thinking largely in terms of such participating in the community's decisions. The Greek *polis* knew little of the freedom that is independence as far as the individual is concerned; there were no bills of rights, and the private life of the citizen of a typical *polis* was anything but free from public interference. A famous account of the Greek *polis* states: "It is a singular error, therefore, to believe that in the ancient cities men enjoyed liberty. They had not even the idea of it. They did not believe that there could exist any rights as against the city and its gods. . . . To have political rights, to vote, to name magistrates, to have the privilege of being archon—this was called liberty; but man was not the less enslaved to the state."[10] But it was a life of constant participation, especially in the democratic cities, where the citizens shared not only in legislation, but in executive and judicial activities as well. This freedom of participation was, for the Greeks, combined with a freedom of independence for each particular *polis.* The countries now emerging from colonial tutelage, whatever their previous cultural traditions, are likewise preoccupied with the freedom of national independence and the freedom of individual participation, but will sacrifice the latter to the former, if necessary. The Greeks felt what the Romans put tersely, as was their wont, when they said, *Inter arma leges silent,* which might in this context be rendered as When group independence is threatened, individual freedom of participation must be suspended. The most radical institutional embodiment of this outlook was the Roman dictatorship, which suspended the entire constitutional machinery for the duration of an emergency.[11] Thus freedom of independence, albeit for the group, was considered primary. I believe that a variety of historical situations suggest that this primacy is of universal application; even in the most liberal countries, most citizens will be ready to surrender the freedom of participation when the freedom of independence of their country is at stake.

[9] Incomprehensibly, Oppenheim, 1961, p. 176, states that it is "misleading" to call this "freedom of participation"; for his text suggests just that.

[10] Fustel de Coulanges, 1889, p. 298. Perhaps the view is a bit exaggerated when it speaks of "slavery" here; yet Burckhardt took a similar view in 1898, p. 80 and *passim.* In any case, the view is fundamentally sound, the *Funeral Oration of Pericles* notwithstanding.

[11] Watkins, a, 1940, pp. 331ff.; Rossiter, 1948, pp. 15ff.; Friedrich, 1937, pp. 210ff., and 1950, pp. 237ff.

The freedom of participation has, in politics, expanded in a significant direction where federal structures provide for the participation of component entities in a more comprehensive community. Considering the highly developed freedom of participation in Greek politics, it is strange that such difficulties should have been encountered in extending it to the intracommunal sphere. But the sense of communal independence was evidently so highly developed that the necessary restrictions involved in participating and cooperating in a larger unit were hard to accept. A similar difficulty can at present be observed in the European context; the countries with the most highly developed freedom of participation, Britain and Switzerland, show the greatest reluctance in joining a federal union of Europe. To be sure, other important factors, such as the Commonwealth and neutrality, are also at play, but the sense of national independence, connected with a highly developed scheme of participation, is surely equally at work. Federalism, generally, exemplifies the parallelism between personal and group freedom, if freedom is taken empirically, as suggested (Chapter 32). It is therefore important to explore both for a full appreciation of the political dimensions of freedom.

Freedom of participation, whether by persons or groups, is subject to all the vicissitudes of power, influence, rule, authority and legitimacy. We need not explore these subjects here in detail again. It is important, however, to remember that all these political relations involve interference of some kind with the personal preferences of him who so participates; they engage him and commit him, and at the same time frustrate and defeat him. At such times especially, but not only then, the man who freely participates in a political community feels the need of withdrawing, of being by himself and maybe recuperating for a new spurt of participation. He may concentrate upon his family and professional preoccupations, or he may go to church or club or concert. It is more particularly the family and religious needs of men which have contributed to the rise of the notion of a nonpolitical sphere where personal freedom of independence, private freedom, reigns. Many of man's most cherished values are realized in this sphere, and the community's purpose thus is vindicated by protecting him in the pursuit of these values, interests and beliefs. Evidently, the larger the sphere of this private freedom, the more restricted will public freedom be, and vice versa.[12]

The sphere of private freedom is customarily delimited by bills of rights. Such bills of rights were initiated in the eighteenth century, were at times neglected in the nineteenth, and have achieved a new relevance in our own time because of the challenges to freedom which it has wit-

[12] An interesting study has recently been published by Cassinelli, 1961, in which the author undertakes to show "how the principal political features of the democratic state are interrelated. . . ." His intention is to construct the generalized model of a political order of freedom.

nessed. They have undergone a certain evolution, which is suggested by the terms "rights," liberties," "freedoms," which have succeeded each other as the main focus of attention. When people spoke of rights, they looked toward the individual who must be protected against governmental interference. When they came to stress liberties, the requirements of effective participation in public life had come to the fore, as in twentieth-century America; "civil liberties" became the battle cry on behalf of underprivileged minorities, such as labor, the Negro and the pacifist. Finally, when freedom was substituted, especially during the Second World War, most importantly in Franklin D. Roosevelt's Four Freedoms proclamation, the government's role in supporting the underprivileged in his struggle for a humane existence, the protection of the weak against the strong members of society, was claimed to be the heart of the matter.[13] The emphasis upon protection of the individual in such expressions as "freedom from want" has given rise to the term "social rights." These social rights are, of course, especially important to Socialists and have provided a kind of bridge between the West and the East. Thus the Universal Declaration of Human Rights, proclaimed by the United Nations in 1949, embodies these social rights to a considerable extent,[14] but they are also found in the new constitutions of Italy and Germany, and have made their way even into some state constitutions of the United States. Yet, when the people of Puerto Rico wanted to include them in their constitution, the United States Congress insisted upon their being struck out, on the ground that they were contrary to the American tradition. Some of the speeches made in Congress at the time highlighted the conflict in these conceptions of freedom.[15]

The universality of such concern with human "rights" suggests that the ubiquity of threats emanating from power-handlers is generally recognized. It may be doubted, however, that such freedom of independence for the individual is a genuine concern of the large majority of mankind. The countries with European tradition apart, most men seem to be genuinely concerned with freedom of independence for their nation, as noted. A fair number also are interested in participating more or less freely in politics. Is it surprising that only the European Community has committed itself internationally to such rights? [16]

In view of so variegated a tradition, it would be inopportune to try to enter into details about the substance of such rights. It is clear, however, even from these hints that only the original rights, as embodied for ex-

[13] Friedrich, a, 1942; cf. also Friedrich and McCloskey, 1954, introd., and Friedrich and McCloskey, a, 1960.

[14] Holcombe, 1948; Lauterpacht, 1950; Martin, 1951; Guradze, 1956; Schindler, 1957.

[15] Friedrich, 1959, pp. 1ff., p. 20, fn. 1.

[16] Concerning this, cf. Guardze, 1956, pp. 160ff.

ample in the American Constitution and its early amendments, are clearly concerned with freedom of independence, that is, with private or personal freedom only. It might, however, be argued, and is being so argued, that the more recent trends spring from a realization that such limited concern is unrealistic, since it does not take the social problems into account. This tendency is by no means limited to the United States. The neoliberals of postwar Germany led by Ludwig Erhard stand for a free market economy, but with the important proviso that the government must be ready to protect the free market (as well as other freedoms) whenever concentrations of economic power—that is, monopoly—threaten it.[17] This notion of a governmentally protected freedom brings out forcefully a point to which we shall presently return, namely, that freedom and order are dependent upon each other, and not at all antithetical. This dependence of freedom upon order has often been overlooked. Thus in seventeenth-century England, the idea was alien to the framers of the Petition of Right of 1628. They passionately desired to protect a personal sphere of freedom against the encroachments of a Crown with absolutist propensities. Two rights seemed to them paramount, and remained so throughout the revolutionary period, namely, (1) the right to one's property, and (2) the right to one's religious conviction and behavior. Of these, the first is the more ancient notion; in the middle ages and down to Bodin's writings, a ruler was believed to be bound to respect the property of his subjects. When Georg Jellinek developed the proposition that religious freedom had been the original concern of those claiming personal (in his language, subjective) rights, he overlooked the central role of property.[18]

It is highly significant that religion and property, the ideal and the material sphere of human interests and values, have *both* served as foundations for the demand that a private sphere be recognized which would be "inviolable." Both the ideal and the material sphere were and are held to be important for human dignity; economic dependence upon the rulers of the community was believed to be humiliating by the champions of the bourgeois world. The world has moved away from such absolutes, as far as property is concerned. While the right to private property is still proclaimed in many constitutions, it is usually hedged in by qualifying adjectives or phrases, such as that property implies duties as well as rights which the law shall define. Property is no longer simply and as such included in the private and personal sphere; still some measure of independent ownership is in free societies considered a vital part of the freedom of independence. Other components of this dimension of freedom are the protection against arbitrary arrest, search and seizure; the freedom of expression not only in religion and other basic convictions, but also in

[17] Friedrich, a, 1955, for further detail.

[18] G. Jellinek, 1895, 1927, pp. 42ff.

arts, letters, science and scholarship (academic freedom); the freedom of ordering one's family and professional life as one chooses, except where the public interest is touched, for example, in the mistreatment of children, and the like. The rich and variegated pattern of this personal sphere is evidently not fixed, but varies according to time and place; but what is fixed is the need for such a personal sphere of freedom of independence from public regulation and interference. It is necessary to remember, however, that so important a political thinker as Plato utterly rejected this notion when he set out his famous rule:

> But we think that it is better for every man to be ruled by divinity and insight. It is best, of course, when he possesses that within him, but if he does not, it had better be put over him from without, and then all men, being guided by the same principle, will be equals and friends as far as may be. . . . The greatest principle of all is that nobody, whether male or female, should be without a leader. Nor should the mind of anybody be habituated to letting him do anything at all on his own initiative; neither out of zeal, nor even playfully. But in war as well as in peace to his leader he shall direct his eye and follow him faithfully. And even in the smallest matter he should stand under leadership. For example, he should get up, or move, or wash, or take his meals . . . only if he has been told to do so. In a word, he should teach his soul, by long habit, never to dream of acting independently, and in fact to become utterly incapable of it.[19]

This challenge has given rise to the view that Plato was a "totalitarian." He was not, unless the term "totalitarian" is defined so broadly that even the monastery must be classed as totalitarian. But he was authoritarian and hence rejected completely the notion of personal freedom of independence as a necessary part of a well-ordered community. It is important to remember that in taking this view he had a good deal of human experience on his side, as there have been many political orders which lack such a personal sphere–if not entirely, then to a large degree.

Plato's position was and is often argued in terms of order and justice. Having in a previous chapter (19) explored the general problem of order, we may here concentrate attention upon order in relation to freedom. We mentioned at the outset that freedom depends upon order, as it in turn sets limits to it. This dependence of freedom upon order is, as we said, often overlooked, though in fact quite apparent. Government (and other power-handlers) cannot be kept out of the personal-private sphere without a fairly rigid constitutional or legal order which states the limits and organizes procedures for defending oneself against their infringement. Hence freedom of independence of persons depends upon order. The same is true for communities, and hence a federal union seeking to organize a measure of communal autonomy, that is, freedom of independence

[19] Plato, *Republic* (transl. Lindsay), p. 590.

for the component units of a composite whole, also depends upon a constitutional order. It is equally true (and evident) that freedom of participation depends upon order. For if a number of people are to participate in making political decisions, such participation must be organized, that is to say ordered, so as to be effective. But in both spheres, the private and the public, the personal and the political, the ordering will have to seek to maximize freedom—for any community which cherishes freedom as a primary value. This task of maximizing freedom involves a balancing of the two dimensions of freedom.

Some of the most bitter controversies in our time are due to a lack of understanding of this interdependence of the two kinds of freedom. The two dimensions of freedom cannot be indefinitely expanded at the same time. They cannot be maximized at the same time in the same direction. When the freedom that consists in participating in communal decisions is increased, that is to say, when the communal sphere of decision-making is increased in a community in which the citizens participate in such decision-making, the sphere of independence is thereby reduced. The following reflection will show the reason. If the entire range of selective choices be A, and if these choices be either personal and private (p^1), or communal, political and public (p^2), then A evidently equals p^1 plus p^2. Hence, if A is a determinate number, no matter of what magnitude, an increase in p^1 must mean a decrease in p^2. This is clearly seen in the dilemma of modern collectivization. As spheres of activity are transferred from the private and personal to the public and political, freedom of independence is reduced. If the total of freedom is, under such conditions, to be maintained, it follows that freedom of participation in the public sphere must be expanded. Modern democratic societies provide for such expansion fairly automatically through the provision that all such extensions of the public sphere must be sanctioned by legislative process in which all participate at least indirectly. At times, even referendum procedures are stipulated. But very serious problems have arisen where the popularly elected legislature has granted extensive discretion to administrators. A bitter controversy is raging over these issues.[20] There can be little doubt, especially in view of the large electorates, that in many countries the private sphere is continually being reduced "in the public interest," without a corresponding increase in the public sphere of effective participation. This tendency has given rise to new ways of organizing participation, such as the planning committees of the United States Department of Agriculture, the mixed industry committees of the French planning organization, and the similar bodies developed in the European Coal and Steel Community.[21] All these varied groupings are tentative at-

[20] Robson, 1928 (and later), *passim;* Keeton, 1952, and the literature given there.

[21] Friedrich, 1942, pp. 114ff.; Harbold, 1954, pp. 129ff.; Diebold, 1959, pp. 459ff., 616ff.

tempts at enlarging freedom, that is, at maintaining a minimum of such freedom in the face of multiple invasions of the private sphere.

It has been objected to this general analysis that in certain cases there might be an increase in the freedom of participation which would lead to an increase of the freedom of independence for some and no decrease in the participation of others. The following hypothetical case was advanced to illustrate this point. Suppose a government were to build a dam to bring relief to marginal farmers, as is done all over the world but notably in Egypt, Pakistan and India. Given a situation of widespread unemployment and unused material resources, the projected dam would seem (1) to increase the participation of those who ran the government, (2) to increase the independence of the farmers, hard pressed by their environment, (3) to increase the independence of those formerly unemployed who received additional income. In this type of situation, it is argued, there would be no decrease in freedom equal to the increases. This conclusion is based upon the condition that the government used self-created credit, or "dissaving," which would eliminate the possibility that either taxes or loss of purchasing power would decrease the freedom of independence on the part of other participants in the system. But this condition brackets out the eventual consequences of credit creation and dissaving, namely, inflation or taxes (after a time). What is more important, it overlooks two crucial premises of the analysis given above, namely, (1) that political freedom is expressive of the absence of interference *by other persons*, and (2) that the number of selective choices is a determinate number. If the dynamism of a significant increase in such choices is introduced, naturally the proposition no longer holds. This possibility calls for exploration of innovative freedom, which will be discussed in the next chapter. In short, the case here presented is not one in which the freedom of participation is expanded by the community taking over a part of the sphere of freedom of independence.[22]

The problem of "maximizing" freedom is therefore seen as a problem of balancing various claims to freedom against each other. It has been asserted recently that allegations such as that "democracy maximizes freedom" obscure the problem, which is really said to be that of the "equality of freedom." [23] But both the problem of greater or less equality (Chapter 16) and the problem of balancing claims to freedom involve the issue of the more or less of freedom. This is the issue of the more or less of interference, according to our analysis. Before we turn to it, it may well be

[22] This objection, made a number of times, was ably presented in my graduate seminar by Mr. Leo Byrnes.

[23] Oppenheim, 1961, pp. 206f. "The essential difference between dictatorship and democracy is not that there is little total freedom in one and much in the other, but that freedom, and power as well, is more equally distributed in the latter." But whether this is the "essential difference" or not, it does not dispose of the problem of "maximizing freedom."

helpful to state this interdependence in the form of four simple formulas, relating fi (freedom of independence) and fp (freedom of participation) to a median M. The formulas could be written as:

1. $fi > fp$	2. $fi > fp$	3. $fi < fp$	4. $fi < fp$
$fi + fp > M$	$fi + fp < M$	$fi + fp > M$	$fi + fp < M$

M in all these formulas is a median between the situation where $fi - fp$ is very large and where $fi + fp$ is very small. In this form, these "equations" are merely hints as to the direction which quantitative research may take. This quantifying of freedom is a task which urgently awaits attention. Everyone talks of freedom in terms of "more" and "less," and such expressions are presumably quite meaningful, but they certainly call for specification.

The maximizing of freedom is commonly acclaimed as a self-evident goal of democratic societies. Experience has shown, however, that it is an error to assume that the majority of citizens in existing real political orders desire a maximum of freedom. It is the premise of classical liberalism that all human beings prefer to be in a position of making as many free choices as possible, that is to say, of deciding for themselves rather than following the suggestions or even the command of others.[24] Yet past as well as contemporary experience provided by history, sociology and psychology suggests that human beings desire a *minimum* of freedom, rather than a maximum. All human beings enjoy making *some* free choices, but not many, let alone all. It is only an unusual man who desires to be as fully autonomous as possible. Kant's moral and political philosophy rests upon the fallacious assumption that all men are autonomous, or at least seeking autonomy.[25] In this respect he is representative of the old liberal tradition and its ideals. When tested in a democratic context, where an opportunity for maximizing freedom is provided, most or at any rate many men exhibit a decided preference for values other than freedom, such as justice and security, and a consequent willingness to be content with something decidedly less than the maximum possible. When opportunity for participation is provided, they do not participate, and when opportunity is provided for private activity they do not engage in it.[26] Many men seem

[24] Mill, 1859, *passim.*

[25] Kant (ed. Friedrich), 1949, pp. 187ff., 225ff., xxvi ff. Riesman, 1950, has argued that most Americans (why just Americans remains obscure) can be divided into tradition-directed, inner-directed and other-directed—weird terms for the more ordinary insight that human beings are motivated by custom, conviction and sociability. To these common types he opposes the "autonomous man," a "rare bird," who will act on the basis of rational reflection and free choice; cf. pp. 287f., 311–319.

[26] Erich Fromm, 1941, *passim.* A considerable discussion has developed since. For a review, see Riesman, 1954, esp. pp. 105f. Cf. also Kluckhohn, 1948, pp. 228ff.

to prefer having most decisions made for them, and practically all men prefer to have some decisions made for them. What holds for decisions, holds equally for actions, opinions, and the rest. This tendency of human beings to shirk the more radical freedom, the maximum freedom attainable, is not necessarily to be condemned. It hangs together with man's desire to live effectively, and to pursue his vital tasks according to the rule of the path of least resistance. Overextension in fields not closely related to the immediate tasks in hand may mean lower achievements in these tasks. For a full appreciation it is necessary to go into another dimension of freedom, the freedom of creation, of invention and innovation. This we shall do in the next chapter.

It remains to develop some general propositions concerning the more or less of freedom or interference. The close interdependence of freedom and power suggests that this comparative measurement of freedom is dependent upon the comparative measurement of power. As we saw earlier (Chapter 9), we lack at present detailed and precise indices of power in quantitative terms. By common agreement, it is often possible to state a judgment of more or less regarding power without such quantitative specification. On the basis of our own situational analysis of power, the extent of conforming behavior serves as a rough index. This index is similarly applicable to freedom (in reverse). This approach to freedom has recently been more fully developed.[27] It has been pointed out that such comparative evaluation of "more" or "less" freedom, taking account of the several components of the political situation, may be broken down into several interrelated aspects.[28] Within the framework of our theory, these aspects may be stated thus: (1) the probability of the actors being interfered with, (2) the conflict of values involved, and (3) the scope or extent of the sphere of action, either in terms of the range of activities involved or in terms of the size of the territory and number of people to which they apply. To begin with the last, it is evident that one may speak of someone as "more free" if he can act within a larger territory or in dealing with a larger number of people according to his own preferences. To illustrate, a person who can travel within a large country seems freer than one who is restricted to a small one. People confined to Berlin are less free than those living in the Federal Republic of Germany, and

[27] Oppenheim, 1961, chap. 8, "Degrees of Power and Freedom." This study largely confirms my own studies in this field; see, however, the critical comments above, fns. 2 and 9.

[28] Oppenheim (pp. 183ff.) calls these aspects "dimensions"; if one were to differentiate his use of the term from the one here employed, he might say that Oppenheim's are the quantitative dimensions, while ours are the generic dimensions. However, Oppenheim neglects the third generic dimension of freedom (see next chapter), to which his quantitative dimensions do not actually apply. It would seem that the usage adopted in the text is more appropriate.

the Europeans in the European Community *feel* and *are* more free today, with passports and travel restrictions removed, than they were formerly. The extreme limit of this aspect is a solitary prison cell in which the victim is chained. Again, a person who can transact business with or choose a marriage partner among millions is more free than one who is restricted to a small number; hence all boundaries are limits, reducing freedom, and the countless prohibitions which custom and law have maintained in the history of political communities, and for the very purpose of organizing community, are calculated to reduce freedom. Looked at from this aspect, it would seem that freedom and community are antithetical: the more community, the less freedom. The reverse of this conclusion provides the basis for most philosophical anarchism.

The second aspect of the political situation that affects the comparative evaluation of freedom, that determines the more or less of freedom, is what we called the "conflict of values." That a man can increase his freedom by changing his values is well illustrated by the famous dialogue between Epictetus and the tyrant (see page 164). Any interference, in other words, by which a person is being coerced into complying with someone else's preferences will depend for its effectiveness upon the means of coercion involved. When a man is threatened with loss of his job, if he does not comply with his boss's wishes, he may yet remain relatively free by giving up his job. A ratio between the value of the job and of the action involved in noncompliance will determine his measure of freedom.[29]

The third aspect (the first in our list) is the probability of the actors being interfered with. There always is some small residue of freedom in all but the marginal case of the chained and gagged prisoner. The writer who is critical of the government is more free in Poland than in the Soviet Union, more free in a part of the Soviet Union where the local boss is easygoing or corrupt than in another where he is fanatical and honest. A professor is ordinarily more free to express radical views in one of the great private universities of America than in a small denominational college or a lesser state university. A businessman in most countries is usually more free in matters of sexual life than a member of the clergy, and so forth. These are cases of freedom of independence; but the same reasoning applies to freedom of participation. A person who may choose only between an official candidate and a protesting no, as in most one-party dictatorships, is less free than one who can choose between two or more

[29] Oppenheim, 1961, pp. 187ff., discusses this aspect under the heading of "probability of degree of deprivation." But the deprivation is only one part of this aspect of the situation, referring to those situations where the power to interfere is the power to deprive. It may be the power to reward, and so on.

candidates.[30] A person who can choose his local officials and those of an intermediary level (federalism: Chapter 32) is more free than one who is restricted to choosing the central government. A person who may share in actual legislation through referendum and initiative is more free than one who may only elect representatives.[31] In all these cases, the greater amount of freedom may be expressed in terms of the greater number of actions a particular person is at liberty to take without interferences by others.

But it is only a combination of the three aspects which enables us to speak of the over-all freedom of independence and participation. This would be a simple matter of addition and subtraction if the three aspects could be fully quantified in terms of ordinary numbers. But since this is not the case, the matter is often rather beyond convincing assessment. Is a worker more free in a political democracy where he may vote and otherwise participate in politics, as well as operate freely within his sphere of independence, than another worker in an autocratic political regime ruled by a single party of which he is a member, seeing that the latter can also participate in the control of the industrial plant in which he works? Is an official more free in a parliamentary democracy where his minister is subject to being overthrown by vote in parliament than another official in a presidential democracy? While it would be easy to multiply such examples where an assessment would be very difficult, if not impossible, these comparisons are usually less important in practice than assessment within political orders where changes are occurring. The Negro is more free in the United States than he was thirty years ago, though less free than a comparable white man. A member of the French parliament is less free under the Fifth Republic than under the Fourth and Third. The citizen of the Federal Republic of Germany is more free than the German was under military occupation, not to speak of the Hitler regime. The citizen of West Berlin is less free than the citizen of Hamburg, though more free than the "citizen" of East Berlin, and so forth.

Most of what has been said in the preceding paragraphs of persons applies to groups of persons as well. A trade union is more free in Great Britain than in the Soviet Union, a church more so in the United States

[30] Whether the *number* of choices increases freedom is a complicated question, depending upon the system of representation and the political order of which it is a part; it may be a reduction if the result is a multiple-party system and a consequent barter behind closed doors which determines the actual government. See Chaps. 17 and 27, and Friedrich, 1950, chap. XIV.

[31] This fact explains no doubt, at least in part, Rousseau's hostility to representation; he valued freedom very highly and wanted to "maximize" it for everybody. What he forgot is that the first aspect, involving territory and population, also is involved in an over-all assessment.

than in Italy, a university more free in Western countries than in the Soviet orbit.[32] Since groups take actions and are interfered with in their desire to do so, the phenomenon of freedom as defined has parallel application to them. Having bracketed out the metaphysical problem of freedom of the will and concentrated on what can be observed, reported and analyzed, one may apply the propositions developed in the foregoing to all kinds of groups as well as individuals. As we noted earlier, the freedom of the group may often appear to its members more valuable than their personal freedom; they may consequently be quite prepared to sacrifice the latter for the former, at least up to a point. Since freedom of the group usually increases the scope of freedom of participation, this phenomenon may also be described by saying that men will often prefer greater freedom of participation to greater freedom of independence. The struggle of colonial peoples offers numerous illustrations of this rule. To those who have long enjoyed an adequate amount of freedom of participation in a group which possesses national freedom of independence and hence are primarily concerned with their personal freedom of independence, the extent of the willingness of such formerly subject people to sacrifice their personal freedom for national freedom is often astonishing. The broader view of freedom here developed might serve to explain it. The liberation of creative potentialities through the freedom of invention (see next chapter) also, of course, contributes to it.

In conclusion to this chapter, we wish to recall that all human activity, and more particularly political activity—all human behavior, if one prefers—can be either carried forward at the behest of other human beings, or not. If such action is not engaged in, not because someone else commands it or brings it about by one of the several modes of coercion, but because the actor chooses it himself, it is said to be free. Freedom is the human condition in which one is able to engage in such independent activity. Hence communities as well as persons may be said to be free. But in speaking thus, we should remember that all communities consist of persons, and that the persons of which they consist gain some kind of freedom through the measure of participation, be it ever so limited, which the community provides.

[32] The same point is made a number of times by Oppenheim, 1961.

chapter

21

Political Innovation and Invention: Creative Freedom

Great innovations should not be forced on slender majorities.
Thomas Jefferson

THE TWO DIMENSIONS of freedom, freedom of independence and freedom of participation, have so far been discussed largely in terms of the freedom to choose, to select, to prefer. All these human activities presuppose that there are known alternatives between which a choice or a selection can be made, a preference expressed. But there is another possibility, a new dimension, so to speak, cutting across the other two, which arises when none of the available alternatives is acceptable, either because every one of them conflicts with preconceived values, interests or beliefs, or because experience has shown that none of them accomplishes the purpose which these values, interests or beliefs suggest in the particular situation. There is a very great difference between choosing between alternatives that are known to exist and discovering a new alternative. Such discovery of a new alternative is, as we saw, a creative process (Chapter 4). Innovation and invention are distinct from choosing. Now the freedom of creation, though occurring in the sphere of both private and public, of personal and communal or political life, is distinct from selection in that it cannot possibly be predicted. For in order to predict such an innovation, one would have to be the inventor, which is obviously impossible. Hence this unpredictability of the inventive use of freedom has served to assert freedom as real, beyond the argument of the determinists and the voluntarists. A free action would then be an action which could not be predicted.[1]

The issue involved in prediction may account for a recent increase in the interest in innovation and invention. It is probably also related to the stress on system theory and on the "outside interference" emanating from inventions and other innovations in economic development.[2] Scientists have become decidedly more self-conscious in recent years about the processes and procedures of discovery and invention.[3] The ever widening tendency to organize invention and discovery through research organization has introduced a measure of steady progress into these fields, while at the same time greatly accelerating the rate of induced change. Social scientists have been slow to follow suit, but are beginning to catch up.[4]

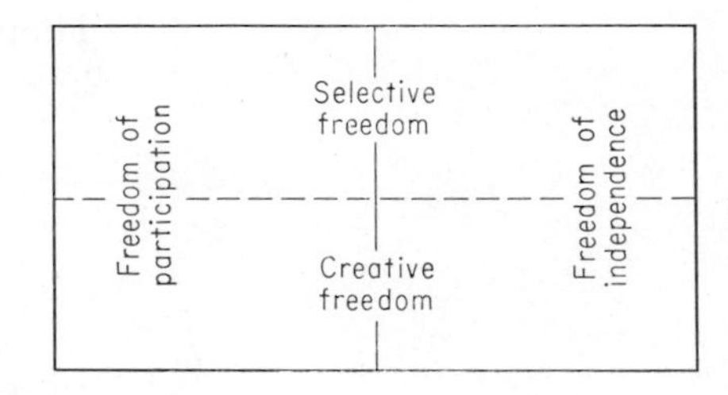

Inventions, innovations and discoveries in the social field are, however, of very great importance and have played a distinct role in the field of government and politics. As we shall show later, political innovation is typically a group process; not the individual "inventor," but the complex process of discussion and negotiation is the seedbed of "new ideas." It

[1] Cranston, 1953, esp. pp. 162ff.

[2] The theorizing of Schumpeter revolved around this issue; cf. Schumpeter, 1934. His inclination to stress the "bureaucratization" of the process, with the attendant claim that the inventor had become "obsolete," is overstressing a significant change involving the "organizing" of innovation in technical fields; in the political and social field, innovation has been organized for a long time, especially through the legislative process.

[3] N. R. Hanson, 1958; Popper, 1934, 1959.

[4] Note the interesting survey by A. de Grazia, a, 1961, including a partial review of the writings. This author addresses himself to "social" invention, but then suggests that "all" invention is "social." (If so, what is the use of the qualifying term?) He is right, if what is meant is that all inventions (discoveries and innovations) are apt to have social consequences, and occur within a definite social setting (the same could be said regarding the political setting). But surely there are marked differences between discoveries, inventions and innovations, if one considers material involved, the maker and his make-up, and the objective or end to be served. It is, therefore, not merely a question of the "high proportion of direct human contacts," as De Grazia suggests, though "human contracts" or relations are the "material" of social inventions, while those particular relations concerned with organization and government are political ones.

has been suggested in this connection that innovation might be distinguished from invention by considering the former a "social change" which has been "deliberately brought about." [5] But the introduction of the aspect of deliberateness, while important, seems too narrow; innovations may be quite unintended and gradual, especially when they occur as secondary and tertiary effects of intended ones. An invention, on the other hand, is typically "deliberate" in that it occurs in connection with a search which is related to "problem-solving." It has been rightly asserted that such problem-solving, and not only necessity, is the mother of invention (as "want" is said to have been its "mistress"). As Dewey wrote, in discussing discovery: "Important conclusions of science are those which distinctly refuse to be identified with anything previously known." [6] Invention, discovery and in general creativity, and the innovations which they foster and beget, are in fact the result of man's most deep-seated drives and manifest his most remarkable freedom. Hence certain of these inventions, such as language, tool-use and the alphabet, have been acclaimed as revealing distinctive traits of man. It is the sublimated creativity which all of them spring from.

The question as to what occasions such inventions has produced a number of interesting answers. It has been difficult to test these speculative hypotheses, most of which have been concerned with individual inventiveness. There can be little doubt that very intriguing psychological issues are involved. One writer has recently suggested that "inventiveness appears to emerge from situations where personal and social conditions of the following types are encountered: high drive (ambition); frequent marginalism; high relationism; and high operationalism." [7] We would prefer to put the matter somewhat more simply, restricting ourselves to the political sphere of operations by suggesting that innovations involving discovery and invention are likely to occur in response to pressing problems resulting from novel situation aspects, provided the political community is receptive to change and has organized procedures for putting proposed changes into effect. Modern legislative process, as already mentioned, amending procedures for the basic order, and more recently "planning" procedures are of this kind. And because of the peculiar nature of political innovation (related as it is to the nature of power, authority and order)

[5] *Ibid.*, p. 17.

[6] Dewey, 1929, p. 184; Stecchini's recent observation that "contrary to Dewey's idea, inventions do not spring from a concern with the solutions of pressing problems" (a, 1961) does not seem valid; he himself argues throughout his paper in terms of problems that inventions solved. Cf. also the interesting pages in Dewey, 1925, 1958, pp. 154–157, weighed down by a quite unnecessary insistence that the discovered object did not "exist" prior to its discovery as an "object of knowledge" which latter is merely "the conclusion of the historical event of inquiry in its connection with other histories" (p. 156).

[7] A. de Grazia, *op. cit.*, p. 8. He there explains these terms.

there should be added to these procedures the opportunities for group discussion. The delineating of these procedures would seem to imply that it might be possible to predict the frequency of political innovation and invention, even though the actual content of such invention remained in the realm of the wholly contingent. We agree that clearer perception of the nature of social invention will permit an abstracting of the inventive elements of the social process. But it would be a dangerous mistake to believe that because of such insight into the path (method) of invention and innovation they are certain to occur; all that seems possible is to provide a favorable climate for their insemination, incubation and growth.

From a political standpoint, such insistence upon the aspect of nonpredictability is undesirable, because the actions of a person which are not interfered with by another, which are not the result of another's preference, may yet be predicted and predictable on the basis of his character, of basic human nature, and the like. That a person would defend himself against a baseless calumny might be generally predicted; yet that he does so may be his own choice and preference, and in no wise due to another's interference, whether by order, command or negotiation, or other influence. It is, in any case, more likely to be true of the inventive dimension of freedom, than of the selective ones, that it is unpredictable. But since inventive freedom plays a very important role in politics, any approach to politics purely in terms of finding generalizations which will provide a basis for prediction is apt to miss some of the most significant aspects of politics, both in the past and in the future. Some time ago, in 1941, a leading social psychologist who had become interested in the psychic conditions under which predictions are made asked fifty social scientists of standing what in their view the world would be like in 1951. In replying to this request, I pointed out that no predictions of this kind are possible, because they have to be made on the assumption that the givens of the political situations remain unaltered by creative innovation. This assumption can, of course, be made as a counterfactual condition, and in making it I ventured a prediction which proved largely correct. However, I would say in retrospect that I was merely lucky; for one of the inventive innovations which occurred, the atomic bomb, happened to intensify the trends which I stressed, instead of counteracting them. The opposite could just as well have happened.[8]

The case of the atomic bomb brings out the fact that inventive freedom can operate in two distinctive ways: by producing innovations and inventions *outside* the field of politics proper which yet vitally affect it, and by discovering innovations and inventions within the area of politics itself. The first of these areas of inventive activity is, of course, by far the larger and might well be called "creative"; it springs up in

[8] Popper, 1957, discusses this problem in relation to historicism.

the cultural sphere of arts, letters, science and scholarship, as well as in the humbler fields of recurrent production in economic life. In an ultimate philosophical sense, the procreative activity must be reckoned as constituting part of the dimension of creative freedom, even though it occurs in response to one of the most insistent urges or compulsions. Generally speaking, creative freedom is no different from other free activities, in the sense stipulated by us, in that it occurs because it must. Yet each time two human beings embrace each other in love and lust, the freedom of bringing into existence something entirely new in all its mysterious potentiality is at work. It is important to stress this human, all-too-human, side of creative freedom, because it explains why even the most autocratic regimes will and must provide a measure of freedom, since their very survival depends upon its continued practice. The senseless absurdity of Huxley's *Brave New World* is nowhere more clearly revealed than in the efforts to escape from the necessity of recognizing the inescapable need of maintaining human creativity intact, no matter what the political order. The reason is, in part, that such creativity benefits not only the individual, but the community as well.

The Soviet Union has made great efforts, with striking results, to maximize this freedom in certain fields of human endeavor. Former attempts to account for achievements of the Soviets in science and engineering by their utilizing the results of science in the free world are generally abandoned today. It is clear that there exists a considerable degree of independence for those who will employ it for creative effort in a variety of fields.[9] Nor is this independence limited to science and scholarly pursuits. It may be substantially more limited and hemmed in by personal prejudices of the power-holders, and more especially the leader personally, but in the interstices a measure of freedom survives.[10] Such "freedom" does not, however, explicitly extend to the political sphere. Here we have instead "the pleasure of having one's action determined," and the consequent "aversion to the habit, ascribed to the intelligentsia, of 'inventing,' that is, of deciding upon a course of action originating in one's thought rather than in the external situations."[11] In spite of this denial, there exists in Soviet thought a strong sense of the range of "unpredictability" of the future, of the indeterminist aspect, especially in regard to the *political* future, which has rightly been insisted upon as in contradiction with basic communist determinism.[12]

[9] Cf. also Polanyi, 1958, chap. IV, pp. 49ff.

[10] Swayze, 1962, has traced the ups and downs in the field of literature; note especially his chap. VI, dealing with bureaucratic controls—read "interferences."

[11] Leites, 1953, p. 77. Leites, in spite of his elaborate exploration of the personal factor in Bolshevism, does not give special attention to the problem of "inventive freedom."

[12] *Ibid.*, pp. 77ff., and esp. p. 92.

In keeping with this "divided mind," Soviet Russia has on the one hand established an elaborate system of controls and direction for science, while on the other hand leaving scientists a fair amount of freedom within this system, the amount varying with the extent to which their views impinge upon relevant aspects of party ideology.[13] Considerations derived from that ideology are counteracted by the great enthusiasm for science which some even have called the Soviet Union's "professed faith."[14] The intense preoccupation with science is deeply embedded in Marxism, which believes itself to be "scientific socialism." But this does not prevent such absurdities as the slogan of the *Journal of Marxist-Leninist Natural Science*, "We stand for party in mathematics," or "We stand for the purity of the Marxist-Leninist theory of surgery."[15] The deleterious effect of any state control of science is patent in such nonsense.

The striking successes of Soviet science in a variety of fields show, however, that these absurdities must not be taken at face value. They do not necessarily mean much in terms of specific tasks with which the scientist is confronted. The range of inventive freedom must be quite considerable, especially in recent years,[16] but it remains rigidly restricted to technical focal areas, and there is a constant pressure of relating it to the planning of the society as carried forward by official agencies. It is, of course, not possible to say at present whether such "freedom of independence" granted for the sake of "liberating inventive freedom" can be indefinitely prolonged without generating a demand for "freedom of participation," though it seems unlikely. The present channeling of such demand through the Communist Party may not prove to be feasible in the long run.[17]

On the other hand, it seems doubtful also that a radically libertarian view which rejects all political coordination or control of science and pleads for its "self-government" can really be justified in view of modern

[13] Thus the Lysenko case showed extensive interference; cf. H. J. Muller, a, 1954; the varied impact of this issue can be seen in such fields as transportation (cf. H. Hunter, 1957), education (cf. Inkeles and Bauer, 1959), and medicine (cf. Field, 1957).

[14] Webb and Webb, 1936, pp. 1132ff. Cf. also entire chap. XI, pp. 944–1017.

[15] *Ibid*., p. 1000.

[16] Cf. B. Moore, Jr., 1954, chaps. 4 and 5. The latter, entitled "Scientist and Artist in the Police State," gives a very discriminating, balanced account, culminating in the proposition that "at both the group and the individual level, the recurring theme in the intellectual's response to the Soviet system is the *search for some minimal degree of autonomy* within the system" (p. 153, italics added). Moore also notes that a restriction to such minimal autonomy might, when it results in intense effort at the job, as is often the case, help rather than hinder the rulers of the system (p. 151).

[17] Fainsod, 1953, pp. 487ff. Schapiro, 1958, esp. chaps. 13, 17, 25. Cf. for most recent developments, Triska (ed.), 1962, pp. 154ff.

weapons development, as well as other fields vitally related to political objectives.[18]

The exercise of inventive freedom in politics proper presupposes participation. In totalitarian dictatorships such participation has, of course, been limited to the party and more especially its *cadres.* But here the tempo of innovation has been considerable. Indeed, in the course of the last forty years, totalitarian dictatorship has itself been created out of beginnings which were conceived in quite different terms. The "dictatorship of the proletariat" of Marxian writings in no way anticipates the actual course of events. Totalitarian dictatorship did not spring ready-made into being in 1917, but was fashioned in the course of extended and violent struggles among those who were trying to "realize" the tasks which the ideology had put before them. These efforts to cope with novel situations give to totalitarian dictatorship its "uniqueness," even though it be readily admitted that nothing is ever "wholly unique," just as nothing ever lacks an element of uniqueness.[19] Correspondingly, innovation utilizes various available elements in new combinations and applications. To those objections against the proposition that totalitarian dictatorship is a unique and novel mode of governing men, usually couched in terms of comparing it to tyranny, despotism and other forms of autocracy, we are ready to concede that totalitarian dictatorship has features in common with these older forms of predominantly coercive government, in other words, that it belongs to a generic category which is perhaps best designated as "autocracy" (Chapter 10).

Political innovation and invention are, of course, by no means restricted to such autocratic regimes; quite on the contrary, the freeing of inventive human energies in modern constitutional orders has generated a continuing stream of such innovations. But these processes are primordial. In a very real sense, the modern state is such an invention, or rather a composite of many innovations. A detailed study of administrative history, for example, reveals how ever renewed efforts were made to deal with stubborn problems of government by new devices such as the differentiation of functions, and the like.[20] Again, the American Constitution was a major and successful effort at political innovation; among its inventions were federalism in its modern form (Chapter 32) and the process of constitutional amendment.

Among recent innovations, two might be mentioned here for illustrative purposes. One is the so-called constructive nonconfidence vote which has provided German parliamentary government with the stability

[18] A strong and persuasive argument in support of this contention is given by Polanyi, 1951, pp. 49ff., in a paper entitled "Self-government of Science." See also C. P. Snow, 1961.

[19] On this issue, cf. the excellent article by Joynt and Rescher, 1961.

[20] T. R. Tout, 1920. Cf. also Friedrich, 1950, chap. 2, for a comparative view.

it formerly lacked. According to this (article 67 of the Constitution of the Federal Republic of Germany), no government, no chancellor, can be overthrown without the hostile majority's electing at the same time his successor. To date, the provision has operated in a purely negative way; no government has been overthrown, because the occasional constellations of opposing groups never consolidated themselves sufficiently to agree on a successor (or even to discuss him). If we study the record, we find that this innovation, anticipated in attenuated form in two state constitutions, Bavaria and Baden-Württemberg, sprang from a determination to avoid the instability of governments under the Weimar constitution and to achieve something akin to British cabinet government. It was realized that the British parliamentary system rested upon the existence of a stably organized opposition, ready and willing to take over the government, whenever the existing majority should disintegrate. Since no two-party system existed in Germany, it was felt that the opposition should be forced to consolidate itself before overthrowing the government. Actually, the inventors of this "constructive nonconfidence vote" overshot the mark they had set themselves. The German system as it has worked so far appears to lack the flexibility of the British scheme, and resembles more nearly the American one, with a fixed term for the chancellor and his government, coinciding with the period for which the parliament is elected. However, there are possibilities of change, and it would be safer to characterize the German system as something of a blend of the British and American schemes. In any case, there can be no doubt that the innovation radically altered the German political scene. It would be interesting to consider the new French constitution from this viewpoint, but the test of time has been too short. Its most interesting innovations are to be found in the sphere of France's overseas dependencies; one article, No. 88, provides for "association." Now association is another innovation of the recent past, a new device in the evolution of federalism. Associational extensions of federal unions have occurred in a number of different places and under varying conditions. It is strikingly illustrated by the status of Puerto Rico within the American system. No such entity as a "free and associated commonwealth" was envisaged by the Fathers at Philadelphia, and no word in the document hints at it. The Constitution speaks in terms of a simple territorial entity, composed of "states and territories." By the notion that an entity like Puerto Rico might be "associated" with it, a more complex system is created. The boundary does not have the same meaning; indeed association in this sense suggests a loosening of the bond of boundary.[21] Association, as a new dimension of federalism, is not confined to this instance, however. It turns up, as mentioned above, as a potential mode of relating

[21] Friedrich, 1959, pp. 17f., and below, Chap. 32.

French overseas territories that seek independence from France. In Europe, highly flexible arrangements for "associating" Greece and other European powers with the Common Market (European Economic Community) have been incorporated in the law and are already being tested. They were also envisaged in the draft constitution of a Political Community. Again West Berlin's curious form of participation in the Federal Republic of Germany is a form of "association"; Berlin has representatives in the federal parliament, but they have no vote, though they recently voted in the election of the president. In all these novel relations, the inventive capacity of men in politics is at work, as it has been in the past.

All those who struggle with the problems of how to organize an effective government for newly liberated peoples need to be aware of the extent and importance of innovation in the field of politics. It just is not true that men have continually moved in a recurrent cycle of political institutions. Of course, there are resemblances between the new and the old, but there is wide scope for inventive enterprise. This means, of course, that the term "progress," now so often decried, has substantial meaning in politics. This meaning suggests continuous adaptation of political processes to new situations with a view to providing maximum opportunities for human development and happiness, if this term may here stand for the feelings accompanying the fulfillment of cherished expectations. The history of government is the story of successive innovations as well as the cyclical repetition of established modes of behavior. These innovations have been devised by particular men at particular times, and are not the result of impersonal forces, except as mediated by the creative potential in man. It is perhaps not too much to say that much government has been invented in the course of time. If we turn to the speculative inquiries of archaeologists, informed as they are by the solid data of anthropologists, about the origin of political institutions, the notion of such creative innovation is reinforced.[22] Institutions are not always invented; they may represent the crystallization of practice through habit and custom (Chapter 3), but they *can* be so invented, and often are. The wider has been the participation in government, and the wider consequently freedom of participation, the more numerous have become the proposals for innovation, as well as their adoption.

The most dramatic occasions of political innovation are, of course, periods of revolutionary upheaval. Generally speaking, the modern world is distinguished by a reasonably favorable attitude toward revolution. This attitude stands in sharp contrast to the views of earlier periods. Plato and Aristotle were preoccupied with how to prevent revolution, and indeed how to achieve a stable, unchanging order. Similar notions predominate throughout the Orient. These views were, however, not ex-

[22] American Ethnological Society, 1958, and below, Chap. 22.

pressive of an actual stability, and were not empirically derived from the experience of such stability, but were formulated in conscious opposition to the revolutionary transformations in the society to which such thought was meant to apply. In this sense, all such thought was an "escape from freedom," the disquieting consequences of creative political freedom being more apparent than its eventual result, the emerging new political order. Alexander, cutting the Gordian knot of how to renew the political order of the dying *polis* by transcending it in the form of an empire, was the true innovator. But he did not live long enough to institutionalize his new conception and, under his successors, it lapsed back into the still older form of Oriental despotism. It was the Romans who in gradual steps transformed the ancient *polis* into a viable empire [23] by a series of innovations. These inventions did not perish with the collapse of the empire, but eventually inspired the builders of the modern "state" (Chapter 30). This process, though gradual, was by no means peaceful; on the contrary it was accompanied by a great deal of violence and bloodshed, and this fact justifies us in thinking of it as a revolution.

For the contrast of revolution and evolution, so much discussed in recent times, and not only among Marxists, may presumably be described by the degree of violence associated with political change (Chapter 34). A number of general analyses of revolution as a political process have been offered by historians and sociologists; they have contributed vitally to our understanding.[24] Their work, however, is based upon a comparative analysis of the English, French, American and Russian revolutions; of these examples, three at least belong to what Rosenstock-Huessy has rightly identified as "great revolutions," in contrast to the strictly governmental or political revolutions. Aristotle's famous analysis,[25] on the other hand, was preoccupied with the political *stasis*, or overthrow. He described it largely in terms of a struggle between the rich and the poor, and their rival conceptions of justice, and sought to fit it into the pattern of a cyclical transformation of the political order, as suggested by conventional Greek notions of the types of rule (Chapter 10). It is obvious that such an analysis cannot be considered satisfactory for an event like the French Revolution. Furthermore, the idea of historical development or evolution called for some recognition of a pattern of progress—a recognition which is, however, in politics made ideologically difficult by the Russian revolution. Rosenstock-Huessy undertook to link the revolutionary pattern of Western history to the growth of West-

[23] Cf. Syme, 1939, *passim,* for a recent treatment of these innovations.

[24] Pettee, 1938; Rosenstock-Huessy, 1931; Sorokin, 1937, III, chaps. 12–14; Brinton, 1938. See also Friedrich, 1950, and references. Some of these are discussed in greater detail below in Chap. 34.

[25] *Politics,* bk. V.

ern nations. He extended the usual scheme backward to include the "papal" revolution of the thirteenth century, and the Reformation of the sixteenth, and then constructed a most intriguing succession of "national" revolutions in the course of which Italy, Germany, England, France and Russia achieved nationhood, that is, a sense of cultural identity. The process now having come to an end, he interpreted the present as "out of revolution."[26] But this is true only, if at all, for Europe and the West, while vast revolutionary movements are transforming Asia, Africa and the rest of the world. In response to these revolutions Europe is being unified, surely itself a revolution of no inconsiderable scope.

To glean the main features of revolution analyzed in Chapter 34 is not our purpose here. Here it is merely a question of linking them concretely to the range of inventive innovation. Even the unlimited great revolutions did not necessarily do much by way of inventing new political institutions. It can happen, but need not do so. The Cromwellian revolution put forward the modern idea of a "constitution" consciously fabricated by human design. The Russian revolution initially produced the "soviet" or "council" (*Rat*) type of government,[27] which it afterward abandoned in favor of a totalitarian dictatorship which is the most striking governmental invention of our time, unsuccessfully imitated by the fascists and at present being tested in the Orient.

When considering the governmental task of the newly liberated nations emerging from a colonial or dependent status, it is usual to argue the case in terms of their adopting either constitutional democracy or the soviet type of government. Experience to date suggests that neither of these forms is really suitable to their needs, though both have passionate adherents. In a number of places, Mexico, Bolivia, Egypt, Tunisia, Iraq and Puerto Rico, to mention some of the more striking examples, a new type of political order appears to be in the making. It is being invented by practical men devoid of dogmatic preoccupations who are trying to solve the problem of a viable political order. This order seems to be characterized by three key elements or components, namely, a predominant party having the function of integrating rather than dividing the people, a key elite of managerial talent, inspired by the party's purposes but preoccupied with the tasks of concrete administration, and finally a plan for economic and social development. This plan is the result of a kind of planning which is less autocratic than the totalitarian planning, and more authoritarian than planning procedures in constitutional

[26] This is the title of the English version, 1938, of the original work cited above.

[27] Hannah Arendt, 1958, has argued that the soviet type of government, abandoned by the Soviet Union, has a great future; she adduces the Hungarian attempt at reproducing it during their uprising in 1957 as evidence. It seems doubtful that this argument really can be supported by adequate evidence.

democracies.[28] It is difficult to classify this type of political order in terms of democracy and dictatorship, for it represents a novel amalgamate of the useful features of both.[29]

More limited is the degree of innovation in the so-called new constitutions of postwar Europe. The peculiar conditions prevailing after the Second World War led to a number of quasi-revolutionary upheavals which were primarily *negative* in character. But they are negative only in the political perspective. By this term we wish to indicate that their promoters were not so much motivated by any enthusiasm for a *novel* and hence more promising method of government, as by a rejection, a negation, of a discredited past and a repellent future under totalitarian dictatorship. The French constitution of 1946, the Italian constitution of 1947 and the German constitution of 1949 are all the outcome of such "negative" revolutions. They all seek to avoid totalitarianism, and the new French constitution of 1958 largely resembles them, except for the further negative feature of rejecting the kind of radical parliamentary democracy of the Fourth Republic. Nonetheless, as already noted, these constitutions embody some novel features which are striking instances of political inventiveness occasioned by a political situation, rather than by an ideology or dogma.[30] Revolution induced by military conquest and occupation and directed toward the rejection of a defeated regime is a particular and curious case of negative revolution. It has recently been skillfully analyzed under the heading of Rousseau's famous dictum insisting that one can "force men to be free." [31] The formula is somewhat misleading. For in both Germany and Japan there were substantial minorities who were very desirous of freedom in all three dimensions, and more particularly of participating in the political order. But the ruthless persecution of these minorities by the Nazi and Imperial regimes had decimated the democratic leadership to the point where these minorities could not expect to carry out the needed revolution, just as they had failed to do in Germany under the Weimar Republic.[32]

The problem of revolutionary elite formation is closely related to that of freedom, freedom to do extraordinary and novel things which the old order seeks to prevent. This proposition is broader than one which would assert that revolutionary elites are committed to that peculiar kind of democratic freedom which seeks wide popular participation in politics. In fact, there is a built-in propensity toward elite formation in

[28] Friedrich, 1942, 1950, chap. 7; Friedrich and Brzezinski, 1956, chap. 18.

[29] The writings on this type of government are rapidly increasing; note the book by Almond and Coleman, 1959, and the articles by C. H. Moore, 1960, and Newman, 1962.

[30] Friedrich, a, 1959, pp. 814ff.

[31] Montgomery, 1957, esp. chaps. IV and V.

[32] Eyck, 1955, pp. 298–306.

revolutionary movements[33] which is the result of the deep-seated sense of novelty of what is being attempted. It is, of course, less pronounced in limited and strictly political revolutions, but even here the notion plays a distinctive role, if only in terms of a conviction that only the revolutionary leadership understands the necessities of the situation. Hence, we repeat that the formation of elites, political and nonpolitical, is closely tied to the desire for freedom in its several dimensions (Chapter 18). As we have pointed out, this desire is not uniform and constant, but varies greatly as between individuals, and in different times and places. A great desire for freedom of participation may be accompanied by a rather limited desire for freedom of independence, and vice versa, and the desire for freedom of invention and innovation may exceed that for freedom of choice, both in politics and outside it. Artistic and intellectual elites are more likely to strive for freedom of independence, as do commercial and industrial elites,[34] whereas ordinary men may be more concerned with freedom of participation. Elite formation is further complicated by the number of groupings in which participation might occur, or from which independence may be sought. Aristotle's famous argument in support of slavery, on the ground that there exist natural slaves,[35] is basically a special instance of such a differentiation. Even in a very open society, therefore, certain persons will be participating much more freely, using their independence much more fully, creating and inventing much more richly than others. These are, indeed, in the political sphere, the persons who correspond to the image of the common man as responsible, communal man, and in that sense constitute a "political" elite. But they are a functional elite, not a governing elite in the sense commonly associated with this concept. Their role is characteristically that of innovators, and the history of the American government provides many impressive illustrations. Proportional representation in its various forms, the different types of referendum and initiative, improved techniques in

[33] It is no accident, but a manifestation of this universal tendency, when the *Communist Manifesto* speaks of the communists as the elite of the proletariat; see above, Chap. 18.

[34] Riesman, 1950, pp. 287ff., 317ff., and *passim*, argues for the autonomous man, as contrasted with the ordinary person in "the lonely crowd." This autonomous man (of Kantian and Christian antecedents) has a difficult time in an "other-directed society," because of what Riesman calls "the fallacy of misplaced participation." But he adds, "perhaps a real opportunity for autonomy lies in a reconsideration of the emotional space left in our society by its impersonality. . . ." He has recently changed his views on this.

[35] *Politics*, bk. I.1 (at end of 1252a and start of 1252b); 5.1254b; 6.1255a and b; and 13.1260a and b. In Aristotle the argument is cast not so much in terms of freedom as of reason; yet both freedom and nobility are implied, as can be seen in chap. 6, where Aristotle comments on the prevalent Greek belief that they are both noble and free "everywhere."

the formulation of public policy—these are some of the more significant. Just recently, the problem of party financing has become more insistent, and a number of different possibilities have been discussed which represent distinct innovations. Among these, perhaps the most ingenious is a scheme under which party finance would be linked to taxation. But in order to preserve the citizen's freedom of choice, as well as the secrecy of his preference, it is being proposed that the citizen receive a kind of chit from the tax authorities for what he has paid and thus be enabled to "contribute" to the party of his choice by turning over his chit to that party, which then presents it to the public treasury for payment. Some people have objected that this procedure would further enhance the dependence of the elected upon the electors, since it would amount to an annual referendum; it is an objection which weighs heavily with those who generally are skeptical about the capacity of the people to govern themselves.[36]

The process of political invention, whether in the *ad hoc* fashion of a gradually evolving system or in the more dramatic revolutionary events of past and present, is not very well known. It resembles, of course, in some respects, other types of invention,[37] but is distinct especially in the degree to which groups of like-minded people, rather than isolated individuals, succeed in it. To implement what has been said above, page 370, we can say that typically political inventions seem to crystallize when politically interested persons, confronted by a situation in which the available alternatives are objectionable from one viewpoint or another (usually being argued by different persons in such a group, but without success), become stalemated. As the deadlock becomes plain for all to see, novel conjectures embodying a new solution are brought forward. Very often, it is not possible to say that one individual or another "has the idea"—though the leader may afterwards be credited with it—because the idea crystallized in the give-and-take of exploring the unknown.[38] Detailed studies of the historical evolution of certain inventions, such as proportional representation, show that such a process may also be carried forward over many years, and by printed word as well as group discussion. But there can be little doubt that the kind of freedom manifest

[36] The matter has been discussed in a number of groups; the writer found most stimulating a seminar meeting at Heidelberg, with Professor Eschenburg as reporter. Cf. Heidenheimer, a, 1958.

[37] N. R. Hanson, 1958. This view superseded by Polanyi, 1958, esp. pp. 123–124 and *passim;* Popper, 1954 (original German, 1934) pays no attention to the social and political field.

[38] This process is negated in such conceptions as the "family of alternatives" (Lasswell and Kaplan, 1950, p. 8) which presume that there are new babies to be born (to stay within the somewhat awkward metaphor). Note the interesting point of A. de Grazia, a, 1961, about the importance of "breaking down" general concepts, such as representation, into discrete elements.

in such activities, though vitally involved in the freedom of independence and of participation guaranteed by the various bills of rights, is a distinct dimension, as we suggested at the outset. In the field of politics, as in other realms of human activity, it plays a decisive role; it moulds the political order. In constitutional democracies, this freedom is potentially maximized in the *political* sphere, because anyone is free to develop new notions concerning the government and to advocate them in the hope of persuading others to join him in getting them adopted.

The unknown potentialities of such political invention make it necessary to be very cautious in speaking of something as "politically impossible." [39] Many actions deemed at one time impossible have eventually proved feasible. What is meant, or at any rate ought to be meant, by "politically impossible" is what is contrary to the nature of politics. Philosophically, three kinds of the possible can be and have been distinguished: the logical, the epistemological and the metaphysical. In the first sense, all that is thinkable is considered possible, which means the exclusion of the self-contradictory. Thus a powerless ruler would be "impossible," because it is of the essence of rule to require power. In the second, and scientifically the most important, sense, that is possible which is compatible "with the formal conditions of experience, regarded in terms of intuition (*Anschauung*) and concept" (Kant) as well as with the recognized body of experience. Finally, the metaphysical or ontological meaning of the possible is that which has the capacity to become something, in contrast to that which already is something. The possible is—and this has been recognized since Aristotle—a kind of being and in a way lies between being and nonbeing. The impossible, then, would be something which can never become actual reality. It is evident, or ought to be, that in the field of politics this kind of impossibility is going to be linked to views on "human nature," if it is admitted at all. For that reason, one finds such impossibilities alleged in writings of the conservatives, but also for instance in Machiavelli. Such views rest upon dogmatic assumptions which defy scientific testing and analysis. They lead into the basic assumptions concerning human nature (Chapter 1).

The obstacles to political action may be the result of what commonly goes under the name of national character. Or they may be related to other givens of a psychological sort, for example, the entire range of issues related to and dealt with by psychoanalysis and psychiatry. A great many of the political procedures envisaged in the age of rationalism, and associated with such names as Bentham and his school, appear today "impossible" because they rest upon erroneous psychology. A good many views of economists and others have not succeeded, or rather, their counsels have not been adopted, because they presupposed men

[39] Schoeck, 1959, esp. pp. 89ff.; Friedrich, a3, 1960.

to be much more rational than they actually are. I would say these are not political impossibilities, but psychological ones. Admittedly, the line is at times difficult to draw, because the political and the psychological spheres are so very closely bound up with each other. But unless an effort is made to exclude those numerous issues which are strictly psychological, the realm of political possibilities (and impossibilities) is so greatly expanded as to become quite unmanageable.

There are strictly "legal" impossibilities. Thus it might be alleged that a certain proposed policy in the United States is "impossible" because the Constitution of the United States leaves certain fields, such as *labor*, largely to the states. There are in any constitutional system many such "impossibilities." These impossibilities, though political realities, ought not, strictly speaking, to be called "political impossibilities," because the obstruction is *legal*, not political. Politically speaking, laws and constitutions can be changed.

At this point a couple of illustrations may help. It is often proposed by well-intentioned persons of good economic insight that free trade should be substituted for an established system of tariffs. We need not specify the many different forms this proposal has taken in the past. If handled thus, such proposals are "politically impossible." For such a free trade policy would have to be enacted into law, and hence would have to pass through the established legislative channels. These channels operate according to the well-known ways of parliamentary bodies, responding as they do to pressure. The whole range of political influence comes into play (Chapter 11). Hence, in many situations, the so-called general or public interest of such inchoate conglomerates as "the consumers" will be very ineffectively defended because they are inactive, whereas rather more specific interests will be very effective.[40] It is politically "impossible" to realize the general interest in such a situation as that of tariff legislation, where the special interests involved are very sharply affected, by merely enunciating this general interest in the form in which this is usually done by scholars and other well-meaning persons. But there are political situations where it may become possible.

A similar situation arose in France under the Fourth Republic vis-à-vis Algeria. Any number of schemes were set forth for handling the problem, but the usual statement accompanying such a proposal was that it was "politically impossible." They were that because the French parliament and the French parties operated in particular and well-known ways which constituted responses to the preferences of particular groups in the total electorate which forestalled the adoption of such schemes.

[40] Cf. *Nomos V*, 1962, for a many-sided exploration of the "public interest." It is one of the key problems of transforming invention into innovation to link it to "public interest."

As long as the French democratic institutions operated the way they did, many things otherwise desirable remained impossible. Now under De Gaulle it may be different. Similarly, when the "reform" of the constitution proved impossible, a revolution brought forth a new one.[41] This complex situation illustrates the familiar proposition that it is rare indeed for any one man or group to surrender voluntarily power he possesses, and to do so without any *quid pro quo* (Chapter 9). That, incidentally, is behind the patent fact that the so-called reunification of Germany is "politically impossible." Why should the Soviet Union surrender the power it wields through the East German Republic?

"Impossibilities" of a truly political kind also *impede* the unification of Europe; the difficulties are mostly of this type. A united Europe would do away with deep-rooted vested interests, especially of certain sectors of the government bureaucracy and the economy. But do the political "impossibilities" suffice to make the unification itself impossible? Do they prevent it? The range of creative potential in the field of politics is so large, the number of possible inventions and the possibilities of superior leadership so great, that one hesitates to conclude thus. There have been numerous occasions in the past when what seemed impossible has been made possible by superior effort and innovation. The example of Puerto Rico demonstrates the point. Not many years ago, the situation of this overcrowded, badly led island possession of the United States in the Caribbean Sea seemed all but hopeless.[42] Most men studying the situation around 1938 to 1939 would have been inclined to say that both politically and economically the prospects of Puerto Rico's becoming a viable political and economic society were very poor. Yet due to remarkable leadership and bold inventiveness, expressions of creative freedom of a high order, this overcrowded island has become an associated commonwealth of the United States, with autonomous status and a thriving economy. The "impossible" was made possible.[43] Such cases demonstrate that one has to be very careful in arguing political "impossibilities." Unless it can be clearly shown that a well-established generalization is involved and the facts effectively related to it, it is wiser to speak of improbabilities.

One is nevertheless not justified in abandoning the category of the politically impossible just because of these cases of inventive freedom. For one thing, it always takes time for such inventions to crystallize. The time factor is of decisive importance. Most statements of the "politically impossible" would be more nearly correct if they were enclosed in specified time brackets. It might well have been sound beyond peradven-

[41] Friedrich, a, 1959; Goguel, a, 1959; M. Harrison, a, 1959; Kirchheimer, a, 1959; Wahl, a, 1959.

[42] Tugwell, 1947.

[43] Friedrich, 1959, pp. 31ff.

ture of a doubt to say in 1957 that a "solution" of the Algerian problem was impossible within the next twelve months or two years, and quite unsound without such time limit.

I would conclude that apart from the logically impossible, which results from self-contradiction, the range of the scientifically demonstrable "political impossibility" is very limited, if the sphere of the metaphysical is excluded. If it is included, and dogmatic views concerning human nature are admitted, the range will include all those matters which happen to be incompatible with the alleged "laws of human nature." For only what is contrary to nature is existentially impossible, and this realm is politically very flexible. Hence the statement "This is politically impossible" ought always, or nearly always, to be qualified by reference to the conditions and the period of time to which it is supposed to apply.

For the rest, invention and innovation have a distinct role to play in any political order. They are likely to be considerable wherever participation in politics by sizable groups of persons is effectively organized. It is a matter of setting free their creative energies in the political sphere. But while general participation in politics multiplies the inventions, it may prevent their realization, because of the difficulty of winning a sufficient amount of general public support. As a result, a sizable minority, operating either as an elite or as effective support for its own elite, may be more efficacious in transforming inventions into innovations. Thus such a minority may enjoy the fruits of creative freedom on a larger scale than do the members of a free society. In the latter the freedoms of independence and of participation have been effectively organized, but the inventors of novel devices which would serve the political order encounter much opposition from the other more effective participants. Creative freedom, because less dependent upon a particular political order, proves the most universal form of political freedom. Through long ages the belief in stability of the political order as an ultimate goal prevented the recognition of this striking conclusion.

part IV

The Governing Processes and Their Modes of Operation

part IV

The Governing Processes and Their Modes of Operation

chapter

22

Founding the Political Order

Quanto sono laudabili i fondatori d'una repubblica o d'un regno, tanto quelli d'una tirannide sono vituberabili.
Machiavelli

LEGALIST AND HISTORICIST notions have obscured the fact that a political order has to be founded, that it does not come into being by "processes" or "tendencies" or "forces." A particular person or group of persons has to act, and act politically, has to *organize* a government in order that a political order arise. Political theorists from Plato to Rousseau have recognized this primordial fact of politics. They have tried to rationalize it in various ways, relating it either to a search for justice (Plato), to the builder's art (Machiavelli) or to some sort of contract (natural law writers). The founders of states have been glorified and indeed deified; Solon, or Lycurgus, the *nomothetes* (or giver) of the basic law of the ancient Greeks, Moses, making the will of God manifest, or indeed the Pilgrim Fathers, drafting and adopting a solemn covenant for a godly community, are merely archetypes of a recurrent experience.

Any particular political order is given concrete form by the functions it serves as it seeks to realize the values and purposes for which it exists. Such values, purposes and functions exhibit an infinite variety in detail and specification; yet they permit of fairly general description in terms of what is common to political communities throughout man's experience. Values and beliefs may range from the simple and material to the complex and spiritual. Varieties of food and varieties of religious belief present a colorful spectacle of potentials of motivation. But the base line of political functions is recurrent, and consists of four which are found throughout all political experience. Defending the community, settling disputes between its members, making rules for all to follow, and carrying on the work which such rules imply: these are the basic functions as embodied in the military and diplomatic establishment, the judiciary, the lawmakers, the administrators (bureaucracy). Negotiating all kinds of political bargains and providing for an orderly succession of rulers completes the basic design of the concrete political order—any political order. The simplest way to deal with the matter of government as thus delineated is, of course, to find some one individual who will attend to the four functions and who will select his successor, and this is indeed the primitive system of the king-priest extensively studied by anthropologists. Humanity has tried to return to such a system under various guises, such as the Roman Emperor or the totalitarian dictator. Theorists of such diversity of outlook as Plato, Dante and Hobbes have sought to construct a rational underpinning for the rule of the One who would fulfill such a role. The actual course of development has, however, been toward the *differentiation* of functions as political communities have grown in size and complexity, positing thereby the problems of both integration and succession. In the following chapters it is proposed to deal with these prime functions, but to treat them as an interrelated whole.

It is a curious fact that the issues which must be faced when dealing with these functions today are recurrent throughout the history of man's struggle to achieve and maintain a political order. But before they can be adequately set forth, the process of founding a political order calls for more detailed, descriptive specification. How basic this process is for all political theory can be seen from Plato's argument in the early part of *The Republic*. In order to have his interlocutors understand the role of justice in the elaboration of a political order, Socrates makes them retrace with him the founding of a *polis*—an enterprise familiar to all Greeks from the recurrent colonizing in which all vigorous Greek cities engaged. Socrates seeks to show that unless higher values than the mere satisfaction of bodily needs are realized, the newly founded city will be a community of swine rather than men. "For I suspect many will not be satisfied with the simpler way of life . . ."; there then fellows an elaboration of all the refinements which produce that "state at fever-heat," as Socrates calls it. The discourse soon arrives at the need for guardians and the virtue they must possess, and the education by which alone they can acquire it—all this to show "how justice and injustice grow up in a *polis*." Corporal and cultural education and the ranges of philosophical understanding involved fill the remainder of the work, as everyone knows. The problem of *founding* a city was explored further by Plato in the *Statesman* and *The Laws*, the one stressing the role of creative founder, the other the rules which a sound foundation presupposes. These three approaches suggest the three constituents of the founding of a political order: the establishment of a community of human beings bound together by common values, interests and beliefs, the initiating effort of the leader, and the rules which specify the range of human behavior which the governing of such a community (including the conduct of the governed) calls for.[1] All three are discussed by Plato, however, not in terms of the *political* process, but in terms of the qualities of the human beings involved in the process. His discussion is, in a dynamic sense, apolitical.

Similarly, the natural-law schools, though vitally aware of the need of facing the origin of political communities, avoided a realistic appraisal of the founding processes by positing a more or less *spontaneous* occurrence: the social contract. The several doctrines of such a contract, though by some put hypothetically, rather than asserted to be historical description, claimed that political orders arose as human beings faced the dangers of a state of nature depicted, if not as a state of war (Hobbes), then at least as a state of insufficiency (Pufendorf), insecurity (Locke) or loneliness (Rousseau). Rousseau, to be sure, discussed the "institution" of government, that is to say, of the political order. He thought the act was complex and composed of two others, the establishment of the law and its execution.[2] For this "establishment" of the law, he provided by resuscitating the notion of the *nomothetes*, the legislator, the giver of the basic law; for "in order to discover the rules of society best suited to nations, a superior intelligence beholding all the passions of men without experiencing any of them would be needed."[3] This undertaking seems to Rousseau so difficult that he exclaims: "It would take gods to give men laws." Recalling the great name of Lycurgus, he insists that such a legislator-founder should merely draw up (*rediger*) the laws, but should have no right to legislate; such legislating is reserved to the people expressing the general will. He recalls that Greek cities entrusted this drawing up of their basic law to foreigners and that the republics of Italy have followed their example; he also speaks of Calvin in this connection in highest terms of praise, who though a foreigner "played a large part" in the codification of Geneva's laws. In order to solve the problem of how to secure the assent of the people, such founders, being unable to appeal to either force or reason, must have recourse to another source of "authority": the gods. The fathers of all nations have had re-

[1] These three basic tasks were discussed above in Chaps. 8, 9 and 15.

[2] Rousseau, 1762, bk. III, chap. 17. These terms correspond precisely to those used by Althusius, who speaks of *constitutio juris* and *executio juris* (*Politica*, 1603, 1614, chap. XIX). Hobbes, by contrast, speaks of the "institution" of a commonwealth when describing the contract (*Leviathan*, chap. 18).

[3] Rousseau, bk. II, chap. VII.

course to "heavenly intervention" and to "honoring the gods" by attributing to them their own wisdom. "This divine reason which rises above the capacity of ordinary men is that whose decisions the legislator puts into the mouth of the immortals. . . ." But in truth the "great soul" of the *legislateur* is the true miracle which ought to prove his mission. It is evident that Rousseau is thinking of genuine capacity for "leadership" (above, Chapter 9) from which he distinguishes at once the spurious kind of the impostor who fraudulently appeals to the gods.[4] Sound political theory admires in the institutions which such founders build the "great and powerful genius" which is capable of constructing an enduring political order.

In the course of this discussion, Rousseau harks back to Machiavelli and to Montesquieu, who adapted Machiavelli. Machiavelli had stressed the importance of religion in the founding of Rome. "In truth, there never was any remarkable lawgiver amongst any people who did not resort to divine authority, as otherwise his laws would not have been accepted by the people . . . thus did Lycurgus and Solon. . . ." [5] But these reflections merely rounded out distinct notions about the founding of a political order with which Machiavelli had opened his *Discourses*. He of all the classical political theorists was perhaps most alert to the founding process. This is understandable enough, since he considered the political order, the state, a work of art.[6] In keeping with his perspective, he is primarily concerned with the founding of "cities." They may be founded by natives of a country or by foreigners. In speaking of the founding of cities by natives, he seems essentially to be describing the process known in Greece as *synoikismos:* "the little security which the natives found in living dispersed; the impossibility for each to resist isolated . . . ; the difficulty of uniting in time for defense . . ." These he thinks were the motives for founding cities. He mentions Athens and Venice as examples; he also speaks of Moses. Foreign invaders founded cities either as freemen establishing a colony to relieve overpopulation, or to secure control of a territory; they might also do so as the subjects of a ruler. Cities established as monuments to a ruler's glory, such as Alexandria or Florence, had not much prospect of making progress. There follow reflections about a desirable location, such as are already found in Plato and Aristotle, and the familiar argument that Rome's greatness was maintained by the discipline imposed upon the people by severe laws which neither fertility of the soil nor other debilitating conditions could destroy.

[4] Rousseau's argument must not be confused with that over "charismatic leadership," to which it is evidently related.

[5] Machiavelli, *Discorsi,* bk. I, chap. XI. The argument is continued and elaborated in succeeding chapters. For Montesquieu, see *Grandeur et Decadence des Romains,* chap. 1.

[6] Cf. Friedrich, 1957, chap. 2, and the literature cited there. Machiavelli's views are set forth in *Discorsi,* bk. I, chaps. 1, 9 and 10.

Machiavelli is, however, convinced that the founding (or refounding) of a political order is the work of one man. Trying to justify the murder which Romulus committed at the founding of Rome, Machiavelli observes that "a sagacious legislator of a republic, therefore, whose object is to promote the public good, and not his private interests, and who prefers his country to his own successors, should concentrate all authority in himself; and a wise mind will never censure any one for having employed any extraordinary means for the purpose of establishing a kingdom or constituting a republic." "To found a republic, one must be alone"; this is the conclusion Machiavelli draws from a further review of historical experience. History does not, however, fully bear him out. In a number of instances, notably the United States, not one but a number of men were involved who effectively wielded the constituent power. Nonetheless, in the past numerous cases occurred of a political order being brought into being by a single individual. It is a case of initiating leadership, as discussed earlier (Chapter 9).

It is clear that all past theoretical discussions are based upon more or less legendary events, building upon the mythology of the Mediterranean cities. Such founder myths were started almost immediately after a new city had been established.[7] Similar tales did not attend the organizing of the body politic in medieval Europe, though certain stories, like those of King Alfred, resemble them. In keeping with this "heroic" view of the foundation of a political order the theories built upon them lack specific and precise detail. Apart from such legends as the killing of Remus, or the flight of Aeneas, and the reference to the importance of religion in gaining acceptance for the particular principle of order, we learn very little about the political process involved. The actual "histories," that is to say, the legends, are not very revealing, either. In Aristotle's *Constitution of Athens,* there is given at the outset a description of the ancient order, both before and after Draco, but the process by which this order came into being is not detailed. As for Solon himself, we only learn that he was a poet who "fought *for* both parties *against* both parties"; in other words, Solon rose above the parties and achieved such authority that he was "entrusted with full powers to act"; he then proceeded to create a new political order by giving Athens a new constitution or basic law, and then "departing on a journey." Aristotle thinks that Solon could easily have set himself up as a tyrant, but he did not wish to; instead he set himself "against both parties" in order to save the country and to give it the best laws possible at the time.[8] Thus Solon appears to have acted in some ways as Rousseau wished the *legislateur* to act, though he clearly not only drew up but enacted the basic laws he considered right.

[7] J. Burckhardt, 1930, vol. I, pp. 69ff.

[8] Aristotle, *Constitution of Athens* (ed. Fritz and Kapp, 1950), chaps. 1–12. Bury, 1937, pp. 173ff., follows this account.

The situation is similar in the case of Rome. We do not know what actually happened at the founding of the city, but indications are that a synoecism of villages on the various hills took place as a defensive measure. How it was accomplished we do not know. There was no Romulus and no Remus, and Machiavelli's speculations about the one murdering the other and being justified in doing so resemble the proverbial metaphysician looking in a dark room for a black hat that isn't there. There was no migration of Greeks or Trojans from overseas; Rome was a Latin city about whose foundation we know nothing. The "endless variety of foundation legends" ties in with the "Greek story-telling faculty" which "supplied mythical founders to all cities that lacked an authentic record."[9]

The only valid proposition which can be distilled from this record of past experience is that the founding of political orders is shrouded in uncertainty, and that it serves as a fertile ground for political myth-making (Chapter 5). This latter proposition can be tested in the light of more recent events; even in cases where the record is reasonably clear and well established, such as the founding of Plymouth and the Massachusetts Bay Colony or of other modern political orders, legends and myths have persistently prevailed. The most persistent feature of such myth-making is precisely the exaggeration of the role of one individual (or at times several), investing such a person with more or less heroic stature. Thus the older theories stressing this role (as did Machiavelli) are really distilled from these myths which they tended to accept bona fide as descriptive of these foundation processes.

A curious derivative of such myth-derived theories is the notion, recently developed by an American political scientist, that the founding of a political order is the source of genuine authority.[10] Building on the Greek and Roman foundation myths, and on what Plato, Aristotle, the Christian Fathers, Machiavelli and Robespierre made out of them, this theory considers not "authority in general" but "the very specific concept of authority which has been dominant in our history," which is said to be rooted in a "foundation experience," but is actually rooted in the myths which are derived from a foundation experience and which embody the values, interests and beliefs of the new political order which in turn provide the basis for reasoned elaboration to which "authority in general" is related (Chapter 12). It is the new order, in other words, and not the founding of the new order, which provides the basis for the new authority.

The difficulty which has in the past prevented an adequate analysis

[9] Cary, 1945, pp. 34ff. Cf. also Voegelin, 1957, chap. 4; Bury, 1937, chap. I.
[10] Arendt, a, 1958.

and understanding of the founding of a political order has sprung from confusing the political *community* and the political *order*. Political communities are not founded; they come into being by a process which has been described earlier (Chapter 8). It is only the political order of such a community which needs to be founded, or as another, more legal approach puts it, "instituted." Decisions have to be made about the *governing* of such a community, about who shall rule and in what manner, and these decisions may either be preferential choices between known alternatives or innovations (inventions) striking out along new paths. Revolutions which destroy an older order therefore precipitate the founding of a new one, though the community may to a large extent persist. The degree of the transformation of the community itself will determine the extent of novelty of the new political order as well. But such transformations may go very far without any corresponding change in the political order. A political order may be very stable, in spite of great social instability, and there is nothing surprising in this well-known fact. Community and political order need to be clearly distinguished from each other, and the founding experience must be recognized as referring only to the latter. This founding experience cannot, of course, be recognized, if it is assumed that the political order (*Staat*) precedes the communal living of man,[11] but the evidence at our disposal suggests that men can and do live together in communities which are not in fact *governed*, that is to say politically ordered, though such communities are the exception rather than the rule. They are considered to be "tribes without rulers" and to recur under specific cultural conditions, more especially "segmentary lineage systems." [12]

Unfortunately, though understandably, the founding of a political order has not been studied extensively by anthropologists. Some have been content to recite the mythical tales which are ubiquitous in connection with the founding process. In a few cases factual historical data have been developed.[13] Among the published myths some purport to describe the original founding of a new political order,[14] others are concerned with the revolutionary transformation of an existing political order, or rather the founding of a new political order for an established

[11] This is the position of Eduard Meyer, who claims it to be the "historical" view, as contrasted with the "liberal" prejudice of anthropologists and sociologists (1884, 1910, vol. I, par. 5). Actually, his position is purely speculative, in the tradition of Hegel and Treitschke, and not based upon history at all. History, including his own, records innumerable "foundations" of political orders, and what has thus been founded again and again is not very likely to have preexisted. For the anthropological view, stated as a matter of course, cf. Linton, 1955, p. 125.

[12] Middleton and Tait, 1958, esp. introd. Cf. also M. G. Smith, a, 1956.

[13] Note especially, M. G. Smith, 1960; Nadel, 1942, 1961.

[14] Cf. for example, L. H. Morgan, 1901, vol. I, p. 57; Evans-Pritchard, a, 1948, p. 9.

political community which persists.[15] Founder myths need not be wholly consistent. At least one instance has been analyzed where they were in partial conflict with each other; [16] it is probable that further research would show this sort of conflict to be recurrent, since it can also be observed in the contemporary world, where in various organizations different legends as to their origin persist (see below). The existence of written records has enabled anthropologists to describe the establishment of a number of political orders by conquest, especially where it proved possible to document such events further by information from nonindigenous sources.[17] While these bits of data are suggestive of processes similar to those known to have occurred in historical times, they are too fragmentary to shed any significant additional light upon the dynamics involved in the founding of a political order. It is not very likely that much additional material of sufficient detail will come to light for these processes, as contrasted with the founding processes now in progress in Africa and elsewhere.

Since anthropological and earlier historical records give us so little in the way of clues about the founding of a political order, it is clear that recent history and contemporary evidence must be used. Presumably, modern evidence will also provide hypothetical indications about the actual founding processes at earlier periods. But before we turn to some of this evidence, one contemporary theorist deserves mention who has given special attention to the founding process. He has, partly in light of his understanding of the entrepreneurial role in economic life, offered a general description of the *entraîneur* (trainer, pacer).[18] He insists that in the formation of groups which are to act effectively together, there must always be someone who takes the initiative and brings people together for such group action. It is this capacity for inducing human beings to form groups and to act collectively which this author wishes to call "authority." [19] It is actually the capacity for reasoned elaboration which enables a person to secure another's consent, and it is only one of the possible lines of such consent to form a group, and a special instance of such consent to found a political order. Nor is such consent vital to foundation. A political order may be founded not only on consent, but on coercion as well. In keeping with the nature of power,

[15] Cf. for example, Jomo Kenyatta, 1953, p. 186.

[16] Mair, 1934, p. 162.

[17] These studies refer to relatively recent events. Cf. for example, M. G. Smith, 1955, pp. 165ff.; Busia, 1951, pp. 4 and 14; Gluckman, in Fortes and Evans-Pritchard (eds.), 1940, pp. 25–26.

[18] B. de Jouvenel, 1955, pp. 50ff.; a, 1958.

[19] *Ibid.*, 1955, p. 45: "*J'appelle Autorité la faculté d'entraîner le consentement d'autrui.*" This view differs from, though it has a certain kinship with, the notion of authority developed above, Chap. 12. Cf. also the same author's view of 1947, pp. 140ff.

it is usually founded with the aid of both consent and coercion (Chapter 9). But in any case, the formation of the group, as contrasted with the founding of its *order*, may be and usually is the result of spontaneous and gradual processes; it does not require a founder, and this author's tendency to insist upon the role of a *single* trainer or pacer resuscitates the ancient notion of the heroic founder which we have seen to be universally prevalent.

It is obvious, and implied in all that has been said so far, that founding the political order is related to political leadership; it should be equally apparent that founding the political order demands the type of political leadership we called "initiating" and to which the followers respond by imitating (Chapter 9). Not all initiating is, of course, founding; when legislation is proposed and drafted, when new policy is formulated, when new modes of executing policy are put forward, to mention only the most important modes of such behavior, initiating leadership comes into play. But the founding of a political order, or organization, is the most dramatic role which initiating leadership can play in politics. It would be a grave mistake, common enough as it is, to assume that because initiating leadership plays a crucial role in the founding process, it is the sole or even the primary cause of such founding. The founding of a political order, like the founding of an organization, presupposes a disposition on the part of the following to let such founding occur. This proposition follows from the dual nature of the power relationship. Before drawing any definitive conclusions, though, it is necessary to review some concrete experiential data, that is, to analyze specific cases of founding. And since there appears to exist some significant parallelism between the founding of *any* organization and the founding of the particular organization which is called a government or system of rule, let us first study the founding of an organization, such as a commercial company, a college or a club.

Any such founding presupposes a disposition on the part of a group of human beings to secure by concerted action what they cannot secure by separate action. Such a disposition may be conscious and known to the participants to a greater or lesser degree, or it may be wholly subconscious. It is one of the most serious errors to suppose that it must be conscious. It is this error which has led to the overestimation of the role of leadership in the founding of organizations. Whether conscious or not, the disposition toward concerted group action results from the sharing of values, interests and/or beliefs by the members of the emergent group. Communication between them manifests and, to some extent, precipitates a tension which may take the form of action proposals. As often as not these proposals are made by persons who are intellectually alert, "idea-men" who are capable of the feat of imagining "what might be that is not." These persons are not necessarily, nor even usually, the persons who possess the capacity for initiating leadership. But as the communications become more numerous and the disposition to act becomes more pronounced, persons with such capacity are stimulated into gathering the members of the group, or more usually some part of them, and proposing that a specific action be taken and that an organization be formed to attend to it. By such a proposal the proposer places himself in the position of leadership which may forthwith be formalized by acclamation or election. It is, of course, entirely possible that the particular individual who acts as proposer was also among the early talkers; indeed he may himself have been aggressively engaged in communicating with his fellows about the need for action. But this combination of roles is neither necessary nor typical, except in particular cultural contexts and fields of activity. Thus the founding of a commercial company to seek profits by engaging in a particular activity is more often the result of a single person's initiative than is the founding of a trade union or a club. The reason is that only he may perceive at the outset the possibility of making money by pursuing a certain activity; he may even have engaged in this activity by himself and later, through his success, attracted others into joining him in the endeavor. But in the forming of a club or a professional group, the person who steps forward and assumes the role of initiating leader more nearly resembles the additional crystal that is dropped into a concentrated solution than the billiard stick that pushes the balls. Whatever the specific procedure, it is the shared interests, beliefs and /or values which condition the founding process in its concrete course among a particular group of persons.[20]

In modern times, the founding of political orders has rarely been the work of a single individual, though one man may have played a predominant role. Washington is called "the father of his country," but who would gainsay the roles of Hamilton, Jefferson and the other "fathers"? In the case of Israel, Chaim Weizmann certainly stood out, but who would say that he was the "founder" of Israel? [21] Puerto Rico's new order assuredly owes much more to Luis Muñoz Marín than to any other individual, yet the founding of the order was the work of many men, though the founding of the party to which most of them belonged was truly his work.[22] Finally, the founding of the Federal Republic of Germany, certainly the largest political order founded in the postwar period, resulted from a complex process in which not only

[20] The large body of writings on the history of entrepreneurship, corporations, trade unions and other organizations, large and small, all are able to contribute to our understanding of the founding process described in the text in its most general aspects. Organization theory is in urgent need of making fuller use of this body of empirical data.

[21] Weizmann, 1950; Hurewitz, 1950; Halpern, 1961.

[22] Wells, 1961.

Germans but Americans, British and French had a hand.[23] The "founding" of a United Europe is still in its embryonic stage, and the number of persons who have contributed significantly is already no longer countable on the fingers of both hands. These processes are further discussed below. But even this evidence from constitutional systems stands in some contrast to the totalitarian ones; Lenin in Russia, Mussolini in Italy, Hitler in Germany, Mao in China, to mention only the outstanding examples, each played a decisive role in founding the particular totalitarian order over which he ruled.[24] In the newly organized "nations" of Asia and Africa, the role of single leaders has in many cases been decisive, especially when freedom had to be won by fighting the colonial power. Where this "heroic" leadership has been needed, a tendency toward dictatorial rule has usually resulted, as in Ghana, Guinea, Egypt and Indonesia, to mention some prime examples.[25] It remains to be seen, and seems somewhat doubtful, whether the arbitrary division lines enclosing these countries—resulting from compromises between the rival claims of the European colonizing powers—will become true boundaries of effectively integrated "national" states. They cut across tribal associations of long standing; certainly no one considering Africa as a whole and trying to divide it in a meaningful way would ever have adopted many of these lines. Until the Europeans came and "partitioned" Africa, the continent had, since time immemorial, been largely governed along tribal lines, and the kings, priests and elders had been meaningfully representative of their people. As one leading expert has said: "The aims and methods of tribal government were familiar, and in many cases the people themselves shared in forming decisions which might affect the welfare of the tribe." [26] The Europeans changed a good deal of that. As overlords, they began promoting change, expansion and intertribal peace. At the same time, modern governmental machinery made its appearance. "The running of machinery presupposes the existence of designers," [27] and the founders of these political orders were alien and unrepresentative. There was, consequently, a mixing of tribes: ". . . people of common tribe and tongue found themselves living on opposite sides of a boundary, and compelled to learn the quite different ways, laws and languages of their newly acquired rulers." The machinery of administration used by the colonial powers

[23] Golay, 1958, chap. 1. In spite of its title, this work lacks appreciation of the founding process.

[24] Wolfe, 1948; Bullock, 1952; Germino, 1959; Schwartz, 1951.

[25] Kimble, 1960, vol. II, chaps. 14, 15 and 21. Spiro, 1962, esp. chaps. V and X. Note also the several HRAF studies, as well as Carter (ed.), 1962.

[26] T. R. Batten, 1948, 1960, p. 113.

[27] Kimble, 1960, vol. II, p. 303. The following quotation is on the next page. On pp. 307–353, this author gives a good review of the several systems of rule established by the European powers.

was very simple; much simpler even than the type of administrative autocracy which had served in Europe in the days of the emergence of the modern state. It is, therefore, natural that native rule should have developed a preference for some species of dictatorial system. The problem of how to integrate effectively the several tribes into one people must have priority if they are to maintain their sway. Founder myths are making their appearance.[28]

The situation was, of course, very different in the case of Israel. Here an ancient nation which had maintained its cohesion and national identity for nearly a thousand years while dispersed among other nations —a feat of unique impressiveness in the annals of politics—reestablished itself and its political order in the course of a process of complex international negotiation and against the violent opposition of the Arab nations who had been in possession of the land of Palestine for centuries. This is not the place to recite this dramatic story. Its ideological dimension has only recently been told.[29] What matters here is that the political order as such came into being by way of concrete political action. After the United Nations had adopted on November 29, 1947, the partition plan which gave part of Palestine to Israel and left the remainder in Arab hands, the members of the Arab League made war upon the Israelis in the hope of preventing the establishment of the new order. After a protracted period of anarchy, Israel was proclaimed on May 15, 1948, a sovereign and independent state. Israel won its survival by the defeat of the several Arab armies, and organized itself more or less *ad hoc;* pleas for the adoption of a formal constitution did not meet with success. Here the founding of the new order emerged from the ordeal of war and therefore presents the strange picture of a people defending their political order in the process of its being founded. Since the extended negotiations leading first to the establishment of the British Mandate over Palestine under the League of Nations and afterwards to the adoption of the partition plan by the United Nations were carried on by representatives of the Jewish people in the Zionist organizations, these leaders must be considered the true founders of the state of Israel. It is a clear case of collective foundation, involving bitter conflicts within the group, including total rejection by some members of the idea of founding such a political order.[30]

If the founding of the state of Israel (1947–1948) was projected and carried out within the framework and to some extent at the suggestion of the United Nations, that of the German Federal Republic a year later

[28] Melady, 1961, gives an instance of such myth-making.

[29] Halpern, 1960, is both thorough and aware of the imponderables, while an avowed partisan in the struggle.

[30] Dunner, 1950, chaps. 6 and 7; Manuel, 1949, chaps. 6–8; García-Granados, 1948, *passim;* Hurewitz, 1950, esp. chaps. 10, 12, 15, 22 and 23.

occurred at the beckoning of the Western occupation powers. It was a case of refounding in one sense, since the German community had had a number of political orders before, of course. But unless one wants to consider the occupation regime a *German* political order, which seems hardly to make sense, especially if the breakdown of Allied cooperation after 1947 is taken into account, the work of 1948–1949 constituted a new foundation because it organized only part of the German nation.[31] In many respects, the establishment of the Federal Republic resembled the process by which new states have emerged from former colonial possessions: a foreign power devoid of democratic legitimacy and hence devoid of authority transferred its governing functions, including the constituent one, to native leaders. This decision—which leaders to invest with power—was participated in by the Germans themselves, in contrast to some colonial cases. For the minister-presidents of the several states were elected by the Germans. Still, the establishment of these states (*Länder*) had been the result of action taken by the occupation powers; [32] in a sense this action, defining the boundaries and calling for the election of constitutional conventions (at least in the American and French zones of occupation), was the primary founding act. However, for the main point of the argument we are now considering, this question is not decisive; for in either case the founding act, initiated to a greater or lesser degree by the temporary occupying rulers, was a German act, and it was not an act of an individual but of a "considerable number" [33] of Germans who wished to escape from the condition of servitude which the occupation regime imposed upon them.

This "founding" was a protracted process, partly because it involved the decision to accept the division of Germany, at least for the time being. How difficult this decision was for the German leadership can be seen from the fact that they at first rejected the opportunity offered for founding a German state in the territory of the Western zones of occupation. But they soon were persuaded to change their mind,[34] and therefore a constitutional convention, the Parliamentary Council, was set up by election of the state (*Land*) legislatures. To a considerable extent, the basic law which this Council produced reflected German traditions and experi-

[31] This *political* question is related to the *legal* question of the "continuity" of the German "state," a question which German jurists have answered in the affirmative, though without convincing arguments. Cf. Friedrich, a, 1949, pp. 474ff., and Friedrich and Spiro, a, 1953. The true reasons were pragmatic, as were those of British jurists. Litchfield, a, 1953, rightly speaks of "agent governments."

[32] Clay, 1950; Wells, a, 1953.

[33] Friedrich, 1950, p. 130; cf. also pp. 152f. for the process. Cf. also Litchfield, a, 1953; Golay, 1958, chap. I.

[34] The offer was made July 1, 1948, was rejected July 10, and was in turn accepted July 26. The complex history of what went on during these four weeks has never been written; crucial documents are still classified.

ences, but a measure of Allied interference has deprived it of some of the legitimacy to which it is entitled. Enemies of the German constitutional order both at home and abroad have seized upon this partial interference to belittle the constitution. In any case, the eventual adoption was only a step (though a major one) on the road to an autonomous political order, which culminated in the proclamation of German "sovereignty" in 1955. Throughout the protracted consultations and negotiations, the German chancellor, Konrad Adenauer, was unswerving in his pursuit of the goal which was eventually reached. In the process, the originally intended political order underwent a marked evolution, both by formal action and informal usage; the end of this evolution is not in sight. Clearly the founding of the German Federal Republic was not the kind of "heroic" act which earlier views on the founding of a political order took for granted. It was the result of the complex interaction of many persons and many minds.

A third foundation process of more than local interest is the establishment of the Commonwealth of Puerto Rico in 1952. Puerto Rico had been an American colonial dependency, an "unincorporated territory," since the Spanish-American war at the beginning of the century. While granted a measure of local autonomy which was slowly increased over the years, Puerto Rico endured a political order which was essentially "imposed" by a foreign conqueror who had at first been mistaken for a "liberator."[35] The people were for many years bitterly divided between those who wanted to achieve statehood within the American Federal Union (*Estadistas*) and those who demanded independence (*Independentistas*). While the Puerto Ricans wrangled, the economic conditions of the island went from bad to worse.[36] To escape from this desperate plight, a leader of exceptional inspirational power, Luis Muñoz Marín, founded a new party in 1938, the Popular Democrats, which under the banner of "freedom and bread" replaced the struggle over status by an insistence upon the development of the island, economically, politically and culturally. In keeping with postwar trends, as well as with the partial success of these efforts, a movement for a new status, that of free association, gained ground, actively promoted by Muñoz Marín and the Popular Democrats. Meeting with a certain degree of sympathy in the United States Congress, they were able eventually to work out an agreement "in the nature of a compact" to which the people assented in a referendum. Under this compact the people of Puerto Rico were empowered to elect a constitutional convention, which after months of careful deliberation during the winter of 1951–1952, produced a draft constitution which was

[35] Friedrich, 1959, pp. 57–58; this study contains extended references to Puerto Rican history and government. Cf. Hansen and Wells (eds.), *Annals*, 1953.

[36] Tugwell, 1947.

submitted to the President and the Congress and finally approved by the Puerto Rican people on July 25, 1952.[37]

While the founding of the Commonwealth of Puerto Rico owes much to the effective leadership of Muñoz Marín, he himself has repeatedly insisted that it is the result of the extraordinary collaboration of many minds, both in Puerto Rico and on the mainland of the United States. Furthermore, although the Puerto Rican share was of primary importance, the United States Congress vetoed certain provisions, more especially those dealing with the "social rights" in the bill of rights, and thereby documented its own share in the founding process. It was a regrettable step, comparable to the stubborn interference of Allied occupation powers in the process in Western Germany, and it had the same result, namely, to deprive the foundation of some of the legitimacy to which it was entitled. But it showed again that "founding" a political order can be the work of many hands; the viability of such an order is enhanced by the participation of all those who are concerned in it. It is a process extended through time, and not necessarily completed at a specifiable date.

The political order which is in the making in Europe (as well as in other parts of the world, notably Africa) exhibits the traits which the foundation process has shown to have in the three preceding examples, only to an even more marked degree. It is a process that is far from completed and in which a number of leaders have played a significant role, notably Churchill, Robert Schuman, Adenauer, Spaak and Monnet. Indeed, the process of formalizing the political order has barely begun. A first effort, linked with the abortive attempt at establishing a European Defense Community, produced a draft constitution, but the draft has not been acted upon, and all that remains so far is the organizational framework of the Coal and Steel Community, the Economic Community, and Euratom, now possessing at least a common representative assembly and a common court.[38]

In the case of the efforts at founding a United Europe, of federating the many political units of which it consists (as in similar cases elsewhere),[39] the need of effective cooperation among many leaders to secure the support of the following in divergent political communities is par-

[37] For the details of this process and the quotation, cf. Friedrich, 1959, chap. II. For a criticism and proposals for further change, cf. *ibid*., chap. III.

[38] Bowie and Friedrich, 1954, introd. and *passim;* Macmahon (ed.), 1955, chaps. 1 and 21 by Macmahon; chap. 25 (Bowie), chap. 26 (Friedrich); Haas, 1958, esp. chaps. 1, 2 and 8. Schierwater, 1961, on the assembly; on the court, Valentine, 1955; for the earlier phase, cf. Rappard, 1930.

[39] Cf. Chap. 32 below for further analysis of this process itself; the act of foundation is frequently the culmination of a long period of preparatory efforts, as well as the starting point of an evolution involved in the federalizing process.

ticularly evident. It can and does occur when these several communities have become encompassed by a more comprehensive community whose values, interests and beliefs are shared by many persons belonging to the separate communities. This means that a more or less extended period of communication, of argument and discussion, will precede the founding process in this instance also. The multiplication of such communication contacts has been studied in considerable detail in recent years.[40] It is probable that, in due time, it will become feasible to determine with a fair degree of accuracy the culminating point at which the founding of a political order becomes possible. The rise in the number of such communications in the case of continental Europe in recent years is a striking instance of the approaching potential foundation of an inclusive political order.

These sketches of some recent efforts at founding a political order provide ample evidence for the contention that such political foundation can be a cooperative endeavor, rather than the achievement of a single individual. Indeed, the evidence is so massive that it seems doubtful that foundation has often been an individual's achievement, as proclaimed in legend and past theory. At the same time the role of violence appears to be a different one from what heroic theory asserts. There may be some violence employed in the founding process itself, as happened in the case of Israel. But usually the violence occurs prior to the founding, in the course of the destruction of a preceding political order and the emergence of a new political community or the reemergence of an old one.

Not every political order is "founded," however. The states of England, France and Spain "emerged" as successful monarchical rulers consolidated their kingdoms in the course of many generations, transforming the feudal into a bureaucratic order. Foundation occurs when a violent break with the past confronts a political community with a more or less explicit challenge, namely, with the task of finding its political form. Foundation is, therefore, intimately linked with revolution (Chapter 34), though by no means necessarily so. The revolutions of the twentieth century have engendered a great number of political foundations, both constitutional and totalitarian, and this patent fact might induce one to see them as interdependent. But cases such as Puerto Rico and the unification of Europe show that political communities may produce political movements and leadership which are capable of founding a new political order without a preceding revolutionary upheaval. Whether such founding process is desirable or not, cannot be determined except in terms of the value and belief which is served by it, as the quotation from Machiavelli at the beginning of this chapter suggests. Nations and movements,

[40] Deutsch, 1953, esp. chap. 2; Deutsch, 1957, chap. 2A.

like any lesser organizations, are not "good" in themselves, and to found a robber gang is a criminal conspiracy in most jurisdictions. Still, it will occur in much the same way as the founding of organizations with more laudable objectives. The same reasoning applies to the great political orders and their founders; they may be judged good or bad, but the founding processes of both good and bad are alike.

chapter

23 Defending and Expanding the Political Community

We shall not flag or fail. . . . We shall defend our island, whatever the cost may be, . . . We shall never surrender. . . .
Winston Churchill, June 4, 1940

DEFENSE HAS ALWAYS BEEN recognized as a prime objective of any political order. To be sure, in dealing with the basic drives leading toward war, defense and self-preservation, though often overshadowed by the search for food, procreation, territory, adventure and domination—to use the terminology of a leading work on war [1] —have played a decisive role. In modern warfare they have been absorbed by what might be called the political, the economic, the cultural and the religious motives.[2] But actually war, in the sense of sanguinary fighting, has resulted from these other drives or motives only because one political community was prepared to defend its food, its women, its territory or its independence against an aggressor who attempted to deprive it of these possessions. Thus, all of them are ultimately subsumable under defense in the political perspective.

[1] Q. Wright, 1942, pp. 74ff., 131ff.; besides these five, independence and society (meaning social solidarity) are discussed as basic drives; the maintenance of independence and social solidarity are however aspects of defense of the political community. This study, in two volumes, offers the most exhaustive survey of human experience in this field.

[2] *Ibid.*, pp. 273ff. Cf. also Huntington, 1957.

This general view is substantiated by what is known about war in primitive societies. Much of the research by anthropologists concerned with a particular tribe seems to suggest that the aggressor's outlook is prevalent, but when the detailed motivations are analyzed, the general pattern becomes visible. This statement is not supposed to deny that there are very considerable differences among primitive peoples on this score; there are certainly belligerent and peaceful ones. But as a survey will show, each of the several purposes mentioned is ultimately related to the community's defense. Sometimes the wars aim at reducing the power of neighboring tribes, as in the case of Ganda and Nupe (Africa), where considerable territorial expansion ensued, but where such expansion provided, so they thought, a protective belt—a pattern of thinking which still persists, for example, in the Soviet Union.[3] The "wars" between Bushmen and Hottentots who fought over boundaries were quite in line with the general and recurrent situation.[4] The American Indian presents the observer with the most striking instances, also recurrent though they be in human history, namely, the positive cultural function of warlike activities when war becomes the focus of interest. It is the world of the *Iliad* and of the *Song of the Nibelungs*, as well as of the Masai (Africa) and many others. Even here, some political motivation, such as avenging a wrong, is involved; but since participation in warfare is essential to political advancement, the defense of the way of life is the core of military combat; territorial or other material community interests are of minor importance.[5] There may be marginal cases, where even this motivation is lacking. All in all, explicit or implicit defense of the community appears to be the heart of the matter for primitive societies, as well as advanced ones.

Such defense may anticipate bloody contests by appropriate political means, more especially diplomacy. Diplomacy is the art of avoiding armed conflict by negotiation (Chapters 11 and 27). The *ultima ratio*, or last resort, of all effective diplomacy is, however, war, and diplomatic effort could not succeed if its negotiators were known to be obliged to buckle under if a threat of force were made. Hence the study of how men have defended their political communities is primarily a study of war. Such study must explore the problem of reason of state as the background for an exploration of the different forms of war. It must consider the conceptions of strategy which have been derived from them and relate these conceptions to the contemporary issues, as highlighted by the debate over limited war and arms control.

The reason for putting the defense of a political order first is that

[3] Mair, 1934; Kenyatta, 1953; Evans-Pritchard, 1940; Busia, 1951; M. G. Smith, 1960; Nadel, 1942; Coon, 1931; A. Musil, 1928.

[4] Schultze, 1907; Schapera, 1930.

[5] Speck, 1945; Swanton, 1928; Lowie, 1935; Holmberg, 1950.

no matter what its internal ordering, any political order has to be and will be defended. The survival of the order, threatened continually by external and internal enemies, cannot be repudiated by anyone who belongs to the community; if he does, he places himself outside the community and the order and becomes an enemy. The full appreciation of, as well as the overemphasis upon, this predominant concern of all politics, is the distinguishing feature of Hobbes's political theorizing. Treating the search for survival of individual and group as a "fundamental law of nature," he derived his radically authoritarian "Leviathan" from this premise. No one before him or since his time has ever done the same. Plato and Aristotle were curiously indifferent to the problems of defense, though the task is assigned by Plato to a special elite. He, like Aristotle after him, addressed himself almost exclusively to the discussion of defending one *polis* against another; the trauma of the Persian wars appears sublimated in a blithe assumption that no "natural slaves" can challenge, let alone seriously threaten, the survival of the world of the *polis*. In any case, the defense is seen entirely in terms of military combat. The tasks of diplomacy are hardly touched upon by either. It was Thucydides who explored these problems for the first time in terms of the survival of a political community. As a consequence, he "discovered" the problem of "reason of state," to which diplomacy inevitably leads.

"Reason of state," or *ratio status*, classically embodies those rules for the rational conduct of government which will insure its survival. It is in this sense the core of Machiavelli's work; for in both *The Prince* and *Discourses* the discussion returns again and again to various aspects of such survival. But these mere rules of expedient conduct are only one side of reason of state; the other side, and much the more specific side, consists in the justifications, the "rationalizations," as it were, of such conduct when it comes into conflict with the other values and beliefs prevailing in a particular community. It is this side which Machiavelli almost completely omitted, because he adopted the position that the political order is man's highest achievement and that, therefore, all that was necessary for building a state was "beyond good and evil," a work of art.[6] It was, therefore, no real problem, but purely a matter of rhetorics, of propaganda and psychic manipulation. For anyone sharing Machiavelli's outlook, there is similarly no problem; reason of state is not a problematic but a dogmatic set of rules of conduct. The totalitarians are in this position. For the Fascist the state is the highest value, for the National Socialist the racially defined folk, for the Communist the classless society. Lenin characterized morality as a bourgeois prejudice, and Marx and Engels preceded him in taking similar positions; it is simply a

[6] Meinecke, 1924, bk. I, chap. 1; Friedrich, 1957, chap. 2 and literature.

raison de classe in analogy to *raison d'état*. All dealings with the totalitarians are so perplexing for men to whom reason of state is problematic, because totalitarian convictions provide a basis for pure expediency in terms of reason of state or reason of class.

The defense of a political order against an enemy with such views is much more difficult than it is against an enemy who shares one's own ethical convictions or some other moral scruples. This would be true even if the enemy had no revolutionary designs for the overthrow of the order to be defended. The elaboration of international law since the time of Grotius, and more particularly of rules of conduct in war and peace, was essentially an effort to escape from the more extreme forms of conduct considered purely in terms of their efficacy in securing and maintaining power; the breakdown of international law in the twentieth century was an inevitable consequence of the reappearance of the conviction that the state (or class) embodied the highest value.[7] The constellation is aggravated by the revolutionary expansionism of the movements which are built on such convictions.

The complications which the rise of totalitarianism has introduced into the defense pattern, and which are reminiscent of problems which also plagued earlier revolutionary periods and more especially the age of religious wars (1540–1660), must not blind one to the common underlying design of defending the political community at all times and in all places. This, to repeat, consists of two related undertakings: diplomacy and war. To be sure, the celebrated aphorism of the great Clausewitz that "war is the continuation of policy (*Politik*) by different means" hides rather than reveals the important insight that both serve the defense of the political community.[8] Clausewitz himself perceived this, when he wrote: "War is nothing else than the continuation of political transactions intermingled with different means. We say intermingled with different means in order to state at the same time that these political transactions are not stopped by the war itself, are not changed into something totally different but substantially continue, whatever the means applied may be. . . . How could it be otherwise? Do the political relations between different peoples and governments ever cease when the exchange of diplomatic notes has ceased? Is not war only a different method of expressing their thoughts, different from writing and language?

[7] In terms of value analysis, as given in Chap. 2, it is possible to state thi situation as one in which a monistically conceived hierarchy of values prevai the highest value being a particular power configuration.

[8] Clausewitz, 1832, vol. I, p. xviii; cf. also vol. III, p. 121. Rothfels, 1920; also Rothfels, a, 1943, where it is pointed out that Clausewitz gave much weight to the political aim, though his position is not unequivocal. The quotes in the text above are found on pp. 105–106. This statement is considered by Rothfels to be "the most elaborate and mature form."

War admittedly has its own grammar, but not its own logic." [9] But this, a true insight, is overstated in a military perspective which distorts the specifically political dimension. It is therefore not surprising to hear Clausewitz also tell us that "the political end is . . . no despotic legislator. It must be adapted to the nature of the means and consequently may often be totally changed. . . . Strategy in general and the commander in chief in particular may demand that the political aims and tendencies shall not conflict with the peculiar nature of military means, and this demand is by no means a slight one. . . ." [10] This may refer merely to what is militarily possible or again to some of the more irresponsible political influences. But the basic goal of defense is a given which transcends all military exigencies. Political and military considerations are intertwined in complex ways, but in the last analysis the political must and will prevail, even in the military field.[11] This is true even in the most autocratic regimes, indeed perhaps especially there; it may well engender the destruction of the political order, but to surrender this ultimate power to the military certainly would.

That the military establishment may also serve to expand the political community is obvious. Yet defense is the more crucial and the more universal phenomenon: every political community has to defend itself, but not every such community has to expand. Hence, expansion may be treated as a subordinate goal, at times rationally related to the goal of defense, at other times transcending any such link to defense needs. In the subsequent analysis, expansion will be treated in this perspective. It has, to be sure, been argued by a number of writers that expansion is a "natural" propensity of political communities (that is, states), but more careful analysis of the facts reveals that such assertions are not supported by adequate evidence. Expansion is a "cultural" phenomenon, resulting from certain value dispositions and beliefs prevalent in particular political communities at particular times.[12] The contrary assumption is a

[9] Clausewitz, 1832, bk. VIII, chap. VI, sect. B.

[10] *Ibid.*, bk. I, chap. 1.

[11] Rothfels, 1943, maintains that Clausewitz had in mind "the vital character of military decisions" and that he "had struck upon a fundamental verity which has proved true under every form of government." He adds that "even democracies have faced and will face situations in which military agencies are bound to overrule political considerations." Stated thus, the proposition contains a *non sequitur:* for obviously *more urgent* military considerations will outweigh *less urgent* political ones; but in the last analysis, the decision as to the relative urgency will be a political (civilian) one. Clemenceau and Churchill, among recent statesmen, are known to have thus insisted.

[12] Ratzel, 1923, pp. 59ff., from whom the doctrines of the "Geopolitics" school are in part derived. More recently, Carl Schmitt, 1950, has argued similarly that *Landnahme,* the taking or occupying of land, is the "constituent act of international law"; we read that "Alle Völker aller Zeiten, die in neue Räume aufbrachen und

result of the organismic fallacy which made the correct observation that political communities tend to grow the basis of an assertion that states are organisms; on this basis of an asserted "organic nature" it proceeded to argue in terms of a crude simplification of Darwin's theory of evolution and the "survival of the fittest." [13]

War is more basic than diplomacy, if man's total history and more especially the conduct of government in primitive communities are considered, but it is not, therefore, "natural." Indeed, from a moral standpoint, Kant's dictum, derived from the categorical imperative, that "there shall not be war" stands unchallenged if the personalist value system, implicit in several of the world religions, notably Christianity, Buddhism and Confucianism, is accepted. Psychologists have been at odds over the question of whether war is endemic (inborn) in human nature, but the better evidence appears to be on the side of the negative.[14] But the defense of themselves, including their kin and what "belongs" to them, is in fact "inborn." Natural law has recognized a "right" of self-defense, no matter how it was conceived, whether ethical, prudential or religious. Such "natural law" or "right" is evidently only an imperative or normative formulation of an existential judgment of broad universality: men have always defended themselves, and so have political communities. What is more, they have been inclined to disregard moral and legal restraints when such defense was calling for radical action: *Inter arma leges silent.* War in the sense of lethal combat is the most radical form of such defense. But this sense is by no means the only one. At present, expressions like the "cold war," the "war of nerves," and so forth suggest readily that war may be carried on by other means than weapons designed to maim and kill the enemy. We may distinguish three major forms of

---

auf ihren Wanderungen sesshaft wurden, griechische, italische, germanische, slavische, magyarische and andere Sippen, Stämme und Gefolgschaften, haben Landnahmen vollzogen, und die gesamte Kolonialgeschichte ist ebenfalls nur eine Geschichte raumhaft bestimmter Gründungsvorgänge, in denen Ortung and Ordnung sich verbinden" (p. 50). Schmitt links these thoughts to the etymology of the word *nomos,* deriving it from *nemein* to herd, to fence in. Since *nomos* is originally (in Homer) a feeding place, a fenced-in pasture for cattle, there is indeed something to Schmitt's argument, considering that *nomos* eventually comes to mean not only custom, but law.

[13] Treitschke, 1916, vol. I, pp. 15ff. and 45ff., and Seeley, 1896, pp. 53–76. Cf. also Mackinder's work, esp. 1919, which implies the organic notion. For a critical appraisal of the geopolitical writings see Whittlesey, 1939, Dorpalen, 1942, and Spykman, 1942. Cf. also Whittlesey, a, 1942.

[14] Murphy (ed.), 1945, esp. pp. 3–50. On p. 20 we read: "If man can live in a society which does not block and thwart him, he does not tend to be aggressive; and if a society of men can live in a world order in which the members of the society are not blocked or thwarted by the world arrangement as a whole, they have no intrinsic tendency to be aggressive."

warfare: military, economic and political (psychological). Clearly these three forms correspond to the three forms of coercion (Chapter 9): physical, economic and psychological. There exists an evident relationship among the three; they supplement each other, and may even, under certain conditions, replace each other. When armed combat appears either impossible or highly inadvisable, the two other forms of fighting are likely to be intensified. This at present patent drift in the world at large is nothing new; it has happened under a great variety of conditions.[15] More especially, political communities and powers which were for various reasons militarily weak have relied upon economic and psychological weapons for their defense; they are the arms of small powers and of such bodies as the papacy.

War has often been fought with all the means at the disposal of the warring social groups. Clausewitz' famous formula, mentioned earlier, really meant that politics in his view consisted of strife and struggle, and that when such strife and struggle became violent, then the tensions became so strong that people would seize arms and try to kill each other. But politics is not entirely or even primarily strife and struggle, is not only a matter of identifying the enemy,[16] as we have seen. War is therefore *not* the *continuation* of politics, let alone of diplomacy, but rather its *abandonment* in favor of violence.[17] From primitive warfare, precipitated by survival interests such as the defense of grazing grounds or farm lands needed for the existence of a political community, to the sophisticated warfare over whether a country like Korea is to be communist or not, that is, in defense of one ideological and social system or another, or whether a country like Bohemia is to be Protestant or Catholic, that is, in defense of religion and other convictions or beliefs, war has not merely been "an act of violence for the purpose of forcing the adversary to bow to one's will,"[18] but an effort at defending what appeared of vital importance to the survival of a particular community, or several of them. Civil war is the result of a split in the political community; if such a split is reasonably well defined territorially, the chances of civil war are greatly increased.

War, like any other social phenomenon, may be characterized primarily in terms of ends (teleological definition), or in terms of effective causes (etiological definition); its character may be specified in respect to the participants, or to the methods employed, or to the effects. Depending upon which standpoint is selected, different classifications suggest themselves, and there is no particular advantage to be gained by reviewing

[15] Q. Wright, 1942, vol. I, part II.

[16] Schmitt, 1932, *passim,* presents the most challenging statement of the thesis that politics is the relation of friend and enemy.

[17] That a political setting continues is, of course, obvious, as suggested above.

[18] Clausewitz, 1832, 1857, 1937, bk. I, chap. 1.

all the possible "definitions." [19] But some suggestive classifications may well be mentioned here. One leading author relates "stages of war," to the "level of civilization" and speaks of "primitive, historic and modern" warfare.[20] This approach brings out the fact that war changes with the cultural transformation of society. War depends upon social and industrial organization. The organization of political communities is frequently accompanied by warfare (Chapter 22). War unites a political community, and only the imperatives of war lead many people to cooperate.[21] As H. G. Wells once said: "When the contemporary man steps . . . . into the barrack-yard, he steps to a higher social plane, into an atmosphere of service and cooperation and of infinitely more honorable emulations." [22] Thoughts like these recall Hegel's well-known expostulations about war as the final test of the vitality of nations and civilizations, making "world history the world court." Such romanticizing of hardihood, valor, gallantry and sacrificial devotion obscures and confuses the role of war in the forward march of civilization. It may be compared to the role of illness in maturing human personality, which cannot be doubted but which has hardly ever persuaded people of the wisdom of injecting typhus bacilli into healthy persons in an effort to ennoble them. The changing pattern of war at different levels of civilization has had a profound effect upon the political order regardless of the sometimes ennobling, sometimes crushing, impact upon human development.

Another suggestive way of differentiating between several kinds of war is to correlate the end or objective of a war with the methods em-

[19] Grob, 1949, presented a critical survey of recent usage in international law.

[20] Q. Wright, 1942, vol. I, part II, esp. chap. IV. Cf. also most recently Waltz, 1959, for an analysis of the relation of etiology to ideology.

[21] This fact led William James, in a famous essay, to call for a "moral equivalent of war." In it James, an avowed pacifist, insisted that "militarism is the great preserver of our ideals of hardihood, and [that] human life with no use for hardihood would be contemptible." He added that "there is a type of military character which everyone feels that the race should never cease to breed, for everyone is sensitive to its superiority." He thought that this "martial" character "could be bred without war." Instead of fighting men, youths would be enlisted to "fight nature." This idea of a "labor service" has played a certain role in the thought of social reformers, among whom Rosenstock-Huessy might be mentioned as outstanding. See his work of 1956–1958, esp. I, p. 232, and the many special studies given in the bibliography of his book, 1959.

[22] Cf. for this viewpoint also the work of Huntington, 1957, who in speaking of the military ideal contrasted the anarchic pluralism of the Main Street of Highland Falls, "the incredible variety and discordance of small-town commercialism" with the "ordered serenity" of West Point. "Beauty and utility," he thought, were "merged in gray stone." Rather surprisingly, he suggested that "the spirit of West Point is in the great, gray Gothic Chapel, . . ." calling to mind Henry Adams' remarks at Mont-Saint-Michel on the unity of the military and the religious spirit. He concluded that "West Point embodies the military ideal at its best; Highland Falls the American spirit at its most commonplace" (pp. 464–465).

ployed in fighting it. Thus, wars of conquest waged by a power of superior strength are characterized by methods which seek to destroy the ruling group of the conquered people in the shortest possible time and with minimum loss. Colonial wars have usually been of this description; so have a number of wars of the totalitarian powers in our time, such as the Soviet war against Finland and Hitler's wars against Poland, Yugoslavia and Greece. By contrast, wars over questions of dynastic succession have been fought with great caution and often were expected to yield the desired result by means of the nuisance value which they possessed. Wars over trade have also been distinguished by relatively mild methods. Since the object in such wars is economic advantage, there is little sense in expending more than the expected gain. By contrast, wars over religion and over ideological issues have exhibited the most ruthless methods. The bigotry of each side in such wars portrays the enemy as subhuman, and hence the war is pictured as a crusade, usually a divinely ordained mission to exterminate the infidel, the heretic or the criminal. Besides the well-known examples of our own time, such conflicts as the religious wars in sixteenth- and seventeenth-century Europe, the wars against the Waldensians and other "heretics," the Crusades proper and the wars of Moslem believers come to mind. In approaching war with this type of classification in mind, it is easy to lose sight of the basically defensive posture of a good many of these bloody encounters. As mentioned before, in virtually all instances of dynastic, trade and religious wars, the defense of a political order has not only been a pretense, as the skeptic is inclined to argue, but a key factor both in causing the war and in providing the fighting communities with their primordial goal. Only wars of conquest must be excepted from this observation; there can be no question that such wars have occurred, but only those who were being attacked waged them in defense of their political orders.

An American political scientist undertook to systematize these observations by suggesting a tripartite division into absolute war, instrumental war and agonistic fighting; [23] by the last-named he meant prestige wars. The end or purpose of these would be, respectively: annihilation, advantage and glory. It is not pretended that these types are found in their pure form, but different types of war are believed to approximate these pure forms. Because of their several natures, each of these types exhibits characteristic features. Absolute war is unrestricted and unregulated war; agonistic fighting is regulated according to norms; instrumental war may or may not be restricted according to considerations of expediency. It is apparent from such a typology of war that by no means all wars are defensive, and that the expansion as well as the defense of a political order may be involved. From the political standpoint (rather than the

[23] Speier, a, 1941; Speier (and others), 1939.

military one), a general distinction between defensive and nondefensive warfare (and diplomacy) may be more fruitful.[24] Nondefensive war has, in modern times, been increasingly condemned, and such condemnation has crystallized in tentative legal norms "outlawing" this type of war, but that does not mean it has disappeared, either actually or potentially, but rather that even the most patently nondefensive war, such as Hitler's war against Poland, is dressed up by legal subterfuges as "defensive." The difficulty with this outlook is that modern weapons development favors the aggressor, because of an increasing imbalance in favor of weapons of attack, quite apart from a long-standing presumption in favor of attack as expressed in the familiar adage that "attack is the best method of defense."

If not all wars have been fought with all the means at the disposal of the warring political communities, wars of defense in which the survival of the community is at stake usually have. Since all war may turn into such a contest for survival, the potential of its becoming a total one is always present.[25] It is an erroneous modern view to assume that economic and psychological features of war are novel; novel are the technological ramifications of such economic and psychological warfare. Weapons have undergone continuous change in all the dimensions of war, and it is possible to speak in all ages of three dimensions of warfare, mentioned already: the military, the economic and the political (psychological). Each of these modes of fighting has, of course, its peculiar methods, adapted to the means of force and coercion employed. Force, designed to bend an enemy's conduct to one's own preferences, is the quintessence of all warfare, whether military, economic or mental. Which of the three dimensions happens to be the most important at any particular time is a matter depending upon the general situation, the constellation of powers, the technology of weapons, the foci of ideologies and the economic resources at the disposal of the combatants. It has proved of decisive importance to provide an integrated high command. For only such a high command dealing with all three levels as an integrated whole can carry on modern war with maximum efficiency and effectiveness, at all times. The "posture of gladiators" Hobbes spoke of in discussing the relations between sovereign states in the seventeenth century is still very apropos, but it overemphasizes the strictly military aspect. Each dimension of warfare has its own advantages. The great advantage of the military dimension lies in its decisiveness, the advantage of the economic dimen-

[24] We say "nondefensive" rather than "aggressive," because the term is less prejudicial, and not all nondefensive wars are aggressive, as Speier's category of agonistic fighting clearly shows. Cf. also Delbrück, 1900 and later, *passim,* and Craig's critical appraisal in Earle (ed.), 1943, chap. XI.

[25] This very general proposition seems to me the basic objection to the ingenious proposal for limited war contained in Henry Kissinger's work, 1957.

sion in its calculability, the advantage of the psychological dimension in its "cheapness," both in manpower and in fiscal outlay. An over-all rule in the political perspective of war as a means for accomplishing both defense and expansion might be stated thus: depending on the prospect of achieving the desired result, psychological warfare is preferable to economic, and economic to military warfare. Curiously enough, modern democratic states, including the United States, have expended efforts in the inverse ratio to this rule. Maybe that is why they have lost one position after another to the totalitarians.

In the strictly military dimension, past history has been shaped by warfare on land and sea. Before considering the novel problems arising from air warfare, one or two problems of political relevance regarding the other two should be considered. There have always been land powers and sea powers, and there has always been disagreement on the relative importance of them. If the world's great empires, from Egypt and China to Rome and modern Europe, are made the basis of a generalization, it would seem that land armies have been much more often the basic instrumentality of successful warfare than navies. Yet it is the opposite contention which has had great vogue among writers on strategy. Alfred Thayer Mahan's celebrated contention was that sea power is decisive in modern warfare.[26] He thought that "sea power was vital to national growth, prosperity, and security." His analysis is cast in terms of six fundamental factors: "geographical position, physical conformation, extent of territory, population, national character, governmental institutions." This view has been vigorously questioned and cannot be maintained in the light of all the evidence.[27] But neither can the opposite view. Island position and various other factors, including the importance of trade for the economy, play a vital role. Mahan's doctrines were developed from a history of the rise of British sea power, and their broad generalizations are not applicable to situations differing radically from that of Great Britain. Indeed the Athenian empire is the only close parallel in world history to British imperialism, and it proved admittedly feeble in its efforts to ward off the land armies of Sparta and Macedon and later of Rome. Other striking examples of naval power are provided by Venice and the Netherlands, though neither achieved the predominance of Britain or Athens in their respective spheres. Mahan himself was admittedly inspired by his studies of the Punic Wars and more especially by Mommsen's conclusion that Hannibal's defeat was the result

[26] Mahan, 1890, 1892, *passim;* cf. also the commentary by M. T. Sprout, in Earle (ed.), 1943, chap. 17. The quotations are from this chapter, p. 418.

[27] For example, Mackinder, 1930, chap. 20. Cf. Strausz-Hupé, 1942, who wrote that geopolitical doctrine "is the most extreme negation of Mahan's theories" (p. 246).

of lack of naval power.[28] Assuming this to be true, it would merely show that when a political community engages upon a conquest involving distant communications across the sea, naval power is paramount. There are, however, other instances in which the lack of sea power seemed to be decisive in determining the failure to survive. Thus the fall of La-Rochelle, high citadel of French Protestantism in 1628, was related to Richelieu's successful effort at cutting the impregnable fortress city's sea communications. The crucial importance of sea power was, however, the result of a lack of adequate land power. Had the Protestants been sufficiently strong to withstand the onslaught of the royal forces on land, sea power would not have been vital to their survival. This and many other examples tend to show that except in the case of islands depending on foreign trade, sea power has been only supplementary to land power in the *defense* of political communities. It has been more vital to the *expansion* of such communities whenever that expansion called for traversing the sea. These seemingly banal conclusions need stating, because much writing on military strategy in the wake of Mahan's challenging work has obscured them. The reasons for their cogency are not far to seek. It is land upon which political communities are based, and it is therefore the taking of land which ultimately spells their destruction.

Weapons of warfare will succeed within their appointed sphere, and natural conditions of geography will limit the possibilities of armies and navies. The broader the land base of a given power, the less will it depend upon naval successes; islands, since they are surrounded by water, will necessarily focus attention upon naval weapons as a method of both offensive and defensive warfare. There has been a tendency to overlook the parallelism of development in the two fields, and more especially to recognize the aggressive and militaristic potential in naval armament, on account of the particular consequences of this development in England. These consequences were of decisive importance in the evolution of English constitutionalism. The absence of a standing army during the period of the emergence of the modern state (1500–1650) deprived the British rulers of the means of force and coercion which enabled their continental counterparts to destroy the opposition of local powers, the estates and the independent cities. But on the other hand the navy did engender the same administrative problems which the army caused in continental European countries. From Henry VIII to Cromwell, central administrative control evolved until finally the navy became the mainstay of English central administration. Defense of the island kingdom in combination with overseas expansion constituted the goal of these efforts and the core of British strategic thinking.

[28] Lamb, 1958.

A third dimension has been added in this century by the development of aerial weapons. These weapons have been the subject of heated strategic debate ever since their first appearance. A striking expression of the technological age, these weapons have seemed to some the most important for a decisive victory in the "air age." Some have even insisted that superiority in the air will give victory in a very short time. Others have claimed that the airplane is significant only as a combat instrument, but that by itself it cannot achieve decisive results. Experience during the Second World War is by no means conclusive. The capacity of the airplane to reach the enemy's lines of defense and destroy vital centers of production played a significant, but not a decisive, role until the arrival of the atomic bomb. Even its decisive impact upon the Japanese may have been at least in part psychological and hence a parallel to other well-known examples of the importance of the surprise, for example, the appearance of elephants in the army of Carthage which put the Romans to flight, though not for long.[29] Very recently the importance of aerial weapons has suffered a significant decline due to the development of long-range missiles; indeed the fantastic pace at which weapons development is going forward at present has made all previous thought about the relative importance of one or another arm obsolete. The choice of weapons systems has multiplied a hundredfold, and more than one leading authority has argued that the older notions of the role of the army, the navy and the air force in terms of the particular dimension, land, sea or air, in which the specific arm operates, have become completely untenable, since the weapons systems so continuously interact that they can be considered and decided upon only in one all-embracing strategy.[30] This conclusion is actually suggested by the entire history of defense efforts. No argument about the superiority or decisiveness of one kind of military power, whether land, air or sea power, over the others, nor indeed over economic and psychological warfare, is borne out by experience, if a sufficiently broad and comprehensive view of this experience is taken. In the political perspective, the various weapons must be seen in terms of the particular requirements of security and survival, and/or of expansion and conquest, depending as such requirements do upon the totality of resources, both human and material, which are at the disposal of the political community for which the strategy is to be devised.

At this point in our analysis, a word needs to be said about the con-

[29] Cf. for a careful evaluation of the value and disvalue of the bombing of industrial centers *The Strategic Bombing Survey*, 1946. Its conclusions have never been seriously challenged. Recently C. P. Snow, 1961, has confirmed them in a striking, though perhaps somewhat exaggerated, way.

[30] Kissinger, 1957, chaps. 5 and 12, also documents listed and bibliography; Bush, 1949; Osgood, 1957.

cept of strategy, especially in its relation to tactics and foreign policy. Clausewitz' distinction between strategy and tactics in terms of the actual fighting, as contrasted with the object of war, has been much discussed and argued about, but contains the vital political distinction in terms of the prime objective of defense.[31] Strategy cannot be separated from a community's general foreign policy because it is oriented toward the "purpose of the war," that is to say, toward the congeries of values, interests and beliefs for the defense or expansion of which the war is being waged. It is the defense or expansion of these objectives which brings on the war.[32] The defense is the stronger posture, militarily, too. The defense is the stronger form of warfare, because it is easier to preserve than to make gains.[33] But this is true only if it rests upon a sound strategy of defense, defense as it ought to be. Such a defense presupposes "a most careful preparation of all available means, an army which is soundly trained for war, a military leadership which does not await the enemy in perplexed and confused uncertainty, but with quiet determination, fortifications which are ready for a siege, and finally a healthy nation which does not fear its enemy any more than it is feared by the enemy."[34] These thoughts seem as sound today as when they were penned by a theorist who had watched the military operations in the wars precipitated by the French Revolution, and the eventual victory of nations defending themselves and their heritage against a foreign conqueror. Bonaparte had claimed to be "peace-loving" in his desire to impose a revolutionary doctrine upon France's neighbors by force of arms, as have Hitler, Stalin, Khrushchev and Mao in our own time. Defense is indeed the stronger form of warfare, provided the political community realizes the magnitude of the task involved.

At this point, another important argument touching the heart of strategy deserves mention: the question of whether to adopt a strategy of annihilation or a strategy of exhaustion. The issue is at the very heart

[31] Clausewitz' definition is as follows: "die Taktik [ist] die Lehre vom Gebrauch der Streitkräfte im Gefecht, die Strategie, die Lehre vom Gebrauch der Gefechte zum Zweck des Krieges." 1857, bk. II, chap. 1, p. 89. In the sequel, Clausewitz points out that the many ancillary activities which are nowadays referred to as logistics are part of neither tactics nor of strategy. In a technological age, this position is untenable; logistical tasks are part of both, or, to put it another way, logistics has its own strategy and tactics.

[32] *Ibid.*, bk. VI, chap. I, p. 143, points out the paradox that the conqueror is "oft friedliebend" (often peace-loving), because he would gladly "enter a foreign state quietly"—Clausewitz is referring to Napoleon's protestations to this effect—but "so that he [the conqueror] cannot do it, the defender must be ready to wage war."

[33] "Erhalten ist leichter, als gewinnen," and "die verteidigende Form des Kriegfuehrens ist an sich stärker als die angreifende." (*Ibid.*, bk. VI, chap. I, pp. 124–125.)

[34] Clausewitz, 1857, p. 144. Translation my own. Presumably Clausewitz would include the navy and air force as well.

of contemporary discussions in this field; for the strategy of exhaustion is implied in the preference for a cold war in the nuclear age. Nuclear weapons have conjured up possibilities for a strategy of annihilation on a hitherto undreamed-of scale, but these very possibilities have reinvigorated thought in support of a strategy of exhaustion.[35] These terms do, of course, in their original meaning both refer to military operations proper. In the strategy which seeks to gain victory through exhausting the enemy "the battle is no longer the sole aim of strategy; it is merely one of several equally effective means of attaining the political ends of the war and is essentially no more important than the occupation of territory, the destruction of crops or commerce, and the blockade. . . . In certain periods of history, because of political factors or the smallness of armies, it has been the only form of strategy which could be employed." The significance of this theoretical exposition of a strategy of exhaustion was that it recognized the variability of strategic concepts and their dependence upon politics, that is, the peculiar nature of the political order concepts involved.[36] The strategy of exhaustion leads to the employment of limited war, which has once more become of vital significance on account of nuclear weapons.[37]

One aspect of this basic problem deserves further exploration not only because it has played a continuing role in the discussion of writers on military affairs, but because it touches the very core of the political community's defense, and that is the issue of the "citizen army." No less a political thinker than Machiavelli made the advocacy of such a citizen army the very core of his military theory. He has been vigorously condemned for his theorizing, and the collapse of the Florentine Republic, as his citizen contingents fled before the French professionals, has been laid at his doorstep. Nor can there be much doubt that Machiavelli greatly underrated the difficulty involved in organizing a citizen army under the civic and technical conditions prevailing in the Italy of his time. But was there not something prophetic in his vision of such an army, as he dreamed of the rise of a republican state in the image of classical antiquity? Was not the modern constitutional democracy truly anticipated in Machiavelli's reflections? [38] Machiavelli saw the citizen army as a vital manifestation of that "healthy nation" which sound defense strategy

[35] The dichotomy of these two strategies was developed by Delbrück, especially in 1890. It should be noted that he did so in controverting Clausewitz' emphasis upon the strategy of "annihilation" (a mistranslation, for the German term is *Niederwerfung*, which means defeat rather than annihilation). Cf. also Craig, a, 1943, pp. 272ff. The quotation is from this study.

[36] For illustrations, cf. Delbrück, 1900, vol. I, pp. 101f. (evaluation of Pericles versus Cleon) and vol. II, p. 394 (evaluation of Belisarius).

[37] Kissinger, 1957, chaps. 2–7. Kissinger has since changed his position; cf. 1961.

[38] Machiavelli, *Dell'Arte della Guerra* (1521; my edition, 1550); cf. Delbrück, 1900, vol. IV, chap. 6.

calls for. Other political theorists have given vent to similar ideas, notably Rousseau who in *La Nouvelle Héloïse* insisted that all citizens must be soldiers by duty and none by profession. This sentiment became the basis of the *levée en masse* of the French Revolution when the masses rose to defend their *patrie;* on this experience Napoleon built his victories. In response to Napoleon's achievements, the rebuilders of Prussia's military might, Scharnhorst and Gneisenau, developed the universal military service notion, the *Volk in Waffen*, which has since been adapted and adopted by all modern nations. It is generally recognized and acknowledged as the military manifestation of democracy.[39]

The difficulty with much of the discussion has been that two quite divergent strands of argumentation have been intertwined and often confused. One argument asserts that a citizen army will be a more effective army, for various reasons, including patriotism and morale. The other argues that such military participation of the citizen will have beneficial effects upon the conduct of a democracy, because of the commitment such sacrifices entail. This latter argument, of course, lost a good deal of its former appeal during the First World War. The conditions of technology seemed to preclude individual combat and the display of personal valor for most of the participants, many of whom were more or less helpless victims of a vast machine process.[40] The most recent developments have produced a countertrend. Already during the Second World War, individual capacities were becoming important again. This trend has continued since then. It is likely that a nuclear war, fought without any definite front, will call for exceptional self-reliance of soldiers of all ranks. This personal valor seemed basic to William James, and he used it as the starting point for his argument in favor of a "moral equivalent of war"; he found such an equivalent in dangerous and strenuous exertions of young men on behalf of the common good.[41] More decisive, at least within the context of a discussion of defense, is the first question. Here the answer is not the same, but depends upon various circumstances, more especially weapons technology, as they affect strategy. As Machiavelli and his Florence learned to their sorrow, a citizen army was no match for the professional army which the new techniques were inducing monarchical rulers to put into the field. Such

[39] As such, it turns up not only in Rousseau but in Kant's essay on eternal peace, where the philosopher argues that standing armies are an invitation to war, whereas an armed people will oppose it.

[40] The attempts of writers like Ernst Jünger to distill a specific pathos from this kind of involvement in a *Materialschlacht* are romantic at best, and have been abandoned by Jünger himself. Portrayals such as that given in Mailer's *The Naked and the Dead* come closer to the moral *nihil* of technological warfare. The problem is discussed in Wright, 1942, vol. I, chap. 10.

[41] Cf. above, fn. 11, and specifically, Frederick Stern, 1957, chap. 6 and *passim*.

an army served Rome in her Republican period very well, as it had Athens and Sparta at an earlier age. It has done so again in the last few generations, but the argument for a professional army or at least a strong professional core has continued to attract followers, and modern armies tend to be a combination of the two, the professional element being especially important for the officer corps, as well as for those services in which the technical element predominates (navy, air force, and so on).

chapter

24

The Settling of Disputes

If one man sin against another
the judge shall judge him.
I SAMUEL 2:25

A judge should not be a youth but old.
Plato, THE REPUBLIC, III

If thou be a severe, sour-complexioned man,
then I disallow thee to be a competent judge.
Izaak Walton, THE COMPLEAT ANGLER

THE SETTLING OF DISPUTES is the primordial internal function which a political order has to perform, antedating the making of rules and the application of such rules in administrative work. The modern view has tended to assign to it third place, and to see the judiciary as the main form of it. Such judges, being enjoined to "apply the law, not to make it" (*Judicis est jus dicere non dare*), a principle not only of the Roman law but fairly universally proclaimed, are seen as the helpmates of the lawmakers, the supposedly "sovereign" legislature. Such a view is formalistic and overlooks other than strictly judicial forms of settling disputes.[1] Wherever even in modern communities deep and vital conflicts of interest divide powerful groups, or even individuals, the ancient function of settling disputes by negotiation comes into play. Its most striking field of operation in industrialized nations is that of conflicts between management and labor. Here mediation and arbitration have come to play a decisive role (below, Chapter 27). But there are others.

The legendary figure of the king under the oak tree, dispensing justice, is the symbol of this primordial function. In the medieval perspective, which is the human situation in many ages and under many

[1] For a typical view, see Barker, 1951, p. 97.

conditions, the "law" is there to be ascertained and pronounced. In the life of primitive man, such enunciating of the law is the main function of the ruler, be he priest or king. Where no such ruler exists, the elders may act, or the community at large. Llewellyn and Hoebel have described such a procedure very vividly in *The Cheyenne Way*.[2] A man whose horse had been taken without asking by a friend who did not return it wanted to know what to do. He asked the Elders: "Now I want to know what to do." They sent for the friend, and in the light of his report, which the Elders accepted as a basis for settlement, they said: "Now we have settled this thing." But they were not content with having done so. They went on and made a new rule that no horses should hereafter be borrowed *without asking*. This tale shows both the intimate link and the contrast between the settling of disputes and the making of rules. By its very functioning a court is a rule-making body, even as it interprets rules, and it is in keeping with this universal fact of political order that the representative body of the kingdom should be titled: The High Court of Parliament.[3] And that the corresponding French bodies should have developed into courts rather than legislatures was logical enough, even though fatal to the development of constitutional democratic government. It was logical, because the original function had been that of settling disputes.

Associated with all such efforts at settling disputes is the notion of justice. Indeed, in a political sense, one might even be tempted to define "justice" as that which is settled by judicial procedure. The relation between justice and law has been explored at an earlier point (Chapter 15). It was developed in terms of authority and legitimacy and related to equality, representation and responsibility (Chapters 12 to 14, 16 to 17). But the problem of how justice is to be found was left aside. From the governmental viewpoint, the maintenance of justice is closely related to the task of maintaining internal peace and order. Unless people can be reasonably certain of securing what is theirs through a process of adjudication, they will undertake to secure it themselves, if necessary by violent means. The failure to settle vital disputes authoritatively is the signal of the breakdown of a political order. Each settlement contains a potential rule which may or may not become a precedent, depending upon the circumstances. There can be little doubt that the rule-making function as distinct from the judicial function grew out of the latter in a slow process, whether the people were Cheyenne, Athenians or the nations of the modern West. From the legal viewpoint, perhaps the most significant development was the clear separation of the two functions. This view

[2] Llewellyn and Hoebel, 1941, p. 127.

[3] In Massachusetts, too, the legislature is called the "General Court." Professor Hoebel is quite right in arguing that the Elders of the Cheyenne constituted a "court" (*ibid.*, and 1954, p. 24).

was explicitly stated by Montesquieu, who, generalizing from English and to some extent other European practice, observed in *The Spirit of the Laws:* "There is no liberty yet, if the power to judge is not separated from the legislative and executive power. . . ."[4] It seems more than doubtful, in light of anthropological evidence, that this proposition is correct in such generality; indeed, as we have seen, no political order is ever completely devoid of liberty. It is a question of more or less, and of the kind of liberty, and whether political or other (Chapters 20 and 21 above). If then the distinction and separation of the legislative from the judicial power is not to be assessed in terms of the presence or absence of liberty in general, what is its significance? It is to some extent a matter of the degree of liberty: the more clear the distinction and separation, the more secure and the more extensive is the scope of political liberty. But this proposition in turn cannot be maintained in its abstract generality; for the "tyranny" of judges, that is, the irresponsible use of their power, may actually curtail liberty and not only the liberty of participation, but also the liberty of independence. For in a complex pluralistic society, the balancing of the liberty of different individuals and groups becomes ever more difficult. Kant's famous formula about the coexistence of the liberty of one with the liberty of all others often presents seemingly insurmountable hurdles to its realization.[5] We shall return to this problem below.

If the function of settling disputes is considered as a process of government, what are its main components? Basically, three "persons" are involved, the accuser, the accused and the settler of the dispute. In order to function effectively, the settler, or arbiter, needs power, authority and legitimacy. The accuser will not turn to him if he does not think he is entitled to rule, that is, to determine the issue at hand; neither the accuser nor the accused will listen to the verdict unless the settler has authority in the sense of a capacity for reasoned elaboration in terms of the values and beliefs, as well as the interests, of the community (its law); and accuser as well as accused may try to evade the verdict if the settler does not possess or is not backed by the power to enforce the verdict he has rendered. In the Cheyenne case, the Elders add that they will whip a man who does not submit to their verdict; whatever the punishment, it merely incorporates the enforcement potential of the dispute-settling function.

This basic model of dispute-settling shows that it does not presuppose a rule which the dispute "settlers" are applying. They may do so; but they often do not. One of the most important distinctions between different

[4] Montesquieu, 1748, 1835, bk. XI, chap. 6—the famous chapter in which he discusses the British constitution.

[5] Cardozo, 1928, pp. 94ff., develops this paradox of liberty.

modes of the settling of disputes is in fact related to the presence or absence of rules. If there are no rules at all, we may speak of expedient settling, if only broad general rules, of discretionary settling, if detailed rules, of judicial settling. However, even such judicial settling of disputes often involves an element of newness, of interpretation which may be either restrictive or broadening. This question has been central to the discussion of the principle of *stare decisis.* Although this is a rather sophisticated product of juristic thinking, it may be well to consider it presently. But before we do so, it seems desirable to explore somewhat further the expedient and discretionary settling of disputes.

Expedient settling of disputes will hark back to the values, interests and beliefs of the community. It may merely compromise the positions of the contestants; or it may undertake to transcend them by absorbing them into broader values, interests and beliefs. Typically, in conflicts between management and labor, modern industrial relations practice seeks compromises, wherever possible, but appeals to broader community interests where no effective compromise can be reached.[6] Because of such reference to general values, interests and beliefs, the settlers of disputes involving judgments of expediency need, in adjusting basic communal positions, considerable authority, as well as clear legitimacy and firm power behind them, if their settlements are to prevail. This range of issues urgently calls for quantitative exploration, which it has not so far, to my knowledge, received.

Discretionary settling of disputes calls for the exercise of discretion, obviously. What is discretion? Discretion may be defined in various ways, but what it always involves is (1) the notion that a choice among several alternatives can, indeed must, be made, and (2) the notion that such a choice is not to be made arbitrarily, wantonly or carelessly, but in accordance with the requirements of the situation.[7] The concept of discretion usually involves the further notion that it comes into play within a framework of rules, implementing them, elaborating them, carrying them through. Thus a court, when using discretion in imposing a penalty, is acting within the framework of the rules of the penal law according to which the criminal has been adjudged guilty; similarly, a regulatory body, in fixing a rate, is acting within the framework of rules of law establishing the regulation. When a court or a commission or an administrative official, arbitrator or mediator acts in accordance with such general standards as "reasonableness" or "good morals," it or he is supposed to do so within a range typically fixed by law or custom, including precedent.

Discretion comes into play whenever no specific rules or principles

[6] Fuller, a, 1957, draft. Cf. also Stevens, a, 1958; Taft, 1954, chaps. I and VIII.

[7] Friedrich, a, 1958, pp. 40ff. For discretion as a personal trait of officials see below, Chap. 26.

can be or have been formulated, while at the same time mere whim, that is, the failure to recognize broad rules of conduct, cannot be allowed. Situations of this type are recurrent in the settling of disputes, whether on the primitive level of traditional wisdom or on that of the highly articulated forms of judicial procedure. As just indicated, discretion is by no means restricted to such situations, since it also plays a vital role in administration. But the operation of discretion in the settling of disputes is inherent in the very process; presumably no dispute would have arisen if there were no room for disagreement about a given situation and the rules which apply to it. If there were no alternative courses of action open to the arbiter of a dispute, evidently he would not be operating; for unless he might either decide for A or for B, or decide upon penalty *x* or *y*, or transcend these possibilities by deciding as Solomon did, the role of the settler could not be played. Discretion is therefore inherent in the function of settling disputes.

At the same time, it will be generally assumed that a person vested with power to exercise discretion will be able to give reasons for what he has done. These reasons are likely to be persuasive, rather than conclusive. There will be room for disagreement. Therefore, authority is important as the believed-in capacity for reasoned elaboration of the grounds upon which the settlement is presumably based. We have shown that such reasoning by authority relates what is said to the values, interests and beliefs of the community. Such reasoning may be elaborate and public, or it may be brief and/or confidential. The court systems of civil-law countries are based upon the latter procedure, those of the common law upon the former. Courts in France and Germany usually restrict themselves to a brief recital of the legal provisions in a code or statute upon which the decision is based. But not always; the (Supreme) constitutional court of the German Federal Republic has in recent years developed the technique of elaborate reasoning in support of its decisions, although dissenting opinions are still lacking.[8] The integration of the decisions of the several courts in the hierarchy is achieved under such a system by the discipline exercised by the Ministry of Justice, which may inquire into the reasons for a particular decision and may penalize judges who do not conform to its views in various ways.[9] The lower court has only very limited discretion; the ministry assumes that the judge will use good sense, experience and precedent. It will also expect the subordinate to be able to "explain" what he has done if for any reason it finds that a particular decision ought to be subjected to review.

[8] This practice of the Supreme Constitutional Court has come in for much adverse comment by German jurists; cf. R. Taylor Cole, 1958, pp. 287ff.; McWhinney, 1956, 1960; Dietze, 1958, pp. 123ff.

[9] Ensor, 1933, chap. 4, esp. pp. 80ff.; cf. also Goodhart, 1934; Allen, 1927, 1958, chap. 3.

In common-law countries, the reasoning is built upon "precedent." Now precedent is a very general guide of action in all spheres of life, not only in government and politics. The very specific mode of using precedent in judicial proceedings is embodied in the doctrine of *stare decisis.* Literally, it means, stay with the (previous) decision. Actually, it should rather read, stay with the *ratio decidendi*, the reasoning of the decision; and if at all possible, give the *ratio decidendi* in a comparable case the benefit of the doubt. The ground for this rule is the same as for all precedent in life. "It takes time and effort to solve problems. Once you have solved one it seems foolish to reopen it. . . . Both inertia and convenience speak for building further on what you have already built; for incorporating the decision once made, the solution once worked out, into your operating technique without reexamination of what earlier went into your reaching your solution." [10] As Mr. Justice Cardozo once put it, the power of precedent is the power of the beaten track. However, the track is often not as beaten as is pretended. In England, the House of Lords considers itself bound by its own decisions,[11] yet has developed the art of "distinguishing" in an effort to escape from unwelcome ones, to such a degree that in the view of one authority the rule appears rather "amorphous." [12] The same writer reports that the Supreme Court of South Africa "has laid down the general rule that it is bound to follow its own decisions, but that it may depart from this rule, when 'it is clear that the decision is wrong' or arrived at 'on some manifest misunderstanding,' or where there has been 'something in the nature of a palpable mistake,' or 'where a court is satisfied that its previous decision was wrong,' or 'more particularly where the point was not argued.' " [13] Obviously these are very vague and uncertain criteria, as is the "distinguishing" which rests upon the notion that "the case must be limited so as to fit all the facts held material" to the case. Judges are, of course, continually reminded of precedents by counsel, who will try to make the most of them in the interest of their clients. At the same time, the reading of counsel's briefs in any case will show how radically divergent precedents are apt to be, and how invariably the notion of "following" precedent is preceded by the discretionary selection of those precedents which are to be followed. The pleadings of opposed counsel cannot but heighten the judge's sense of responsibility as he confronts the particular situation of the case in

[10] Karl Llewellyn, 1930, 1951, pp. 64–65.

[11] *London Street Tramways v. London County Council*, 1898, A. C. 375, cited by McWhinney, 1956, 1960, p. 17.

[12] McWhinney, 1956, 1960, p. 17; cf. Goodhart, 1931, pp. 26ff. For the U.S., Oliphant, a, 1922, pp. 215ff.; K. N. Llewellyn, 1933, esp. pars. 1–17; Radin, a, 1933, pp. 199ff. Cardozo's remark is in 1924, p. 62; cf. also 1921, pp. 29–30. For a comparative view, see Goodhart, 1934.

[13] McWhinney, 1956, 1960, p. 18; the next quotation is from p. 55.

hand and seeks to determine whether this situation is novel or covered by "previous" decisions. It would be foolish indeed to assume that a case can be "decided" on the basis of precedent, except when the judge has *first* decided to admit the precedent as ruling the case—a decision in which the "distinguishing" of the House of Lords, as well as the several criteria of the Supreme Court of South Africa just cited, may be involved. Other high courts have evolved corresponding rationalizations. Thus the principle of *stare decisis*, while seemingly directed towards stability, actually makes for change as well. It does so by dint of two radically divergent interpretations of precedent which have been called the "strict" and the "loose" view, involving a narrow or a broad interpretation.[14] According to the strict view, the judge must make certain just what it was that the precedent decided; he must confine the case to its particular facts and the reasoning focused on them. This view is applied to unwelcome precedents. It is the technique for "freeing" the lawyer and the judge of precedents. The loose or broad view, on the other hand, maintains that the court has decided any or all points on which it chose to rest a case, no matter how broad the statement. This loose view accordingly provides lawyer and judge alike with a technique for capitalizing on welcome precedents. A strictly rationalist approach might therefore be tempted to dismiss the rule of *stare decisis* as so much gibberish.[15] Against such a view, Cardozo maintained that adherence to precedent should be the rule and not the exception.[16] For the role of reasoning and therefore of persuasion is more complex, and any decision which is argued on the ground of careful reasons will appear less arbitrary than a mere expression of will. The *function* of the rule of *stare decisis* in such political perspective appears to be to oblige the judge to maintain his authority by a display of his capacity for reasoned elaboration. This argument is reinforced by Cardozo's view that "objectivity" in a judicial process can be stated thus: "In such matters the thing that counts is not what I believe to be right. It is what I may reasonably believe that some other man of normal intellect and conscience might reasonably look upon as right." [17]

Appeals to such general standards as justice and natural law serve this purpose. "Acquiescence in such a method has its basis in the belief that when the law has left the situation uncovered by any pre-existing rule, there is nothing to do except to have some impartial arbiter declare what fair and reasonable men, mindful of the habits of life of the community, and of the standards of justice and fair dealing prevalent among them,

[14] K. N. Llewellyn, 1930, 1951, pp. 60ff., pp. 63ff.; 1933, par. 16, pp. 44–46.

[15] This was the inclination of some of the "realists"; cf. Jerome Frank, 1949, pp. 63ff. Llewellyn's view, 1930, 1951, appears more balanced. Cf. also Stone, 1946, pp. 166ff.

[16] Cardozo, 1921, p. 149.

[17] *Ibid.*, p. 89.

ought in such circumstances to do, with no rules except those of custom and conscience to regulate their conduct." [18] Against this, "it may be urged that the language of judicial decision is often determined by pious platitudes. But do not pious platitudes likewise determine actual decisions?" [19] Neither the reasonings derived from the generally held and hence necessarily somewhat platitudinous notions of a community (for what does platitudinous mean but generally held?), nor those related to "natural law," "justice" and other belief systems, nor those based upon precedents, can be understood in their political function if assessed in terms of a reasoning derived from notions not generally held and without regard to precedent.

Ever since Bentham bitterly criticized Blackstone's tradition-bound inclination to justify such a procedure,[20] it has been quite clear that the only alternative is an arbitrary decision by a power-holder, such as a parliament which bases its decision upon the will of the majority; in lieu of a *ratio decidendi* in terms of preceding *thought* there is put forward a *ratio decidendi* in terms of the preferences of the majority.[21] Since behind the former there often hide the preferences of a minority, the basic issue of majority rule readily arises in this context, as it did in the conflict between the United States Supreme Court and President Roosevelt in the thirties.[22] Admitting the possibility of such miscarriage of the function of settling disputes (inherent in the very act, as we have indicated), it is nonetheless important to see the rule of *stare decisis* as the public mode of following precedent, and to appreciate the following of precedent as an important, indeed ineluctable, procedure in any political order.[23]

The following of precedent, whether organized according to *stare decisis* or according to hierarchical discipline, operates to organize the political and other behavior through the heightening of influence which it brings about in accordance with the rule of anticipated reactions (Chapter 11). The maintaining of the continuity of the legal system by binding the settlers of disputes to what their predecessors have done is greatly facilitated if those affected by future potential decisions can reasonably effectively anticipate what these decisions are likely to be. Everyone knows that many disputes are in fact prevented from developing to the point where a settlement by formal procedure becomes necessary, because

[18] *Ibid.*, p. 142.

[19] Morris Cohen, 1933, p. 217.

[20] Bentham, 1776, *passim;* Blackstone, 1765, introd., sec. 2.

[21] Fuller, a, 1946.

[22] Schlesinger, 1960, pp. 447–496, gives a masterly general analysis of the background of this conflict.

[23] It would be highly desirable to have some quantitative assessments of the extent to which either one or the other of the two views of *stare decisis* comes into operation, and how this quantitative distribution is correlated with the issues in the cases, classified according to interests and belief groups.

a potential contestant is advised (or recognizes, himself) that "the precedents are against him." Here again, it would be both possible and highly desirable to undertake some quantitative studies in order to determine the range of operative influence. Everyone knows (or ought to) that the mere establishment of an effective arbitration or mediation procedure will often reduce the amount of conflict, and the same holds *a fortiori* for courts.

The foregoing analysis shows that the difference between judicial and discretionary settling of disputes is a matter of the degree of importance attached to preexisting rules and precedents. But even in the expedient settling of disputes, rules and precedents intrude themselves quite often whenever the settler decides to have them do so. The distinctions drawn between the three models ought therefore to stress the *degree* to which the arbiter or settler is bound by rules, which is a matter also of the degree of specificity of the rules to which he is subject. English and American law has recognized for a long time that judicial proceedings in the formal and strict sense are subject to detailed procedural rules, such as those of due process of law in its original meaning under the American Constitution, tracing back to Magna Carta.[24] We shall discuss below the doctrine of judicial review which sprang from it. Here the general proposition can now be formulated that the three models of settling disputes exhibit a significantly changing ratio of power and authority, the expedient settling of disputes calling for most power and least authority, and the judicial for most authority and least power. The first model is therefore characteristic of the more autocratic forms of government, the second for the mixed and intermediate forms and the third form for constitutional governments; but, of course, all three occur in all forms of government, as previously stated. Their employment depends to a large extent upon whether preexisting rules (and precedents) are available in the field of social life where the dispute occurs.

A difficult set of questions arises when the judicial and other dispute-settling officials are confronted with a dual or plural set of legal rules and precedents. This situation presents itself when a political community, as a consequence of war and/or conquest, comes under the sway of another. In colonial territories, as well as under military government, some kind of balance has to be struck if the most egregious kind of injustice is to be avoided. In some cases, as was done in the Belgian Congo, the judiciary is split, and both native and European courts are provided; a similar situation occurred in occupied Germany.[25] The British developed an interde-

[24] McCloskey, 1960, for a recent statement; cf. esp. pp. 121ff. Cf. also Friedrich, 1950, chap. VI.

[25] Loewenstein, a, 1953, in Litchfield (ed.), pp. 236–262, describes the reconstitution of the German judiciary rather than the dual system before 1949; for this last see W. Friedmann, 1947, chap. 10.

pendent system, with African courts at the local level, subordinate courts, handled by local magistrates, Her Majesty's High Court with full jurisdiction, civil and criminal, over all persons, and a further appeal to the Judicial Committee of the Privy Council. All these courts settle disputes on the basis of "the common law of England, the doctrines of equity, and all statutes of general application" since 1902, with, however, the qualification that in all cases "to which natives are parties, every court shall be guided by native law as far as it is applicable and is not repugnant to justice and morality. . . ." Furthermore, "substantial justice" should always be done "without undue regard to technicalities of procedure." [26] Similarly in French colonies, in spite of heroic efforts to apply the *Code Civil* and other French law, "the form of justice practiced . . . remained a careful blend of the French code, indigenous custom and, where it applied, Koranic law," one recent analysis reports. Some such compromise is inescapable under conditions of dual or plural law.

It remains to add that judicial methods, especially in the matter of taking evidence, are or ought to be akin to the spirit of science and the search for objectivity characteristic of science in the broad sense. This kinship has recently been commented upon, again from the scientific side, by a philosopher of science, who writes: "There is, therefore, strictly speaking, no possible contradiction between the factual findings of a court of law and those of scientific and ordinary experience. . . . The relation between observed facts and legal facts is similar in principle to that between factual experience and an art based on such experience, or between empirical facts and mathematical conceptions." What interested him especially was that "the procedure of the law courts prescribes the observance of strictly impartial agnostic *doubt* in respect to a specified range of topics." [27] This sort of prescription calls for a "will to believe" that "originates in the will to do justice." The subtle and elaborate law of evidence is deeply rooted in notions of a just order, as witness the recent bitter controversy as to whether information secured by wiretapping or lie-detectors ought to be allowed as "legal evidence" or not.[28] At times, as in the case of Sacco and Vanzetti, such laws of evidence can be made into a bulwark of highly prejudicial evaluations.

Let us now return to the other two figures involved in the triangle of settling disputes, namely, the two contenders we called the accuser and the defender (or accused). Law has in many cultures distinguished be-

[26] Kimble, 1960, pp. 325–326, referring to *Uganda*, 1958, H.M.S.O., pp. 143–147 and 95. Belgian and other colonies are discussed in chap. 21 on "The Machinery of Government." The next quote is from p. 348. Why this sort of arrangement does not function is vividly portrayed by Richard Llewellyn, 1961.

[27] Polanyi, 1958, pp. 277–279; it should be remembered in this connection that Polanyi argues for the *personal* factor in all human understanding.

[28] Westin, a, 1952; cf. also extended bibliography by Tompkins, 1955.

tween the private and the public accuser, that is to say, between disputes arising between private persons, between public and private persons, and finally between public persons, that is, the respective spheres of private law, criminal law and public law.[29] These subjects are surrounded by a vast amount of detailed legal lore, and it is difficult to steer clear of these formal entanglements. In the political perspective, the disputes are the more important when they involve public persons. It is not correct to say, as is often done in legal works, that these are the only cases involving the public interest. For all settling of disputes is "in the public interest," and in some instances the settling of a private law case may be of vastly more interest to the public than a public law case. But it is of importance to know whether the accuser and/or the defender are public persons,[30] because of the power they possess and the role they therefore play in the political and governmental process. Such a rule as that "the king can do no wrong," with its consequences in the history of English law and government, has significance in this context.

In a dispute in which the violation of a private right is being claimed by the accuser, the defender will either claim that no such right exists or that he did not violate it. Whichever might by the arbiter (settler) be found to be the case (or its opposite), no public persons are ordinarily involved. The political dimension is only indirectly touched, as the issue involves only the maintenance of law and order in general.

In a dispute in which the commission of a crime is being claimed by the public prosecutor, the defender will either claim that the act committed was no crime, or that he did not commit the act. Whether the act at issue is a crime or not is a question which can be settled only by reference to the law. Such law may be highly formalized, as it is in advanced legal systems, more especially in what the Germans call a *Rechtsstaat,* that is, a government according to law, or it may be quite informal and correspondingly uncertain, as it usually is in primitive societies where "custom is king." Not all custom is, of course, law, but there are such customs. In the instance of the Cheyenne Elders cited earlier the rulers made the "borrowing" of another's goods without permission of the owner a forbidden act when they enunciated the rule; they at the same time provided a sanction for returning such goods, though apparently no punishment for not having done so. They said only that "if the taker tries to keep them, we will give him a whipping." But no doubt, if they had found the rule frequently violated, they would have taken the further step of providing for suitable punishment of the act itself.

[29] For the stress on persons, see above, Chap. 1, and Hohfeld, a, 1913, and a, 1917.

[30] We are deliberately using the terms "accuser" and "defender," rather than "plaintiff" and "defendant," so as to avoid all pretense of dealing with legal problems rather than the broad political models.

What is forbidden may be settled by customary law.[31] Such customary law cannot be defined in terms of norms which are maintained by coercion on the part of the legitimate ruler. Much law is of this sort, but its distinctive character is that it is a rule of reason, that is to say, is related through persuasive (authoritative) reasoning to the values, interests and beliefs of the community, and deals with interpersonal relations. To determine whether a given act violates such law is obviously a matter calling for the highest ability that can be brought to bear upon the question by minds who fully understand the rules which are the expression of sound reasoning in the premises. A settler or arbiter, a kind of "court," if you please, is therefore essential;[32] essential, that is, to determining whether a crime has been committed. Thus the rule *nulla poena sine lege* (no punishment without law) could be restated as *nullum crimen sine judice*. It presupposes the role of the judge in settling disputes concerning the *meaning* of the rules of law.[33] It incidentally eliminates the difficulty encountered in the trial and conviction of the "war criminals" which the older rule raised. In several respects there was no law which dealt with the actions and deeds committed by the Nazi leaders. They nonetheless were considered crimes according to customs which a court could, by a process of reasoned elaboration, firmly link to the values, interests and beliefs of the community of nations, for which it spoke. But such an argument does not, of course, dispose of the objection by liberal legal philosophy which asks for much more than the simple formula *nulla poena sine lege*, namely, that no punishment shall be inflicted unless such punishment is laid down in explicitly formulated formal law. For it is

[31] In anthropology, a controversy over primitive law was raging some years ago which contrasted "custom" with "law." This controversy is reviewed by Hoebel, 1954, pp. 20ff. Cf. Hartland, 1924; Seagle, 1941; Malinowski, 1926. It cannot be settled by stressing the element of "coercion," as was done by Hoebel, following Hohfeld, Radin and Ihering. Cf. Friedrich, 1958, chap. 21, and above, Chap. 16.

[32] In spite of the criticism contained in the previous note, I agree with Hoebel's argument on the role of a court, 1954, pp. 23f., where one reads: "Some courts are difficult to identify." Whether one ought to go as far as to say that even "if an agreed party . . . must carry through the prosecution without the intervention of a third party, there will still be a 'court' if the proceedings follow the lines of recognized and established order. . . ." (*ibid.*, p. 25) seems doubtful; Hoebel is perhaps stretching a good point.

[33] This is the sound kernel of such extravagantly normative statements as that of Salmond, 1924, that it is "to the Courts and not the legislature that we must go to ascertain the nature of true law" (p. 49). Or again: "English law is nothing but the body of rules recognized and applied by English Courts . . ." (p. 113); cf. contra, Cardozo's sane statement: "The rule that fits the case may be supplied by the constitution or by statute. If that is so the judge looks no farther. . . . The constitution overrides a statute, but a statute, if consistent with the Constitution, overrides the law of judges. In this sense, judge-made law is secondary and subordinate to the law that is made by legislatures . . ." (Cardozo, 1921, p. 14).

such highly formalized law which an advanced legal system recognizes. The difficulty arose because the seizure of power by the National Socialist leaders constituted in effect a breakdown of this advanced legal system and the return to a much more primitive system in which the place of "king" is taken by an alleged "people's feeling" or *Volksempfinden,* i.e., custom.

A dispute in which one public person accuses another public person of abusing his power can occur only under a constitutional system. For only in such a system are public functions made the subject of law (Chapter 15). Such law need, of course, not be formalized in a constitutional document. But unless it is justiciable, that is to say, unless it can be made the basis of some sort of lawful judicial settlement, a constitution cannot be said to exist. The pocket veto which the United States President practiced for many years, when eventually challenged, became the subject of a case before the Supreme Court, and it was only then settled definitively that such a veto was within the rightful exercise of the presidential office.[34] Medieval constitutionalism had depended upon the ecclesiastical authorities as the ultimate arbiter of questions in which several public persons were involved. This was partly due to the fact that high ecclesiastics, notably bishops, were themselves such public persons, through membership in representative assemblies such as the English Parliament. But it was also due to the notion that only law which was in accord with natural law was truly law, and the ecclesiastical authorities were charged with the interpretation of natural law as an emanation of eternal law,[35] even though rulers must "enact statutes which are particular determinations of the natural law." Therefore, when the ecclesiastics lost their authority, in the sequel to the breakdown of faith eventually formalized in the Reformation, a serious crisis resulted from the disappearance of the arbiter. Since no one could settle the disputes, the estates (through representative assemblies speaking for them) took up arms against the ruler and against each other. From the succession of religious wars and revolutions in France, Germany, England, and elsewhere, there seemed no escape but the establishment of one ultimate arbiter. Hence the doctrine of sovereignty (Chapter 30).

In turning to such a view, Europe adopted an ancient position. For much more commonly the highest ruler, such as the Chinese Emperor, is the ultimate arbiter in settling disputes between several public persons, as he is in disputes between private persons. In this case, as in the corresponding case of a totalitarian dictator, the settlement will typically

[34] U.S. Supreme Court, 1929; cf. also Swisher, 1943, pp. 784ff.

[35] Thomas Aquinas, in his *Summa Theologica,* stated the matter most authoritatively, I.II.q.92.arts.1 and 3, where St. Augustine is quoted with approval. Cf. also q.94 for the discussion of natural law, and II.II.q.147.art.3, as well as q.60.art.6 and *De Regimine Principum,* I.chap. XIV.

turn upon the expedient preference of the ruler rather than upon actual or alleged rules of law. Of course, precepts of ethics and manners may be developed to such an extent that they will suffice as a substitute for law in providing detailed rules of conduct, as was the case of the Confucian doctrine of *li*. "*Li*," we read in Confucius, "is the principle by which the ancient kings embodied the laws of heaven and regulated the expressions of human nature." Among other things, it dealt with court audience and the exchange of diplomatic visits. It was "the principle of rationalized social order and through it everything becomes right in the family, the state and the world." [36] Priests at the temple, high ministers at court, and elders at the college where the doctrine is taught—these were all provided for. "The reason the Sage is able to regard the world as one family and China as one man is that he does not make *arbitrary rules*, but tries to understand human nature, to define human duties. . . ." [37] In light of such a doctrine, the ruler as supreme arbiter remained within a set of precedents and therefore really assumed a role comparable to that of a supreme judge. The settling of disputes even between public persons was not simple expedient settling, but a discretionary settling, since the rules were very general. The reality, to be sure, was usually autocratic.[38]

As stated previously, only within a constitutional system can the settling of a dispute between public persons become a judicial settling. This aspect of judicial review, in the classical sense of a review of the constitutionality of legislative acts, is the politically basic one. For whenever private persons appear as accusers of public persons, as is, of course, the case wherever the issue is over individual rights or liberties, the range of lawful power of such public persons does not constitute a dispute between public persons.

Genuine disputes between public persons result from the "separation of powers," so called, whether functional or territorial.[39] For every such division of powers assigns specific powers to particular persons holding legally defined offices which make them *public* persons; thereby it engenders the potentiality of disagreement and conflict over the meaning of the terms employed. It is an inescapable feature of the conventional scheme that the sphere of the arbiter himself cannot be thus delimited. The judiciary has recommended itself to constitution-makers for this function as the "guardian" of the constitution, because it is a power

[36] Confucius (ed. Lin Yutang), 1938, p. 229.

[37] *Ibid.*, p. 234. See for a discriminating discussion of the relation of this ideal to reality, De Bary, a, 1957. Contra, Wittfogel, 1957, chap. 4. For a similar situation in ancient India, see Drekmeier, 1962.

[38] Even if Wittfogel, 1957, chap. 4, goes too far in calling such power "total," the settling of disputes was "expedient" most of the time.

[39] Cf. Friedrich, 1950, chaps. X and XI.

which in a certain sense is *not* a power (it is *dans une façon nul*, in Montesquieu's famous phrase to which Hamilton referred in *The Federalist*),[40] because it can make decisions only when asked by a disputant to do so. In our present perspective, a judge as arbiter can settle only disputes between others. That this evaluation of the judges' power was somewhat unrealistic, the history not only of the United States Supreme Court but of other tribunals has shown in ample measure.[41] To be sure, they cannot arrogate to themselves the more specific executive and legislative functions, but there exists considerable scope for "judge-made law" and for at least negative participation in policy determination. The desegregation decisions show that even positive policy-making decisions may be fashioned by the judiciary. The same can be observed in other constitutional orders. Thus the German Constitutional Court has in several important instances determined policy in responding to cases in which one public person disputed another's right to take action. Most recently, it denied the Federal Government (Adenauer) the right to institute a federal television program on the ground that it invaded the states' (*Länder*) right to complete cultural autonomy.[42] Similar cases have occurred in Canada, Australia, India, and elsewhere; for federalism, with its territorial division of powers, is particularly prone to precipitate such conflicts. For this reason, opponents of judicial review of legislative acts have always been much more ready to concede the need for a final judicial arbiter in issues concerning federal-state relations, including the review of state legislation (Chapter 32).

Classical judicial review, which makes the final judicial authority the arbiter of the power limits of federal legislation is, however, only a logical outgrowth of the federal dispute-settling function. For if it is inherent in the logic of a federal constitutional order to set up a judicial body to settle disputes as to the division of authority between the federal government and the states (or other component units such as provinces, Länder, cantons, and the like), it would hardly do to exempt the federal legislature from such settlements. Once, however, the legislative supremacy is thus "limited," it is difficult to see why the same reasoning should not apply to the functional as well as to the territorial division of power. The usual argument is that the constitution needs a guardian, and that a court is the safest guardian. But politically it is more nearly cogent to argue that disputes must be capable of settlement in a constitutional as much as in a nonconstitutional (autocratic) regime. And since the determination of such disputes involves the interpretation of

[40] Dietze, 1960, *passim*, but esp. pp. 171ff.
[41] Cf. citation above, p. 427 fn. 8.
[42] Reich, unpublished dissertation, Harvard University, 1960.

elaborate legal norms which a constitution contains, the strictly functional argument in terms of the specialization of functions calls for a judicial arbiter.[43]

The institution of judicial review in the classical sense frequently substitutes the judgment of judges for the judgment of the elected representatives of the people when doubt exists regarding the meaning of a constitutional provision. It is not often a question, however, of anything like the "manifest tenor," in Marshall's memorable phrase, but usually of the doubtful meaning or actually even of "gaps" in the constitution. Arguments such as those derived from the "intention of the framers" are more often than not a gloss upon the original text; for the intention of those writing constitutions either cannot be ascertained or in certain instances could not even have existed. Technological progress alone excludes such intention in many cases. Precisely because constitutions are meant to be basic law lasting over a considerable period, their principles cannot be narrowly construed in terms of the passing situation at the time they are enacted. In this connection, the observation of Judge Cardozo that "new times and new manners may call for new standards and new rules" is apposite, since it was written with precisely such constitutional interpretation in view.[44]

The role of the United States Supreme Court in settling disputes arising under the Constitution has obscured the role of Congress in interpreting the Constitution. The same holds true for other countries, though to a lesser extent. Only in systems with a centralized government of the parliamentary type and without judicial review is the constitutional role of the representative body readily recognized. The above-noted participation of judicial bodies in policy-making is paralleled by a constitutional role of the legislative bodies. "The United States Congress, in deciding policy questions, necessarily rules simultaneously on Constitutional questions," a learned author has recently reminded us, adding that this "is less clearly understood." [45] In doing so, such bodies may be settling disputes between private persons, especially large groups of such persons; but they may also determine the disputes arising between public persons, especially in a federal system, but in others too. Proposals on the part of disaffected legislators for "curtailing the power" of the United States Supreme Court are only an instance of such recurrent roles. Property and other basic interests may be involved in such settlements. It is clear from even these casual remarks that the settling of disputes is not limited to the courts; besides legislatures, administrators participate in this vital function. It is not their primary role, but it is a part of their governing func-

[43] For a more elaborate argument cf. Friedrich, 1950, chaps. XI and XII; also the literature given there.

[44] Cardozo, 1921, p. 88.

[45] D. Morgan, 1959, p. 1.

tion. The real differences between the three traditional parts of a constitutional structure are not in terms of the settling of disputes as such, but in terms of the particular kind or mode of such settling. While the judiciary engages in judicial settling, the legislature does the expedient settling, unrestrained by any rules, unless they be the "law of nature"; the executive (administrator) finally finds his work including much discretionary settling of disputes—discretionary, that is, within the broad boundaries of the rules laid down by the legislature and the precedents in judicial settlements of disputes.

A deviant form of all three types of dispute-settling, and essentially a perversion of the judicial and discretionary types in the interest of expedient settling of disputes involving a presumed "public interest," is so-called "political justice." Such political justice, according to one recent broad-gauged appraisal, has as its aim "to enlarge the area of political action by enlisting the services of courts in behalf of political goals."[46] The author adds that "those instrumental in such submission seek to strengthen their own position and weaken that of their political foes." They do so, in our terms, by mobilizing the authority of courts for the purpose of legitimizing the exercise of power against their political adversaries. It is evident that any political regime will be engaged in doing what it can to win a dispute which involves its own existence. That is, its very survival. "Justice" in such phrasing is related, as usual, to the values, interests and beliefs which the community cherishes in whose name such political justice is rendered (Chapter 14). Considering the rival claims which are advanced in the name of justice, it is surely true that "the authority of the trial neither adds to nor detracts from the fundamental justification of such political claims, namely the justness of the cause."[47] What the political trial does prove is what the clear delineation of rival claims of justice always proves: the existence of two political communities deeply divided by incompatible values, interests and beliefs.

At this point, a few words need to be said about administrative "justice," that is, about the settling of disputes between public persons (the government and its agents) and private persons, or public persons (such as officials) in their private capacity. It has been claimed that the appearance of such administrative law, that is, the exercise of quasi-judicial functions by administrative agencies in limited fields, means the disappearance of the "rule of law" or of the "supremacy of law" (*Rechts-*

[46] Kirchheimer, 1961, p. 419.

[47] Kirchheimer, 1961, p. 430. The author seems to be deeply troubled by the absence of a final yardstick, some sort of absolute justice unrelated to political community, although he clearly recognizes that neither the accuser nor the defender could "play his role" except on the assumption that he knows what "justice" is, that is, what acts are "just." They do know it.

staat).[48] Indeed, in Continental Europe it is through such administrative courts alone that the rule of law, the *Rechtsstaat*, or government according to law, can be made secure.[49] The development of such courts was an achievement of the constitutional era. For it does not signify the supremacy of administrative officials over the law, but its opposite, their subjection to it, which is achieved by subjecting their conduct to legal rules, while at the same time also making their own position vis-à-vis the government secure in terms of such rules. The central concern of administrative law has been the legal circumscription and limitation of administrative discretion. Thus the first principle of administrative law is that no administrative measure which imposes a burden upon anyone can be taken without legal authorization. By this principle, discretion is carefully circumscribed. The exercise of judicial functions by administrative officials is transformed into the judicializing of administrative conduct through subjecting it to a special group of judges, the administrative courts, culminating in the *Conseil d'État*, in France, and corresponding bodies in other Latin countries; in Germany the *Bundesverwaltungsgericht* coordinates the work of the courts of the several *Länder*. These bodies are responsible for the fact that large areas of administrative activity are actually "judicialized," that is to say, these activities are transformed into a judicial as contrasted with a discretionary settling of disputes.[50] How far such "judicialization" may be safely carried is difficult to say. Karl Loewenstein has wisely commented that "to raise the judge high above the policy makers and the people is a mark of either a very mature or a very primitive political civilization." [51]

In conclusion, be it said that the settling of disputes corresponds in basic importance to the defending of the political order. Indeed it constitutes the defense of the political order internally. Through it justice is continually reinterpreted and recreated. Without it, there can be no internal peace. Time and again, it has served as a unifying agent in efforts to cement a more comprehensive political community and thus as the pathfinder of a more inclusive political order. Herodotus' famous tale of how Deioces united scattered villages by being an upright judge is para-

[48] Dicey, 1885, 1926, chap. XII; contra, Robson, 1928, 1951; Dickinson, 1927. See also for the Continent, Waline, 1930, 1949 and 1944; W. Jellinek, 1928; Harnack, 1936, chap. 8; Forsthoff, 1950, 1958.

[49] Gneist, 1872, 1879, *passim*, argues this position persuasively, as was done by Robson with reference to the *Conseil d'État*, 1928, 1951.

[50] The *Conseil d'État* and similar bodies combine judicial with strictly administrative duties, whereas the German courts (and similar bodies elsewhere, as in Switzerland) specialize in the judicial dispute-settling work. Cf. what is said in Friedrich, 1950, pp. 114–115; to the literature there cited should now be added *Études et Documents*, 1947, published annually by the *Conseil d'État*.

[51] Loewenstein, a, 1953, p. 262. Cf. also his penetrating discussion in 1957, pp. 256ff., where the danger of a "judiciocracy" is depicted and analyzed.

digmatic and paralleled by similar deeds elsewhere. The growth of medieval kingdoms, in England, France, and elsewhere, is linked to the activity of royal judges expounding a "common" law which would hold for all and thus establish peace throughout the land.[52]

We witness at present a similar process on the level of world order. The process of such settling of disputes is profoundly affected by whether it proceeds in the light of preexisting rules or not. In this connection, the process may typically be distinguished according to whether it constitutes expedient or discretionary or judicial settling. Generally speaking, the development proceeds from the expedient to the judicial form or type of dispute-settling, as a political order or one of its subdivisions is in process of integration or consolidation. When a community and its order are in the process of disintegration or dissolution, the reverse sequence can be observed. Finally, it should be clearly recognized, in considering modern government, that the settling of disputes, while primarily a function of the judiciary, is not limited to it; that more especially the non-judicial types of settlement are likewise performed by the legislature and the executive. Thus one might say that "the extension of judicial methods is a concomitant of civilized government." The view, often heard at present, that the judicial function is at variance with the requirements of democracy is therefore unsound. On the contrary, a democracy can hope to operate successfully only if the fair and unbiased administration of the rules which the people through its representatives have established is taken care of by a judiciary which operates according to the methods of judicial settling. Only then can justice be achieved in a democracy. And as *The Federalist* noted: "Justice is the end of government. It ever has been and ever will be pursued until it be obtained, or until liberty is lost in the pursuit." Such an alternative is in the modern world suggested by totalitarian dictatorship, in which judicial settling of disputes has once more been largely superseded by discretionary or even expedient settling—the so-called political justice of the autocratic ruler, which is in fact neither just nor political in the broader sense.

The mode of judicial settling of disputes, as developed in advanced political communities, allows for many different ways of approach—ways which will be expressive of the literary and personal modes of behavior prevalent in different communities. These differences in all their subtle complexity may be adumbrated in terms of style. This subject, fascinating in its ramifications, has recently been subjected to a searching analysis by a comparison of the Swedish, German, British, American, Canadian and French judicial opinions.[53] The general conclusion which emerges

[52] Friedrich, 1950, chap. VI. The story of Deioces is found in Herodotus' *Persian Wars*, bk. I, chaps. 96 and following.

[53] Wetter, 1960, *passim*, but esp. part I.

is that the authority of such judicial opinions depends to a considerable extent upon such qualities of stylistic form.

In summing up what has been shown in regard to the settling of disputes, we may say that such dispute-settling is perhaps the most basic kind of political process, without which political order is inconceivable. In fact, it appears a prime function of a political order to provide for this process, one way or another. It was shown that the basic design of this process consists of an accuser, a defender and a settler, and that the settler needs power, authority and legitimacy in order to be effective. We explored the distinction between discretionary (including expedient) and judicial settling of disputes, and analyzed the issues which discretion presents. Included in this analysis is a sketch of the role of precedent. Some further considerations of the role of accuser and defender led into the question of private as contrasted with public persons involved in disputes; only a constitutional system can judicialize disputes between public persons—one of its key advantages. The rules associated with the "separation" of powers, both functional and territorial, are closely connected with this process, judicial review. Some comments on "political" and "administrative" justice concluded the analysis.

chapter

25

The Making of Rules

Obtruding false rules
pranked in reason's garb
Milton

The golden rule is that
there are no golden rules.
Shaw

"THE MOST CELEBRATED system of jurisprudence known to the world begins, as it ends, with a Code." Thus Henry Maine opened his celebrated study of ancient law, referring of course to the Romans. A code here stands for a collection of written rules. As was pointed out earlier, in the discussion of law (Chapter 15), actions which embody a command of a general nature, if enforced, possess a very special significance when rule is legitimately exercised by a person possessing authority. For such a command, applying as it does to many persons at different times and in different places, really encompasses a great many commands which would have to be reiterated over and over again if no such general command were possible. But we also pointed out that this conventional "command theory" of law presents great problems because of its gainsaying of reason. By linking law to authority, as the capacity for reasoned elaboration, we undertook to build into such a command theory a rational element which gives it an existential dimension. Without such authority, we said, a command presented as a law is existentially defective and correspondingly reduced in its ability to oblige. We also showed how such an approach helps to avoid the difficulties which are involved in the antithesis between a normative and a "realistic" or purely behavioral approach to law in terms of prevailing custom and habit. This view of law as consisting of general commands or imperative rules when issued by a legitimate ruler possessing authority, provides the basis for a generalized theory of the *making* of rules. It is evident that this goes beyond the conventional notion of a *legislative* power seen as *the* law-making power which is to be distinguished from the executive and judicial power. All three powers share in the making of rules, as they do in the settling of disputes as was shown in the previous chapter.[1]

The making of rules is based, then, upon institutionalized power, that is, rule. It is not only so based, but constitutes one of the key manifestations of such power. Power, we saw, is a relation among men which manifests itself in the behavior of following (Chapter 9). Men follow another man when they do what he wants; their behavior *conforms* to *his* wishes. But we also saw that this relation does not necessarily mean obedience to commands, though it often does. For power may originate in either coercion or consent. It is characteristic for the situation in which rules are made that commands are involved and hence coercion is needed to provide the sanctions which ensure the enforcement needed so that the rules can be said to exist. The harsh sayings of such writers as Hobbes and Ihering, stressing the importance of the "sword," have their good grounds in this constellation.

If we now ask how such rules are *made*, several elementary models of rule-making are discovered. In order to do this, certain basic aspects of rule-making need explicit statement. First of all, such rules are typically either *decisions* of a rule-maker or ruler (Chapter 3) (though with regard to rules resting upon custom or habit the original decision-making may be obscured or lost from sight), or they may be merely enunciating a custom that has become regular or routine behavior. Second, such rule-making may be by one, or by several persons, or it may be by many or all. Third, rule-making may be distinguished with a view to the political constellation within which it arises: rules may be made with the purpose of preventing conflict, or of outlawing certain behavior, or of providing for various kinds of public policy. Fourth, rules may be made (1) incidentally within the decision rendered by a judge or other settler of disputes, or (2) by another kind of ruler. The latter kind of rule-making may either be magisterial and without reference to the views of others, or it may be consultative and with such reference. In contrast to the rule-making by a superior ruler, rule-making may be the result of the cooperation through deliberation of most of the persons to whom the rule is to apply—deliberative rule-making. A special case of this sort of rule making is deliberative rule-making by elected representatives, familiar as the democratic legislative process.

[1] For a radically divergent view, see Barker, 1951, pp. 89ff., who would go so far as to identify the state and law (p. 89).

Common to all these processes is the enunciation of imperative sentences having the form: All persons of a specified kind shall take specified actions under specified circumstances or suffer specified sanctions if they fail to do so. To suggest a generalized formula:

$$p\,!\,af(c)$$
and
$$p\,!\,sf(\text{non-}a)$$

where $p =$ person
$a =$ action
$c =$ circumstances
$s =$ sanction

Such imperative sentences can be rendered in declaratory form if their existential dimension is to be indicated; they then read that specified sanctions will be applied to specified persons if they do or do not take specified actions under specified circumstances.[2] If the declaratory form is employed, it too can be embodied in a simple formula, namely:

$$s \rightarrow p = f(p) \rightarrow af(c)$$

These formulas are abstract statements about rule-making which indicate that it is concerned with persons, actions, circumstances and sanctions. All these entities have been discussed in earlier parts of this study and do not present any special difficulties. If, therefore, with these constituents of rule-making firmly in mind, we now approach the several models suggested above, an over-all view of rule-making should be possible.

Abstractly considered, and taking the four constituents into account, an excessively large number of models would result from the calculus of combinations and variations. But by restricting our choices to decisional models, by excluding the third constituent which deals with the purposes, objectives or goals of rules—we shall return to these at the end—we arrive at four basic types or models of rule-making, each of them subdivided into two subtypes. One of these models is distinguished by the situation from which it arises, whereas the other three are characterized by a distinctive procedure. The situational one of these models is rule-making by one or several persons, growing out of the settlement of a dispute; it might be called postdisputational, or, to take its most important subform, postjudicial. A subtype would be postdisputational rule-making by many (all), that is to say, by the "ruled," after settlement of a dispute; this is common in tribal and other forms of primitive cooperative political orders, but also in many organizations at annual meetings and the like. The second model is rule-making by one or several who occupy the position of a ruler, which is at the same time without reference to the

[2] This is a concrete aspect of the interrelationship between valuational and existential judgments discussed above, Chap. 2.

views of others; it is the magisterial form of rule-making par excellence, and might be subdivided into monocratic rule-making by one magistrate, and committee rule-making by boards, commissions, and the like. Both these models are extensively found in business and other private organizations, but also on the executive level of the government, especially as concerns the internal organization of such offices, and where it is expressly authorized by the law. The third model of rule-making is that by one or several who occupy the position of ruler (in the executive field) but who proceed with more or less extensive reference to the views of others. It may be called the consultative type of rule-making. It is found in government where the general public is concerned, and in democratic societies is often adopted when the magisterial could be used; it is also common in international organizations such as the International Labor Office, UNESCO, OECD, and so on. It may also be subdivided into a monocratic and a committee type. Fourth, there is rule-making by the many cooperating with each other in open deliberation and discussion, not after a dispute but in response to common needs. It is the assembly type of rule-making—policy-making—of direct and representative democracy and could be called deliberative rule-making. An important special case is that of a large body of representatives acting on behalf of the rest, but elected by them and subject to recurrent challenge in open elections. This, as we said before, is the special model which most writers have in mind most of the time when they speak of rule-making in terms of the modern legislative process. It needs to be seen in the perspective of the rest. A more detailed consideration of each of these four models follows.

The postdisputational or postjudicial model of rule-making must not be confused, though it often is, with the emergence of rules in the context of the judicial process of settling a dispute, incidental to the observation of precedent, as described and analyzed in the last chapter. The model is, like all the models here discussed, as we said, a *decisional* model in the sense that those engaged in the rule-making decide upon a rule, not upon a case like the Elders of the Cheyenne tribe. It is more usual as a sequel to informal types of adjudication than to formal judicial process. However, the famous procedure of the Roman *praetor peregrinus* who formally announced the *rules* in light of previous decisions is a significant instance of such rule-making. It was and is quite common in any sort of monocratic setup such as characterizes a monarchical political order. Rulers of this type very frequently announce a rule after having had to settle a dispute. This kind of rule-making springs very naturally from the fullness of power which such an individual or small group enjoys. It would seem that this is done not infrequently in totalitarian dictatorship, either by the individual or by a small group such as the Politburo. We find that such postjudicial rules do not necessarily embody the decision's main principle. On the contrary, the decision often provides the reason for making a rule which will forestall the recurrence of the situation which caused the dispute and made the settlement necessary. This pattern is found on many levels, from the domestic rule of the father who lays down that the boys whose fight he had to settle are never again to use a particular room at the same time, to the edicts of the English (and other) kings.[3] It is inherent in the reasoning upon a dispute and grows out of the self-evident interest in preventing its recurrence. To say that "the earliest notion of law is not an enunciation of priciple, but a judgment in a particular case" [4] means obscuring this close relationship between the task of settling disputes and that of making rules—two tasks which do not follow each other in time, though they are equally basic and constituent of all political order. Nowadays, when the judiciary is supposed to be neatly separated from all explicit rule-making (which is not the same as law-making), such post-disputational rule-making of one or a few occurs mostly in the executive branch after the settlement of a dispute, say, in labor arbitration, either in the form of ordinances and the like, or in the form of rules and regulations (and their amendment). They thus merge with magisterial and consultative rule-making.

But before we turn to these models, a word needs to be said about postjudicial rule-making by the many (all). This model may seem difficult to picture in modern government, but is actually quite common wherever "direct democracy" "responds" to judicial decisions. When the Congress adopted the income tax amendment, after the Supreme Court had held such legislation unconstitutional, it engaged in such postjudicial rule-making. In Athens, where the courts were extensively participated in by the people, and where judgments were often rendered in open assembly, rules could readily be adopted after such proceedings were completed. A similar type of action can often be observed in smaller organizations. Thus party congresses, notably those of thoroughly democratized parties like the British Labor Party, will often after reaching the settlement of an extended dispute adopt a rule (policy) which is to guide party behavior afterwards, including the behavior of members.[5] An annual meeting of a professional society will at times see a member rise after a controversy has been settled and propose then and there that some rule or regulation, some amendment to the bylaws, be adopted to forestall the recurrence of the conflict.

[3] For illustrations cf. Stubbs (9th ed., rev. Davis), 1921, pp. 257ff.; for France, see Olivier-Martin, 1951, pp. 221ff.

[4] Dwight in his *Introduction to Maine*, 1861, 1873, p. xv.

[5] Cf. Labor Party, 1949, pp. 119ff., where various members demand changes in rules. Cf. also 1959 and 1960.

Vastly more important in the history of government is the second type, *magisterial* rule-making by one or several persons in an executive or administrative position, which is done without referral to the views of others. It goes without saying that such magisterial rule-making takes the view of others *into account*. What we mean as a distinguishing trait of this model of rule-making is that the rule *qua* rule is not referred to others. Thus orders and ordinances, rules and regulations of administrators and executives, when not referred to someone else, are typical instances of this kind of rule-making. Any commercial corporation will exhibit this type regularly. In a recent report of General Electric to the stockholders, this sort of rule was made public because the court decisions against a number of officers and employees had raised the question as to whether their malfeasance was a company responsibility. Although having to concede legal responsibility toward outsiders, the company stressed that a series of directives as well as general instructions had enjoined its officers and employees "to comply strictly with the antitrust laws." [6] This rule was mandatory and enforced by severe sanctions. No man, from the ancient tribal chief to the administrator of a large organization, private or public, has been able to operate without this magisterial type of rule-making. It is particularly adapted to all situations in which the value and the objectives to be realized are generally agreed on and the technical problems involved are a matter of expert knowledge. Usually the rule-making results directly from the necessity of directing the activity of a considerable number of persons *belonging to the organization* and moulding their behavior along suitable lines. Magisterial rule-making is the type for internal organization affairs. It is also often found where only short-run operations, such as occur in an emergency, oblige the person in charge to dispense with consultative processes. Rules of this type rest more often on power than on authority; they frequently contain an element of the arbitrary and spring from the fact that *some* decision must be made. Employees cannot arrive at different times if the work is to proceed smoothly; the question as to when they arrive may disregard the preference of quite a few, and consultation would only aggravate the issue; yet *some* decision has to be made. This is one of thousands of illustrations that could be given in order to demonstrate how this kind

[6] General Instruction No. 2.35, November 18, 1946. It was reissued several times; the statement of 1954 is quoted as saying that "no employee shall enter into any understanding, agreement, plan or scheme, expressed or implied, with any competitor . . . nor engage in any conduct which in the opinion of the Company's counsel violates any of the antitrust laws." The company stresses that its rule went beyond the injunctions of these laws, that it was a pioneer in issuing such a directive. It further describes the disciplinary action taken against the offenders. See *Report to the Stockholders* in calling the annual meeting, March, 1961. It is clear from the context that the issuance of such rules is common practice not only in that company but throughout the industry.

of decision is bound up with the operating of any organization whatsoever.[7]

Whether such rule-making takes the monocratic or the committee form is often a matter of convenience, but there exists a definite rationale for choosing either one or the other. Often, of course, the rationale springs simply from the form of rule that prevails. But where an alternative is possible, the choice depends upon whether the activity is primarily an executive one, with rule-making incidental to the operation, or is non-executive. Many organizations, notably state governments and universities in the United States today, are overloaded with committees, boards and commissions, where a monocratic director would be more suitable. This misdirection of effort springs from a vague feeling that committees are more "democratic." As long as their rule-making is magisterial, there is no good ground for this view. Both monocratic and plural decision-makers are democratic to the extent to which they are responsible, either through election or otherwise (Chapter 17), to the persons to whom their decisions, including rules they make, extend. A faculty committee which is not elected by the faculty but appointed by the "higher powers" is no more democratic than a single "administrator." The same holds for other organizations, including governments. It may, however, be better to forestall the demand for a democratic arrangement, because it enlarges the circle of those participating in the exercise of power. To the extent to which it does, it should, in terms of the typology of rule (Chapter 10), be classed anyhow as a step toward aristocracy, or oligarchy if the old Aristotelian classification is used. Whether there are sound reasons for putting a committee rather than a single person in charge depends upon whether the function to be taken care of is primarily one of making rules or primarily one of taking measures in specific instances. If the former, a committee is often indicated, because rules in the nature of things affect a large number of persons, last over considerable periods of time, and must usually be made "public." The authority of a rule is ordinarily enhanced by a committee issuing it, which is helpful in all three respects. If dispute-settling is also involved, the argument for a committee is thereby reinforced.

In contrast to magisterial rule-making, the third type, consultative rule-making, is practiced where the rules concern primarily persons beyond the organization, where there is a considerable time span involved during which the rules are intended to hold, and where there is no urgency about their adoption. It is not always sharply differentiated from magisterial rule-making; it is often engaged in by the same person or group which also practices the latter; but it is quite distinct as a model, with its own dynamics. Consultative rule-making typically seeks to gather the

[7] Dahl and Lindblom, 1953.

reaction of those affected most by the rules that are being fashioned. The county committees developed by the United States Department of Agriculture for consultation with the farmers about impending rules are characteristic instrumentalities for consultative rule-making. So are a considerable range of advisory bodies, such as the bodies known as "economic councils" and the like in European government; more recently, the European Coal and Steel Community and the Common Market have developed an elaborate setup of this type.[8] It has been a recurrent illusion to think that such consultation can be detached from the interests of those consulted. Thus the Consultative Committee of the ECSC was conceived as "a loyal help-meet of the High Authority, giving technical expertise and wisdom to its decisions through the quality of the advice tendered by its members, considered as independent experts."[9] A qualified observer has rightly commented that "never have the steelmen or the leaders of the coal firms who sit in the Committee felt themselves to be the aides or technical councillors of the High Authority. On the contrary they have considered themselves representatives of their professional organizations, and have thus defended corporative viewpoints." Nor is this a peculiarity of the business interests represented; labor and consumer representatives have acted in this same manner.

Candor, as well as political experience, suggests that consultation is intended to provide the parties interested in the rules with a voice in the process of making them. Those preoccupied with the public or common interest have, therefore, been almost invariably disinclined to advocate the consultative process of rule-making. Far better to secure a bureaucratic elite which would make the rules without any reference to those affected by them, who presumably do not understand their own interest! Such is the usual notion of those who advocate such an elite. As against this sort of belief, the practice of consultative rule-making rests upon the notion that "decisions that are the product of a process of full consideration are most likely to be decisions in the public interest."[10] Within a democratic context, such conduct as is exhibited in the consultative model of rule-making recommends itself to rule-makers whenever the failure to enlist at least the partial support of those affected would imperil the eventual survival of the rule made. The reason is that there is the possibility of the rule-maker being overruled on the higher levels of decision- and rule-making which a democratic system provides. Thus consultative rule-making is embedded in deliberative rule-making.

Deliberative rule-making, the fourth model we identified at the

[8] Friedrich, 1950, chap. 22; Haas, 1958, chaps. 9 and 10; also arts. 193–198 of the Treaty on the Common Market, organizing the consultative "Economic and Social Committee."

[9] Haas, 1958, p. 475; the next quotation, *ibid.*

[10] Schubert, 1960, p. 205.

outset, is the rule-making by the many cooperating with each other in *open* deliberation and discussion about common needs calling for public policy. It is the assembly type of rule-making of direct democracy, as we said. To Rousseau and other radical democrats it seemed to be the only kind of legitimate rule-making when the rule is to have the force of law. He therefore excluded representation (see above, Chapter 17). This view results from laying great stress upon the value of law and a corresponding disvalue upon the coercion associated with it. In order to escape from the dilemma, it is argued that only a rule adopted with the effective cooperation of nearly all to whom it applies (excluding minors, imbeciles *and*, until recently, women) can entitle the maker to use the coercion which the enforcement of the rules of law calls for.

Considering the emphasis which has recently been placed upon past practices of deliberative rule-making in the tribal usage of the peoples from which the emergent nations are now being fashioned,[11] it is surprising how inadequately this process has hitherto been observed and described by anthropologists. Often there is merely some such general statement to be found as that "toward evening everyone would drift over to the assembly place . . . the elder ones would sit and talk; questions would be thrashed out, and at the end of the evening the point would be settled." [12] Are we to assume that the proceedings are like those of the evenings New England selectmen spend with their fellow townsmen? The description would certainly fit. Not infrequently unanimity is the rule of such deliberations. These, too, concern specific measures more often than the making of rules, but rule-making is certainly included.[13] Time and again the merging of the executive, legislative and judicial authority seems to have prevented any further inquiry into whether there are peculiar features of such rule-making.[14] Deliberative rule-making seems to be intermingled with discretionary and consultative forms, the latter definitely predominating.

In terms of human experience, this submodel of rule-making is marginal—the exception rather than the usual procedure. The reason for this is not far to seek. Not only does it severely limit the size of the political order, thereby creating insoluble survival problems, but it also brings on problems of corruption which go under the general heading of "demagogy." Demagogy is classically the misleading of the many in order to entice them into making rules which are unsound. The methods were analyzed by Aristotle in his *Art of Rhetoric*, which summed up two centuries of Sophist teaching in the field of "making the wrong seem right, and the right wrong." Whether these dangers are as great as they

[11] Note, for example, Kenyatta, 1938; Nyerere, a, 1961.

[12] Linton, 1939, p. 161; similarly, Warner, 1958, p. 585.

[13] Wallace and Hoebel, 1952.

[14] Cf. L. H. Morgan, 1901; Noon, 1949; Middleton, 1958; M. Mead, 1930.

turned out to be in fifth-century Athens may well be doubted in light of much contrary experience. Ever since Plato made his impassioned indictment of Athenian democracy, the points have constituted a recurrent theme in political thought. Actually, the conditions of Athens were quite unusual and in some respects extreme. For the Athenian *demos* was not only participating in the making of the rules, but also in their administration. It manned the courts and assumed complete control over short-term executives. The objections to such an experiment arise rather from the complete merging and concentration of power in the hands of a thus unrestrained multitude than from their failure in the field of rule-making. Where the many are restricted to such rule-making, the experience has been substantially more satisfactory. Not only in the Swiss cantons and the New England town meetings, but in a considerable variety of other comparable bodies the many have shown themselves capable of satisfactory rule-making, especially if adequate procedural safeguards, such as the "moderator" of town meetings, are adopted.[15]

Lord Bryce once wrote that of three or four types of systems of local government which he had described in his *American Commonwealth*, "that of the Town or township with its popular primary assembly has been the best. It is the cheapest and the most efficient; it is the most educative to the citizens who bear part in it. The town meeting has been not only the source, but the school of democracy."[16] It could, of course, be "best" without being good, and the rules which result from its deliberations could be inadequate, to say the least. But anyone who has participated in the work of such assemblies will, I think, be inclined to agree that while far from perfect, they provide a feasible model of rule-making. Being suited to the "intimate" community and the small organization, rule-making by the many tends to be rather conservative. The inertia which argues against the leaving of familiar paths of behavior is ever present, because many of the participants do not spend much time on the issues involved. This kind of rule-making is therefore the despair of all radicals and technical specialists whose more "rationalist" proposals and schemes are apt to be rejected.[17] The experiences with a modern adaptation of rule-making by the many, namely, the referendum and initiative, have tended in the same direction, though some rather striking instances of demagogic corruption have also occurred. In any case, the referendum is not fully a model of deliberative rule-making because

[15] Friedrich, 1942, pp. 121ff. For a graphic descriptive account, see Gould, 1940. But the role of the moderator deserves a more detailed behavioral study and a critical appraisal because of his importance for the understanding of deliberative rule-making.

[16] Bryce, 1924, vol. I, p. 626.

[17] G. Hicks, 1946, has described very vividly his own experiences in such a context.

of the absence of face-to-face encounter with its give-and-take of argument, although modern mass media have produced some interesting substitutes, such as the "letter-to-the-editor" column and the radio and television debates with open participation of the public.[18]

Rule-making by the many is rather unsatisfactory from a technical standpoint, whether the technique involved in the rules be engineering or law. In referendum procedures this handicap can be reduced by adequate preparation, but in the town meeting model it is difficult to maintain a technical rationale as against the common sense and common speech of the crowd. This fact has resulted in a virtually complete failure of the rule-making function of stockholders' meetings, although these are said to be the "ultimate" determiner of company policy. Nothing could be further from the truth. Stockholders have largely abdicated any such function, and whenever they attempt to exercise it, they are almost invariably opposed by "management." But since the bylaws of company charters usually make certain actions on rules mandatory, stockholders are still *pro forma* consulted prior to voting. The student of political process is obliged to conclude that the technical nature of most such company rule-making precludes the effective exercise of the rule-making power by the stockholders at large. If this conclusion is sound, corporation law needs to be revised to provide for some other kind of safeguard for stockholder participation in such rule-making as calls for it, or for the abandonment of the fictions involved.[19]

Far more important than direct participation of the many in rule-making is the model where the many are represented by a small number among them for the purpose of rule-making. It is the quintessence of the legislative process in constitutional systems, and the remainder of the chapter will be devoted to this crucial subject. By transforming an electorate running into the millions into an assembly numbering only hundreds, both the legal and the engineering techniques involved in rule-making for an industrial mass society can be more properly attended to. Before turning to the broad features of this democratic process, a few words may be said about the totalitarian make-believe of such bodies as the *Reichstag* under Hitler and the All-Union Congress of Soviets and comparable bodies in other Communist states. These are not engaged in deliberative rule-making in the sense here used. They are organized for purposes of acclamation of the rules decided upon either in magisterial or consultative processes. Perhaps in view of the spreading of such modes of procedure in rule-making, we should differentiate a distinct model in which such acclamation is added to the magisterial or consultative rule-

[18] Friedrich, 1950, chap. 25, esp. pp. 550–557. There is also much further literature.

[19] The issue is under active discussion in a number of countries, including the United States and Germany.

making, and call it by some specific name. But I do not think so. For the acclamation adds nothing to the content of the rules; it is an event completely external to the rule-making process itself. Primitive government has at times sought this type of acclamatory approval; it is so reported about some of the primitive Germanic tribes.[20] Its purpose is not related to the rule-making process as such; to the extent to which it is not meant to deceive the public into believing that a deliberative democratic process is still in use, such acclamation serves to buttress the legitimacy of the totalitarian rulers by suggesting that they are entitled to make such rules. Among their own following it may also enhance their authority.

Rule-making by a representative body, acting on its own, is radically different from such acclamatory proceedings, though a superficial similarity could deceive one. After all, the majority party in the British House of Commons similarly seems to "acclaim" what the government leadership, which is its own, has worked out in the way of legislative proposals. Again, in Tudor times the Parliament largely ratified what the King (or Queen) and his ministers proposed. But the history of British parliamentary procedure reveals that the crucial issue has always been how to protect the opposition and the minority or minorities so as to secure freedom of debate which alone could assure the deliberative character of the rule-making.[21]

Whether the British Parliament is still a deliberative body or merely acclamatory at the present time, has been hotly contested.[22] For our present purpose, the answer is not as important as the fact that Parliament has been a deliberative body for a long period and may therefore be considered to represent the archetype of the deliberative type of rule-making. In any case, there are many others; the legislative bodies of the British Dominions, of the United States, of France, Germany, Italy and the smaller states of Western Europe all have engaged in deliberative rule-making. From this extended experience, which needs to be seen as unrelated to the particular kind of governmental pattern, whether of a parliamentary, presidential or council type, certain very general conclusions can be drawn.[23]

[20] Tacitus, *Germania.*

[21] For the background of "freedom of debate" cf. Chafee, 1956, chap. 1.

[22] One author has gone so far as to claim that Parliament has ceased to be a "thought organization" (Finer, 1932, and later editions). For two generations critics have asserted that it was a "rubber stamp" or a "voting machine." Keeton, 1952, speaks of the "passing of Parliament" in connection with "the menace of delegated legislation"; a generation earlier, Muir, 1930, had stated "that the time-honoured description of Parliament as the effective legislative body has ceased to be in any valuable sense true" (pp. 32–33). For a more balanced statement cf. Jennings, 1940, chaps. VII and VIII, and Morrison, 1954, chaps. X, XI.

[23] For a more detailed account of these problems cf. Friedrich, 1950, chaps. XVI and XVII. There also is much additional literature cited there. Cf. also Cassinelli, 1961, chap. 5.

Speech and debate are the key to deliberative rule-making, as they are the basis of all parliamentary work of which rule-making is of course only a part, though an important one. But such speech and debate must be ordered and directed toward the goal of reaching a decision; hence rules of procedure are vital ingredients of such speech. These rules of procedure, notably in the British Parliament, were evolved over many generations, beginning in medieval times. There are many variations in detail, expressive of particular national traditions, ways of doing things and forms of government. In the British case, the evolution of these procedural rules closely paralleled the development of parliamentary government. Legislation by bill rather than upon petition having been worked out before the reign of Elizabeth, procedure thereafter successively established the rights of each participant in the debates and decisions, the separation of the Speaker's position from the Crown as part of the prevention of the Crown's influence upon the deliberations of the assembly, and the protection of the opposition, that is to say, the minority's role in the work. These were the main accomplishments of the aristocratic period. After 1832, when representation became more broadly democratic, and the forward march of industrialization called for an increasing amount of legislation, procedural changes were made in order to expedite business and to prevent useless rhetoric. Rules for debate and such devices as the question were then developed. The abuses of obstruction in the latter half of the century, as well as the change in party organization, called for closure and similar devices, which meant a decline of the deliberative method of rule-making in the interest of effective party support for the government. These trends have continued to the present and have occasioned the criticism already mentioned.

Similar tendencies can be observed elsewhere, especially in the United States; they are often associated with the rise of a specialized committee system, alien to the British Parliament. For the committees in the House of Commons are nonspecialized bodies. The specialized committee, as it is found in the United States, France, Germany and other countries, tends to preserve the deliberative process of rule-making intact. As one experienced writer said: "This process has been a matter of convenience, a natural development of orderly system, not begun with any deliberate purpose; . . ." [24] and he continued: "No man is the same in private and in public. The more numerous the observers and auditors, the less the frankness, sincerity, confidence. Universal experience tells us that in all manner of conference and deliberation, we reach results more speedily and satisfactorily if those persons directly involved are alone." The issue of publicity which is here raised deserves fuller exploration. But before we consider it, some further points concerning the committee

[24] Luce, 1922, chaps. IV–VIII. Cf. also Young, 1943, 1958, esp. pp. 129ff., 140ff., 159f., and 274ff.; also Bailey and Samuel, 1952, *passim.*

system deserve mention. Other factors than the problem of effective rule-making entered into the development of committees. The increasing technical complexity of legislation, as well as its amount, called for a division of labor. The former notion of the representative as the nonspecialist who like his electorate would render judgment upon all matters calling for rule-making, slowly made way for the opposite view, namely, that a representative should acquire, if he does not already possess, specialized knowledge in a few fields of rule-making.[25]

Referring all bills immediately to a committee, without any consideration at large, as in the United States, or only a cursory one, as in other countries, leads to the "killing" of many proposals in committee. Critics often forget that many of these bills could not even get introduced into the House of Commons. Nonetheless, this method of choosing between various measures proposed is a far cry from the deliberative process. It would seem more in keeping with it if the assembly itself decided which particular proposals to take up, but under present rules such a procedure does not seem feasible. The key role of the Rules Committee of the House of Representatives of the United States Congress was meant to counteract the overweening position of the Speaker earlier in the century; a recent revolt has reversed this trend.

Committees in American legislatures hold hearings in order to secure information beyond that furnished by the departments of the government. Such hearings may be either public or private. The nonpublic hearing is defended on the ground that witnesses can be induced to testify more readily and more confidentially. Anyone who has ever testified before such a committee is likely to have done so as a partisan of a particular line of policy; he is either for or against a particular rule that is in the making. As such, he contributes to the deliberative process, especially as committee members avail themselves liberally of the opportunity to ask questions, often friendly if they share the witness' views, hostile if not.

The deliberative process in committee produces extensive changes in all major legislative proposals. In contrast to Britain, where the bills the government puts forward are usually altered only in minor detail,[26] in the United States every piece of major legislation, even if introduced with the full support of the President, is profoundly affected by the committee's work upon it. And not only the committee's; especially if

[25] In some countries, notably Germany, this tendency has been carried to the questionable length of having public officials from particular services, such as the post office, sit on the parliamentary committees concerned with their field; obviously such an arrangement tends to destroy the deliberative model and to return to a magisterial one. Cf. Friedrich, 1950, chap. XVII.

[26] Jennings, 1940, notes several instances where major changes were made, or the bill even withdrawn (pp. 224ff., esp. p. 230). See also Allen, 1927, 1958, chap. 6.

the committee has been divided, the different positions will be fought over on the floor of the Senate and House. The same holds for other legislatures with a developed committee system, notably France and Germany. The vigorous and majority-supported leadership of both De Gaulle and Adenauer has caused a certain reduction in the range of deliberation; especially the former and his former Prime Minister, Debré, have tended to assume a rather authoritarian leadership, making use of the threat of dissolution. But even so, the criticism and debate continue to affect rule-making, if not explicitly, then by way of anticipated reaction.

This is not the place to consider the problems of membership, size and number of such committees, even though they make an appreciable impact upon the product of such deliberative rule-making. But before a rounded assessment can be made, the problem of publicity must now be more fully considered. That law ought to be public has been the view of most writers; for to expect someone to obey a norm which he does not know arouses an elementary sense of injustice—and to punish him for not obeying it, even more so. But whether the law-making, the rule-making process, ought to be public is quite another matter. Certainly it is a fact that it has not been public for long periods, and there are weighty arguments against publicity, such as the view just cited above. However, the contrary view has been much more widely advocated, if not held, under democratic conditions. The most radical and forthright argument was developed by Jeremy Bentham in the beginning of the nineteenth century. In *An Essay on Political Tactics* he asserts at the very opening the vital importance of publicity. "Before entering into the details of the operations of an assembly, let us place at the head of its regulations the fittest law for securing the public confidence and causing it constantly to advance towards the end of its institution. This law is that of publicity." [27] He would presumably exempt foreign affairs, "where publicity would favor the projects of an enemy," but we are here concerned with the rule-making process. In support, he gives the following reasons for the value of publicity which seem to him patent. First, to constrain the members of the assembly to perform their duty, second, to secure the confidence of the people, and their assent to the measures of the assembly, third to enable the governors (rulers) to know the wishes of the governed, fourth, to enable the electors (electorate) to act intelligently in elections, fifth, to provide the assembly with the means of profiting by the information of the public, and sixth, to give amusement. Bentham reduced the objections to publicity to one, that "the public is incompetent to judge of the proceedings of a political assembly." This objection he rejects; for he thinks that the public will judge, whether

[27] Bentham, *Works*, vol. II, pp. 310ff.

informed or not, because it wants to. He argues further that those who judge (and that is apt to be a majority) will form bad judgments upon incomplete information. To deny people such information is like saying: "You are incapable of judging, because you are ignorant; and you shall remain ignorant, that you may be incapable of judging." This argument might hold if men were entirely rational. But their reasoning is in fact embedded in a congeries of only partially rational values, interests and beliefs, which renders the problem of publicity much more difficult. Most importantly, however, Bentham errs in arguing almost entirely in terms of the electorate and what a lack of publicity might do to them, rather than in terms of the rule-making process itself. For surely the first argument may be discarded; talking "to the galleries" or "out of the window," which publicity of the proceedings invites, is not "the duty" of an assembly. As for the second, the confidence and assent of the people were not lacking in England when proceedings in the House of Commons were completely secret, nor are they lacking in the United States where much of the deliberative work is done in committees from which the public is excluded. As for the third and the fifth reasons, there are and were much better ways, not only with modern mass communications but even in the time of Bentham, for learning the wishes of the governed, and all the assembly needs to know for its work it can certainly read in the newspapers and learn from the constituencies. Thus only the fourth reason, namely, to enable the electors to act intelligently in elections—if we leave aside the sixth one as frivolous—seems to possess intrinsic merit. There can be little doubt that the more fully publicized a legislative proceeding, the more fully informed will the public be about it. In recent years, proposals in favor of broadcasting legislative sessions have advanced with this argument in mind. It is, however, arguable that this advantage is outweighed by the disadvantage which such publicity entails for the rule-making process itself. This aspect of the matter Bentham gave little attention to, in spite of his insistence that the true purpose of rules of procedure is to produce a majority and thus to aid in reaching a decision. It is perhaps significant that he never participated in parliamentary work.

Before considering the arguments further, let us face the fact that the deliberative process of rule-making has either been protected against publicity or it has been largely abandoned. In Britain rules are made in a magisterial and/or consultative process presided over by the Cabinet, and extended (for purposes of consultation) to the party and its Clubs. Party congresses in which a general program of policy is thrashed out in open debate provide a degree of deliberative process, but it is rarely extended to the rule-making as such. In the United States, France, Germany and elsewhere, as we have seen, the deliberative process has been maintained, but in committees from which the public is often excluded.

It is therefore undoubtedly correct to say that "legislation, as we nowadays conduct it, is not conducted in the open. It is not thrashed out in open debate upon the floor of our assemblies. It is, on the contrary, framed, digested and concluded in committee rooms. . . ." [28] This mode of work may have serious disadvantages; it gives the interests which "lobby" for legislation an undue advantage, for one thing. But the "justification for privacy is that its absence would enure to the injury of the public business." Why? Because it is of great importance in the rule-making process that all relevant arguments be set forth and discussed. This will not be done if the representatives must consider at every turn the reaction of the public and try to anticipate it. The making of rules is very difficult, since past shortcomings in the legal and political order have to be realistically analyzed and remedies have to be projected on more or less hypothetical expedient grounds. All rule-making deals, as Aristotle already knew, with contingent matters which often exhibit secondary and tertiary effects that are very hard to prognosticate. One could say that a certain degree of privacy is called for by the nature of the deliberative function, while it is at variance with the representative one. As one very experienced American legislator put it: "When a man thinks his words are to be repeated, he has an eye to the ultimate consumer. Instead of talking solely to those who are to make the immediate decision, he frequently talks with remote effects in mind. This would turn a public committee conference into a sparring spectacle for personal or party advantage." [29]

We are confronted with a conflict of values and interests. In order to strike a balance, the committee system has been evolved. The British Cabinet [30] and party procedure is another way of reaching a compromise; characteristically, the argument for cabinet secrecy is that the ministers "have one duty above all others: it is to speak the truth as they see it and pursue the public interest as they see it without fear." In either case a measure of privacy is provided for the deliberative process of rule-making. But the competing value of publicity is also recognized by the provision for an ultimate, if somewhat cut-and-dried, debate of the committee reports in the whole house (as well as public meetings of the committees). Thus the American Congress, the British Parliament, the

[28] Luce, 1922, pp. 150–151; the next quotation *ibid.*

[29] *Ibid.*

[30] So strong has been the propensity toward privacy (secrecy) in the case of the British Cabinet that only a summary is kept of the proceedings. That this is not quite as rigorous a prohibition as it once was can be learned from Morrison, 1954, who writes: "It is the summary of discussion that presents the most difficult task . . . judgment is needed in summarizing what the Ministers have said . . . the essentials of all points of view expressed are summarized with much accuracy and fairness." (Pp. 12–13.) The next quotation *ibid.*

French *Assemblée* and many other legislatures (rule-making bodies) provide for public debates *as well as* private deliberations.[31]

It is beyond the purpose of this book to discuss in detail the various institutions of parliamentary procedure, such as questions, interpolations, closure, and the rest, important though they be to parliamentary work. They all seek to organize and channelize discussion and debate and are as such patterned in accordance with the kind and amount of work done. But their functioning basically depends upon the existence and persistence of a measure of cohesion in a political community. When and to the extent that such community breaks down, all these devices become tools in the hands of the enemies of the political order, who will employ them for the purpose of obstructing the work of such an assembly, not *only* in its rule-making, but particularly in that field. Especially those who seek the destruction of a particular political order will go far in the direction of abusing the procedural devices of a deliberative assembly. From their point of view there is no ground for deliberation. This happened when the Irish opposition had decided to seek Irish home rule and eventually independence. In 1881, at a crucial juncture in that struggle, after the House of Commons had been treated to five days of obstruction, the Speaker called a halt by closing the debate on his own authority, and in a brief statement explained his reasons. "The dignity, the credit, and the authority of this House was seriously threatened, and it is necessary that they should be vindicated. Under the operations of the accustomed rules and methods of procedure, the Legislative powers of the House are paralyzed. A new and exceptional course is imperatively demanded; and I am satisfied that I shall carry out the will of the House, and may rely upon its support, if I decline to call upon any more members to speak, and at once proceed to put the question from the Chair. I feel assured that the House will be prepared to exercise all its powers in giving effect to these proceedings." Technically, this was the beginning of closure; actually, it was a striking case to show that the more a community is at one, the safer it is to allow it to bicker, to paraphrase a well-known statement of Balfour.[32] The history of the downfall of the Weimar Republic is replete with instances of such obstructionist tactics by Communists and National Socialists alike.[33]

Put abstractly, the proposition might be stated thus: the deliberative

[31] Recently, C. P. Snow has created a stir with his observations about "secret" politics, and more especially committee politics (which he distinguishes from "hierarchical," that is, bureaucratic, and "court" politics). These observations, especially in their lumping together of such politics in constitutional and totalitarian orders, smell a bit of the "lamp." Surely on Snow's own evidence there is a vast difference between the decision-making of committees set within the framework of a public and political responsibility to Parliament and the public, and decision-making not so framed. Snow, 1961, pp. 1–2.

[32] See for this Redlich, 1906, 1908, vol. III.

[33] Bracher, 1957.

process of rule-making, especially by a representative assembly, can function adequately only when a minimum at least of agreement on the values and beliefs of the community can be presupposed. The minimum is pragmatically signalized by the absence from a representative assembly of groups which are prepared to employ parliamentary procedure not for getting the work of rule-making done, but for preventing its getting done. In that case, a political order can be preserved only by substituting magisterial or consultative processes of rule-making, or by removing or silencing the disruptive elements. This general insight is at the basis of the outlawry of "subversive" movements and parties in many contemporary states. Such employment of the rule-making process puts the deliberative mode in jeopardy, even while it seeks to preserve it; but there may be no alternative if the political order is to be maintained. The Weimar Republic recoiled before such a prospect; the Basic Law of the Federal Republic transferred the decision to the government, as accuser, and the Constitutional Court, as settler of the dispute. It seems a more appropriate way of dealing with subversive groups than outlawry by those representatives who are not part of such movements.

The case of the British Speaker just recited shows that the presiding officer is decisive for the functioning of the deliberative mode of rule-making. As in other power situations, an ultimate arbiter is needed if political order is to be kept intact. Such a presiding officer as the Speaker of the House of Commons, the President of the French *Assemblée*, and other public persons of this type, down to the moderator presiding over a town meeting or an individual put in charge of any other gathering, are assumed to possess the penultimate right to intervene when the discussion and debate get out of hand. This power is implicit in all their intermediate discretion, such as "recognizing a speaker" or "ruling on" the propriety or impropriety of some act or word. In order to heighten their authority and give their decisions the weight of a settler of disputes, such presiding officers have been surrounded by more or less pomp and circumstance. Within the charmed circle of a deliberative assembly they are rulers, and subject to all the general laws of rulership (Chapter 10). From this fact has sprung the notion that the presiding officer should be "neutral," and should not even participate in the discussion (Bentham). His role has been likened to that of the obstetrician who assists, but does not direct. His power is all procedural, all over the how, not over the substance of what is said. "Any influence whatsoever that he possesses over the acts of the assembly, otherwise than subject to the immediate control of the assembly is just so much power taken from the assembly and thrown into the lap of this single individual." [34] There is much experience back of this notion of absolute neutrality; but it does not possess universal

[34] Redlich, 1906, 1908, vol. II, p. 168, citing Bentham, *Essay on Political Tactics.*

application. The American Congress and state legislatures have developed the institution of the speaker without trying to neutralize him, and with conspicuous success. The explanation is to be found in the difference between the two political systems. In Britain (and systems modeled on the British design) the government provides the legislative and hence the rule-making leadership, its ministers being present in the House. The presiding officers may, therefore, assume a role of almost complete neutrality. In American assemblies the ruling party needs leadership to assume the direction of the assembly; hence, the speaker seems the natural person to assume this function. But the need for an impartial umpire is so great that recurrent attempts have been made to have others, such as the floor leader, take over, especially since the President has become increasingly active in promoting a legislative program. Thus the Speaker could become neutral; but American politicians have not shown much inclination to do so. As long as the minority is solidly and effectively organized to defend its position, a presiding officer can effectively function as director of the rule-making process even when he has party background and support. Marvellous as is the dignity and authority which tradition and deliberation have conferred on the Speaker in the House of Commons,[35] it may well be doubted that more recently established political orders could hope to copy this institution effectively. What they can do is to organize effective leadership of the rule-making process by providing for a presiding officer who possesses ultimate authority and power over the proceedings.

In advanced contemporary political orders the process of rule-making is seen by many as submerged in that of policy-making. Actually policy-making is a much more general aspect of politics (Chapter 3) which may be manifest not only in rule-making, but in dispute-settling and measure-taking as well. Still, even today a good part of the most important policy decisions have to be transformed into rules (legislation) before they become working features of the political order. Thus the American policy decision in favor of social security was not operational until the requisite legislation was on the statute books. While law-making has ceased to be looked upon with awe, as it was in the seventeenth to nineteenth centuries, and is no longer seen as the very acme of politics, it continues to be of universal importance and is practiced wherever a functioning political order operates.

In summary, we may therefore say that rule-making is a basic political process, that it proceeds in four distinctive ways constituting typical models. These we designated as postjudicial (or more generally post-disputational), magisterial, consultative, and deliberative, suggesting a number of submodels besides. These models result from various combina-

[35] Jennings, 1940, chap. III, esp. p. 62.

tions of the four constituent elements of all situations of rule-making: persons, actions, circumstances and sanctions. In advanced political communities based upon cooperative procedures of government, the deliberative model is by far the most important, but the other models are by no means absent. They predominate in autocratically ruled communities. But the deliberative model becomes unworkable when the political community disintegrates or becomes divided by subdivisions which develop in anti-communities (Chapter 8). Since rule-making cannot be abandoned, one returns to the simpler models of consultative and eventually magisterial rule-making. The latter is typically associated with the taking of measures, and to this topic we now turn.

chapter

26 Taking Measures and Carrying On: Bureaucracy*

Away with the cant of "Measures not men." . . . If the comparison must be made . . . men are everything, measures comparatively nothing.
Canning, in the House of Commons

"A sound Conservative government," said Taper, musingly. "I understand: Tory men and Whig measures."
Disraeli, CONINGSBY

THE VAST BUREAUCRATIC structures of modern states with their tens of thousands of officials make them the "core of modern government." [1] But not only the government possesses a bureaucracy; any organization exceeding the size of the face-to-face group needs a bureaucracy, that is, a number of persons who will attend to the activities for which the organization exists. When looked at in this broad perspective, the bureaucracy becomes in a sense identical with the more active members of any given organization.[2] If that is the most general sense of the concept of bureaucracy, it becomes problematic what such

* The discussion of this chapter is concerned with the primary *function* of the officials constituting the bureaucracy, and the processes and behaviors involved. For corporate substance and its elite position see above, Chap. 18.

[1] This is the phrase suggested in Friedrich, 1937, 1950, where in chaps. 2 and 19 the functioning of this sort of complex bureaucracy is described and analyzed. Cf. also Merton et al., 1952, for a number of studies exploring the critical problems of this category of phenomena.

[2] In the case of commercial companies, this view requires the inclusion of the customers in the organization as the "less active" members, as is done by Barnard, 1938, chaps. 6 and 7, and many others; in the case of universities, students and other beneficiaries of teaching and research activities would similarly be part of the organization.

an expression as "bureaucratization" actually means. It would seem that in its general sense it means that in more and more spheres of life there exists a distinction between the "more active" and the "less active" and that each person is active in only one organization in the full sense of being a bureaucrat therein. Hence the sense of "alienation" and of "isolation" which is said to be associated with this development,[3] though also with the mere size of organizations. Total bureaucratization is a feature of totalitarian systems; it is the culmination of this trend. But before further elucidating these problems, we need to elaborate the basic issues associated with the function of taking measures and carrying on the work accruing in a political order. The previously discussed functions of defending the political order, of settling disputes and making rules, do themselves often involve the taking of measures. As stated before, these functions do not represent separate boxes between which human activities linked with a functioning political order can be divided and in which they can be stored away. They constitute an interrelated whole, namely, that order itself, and they are distinguished from each other by the kind of acts or behavior they consist in.

The "taking of measures" is a term meant to designate the concrete acts in a specific situation which constitutes a challenge to the political order. Measure-taking is a response to a challenge. It may occur in consequence of a rule that has been made, or prior to the making of a rule, or separate and apart from any rule-making. It may also occur as a follow-up to the settling of a dispute, in conjunction with arranging for such settlement, or again apart from it altogether. Whenever a more active member of an organization acts directly and concretely in a specific situation, not by settling a dispute nor by making a rule, he is "taking a measure," he is "carrying on the work." A customs man collecting a fee, a policeman arresting a vagrant, a university professor giving a lecture (in a public institution), a chief executive signing a bill, a superior issuing an order to his subordinate—these and thousands of other similar acts are part of this particular function of government. It will be readily seen that while public administration provides the bulk of such acts, the totality of such acts is not coextensive with the field of public administration.

What are the distinctive features of all these acts? They are the acts of the more active members who are said to "hold an office" and hence are called "officials" of the government. They are responses to a challenge: a person wants to bring goods across the border, another wanders about aimlessly, a third wants to learn, a group has steered a rule through "chan-

[3] It was stressed by Hegel as a feature of modern work conditions and elaborated upon by Karl Marx; *Entfremdung* has since been the subject of much Marxian commentary; cf., for example, Kojève, 1947, and Popitz, 1953; Franz Neumann, 1940, 1944, pp. 365ff. Franz Kafka has offered striking literary sketches of the human situation vis-à-vis bureaucracy.

nels," a letter of complaint has arrived in an office—these and countless similar challenges confronting the political order from day to day have to be met by appropriate responses. Such responses are appropriate if they "meet" the challenge by deploying the "power" at the disposal of the official. The settling of disputes and the making of rules are also responses to challenges, of course; but they meet the challenge not by a concrete measure, not by the action of an individual. Instead the former function indicates what would appear the right action for those to take who are engaged in the dispute, while the making of rules states what action shall in future be taken by persons in defined situations. In so far as measures occur in the execution of such rules, that is in so far as they "apply" a rule, they constitute judgments which bear a certain kinship to the judgments which occur in the settling of many disputes wherein rules are applied, namely, the judgment (1) concerning the "meaning" of the rule, and (2) regarding the concrete situation. This makes it at times difficult to distinguish between the taking of measures and the settling of disputes in highly elaborated systems where the problems of administrative law present themselves. But the fundamental difference between the two forms of governmental (and other organizational) activity is nonetheless there. Hence the attempt of certain political philosophers to relate the separation and distinction of powers to the pattern of a syllogism is applicable only to those particular political order systems which may be called constitutional: "a government of laws and not of men," as the slogan has it.[4]

In their attempt at formulating a general theory of social action, a group of social scientists, not especially concerned with government, pointed out that "in the theory of action the point of reference of all terms is the action of an individual actor or of a collectivity of actors." When describing an action, we are concerned with the orientation of that action.[5] Orientation calls for objects, the values, interests and beliefs in terms of which the action proceeds. Actions of the kind involved in measure-taking are oriented toward a particular kind of social object, governmental or political, in the sense of being positively related to the values, interests and beliefs of the members of the political community concerned. It cannot, however, be existentially asserted that all the measures taken by a particular individual actor or group of them are necessarily so

[4] Kant, in his *Rechtslehre,* made this suggestion, par. 45. Each state, he wrote, contains three powers, that is, it contains the general and united will in three persons: sovereignty, or the power to rule, in the person of the legislator; the executive power in the person of the governor (according to law); and the judicial power (giving to each his due according to law) in the person of the judge—"like the three propositions in a practical syllogism: the major premise [being] the law of that will, the minor premise the order to act according to the law, that is, the principle of subsuming one to the other, and the conclusion, which contains the judicial decision [the sentence], of what is right."

[5] Parsons, Shils, et al., 1952, p. 4.

oriented; they are apt to be and supposed to be, but they *may* not be. In this perspective, and because the orientation of the action cannot be made the criterion for determining its classification, measures of the order here under consideration can only be defined in terms of the *person* taking them. Hence the emphasis on the official or agent of the government or party or whatever other political unit is under consideration. The office which the official occupies is the complex of measures which are supposed to be taken in the pursuit of a particular set of objectives which constitute the function which the office serves. It defines the "role" which the official is meant to play in the political order.

It is therefore not surprising that we find officials (and a collectivity of such officials, to be designated as a bureaucracy) as a rule even in primitive societies. Anthropologists have recently addressed themselves to investigating some of these structures. Thus we read that "bureaucratic institutions did exist in Africa prior to European control." [6] But this statement is at once qualified by the remark that "perhaps it would be wiser to say that in some areas there was a strong tendency toward the development of appointive offices which served as agents of the central power." Such a development is not essential to the emergence of bureaucracy. The offices could be elective, and still be "bureaucratic"; again, they could fail to serve as agents of a central power and yet be bureaucratic. It is necessary to guard against such one-sided views by keeping clearly in mind that it is the broad function of *taking measures* believed to be oriented toward the objects of a given political order—the values, interests and beliefs of its members—which constitutes a bureaucracy. What we find, of course, is that in many of the more primitive, smaller communities the functions are merged. But the fact that a particular "chief" or subchief engages in judicial and legislative work does not alter the fact that he also and perhaps primarily takes measures; when doing so, he is part of a bureaucracy.

In his interesting study of Busoga bureaucracy, an anthropologist has not employed the terms in this fashion, but has rather associated the notion of bureaucracy with the coming in of British colonial administration.[7] He associates the notion of bureaucracy with the specific development of a system of offices occupied by persons without regard to their family ties, and rewarded by money in the form of salaries. This system did not arise locally, but was brought in by the colonial administration, as in so many other African territories, and it would, therefore, be more accurate to speak of British bureaucracy in Busogaland. If a developmental construct is made the basis of the concept of bureaucracy, and if this developmental construct is built upon European development, this procedure

[6] Colson, a, 1958, p. 42. Cf. also Fallers, 1958.

[7] Fallers, 1958, esp. chaps. 6 and 8.

can be justified. We prefer a broader basic approach. I should myself be inclined to argue that the system of "client-chiefs" which this writer so vividly describes is a particular form of bureaucracy; it certainly is regularized, centralized, hierarchical and based upon notions as to qualification for office which are deeply rooted in the values and beliefs of the Bantu people. Qualification for office is likely to be tied in with cultural considerations, anyhow. Among other elements, the question of charismatic call enters here. Especially in ecclesiastical organizations, but also in political organizations which do not clearly separate the secular and the religious spheres, such charisma may be decisive as a qualification for any office. Similarly, racial considerations may be important ingredients in the qualifications for office. (For the problem of charisma see above, Chapters 9 and 10.) The problem involved here cannot be evaded by oratory about the "best man for the job," because this kind of argument begs the question as to what constitutes goodness.[8]

Instances like these raise the question as to whether a developmental model of bureaucracy exists and can be empirically ascertained and detailed. Max Weber, in his well-known discussion of bureaucracy,[9] asserts it by employing the concept of a "fully developed" bureaucracy. Such a concept of full development embodies, in fact, a "normativization" and to some extent an "idealization" of the actual development which the administrative services underwent in the modern Western state. The terms which Weber employed, while highly suggestive, were not sufficiently and carefully related to the empirical evidence, because of his method of constructing "ideal types."[10] An empirical and comparative inquiry leads to a somewhat different construct, which will be discussed below. First there is required an answer to the question of whether the development of officialdom in other cultural contexts is sufficiently alike throughout for us to derive from such developmental tendencies a universal norm. I believe that such a proposition can be validated for the organizational aspects of this development; for the behavioral aspects the evidence is somewhat more contradictory.

The organizational aspects which stand out in the development of bureaucracy are three: hierarchy, differentiation and qualification. Hier-

[8] In composite political orders containing several nationalities, whether one belongs to one or another of these nationalities is necessarily a factor in the selection of officials on the basis of qualification. Cf. Friedrich and Cole, 1932, chap. 4, and Cole, 1949, chap. 5. Cole there also discusses the "veteran"—another culturally conditioned category which sets up a yardstick for qualification other than technical proficiency.

[9] M. Weber, 1925, part I, chap. 3, pars. 3–5, 126–130, and part III, chap. 6, pp. 650–678; the latter in translation in Gerth and Mills, chap. 8, pp. 196ff. For critical comment cf. Friedrich, a, in Merton et al., 1952, pp. 27ff. Cf. also T. F. Tout, 1916, pp. 192ff.; Bendix, 1954.

[10] See for that, Friedrich, 1961, pp. 19f.

archy means centralization of control and supervision (in which ought to be included any "centrally directed" decentralization, of course). The differentiation is one of offices and functions, or what sociologists would call roles. Qualification refers to these functions or roles and requires that the person playing a certain role must be qualified for it, typically in highly developed bureaucracies by adequate preparation and education. Thus, the evolution of bureaucracy in China exhibits these three traits very clearly, although the underlying political and social philosophy based upon Confucian ethics produced radically divergent behavior patterns on the part of the persons engaged in the taking of measures.[11] There was a "permanent table of organization cast in functional terms." There were typical distinctions, familiar from European administrative history, into household and public functions, central and provincial tasks, and the central administration "was portioned among a manageably small number of departments, each with specific and well-defined functions." A hierarchical "chain of command" structured the entire organization and placed it under the emperor as the more or less active head. It was centralized, but with controlled features of decentralization throughout the vast territory. Finally, of course, as everyone knows, China developed an elaborate system of education intended to qualify men for public functions by imbuing them with the spirit of Confucianism. Competitive written examinations tested the thoroughness of the education, and they were followed by other examinations for appointment and promotion. These were implemented by merit ratings and other devices intended to test the qualification for office.[12]

It would appear that similar developments may be traced in the bureaucracies of India, Egypt and other large governmental organizations. We are therefore justified in looking upon these three traits or characteristics as inherent in bureaucratic organization. A consideration of the function of taking measures reveals the inherent rationale. Since such measure-taking is addressed to specific situations whose challenge the action responds to and seeks to meet, absence of hierarchy would result in confusion and possible contradiction, as the same challenge met with different responses on the part of different officials. Such contradictions would arouse a sense of injustice, since justice presupposes the treating of equals (persons and situations) equally (Chapter 14). Likewise, the ab-

[11] It is therefore hardly surprising that M. Weber, with his Western model in mind, claimed it not to have been a "pure" type. The description above follows Pelzel, a, 1958, p. 54, to some extent. Cf. also Wittfogel, 1957, pp. 336ff.

[12] Pelzel, Wittfogel and others following M. Weber confound the behavioral aspects with the organizational ones, and thus conclude that the bureaucracy was less rational than the pure type. Such an evaluation identifies Western "rationality" with all reasoning, whereas the "reasoning" from Confucian principles necessarily leads to different results. Cf. Liu, a, 1959.

sence of a differentiation of offices and functions would mean that similar, even identical, situations would be treated by a number of officials, with consequent loss of consistency and waste of effort. Indeed, the differentiation of functions is merely a special instance of the universal law of the division of labor as developed by sociology and economics.[13] Finally, the effective handling of a measure is so obviously dependent upon the knowledge and understanding of the situation to which it responds that once the situation becomes recurrent, as it does in all operations of any size, the qualification principle appears as a matter of course. As can be seen from even these cursory remarks, the three aspects of the organizational development of a bureaucracy are not merely ascertainable by empirical evaluation of the evidence of the growth of bureaucracy, but can as readily be derived from the rationale of the actions involved.[14] We may therefore presume that wherever the need for the regular taking of measures brings a bureaucracy into being, bureaucracy will follow the developmental pattern toward hierarchy, differentiation and qualification.

The problems presented by the behavioral aspects of bureaucracy are considerably more complex, and although a certain similarity is observable, the behavior of bureaucrats varies widely in time and place without there being any clear-cut pattern of development. Nor is this fact to be wondered at. The behavior of all persons in a particular cultural context is bound to be moulded by the values and beliefs prevalent in that culture. Thus the Chinese official, motivated by the doctrine of Confucius and his followers, will be much more concerned with good manners than the Swiss official, while the latter, motivated by the teachings of Christianity and more especially (typically) by a Protestant and Pietist version of Christian beliefs, will be much more concerned with honesty and duty. Certain behavioral traits are, however, so advantageous for the efficient and hence successful performance of actions on behalf of the government that they will tend to impose themselves even against considerable handicaps deriving from culturally determined values and beliefs. Careful studies of bureaucracy, not only modern Western, but historical forms in various cultures,[15] tend to confirm the generalization derived from Western his-

[13] Arthur Salz, in his interesting article on the subject in *ESS*, starts from the proposition that "specialization is a technical term for all those phenomena usually subsumed under the phrase division of labor." The proposition can be reversed, as in the text. Cf. Durkheim, 1893; Marshall, 1870 (8th ed., 1922), bk. 4, chaps. 7–9; Schmoller, 1919, vol. I, pp. 346ff.

[14] Thus these phenomena provide a striking illustration for J. S. Mill's inverse-deductive method, which correlates empirical evidence with "the facts of human nature." Further evidence for the argument advanced in the text may be derived from a systematic examination of the rationale in terms of the several basic traits delineated in Chap. 1 above.

[15] Eisenstadt, a, 1956; a1, 1958, and a2, 1958; Corpuz, 1957; Cole, 1949; Liu, a, 1959.

tory that there are several behavioral traits that any government is apt to cultivate in a bureaucrat. Among these, the most important are objectivity, discretion, precision and consistency. In all four of these traits, the inner rationale is not difficult to discern, as it is clearly and closely related to the measure-taking function of administrative officials. These traits are also found among other than governmental bureaucracies. *Objectivity* is the quality which enables a person to transcend his personal views and prejudices and to see the "object" or situation "as it is." Since such objectivity will obviously lead to the taking of more nearly right actions, it will assist the measure in succeeding. It will also minimize controversy and conflict among the members of an organization.

Discretion is the quality which enables a person to be discreet, that is, to speak only of matters which will not embarrass himself, his associates and superiors. The need for discretion has repeatedly led to the adoption of some radical norm of secrecy, such as is expressed in the term "official secret." The adoption of norms of this type runs counter to the rule of publicity (Chapter 17) which dominates democratic societies, but it has recommended itself to governments and others as an inescapable means of counteracting a natural human tendency to communicate with family and friends about matters that are of special interest. The disadvantage of such talk is very considerable, even when the matter does not concern a foreign power, especially a hostile one. Therefore, discretion on the part of officials, though not necessarily secretiveness, will contribute to the effective functioning of the organization under all conceivable circumstances.

Precision, or accuracy, is desirable in all goal-directed actions. The arrow hitting the bull's-eye is the symbol of this desirable trait in all actors. Sloppy and careless measures are apt to be self-defeating. This trait of precision is particularly evident in technical operations. It affects, however, all kinds of activities. In officials, it particularly matters to all kinds of communications. A clear and precise answer to a question is appreciated not only in parliament, but by every member of the public. It may mean the difference between success and failure in interoffice communication. The need for and desirability of precision is so great that it often leads to pedantry and officiousness—familiar vices of all officials in positions of power.

Finally, *consistency* is paramount whenever someone is entrusted with the taking of measures, because erratic conduct not only arouses indignation among those thus treated, but "rocks the boat" in the sense of producing widely varying results and consequent disorder and confusion. The value of consistency has therefore always been recognized in all sorts of situations, and the governmental instance is supported by a great deal of evidence. Consistency has more especially been sought in the field of foreign affairs, where some writers have elevated it into an eternal principle of good policy.[16] But consistency, like the other behavioral traits, has its limits, and can become a vice if exaggerated. As the great Mommsen once wrote: "One can lose the right way by remaining too long on the straight path."[17]

Now all four of these behavioral traits may be comprehended under the general concept of *discipline*. Discipline is the means by which these traits are cultivated; after an initial period, self-discipline supplants discipline imposed from outside or from above. But men rarely rely exclusively on the self to produce the discipline which the effective functioning of a bureaucracy calls for. Nor would it be safe to do so. Long-established rules of prudence in the matter of discipline have been reinforced by the findings of modern psychology and its explorations of the "subconscious." It is not necessary to adopt a radical psychoanalytic position in order to appreciate the bearing of these studies upon the failures of the self in adjusting to the requirements of organization, and the consequent need for discipline.[18]

Almost all administrative hierarchies have well-defined rules of discipline according to which acts of supposed insubordination and other deviations from the approved conduct of officials are judged. It is therefore a sound scientific proposition to say that some rudimentary discipline is inherent in any hierarchy. What kind of conduct would be thus enforced is partly a question of the general beliefs prevailing in a particular political community. Officials are punctual in Britain and Switzerland, they are tardy in more southern latitudes. This seemingly small matter actually is expressive of a great many other detailed features of official conduct. Evidently it cannot be detached from cultural context, and such a yardstick as "rationality" is likely itself to be culturally determined, as it expresses a particular religious and convictional background which shapes the notion of what reason and rationality demand. This point, once made, is too obvious to require further elaboration, but Western students of bureaucracy have been inclined to overlook their own culture-bound notions of what is rational. The rationality of an administrative service cannot be wholly detached from the human context within which occurs the reasoning to which such rationality refers.

There is, however, a rationality in *things* which is derived from their

[16] Friedrich, 1938, chap. 5, where the difficulties resulting from the built-in partisanship and hence discontinuities in democratic governments are analyzed. Cf. also Morgenthau, 1948, 1954.

[17] Mommsen, 1864–1879, vol. II, p. 25: "Man kann auch dadurch vom rechten Wege abkommen, dass man zu lange auf dem geraden Pfade bleibt."

[18] The reverse danger for the development of the self through excessive adaptation, as depicted in analyses of the "organization man" and the "other-directed man," need not concern us here, though it has been a threat to humanism in all ages. Cf. Riesman, 1950, and Whyte, 1956; also Viereck, 1956, for a virulent counterargument and protest.

very nature and which imposes itself upon the human who tries to deal with them. It is the ultimate given which Machiavelli and the Renaissance so rightly insisted upon as the *necessità* inherent in the situations with which the person in politics is confronted. Technical considerations apart, there is much that imposes itself by dint of what particular situations call for. A basic proposition is that discipline is the more severe, the more dangerous and difficult is the task confronted by the organization, the requirement of speed being one of these exigencies. An army at war and business enterprises in highly competitive fields offer such examples of severe discipline; for the purpose of the entire enterprise or organization is likely to be defeated by delay and deviant conduct. The interrelation is fairly complex, because the degree of pressure for ironclad discipline must be related to the extent to which the conduct required by the discipline deviates from conduct under ordinary circumstances. At this point, the issue of "reason of state" arises—the disciplining of action on the part of all those concerned with taking measures on behalf of the community for the success and survival of the organization. Such "organization rationality" encounters much greater difficulties in a free society, the established constitutional mores of which are in conflict with what the situation demands, than in autocratic societies, especially those which, like the totalitarian regimes of our times, have emerged from and are dominated by revolutionary movements based upon a totalitarian ideology (Chapters 4 and 7). Old slogans such as the saying about ambassadors being "gentlemen going abroad to lie for the good of their country" provide folkloristic insight into this complex issue.[19]

It would be most interesting to have detailed empirical studies on the correlation between degrees of exigency and rigor of discipline as a guide to action, but most of this field is dominated by traditional notions, many of them outdated. The unforeseen secondary and tertiary effects of wrongly applied discipline have, in fact, produced a disinclination to face the problems of discipline at all, treating it as a taboo related to the equally dreaded "authoritarian personality" (Chapter 12). If one studies the history of administrative services, one cannot help being impressed with a change from severe to relaxed discipline. This is undoubtedly sound and related to the "progress of civilization" toward a more humane society. It is however also a consequence of the stabilization of society which reduces the conflict and thereby permits organizations of all types, but more especially governments, to operate with regard to ultimate rather than immediate satisfactions, and to perform their activities largely in conformity with the prevailing ethics of the community. The comparatively static condition of most governmental activities during peace and prosperity in the modern West has made it possible to subject all disciplinary

[19] For a discussion see Meinecke, 1924; Friedrich, 1957.

action against derelict officials to fairly elaborate judicial procedure. The main purpose of such procedures is to protect the official against the arbitrary exercise of the disciplinary power. Punishment of such an official cannot take place until he has been subjected to a regular judicial proceeding. Such elaborate procedure is not likely to be politically feasible under less settled conditions, except for the most severe sanctions such as removal from office. We shall elaborate this point below in connection with the discussion of how to bring about responsible conduct. Here we must first consider another issue, namely, that of morale as a supplement to discipline.

The discipline of administrative organizations is intimately related to their morale. When morale is high, the problems of discipline are greatly reduced. Morale and the need for discipline stand in inverse relation to each other, or more correctly put, morale helps to convert external discipline into self-discipline. The self, caught up in the feeling of dedication to group purposes, values and beliefs, adopts and imposes upon itself those behavioral rules of conduct which the conduct of the organization requires of him. Morale is indeed this sense of dedication to group ends. Military men have always been keenly aware of the importance of morale for achieving effective cooperation in fighting as well as other military activities, and they have under all kinds of cultural conditions developed elaborate techniques for developing and maintaining such morale. It is much more than "group persistence in the pursuit of collective purposes." [20] Such group persistence is one of the consequences of good morale, but morale itself depends upon an emotional commitment to shared purposes and ends, values and beliefs. Therefore, morale is intimately tied to situations which arouse and maintain such emotional commitment and loyalty, including inspirational leadership, a sense of common danger and an impressive ritual for the effective symbolization of such values and beliefs. The behavior of military and other fighting organizations works, of course, with all three of these components.[21] Civilian organizations and governmental units usually have to depend primarily upon the first of these factors. The capacity of superiors to inspire confidence and an emotional commitment to the task in their subordinates is therefore a crucial trait in all administrative hierarchies. The work could not be carried on without it. Modern students of administration have for this reason given increasing attention to cooperative techniques. Such techniques have proved especially important in international administration and in technical assistance programs in which the morale is difficult to develop and maintain because of the cultural diversities affecting the key behavioral traits of good dis-

[20] Lasswell in his article on "morale," in *ESS*.

[21] For a detailed empirical study of these several features of the morale situation, cf. Stouffer, 1949, esp. vol. II, pp. 105–191.

cipline.[22] Cooperative techniques of administration turn upon a true understanding of the nature of authority and of the importance of the capacity for reasoned elaboration (Chapter 12). It is a matter of making sure that the subordinates understand the reasons for the proposed action or policy decision. The problems of communication are often quite considerable, but they can be overcome in suitably cooperative patterns of administration.[23]

After these general observations on discipline, the discussion of the four behavioral traits, objectivity, discretion, precision and consistency, may be expanded. Objectivity, or disinterestedness, is closely related to expertness. Every craftsman is what he is by dint of his thinking in terms of the objective requirements of the particular job in hand. All taking of measures to get a job done will be operationally satisfactory to the extent that the measures are oriented toward a disinterested appraisal of "the facts." This simple statement of the matter at once reveals that its simplicity is deceptive; as has been shown, and is now generally recognized, there are many fields of activity in which the facts are not all apparent, let alone obvious. Governmental activity is value-oriented, and the valuational dimension is, especially in a pluralistic society, fraught with contradictions and conflicts of viewpoint. It is therefore much easier to state the trait of objectivity negatively in terms of disinterestedness, by specifying the interests which the operator *should not* allow to interfere. Broadly speaking, these would be the "private" interests which the public does not recognize as public. Thus in the typical Western Christian community the bias of family resulting from that interest should be avoided. There are however even here considerable variations, not only throughout Western society, but even within particular national communities. Another interest which is said not to be permissible is the interest in private monetary gain, and the broad norm of "honesty" is put forward in support of this view. But what if the official's action benefits not only him, but the class to which he belongs? A third private interest which is considered contrary to objectivity is that in a particular religion and its convictions. But here again the exclusion of the "interest" applies only in the case of minority groups, whereas the majority religion is not only supposed to be a justified interest, but is frequently made a prerequisite of qualification for office. Nor is this to be wondered at when the nature of political community is borne in mind (Chapter 8).

All these instances show that objectivity or disinterestedness is far from easy to circumscribe, nor will it do to call it an "ideal"—neither complete objectivity nor disinterestedness is wanted in a public official.

[22] Cf. Moulin, a, 1958; and Racine, a, 1958. Cf. also Montgomery, et al., 1959, for interesting case material.

[23] Cheever and Haviland, 1954, pp. 390ff.

For he must also be committed and vitally concerned. This issue has in recent years been argued especially in relation to certain phenomena such as the "neutrality" of the German officials and army officers. Here a group of men, raised in the tradition of objective disinterestedness, refused to take sides in the political conflicts that were rending the nation, and thus helped to make it possible for a subversive movement to overthrow the constitutional regime. Against such a position, it is argued that a public official *must* be committed to the political order of which he is a part. If this argument is sound, and we think it is, then the range of values implicit in the regime calls for the requirement of objectivity being expressed more precisely. It will be necessary to say that objectivity calls for considering the situation objectively within the framework of value reference provided by the organization or group. It is not absolute, but relative to the political order itself.

One is led into similar reflections when considering the trait we called discretion, or discreetness. Discretion, we said, is the quality which enables a person to speak only of such matters as will not embarrass himself, his associates and his superiors. The conflict with democratic beliefs, already noted, has led many writers to overlook the problems of discretion. Rules and regulations about secrecy have, however, always been important in connection with the taking of measures. It is an important facet of the distinction between it and rule-making; for rules must in the nature of things be made public, since it is manifestly unfair to expect anyone to follow a rule which he does not know about. In constitutional government, the actual process of rule-making itself is to a considerable extent public (above pp. 457ff.), but the rules themselves always have to be. Measures need not be; their specificity permits a varying degree of secrecy. Most private organizations also practice secrecy with regard to most of their work. Conversely, it is an important weapon in the hands of the government, if the need for control arises, to oblige such organizations to make public such matters as the sources of funds and expenditures.

The extent of what is to be kept secret varies between organizations and among different services of the government, and depends upon the nature of their work and the competitive or fighting position they are in. That commercial and industrial enterprises wish to keep secret their trade or manufacturing specialties is obvious. That a trade union wishes to protect its strategy from being known to the management it is fighting is equally apparent. Organizations engaged in propaganda are usually eager to keep secret the source of their funds, and organizations financing propaganda, their expenditures. When it comes to governments, the need for discretion is most apparent in the field of foreign relations, which in modern times has included an ever widening range of activities. But even in the strictly internal administration, the rivalries between different groups, the needs of situations in which the government is fighting crime, and the necessity of protecting the privacy of individuals in such fields as taxation and health indicate the range of issues the problem of discretion raises. The progressive inclusion of more and more aspects of industrial production in weapons manufacture has led to a very broad definition of official secrets, not only in private industrial plants, but in universities and research organizations, both private and public.[24] There is a certain danger in this development. It produces a tendency to distrust the government, because discretion provides a cloak not only for keeping secret those matters which should not be publicized, but also others which should. This argument applies not only to corrupt practices, but also to the airing of public policy issues. Dramatic instances, such as that of Admiral Sims's criticism of United States naval policy or "Billy" Mitchell's attack on air policy,[25] illustrate the need to set aside discretion when the issue is of sufficient importance. But the extent to which such criticism can be permitted presents one of the most delicate problems of administrative management. Generally speaking, public critics of their superiors have usually had to pay for their boldness by the loss of their position, or at least of promotion. This particular issue can, of course, arise only in constitutional systems where the public is supposed ultimately to determine public policy. Autocratic systems do not invite similar public criticism, because the public is not supposed to participate in the making of public policy anyhow. They are, however, as much afflicted as constitutional governments by another consequence of secrecy, and that is the tendency of persons on the inside to lose their sense of perspective and to believe that information is the more important the more secret it is. This distorted notion is the cause of much faulty intelligence work. It produces the further consequences that public officials, instead of concentrating upon the basic issues involved in policy decisions, become preoccupied with the "latest" inside reports.[26]

Discretion is, in view of all the foregoing, a desirable trait only if it is operative within limits. To determine these limits would be highly desirable, but to date it has been left largely to "feel"; enactments such as "official secrets acts" have furthered this tendency by inclusive and undiscriminating definitions. The continental tradition of the *Amtsgeheimnis* is similarly crude. It is clear, however, from what has been said that discretion is a needed trait of bureaucracy, and that its sphere of desirable

[24] Illustrative of this general trend are Britain's *Official Secrets Act*, 1939, and in the United States the *Espionage Act*, 1917, and the *Alien Registration Act*, 1940. The postwar intensification of the cold war in the fifties has produced the even more stringent U.S. *Internal Security Act*, 1951.

[25] Morison, 1942, pp. 183ff., Kittredge, 1921, *passim;* Burlingame, 1952, pp. 150ff.; Gaureau and Cohen, 1942, pp. 118ff.

[26] The "inside dopester" psychology, which also afflicts, for example, the investment field, has been commented upon with sagacity by C. P. Snow, 1961, pp. 72–73.

application depends upon the tasks, the situations and the nature of the political order.

Precision and consistency are closely related traits; a man who is precise is likely also to be consistent in the actions and measures he takes. We noted already that imprecision in speaking and writing leads to faulty communication, and such faulty communication impairs the activity, whether it be internal or not. If the subordinate does not understand what he is being asked to do, if the superior does not understand what is being reported to him, if the member of the general public fails to learn what is expected of him, these are so many breakdowns of administration; indeed the intended measures do not take place under such circumstances. The likelihood of such faulty communication is greatly increased if the actions involved are erratic, that is, lacking in consistency. Predictability is an important part of the smooth functioning of a bureaucracy, both in its internal and external dealings.[27] Such predictability is dependent upon precision and consistency as established traits of the bureaucracy. It results to a considerable extent from the knowledge (expertness) of the officials. For evidently a person who knows that a certain effect follows a particular cause or who understands the interacting concomitants of a given situation in their recurrent regularity will speak and act accordingly, regardless of the peculiarities of the situation. Such precise knowledge of a particular field of governmental activity is therefore a prerequisite not only for rendering an informed judgment concerning administrative actions in this field, but also for acting effectively, that is, for taking the needed measures in a precise and consistent way. This fact often arouses the hostile response (anger, indignation, and so forth) of the uninitiated outsider, and the familiar outcry about "red tape" and "paperasserie" is the result. For the consistent application of a rule, for example, closing the Post Office at a particular hour, appears as wanton "red tape" to the man who arrives a minute after the hour to deliver a (to him) important package. This trite everyday example depicts in its essentials the recurrent conflict between the regularity of the measures taken on behalf of an organization and the specific and detailed human situation to which it is applied. It reveals that precision and consistency, too, have a limit beyond which the heuristic value declines–they become "vices" rather than "virtues." The rigidity and pedantry of officials, not only of the government but of all large organizations, often produces very real handicaps and thwarts the effectiveness of the measures which are being taken. It has been said that a good administrator is one who not only knows the rules and follows them, but who also knows when to disregard them. We need detailed

[27] Some interesting work on the communication aspect of this problem has recently been reported by Deutsch, 1962, chaps. 4 and 6, but the issue of consistency as such has not been included in these analyses.

studies of the operation of this principle which would show what are the situations and conditions under which a discarding of consistency is sounder than its maintenance.[28] Similarly, we ought to know much more than we do about the degree of precision called for under varying conditions of measure-taking. There can be little doubt that the more fluid, not to say revolutionary and novel, the situation is in which the administrator finds himself, the less valuable are precision and consistency as traits of the bureaucrat. In highly stable conditions, the obverse would be true. Similarly, we may surmise that in a homogeneous context, where the values, interests and beliefs of the community are effectively integrated, consistency and precision will be more desirable, as well as more easily attained, than in a community of divided loyalties and extended heterogeneity.

This thumbnail sketch of the behavioral traits found in a bureaucracy shows that they do not allow of a simple one-directional developmental construct such as Weber's notion of a "developed bureaucracy" implies. For the traits themselves are not absolutes which can be treated in such a perspective. They are qualities of which a certain amount is desirable and found in actual administrative setups; they are closely interrelated traits of those in charge of taking the measures which the functioning of the political order requires.

It remains to draw the conclusions of the foregoing analysis for a general theory of bureaucracy. Such a theory must be seen within the general framework of decision-making outlined at an earlier point (Chapter 3). It was there said that a decision is a choice between one or several alternative courses of action or inaction suggested by a problematic situation. It is obvious that whenever a measure is taken, such a decision is involved, and the four behavioral traits of a bureaucracy that have just been delineated are traits which help rather than hinder such decision-making; the choice between several possible courses of action is assisted if the person making the decision is objective, discreet, precise and consistent. Cultural traditions which are adverse to the development of these traits will impede the establishment of an adequate bureaucracy and may have been responsible in the past for the failure to develop one.[29] Since industrialization requires an ever larger number of qualified bureaucrats to man the enlarging organizations, the educational problems may become formidable and raise the question of fundamental changes in the pattern of cultural values and beliefs. Several recent novelistic treatments of this issue, portraying as they do the clash of cultural traditions in their impact upon the tasks of an advancing industrial society, provide no real solution, because some optimistically assume that the problems of culture

[28] Cf. the interesting case in Montgomery, 1959, pp. 204–15.

[29] Corpuz, 1957, has given a good analysis in these terms for the Philippines.

conflict can be avoided by sticking to the simple problems of everyday living such as using a long-handled broom, while others pessimistically suggest that the reforming enthusiasm of Western (American) persons necessarily do more harm than good by disturbing the cultural equilibrium.[30] Actually, only some such procedure as the colonial powers employed in developing native talent for the vast tasks of measure-taking (and thus making an industrial society possible) can do the job. Once the impetus provided by the power potential of a colonizing power is no longer actively engaged in such a process, the most viable alternative for providing the needed incentive of cultural transformation seems to be the inspirational leadership of a person building a single mass party with the capacity for effective integration. Such has been the process in a number of different countries and contexts. One of the most striking instances is that of Puerto Rico, where after a period of stagnation, even decline,[31] Muñoz Marín succeeded in building a broad popular support for a party concentrating on economic development within a suitable framework of constitutional freedom. The results have been remarkable, and the role of Muñoz Marín decisive, but inadequate attention has been given to the role of a bureaucratic elite who have been prepared to abandon the traditional cultural attitudes impeding effective administration and have developed the syndrome of behavioral as well as organizational characteristics of an advanced administrative system (Cf. Chapter 22). Comparable trends can be observed in a number of other countries, including Egypt, India and Tunisia.

The growth of such a bureaucracy, culturally conditioned as it is, has itself then cultural ramifications. This consequence of modernization has often been overlooked. It was perhaps natural for people to assume that it would be possible to take over the technical and industrial achievements of the West without getting involved in the culture of the West, or at least in those aspects of Western culture which are closely related to the organizational and governmental conditions of these achievements. These are, however, closely bound up with each other. Hence more recently "foreign aid" has had to face the fact that administration was vital if such aid was to achieve lasting results. A large number of projects have been initiated through institutes and schools of public and business administration to provide the missing link. Unfortunately, these have often themselves not been inspired by any real insight into the basic conditions of Western administration, and hence have tried to bring techniques to persons who had not yet achieved the basic adjustments which the be-

[30] Burdick and Lederer, 1958, is a striking instance of the first; Greene, 1955, of the second variety of approach.

[31] Tugwell, 1947; cf. Friedrich, 1958, for the sequel.

havioral traits presuppose and upon which the elaboration of the organizational features of the existing bureaucracy depends. As a result, the graduates of such schools have gone forth to engage in the taking of measures which were derived from decisions inspired by the traditional cultural alternatives, rather than those "hidden" alternatives which an advancing industrial society calls for. Therefore, to repeat what was just said, only the inspirational leadership of an integrative mass party with an appropriate ideology of programmatic change can provide the needed incentives for such a new bureaucracy.[32]

The feedback of a bureaucratic development has long-run implications which have occasioned the extended discussion over bureaucratization alluded to at the outset of this chapter. If an ever larger number of persons in any given society develops the traits which an operative bureaucracy calls for, such persons will in turn constitute an ever larger subculture. This subculture as it expands tends to engulf the culture as a whole. The most striking instance can be seen in totalitarian societies at the present time. In countries such as the Soviet Union everyone, except the "toilers in factory and field" (and even these, in a sense), has become a bureaucrat. Thus totalitarian societies engender total bureaucratization; all persons are caught up in one all-engulfing organization which encompasses the party and the government.[33] The earlier view of nationalization and socialization had overlooked this organizational aspect of the matter. It has revealed itself in this century as a formidable force, making for drabness and lack of differentiation in personal development.

A centrally directed and planned economy requires a very large number of public officials; indeed, since all economic functions are part of the public enterprise, a distinction is difficult to draw between functionaries and others; every function is a public function. Such total bureaucratization is implicit in the socialization of all economic activity, but it was accomplished under National Socialism through the process of *co*ordination (*Gleichschaltung*), which was also a process of *sub*ordination of all organizations, economic, cultural and even fraternal, as well as political. By this procedure, the National Socialists sought to apply what they called the leadership principle throughout the political community. According to it, the presidents, chairmen, secretaries, and so forth, all became "leaders" of their organizations who were appointed by the government; as such they exercised the same kind of "limitless," that is, "ill-defined," power within their organization which Hitler claimed over the system as a whole, and conferred upon his subordinates throughout the hierarchy. It is apparent that this process of assimilating all intermediary

[32] Cf. Wilhelm, a, 1955; Montgomery, a, 1959, pp. 322ff.; C. H. Moore, a, 1960.
[33] See Friedrich and Brzezinski, 1956, chap. 19, and the literature cited there.

organizations to the governmental bureaucracy made them in effect part of it.[34] In Italy, the corporative "state" served a similar purpose, as far as the economy was concerned; all organizations, whether business corporations or labor unions, were made part of one hierarchical structure with the Duce at the head.[35] The Soviet Union has developed yet another term, "democratic centralism," to designate the total bureaucratization. In all these totalitarian systems there exists, however, a recurrent conflict between the party bureaucracy and the governmental bureaucracy. In the last analysis, the dynamics of these orders makes the party bureaucracy, the *apparatschicki* of the Soviet Union, the predominant bureaucrats whose measures take precedence.[36] Nonetheless, the sharp dualism of party and governmental bureaucracy creates serious problems of the two bureaucratic cadres fighting for supremacy. It is probably too much to say that this conflict constitutes an abandonment of the centralization of control which was shown to be constitutive of a bureaucracy, but it unquestionably endangers it. The continuous struggle over "decentralization" in the U.S.S.R. is part of it.

Such a development endangers the very goals for which the bureaucracy was originated. The recurrent organizational breakdowns, such as are portrayed by the struggle in the Soviet Union over centralization and decentralization and over the cult of personality, are merely reflections of the underlying issue of "excessive" bureaucratization. Hegel may have been wrong in favorably contrasting the highly developed Prussian bureaucracy with the British constitutional order in which the bureaucracy was honeycombed by corruption.[37] But the British paid him the (unintentional) compliment of reforming their civil service later in the century and thus supplying the "neutral" and "objective" public service which Hegel had considered an essential feature of a well-ordered political system. But Hegel was more certainly right in insisting that this bureaucracy ought to be restricted to a limited field of public decisions, leaving the remainder to "civil society." He was speaking in the tradition of liberalism and Christianity, and his culture-bound argument is based upon metaphysical reasoning which does not convince or even persuade us any longer. But it contains an important kernel of truth, which it owes to its being a manifestation of empirical facts, that is, of experiences which possess historical validity. These experiences were embodied in the administrative services of the modern Western state for which Hegel spoke better than he knew. Marx's bitter denunciation of bureaucracy failed to take into account the universal kernel of truth which Hegel's tradition-

[34] Franz Neumann, 1942 and 1944, pp. 365ff.; G. Reimann, 1939, chap. 14; Morstein-Marx, 1936, pp. 114ff.

[35] Salvemini, 1936, *passim;* Schmidt, 1938, *passim;* Germino, 1959, pp. 42ff.

[36] Fainsod, 1953, pp. 152ff.; B. Moore, 1954, esp. chap. I; Djilas, 1957, esp. pp. 70ff.

[37] Hegel, 1832, 1956 and 1833, 1955, pars. 289ff.

bound and hence class-influenced arguments contained. By imagining that a future socialist society could escape from the universal need for administration, for the taking of measures in the sense here described, Marx and his followers laid the foundation for an over-development of bureaucracy. Marxism in practice has meant total bureaucratization, which has brought about a society diametrically opposed to the free society Marx himself had dreamed about in which the state would "wither away" and there would be only "administration." For it is precisely this function which has been the universal task of all bureaucracies in the broad functional sense here suggested. There cannot be any political order, socialist or other, in which there is not a taking of measures for public purposes.

chapter

27 *Negotiating a Political Bargain*

A bargain is a bargain.
ENGLISH PROVERB

It is generally better to deal by speech than by letter; and by the mediation of a third man than by a man's self. . . . In all negotiations of difficulty, a man may not look to sow and reap at once; but must prepare business, and so ripen by degrees.
Bacon, ESSAYS, XLVII

SO FAR WE HAVE DISCUSSED the operations of persons participating in the governing process as if they operated as part of an integrated whole, the government and its various subdivisions. Their power, while both consensual and coercive, was predominantly seen as flowing through a center and thus possessing unity. But as we saw earlier in the analysis of power and more specifically in the course of the discussion of influence (Chapters 9 and 11), the entire field of operations involving negotiation and compromise provides occasions for the exercise of power in which consent and constraint are intermingled. Power in such situations manifests itself in proposals and counterproposals and all the other techniques of diplomacy. It also manifests itself in threats and counterthreats and the complex maneuvers of the "strategy of conflict." [1]

[1] This suggestive term provides the focal point for Schelling's brilliant analysis, offered in 1960. As will be seen, the discussion which follows owes much to his work, but it will be less concerned with the aspect of deterrence (threats) and will treat as much of the negotiation inside political systems as of their projection outward. It will also draw to a larger extent upon historical materials—a great many of the most penetrating insights into the tactics of negotiation having been developed by "political" historians.

The kind of power situations which produce bargaining are more or less balanced. Typically, such a situation produces a confrontation of power-handlers and -holders who are to a degree independent of each other, but who pursue aims and who have interests that may be common, complementary, divergent or mutually exclusive (contrary).[2] Negotiating a bargain will suggest itself to such relatively independent power-handlers in all these instances. The most characteristic "field" for such operations is, of course, an assembly in which one or more of the functions of government are at stake. In modern constitutional systems, the legislative body has developed elaborate regularities of behavior embodied in rules of procedure, whether explicit or customary. Such rules have been evolved over long periods and testify to the importance which attaches to the art of negotiating an effective bargain. In a sense these rules of procedure constitute an internal parallel to the elaborate codes of diplomatic conduct which formalize the relations between states. There is nothing fixed or final about either of these sets of rules; they continue to evolve in response to shifting constellations of power and technology. They also seem to some extent affected by other cultural factors, but the relation is not clear, and has often been overstressed.

It has been suggested that negotiating should be clearly and sharply distinguished from bargaining. Thinking in economic terms, where a bargain in the market place need not entail any kind of negotiation, an economist has recently pointed out that "only certain exchange transactions are featuring negotiation, although all may be viewed as instances of bargaining." [3] This would mean that negotiation is a species of bargaining. But when one considers that a bargain may be negotiated, but not a negotiation bargained, it becomes clear that negotiating is not a kind of bargaining, but a particular procedure adopted in seeking to arrive at a bargain. Typically, negotiation involves meeting with other power-handlers or their representatives, either in person or by direct communication (in writing or by telephone, for example), and putting forward proposals and counterproposals in a process of give-and-take involving

[2] The incomplete analysis of the variety of possible interests is one of the few weak points in Schelling's work; cf. esp. p. 11, where only conflicting and common interests are mentioned. As far as these two situations are concerned, it may be best to see them not as absolute alternatives, but as spread over a scale with completely exclusive (contrary) and common interests as the two extremes. In the middle would be situations where the gain of one side is indifferent to the other.

[3] Stevens, a, 1958, p. 78. For the recent increase in interest among economists in these processes, cf. also Chamberlain, 1955, and Shackle, 1949, chap. VI. Stevens seeks to develop a general theory of negotiation on the basis of negotiations in labor relations (union contracts); he recognizes that concurrent principles may govern negotiation in intranational and international political relations. His "formal analysis is intended to be applicable to negotiations of many sorts." See for further comments on this score below, p. 499.

all the different ways in which power may be employed. Negotiation may employ the threat, but the threat is typically a tool of deterrence which may also lead to a bargain, but not by negotiation.[4]

Negotiation is often surrounded by a great deal of ceremony. Such ceremonial does not only serve to set the stage, but also allows for a degree of formalizing the relation between the negotiating powers. The peace pipe which Indian chiefs used to smoke with emissaries from other tribes before entering into a negotiation is a vivid symbol of this dual function of the negotiation ceremonial. Such ceremonial may then in turn become the subject of protracted negotiation. Before the peace negotiations after the Thirty Years' War could begin, many months were consumed in trying to iron out the ceremonial questions of precedence and who could talk with whom. While the war went on its weary way, Spain and France and Hapsburg wrangled over who could sit where, and eventually a compromise had to be arranged according to which negotiations were carried on in two separate cities. If a general peace conference were to be arranged now, similar questions would have to be resolved; for as the Geneva Conference showed, the question of how to treat the East and West Germans would be crucial, as would that of who might represent China. Diplomatic codes are meant to reduce the need for this kind of bargaining as much as possible.

We have spoken of a balance of powers as typical for the setting in which negotiation occurs. This is actually a rather inaccurate way of describing the situation, if "balance" is meant to refer to the comparative power status of the negotiators. Many negotiations are carried on between powers and power-handlers of very unequal status. It is the constellation which determines whether a particular issue is negotiable or not. In fact, frequently the near equality of the power status of the negotiators may make it especially difficult to negotiate effectively, as the negotiations concerning the limiting of the arms race and the restricting of nuclear weapons have painfully reminded us. What then are the features of a political constellation—or, analogically and *ceteris paribus*, of economic and other social ones—which invite negotiation as an effective mode of operation? They are four.

Besides two or more powers, there needs to be a pattern of interest (objective) that affects both (or several) parties. Such an interest pattern is typically composed of shared and conflicting interests. The shared ones may be common or complementary, the conflicting ones may be divergent or contradictory or even mutually exclusive. Thus the protracted negotiations at the end of a war which are meant to establish peace are characteristically informed by all five of these interests: the common interest being the reestablishment of nonwarring relations between the

[4] Much of Schelling's work is concerned with this mode of bargaining, which may be called a kind of tacit bargaining.

states concerned in the negotiations. Complementary are those interests, such as the reestablishment of trade, in which effective exchange of goods and services benefits the contractants; conflicting are the interests of victorious allies who may disagree on how to share the territory or reparations of the vanquished; contradictory are the interests of victor and vanquished in territory and other spoils. Any great peace conference provides ample evidence for the complex pattern of interests and the enormous range of negotiation involved in their accommodation.[5]

Besides the powers and pattern of interest, there needs to exist a minimum of community (Chapter 8) and that corresponding minimum of mutual confidence which is presupposed in all promises. Oftentimes, the negotiating parties have a great deal more confidence than this minimum required for negotiation. It is also frequently possible to increase this confidence by the method of negotiation itself; indeed sometimes negotiations are initiated in the hope of finding a common ground that would provide a basis for broader agreement. This hope has no doubt been involved in the protracted *pourparlers* in connection with the limitation of armaments and the settlement of the Berlin situation. As these instances show, there is always present in such cases the danger that the opposite result might ensue: long discussions leading to no satisfactory basis of negotiation enhance the tension and aggravate the conflict which the negotiations were supposed to resolve. It must however be remembered that even though there never were any real expectation of concluding a satisfactory agreement, powers find themselves at times obliged, or if not obliged then at least persuaded, to initiate negotiations simply because other members of the larger community expect that an effort be made to discover a satisfactory settlement.

Finally, negotiation presupposes that the issues at hand are sufficiently flexible, and that as a consequence there is sufficient ground for assuming that a substantial improvement might result for each party to the bargain by entering into negotiation. When parties in a multiparty system enter into coalition, they are in effect concluding a bargain after extended negotiation. One of the strictly numerical aspects of these bargains is the number of cabinet posts which each may receive. Logic might suggest that this number should be proportional to the number of votes each party received in the election or that it commands in the assembly. But while this may be the eventual outcome, it often is not. One of the parties may be more eager than another to be in the government; a small party may be the least eager, and yet essential for a majority; talent might be unevenly distributed among the several party aspirants, and so forth. Protracted negotiations are required before the question can be satisfactorily settled for all concerned. The shared common interest in forming a government, their complementary interest in each having some posts,

[5] Nicolson, 1933; Hill, 1905, pp. 282ff. and 537ff. for Louis XIV and Frederick II.

and their contradictory or even mutually exclusive interest in a particular ministry all come into play. But of course, it is not only a question of the number of posts, though this is usually the toughest issue; the outcome has over the years occasioned an increase in the size of cabinets as such negotiators have tried to accommodate conflicting demands. There is also the question of which party gets what posts, which in turn is linked with the problem of the policies to be pursued by the coalition. Having fought each other in the election campaign, and in this connection stressed the divergence of their policy preferences, rival parties are often hard put to find satisfactory formulas for a common policy. Policies may be traded against posts and a bargain may be struck at the expense of the electorate.[6] What is patent, and what illustrates the fourth condition (flexibility) of the effective operation of negotiations, is that each party enters into the fray with a distinct hope of securing a maximum number of posts of highest significance, while keeping its policy program virtually intact. Its inevitable failure to do so creates a mortgage of ill-will toward its partners and of disappointment and suspicion among its following (including disappointed job-seekers), which dooms a coalition to being a weak government.[7]

The flexibility of the situation and the expectations built upon it by the negotiators suggest that numerous decisions will have to be taken in the course of a negotiation. These decisions are interdependent in that what one of the participants decides will necessarily affect what the other does. Game theory, which has yielded striking results in situations of "pure conflict," has not produced comparable insights where conflict is mixed with sharing and where a communal bond unites the antagonists. "Though the element of conflict provides the dramatic interest, mutual dependence is part of the logical structure and demands some kind of collaboration or mutual accommodation, . . ."[8] it has been said. This interdependence is not of the mechanical order of interdependent vari-

[6] These processes have only recently been subjected to a detailed scholarly analysis in a series of studies conducted under the direction of Professor Dolf Sternberger. See his own work, 1956, as well as the related ones of Roth, 1951, Neunreither (MS), 1956, and Wildenmann, 1954.

[7] The argument that therefore a multiparty system is to be avoided at all costs often overlooks the fact that a single party is obliged to engage in similar negotiations to accommodate sectional and professional divergences in its own ranks. It nonetheless has the great advantage of a negotiation within the context of the stronger communal bonds which the party as such provides. The argument should therefore focus on this aspect of the matter.

[8] Schelling, 1960, p. 84. Cf. the entire chap. 4 of this work for an attempt at developing a theory of "interdependent" decision. I would suggest that these situations are indeterminate "games," partly because it is not a matter of the structure of such situations being "logically" what it is, but *existentially* so; and partly because the psychological factors involved, such as expectations in infinite regression, defy mathematical analysis. There is nothing necessarily quantitative about a psychological given. See also the interesting analysis in Iklé and Leites, a, 1962.

ables, but turns upon complex patterns of unpredictable feedback. The conclusion of any negotiation is hence unpredictable and indeterminate.

The indeterminacy of genuine negotiations—there are of course instances where negotiation is put on for facade effect, while in fact all parties have agreed and are putting on a show—places a very high premium upon the skill of the negotiator. Not only the effective deployment of the various open power resources at his disposal (or at the disposal of his principal, if he is an agent), but also the adroit use of influence and the anticipated reactions associated with it (Chapter 11) are part of such skill. Besides these power resources, authority and legitimacy play a significant role in the effort at persuasion which all effective negotiating involves (Chapters 12 and 13). Does the negotiator speak with authority? Does the power or powers he represents possess legitimacy? These and related questions may determine the success or failure of a negotiation. The secrecy to which a great deal of effective negotiating is subjected is characteristically motivated in part by a desire to avoid all questioning of the authority and/or legitimacy of the negotiators. A negotiator may lose out if his right to offer or even to discuss certain terms becomes the subject of public controversy. This circumstance often prevents, in cases where hotly contested issues are at stake, the opening of negotiations in spite of urgent necessity; no one cares to take the risk which premature disclosure would entail. A posture of threats and counterthreats which are openly avowed and in keeping with the prevailing values and beliefs may recommend itself to the antagonists in spite of their possibly greater chance at mutual accommodation in the process of negotiating a practical bargain. The Berlin situation provides a striking illustration; a number of plans for mutual accommodation have been put forward by private parties, but they have not so far become negotiable, because of the dangers involved in any kind of publicity, even by way of rumor.[9]

It has at times been suggested that bargaining is the typical mode of procedure of traditional societies, while "conventional" ones use "legal" modes which are adopted by convention.[10] A contrast of this kind cannot readily be maintained. Negotiation is a very ubiquitous mode of political operation in every kind of political system. Many a major decision is preceded by negotiating for a bargain by the affected parties. This fact is of particular importance in the field of legislation and policy formation. Not only do officials of the various departments of the administration

[9] There is, of course, also the danger of suggesting weakness, which Schelling, 1960, pp. 36f. and elsewhere, notes, but this danger could be coped with by adequate postures of a military nature.

[10] Binder, 1962, pp. 227ff. This author recognizes of course that bargaining is not an "exclusive" feature of traditional societies, but he believes it to be "often restricted to electoral and parliamentary operations" in a conventional system, while in a traditional one "it permeates all phases of political life" (p. 228). As our illustrations and analysis show, it is the same with other systems. The difference is not in the fact of bargaining, but in the "terms of trade."

negotiate with each other in more or less formal procedure, but they in turn negotiate with the legislature and the affected interest groups, which in their turn negotiate with each other. In the course of such multifarious activity a great variety of bargains are struck, all involving "interdependent" decisions. This fact is patent in constitutional systems, where much of this negotiating is attended by extensive publicity (in spite of the secrecy which surrounds much of the detail); it is demonstrable in autocratic systems, including totalitarian dictatorships, whenever the documentary records become available for research. This fact has been obscured by the ultimate decisional power of the dictator; but the various power-holders and -handlers who operate on the lower echelons of the hierarchy are continually engaged in far-flung negotiations.[11] Whenever the four features of the constellation that have been described are present, negotiations are likely to take place. The situations are of the greatest variety, but in certain fields the modes of operation for carrying them on have been formally institutionalized to a considerable extent. The elaborate rules of procedure which modern parliaments have evolved (and which have, like Robert's *Rules of Order*, been followed by many other bodies) are such institutionalized operational codes. Their ultimate purpose is to enable a composite group to reach a decision, that is to say, to strike a bargain between contending participants. In the words of the Marquess of Hartington, spoken when discussing closure in the House of Commons in 1882: ". . . the privilege of speech is a privilege which the House permits to be exercised for its own instruction, for its own information, in order to form its own opinion, and . . . is not a personal privilege to be used irrespective of the convenience and efficiency of the House. . . ." It is the business before an assembly such as this that determines the rules governing speech and debate. Confronted by such formalization of the negotiating process, the parties at interest invariably retreat into more confidential and less formal settings, such as committees, party caucuses, and the like. For the compromise which must be reached if the bargain is to be struck is hindered by such formal proceedings. But when the record is inspected (provided there is one), it turns out to be a record of negotiations following their characteristic course. Even so confidential a body as a cabinet spends a great deal of its working time in negotiations among the members[12] which are subject to certain restrictions, usually of a conventional sort. Thus threats, which are an important factor in international and party political negotiations, are usually excluded from negotiations in groups which have close communal bonds. Techniques of negotiation may, however, themselves pro-

[11] Cf. Friedrich and Brzezinski, 1956, and literature cited there.

[12] Morrison, 1954; biographies like that of Disraeli by Monypenny and Buckle, 1910–1920, provide excellent illustrations. For a comparative analysis of parliamentary procedure, cf. Friedrich, 1950, chap. XVII.

vide opportunities for at least the threat of breakdown. A most striking illustration is the filibuster in the United States Senate.

Whereas publicity is the typical feature of negotiations leading to rule-making, even though often circumvented in the early stages by both ministerial and parliamentary power-wielders, negotiations accompanying the administrative process and culminating in the taking of specific measures are usually secret. To the extent to which they concern personnel this secrecy is necessary and imposes itself out of regard for the unsuccessful candidates. Personnel choices are especially difficult to negotiate where professional and personal qualifications are intermingled. The design of this type of negotiation is familiar to professors, since most of them have had to participate in complicated negotiations for the promotion of their junior colleagues and the calling of outsiders. The initiation of the negotiation is automatic when a vacancy occurs. After a search, various proposals are put forward and debated at length in the in-group of professionally competent judges. The negotiation proceeds on the not always realistic premise that all the participant negotiators are equally competent to form a professional judgment and that all are motivated by the desire to secure the most competent man. But judgments differ and call for a subtle process of mutual persuasion, often involving all the devices characteristic of political bargains. After agreement is reached, another round of negotiations is frequently involved in securing the assent of colleagues in other fields sitting on a superior body, as well as that of the administrators. Eventually, after all these several power-holders have reached agreement, a final negotiation is needed to secure the acceptance of the post by the person who has been chosen. This familiar procedure is recalled in its broad outlines because it is a close analogue to what goes on in administrative offices of government on all levels. The entire process is nonpublic in most instances, although there exist points at which a broader public is taken into confidence. The interests to be compromised are constitutive of the academic or other professional community which is confronted by the need for action; contrary to what is often assumed, the nonpersonal nature of the interests, as well as their completely nonquantitative character, often sharpens the conflict. Unless great care is taken, such negotiations may embitter the personal relations in such a professional group and have a long-range disruptive effect which is more damaging than the choice of a less competent man. The result is often a compromise in favor of the colorless candidate whose major qualification, apart from an average competence, is his lack of enemies.[13]

[13] This process has been perhaps most skillfully described by C. P. Snow in a number of novels dealing with academic appointments, notably *The Masters*, 1951, and more recently *The Affair*.

But the choice of personnel is only the most dramatic of the types of decision which involve in-group negotiations. It helps to uncover a distinctive aspect of most negotiating for this sort of bargain, and that is the preoccupation with the balance of power within the group itself. Economists have, in their interesting studies on negotiation and bargaining, given relatively little attention to this aspect. For typically the bargaining in the market place is object-related; a house is bought for a certain price and the bargain is concluded. Neither party is likely to have further dealings. But in closed groups—and this holds for legislatures as much as for administrative units—the success in negotiating bargains becomes itself a factor in the evolving power struggle. Recurrent effective bargaining gains a man a predominant position, and enhances his authority as well as his power; it may strengthen his influence to the point where negotiations become facade for a decision which he actually makes on the basis of consultations thinly disguised as negotiations. As a consequence all such negotiating is subject to the general propositions concerning power and influence developed earlier (Chapters 9 and 11).

It will be readily seen that negotiations in such closed groups as academic departments bear a closer resemblance to international bargaining than does the bargaining in the open market and similar constellations. Typically, the participants cannot escape from the closed group. They may adopt a policy of isolation, but such isolation is rarely "splendid" in the long run. Failure to share in the rounds of negotiation which precede a political bargain simply means loss of status and eventually loss of position altogether. It is a counsel of despair.

Before we turn to a more general statement of the negotiation procedure it seems therefore advisable to deal with some specific points concerning negotiation in international operations. It has been rightly observed that bargaining is not restricted to adversaries; that it also occurs among allies and friends.[14] We are prepared to go further and assert that it more frequently shapes the relations between allies than between adversaries. As a typical example, we might take the negotiations involving the entrance of Great Britain into the Common Market.[15]

Once the British government had reached the decision to enter the Common Market, if possible, a number of special issues presented themselves, more particularly those arising from existing Commonwealth relations, from the commitments made to the participants in the free trade area (EFTA), from the needs of former dependencies and from the precarious position of British agriculture. The situation was further complicated by the considerably less than enthusiastic response to this plan

[14] Schelling, 1960, *passim.*

[15] Young and Robinson, a, 1962, have given an interesting analysis of these negotiations as a case in decision-making.

on the part of De Gaulle, and the critical and unhelpful attitude of the opposition party in Great Britain. All these issues had to be handled and compromised in protracted negotiations, if the original intention of the British government were to be realized. Fortunately, the United States maintained its favorable attitude toward the move in spite of certain obvious economic disadvantages; indeed the United States government seized the initiative and secured from the Congress broadened powers of negotiation in the foreign trade field, in order to be able to cope with the range of issues involved. In the end, no bargain was struck, though the negotiations had granted more to Britain than anyone would have predicted, and yet notably less than Her Majesty's government had hoped to secure. No comparable negotiated bargain is conceivable with the Soviet Union or Red China. The respective positions are too rigidly fixed, and the communal bonds are too feeble to provide leeway for effective negotiation, even though the common interest in the avoidance of nuclear war and of the armaments race is very great.

While the avoidance of war has always been a primary task of diplomacy, it could also in the past be employed for the preparation of war. The strategy of men like Richelieu and Bismarck was often directed toward isolating a potential enemy prior to mounting the armed attack; at other times it was more or less openly concerned with persuading nonparticipants to enter the fray. Negotiating for such purposes usually involved a bargain over the spoils. As late as the First World War, several secret treaties had been concluded by some of the Allies for the partition of territory of the enemy, and in a sense the Yalta Agreements turned out to be the same sort of thing. Although palpably concluded merely for the purpose of providing for the postwar administration of conquered Germany, they actually resulted in the partition of the country and the forcible annexation of large parts of it. Negotiations of this type are always secret and often entered into with a mental reservation explainable by the duress caused by the war, and eventually rationalized by the doctrine of "reason of state." All diplomacy is shot through with such rationalization; hence the ancient quip about ambassadors who are gentlemen sent abroad to lie for the good of their country. This contains an overstatement of a good point; for a great deal of diplomatic talk may seem like lying, but is actually conventional phrasing in terms which are fully familiar to the persons communicating with each other. Indeed this technical language of intergovernmental communication is the formal bond of the international community of which it forms a part. The decline or disappearance of such community can have rather serious consequences, as the reckless language and other conduct of the totalitarians in the twentieth century have shown. Their failure to observe the niceties of international communication has greatly complicated all negotiations. The constant use of violent language and the employment of propagandistic slogans which had by mid-century become commonplace, not only between the two hostile camps, but also within them, still handicaps the traditionalist powers which are more reluctant to adopt the new "style" of diplomacy by "threats."[16] Many of these "threats" have become empty through constant reiteration. Even pounding the table with a shoe may not alter that.

But whether the language is smooth and conventional or rough and revolutionary, whether the techniques of negotiation are well established and generally agreed or novel and surprising, no art or craft of negotiation could hope to eliminate conflicts of interest, nor proceed without a community of such interests. All fields of activity in which negotiation is employed are subject to continual change, and the techniques will have to be adapted to the newly emerging persons and processes. Foreign policy, more especially, cannot be carried forward according to some fixed and static pattern, but must respond to the emergence of new powers, new technologies, new values, interests and beliefs. It is this element of contingent change, of evolutionary or revolutionary transformation, which prevents the "game" of diplomacy from corresponding to the fixed pattern of a mechanical "game theory."[17] Time and again, new factors are brought into the negotiation, such as new information; indeed not only information, but the innovative discovery of a new "line" or a new "approach" may provide the decisive turn in such a negotiation (Chapter 21).

Does this mean that no systematic analysis of negotiation, no "theory" in the descriptive sense, is possible? Far from it. Indeed, some of the aspects of such a theory have already been touched upon at various points in our discussion. In the remainder of the chapter, we hope to systematize these points.[18] In all negotiations, the bargaining power of the negotiators

[16] Cf. Friedrich and Brzezinski, 1956, chap. 10; cf. also the comments in Friedrich, 1950, chap. IV. Satow, 1917, gives an over-all view of the traditionalist position; for a more recent view cf. W. Gould, 1957, chap. 9; for the problem of the international official, cf. Hill, 1947. A careful analysis of the changes in the language of diplomacy is urgently needed, including a quantitative, word-count type of analysis in terms of "challenge and response."

[17] There is recognition of this limit in Schelling, pp. 97–98, where in the context of a discussion of "the nature of the intellectual process in coordination" and the resulting "strategy of coordination" he observes: "This corner of game theory is *inherently* dependent on empirical evidence." Stevens, a, 1958, goes a step further and rightly remarks: "In this writer's opinion, the game theory format is essentially inappropriate to the analysis of negotiation. . . . Game theory emphasizes a rationality-type solution with the calculation of optimal strategy. . . . But in most negotiated, purposive games, precisely the major task of the exchange of information during the negotiation is to change the negotiators' perception of the values comprising the pay-off matrix." Pp. 96–97.

[18] Our analysis is suggested by Schelling, 1960, chap. 2 (first published in article form in 1956), but deviates from Schelling's.

is of prime importance. This power is not necessarily identical with the total power of those engaged in a negotiation. Part of their power may be tied up elsewhere, or it may not be available and capable of being mobilized for the particular negotiation. If the leader of a party is obliged to heed certain factions in his following (or is believed to be thus limited), his ability for negotiating a coalition may be severely handicapped. If a power is greatly influenced by what effect its actions might have upon third parties (or is believed to be thus constrained), it may not be able to deploy its basic power. This is the situation of the United States vis-à-vis the U.S.S.R. concerning Cuba, because of Latin America. Yet, there may be a point at which such secondary considerations are set aside and the full power comes into play, creating a major uncertainty for the other negotiators which can be skillfully exploited. Thus, as in all power relations, actual and potential bargaining power need to be considered. The bargaining power may also be greatly influenced by the extent of the commitment of the negotiators. In both the Berlin (1948) and the Korean conflicts, a major difficulty was introduced by the fact that the United States did not apparently "get across" to the U.S.S.R. the extent of her commitment (did she try?). Commitment may have to be demonstrated by some concrete step, and even then doubts may remain. Many persons in the European Community of the Six were not at all sure of Britain's commitment to entrance; in view of past experience these persons suspected that the British merely wished to disturb the development of the Common Market. Indeed, even in 1962, after the efforts made by the British government to negotiate entrance, the doubts which remained in the mind of De Gaulle helped to produce failure. Commitment is therefore a decisive aspect of the bargaining power of negotiators. For if they are not committed, or not believed to be, bargaining power is greatly reduced. Therefore, one might say that the situation "depends not only on incurring commitment but on communicating it persuasively to the other party." [19]

A number of factors affect the extent of the commitment. One is the use of a bargaining agent with explicit and perhaps difficult instructions. The objection to an explicit mandate given by a constituency to its representative in a legislative assembly finds part of its justification in the difficulty it creates for effective negotiation (Chapter 17). But as we have seen, in spite of constitutional norms demanding that such a representative be "only subject to his conscience," the very tendency of elected persons normally to desire reelection causes them to be tied to their constituency, if merely by the anticipation of their reactions. Other

[19] Schelling, 1960, p. 28. Schelling adds that it is not easy to convince the other party that such demonstration may be available to one side and not to the other, and that all commitments raise the danger of overcommitment, stalemate or breakdown being the result.

agents, such as the representatives in international conferences, are usually thus tied, and Burke's famous contrasting of ambassadors "of different and hostile interests" with the people's representatives highlights the situation. We have here a mutual commitment, however, and a government which made it a practice to disavow its agents would soon find its bargaining power substantially reduced.

Overcommitment may also result from excessive or untimely publicity; on the other hand, a measure of publicity is part of an effective commitment. In dealing with its several publics, the British government negotiating for entrance into the Common Market had to find the narrow path which provided adequate commitment to satisfy its negotiating partners, while avoiding overcommitment in the eyes of the opposition at home or the Commonwealth nations abroad; conversely, it had to commit itself sufficiently to the Commonwealth views, in negotiating the issue with them, without scaring the members of the European Community. A nice balance had to be struck between too much and not enough publicity, between too much and not sufficient secrecy. Would it be possible to assign to these comparisons definite quantitative specifications? It seems more than doubtful.

Negotiations may be affected by the fact that the same power may have to carry on similar negotiations with a number of powers. Some of the more egregious "mistakes" in the handling of Marshall Plan funds are traceable to the fact that conditions which might be imposed upon a minor and politically inept power could not be asked of Great Britain. Yet to grant palpably less to one power than to another, to impose conditions on one and not on the other, may have very serious consequences. Negotiations in connection with foreign aid continue to be bedeviled by such difficulties. A way out appears to be the leaving of the initiative in opening such negotiations to those receiving aid, and asking that they specify in detail the projects for which the aid is needed; but touchy issues of international prestige are involved in such an approach.[20]

There is a great difference between the kind of negotiation involved in the limitation of armaments, or in the legislative decisions of a representative assembly, and in negotiations directed toward a single settlement such as a peace treaty or the adoption of a constitution. For negotiations of the first sort I should like to propose the term "chain" rather than "continuous" negotiation—the term used by Schelling. In them the problem of precedent is a recurrent factor affecting the mode of operation. Linked to it is the problem of long-range effects: a negotiator can more easily afford being disagreeable in a single-throw negotiation

[20] Montgomery, a, in Braibanti and Spengler, 1961, pp. 243ff., and Roepke, a, in Hunold, 1961, pp. 11ff., esp. pp. 48ff. Cf. also Montgomery, a, 1960, and *Public Policy* XI (ed. Friedrich and Harris), 1961, *passim*.

than in an extended chain of negotiations. Failure on the part of the totalitarians to appreciate this aspect has resulted in virtual stalemate on a number of fronts where chain negotiations are unavoidable.[21]

In all negotiations, the agenda are of vital significance. If partner A is more ready to settle with regard to issue *x*, and partner B with reference to issue *y*, the outcome of the entire negotiation may be vitally affected by which is put first. It may mean a difference not only in the terms, but also in the eventual success or failure. In tight and unpromising negotiations, a large part of the effort may be concerned with the agenda. The issue has recently been highlighted in connection with the so-called summit conferences; experience has shown what systematic analysis could have suggested, namely, that it is unwise to enter that kind of conference without an agreed agenda which has been negotiated in regular diplomatic procedure. Actually, diplomacy by conference is apt to break down unless agreement on agenda precedes it. In the Moscow Conference of March, 1947, the Western Allies hoped to achieve agreement on a German government, while the Soviet Union hoped to secure agreement on substantial reparations which the Allies were unwilling to concede. Much time was consumed in determining whether and when to treat the second item. The virtual breakdown of the conference was veiled behind an agreement on previously agreed subjects, including denazification, which were cast in standardized terms and not meant to be put into practice.[22] If it had been possible to work out an agenda beforehand, there is a chance that better results might have been achieved.

In all negotiation, the possibility of offering some compensation outside the immediate range of agenda must be considered an opportunity for achieving a bargain which might otherwise be impossible. Where the matter to be negotiated is quantifiable, such compensation is more easily determined than in the kind of issue which political bargains involve. Nonetheless, compensation is continually practiced, as the phrase "logrolling" suggests. Any negotiator who can afford to is well advised to come to the conference table with some compensatory object in the back of his mind which he might introduce into the discussion at the point of threatened breakdown. Often, in international political situations, an offer of trade advantages might "do the trick," as in legislative bargaining of the executive with members of an assembly a timely offer of a job to a retainer of the legislator to be won over might help. It has been hinted, for example, that the United States Federal government made the appointment of a "soft" attorney general part of a behind-the-scenes deal

[21] Davison, 1958, provides a striking illustration of the interaction of the two kinds of negotiation.

[22] Clay, 1950, pp. 145ff.; cf. esp. pp. 152–153.

which resulted from the negotiating of the handling of desegregation under Eisenhower;[23] whether true or not, it is typical of the kind of compensating offer which resolves a political deadlock. In this connection, it is certainly correct to point out that "it may be to the advantage of one party to keep a bargain isolated, and to the other to join it to some second bargain." Thus, the refined rules regarding amendments to be offered to a motion are the result of long experience with this problem and are inspired by the hope of keeping within bounds the desire of some parties to complicate the negotiation to the point where it becomes unmanageable.

These reflections engender a more general comment on parliamentary technique. The rules of procedure constitute a pattern which is shaped by the main business before the parliament. This basic point is well illustrated by the history of British parliamentary procedure.[24] Leaving aside the earlier story, we can briefly summarize the development in terms of four periods. During the time when the Commons were engaged in a struggle to curb the Crown, they sought to prevent the exertion of undue influence by the Crown's ministers over the deliberations of the House. Perhaps the most important achievement of this phase was the securing of each member's full right as an individual participant in the debates and decisions. Separate readings of bills, and the gradual separation of the Speaker from the Crown were others. The second period, after 1688, when the House was divided into two oligarchic factions, especially under and after Walpole, bought the provisions insuring the opposition a fair share of the time of the House, in other words, protection for the minority. Among the new technicalities was the employment of the committee of the whole, especially for budgetary questions, but there were many others besides. Procedure could be concerned with encouraging opposition, because there was little inclination to obstruct. In the third period, after the Reform Act, and down to the late seventies, the House of Commons, having become the center of the British system, faced an ever widening scope and an ever increasing burden of business. Conservatives and Liberals were the fairly evenly matched contenders over the rate of change required. As industrial, social and imperial problems multiplied, procedural reforms sought to expedite business and to prevent debate from being mere rhetoric. Hence, a multitude of rules of debate and the technique of questioning were developed. Finally, in the fourth and last period, the Irish obstruction and the rise of a third party (Labor) raised the issue of how to restrict obstructive minorities. At the same time, the government (Cabinet) came to rely more and more upon

[23] Peltason, 1961, pp. 52, fn. 34.

[24] Redlich, 1908, esp. vol. II, pp. 115ff. Cf. also Jennings, 1940, esp. chap. X. The point is developed in Friedrich, 1950, chap. XVI.

popular as contrasted with parliamentary support, the party organization and the caucus supplanted parliamentary control. Therefore, the problem of procedure became how to insure to the government adequate control over parliamentary work. Closure and various other devices for expediting parliamentary business were adopted to deal with the problem.[25] This sketch indicates clearly how procedure corresponds to the particular business in hand which requires negotiation. It shows that the major features of negotiation we have mentioned—compensation, agenda, the chain, the "cross and overlap"—all have played their role in shaping the evolution of parliamentary procedure.

It remains to deal briefly with the genetic (as contrasted with the morphological and operational) theory of negotiation. Why does it take place and why does it come to an end? In any given situation either party (power-handler) may have a choice of several alternative modes of procedure besides negotiation. In the present cold war situation of the United States and the U.S.S.R., for example, either may go to war, or may surrender to the other side in Laos, Berlin or Cuba. Why do they choose negotiation? Presumably because the price of the other alternatives, of the other possible "solutions," is too high. But negotiation does not occur only in response to such problems of avoiding undesirable alternatives. When party leaders decide to negotiate about a coalition government, there may not be any alternative possibility, although the formation of a minority government may be logically conceivable; if however the president or king who has to lend a hand in forming the government refuses to appoint such a minority government, negotiation may become imperative. The same situation prevails where negotiation between several department heads is ordered by their superior in an administrative organization, such as a government, an enterprise or a university. It seems therefore necessary to distinguish between such an imposed or involuntary negotiation and a voluntary one. The decision of the superior to have it thus constitutes so to speak the equivalent of the decision of the parties themselves to avoid other and less desirable alternatives. Now it may be said that in such a case it is simply the superior who makes the decision to avoid such alternatives. But while this may be true, it is not necessarily so; there may in fact not be any alternatives if action is to be taken.[26] In short, negotiation may start because one of the partners (or both) is convinced that alternative courses in a situation requiring action of some sort are more disadvantageous; or they may start because

[25] Jennings, 1936, esp. chap. XIV; cf. also Morrison, chap. VI.

[26] Stevens, a, 1958, does not consider this possibility. This is natural enough, since he develops his theory of negotiation on the basis of union-management relations. It is the major limitation of his interesting study. I would add that the psychological-choice-theory model which he adapts for his purpose seems to me too cumbersome, both analytically and linguistically, for our more general purpose.

a superior orders a negotiation for a variety of reasons related to organizational needs.

It remains to ask how a negotiation may end. Obviously it may end in a political bargain, a compromise. Typically, a compromise consists of a range of concessions on both sides, as we illustrated earlier in discussing a coalition negotiation. It does not seem to make much sense, politically, to speak of a "unilateral" compromise,[27] since it is not, truly speaking, a "compromise" but rather a concession that is somewhat less extensive than the original proposal or demand of one of the powers. Thus if the Allies agreed to reduce their troop contingent and to abandon RIAS (their broadcasting station), while the Soviet Union made no comparable concession, this "solution" to the Berlin crisis would not be a compromise but a concession. Concession is a second possible outcome of a negotiation. In fact, in many political situations, such a concession rather than a compromise is the hoped-for outcome of a negotiation, as far as the stronger power-holder is concerned. He prefers to secure at least part of what he could force upon the weaker party by negotiating for such a concession.

Besides concessions and compromises, whether bilateral or multilateral, the end of a negotiation may be breakdown. Since relations between power-handlers may be considerably worsened by such a breakdown, it is generally preferable not to enter into negotiations unless there is a reasonable prospect of some kind of concession or compromise. In the case of involuntary negotiations, such an outcome is often insured by the determination of the negotiators to avoid incurring the displeasure or more severe sanctions of their superior. The place of such a superior may, as a matter of fact, under democratic conditions of rivalry, be taken by the general public—internationally even by the "world public." This may be true even though it is a matter of voluntary negotiations. Indeed, as noted before, it may under such conditions become preferable to negotiate regardless of the prospect of the outcome. In such situations, there often will result a "noncompromise" outcome.[28] Since the distinguishing characteristic of this outcome of a negotiation is the continuing disposition of the negotiators to resume negotiations under more favorable circumstances, we might positively call such an outcome a projection. Such a projection may, under certain conditions, turn into the chain type of negotiation if repeated over a longer period. At least it would appear so in retrospect. When projection becomes impossible, the result

[27] As does Stevens, a, 1958, though he appears much more concerned with what he calls bilateral compromise, and rightly so. However, in that perspective, a multilateral compromise should be recognized in addition as an important type in political negotiation.

[28] This term seems to have been coined by Stevens, a. 1958, pp. 94f. He distinguishes two types, which he does not denote by specific terms.

is breakdown. While usually undesirable, breakdown may have its uses where a demonstrated inability to reach a compromise may strengthen the cohesion of one or more of the groups associated with and supporting the negotiating power-handlers. Indeed, in political situations, this possibility may at times be the primary objective of one of the negotiators. Such a negotiation is, in terms of the over-all theory of negotiation, fake. But since this objective may be one of several, such fake negotiations can not be excluded from an over-all theory. Political observers have for a long time been aware of the fact that breakdown has an effect upon the negotiators. It is failure and as such politically undesirable and to be avoided. As a seventeenth-century commentator observed: "Negotiators almost always abandon the interest of their principals for that of the success of the negotiation, which gives them credit for having succeeded in their undertaking." [29] This is an overstatement of the built-in desire of negotiators, like all power-handlers, to succeed in their task. The interest of the principals is usually involved in this task and cannot therefore be looked upon in isolation from the negotiation itself. While it surely takes two to make a bargain, there is also no bargain without wine, as the Romans said.

[29] La Rochefoucauld, *Maxims,* 1665.

chapter

28

Succession and the Uses of Party

There is no perfection of government, where the disposing of the Succession is not in the present Sovereign.
Hobbes

What should we do with a party, that is with a collection of asses, who swear by us, because they take us for asses like themselves?
Engels to Marx, 1851

In any political order, one of the most basic problems is that of succession. It is a problem which cannot be escaped, because all men are mortal. The elaborate rites which attend the death of a priest-king are as expressive of the poignancy of the issue as the anxious question in advanced modern political communities: "What after De Gaulle?" "What after Adenauer?" "What after Nehru?" In some sense it is not too much to say that the history of government has highlighted this problem, and various alternatives have been evolved in order to cope more effectively with the hiatus caused by the death of a ruler. Modern constitutionalism is an attempt to eliminate the issue by organizing an alternation of ruling groups at regular intervals, but as the above questions indicate, it has succeeded only to a limited extent. In any case, the regular elections provided for this purpose have contributed to the development of political parties; yet the succession issue arises in their midst as well. In totalitarian one-party systems it is the party which apparently gives continuity to the regime, and which must seek to solve the question of succession within its own cadres. The limited experience to date suggests that only partial solutions have been found so far, and they have not been formalized. But there can be little doubt that in both constitutional democracies and totalitarian dictatorships the party is vital to succession, and it will be shown that only within this context can a satisfactory general theory of the political party be given. Past theories have neglected this aspect, and have therefore been unsatisfactorily preoccupied with power and its manipulation.[1]

Succession is, of course, related to the general typology of political systems. Indeed, past typologies have suffered from a lack of consideration of this aspect of the matter, at least explicitly. To be sure, the Aristotelian (and general Greek) typology in terms of the number of rulers and of the lawfulness of their rule suggested that succession was a matter of course; nowhere does the static character of this typology appear more striking than in the assumption that whatever the number of rulers, their sons will presumably carry on as effective power is turned over to them. There is virtually no comprehension of the elaborate system of charismatic investment which characterized a good many Oriental despotic monarchies, as became apparent when the Roman emperors, confronted with the problem of how to maintain their rule, found themselves persuaded, eventually, to "deify" their rule. If we inspect the typology we sketched, and consider that succession raises the issue of legitimacy in its most acute form, any title to rule at that juncture being put into jeopardy, the complications of the problem are at once apparent. How are we to maintain the political order when the ruler is dead?

If we consider the baker's dozen of types of rule, and the forms of succession to which they are subject, we can identify the following types of succession: (1) charisma, (2) heredity, (3) wealth or some other kind of "objective" quality, (4) election, (5) force. These five types of succession often occur in combinations, such as the hereditary wealthy class in Venice, or the combination of election and force in totalitarian systems. Succession is, of course, a problem at all levels of government and in other organizations; but we are hereafter going to concern ourselves primarily with succession as applied to the apex of the governmental hierarchy, the ultimate ruler or rulers who constitute the type of rule which the succession is to secure and maintain. Obviously, as just remarked, succession will be closely linked to legitimacy. But while the belief in the goodness of the title to rule certainly favors the succession of him who commands such belief, the role of force and the uncertainty of the "signs" signifying the possession of charisma, as well as the complexity of kinship relations and the consequent uncertainties of title (wars of succession!), ought to serve as a reminder that the two questions refer to separate and distinct political phenomena. Even elections may occasion perplexing uncertainties if the suspicion of fraud appears or the election

[1] This holds as true of my own theory as given in Friedrich, 1951, chap. 20, as of others, such as Weber, V. O. Key, Jr. and Neumann. These views will be discussed below.

is boycotted by significant portions of the electorate—to mention only two of the more frequent occurrences. The exclamation *Le roi est mort—vive le roi!* betrays in its very assertiveness the sense of anxiety which seizes any political community when its ruler passes away.[2]

Succession based upon charisma presupposes the belief in a divine being on the part of both the ruler and the ruled. In marginal instances, such as the Roman Emperor Diocletian, such historical evidence as we have seems to suggest that he himself did not believe in his own divinity, but the complexity of the belief system in the late Roman Empire does not permit the drawing of firm conclusions.[3] The preference of a divine being is, of course, not very readily ascertained, and different political orders have evolved a variety of signs which might suggest such preference. Among the Chinese, pragmatic as has been their bent for many generations, the indication of divine favor was strictly in terms of success in avoiding floods, famines and foreign invasions. Since all three of these calamities did in part, at least, result from a failure of imperial administration, the charismatic type had an admixture here of an "objective" basis. To this must be added as a further complication the fact that within dynasties the hereditary type appears to have prevailed throughout.[4] In many more primitive societies similar "signs," especially good weather and good health, have served to indicate the charismatic ruler, often in combination with the hereditary basis. Where priests and rulers become separate, as in ancient Israel, the priesthood often presumes to be able to discern who possesses the divine calling; charismatic and hierocratic elements thus become intertwined. The role of the priesthood is, in a sense, inherent in charismatic succession, because of its reference to the divinity. Thus when Charlemagne sought papal approval for his rulership, he acted upon a sound instinct, since his hereditary claim was weak. However, the charismatic turn given the imperial office by this precedent was destined to prove a stumbling block fatal to quite a few of his successors.

The most extreme form of charismatic power is, of course, that based upon the belief that the king or ruler *is* himself a divine being, an incarnation of a god. The ancient Egyptians believed that the Pharaoh was an embodiment of the god Horus; similar beliefs prevailed in various parts of Africa, notably among the Loanga, in Ganda, Ruanda and Landa. In all of these cases, the king was called "God" or "Almighty" and was venerated as such.[5] Such beliefs raised a peculiarly grave problem of

[2] We exclude from our discusssion the complicated legal problems of the so-called "succession" of states in International Law. Cf. D. P. O'Connell, 1956, and W. Gould, 1957, chap. 14.

[3] J. Burckhardt, 1853, 1949, chap. 2; cf. article by Hocart on "deification" in *ESS*.

[4] Wittfogel, 1957, pp. 87ff., 128ff.

[5] Frazer (ed. Gaster), 1959, p. 126; Hocart, *op. cit.*, and 1927.

succession which not infrequently led to the practice of killing the ruler when he showed signs of failing, or even after a specific interval. Numerous instances of such practices were recited by Frazer the general accuracy of which has not been questioned by more recent research though interesting clarifications in detail have been made. To give one example suggesting the major themes involved: "The people of the Congo believed that if their pontiff, the Chitome, were to die a natural death, the world would perish, and the earth, which he alone sustained by his power and merit, would immediately be annihilated. Accordingly, when he fell ill and seemed likely to die, his prospective successor entered his house with a rope or club and strangled or bludgeoned him to death." [6] As previously pointed out, the variety of signs by which the new charismatic ruler might be recognized is great, ranging all the way from physical prowess to priestly approval. It has been pointed out that "ancient and primitive peoples tend to articulate this parallelism [between ruler and god] under the figure of genealogical descent or actual conferment of properties and status." [7] In this connection, the notion seems to be prevalent that divine status is "conferred," and by such symbolic acts as unction is "rubbed into him." Whenever such symbolism appears, it obviously facilitates the manipulation of succession if those in charge, such as a priesthood, are able and willing to "confer" the powers which the ruler is supposed to possess.[8] The rather plentiful data on succession in primitive societies (see above, Chapter 9) suggest that succession is often based on a combination of grounds. One ground may be more important than another, or it may be a necessary, but not a sufficient one. Another significant observation is that such formally acknowledged grounds are at times disregarded in practice.[9] At times the combinations are rather ingenuous, as when three dynasties compete for the succession and the Elders select the man they believe would make the best ruler.[10] Straight election and outright heredity are also found.[11]

Heredity and election, the two principal modes of insuring succes-

[6] Frazer (ed. Gaster), 1959, p. 225. Under the heading "The succession of Kings and seasons" Frazer on pp. 223–249 (pars. 189–200) has compiled a great variety of instances of this mode of insuring charismatic succession by eliminating the ruler who might be in the process of losing his charisma—a procedure which may in part be explainable by the primitive belief in the immortality of gods, if not of men.

[7] Gaster in an "additional note," 1959, p. 126.

[8] On charismatic power, cf. Friedrich, a, 1961.

[9] Schapera, 1930.

[10] Nadel, 1942, pp. 33 and 88; for similar arrangements among the Ashanti, see Busia, 1951, pp. 97–98; among the Hausa, M. G. Smith, 1960, p. 83; among Bedouins, A. Musil, 1928, p. 50.

[11] For election see, for example, the Comanches, Wallace and Hoebel, 1952, pp. 24 and 210–211; for heredity, Burrows, 1949, p. 98; Malinowski, 1922, p. 66; 1935, pp. 39–40; Fortes and Evans-Pritchard, 1940, pp. 101–102; Leinhardt, a, 1959.

sion, stand in an interesting relationship to each other when considered in the light of the governmental enterprise. It has been remarked that while heredity favors the certainty of having a successor, election is more likely to secure a qualified one.[12] Indeed, it might be argued that this contrast constitutes the key to comparing hereditary monarchy with various republican regimes, and that hereditary monarchy "goes farthest in its willingness to sacrifice personal ability to the interests of a secure and prompt succession." This argument will hold only where no charismatic element enters the succession, which actually was the case for many hereditary monarchies. Furthermore, the very serious problems which were encountered in connection with pretenders and the complexities of descent, once there did not exist a clear case for an eldest son, suggest that the seeming certainty proves illusory in many instances. On the other hand, although there have been many uncertainties in connection with modes of election, and, in the case of oligarchic structures, factional fights endangering the succession, the development of modern mass parties has in stabilized constitutional democratic regimes provided for a certainty of succession far surpassing that of hereditary monarchy. Even the Hayes-Tilden controversy which engendered an elaborate aftermath of moves and countermoves was eventually "settled" by the Supreme Court in accordance with the rationale of party, and earned the Court the rather derogatory epithet that it "follows the election returns." Actually, the epithet does the Court scant justice: it did not *follow* the election returns, but substituted its own judgment for the uncertainty of these results. Nor can it actually be said, on the record, that the succession of American presidents exceeds in ability the comparable British or French monarchs. Great kings follow weak ones, but allowing for the paradoxes of any such comparison, it would seem that on empirical grounds one serves as well as the other as far as over-all capacity is concerned. The real contrast lies elsewhere, namely, in the length of time that a political community is committed to a poor ruler. As just mentioned, some primitive societies have coped with that difficulty by providing for the killing of the king after a certain period, such as twelve years. Apart from the fact that this procedure may do away with a good ruler prematurely, it does not recommend itself to modern political thought. Perhaps the American constitutional amendment decreeing a limit of two terms for a president should be viewed as a civilized analogue. In any case, practically all systems based upon election have provided for rather brief intervals, two to seven years; and such a period, say, five years, is a much safer risk on a poor choice than an entire generation on a bad king who may thwart the community's life and development. In feudal kingdoms, a safety valve was provided by the notion that resistance was justified against a bad ruler, but this safeguard worked more effectively against the tyrannical abuse of power than

[12] Watkins in his article on "Succession" in *ESS*.

against its nonuse or misuse by an incompetent ruler. Generally speaking, no mode of succession can *insure* a competent ruler, but the competition of *two* parties in rivalry for public support gives the best chance of providing him, because of their strong organizational interest in doing so, and because they provide a trial ground in their own internal politics. These reflections clearly show that the party has a crucial function in republican, constitutional regimes by providing for the succession, and it is therefore appropriate to develop the theory of party in this context.

Parties ought to be seen, then, in the perspective of the basic function of ensuring the succession—a point which is at times overlooked, though the theory of the British two-party system of parliamentary government has usually been stated in terms which make this function quite apparent. Indeed, the British system has, on this account, been contrasted with Continental European systems as "true" or "genuine." Leaving aside those issues relating to parliamentary government,[13] it is clear that a general theory of political party will be compatible with this perspective. To delineate such a theory, the following propositions may serve as a summary of such a comprehensive theory.[14]

While it is true that the role of party differs from country to country, and that a "definition" derived from one may exclude others, the very use of a common term suggests the existence of a common genus of which the many different species are concrete manifestations. It is the task of the theorist to identify this genus, while fully recognizing and to some extent even elaborating upon the species which are most important. It goes without saying that parties, like other political institutions, reveal their nature in the functions they serve in the political and more especially in the governmental process. One of these functions we have just come upon; it is the function of providing for the succession of rulers or governors under a great variety of conditions ranging from an orderly constitutional system to tyrannical forms of autocracy. But the function of parties goes well beyond this intermittent function of providing for the succession of rulers and is related to the process of government in its

[13] Redslob, 1918, 1924, *passim*, is perhaps the best-known exponent of this view, which has become newly important in connection with the arguments over the constitution of the Fifth Republic, since this constitution was inspired by similar views.

[14] The following is based upon Friedrich, 1950, chap. XX, revised in the light of more recent work, esp. S. Neumann, 1956, particularly the introd. and pp. 395–421; Duverger, 1951, 1954; Lavau, 1953; Livingston, a1 and a2, 1959; Leibholz, 1952, and a, 1951; Lipson, a, 1953 and a, 1959; Lipset, 1960, chap. 9; D. R. Rustow, 1955, chaps. 1, 3 and 5; V. O. Key, Jr. (4th ed.), 1958, esp. chap. 8, which contains a skillful digest of recent writings in the field in America. He rightly praises as comprehensive Leiserson, 1958, but does somewhat less than justice to "general political theorists," of whom he alleges that they have "given scant attention to the party processes." I would not say that of the theorists with whom I am familiar, from Burke and Weber to our contemporaries.

entirety. Parties have the function of integrating the multitude of interests, values and beliefs which exist in a political community into either one or several programs often elaborated into comprehensive ideologies. Such ideologies criticize, as we have shown (Chapter 4), the existing state of things and propose ways of changing them. In this process of integrating the community, they develop leaders, and a second function of parties is the providing of leaders for the government of the community. Looking at it from the viewpoint of the members of such a party, one can say that a party is a group of human beings, stably organized with the objective or purpose of securing or maintaining for the members ideal and material benefits and advantages, and that in order to do so, a party also seeks to have its leaders become rulers, that is to secure or maintain for its leaders the control of a government.[15] If parties other than *political* parties are to be covered by the theory, one can speak of the control of "organization" rather than government. All the three major functions of any, but more especially of a political, party, can be performed only if the human beings composing it are stably organized. It is this fact of stable organization which distinguishes a party from cliques, factions, juntas and other similar groupings of a temporary character. This distinction has often been overlooked, and many historical phenomena have been called parties which were really factions. The matter is of some theoretical importance, because parties may themselves be divided on a more or less stably organized basis. If the divisions are fairly permanent, such parties within parties deserve to be recognized as such; they may oblige us to interpret a seemingly one-party situation as actually a two- or multiple-party one.

In speaking of parties, we directed attention to the fact that the leaders are to become rulers through whom the party is to secure and maintain the control of the government. It is vital to put the matter thus, and not to speak, as is often done, of gaining power. Many groups other than parties are organized with a view to gaining power, such as interest groups, mass-communication companies, and so forth. They are distinguished from parties by not seeking rulership or control of the government through acquiring posts therein.[16] It is thus a particular kind of control, namely, personal control—or rather, conduct—of the government itself, which distinguishes a political party from other kinds of power-

[15] This way of putting the matter, which was used by Friedrich, 1950, chap. XX, is a modification of the theory expounded by Max Weber, 1922, part I, par. 18, and part III, chap. 4. The latter, in keeping with Weber's general tendency, is a theory cast in terms of the psychology of the human beings involved. It seems to me more appropriate, within the context of political theory, to state the position in terms of the functions the party serves in the political order. But the one set of propositions does not invalidate, but complements, the other.

[16] This crucial point is the main difference between the above and Max Weber's theory, though the matter of recruitment also is important. For the distinction between power and rule, see above, Chaps. 9 and 10.

seeking organizations. What is here involved is the function of succession, intimately related to the function of integration.[17]

Parties, because of their close relation to the government which they wish to operate, tend to evolve a structure that closely corresponds to the governmental structure. Thus if the government is patterned federally, the party organizations will tend to be "federations" of local parties, as is the case in the United States, Switzerland and Germany—each case faithfully reflecting the degree of federalism prevalent in the particular country. An extreme instance is provided by the slow development of supranational party organizations in the Community of the Six which comprises the Common Market in Europe.[18] In this instance a more comprehensive organization is seen emerging from the separate national organizations in response to a supranational governmental structure, even though a very feeble one at present. Similarly, the structure of government in the realm of the executive tends to mold party organization; the more integrated the executive structure is, the more integrated will be the party structure.

It should be remembered, however, that the structure of the government is not the only factor affecting party structure. Party organization also responds, of course, to internal forces and the total situation in which a party finds itself. Thus a party with a revolutionary goal will be more autocratic than one which fits readily into the existing society. Again, the more advanced the democratization of a political community, the more democratic will the internal structure of parties tend to be, and in spite of Roberto Michels' alleged iron law (above, Chapter 18) parties with a radically democratic ideology such as the British Labor Party or the present-day German Social Democratic Party will be more inclined to "practice what they preach," that is to say, will develop intraparty institutions based upon cooperation and participation of the membership, than parties not so motivated. What Michels overlooked in his well-known and overrated study is the fact that the German Social Democratic Party under the German Empire, to which most of his factual data refer, was operating within a setting rather unfavorable to its objectives, hostile to its ideology and favorable to autocratic leadership. The more extreme cases of the Russian Socialists and more particularly the Bolsheviks was skillfully analyzed by Lenin, who however also generalized perhaps too much from his limited experience.[19]

The inherent trend toward autocracy in party organizations has in

[17] It has rightly been pointed out that it is *not* the function of a political order as such to integrate and in the process adapt a community to successive stages in its development; cf. Almond, in Almond and Coleman, 1959, p. 5, but his criticism does not go far enough.

[18] Haas, 1958, chap. 11; Schierwater, 1960, part II, chap. 2.

[19] Cf. Michels, 1911, 1915 (English ed.); for Lenin see below, pp. 30ff.; Lenin anticipated and repudiated Michels' argument. Cf. also A. G. Meyer, 1957, chaps. 1–5.

turn caused a variety of efforts to decree democratization, that is, to provide by law for various democratic features, such as publicity, free elections and program control by the members. The American scene is rich in such endeavors, including legislation about primaries, publicity for contributions and other aspects of party finance, and the rest.[20] The German Federal Republic has been struggling unsuccessfully during the first ten years of its existence with the task of similar legislation. As is usual in Continental European legislation, instead of an *ad hoc* solution of one problem at a time, a comprehensive code has been attempted. The result has been failure to act. By contrast, Great Britain has been concerned with certain aspects of party finance, such as the money spent in elections, but has left internal party structure to evolve gradually, in keeping again with British constitutional ways.[21] One very important special aspect of party finance is the question of participation by government officials in such financing. The Federal government of the United States has been firm in restricting Federal officials to making voluntary contributions but forbidding them any other kind of participation, especially the soliciting of funds.[22]

Such passive participation of public officials in "democratic" parties is in striking contrast to the totalitarian policy of forcing officials into the party and exacting vigorous and active participation in its various phases. Where a single party occupies a dominant position, though permitting other parties to criticize and share in legislation, as in many of the newer states, it is well-nigh impossible and perhaps even undesirable to insist upon the strict "neutrality" of public officials, especially where the dominant party embodies a movement of national liberation. They should be committed and actively concerned, and a party benefiting from participation will not necessarily be totalitarian or even autocratic. But there is a real danger, nonetheless, that it may become so.[23] The emergence of single political parties of a nonautocratic and nontotalitarian stamp suggests a

[20] Key, 1958, chaps. 14–16, 18; Heard, 1960.

[21] *Final Report of Committee on Electoral Law Reform*, Cmd. 7286, 1947. Cf. also *Representation of the Peoples Act*, 1948, the provisions of which embody the results of a long evolution. For Germany, cf. Breitling, a, 1961.

[22] See the Hatch Act of 1939, extended in 1940 to all local officials administering any program to which Federal funds are contributed. The broad provisions of the act have been interpreted by the Civil Service Commission, which has evolved the principle of the act over a number of years and embodied it in Rule I, section I, of its rules; see Form 1236, describing the prohibited activities, under #20. They form part of a comprehensive code, limiting participation of officials in party activity to strictly passive membership.

[23] Almond and Coleman, 1959, pp. 109–114, 185–208, 286–313, 391–415, 479–511, describe the party systems in Southeast Asia, sub-Saharan Africa, South Asia, Africa, the Near East and Latin America, distinguishing (rightly, I think) the autocratic (they say "authoritarian") one-party system from the nonautocratic one. Cf. above, Chaps. 9 and 10.

compromise between the need for integration and the objective of democratization. Much depends upon a recognition of this compromise within the democratic ken.

A special but very important aspect of the relative degree of democratization of a particular party is its method of recruitment of members. Some time ago, it was common to include "free recruiting" among the criteria by which to identify political parties.[24] Such a criterion is inadmissible, because it would oblige one to insist that a great many parties, notably all totalitarian parties, were not parties. The term "recruitment" is unfortunate in this context, anyhow, as it suggests primarily an activity on the part of the party, whereas what needs to be stressed is the freedom of anyone to join the party if he feels so inclined. "Free adherence" or "open membership" suggest themselves as more satisfactory terms to describe the situation. Like all questions of freedom (Chapters 20 and 21), such freedom is a matter of degree. As such it is important in providing a significant distinction between parties that are relatively open and others that are relatively closed. The Democratic Party in the Southern states of the United States has been closed to Negroes, but is open to others. So are parties in other parts of the United States which, however, also admit Negroes and therefore are "more open." The exception is the Communist Party, which was closed whenever it had a legal existence; presumably it is even more closed now. The greater or lesser openness of a party may affect its size, because any standard will exclude some persons. It is doubtful, however, whether this proposition can be reversed to say that whenever party membership is limited, the party is less open. For such lack of membership may be the consequence of lack of interest on the part of the public. Indeed, "openness" is never complete; even very open parties with large membership, such as the British Labor Party, reserve the right to expel a member and have done so from time to time.[25] Since parties are organizations with distinctive interests of a very general sort, they can ill afford to be infiltrated by pseudo-partisans whose true objective is to divide and weaken the organization. This possibility constituted no serious problem in the halcyon days of liberalism; it has become a very real threat wherever totalitarian movements have appeared. But before we turn to these and related problems, it seems desirable to explore the issues posed by the "interests" themselves.

We said that a party has the function of integrating interests, values

[24] Max Weber, part III, chap. 4, 1922, as cited above. Weber weakened his argument by qualifying the "free" as "formally" free; as so often, he presumably seeks to meet objections by retreating behind a legal facade; it invalidates the argument for political science if the recruitment is only "formally" free, that is to say, in fact often not free.

[25] Cf. Burns, a, 1950, and the personal account of Zilliacus, 1949. See also Labor Party, 1949, 1950.

and beliefs, often by developing ideologies (Chapter 4). The integration of values and beliefs turns upon the nature of values and beliefs; as a result it differs markedly from the integration of interests. What really happens is that values as well as beliefs are continually being elaborated and transformed through the concrete experience of the members of a political community (Chapters 2 and 6), not uniformly and in unison, but within the context of individual and group life exhibiting a vast diversity of experience. From the highly personal sphere of sex and family, food and fashion to the development of science and technology, ever-new problems are presented by the transformation of values and beliefs which call for reintegration if the community is not to fall apart to the point where even communication becomes difficult, if not impossible. But while value and belief integration are elusive and long-range, the integration of interests is more tangible and demonstrable. The ideal advantages which some older definitions of party emphasized to the exclusion of others are at least in part embedded in those values and beliefs which the party seeks to realize and which it must as a precondition continually reintegrate. They are not as readily distinguished from the "material" advantages as might be supposed; the ideal and the material tend to be closely intertwined, and the concept of "interest" serves the purpose of comprehending them in their interrelationship. Every interest group inclines to view its interest in an "ideal" as well as "material" perspective: farmers are said to be the backbone of the nation, businessmen the pathmakers of industrial progress, workers the basis of national wealth, scientists the protagonists of technical advance, scholars and artists the mainstay of culture, and so forth. Nor are these empty or idle claims. Each has a foundation in demonstrable fact. Yet the ideal projection ought not to be allowed to hide the "material" advantage which a group standing for that interest seeks to realize. In multiparty systems, broad economic interest groups are frequently organized as separate political parties, such as workers', farmers' or even real estate owners' parties;[26] in two- or three-party systems such interests are united through *ad hoc* compromises in parties which must seek to appeal to a sufficiently large constituency to win, if possible, a majority of the votes. It is usually easier to arrive at a compromise between interests that are stated in material terms than between those which insist upon an "ideal" projection of their interest. Material interests may often be reduced to monetary terms, which being quantitative permit averaging or compensating. Thus, the bitter struggle over farm interests between the Six composing the European Community was virtually irresolvable as long as the parties to the conflict insisted that the farm group must remain intact because farmers are the "backbone of a healthy people." The con-

[26] Cf. Friedrich, 1950, chaps. XXI and XXII, and the literature cited there. More recently the same view in Lipset, 1961, p. 32 .

flict could be compromised when the material interests of the human beings involved were spelled out in explicit terms and fair compensation was worked out. The solution may now be "idealized" or "rationalized" in terms of the broader community of Europe of which the European farmers taken as a whole still constitute the "backbone," even though the proportion of French to German farmers may have been considerably altered.

Whether interest groups are identified with parties or operate within them and behind them has significance primarily in terms of what is considered the major, or even exclusive, function of a political party. For parties may be seen as functioning to represent the electorate, indeed the individual members of the electorate, or they may be seen as integrating the electorate in its various subdivisions. It has been claimed by some that parties have moved from being parties of representation to being parties of integration, and stress has been laid upon the shift from the former to the latter function. "Instead of a party of individual representation, the contemporary society has produced increasingly a party of social integration." [27] There can be no question that a shift has occurred in this direction, that parties are *more* and *more* preoccupied with integration rather than representation, but basically they have always been both *to a certain extent.* The integrative function is especially pronounced in systems where one party predominates, more particularly in "new" states where the party actually serves the function of bringing a nation into being (see below). Actually, it is not so much the shift from representation to integration, as it is a shift from integration of a part of the electorate, such as the Tories, Whigs, Conservatives, Liberals and Laborites, to the integration of the larger part of the people. The shift is manifest in the "old" democracies by the near identity of parties and their consequent tendency to win or lose on the basis of a shift of a minute section of the electorate. The recent American presidential elections are as much an illustration of this trend as are British ones. In contrast to American parties, British parties used to be praised for their "standing" for programs, and elections were said to be fought on issues. But numerous observers have, in recent years, noted the change.[28]

If we consider both the function of representation and the function of integration in terms of the broader function of providing a link between the voter and the government, between ruled and rulers—a function which totalitarian parties seek to fulfill as much as do democratic ones—it becomes clear that these two functions while distinguishable are not actually separable. Only because the party represents the individual voter

[27] S. Neumann, a, 1954; also the same author, 1956, pp. 403–405. Quotation is found at p. 560.

[28] Lipson, a, 1956; a, 1959; Eckstein, in Beer-Ulam, 1958, chap. 12.

and the interest groups in which he participates is the party in a position to integrate these interest groups, and unless the party integrated these groups, it could not hope to represent the individual voter. This follows from the very nature of representation as shown earlier (Chapter 17). But whether a party integrates only those voters who share a certain ideology, as was in the past frequently the case in the multiple-party systems (even here a considerable amount of integration was called for since the adherents of the ideology usually belonged to different interest groups), or whether it integrates a part large enough to approximate a majority, or whether it finally seeks to integrate the entire people and achieve a predominant status and consequent permanence, that is the really significant question and the one which allows us to speak of phases in the development of parties. It would appear uncertain to what extent, however, we are justified in taking the British pattern as a model.

The most significant feature of party history appears to be that it begins with one party. In many of the new nations one party of national liberation and integration has appeared. This fact has given much concern to the adherents of the doctrine that the model of a well-functioning democracy calls for a two-party system save under exceptional circumstances.[29] A consideration of European party systems, especially the British, could have relieved them of some of this anxiety. Historically speaking,[30] parties in Britain started to form in the course of the seventeenth century. The degree to which organization is stressed in defining a party will to some extent determine how late one places the beginning. There surely is no definite date which could be given. Factions, such as the partisans of the Red and the White Roses, can be included only by unduly broadening the meaning of party, that is, by omitting the crucial feature of ideology. It was under James I that the Puritans definitely acquired the typical characteristics of a party as defined above; they certainly sought control of the government, though they did not often admit it. The Puritans developed in opposition to a monarchical government that rested upon tradition and law; their aspiration could easily acquire the flavor of conspiratorial activity, and their opponents did not form into a party until the Puritans had come into power and were operating as party government.[31] But to the Puritans, the Royalists (Cavaliers) appeared in

[29] Much writing on political parties is cast more or less in terms of this frame of reference, from Ostrogorsky to the recent past. It still exerts a good deal of practical influence, in spite of the experience in many countries. Holcombe cautioned against this view in the *ESS* as early as 1933. Cf. S. Neumann (ed.), 1956, for a balanced picture.

[30] Admittedly, there has been a great deal of controversy over the origins of British parties, and the matter is far from settled; cf. W. C. Abbott, a, 1918; Trevelyan, 1926, and Hexter, 1940, esp. chap. III.

[31] Hexter, 1940, ch. I. Duverger, in keeping with his stressing of the organization, would deny the existence of parties before 1850 (Duverger, 1954, pp. xxiiif.).

turn as antigovernment, and it was not until after these violent revolutionary experiments (including their echoes during the Restoration) had run their course and proven abortive that the English people settled down to the "peaceful coexistence" of Tories and Whigs as parties with large-scale organized support alternating as rulers in control of the government. Bolingbroke's denunciation of parties and espousal of a "patriot king" was a sort of swan song of the old antiparty sentiment, and it was only in that period that writers like David Hume and Edmund Burke began to understand the role and function of party.[32] As is well known, Washington did not yet appreciate the value of parties in a free government, but thought of them in eighteenth-century fashion as factional divisions and detrimental to a free government.[33] Two parties were actually operating at the time, and Washington was the leader of one. His administrative practices and more especially his appointments clearly show it.[34]

Whether a one-party system develops into a two-party one appears to depend upon many circumstances, one of which is the electoral system. Whenever a simple majority is required, the rival groups tend to coalesce into two, each one of which has a reasonable prospect of gaining a majority. The pressure for effective compromise to bring about such a result is inherent in this kind of political situation.[35] But if there are several constituencies, these pressures will work only if the population is homogeneous; otherwise the two parties in one jurisdiction will differ from those in another. Furthermore, the labels may hide significant differences; some of the complexities of the American party system are the result of such heterogeneity.

If the electoral divisions are reasonably permanent and have strong emotional and ideological overtones, a multiple-party system may give better results than a two-party system. For the "crisis of politics" as Bagehot called it is transferred to the level of professional politicians who in coalition negotiations can organize effective compromises for practical political purposes which would be difficult on the electoral level.[36] Expe-

[32] Bolingbroke, 1734; Hume, 1741, chap. 8; Burke, 1770. Note also the opening sentence of Burke's "Observations, . . ." 1769: "Party divisions, whether on the whole operating for good or evil, are inseparable from free government." Hume still denounced parties, though he recognized their role.

[33] Gilbert, 1961, shows clearly that this was Washington's sentiment, though approved, of course, by Hamilton and hence included in his revision of the draft; cf. esp. pp. 123ff.

[34] L. D. White, 1942, esp. pp. 271ff.

[35] The vast literature on electoral systems, and more especially the writings of the opponents of proportional representation, contains an elaboration of and empirical support for this proposition. Note esp. Hermens, 1941, and Friedrich, 1950, chap. XV, for an extended bibliography; cf. also above, Chap. 17.

[36] Goetz Roth, 1954, presents an interesting general analysis of the workings of the German system of coalition government based on data from one state; cf. esp. pp. 82ff. A broader, but briefer, treatment in Sternberger, 1956, pp. 101ff.

rience suggests, however, that under such conditions it is advisable to avoid the so-called parliamentary system of government. For this system calls for stable party support of the government in the representative assembly, and such support is difficult to maintain when the governing parties are held together merely by a coalition agreement,[37] unless the opposition is obliged to do likewise and reach an agreement before they can overthrow the government.

It has recently been argued that "in 1850 no country in the world (except the United States) knew political parties in the modern sense of the word" and that hence parties are part and parcel of the process of democratization.[38] The same writer has also suggested that there were essentially two different processes, one in which parties originated from the coalescing of parliamentary groupings and electoral committees, the other where parties were started by separate and distinct groups such as trade unions, churches and ideological movements. The former exhibit a more pronounced parliamentary leadership and a decentralized pattern of organization; the latter subject the parliamentarians to more or less rigid control of the party regulars and their bureaucracy, and subject the local groupings to centralized direction and control. He believes that these divergent origins continue to mould, and help to explain much in, the behavior of parties. It is evident that these divergences play a certain role, but it does not seem that they are important as compared with the basic characteristic of parties as organizations of voters (therefore presupposing an electoral system, whether restricted or not) for the purpose stipulated above.

Duverger has also suggested that political parties may be roughly differentiated into three types,[39] the middle class cadre parties, composed of notables and preoccupied with political questions, the socialist parties of Europe, based on a dues-paying mass membership and concerned with ideology and education (indoctrination) as well as politics, and the "totalitarian" parties (communist and fascist) based on autocratic leadership, centralized direction and claiming to direct "the whole human being" in the pursuit of its political goals. There can be no doubt that parties have been evolving in this direction, but as we show elsewhere, and as is admitted quite readily by this author, the distinction must be qualified not only by other "types," but also by a variety of overlaps. To approach the problems of party from the side of structure and organization, rather

[37] Adenauer's government during the first German legislature, 1949–1953, does not contradict this rule; for under a new provision of the constitution the chancellor cannot be voted out of office except by a coalition which has agreed on a successor —a condition which has proved unrealizable so far. The so-called "constructive nonconfidence vote" may, however, at some point, become a factor.

[38] Duverger, 1954, pp. xxiv.

[39] *Ibid.*, chap. 1.

than the human persons, their values, interests and beliefs, complicates the analysis and obscures the vision.

In connection with organization aspects of party analysis, the degree of centralization has seemed important and has received a good deal of attention (see also Chapter 32 below). We have already pointed out that, generally speaking, parties will be as decentralized as is the government, and for a simple reason related to their function and purpose, namely, to secure control of the government by electing its leaders. American parties, like Swiss and German parties, have to be able to win state as well as federal elections.[40] In view of this aspect, parties generally show some measure of decentralization, because of the universal acceptance of local self-government (Chapter 29). But, of course, it is not only a matter of the structure of government, but also one of social structure. If a political community is markedly divergent in its composition, in terms of class, nationality or religion, and if such divergences are territorially localized, parties will exhibit a measure of decentralization even if the governmental structure is not federal, lest the divergences lead to multiple party formations. This they will do if parties fail to recognize these divergences by a measure of decentralization. Even in a totalitarian system, these pressures are at work, as manifest in the local "satrapies" under Fascism and National Socialism, as well as in recent developments in the Soviet Union.[41] The responses to both social and governmental structure result from the political function of parties, that is, the uses to which such political organizations are put; hence the evolution of the polity will naturally be reflected in them. Integration as contrasted with representation is one of these evolving objectives of party.

The problem of integration as against representation, linked as it appears to be to that of the interaction between the general social structure and parties, has given rise to movements, often called parties, which, while not *necessarily* totalitarian, have frequently been that. In France, De Gaulle's hostility to the old-style French party of highly individualized representativeness made him stress that his followers constituted a movement "reassembling" the French people, thus highlighting its

[40] The American case has been convincingly documented and argued again recently by Grodzins, a, 1960, taking issue with Schattschneider et al., 1950.

[41] For the governmental versus the social structure, cf. Lipson, a, 1953, as well as S. Neumann (ed.), 1956, esp. the chapter by Schattschneider who would transcend the dichotomy by reference to the "function of the political system." With this approach the analysis here given agrees, of course, though it seems preferable to speak of the specific function of parties in a political order; a system as such does not have a function, except to function. Nor do I agree that recognition of the adaptation to social and government structures does as such mean a static as contrasted with a dynamic approach. "Static" is in any case a pejorative term which it is well to avoid in such discussions; there are more and less flexible factors determining party as they do all other organizations.

intended integrative function. It has not so far become totalitarian. In Italy, as well as in Germany and other countries, the emphasis was likewise on integration of the nation, though the movement was cast in the form of a party organized to compete with other parties; when it achieved power, it proceeded to liquidate them on the ground, among others, that they divided the nation. In many of the newly established nations movements of that sort have been organized as parties, with the avowed goal of first liberating and then organizing the national community.[42] Stressing the traditional importance of discussion in African communities, one of their key leaders, Julius Nyerere, recently stated this position rather forcefully. It may be summed up as follows. The two-party system is only one kind of democracy, related to a struggle between the "haves" and the "have-nots"; the existence of classes in a society results in corresponding parties, and has no application to Africa where "the idea of class is something entirely foreign." Reinforcing this argument from tradition by an argument from emergency, Western peoples have also formed "national unions" in such situations. Once independence is achieved, the supreme need is a task for all, "the building up of the country's economy, the eradication of disease and the banishment of ignorance and superstition." It calls "for the maximum united effort by the whole country . . . there can be no room for difference or division." "This is our time of emergency," he insists. As long as there is free discussion and the citizen has the right freely to share in choosing the government, the essentials of democracy are, in his view, fulfilled.[43]

It has at times been held that this type of organization should not be termed a party, but recognized as something radically different from the parties of the liberal democratic state engaged in free competition and based on open membership. But apart from the inconvenience in political analysis of refusing to call something by the particular name by which it has come to be known—it forces one into saying the Communist Party is not a party—the real difficulty is that these organizations do have some of the primary functions which characterize a party, notably providing for the succession and linking the ruled with the rulers by representation and integration. As a result, the suitable lines of distinction to be drawn are those between different kinds of party, notably between democratic and totalitarian parties. Among the criteria, those of internal organization are important, but even here caution is required, since, for example, greater participation of the members is provided in some totalitarian than in some of the oldest "constitutionalist" parties.[44]

[42] C. H. Moore, a, 1960. See also fn. 45 below.

[43] Nyerere, a, 1962, pp. 185–86.

[44] On the basis of this kind of distinction, one author has gone so far as to group all political orders in which this kind of party is central as "movement states." Tucker, a 1961. Such a lumping together of political orders of a totalitarian and nontotalitarian character is not desirable; not only does it confuse our understanding

Thus after distinguishing between primarily representative and primarily integrative parties, including movements of national liberation, we need to distinguish all these "democratic" parties from autocratic and more especially totalitarian parties. It is important not to overlook that autocratic parties are not necessarily totalitarian. The distinction can *either* be made in terms of ideology, which would mean that an autocratic party would be considered totalitarian *if* it espoused a totalitarian ideology (Chapter 4), or it can be made in terms of its functioning role within a totalitarian regime. A number of national liberation and/or integration parties have been rather autocratic without either espousing a totalitarian ideology or functioning as the mainstay of a totalitarian regime, such as the parties in Tunisia, Morocco, Bolivia and Mexico, and in a number of African states.[45] But such autocracy is a matter of degree and often difficult to determine with any kind of precision. The very nature of power and influence being what they are (Chapters 9 and 11), neither extreme autocracy nor radical democracy is likely to prevail for long under free competitive conditions; they constitute marginal instances in the life of parties. It is only when the party becomes a functioning part, and indeed the central part, of an autocratic totalitarian system that the autocratic character of the party becomes permanent. Such party autocracy may be disguised by a variety of acclamatory devices, such as the *Reichsparteitag* of the Hitler regime, or the party congresses of the Soviet Union. Such devices do provide for a measure of participation, even in the formal legitimizing of decisions arrived at by the leadership. Such participation has the characteristics of a ritual ceremony; independent individual and group initiative are nearly completely absent.[46] Characteristically, "decisions" are taken unanimously. "Essentially the Congresses have become a rally of Party and state functionaries who assemble to applaud and ratify the policies proclaimed by the ruling group," wrote one leading authority in the Stalin era; there is little sign of any significant change in the latest Party congress.[47] Such a ritualistic outlook on participation in basic decisions is compatible with a vigorous insistence on self-criticism, and indeed criticism at lower echelons of the Party. The

---

of totalitarianism, but it also prevents a grasp of general trends in democratic party development.

[45] C. H. Moore, a, 1960; Safran, 1961; cf. also Almond and Coleman, 1959, in which each section contains a chapter on integration. In commenting on Southeast Asia, Pye in his section comments that "to a very great extent, the basis of national integration was the personality and views of the dominant leaders in the independence movement." It is only natural that this fact should lead to a prevailingly autocratic pattern of party. Cf. for Mexico and Bolivia esp. pp. 517–518. The autocratic (misnamed "authoritarian") character of the efforts at integration (not limited to parties) is noted on pp. 530–531. Cf. also Blanksten, 1951, pp. 32–33.

[46] Fainsod, 1953, p. 183, where the author speaks of "mass manipulation rather than spontaneous and creative acts of mass participation."

[47] Fainsod, a, 1961; the quotation is from p. 187. Cf. also Schapiro, 1960.

Soviet practice in this respect has undergone various transformations, but the basic line has never changed; criticism continues to be one of the major duties of a Party member. A good deal of such criticism has, however, itself somewhat the quality of a self-castigating ritual.

Before we extend the general analysis of the totalitarian party, it seems well to consider Lenin's views on the necessity of an autocratic leadership for the Bolshevik Party he was directing. For he was the first to formulate, if not to apply, the operational principles of such a party with laudable candor. By his insistence on discipline and subordination, comprising the total acceptance of an ideology clearly totalitarian, he fashioned the first totalitarian party concept. In his *What Is to be Done?* Lenin outlined in 1902 the rigidly autocratic frame which the Bolshevik movement was to follow. "Everyone will probably agree that 'broad democratic principles' presuppose the two following conditions: first, full publicity, and second, election to all functions. . . . No one would ever call an organization that is hidden from everyone but its members by a veil of secrecy a democratic organization." These are two main criteria by which to distinguish a democratic from an autocratic party. The third criterion is, as we said, free recruiting; a democratic party is open. If an autocratic party has a totalitarian ideology, it may be called a totalitarian party. Lenin would no doubt have preferred to call it revolutionary; but since both a revolutionary and a totalitarian ideology call for a total destruction of the existing and the construction of a totally new and different society, the difference between these two terms is not important for the purpose in hand. It is, however, significant that a re-emphasis of the Party under Khrushchev has been accompanied by a revival of the world-revolutionary thrust of the ideology—never forgotten, to be sure, but soft-pedaled in the later Stalinist period. Since this revolutionary thrust is directed at the outside, it would be awkward to call the Communist Party of the Soviet Union a revolutionary party today; perhaps one could most appropriately say that a totalitarian party is a revolutionary party which has come to function as a part of a totalitarian regime.[48] Besides the rejection of the democratic principle for the

[48] Lenin speaks in *What Is to be Done?* of "professional revolutionaries," of whom it is irrelevant to say whether they are workers or not. Cf. secs. (d) and (e); in the latter section the quotation is found. Many of Lenin's important writings on party are in a German collection, 1958. The essay cited above is found in his *Selected Works*, 1943, vol. II, esp. p. 152, where the passage is located. Lenin himself adds the principle of "careful selection" to the other two as contradictory to the democratic principle (*ibid.*). In the following paragraph Lenin delineates the operation of the German Social Democratic Party in a "land of political freedom," giving a classic description of a democratic party, with its publicity, free elections and free recruiting. He incidentally here and elsewhere answered Michels, before the latter ever wrote, by ridiculing those who thought that a small leadership violated the democratic principle; see sec. (c).

Party, which Lenin believed necessary under the Russian autocratic regime—here too we have an instance of the effect of the form of government upon the mould of party, including the revolutionary opposition—he clearly perceived the importance of ideology. Hence his insistence that a news organ must be the heart of such an organization. "Such a paper can and must be the *ideological* leader of the party," Lenin wrote to a party worker in 1904.[49] Ideological unity seemed to him the heart of effective organization, and organization is crucial: "The proletariat possesses no other weapon in its struggle for power than organization," he insisted again and again, and such organization must be centralist and bureaucratic, rather than the opposite. The expounders of local autonomy and democratism are the enemies of revolutionary socialism, they are exposed to the danger of anarchism and of "primitive" democracy. In this connection Lenin refers to the analysis of the Webbs, who had noted that while trade unions in the early days had subscribed to such "primitive" democracy, they gradually learned that professional experience and leadership, as well as central direction were essential.[50]

The clear recognition of centralized, autocratic direction, as well as ideological orthodoxy and selectivity in membership, has remained the core of such autocratic parties as the Communist Party of the Soviet Union. These traits are at least in part the result of the fighting position of such groups; first the fight against competitors within the movement, then against other parties, finally against enemies of the regime and the outside world. In the mature totalitarian regime the role of the party is a different one[51] from that in a democratic society, even though several functions are similar, as noted above. While Mussolini's well-known phrase describing the party as the "capillaries" of the body politic refers to the functions the totalitarian party shares with the democratic one, actually the party constitutes the elite of the totalitarian political order (Chapter 18). It provides the following for the leader and it monopolizes the selection of such leader or leaders. By providing the one and only road to power and rule, it eventually acquires a formidable attraction for all persons with any desire for power, any *gout du pouvoir*. Mussolini's formula of "believe, obey, fight," and the National Socialist slogan of the marching column are only one side of the coin, of which the other reads

[49] *Ibid.*, p. 112 (1958), pp. 139ff. Lenin's draft of the Party statutes is given. Here, too, we find the clear recognition of the ideological leadership of a central organ. It was drafted in 1903. The same theme is in "One Step Forward, Two Steps Back," esp. pp. 185ff.

[50] Webb and Webb, 1897 (1902), chap. 1. Lenin, *op. cit*, pp. 335ff. The same themes appear again in Lenin's appeal for the reorganization of the Party in 1905 *ibid.*, pp. 422ff. and later. Actually, the Webbs had not "learned" what Lenin claims, but had insisted on "representation" instead of "primitive" democracy (p. 21).

[51] Friedrich and Brzezinski, 1956, chap. 3.

"preach, command, lead." For in face of the rest of the populace, the party exhibits all the traits of a fighting brotherhood, demanding great sacrifices in return for status and power. Phrases like "to enter the sacred door of the Party one must be spotless not only in his public life but in his personal life as well" are repeated over and over again.[52] A great deal has become known through careful research in recent years about the behavior of party members on various levels of the hierarchy in comparison with the rest of the population, both in the Soviet Union and other totalitarian regimes, whether communist or fascist.[53] The total identification of the party with its leader, the radical ideological commitment, the autocratic cast of the organization, described as "democratic centralism" in the Soviet Union and as *Volksgemeinschaft* in Germany (to mention only two leading instances of terminological confusion), which is the same in all totalitarian regimes, must not be allowed to obscure the significant contrasts which have existed and which continue to differentiate such totalitarian parties from each other. Not only is this true as between Fascist–National Socialist and communist parties, but it also occurs within the communist camp. This is to some extent a result of different styles of leadership, as the personalities of Stalin, Mussolini, Hitler, Khrushchev, Mao, Tito and Gomulka express themselves in their actions and are imitated by their following.[54] But it manifests itself most strikingly in the relation of party and government in different totalitarian regimes. For the party may be above, on a par with, or below the government; but there are several reasons for treating the degree of party supremacy as a test for the degree of totalitarian maturity. To be sure, in the phase of extreme personal predominance of Stalin, which many consider the most totalitarian phase of the Soviet Union, the Party lost a good deal of its position, as symbolized by the absence of Party congresses for over a decade (1939–1952). It seems more appropriate to argue that this "despotic" phase of Stalin's was a corrupt or perverted phase, corresponding to similar perversions in other kinds of autocracy. Tsarism and the absolute monarchies of Western Europe are not fairly described

[52] All this is described in greater detail *ibid.*, chap. 3. Cf. also Fainsod, 1953, chaps. 7 and 8; these descriptions should be implemented by the general analysis of daily life in the Soviet Union in such works as Inkeles and Bauer, 1959, esp. chaps. 4–6 and 9–11.

[53] Note esp. Fainsod, 1959, which is based upon a careful examination of the Party records of Smolensk, 1917–1938, as far as they were preserved. In matters of detail, they cannot be considered as descriptive of present conditions; but they contain a basic matrix against which to project the data of such studies as those of Inkeles and Bauer. The twenty-second Party Congress seems to confirm this report; cf. Fainsod, a, 1961.

[54] That this is a common phenomenon in organizations of all types has been shown above, Chap. 7; the interaction of such personal style and the organization objectives and situations has been quite inadequately investigated so far.

in terms of the abuses practiced by their most corrupt rulers, any more than democracy can be properly described in terms of Tammany Hall. If seen in this perspective, the relatively subordinate position of the Italian Fascist Party in the early days of the regime, and its parallelism in Hitler's Germany correspond to an early phase, superseded by the emergence of the party as predominant in the totalitarian consummation.[55] Thus, the difference in totalitarian parties reflects not only the personal style of the leader, but also the national traditions, especially in the governmental sphere.

By way of conclusion, we might say that it is this predominance of the party in the totalitarian system which gives it the decisive role in the crisis of succession. As we said at the outset of this chapter, one of the key problems of any political order is how to provide for the succession. In modern states which no longer can depend upon hallowed tradition and religion for sanctioning blood descent or anointment, such succession depends upon constitutional rule and party-directed electoral choice. Democratic, autocratic and more especially totalitarian (revolutionary) parties, by linking the rulers and the ruled through ideology and organization, representing the individuals and groups as well as integrating them into larger units for effective political action, provide the underpinning for the several functions involved in governing men which have been analyzed in earlier chapters.

[55] Germino, 1959, esp. pp. 26ff.

part

V

Ranges and Levels of Government

chapter

29

The Local Community, Tribe and Region

All high culture is city culture.
The peasant way of life is the truly human,
appropriate to man's nature.
Alexander Rüstow

THE CONCRETE POLITICAL order which we have been discussing may recur on several levels of community: the intimate local community, the region, the nation or the empire. We have had occasion to cite experience from one or another of these levels as the several aspects of the concrete political order were analyzed. It is necessary to consider the several levels in turn, since they present distinctive political problems. In doing this, we ought to remain aware of the fact that the term "levels of government" contains an implicit analogy which deserves brief comment at the outset; for governments are not spatial entities as such, to which the concept of level applies in the first and basic sense. In using this term for designating a particular range of governmental operations, we make the assumption that the several levels may be treated *as if* they were disparate, like boxes piled one on top of the other. In point of fact, governments never are thus sharply separated from each other; the human beings operating on the several levels constantly interact. Still, since the category of "higher" and "lower" can suitably be applied to government, depending upon whether the power a government wields extends to a more or less extensive sphere, the expression "level of government" has a distinct and verifiable meaning, namely, this range or spatial extension of its power. Consequently, there could be theoretically as many levels as there are spatial extensions, in short, an infinite number. But in point of fact and for practical purposes, there are only four levels which are generally acknowledged. These are determined by the community which occupies the space to which the level applies: the local community, the tribal or regional community, the national community, and the imperial and potentially the world community. To these four levels our discussion will therefore be restricted, to be implemented by a discussion of the special problems of federalism as the process of linking autonomous communities of a lower level to constitute a higher one.[1]

Having previously been the subject of extended exploration (Chapter 8), community does not need further elaboration at this point. Suffice it to recall here the following. In the first place, we are dealing primarily with the political community, or, to put it more precisely, with the political dimension of community. This dimension has throughout the ages, as we have shown, been a central concern of political thought. Three great debates have raged as to what constitutes community: Is it a community of law or love? Is it organic or purposive? and finally, Is it simply there as an existential given, or is it willed? We showed how these antitheses need to be resolved and community seen as characterized by all six of these stipulations. It was noted that the increasing insistence upon community in a variety of contexts is due to a special constellation wherein a substantial measure of common unity is manifest in the sharing of values, interests and beliefs, yet lacks, or is insufficiently provided with, effective organization. In the chapters which follow we shall explore the issues presented by this constellation on the several levels of government. In the present chapter the following problems will be taken up: (1) the contrast of the urban and the rural community; (2) the origin of the city, including synoecism and related phenomena; (3) the optimal size of local communities; (4) *polis*, metropolis, megalopolis, necropolis (Mumford); (5) the medieval city and its struggle with feudalism; (6) the role of the city and other local communities under modern government; (7) the metropolitan problem, including the breakup of the metropolis and the use of federal solutions; and (8) regions and their use: federalism.

(1) Since time out of mind, the contrast between urban and rural communities, between city and village, has been of decisive political as well as cultural importance. If the contrast is stated in terms of size, then the village is the intimate community with at most a few hundred families, all of whom know each other, as compared with the anonymity of urban conglomerations.[2] If the economic life that is the primary occupation of

[1] To label the first three "parochial" as does Niebuhr, 1959, and then to contrast them with the fourth seems both misleading and prejudicial.

[2] Plato's notion, as described in *The Laws*, that a citizenry of 5,040 could know each other well enough for the purpose of communal existence in his model *polis* surely is entirely unrealistic, though often repeated since. Cf. for an appropriate criticism of his entire scheme, as far as the urban community is concerned, Lewis Mumford, 1961, chap. VI.

the inhabitants is stressed, then the village is seen as a congregation of farmers as contrasted with the rich variety of trades in a city. Such a city is, of course, admittedly dependent upon the villages surrounding it for its basic foodstuffs, unless they can be imported from afar. Another related antithesis is made in terms of culture: the village is rude and simple in its pursuit of traditional ways, and preoccupied with elemental life functions, while the city is refined and progressive, yet also inclined toward corruption in its cultivation of all the arts and sciences.[3] But from a political standpoint, all these differences and contrasts fade into insignificance—they are of minor importance when seen in the perspective of the natural propensity of the village toward cooperative modes of government, a kind of primitive democracy, compared with the aristocratic, oligarchic, monarchic and even tyrannical bent of the city.

There was a time when this fact was viewed in the romantic light of a "Germanic" versus a "Roman" legal tradition.[4] But it has long since become clear that this conflict between Germanic and Roman legal principles was merely a special instance of a much more universal phenomenon.[5] The great peasant revolts of the fourteenth to sixteenth centuries in England, France and Germany were all attempts on the part of villagers to recapture ancient modes of living and of governing themselves which the rising city culture and its monarcho-aristocratic concomitant in government threatened to destroy; after the failure of these revolts, the village was in fact reduced to impotence until its reemergence as a political factor in the nineteenth century.

These basic political differences between village and city have been obscured by the role which the peasantry has played in the rise of dictatorial regimes in modern times. There can be little doubt that the peasantry has been a decisive factor in providing mass support for these movements and regimes, but the meaning of this phenomenon is rather complex.[6] It is related to the anticapitalist and hence antiurban outlook of the villagers, and to the measure of acceptance of authority in the rural context (in the strict sense developed in Chapter 12 above). Even more important is the strong attachment of the peasantry to the soil. "Since the farmer's entire existence depends upon his place of birth, the 'fatherland' or *patrie* becomes an inseparable and inalienable part of his personality. The interest of rural folk and the interest of their country are palpably one."

[3] Schorske in Handlin (ed.), 1962.

[4] E.g., Gierke, 1868, vol. I, pp. 1–4.

[5] A. Rüstow, 1950, vol. I, pp. 39ff. and 251ff., who relates the problem to that of culture growth and what he calls the "pyramid of culture." Coste, 1899, pp. 154ff., had already pointed out the importance of numbers for cultural development, provided they are politically organized. He called this "la condition démotique du progrès."

[6] Friedrich, a1, a2, 1937, from which the following quotation is taken.

Yet farmers may also become the backbone of a functioning democracy, partly as a result of the natural propensity of small communities to live cooperatively, and partly through their "defensive" nationalism. This fact is important because of the cultural importance of the peasantry. It is perhaps going a bit too far to claim that "the peasantry embodies from a human viewpoint the last pinnacle in the development of mankind."[7] But it is nonetheless true, as was added by way of justification, that "it has as much proved itself economically and socially in the course of two hundred generations as a human institution can prove itself." The attempts to transcend this achievement in cities are believed to have endangered "the stability and health of the vital situation." This insight is important not only for Western politics, but to an even greater degree for the "new nations." The battle cry of industrialization, while understandable, implies a precipitate urbanization which may destroy the foundation of a healthy democracy and prepare the ground for a communist take-over.

Another complication arises from the fact that not infrequently large urban units are in part or in a way divided into village-like subdivisions. It has for example been said that Paris consists of such a medley of villages, though surely that does not apply throughout the city, as some of the modern fashionable parts and some of the factory districts are devoid of this quasi-rural aspect. But while such village-like subunits may be sociologically interesting and culturally valuable, they do not usually affect the political situation sufficiently to alter the basic political difference between city and village. Such units are too fluid to provide a stable basis for cooperative political relations, unless they become explicit political subdivisions, such as the wards in American cities.[8] A formalized arrangement, such as the *borgo* of the Italian cities, is similar to the wards. The lack of success of efforts made in various countries in recent years to recreate genuine political cooperation on a neighborhood basis bears out this conclusion.[9]

(2) The origin of cities is shrouded in mystery. It used to be seen in the light of the establishment of the Greek *polis* which occurred in more or less violent ways by the uniting of several villages—a process known as *synoikismos*.[10] Recently an author, speculating on the basis of archaeological research, suggested a strictly political interpretation, namely, that "the most important agent in effecting the change from a decentralized village economy to a highly organized urban economy was

[7] A. Rüstow, 1950, vol. I, p. 54; the following quotations, *ibid*. and p. 55.

[8] V. O. Key, 1958, pp. 369ff.

[9] Maste, 1957.

[10] J. Burckhardt, 1898, 1930, pp. 60ff., has described the *synoikismos* vividly and concludes his description as follows: "The building of a polis was the great, the decisive experience of a [Greek] populace."

the king, or rather the institution of kingship. . . ." [11] He continues: "In the urban implosion the king stands at the center: he is the polar magnet that draws to the heart of the city and brings under the control of the palace and temple all the new forces of civilization. . . ." He is inclined to think that we are confronted with a "leap" and that this leap ought to be seen, in the manner of trends of modern biology, as "the rise of modern civilization." [12] Tempting as this hypothesis is, especially to the political scientist, the chances are that while this sort of thing may have happened at particular times and under certain circumstances, it is quite likely and attested to in other contexts that the "founding" of cities occurred cooperatively as well as forcibly. This was the view of an earlier writer, who said: "It is of little account to seek the cause which determined several neighbouring tribes to unite. Sometimes it was voluntary; sometimes it was imposed by the superior force of a tribe, or by the powerful will of a man." [13] He linked such voluntary *synoikismos* to the force of religion: "The bond of the new association was still religion." And he furthermore stressed, and rightly in our view, that these tribes and lesser units which were brought together in a *polis* did not lose their identity; indeed a division of the same kind was decreed in newly founded cities. Therefore "the city was a confederation." These views are to some extent empirically confirmed or at least made probable by the better known process of town formation in the Middle Ages.[14] Here we find both the coercive and the cooperative type of process, as well as mixtures of the two. Nor is this to be wondered at, when one recalls what was said about community formation: the common values, interests and beliefs may be imposed or they may emerge gradually in conjunction with common problems and their solution. These common problems may arise in the politico-military field as problems of defense or expansion, or they may be economically conditioned by a changing technology and the means of production it provides and calls for, or they may crystallize in the cultural field through a common language or other modes of self-expression and personality fulfillment. No doubt capable leadership, especially its inspirational variant, often played a decisive role, but in keeping with our general theory of leadership (Chapters 9 and 10) it

[11] Lewis Mumford, 1961, chap. II, p. 35.

[12] Teilhard de Chardin is cited by Mumford as authority for this view as well as for the further notion that "we cannot follow this change at the moment it occurred, for it is the unstable and fluid form that leaves no record behind." *Ibid.*, p. 33. Teilhard de Chardin, 1959, discusses this matter at pp. 202ff. A. Rüstow, 1950, vol. I, suggests a similar approach, but links it with conquest (*Überlagerung*, i.e., superimposition).

[13] Fustel de Coulanges, 1889 (Engl.), p. 167. The next quotation *ibid.*

[14] A learned controversy raged over this question for many years among European scholars; note the concluding argument in Schmoller, 1922, pp. 35–36, citing S. Rietschel; also pp. 39ff.

must be presumed that such leadership need not have been based upon constraint and force, but may have been rooted in consent and cooperation.

The *synoikismos*, or bringing together of villages, in the founding of Greek and other Mediterranean cities, including Rome, had the consequence of deeply affecting the early political order of cities. To elaborate a bit, the legendary history of the founding of Rome, which probably contains a substantial kernel of truth, tells of the forcible uniting of the several tribes which inhabited the other hills surrounding the Palatine hill on which the Romans themselves dwelt. Thucydides, speaking of ancient Athens, gives a similar account. "Attica," he wrote, "had been divided into separate towns . . . and as long as they had nothing to fear . . . they separately administered their own affairs. . . . But when Theseus became king . . . he abolished the councils and magistracies of the minor towns and brought all the inhabitants into a union with what is now the city, establishing a single council and town hall. . . ." [15] Aristotle, whose account of the early developments unfortunately remains lost, stresses the class struggle, the oppression of the poor by the rich; "there was civil strife for a long time between the nobility and the common people, . . ." he writes at the point where the manuscript starts.[16] It is clear even to the visitor of the ruins of these ancient cities that an elevated spot, such as the Acropolis in Athens or Acrocorinth in Corinth, provided the potential ruler of such a city with the stronghold from which to proceed with the forcible uniting of adjacent villages. Many a medieval city north of the Alps shows a similar structure. The common saying that "city air makes free" belongs to a later phase in the development of cities. At the outset, the city air was probably decidedly less free than that of the surrounding countryside. It has been argued persuasively that religious elements were closely intertwined with the political and military position of these "citadels." [17] It would be surprising if this were not so, considering the all-pervading role of religion in politics until recent times (Chapter 6).

(3) It has always been a problem, politically and otherwise, whether there is such a thing as an optimal size of the local community. The answer to the question "How large?" or "How small?" was likely to be affected by the political outlook and the purpose of those who discussed it. Plato and Aristotle, who were concerned with the classical Greek *polis,* independent within the broad value context of the Greek cultural community, both believed that the community should be quite small, as

[15] Thucydides, bk. II, chap. 15; cf. also the account in Pausanias, bk. I, chaps. 15, 26, 31, 37, and Plutarch's "Theseus."

[16] Aristotle, *Constitution of Athens* (Fritz and Kapp eds.), p. 69. Cf. also the account in Bury, 1900, vol. 2, chap. IV.

[17] Cf. Lewis Mumford, 1961, chaps. IV–V, for a good discussion.

indeed it typically was. It should not exceed, in its active citizenship, a size which would allow face-to-face acquaintance of a large percentage of such citizens, but this seems unrealistic when the figure is given as 5,040, as in Plato's *The Laws* (cf. footnote 2). Aristotle, therefore, believed that the figure should be reduced still further. The Platonic body of citizens would mean, with women and children, about 25,000 to 30,000 people, to whom must be added a sizable slave population, giving us a total of upward of 50,000. This figure seems to have been more or less standard in Roman times as a basis for planning new towns first in Italy and afterwards throughout the empire,[18] although of course politically the position of such dependent cities within the Roman realm cannot in spite of their autonomy be compared with the problems of an independent *polis* of the kind that Plato and Aristotle had in mind. Basically, however, the proposed size *is* in both instances related to the task of self-government, and neglects the problems of defense, security and foreign policy, as Rousseau was to do again when he spoke of the ideal community. In either case, such a figure implies a condemnation of cities such as Athens and Rome. Athens had, in the fifth century, probably a population exceeding a quarter of a million, when slaves are included, though the figures are quite controversial.[19] The underlying thought in both Plato and Aristotle, reflecting presumably a widely held view, we saw to be that too large a size disrupts the communal life and undermines the political order. *Anomie*, or the lack of common values and beliefs, they held to be the inevitable result. Neither of them had any notion that a federation of political units into which too large a city, such as Athens, might be divided, could be the answer to the difficulties. It is evident that the arguments resemble those brought forward against the mass society of our time, though the order of magnitude has changed. Clearly related is the problem of how to keep the local community or make it vital again.

The discussion of what would be the best size for a political community subsided in Rome, except as to the administrative problem mentioned above of how large to make new towns; but the growth of Rome into the vast urban conglomeration of the imperial period caused much concern. Any idea, however, of stopping this growth seemed presumably too utopian to have occurred to many of the practical-minded Romans. The development of megalopolis had already had its day in the great cities of the Near East; Babylon, Nineveh, as well as Alexandria and others of more recent origin, obviously made more and more illusory the kind of political order which republican Rome in its heyday had possessed. The imperial rule seemed to obliterate the need for such intimate

[18] *Ibid.*, p. 209.
[19] Beloch, 1886, pp. 99–106, continues to be the authority.

citizenship as had at one time provided Rome with its constitutional underpinning. Many have speculated why it was that the classical world never evolved the notion of representation which has enabled modern nations to combine the advantages of size with the intimacies of local community, and which has made federal solutions possible. Political inventions, like other creative innovations, are made at the time when they are made because all the factors required are present. Representation, as we have seen (Chapter 17) occurs in the West first of all in the Christian church. Here representation of God, that is, the "making present" of a divine being in the priesthood and more especially in its head, the Pope, laid the groundwork for a secularized version. In any case, medieval political theory resumed the argument which Plato and Aristotle had started. As the classical writings were studied anew, it became a favorite subject of some of the early students of population statistics such as G. Botero, who writing *On the Growth of Cities* [20] discerned natural "checks" to the increase in size, thus anticipating Malthus. Yet, and in spite of the rather unsatisfactory living conditions in the larger medieval cities and the recurring ravages of great plagues, the princely rulers' passion for power suggested the desirability of growth. As noted before, the large city is the concomitant of autocratic political systems, anyhow, and therefore the forward march of monarchical absolutism is accompanied by the growth of a cental city in each monarchy. A leading interpreter has suggested a progression from *polis* to metropolis, to megalopolis and finally to necropolis—the dead city in which there are "magnifications of demoralized power, magnifications of life." [21] He has painted in vivid colors the corrosion from within which destroyed the inner core of Rome's greatness. While his argument is impressive and the warning it contains may well be a lesson of what to avoid, it may yet be doubted whether the problem was primarily one of urban size. If the political order, even though autocratic, had been effective and sound, there is no particular reason why even a city of the size of Rome should not have endured. Chinese cities of that same order of magnitude have managed to exist for many centuries, and the more recent history of the great European cities suggests a similar conclusion. It seems all a question of organizing such a city politically and economically in sufficient diversity to cope with the problem of communal living, that is to say, it is a question of how to structure its "public." An autocratic system, which does not need to organize any effective *political* participation, obviously confronts an easier task than does a free society, but even here the problem

[20] Giovanni Botero, *Delle cause della grandezza delle città*, 1588, transl. into Latin as well as English, and widely influential.

[21] Mumford, 1961, p. 242.

can be solved, as indicated below. All in all, the abstract discussion of an "optimal" size resolves itself under modern conditions into the more flexible proposition that a viable national community needs to be differentiated into numerous smaller communities, that none of these smaller communities should exceed a certain limit without being federally structured into subcommunities, and that a large number of reasonably self-governing rural communities are essential for a nation's vitality, because the cities "devour" people.[22]

(4) The discussion about the size of cities and the contemporary trend to resolve it in terms of an internal, a built-in, breakup into subcommunities and "neighborhoods" has been highlighted by sharply contrasting *polis*, metropolis, megalopolis and necropolis—a developmental construct that bears an intrinsic relation to all of life's processes from birth through maturity to death. Such a vista of the growth pattern of local and more especially urban communities need not be accepted, however, with fatalistic resignation.[23]

When symptoms of corruption multiply, necropolis may be near, "the barbarian" may already have "captured the city from within." The appalling story of Rome's continued expansion and the complete perversion of the live community she once was is familiar enough. But it is the story of the imperial city living on exploitation, not that of merely a large community. It may be doubtful whether such an imperial city can be protected against the fate that befell Rome, though London seems so far to have done comparatively well. In the United States the almost complete lack of local self-government in Washington, the one and only city without any self-government in America, surely requires correction, but the problem is eased by the capital city not being the major industrial center.[24] At the same time, the vigorous program of urban renewal which is receiving increasing attention is at least in part directed toward stopping the "progress" toward megalopolis. It is as significant a feature of urban studies in Britain and on the Continent as it is in the United States. Both London and Paris, not to mention Rome, present in aggravated form the problems of revitalizing local self-government, and the solution is still to be found; there are better prospects in London

[22] Emile Verhaeren, 1908, Mumford, and others have written on the contemporary city as "space eaters."

[23] Mumford, 1961, chap. VIII. Mumford illustrates the cycle by the history of ancient Rome, which by the fourth century "suffered from megalopolitan elephantiasis." Rome, according to Mumford, "remains a significant lesson of what to avoid." The quotes in the text are on p. 242.

[24] Recent efforts to reverse this trend and to develop for Washington a measure of such local self-government are therefore very heartening and a sign of the continued vitality of the democratic spirit in the U.S. Cf. especially, for a recent analysis, *The Government of Metropolitan Washington,* staff study, 1958. U.S. Congress.

than in Paris or Rome.[25] We shall return to these questions below when discussing metropolitan problems.

The vast urban aggregations in the United States have for many years seemed a betrayal of the cooperative pattern of politics; Bryce noted that the government of cities over 100,000 inhabitants tended to be corrupt. More recently, a figure of 400,000 has been named as the upper limit of an effective urban community having a democratically manageable government with genuinely autonomous functions. The movement for workable neighborhood units, spontaneously springing up in a number of countries, including the United States, Britain and Germany, is a significant response to these problems.[26]

(5) These problems of modern industrial society, reminiscent of the Athenian and Roman predicament and paralleled in the great cities of the Orient, are a far cry from the medieval city. The extended controversy over the origin of these urban centers already alluded to [27] has served to bring out that the reemergence of the city cannot be attributed to any one factor, be it feudal lord, bishop, monastery or trading center. Neither a strictly military interpretation in terms of security and protection, nor an economic one in terms of trade and/or craftsmanship will do; all these, and in varying combinations, have had their share in the growth of medieval towns.[28] They were unique in that they succeeded where the ancient *polis* had failed; the principle of cooperative association, as manifest especially in the guilds, permeated all phases of government in the high period of medieval city life; it made them genuine centers of local community life, granting a greater measure of freedom and selfhood to all inhabitants than had ever before been achieved.[29] The monastery

[25] See Robson, a, 1961, and L. J. Sharpe, a, 1961, for a down-to-earth analysis of the Report of the Royal Commission on Local Government in Greater London, 1957–1960, Cmd. 1164–1960; also Robson's magistral work of 1939, 1948, esp. pp. 344ff. Cf. also Robson (ed.), 1954, introd., pp. 25–120; the chapter on Paris, pp. 451ff., by Brian Chapman; and the chapter on Rome by G. Chiarelli, pp. 517ff.

[26] See fn. 9 above.

[27] See above p. 531 and fn. 14. Cf. A. Rüstow, 1951, vol. I, p. 55, for comment on this extended argument.

[28] Pirenne, 1925, overstressed the economic factor; but others including Mumford, 1960, chap. IX, have underplayed it. A. Rüstow, 1950, vol. I, pp. 250ff., would tie such growth largely to the processes of superimposition (conquest—*Überlagerung*); he fails to give due credit to the cooperative aspects of medieval towns as expressed in the guilds and other associations; Rüstow however fully recognizes the cultural importance of the city; it is the focal growth point (*Wachstumsspitze*) of higher culture. Rüstow cites with approval Pirenne as well as Max Weber's sketch about the city; see Weber, 1925, pp. 514ff.

[29] Mumford, 1960, p. 316, wrote: "For the first time, the majority of inhabitants of a city were free men: except for special groups, like the Jews, city dweller and citizen were now synonymous terms." Hence the German saying: *Stadtluft macht frei.* This statement holds, of course, only for the period of guild ascendancy.

was its exemplar, in a way; the honoring of labor and the equality of all workers were its very foundation, as they were to become of modern industrial societies. This measure of freedom was, however, a reality only during the period of open guilds and their predominance. Once the guilds became exclusive corporations and thus the basis of oligarchic control, they threatened the cities with slow strangulation, and eventually the autonomy of these local communities was swept away by monarchical absolutism. Even so, the political order of the medieval towns throughout Europe was the progenitor of modern constitutional democracy.

It has been noted that the medieval city constituted a rejection of the original basis upon which the city had been erected. This rejection is intimately tied to certain basic values and beliefs fostered by Christianity. Even though these cities were far from constituting a Christian commonwealth in the more radical perspective of a brotherhood based on neighborly love, they provided the political framework for a genuine political community of a high order of development (Chapter 8). That they also exhibited the weakness of any isolated community—they have justly been compared to islands, protected as they lay behind their surrounding walls—cannot surprise the political theorist. Community always involves exclusion as well as inclusion; one cannot have the cake of intimacy and autonomy, and eat it too by being wide open to a world beyond. Only a measure of balance is achievable.

(6) As suggested at the end of the discussion of the problem of optimal size, a functioning modern democracy needs effectively self-governing local communities of varying size. The problem of how to provide such local self-government has therefore been a subject of continuing concern in the politics of constitutionalism. A number of the more recent constitutions make explicit provision for this principle which forms part of that organized pluralism of which the protection of the freedom of association and of academic freedom are correlative integral parts, since they also protect "communities."[30] But the problem is not limited to constitutional democracy. A measure of autonomy and self-government was often practiced under Oriental despotism, in India, in China, and elsewhere, and contemporary writings on democracy in these countries have been inclined to hark back to these ancient village democracies in an effort to give democracy a national and traditional sanction.[31]

Actually, these patterns of local self-government were rarely what can properly be called democratic. Rather they correspond to some species of aristocracy or oligarchy and have been called "administra-

[30] Mangoldt, n.d., pp. 57ff., 78ff.; Calamandrei and Levi, 1950, vol. I, pp. 154ff.; cf. also Jaspers and Rossman, 1961, pp. 25ff.

[31] Malaviya, 1956, chap. II; Altekar, 1927, gives a description of village government in part I. The latter author's more general treatment, 1949, 1958, chap. X, is also good. For China, cf. Latourette, 1934, 1947, pp. 41ff.

tion by the honored few," if we may thus freely translate a Weberian term.[32] It is, for example, the system of the much discussed *panchayats* of India. Of these *panchayats* there are two basic kinds, those ruling the castes and those ruling the villages. The latter are typically composed of representatives of the caste *panchayat;* they are neither town meetings nor assemblies of democratically elected representatives, but tradition-based bodies which recruit themselves by cooption. Thus the caste *panchayat* consists of the most important men—their importance being assessed on the grounds of wealth, lineage and caste position. They possess authority in that their judgment is believed to be entitled to respect. But in a village gathering others may speak up in discussions on decisions which vitally affect them; we have spoken of these fluid situations earlier in other connections (Chapters 9 to 11). The desire to arrive at some sort of "sense of the meeting" favors a conservative decision which avoids conflicts with any strongly voiced objection.[33] It should be noted that corresponding propensities may be observed in New England town meetings and similar gatherings, such as those found in the small Swiss cantons. They are also characteristic of faculty meetings in various European countries as well as in the United States. It has been said that "the traditional *panchayat* is supposed to find the 'right' decision within the context of the common culture which all its members share." [34] The same is true of a great many other local bodies, whether in Europe, past and present, America, Africa or Asia.

A considerable variety of patterns of local self-government has developed in Europe and America. But these different types of local community have some important traits in common. For one thing, there is to be observed a steady growth in local government functions which is at times obscured by the generally acknowledged widening of governmental functions at the national level. This growth in local functions has been accompanied by increasing dependence on support by the higher levels of government, and this has brought supervision and control in its train. Road-building, schools and water provision are examples of this trend. It has generated a good many serious conflicts and conjured up the danger of a loss of autonomy, not only in the United States, but in Britain and elsewhere. In the last decade, it has been proposed in Britain to place the assessment of property for local taxes in charge of a national revenue authority; while advocated in terms of efficiency and equality, this raises the threat of a complete loss of the power of the purse, such as has

[32] Max Weber, 1921, 1925, pp. 170f., 590ff., and elsewhere, speaks of *Honoratiorenverwaltung*, a system found widely dispersed in all sorts of cultures.

[33] Such deliberation is claimed by some African leaders to be a kind of democracy; e.g., Nyerere, a, 1962, and above, Chap. 28.

[34] Dr. S. Rudolph in a lecture on local Indian government; I acknowledge my indebtedness to her in discussing these and related matters of Indian government.

existed for a long time elsewhere.[35] For in France and other Continental European countries except Switzerland, there never has existed the degree of fiscal autonomy found in the United States, and it is a source of surprise to practical administrators from these lands to discover that in the United States the budget for local schools is determined by local boards, and a corresponding tax rate imposed upon the community by such a board, locally elected by the citizenry.

It is obvious that the activities of these local governments touch the daily life of most people more directly and intimately than the more distant undertakings of the national government in foreign, military and fiscal policy. Water supply, fire and police protection, sanitation, welfare, roads, gas and electricity, parks, libraries, building regulations, town planning, housing, public transportation, and education, though not everywhere in charge of local governments, in whole or in part, are certainly part of man's most intimate and concrete concerns. They are therefore especially suited for handling in the context of the local community and its cooperative pattern of decision-making.[36]

The great problem is how to maintain local control over these varied services. The availability of adequate financial resources, their adequacy to be determined by the local community itself, is of crucial importance. Unfortunately, many constitutional systems are far too rigid in limiting the taxing power of local communities at the present time.[37] The argument often advanced against such flexible powers is that local communities cannot be trusted with this power. The cogency of the argument has been disproved by concrete experience. And indeed, why should a local community when directly concerned with the cost of improvements as well as current outlay, be less able to control such expenditures than a distant national legislature? The other and more weighty argument is that against inequality. It is indeed arguable that it is unjust for a child in a "good" community to be very much better educated than another one in a "bad" location. Comparable statements can be urged in regard to fire and police protection, sanitation, and the rest. Basically, this argument touches the central issue of freedom and responsibility (Chapters 14, 18 and 19). There will be differences between free communities as there are bound to be between free individuals. As long as there exists adequate freedom of movement, so that the citizen can go to another community of similar social structure, but better facilities, if he does not find his community satisfactory, the basic claim to equality is satisfied.

Vigorous self-governing local communities are, as remarked before, a great source of strength to any political order, democratic or autocratic.

[35] Chester, 1951, esp. chaps. I–XIII and *passim;* cf. also A. H. Hanson, a, 1957.
[36] G. Hicks, 1946, has provided a vivid personal account of it.
[37] For further detail, cf. Friedrich, 1951, pp. 242f.

Under totalitarianism they become impossible, and this fact is one of the basic weaknesses of the totalitarian system. In a democratic system, they provide competent and responsible administration for many spheres of governmental activity which a centralized and centrally directed setup can handle only with great difficulty. They also serve as a proving ground for political and governmental talent on a continuing basis. This fact may be of particular importance in periods of national catastrophe. It is striking how many recent key leaders of the German Federal Republic are former local government men, beginning with Konrad Adenauer, former mayor of Cologne. One might add that after the total collapse of 1945 the local communities were the first to emerge as viable centers of new political activity. Military government could count upon the workers in this sphere for the reestablishment of orderly government.[38]

As stated above, patterns of local self-government are quite numerous. In general such patterns tend to follow the broader constitutional pattern or at least to fit into it; but this leaves considerable latitude for local variations. Speaking of Europe, one recent author,[39] in delineating the local government traditions, has emphasized a major division: those countries which like Great Britain, Germany, the Scandinavian countries and Switzerland have preserved historical patterns of local government, and those which like France, Italy, Belgium, the Netherlands and Greece have by legislation created uniform local institutions based upon general and rational criteria. In any case, a gradual adaptation and rationalization is to be expected, he thinks. In the United States, the characteristic feature has been the great freedom enjoyed by American municipalities, and not only in the home-rule states. Under such home rule, the voters have a varying measure of freedom to adopt their own pattern of local government. The prevailing tendency is toward three primary patterns. The oldest is a mayor-council plan, under which both mayor and council are popularly elected, as are judges and other officials; this pattern broadly corresponds to the gubernatorial system in the states, based as it is upon the traditional doctrine of the separation of powers. The second pattern is the so-called commission plan, under which a small elected body combines the rule-making and managerial functions, each commissioner heading a department for administrative purposes. Third, there is the manager plan, under which all administrative responsibility is centered in a single manager; he is something in between the town clerk in Britain and the burgomaster in Germany. Such a manager is responsible to and supervised by an elected council.[40] All three types have their advantages and

[38] Gimbel, 1961; Wells in Litchfield (ed.), 1953, pp. 57–116; and W. Friedman, 1947.

[39] Biascaretti, a, 1961.

[40] Friedrich, 1950, pp. 151–152.

disadvantages which divide experts and general public alike, but the manager plan is gaining ground.[41]

The special pattern of the New England towns is based upon the town meeting, for which all the voters gather once a year or more to vote on the budget and taxes, elect town officials and decide broad issues of general policy. It embodies an ancient tradition. Lord Bryce's judgment probably still holds; he wrote many years ago: "Of the three or four types of systems of local government [in the United States] which I have described, that of the Town or township with its popular primary assembly has been the best. It is the cheapest and the most efficient; it is the most educative to the citizens who bear part in it. The town meeting has been not only the source but the school of democracy." [42] But this system works only within quite limited communities, and breaks down when the number of voters exceeds 2,000. For that reason, a system of substituting an elected representative town meeting has been adopted; such a system, when implemented on the administrative side by a board of selectmen, as is the genuine type, would appear a distinctive fourth type along with the other three outlined above. If instead it is implemented by a town manager, it merges with the manager plan. In any case, the problem remains how a comparable "school of democracy" may be developed in the vast metropolitan areas or even in the large cities with which many countries are dotted today.

(7) The great metropolitan areas present a most perplexing range of issues. These issues have become more and more insistent in recent years. They are not only political and governmental, but technological, economic and cultural. Efforts to solve them have been made in all major countries.[43] The governmental solutions have been along three major lines, all seeking to provide a greater measure of over-all direction and control, and yet offering at the same time a degree of continuing local participation and initiative. But only one among them really succeeds in doing so, namely, the federal linking of the central urban core with the surrounding suburbia. The creation of special boards and commissions to handle particular problems, like the London Metropolitan Water Board, New York's Port Authority, or Boston's Metropolitan Transit Authority, are merely stopgaps; the necessarily great role of technicians in such a setup has always made them appeal to the engineer and specialist. The simple consolidation or merging of many smaller units into a centralized larger one which seems to provide the politician with power and the administrator with maximum efficiency in a centrally directed chain of command is subject to all those objections which we have indicated

[41] Stone and Price, 1940.
[42] Bryce, 1888, 1924, vol. I, p. 626.
[43] Robson (ed.), 1957 (rev. ed.).

in reviewing ancient and modern critics of the oversized community. That the helter-skelter combination of all these approaches can produce only chaos is shown by what has happened in the New York metropolitan area with its 1,400 governmental units of overlapping jurisdiction.[44] London may get a better deal, because of the fact that it is the direct concern of one key body, the British Parliament. A royal commission has recently put forward significant new proposals which are, of course, encountering the by now familiar objections of local government authorities.[45] These objections, though always put forward in the name of "localism," are in fact apt to assist in destroying it. "In the end," it has been observed, "much will depend on whether the Government realizes that opposition to the scheme by councillors and local government officers, no matter how strong and persistent, does not necessarily mean that the electors are against it or would vote against the Government at the next election." [46] Yet, this observation is made conditional upon the government's "adequately explaining" the proposals for change in London. A contrasting view, concerned with New York, looks for little change of the same kind in New York, because neither the leadership nor yet the electorate of the New York metropolitan region shows much inclination to demand it.[47] The need for developing public opinion to insist upon metropolitan change has been noted by others.

The most promising course in terms of the strengthening of the local community is, we insist, a process of federalizing the metropolitan regions. The range of possible federal solutions is great. Generally speaking, the history of federalism shows that a federal union starts with a loose confederation and is then made to grow into a closer union. In all such metropolitan regions, which are megalopolitan in contemporary politics, it would therefore seem best to organize a metropolitan authority to exercise those functions which are clearly metropolitan in nature. Such an authority would provide the units of management which are needed for the handling of the common concerns of the region.[48] But it is essential that the component units would retain their separate identity and autonomy, and that effective representation and responsible control be provided throughout.[49]

This discussion might well end on a statement made by a leading

[44] Robert C. Wood, 1961; Vernon, 1960; Sayre and Kaufmann, 1960.

[45] Robson, a, 1961. Cf. also the same author's basic study of 1939. At that time, Robson could actually speak of "neglect" of the problem. Though no longer neglected, the problem is far from solved; cf. Sharpe, a, 1961.

[46] Robson, a, 1961, p. 71.

[47] Wood, 1961, chap. 5, esp. at p. 196.

[48] For further detail see Friedrich, 1950, pp. 252ff.

[49] The issue of effective control by the electorate is ably stated by Robson, 1939, pp. 344ff. Cf. also the *Greater Boston Plan* by Friedrich and associates, 1944, as summarized in Friedrich, a, 1945.

writer on local government: "If we wish to preserve and strengthen democracy in this country [Britain], it is obvious that we must reject expedients and acknowledge the necessity for a directly elected regional council for Greater London as the only type of institution which is satisfactory from a democratic view. . . ." This opinion holds true just as much for the United States, which is increasingly assuming the character of a network of large metropolitan regions.[50] It is to be doubted, though, that anything short of a national initiative will bring about such revolutionary changes, and that initiative may, as so often in history, come in conjunction with the challenge of a threat of war and the need for a broadly effective pattern of civil defense.

(8) Between the strictly local community and the "all-inclusive" community of nation or empire, there often exists an intermediary community with distinct political institutions, the region, province, canton, *Land* or state (in the specific American sense). Such intermediary communities may wield substantial powers of government and may be a significant factor in politics. Indeed in the large territorial realms of modern times, such intermediary communities are bound to exist, and their effective political organization is a condition of effective government. At times, as in the case of Germany, such intermediary communities may have a distinctive tribal foundation; the Bavarians, Swabians, Saxons, Hanoverians and Westphalians, to mention only the most important, possess an identity which goes back to the ancient Germanic tribes of the days after the collapse of the Roman empire. There are, to be sure, *Länder* which are based upon other, more recent, communal formations, such as the free cities of Hamburg, Bremen and most currently Berlin, or the *Länder* resulting from Prussian provincial organization, but even here tribal antecedents play a role, as in Hesse and the Rhineland. These communal bonds were sufficiently strong at the beginning of this century to persuade the drafters of the Weimar constitution to open their preamble with the phrase "the German people, united in its tribes. . . ."[51] These tribal communities are maintained and indeed reinforced by marked linguistic peculiarities, the dialects, which are distinctive of course not only in Germany, but throughout the world in countries which unite large populations.[52] The cantonal subdivisions of Switzerland, while not tribally determined, have similar characteristics. Even in France, well-defined regions, with distinctive speech and other features of folk culture, survive to this day, and are familiar to every Frenchman who habitually refers to himself as a *Breton*, a *Normand*, a *Gascon* or a *Provençal*, again

[50] Bogue, 1949, *passim*, for a persuasive demonstration.

[51] A most interesting analysis of Germany in terms of these tribes was given by Diesel, 1931.

[52] On the subject of dialects, see Jesperson, 1925, chaps. III and IV, and the article by E. Sapir in *ESS*, 1931.

to mention only a few of the best-known and most colorful. French culinary culture, probably the most advanced in the world and certainly in Europe, derives much enrichment from these regional differences, reinforced as they are by distinctive wines grown in the locality.[53] The same holds for Italy and Spain.

In India, these regional differences are even more pronounced, as they were in the old Austrian empire, and in Russia. For here, the linguistic differentiation is not merely one of dialects, but of separate languages as far removed from each other as German and Hungarian (both part of the Austrian empire). Thus Hindi, an Indo-germanic language, is totally different from Malayalam, a Dravidian tongue. These linguistic divisions are proving a more significant communal building factor than the formal provincial organization. "The most profoundly perplexing problems are presented in India whose vast and heterogeneous people scatter far and wide on the linguistic map, . . ." a discerning student of these matters has written. He notes that "the close ties between language and the sense of community" made it "inevitable" that these divisions should have "political repercussions." [54] These political repercussions are still in full swing, as India struggles with the question of how to deal effectively with the problems of intermediary community-building so that language and provincial boundary lines coincide. If any past experience in similar situations may be employed as a guide, it can be confidently predicted that no perfect coincidence will be achieved in India any more than elsewhere. It is relatively easy to draw a map, based upon such linguistic differentiation, as has been done for Germany and other countries, but it is far from easy to transform such divisions into viable political structures, because language is only one of the factors entering into community-building.

Similar problems beset the African continent, not only in its entirety, but also in the subdivisions now emerging as new states, which frequently owe their existence to the arbitrary action of colonial powers or to the adventitious results of their rivalry. The effective and traditional African community is the tribe, of which a very large number can be definitely distinguished on the basis of language and other cultural traits.[55] These tribal communities were often cut apart by colonial boundaries. They

[53] The classic in the field of regional studies is André Siegfried, 1913; for a striking recent study of a particular local community, see Wylie, 1957; for broader studies of the interaction between the nation and its tribal antecedents, cf. Gorce, 1934. A vivid appreciation of such differentiation is offered by Distelbarth, n.d., vol. I, pp. 64ff., vol. II, pp. 85ff., and by Luethy, 1955.

[54] Emerson, 1960, chap. VII, has given a lucid analysis of the importance of language in political community-building. The quote is from p. 138. Also, Paul Friedrich, a, 1962.

[55] Murdock, 1959. Although Murdock does not particularly emphasize "tribes" in describing the subdivisions, his is nonetheless the most comprehensive survey.

naturally tend to reunite under "democratic" conditions, that is to say, under conditions in which the people themselves have a voice in their political association in accordance with the unfortunately often sloganized principle of "self-determination." It has been rightly remarked that the "self" of which this principle speaks is frequently in doubt. In most of Africa it is the tribe rather than the nation, or at best the tribe in addition to the nation.[56] These tribal units could be either destroyed or employed as the basis of political organization. It is the question which constitutes the focal issue of African politics; on its solution depends much. It has been observed that "as nations come into being in Africa south of the Sahara they are likely to be plagued with language problems as acute as those with which India and some other Asian countries are struggling." [57] It is evident that only some species of novel ethnic federalism (Chapter 32) will be able to cope with community-building under conditions of marked tribal self-consciousness. In view of the importance of maintaining a genuine community, what appears a disadvantage now may ultimately turn out to be a blessing in disguise.

In conclusion, it can be said that even a brief review of the local community as a political phenomenon argues not only its persistence, but also its vital importance. Our communitarian analysis is confirmed. Local communities are communities of law as well as of love, they are both organic and purposive, and they are existential givens which are yet extensively willed, that is, shaped by design. The contrast between urban and rural communities, while still important, is gradually being submerged by the advance of modern technology. Technology through mass communication knits all communities together in a pattern of interurban relationships. It conjures up the totalitarian threat of depersonalized masses devoid of all community, which though unique in its comprehensiveness is yet only a contemporary version of the megalopolis of ancient Oriental despotism. While the notion of complete political independence has long been discarded for the political community as a necessary or sufficient condition, the speculations of political theorists from Plato to the present about the optimal size of a political community still possess a certain cogency. The realization of their inherent truth depends upon the success in federalizing large urban agglomerations and thus providing for the local community a significant degree of meaningful autonomy with regard to local concerns. The neighborhood movement which has

[56] Fortes and Pritchard, 1940, 1947, chap. I, argue the importance of kinship for political organization, as well as the task of transcending it. They describe two kinds of political organization found in the part of native Africa they studied, those with and those without centralized administrative machinery. Cf. also Kimble, 1960, chap. 21, Almond and Coleman, 1960, sec. 3, chap. V, and most significantly Middleton and Tait, 1958, esp. chap. I.

[57] Emerson, 1960, p. 145.

sprung up spontaneously in a number of advanced industrial nations is an expression of this widely-felt need for effective rebuilding of the local community. Local communities can hope to develop and/or preserve their local autonomy only within the framework of a functioning constitutional order today, even though in the past they were often successful in this endeavor without having such an order to fall back upon. The consequence of this dependence is the need for considerable local variety in shaping local government institutions; unless they "fit," they are likely to lose out in the battle over "authority." But this need for local variation should not occasion surprise or lead to overlooking the many common elements; and if there is less need for formal institutional systematization, certain basic conditions such as representativeness and responsibility must nonetheless be generally fulfilled if local autonomy is to serve its function of building the local political community. Regional subdivisions of large territorial states have their distinct role to play and themselves represent a species of separation of powers and functions; though they may constitute a threat to the autonomy of the local community, they can serve as an important rampart if the two are suitably linked. The same holds, inversely, for the process of federal unification of a number of smaller units; here too the degree of local self-government can be increased and its maintenance be made more secure by anchoring it in the federal constitution of the more comprehensive community.

chapter

30

State and Nation: Sovereignty and Its Limits

Nations have lost their old omnipotence;
the patriotic tie does not hold.
Nations are getting obsolete,
we go and live where we will.
R. W. Emerson

Patriotism is the last refuge of a scoundrel.
Samuel Johnson

STATE AND NATION ARE the Siamese twins which Western culture has begot and which have in turn moulded modern politics. Together they constitute the contemporary political community and its order. While in jeopardy in Europe where they were born, they are still proliferating all over the world. All humans with political aspirations want to build states and nations. What there is of world order has donned the garb of an association of *nations,* presumably *united* only in one thrust, that of being nations. The sentiment which attaches to the nation and its state is among the most powerful today: nationalism.[1] At times, it generates even a pseudo-ideology (Chapter 4), although nation-building does in fact precede all genuine ideology formation which is tied to party divisions of the nation-state, or, as it seems more correct to say, state-nation. For typically the building of the state comes first, and it is within the political framework of the state that the nation comes into being, or at any rate to fruition. This historical sequence needs to be kept in mind as we observe the forming of new states whose rulers are earnestly striv-

[1] Hayes, 1926; Kohn, 1944; Deutsch, 1953; Emerson, 1960, to mention only four well-known works.

ing to weld the populations comprised within such states into nations. In the West, the linkage of the two has become so much a matter of fact and the heritage of the national myth is so all-pervading that the doubt is often expressed: How can these new states succeed when there does not exist any nation to support it? But was there a British, or a French, or an American, or even a Swiss nation, when the respective states came into being? Exceptions, seeming exceptions, such as Italy or Germany, will be explored below. Typically, state and nation grow up together, but the state is the active agent, or rather its builders are the kings of medieval Europe. Exclusive preoccupation with the achievement of these rulers is, however, easily misinterpreted and may then give rise to a "blood-and-iron" type of "realism" which is contradicted by the experience of the United States and Switzerland. In these and similar instances a federal union served as the effective state within which a nation could develop and become united.[2] These precedents are important, if one considers the problems of India and of a number of African states, as well as of Europe. The claim that it will be necessary first to develop a European nation before an adequate political order can be built is as erroneous as that which doubts the workability of such an order without the intervention of a forcible "founder" of the Bismarckian type.[3]

The problem of how national unification took place in Europe is actually quite a complex one, and there can be no doubt that a number of causes, political, military, economic, religious and geographic, worked together to bring the modern nation into being.[4] But these factors, while important, constitute essentially conditions for the political activity of the persons who erected political orders that eventually turned out to provide a framework for emergent communities of the national type. What they did was to erect the modern state.

The state as an institutional manifold and its concept as forged in the sixteenth century developed in response to the challenge presented by the church's secular ambitions. It embodies a political order institutionally divorced from the ecclesiastical establishment. Even where a "state church" survived, as in England, this church is "separated" from the secular political order in terms of authority, legitimacy and representation. This sharp separation of the state from religion and church distinguishes it from the political order of Greece and Rome as much as from the Oriental and African monarchies, and from other Asian and American "polities." The state in this distinct historical sense is almost entirely "Western," and some of the perplexities of contemporary state-building

[2] Kohn, 1955; Deutsch, 1962.

[3] For the first error of judgment, note especially Coudenhove-Kalergi, 1953; for the second, Hitler's outlook is typical.

[4] Cf. Friedrich, 1950, pp. 11ff., and the literature cited there.

are connected with this fact.[5] It is therefore not surprising that the Roman law, the most elaborate formal institutionalization of the political thought of the ancient world, did not develop a state concept. Both *civitas* and *respublica* were clearly religious, as well as secular, collectivities, and to equate them with modern government is a mistake. It took the centuries of struggle during the European Middle Ages to distinguish clearly and to institutionalize separately the religious and the secular community. The state crystallized in the chancelleries of England, France, Spain and other countries, as diligent servants of their rulers forged the instrumentality of bureaucracy for purely secular concerns. This is not to deny that similar efforts had not been made elsewhere at different epochs. Surely the vast bureaucracy of the Roman Empire, as well as of comparable Oriental monarchies, bears a close resemblance to its European counterparts, as we have seen (Chapters 18 and 26). But these vast bodies were held together by an authority and legitimacy which was basically religious, and the power they wielded was consequently permeated by religious notions of what was just and right.

The state was, as already mentioned, conceptualized in the sixteenth century, notably by Jean Bodin, who in his epochal work on the state spoke of it as inseparable from sovereignty. Such sovereignty was obviously the culmination of the claims of "imperialist" writers throughout the Middle Ages who had sought to vindicate the position of the secular ruler as independent of ecclesiastical authority. It was thereafter to be independent also of tradition, whether social, tribal or national. Already Marsilius of Padua had gone a long way toward the notion of an entirely autonomous ruler, and others before and after him had challenged ecclesiastical claims. But the doctrine of sovereignty went further. There is a deceptive similarity between the formulations of the ancients, especially Aristotle and Cicero, and the novel state concept. Aristotle speaks of the *polis* as the "highest" or "most lordly" (*kyriotáte*) of the various communities and associations of men, and Cicero claims for the *civitas* the characteristic of universality.[6] But both are thinking of a religious as well as a political community and its organization, and hence of a church as much as a state. Endless confusion has been the consequence of applying the Aristotelian concept to the modern state, culminating in the "deification" of the state by Hegel and the Hegelians and eventually in its "diabolization" in Fascist and National Socialist thought.[7] Unfortunately,

[5] Note, e.g., the insuperable difficulties encountered in connection with the drafting of constitutions for Pakistan and Israel, both new nations with a powerful religious orthodoxy. For the former, cf. Binder, 1961, and Newman, 1956; for the latter, Dunner, 1950, chap. 8; Hurewitz, 1950; Halpern, 1960, is excellent for the background.

[6] Aristotle, *Politics* I.1; Cicero, *De Republica*, I.25.

[7] Friedrich, 1942, chap. II.

many of the newly emergent states are inclined to follow this pattern, rather than the restrictive views of modern constitutionalism or even communism, which think of the state as something to be transcended and dissolved.

For Bodin, and hence at the outset, the state was "a government of an association of families," which in order to be well governed required a single "sovereign." We therefore see the state "defined" in a way which has nearly universal application; for few are the communities where there is an association of families which does not have some kind of government, that is, some kind of rule (Chapter 10). Actually the state was by the sixteenth century a large-scale organization effectively centralized by means of a purely secular bureaucracy, implemented by some kind of representative body which stood for the "*sanior et melior pars*," the saner and better part of the political community, as Marsilius had put it. It was the function of this representative body (Chapter 17) to assist in the making of rules and to grant a substantial part of the revenue needed for the defense of the realm. As a number of writers put it in the sixteenth century, in this representative assembly of the states the entire body politic was understood to be present.[8] The state *was* a "body politic."

It may be a far cry from these early gropings to the mature subtleties of nineteenth-century jurisprudence as theorists fined and refined the concept of *the* state and its sovereignty.[9] But basically, the position remained the same: the state is the government, reinforced and corporatively enlarged by some kind of notion of the nation as the embodiment of the political aspirations of the people under such government's sway, seen especially in its preoccupation with rule-making. Therefore, a nonjurist and a keen observer of the political scene could, after deliberately discarding all definitions, ask: What does the state want to accomplish vis-à-vis the conflicts and struggles going on in the society? And he might give the answer: The state seeks to direct the struggle of the interest groups into the channels of the positive law. Legislation, the making and maintaining of rules and the subjecting of the interests to such rules, is insistently seen as the primordial task of the state.[10] Such legislation receives its ultimate authority from the existence of the nation as the human

[8] E.g., Sir Thomas Smith, 1583; Bodin, in combating the idea of a divided sovereign, recognizes the "estates" as much as Smith.

[9] Emerson, 1928, chap. II. Most of these discussions were oblivious of the rather different realities of colonial and other empires; cf. next chap.

[10] Ratzenhofer, 1893, chap. 17. Sidgwick, 1903, p. 27, denies that "the characteristic of being a nation is commonly implied in the current use of the term 'state.'" He would insist, on the other hand, that a certain "state of civilization" must have been reached, the crucial characteristic of which is "a clear consciousness of this fundamental distinction between the rights and obligations of the community in its corporate capacity, and those of the individuals comprising it" (p. 26)—a very British way of putting it, behind which hides a broader Western value pattern.

embodiment of a complex aggregate of values, interests and beliefs which manifests itself throughout man's life, from the small items of everyday existence (food, table manners, speech), to the main achievements of cultural creativity (literature, art, science and religion). Thus, such an aggregate of human beings is united not only "by the fact of acknowledgment of permanent obedience to a common government" (as political theorists from Bodin and Hobbes to Austin and Sidgwick maintained), but also by the fact of the acknowledgment of "common objects of their affection," as Augustine, varying Cicero, had once put it, these common objects being those comprehended within a national culture. But what of the polyethnic state? The multinational state?

The problem posed by Switzerland and Canada, the Austro-Hungarian empire and the Republic of Czechoslovakia, by India and Belgium, is a real one, and we shall return to it presently. But it does not truly provide a challenge to the linkage between state and nation. Verbally, the way out is provided by speaking of the components of such a state as "nationalities" or "ethnic groups," but in reality such is the dialectic of the political that the state seeks and must seek to foster the growth of a nation, indeed must posit its potential coming into being, in order to live and be able to fulfill its function of transcending the various opposing groups, including nationalities. This is the idea, the concept, the aspiration. Actually, the state in its true and primordial sense exists where a "sovereign" unites in his hands all the power which is needed to do whatever *he* believes necessary in the interest of the state.

From this sovereign within the state, presently to be more fully explored, must be distinguished the sovereign that is the state itself. State sovereignty in the sense of "independence" from other states is a decisive aspect of the state, as it developed in Western Europe and has become universalized in recent times. Such "independence" does not mean that the state does not depend upon other states for cooperation, or even assistance and protection. For, if that were the notion no state would exist at all. Independence means that the state itself, or rather its rulers, decide whom to cooperate with or be assisted by and to what extent. That is one of the reasons for the strength of "neutralism" in the present world; as long as there are two superpowers to depend on, the "independence" of many states is preserved. They are sovereign to the extent that they can choose, and they cherish this chance, even when their choice seems more or less a foregone conclusion. Furthermore, anti-Soviet Europe may have to depend upon the United States to a large extent, but by uniting the states composing it, it can reduce that extent very materially—one of the motivations behind European union. Independence of this kind is not a unique distinguishing trait of the modern state. The Greek *poleis* were passionately attached to their independence, which they called "freedom," and when they spoke of themselves as "the free" they meant this independence rather than any internal freedom from the order of the *polis* such as modern man cherishes (Chapter 20).

The sovereign whom Bodin had insisted upon was the one who had "the highest and perpetual power over citizens and subjects, unrestricted by laws." [11] Decisive is the ultimate decisional power which lets Bodin say that a ruler or people who possess sovereignty do not have to give reasons, i.e., render an account to anyone except the immortal God; they are not responsible to another.[12] That ultimate decisional power has given rise to the shorthand definition of the sovereign as "he who has the last word," or, in the cumbrous language of nineteenth-century jurisprudence, "he who is competent to determine his own competence." [13] In an era of the rule of law, of a government of laws and not of men, as political rhetoric had it, this last word may be one of self-limitation by which the sovereign people delimit their own power and that of all others in terms of a constitutional order (Chapter 15). But such sophisticated perversions of the meaning of the term are a far cry from the original notion of Bodin, Hobbes and the other theorists of sovereignty, all of whom insisted that a state needed a final arbiter who could decide whatever he saw fit, hopefully in the interest of the commonwealth. It is evident that such concentration of power in the hands of an individual or a corporate body such as a parliament, is incompatible with the key to constitutionalism, namely, the division of power, formally called the separation of powers, both functional and territorial.

The analysis of power and rule (Chapters 9 and 10) has shown that no such complete concentration of power is really possible, that the very nature of power makes it impossible; but it has also shown that power may be more or less concentrated and that types of rules are to some extent characterized by the degree of such concentration. Bearing these findings in mind, it is possible to say that the state is a type of rule in which power is fairly concentrated, potentially at least. The problems which a federal system presents in this connection are dealt with in a later chapter. Here it needs to be observed that the totalitarian reaction of the twentieth century is in part motivated by the reassertion of the state as against the denigration of the state in the liberal age. The curious paradox of the communist version of this totalitarian reassertion of the state in the name of a "wither-

[11] Bodin, 1586, bk. I, chap. 8; we neglect the problem suggested by the different wording in Latin and French. Cf. Mesnard, 1935, bk. IV, chap. 3, pp. 473ff., and McRae, 1962, introd.

[12] "Princeps vero, populusve, in quibus majestas inest, rationem rerum gestarum nemini, praeterquem immortali Deo reddere coguntur." Bodin, 1586. This is the decisive passage which has echoed down the centuries to John Austin's formulation of "no earthly superior" (1832). Cf. Chap. 17.

[13] The once famous *Kompetenz-Kompetenz* of Georg Jellinek, 1900, 1913, was primarily concerned with the location of sovereignty in a federal system, however. Cf. Emerson, 1928, chap. II, esp. pp. 59ff.

ing away of the state" highlights the complexity of the issue: the requirements of the new order call for highly concentrated power, and this only the state can provide.[14] The facts are more clearly apparent in the case of fascism, which frankly exalted the state and even employed a neo-Hegelian rhetoric for ideological purposes.[15] But the reassertion of the state is not limited to totalitarianism. The Gaullist movement is profoundly *étatiste*, or statist, and in the utterances of its protagonists, including De Gaulle himself, the state is written with a capital letter; at the same time the link of state and nation is dramatically manifest.[16] It may be objected, however, that after all Gaullism is a way station to fascism, or a crypto-fascist authoritarianism. This objection seems hardly valid when we remember that "neoliberalism" at least as represented by some of its interpreters calls for the strong state; they argue that because only such a state can act as an effective arbiter among the powerful group interests, especially between business and labor organizations, it is needed to protect freedom and to secure the public interest.[17] What is meant by the "state" in both the Gaullist and neoliberal reaction is, as a matter of fact, a strong government rather than a state in the classical sense; for both viewpoints are attached to the nonconcentration of power. There is nonetheless a thrust in the direction of a sovereign. De Gaulle may, in his constitution, assert the "sovereignty of the people" (art. 2); he conducts his office much in the manner of the classic sovereign, albeit under the aegis of an "emergency" power (art. 16).

As against such statist notions, the prevailing tendency in democratic thinking has been "pluralist." Pluralism challenges the notions of a "monopoly of force" and "indivisibility" of power, the latter associated with the Bodinian concept of a "highest" and "perpetual" power from which it logically derives. It stresses, on the basis of an empirical observation of political reality, that even in a rather centralized state there are several centers of power, but that more particularly in a constitutional and democratic political order a plurality of groups divide power among themselves without its being possible to identify any one of them as the "highest." It is admitted that totalitarian dictatorship seeks to cumulate, and to a considerable extent succeeds in concentrating, power in a single party and its leadership, but such concentration is condemned as highly objectionable, and even the practitioners of such dictatorial rule do not by any means always acknowledge the unity of power as desirable. Only the Fascists

[14] A. G. Meyer, 1957; Tucker, 1961; Friedrich and Brzezinski, 1956.

[15] Germino, 1959; Gentile, 1925; Mussolini, 1933. For the more complex attitude of National Socialism, see Hitler, 1924; and the analysis in Friedrich and Brzezinski, 1956, chaps. 8 and 9.

[16] De Gaulle, 1956, pp. 183ff.; Debré, 1947 and 1957; Debré speaks in the first of these titles of the "death of the state."

[17] A. Rüstow, a, 1959; a, 1929; Friedrich, a, 1955.

have faced up to the issue. Hence even though we observe in contemporary politics a certain reemergence of "sovereignty" in the classic meaning of the term, few are willing to claim that a state depends upon it and is well governed only if it possesses such a sovereign.[18] In the new nations, especially where they confront emergency conditions and/or an autocratic native tradition, there exists a marked propensity to look for a "sovereign," within the broad context of generic consent provided by the nation's newly found freedom. Hence the prevalence of one predominant party led by an inspirational (charismatic) leader.

This brings the analysis of state and sovereignty back to the nation. If the state is typically seen to be the nation legally united as an independent power,[19] the link of state and nation is complete; indeed the two are in characteristically nationalist fashion identified with each other up to a point, provided the nation is an independent power, and provided it is united in law (i.e., through a constitution). Actually such an identification of state and nation is inadmissible; the state *is* not the nation, it rests upon the nation, and when there is not yet a nation, its rulers will strive to bring one into being, because without it the state is not fully developed. It is *merely* a government, merely an apparatus for particular purposes, merely the kind of governance which the fathers of the church and their medieval followers wished to assign to the rulers: the maintenance of peace and order as necessary conditions for the accomplishment of higher aims, justice and salvation, which transcend the government's role. Genuine state-thinking since the sixteenth century seeks to claim for the state a corporate foundation, a new *corpus mysticum*, as a sacred being in its own right: the nation.

But while such a conception is convincing enough for England, France and Spain, it does not appear to fit countries like Germany and Italy, where the development of states, like Prussia and the Hapsburg monarchy, the kingdom of Naples and that of Piedmont, seem to be quite separate and apart from the nation. The nation lives a life of its own, defined in terms of language and culture, that is, letters, arts and philosophy. To account for this divergent development, certain writers proposed a distinction between a *Staatsnation* and a *Kulturnation*, a political nation and a cultural nation,[20] or to put it more precisely, a nation based on a

[18] Laski, Lindsay and Duguit, building on the historical studies of Gierke, Maitland and Figgis, among others, reinforced by the writings of Bentley and his school, are among the protagonists of pluralism. Laski, 1917 and 1921, Lindsay, 1943, Duguit, 1901, and Bentley, 1908, have given classic statements of the doctrines involved. Cf. also Francis W. Coker's discriminating discussion of pluralism in *ESS*.

[19] This is the classic phrase with which Treitschke opens his *Politik*, 1897, p. 13. Treitschke uses *Volk*, but in the sense of "nation."

[20] Bauer, 1907; Renner, 1907; Cobban, 1945; Hugelmann, 1934, pp. 242ff.; Meinecke, 1922, 1928, pp. 3ff. and literature cited there. Cf. Chap. 32 below on the idea of a cultural autonomy, as expounded by Renner and Bauer, and its contrast, terri-

political order and a nation based on culture. Such a distinction seems, from the political viewpoint, not very satisfactory; it appears more in keeping with experience to recognize that both a nation and a state are incomplete when they are not linked. If, as is often done, the state is equated with political order, then of course its distinctive character is obscured, and no such link can be asserted. Typically, the state will seek to expand until it comprises a nation, and a nation will struggle to unify its political subdivisions until it achieves statehood. As Max Weber put it in a forgotten essay: the nation is constituted by "a common bond of sentiment whose adequate expression would be a state of its own, and which therefore normally tends to give birth to such a state." [21] This fact must not be permitted, however, to lead to a voluntaristic notion such as Roberto Michels put forward when he asserted that "nationality does not consist necessarily in either language or religion or a common past, but in the will of the people." [22] Indeed, it is just as pertinent to say that a state does not consist merely in an institutionalized structure of power, that is, a system of rule or government over a definite territory. Nor does it merely possess a predominance of legitimate force within this territory, but it calls for a substructure provided by "a common bond of sentiment" and typically manifest in the body of a nation.

The philosopher of the nation-state, recognized by all, was Jean-Jacques Rousseau. Whether he looked at it from the viewpoint of the individual, as in *Émile*, or from that of the nation, as in the *Contrat Social*, or again from that of particular countries, as in his *Project for a Constitution for Corsica* or his *Considerations about the Government of Poland*,[23] Rousseau stressed the close link between state and nation, between the political community and its order in the specific modern form which was to generate nationalism as a pseudo-religious alternative to Christianity's universal brotherhood of man. Indeed, in the celebrated last chapter of the *Contrat Social* he sketched a "civic religion" which he urged as an essential precondition for a sound and viable political order.

---

torial autonomy. The *Millet* system under the Ottoman Empire provided such "cultural autonomy" for non-Moslem minorities on a nonterritorial basis. Cf. Gibb and Bowen, 1950, vol. I, part II, chap. 14.

[21] Max Weber, a, 1913, as cited by Kohn, 1944, fn. 16 of chap. I. Cf. also his discussion in 1922, pp. 627ff. Weber there asserts that "nation" is a conception which, if it can be made unequivocal at all, cannot be made so by empirically common characteristics of the members of a nation. The discussion is fragmentary.

[22] Michels, 1917; cf. also Michels, 1929.

[23] The first two works were published in 1762, the one on Corsica written about 1765, the one on Poland in 1772; they are found in *Oeuvres*, 1827, vols. VIII, IX; vol. III, pp. 97–270; *ibid.*, pp. 279–409; the *Projet* is found in Vaughan, 1915, chap. II, pp. 330ff. Cf. also Friedrich, a, 1962, and references given there, and the provocative chapter in Sabine, 1937, and Hendel, 1934, esp. chaps. XVIII–XXII.

"True Christians are made to be slaves," he wrote. He thought that there was "nothing more contrary to the social spirit" than the Christian religion. The worst of all the Christian outlooks was that of the Catholic Church; from the "double power" it created, "conflicts of jurisdiction" resulted which "made all good polity impossible in Christian states." Therefore, since religion was essential for the social bond, a "purely civil profession of faith" ought to be required of all citizens, the articles of which the sovereign was to fix. And since it was not possible for anyone to be a good citizen who was not loyal to these principles, the state might banish as unsocial whoever did not believe in them, because he was incapable of sincerely loving justice and the laws.[24] It is evident that the nation-state, while not exactly using Rousseau's words, has shown an inclination to act in accordance with this notion; from the Act of Supremacy (1559) and its various antecedents down to loyalty oaths in contemporary America the propensity of the nation-state to look upon commitment to the values of the political order as vital is observed. Rousseau formulated dogmas of such a civil religion. After suggesting that they ought to be few, simple and stated precisely and without explanation or commentary, he claimed that they should assert "the existence of a powerful, intelligent and beneficent divine being, possessed of foresight and providence; a life to come; the happiness of the just and the chastisement of the wicked; the sanctity of the social contract and of the laws." Such civic religion should also deny intolerance; for intolerance had been a feature of past cults which Rousseau rejected, more particularly tribal religions and Christianity. With intolerant religions eliminated, tolerance should be accorded to all religions which do not interfere with the duties of citizenship. But what else is this but the intolerance of the religion of nationalism which rejects all religions that do not accord with its own outlook? The position taken by Rousseau comes perilously near to that of the totalitarians, all of whom proclaim their tolerance for any but those who disagree with them.[25] Once such a position is adopted, it becomes of course very important to instill these dogmas into members of the political community. It is therefore hardly surprising to find Rousseau entertaining a firm belief that education must be employed for such patriotic indoctrination; it must direct the "opinion and the tastes" of the oncoming generation so that they become patriots by "inclination, passion and necessity." [26]

[24] Rousseau, *Contrat Social,* bk. IV, chap. 8. Rousseau would decree the death penalty for anyone who deceived the state about his beliefs in these matters.

[25] The view of Hobbes, cited by Rousseau, as well as of Hegel and others who followed in Rousseau's footsteps, shows that "secular" or "political" religions are nothing new in our century; cf. Voegelin, 1938. The position is essentially that of Machiavelli, *Discourses,* bk. I, chap. 12.

[26] *Constitution of Corsica* (ed. Vaughan, 1915), p. 33. Cf. above, Chap. 28.

A number of studies have been directed in recent years toward an empirical assessment of the factors contributing to nationalism and the forming of nations. "Nationalities turn into nations when they acquire power to back up their aspirations," a prominent specialist has written, who then proceeds to construct a number of tests for determining nationality. Among these are tests based on transmission and tests based on predictability of behavior, generally linking nationality to phenomena of communication.[27] He has sought to work out measurements for national assimilation, for unity and diversity and for national consciousness and will, sorting out quantitative and qualitative factors.

The analysis leads eventually to a syndrome of factors involved in national consciousness and will. "National consciousness," we read, "is the attachment of secondary symbols of nationality to primary items of information moving through channels of social communication, or through the mind of an individual."[28] The writer then proceeds to delineate the process by which such national consciousness seems to him to come into being, "the early stages of this process" possibly "as automatic as talking prose." It is part and parcel of the national group "setting itself off" and "separating and differentiating itself." The national self, like personal kinds of selves, requires other national selves for its existence. In describing the process as a more or less automatic one, the observer is in danger of overlooking or minimizing the role of the political leader. In building a state and thereby providing the setting for the development of a nation as the needed communal underpinning, such a leader is almost bound to utilize those elements in the underlying population and its cultures which lend themselves to political manipulation and exploitation.

The "national will"[29] cannot become a factor in this situation until a national being has come into existence. Even if will is defined in an extreme operational way,[30] it presupposes a cohesive group of persons whose conduct is motivated by a set of common values, interests or beliefs. Only

[27] Deutsch, 1953, p. 78, and chaps. 5–8.

[28] *Ibid.*, p. 146. After drawing attention to the adjectival nature of symbols of nationality, Deutsch observes that "national consciousness, like all consciousness, can only be consciousness of something which exists." It may "misrepresent . . . existing facts . . . yet behind the distortions . . . there must be materials on which they could be based. . . ." This is very true; the national being is not a figment of the imagination, any more than the individual human being. Cf. above, Chaps. 2 and 4.

[29] *Ibid.*, pp. 151ff.

[30] *Ibid.*, p. 151, thought will "may be described as the set of constraints acquired from the memories and past experiences . . . applied to the selection and treatment of items in its later intake, recall, or decisions," adding that "will is the ability to inhibit, partially or wholly, any further learning." This seems to me too negative a description, though it is true that the habits of communication often make the learning of common values possible.

when these have become "national" in the distinctive cultural sense, including more especially the words, i.e., the linguistic symbols, involved in a common vernacular, can the collectivity be said, in a metaphorical sense, to have acquired a will of its own.

Nonetheless, these studies (and others like them) are of the highest significance for political theory. For they show that the actual processes bear out the premises concerning community and power, concerning values and decisions, which have been developed to account for other political phenomena. In keeping with the dual nature of power (Chapter 9) nations are both built and grown; their development is in part the result of power based on consent and in part on constraint. Nations grow because the values and beliefs of separate population elements converge through common experience in thought and action; nations are also built, because leaders with an adequate amount of power in their possession *decide* to build one and thus to make a community where there was none before. At the same time, these empirical researches also confirm that value and belief consensus is partial and fluid, not total and rigid as the expounders of the doctrine of an "agreement on fundamentals" used to assert.[31] On the contrary, a modern nation is characterized by a rich variety of subgroups cherishing divergent "fundamentals." But this much-needed dissent is overarched by a will to form one national community, a will often reinforced, if not generated, by a need of a related set of communities either to defend themselves against a neighboring nation, or to develop a sufficiently broad economic base such as modern industrial life requires for effective operation. It is significant, in other words, that here as in other spheres of human activity, the paradigm of *one* nation in existence elicits the building of another nation in adjoining territory. Historically, then, it could be argued that the English, the French and the Spanish, politically gifted and in sharp and continuous rivalry with each other, first grew into nations which powerful dynasties built out of the building blocks of disparate tribal units, with the English ultimately in this perspective appearing as the "inventors" of the nation-state. The potency of such a state the Hundred Years' War demonstrated to the French kings and people, who in turn taught the lesson to the Spanish, the Swiss, and eventually the Italians and the Germans. No one can read Machiavelli's passionate appeal in *The Prince* without recognizing that it is the need of defending Italy against France which persuaded the great Florentine to advocate the building of a national state at all costs.

It has been repeatedly argued that nationalism dates from the French Revolution,[32] even though it is admitted that there are scattered indica-

[31] See above, and Prothro and Grigg, a, 1960; and Key, 1961, chap. 2.

[32] Kohn, 1944, chap. I, esp. at p. 3: "Nationalism as we understand it is not older than the second half of the eighteenth century. Its first great manifestation was the French Revolution. . . ." The next quote on pp. 18–19. Contra, and in support of our view, Shafer, 1954, where good evidence is presented.

tions of national sentiment earlier, especially in England. This argument is cast in terms of the proposition that "nationalism is a state of mind," animating a nationality with a common consciousness, but seeking to express itself in "what it regards as the highest form of organized activity, a sovereign state." It seems more accurate to look upon the second half of the eighteenth century as a culminating point of nationalism in France. Similar outbursts preceded it in England in the middle of the seventeenth century, and in Germany in the first quarter of the sixteenth century. A most interesting correlation of these outbursts of nationalism in conjunction with "great" revolutions and the subsequent formation of a nation was undertaken by Rosenstock-Huessy some years ago.[33] In such a perspective, nationalism appears as a universal trend in Western culture which finally was universalized in the sequel to the French and American revolutions. It has since swept the globe, and is still, as we said, gaining momentum among the non-European peoples achieving independence and statehood, even while it is beginning to recede in its cradle, Europe. This decline of nationalism in Europe proper was, however, in this century accompanied by a violent reassertion and overassertion of it in the theory and practice of fascism in its various forms; such fascism is endemic wherever nation states are formed.

Nationalism is not merely a state of mind, but also a political movement and at times something resembling an ideology (Chapter 4). As a movement it generates a new kind of political community, preoccupied with a common cultural heritage, especially in terms of language. In both Italy and Germany the first sweep of nationalism was associated with the birth of a "universal" vernacular language fashioned by Dante and Luther respectively; in England, France and Spain (as well as other countries) the vernacular language crystallized in the course of a more gradual growth. But whichever way it develops, the nationalism and linguistic self-discovery went hand in hand.[34] Not all linguistic communities are nations, let alone groups inspired by nationalism. Yet nationalism and the building of a nation are greatly aided by linguistic community. There are, however, many exceptions, as mentioned: Canada, Belgium and Switzerland among the older European nations; among the newer ones in the rest of the world India, Pakistan and Nigeria might be mentioned to illustrate the multilingual nation-in-the-making. Still, we observe the determined effort of many peoples who have recently achieved independence and statehood to develop or revive a common language, e.g., India, Ireland and Israel. As in other matters of value and belief, so in the field of language variety and differentiation a political order can transcend the dis-

[33] Rosenstock-Huessy, 1931, *passim*. Cf. also below, Chap. 33.

[34] Cf. on language community in general, Deutsch, 1944, pp. 25–28: "a community of language is a community of information vehicles." Deutsch gives some interesting map material and further references. Cf. also Jesperson, 1946, chap. III, esp. pp. 71–73, 105–108.

ruptive effects of excessive pluralism by a greater insistence upon unity in other fields, and thus achieve the necessary degree or at least a measure of mutual understanding. As one great linguist put it some years ago: "The main types of speech in a complex speech-community can be roughly classed as follows: 1. literary standard . . . 2. colloquial standard, 3. provincial standard . . . 4. sub-standard . . . 5. local dialect." [35] He actually undertook to link these varieties of speech to "classes," building on the classic English case; this linkage does not appear wholly valid. The varieties of dialect in Germany, for example, are strictly regional, and the nobleman of Bavaria does not yield in upper-class conceit to his confrere from Thuringia or Hanover. But it is a linguistic community which, even though it extends beyond the country's boundaries to Switzerland, Austria and (formerly) elsewhere, unites the Germans in strong national sentiment.

Indeed, the movement that is nationalism finds many of its most potent symbols in linguistic expresssions, presumably indicating unique qualities, as it does in slogans and poetry. It bears strong resemblance to other forms of exclusive group loyalty, notably patriotism, but is distinguished from such other forms by its concern with cultural self-identity which is most pronounced in literary self-expression. All values and beliefs are colored by this self-identity, and there is associated with it a widespread conviction that only a Frenchman can fully appreciate French literary and other creations, and the same with Englishmen, Italians, Spaniards and Germans.[36] Whether true or not (and I believe them to be untrue), there can be no question that such views are very widespread wherever nationalism is prevalent.

Nationalism is historically tied to the growth of democracy. Indeed, it has been asserted that nationalism was the essential condition for the democratizing of the modern state. Against such a view, it seems sounder to see democracy and nationalism in a "dialectic" relation. As one writer put it, they were "in their origin contemporary movements" and therefore many of the conditions for one also served to condition the other. But the hard core of nationalism was a need for and a belief in a particular kind of community, whereas democracy in its modern constitutional forms sprang from the belief in the common man, or rather the belief in man, and was fashioned to serve the needs of a free and competitive society. Democracy's drive is in the direction of an ultimate constitutional

[35] Bloomfield, 1933, p. 52. On language and politics in India, cf. Paul Friedrich, a, 1962.

[36] One can hear highly intelligent persons engage in such comments as that "only a French person can play Fauré" or "only a German can fully grasp Bach." Passages carrying such an implication are found, e.g., in Spengler, 1923, vol. II, pp. 62ff.; Keyserling, 1922, vol. I, pp. 16f., 244ff., 358ff.; vol. II, pp. 629f., 856f.; and Madariaga, 1952, pp. 18ff. (Engl. 1950).

world order transcending nation, state and sovereignty. It is therefore true to say that the link between nationalism and democracy "created an antinomy which ultimately threatened to thwart the realization of democracy" on a world-wide basis.[37] At least this is so in the European and American perspective. In the newly emerging nations any emergent world order will certainly have to be constructed from the building blocks of states and nations, rather than from the beliefs involved in constitutional democracy, more especially individual rights.

The dialectic of nationalism and democracy is imbedded in much modern thought typified by Rousseau, whose position calls for some further comment. As the prophet of both, he exaggerated each of them and provided them with the common mystique of the "general will." For the general will when operating beyond the local community makes sense only in terms of a nation welded into complete unity by undisputed common values and beliefs held by each and all individuals—all of them *Émiles* after a thoroughgoing indoctrination (see above, and Chapter 33). Or rather, this is true unless there is superimposed the faith in a categorical imperative shaping the will of most individual men in terms of norms of universal validity. These norms are discoverable in the individual's conscience and as a consequence mould the nation's state and sovereignty, founding and eventually achieving a constitutional reign of law, because one of the primary categorical imperatives is that "there shall not be war." But as Hegel observed, in rejecting the Kantian universalism, the nation's self in its identity and seclusion is denied by such an imperative.[38] Yet, the Jacobins' rabid and perfervid nationalism had a universal appeal. In conquering all of Europe, Napoleon still flattered himself as being the executor of France's "civilizing mission." When Hegel thought he recognized Napoleon on his white charger as an embodiment of the world spirit, he justified such missions by allowing many nations in turn to become the instruments of the world spirit in its universal significance for the forward march of mankind at large. To recall these familiar and by now banal formulas serves the function of elucidating the broader meaning of the level of political development which nation, state and sovereignty constituted. The nation has always been one among several, a member of a

[37] Kohn, 1944, pp. 191–192. For the dialectic of freedom, see above, Chaps. 20–21.

[38] In a sense, the philosophies of Kant and Hegel spell out and in their turn pursue to the bitter end, each of them, one of the horns of the dilemma built into Rousseau's doctrine of the general will—a will at once that of a nation that knows no individuals, and that of individuals who know no nation. Cf. Friedrich, 1948, chap. VI, for further elaboration. Cf. also this further sentence from Kohn, 1944, p. 251: Rousseau "taught men that their foremost loyalty was due to the 'national' community, based upon law, liberty, and equality, and held together by a feeling of brotherhood and mutual devotion. Such a community could only be founded on the will of all its members. To educate their will, to create conditions favorable to its formation and duration, became the central task of nation building."

"family," a state confronting other states "in the posture of a gladiator," to recall Hobbes's memorable phrase. All by itself, in the lonely singularity of a Roman or a Chinese or even a medieval empire, the nation and its state as a level of political life, comprehensive and exclusive, could not exist. A boundary is of its very essence.

Nation and democracy both possess strongly normative connotations when described in such stipulative terms as the ones just sketched in keeping with the thought of Rousseau and many of his followers. If these normative aspects are elaborated, nation and democracy are apt to become utopias—idealizing projections of popular aspirations rooted in concrete needs and deeply felt longings. Such utopias carry ideological implications whenever they are cast in terms of a critique of the existing social order and of plans for its reform or reconstruction. This broadening stream of programmatic ideologies, stemming from a utopian base (Chapter 5) can be understood only if it be recalled that the emergence of the modern state is accompanied by the invention of utopias, not only the original one of Thomas More which gave the name to all the rest, but a steady progression down to the pessimistic utopias of our own time.[39] Plato's by contrast was not, and was not meant to be, a "utopia," but a practical proposal for the reorganization of the *polis* and so understood and criticised by Aristotle.[40] The utopia of Thomas More, like those of Andreae, Campanella, and others,[41] were elaborations and fancied projections of the state and its nation, the inclusive and sovereign organization of power, deployed for the goal of achieving human happiness and more especially communal bliss on this earth. Often written, so it seems, half tongue-in-cheek, they revealed by their very exaggerations the pattern of the new structure. Daydreams about what one might do if and when he could do anything, they usually embodied bitter criticism of the existing state, and of the use to which its power was put.

State and nation, power and its glory, had to reach the pinnacle of fulfillment in actual and concrete experience, rather than such utopian daydreams, before the antistate and antination utopia of the anarchists could come into its own. Heralded by the Diggers' small voice during

[39] Huxley, 1932; Orwell, 1949; these have been called "distopias" to suggest their disvalue, but wrongly, because the "noplace" meaning is thus lost; if a single word were wanted, dis-utopia might do. Cf. Kessler, a, 1957, for an interesting comparative analysis of the two books just referred to.

[40] On utopias see Chap. 5 above, and the literature cited there—most of which commits the error pointed out in the text above.

[41] On More, cf. above, Chap. 5, fn. 25; on Campanella, Paladino, 1920; De Mattei, 1933, gives a list of editions of the *City of the Sun,* pp. 83ff., and a brief study of his portraits, pp. 103ff. Cf. also the same author's study of Campanella's political thought, 1927, and P. Treves's of 1930.

the English revolution,[42] anarchism, the radical condemnation of the state and its political order, including its law (Chapter 15), is presented in the nineteenth century as the cure-all of man's troubles. Godwin, Proudhon, Kropotkin, Bakunin and Thoreau—to mention only some of its more important exponents—all seek to save man's true being from the corruption by the state and the nation. Man, "the lone and only one and his own" (Stirner), can achieve the good life only if he rids himself of the Frankenstein of the state. It has usually been overlooked that anarchism as a utopia is the response to the growing power of the state; it does not appear until the sovereign nation state began to exhibit its terrifying potential of dehumanizing man in the name of man's happiness. The negative utopias of our time, expressive of a growing pessimism, have converted this theme into prophecies of doom; whereas all utopias from More to Marx had hopefully looked forward to a better future, these dirges of impending catastrophe look sadly backward to a better past or even present. Writers like Kafka, more despondent than such past utopians, meanwhile have depicted insignificant man as inexorably lost in the maze of a man-made organized activity he does not comprehend.

It is one of the most curious facts in the history of the modern state and man's attitude toward it that those most determined to be rid of it seem condemned to forward its extension. True already of Rousseau and his Jacobin followers, this paradox affects socialism in its many facets. It has been most extensively discussed in regard to Marx-Engels' doctrine of the "withering away" of the state,[43] but it equally affects Owenism and other strands. They all eventually fall back upon the state for accomplishing the extensive reforms their doctrines call for. Therefore socialism, although hardly necessarily "the road to serfdom"—for that depends upon the nature of the state—has certainly proved itself to be the road to more government.[44] Indeed for many who think in the older liberal tradition socialism specifically denotes statism, that is, advocacy

[42] On the Diggers, see Sabine, 1941, introd., and Petegorsky, 1940. The Diggers have usually been called "communist," but this term is misleading, since they are opposed to "big government"—as are all anarchists. The leading authority has commented: "Winstanley's communism stood by itself in the political philosophy of the seventeenth century. It spoke with the authentic voice of proletarian utopianism. . . ." But such "proletarian utopianism" was then and has ever again been anarchic and in favor of the small community.

[43] This celebrated phrase is actually not very frequent in the writings of the founders of Marxism; one of the few places is Engels, 1880, 1935, p. 70, where we read: "The state is not abolished. It dies out."

[44] Cf. Hayek, 1944, *passim;* for a critical estimate see Friedrich, r, 1945; Hayek has since somewhat altered his original assertions about the necessary connection between socialism and totalitarianism; cf. Hayek, 1952, pp. 94ff.

of an expanding role for the state. Nor is this view merely partisan prejudice: socialist parties throughout the world have made themselves in their program and policies the protagonists of ever more numerous state functions. It is only in recent years and as a result of experience with totalitarianism that socialists have become wary of overexpansion in this direction. The most interesting instance of such reevaluation of their position is the great debate over nationalization in the ranks of the British Labor Party,[45] but other socialist parties, notably the German Social Democrats, have also restated their position along less statist lines. This tendency has been coupled with a continued vigorous advocacy of democratization as counterweight to such statism as the political situation requires. (See above, Chapter 20, for the problems of freedom involved.)

Socialism has been a key factor in the totalitarian movements of the twentieth century and the states which these movements have brought into being. In the case of communism, the link with the nation has been, at least on the ideological level, highly "dialectical." In theory the place of the nation has been taken by the proletariat—the masses of the working population, especially the workers and peasants. In actual practice, the radical internationalism of the communist ideology has had to yield to a measure of distinctive nationalism, whether in Poland or China; this has in turn been decried as "deviationism." Even within the Soviet Union there has been recurrent conflict among the nationalities, though the predominant policy has been to recognize them culturally, but integrate them politically and economically. This integration has, however, not been pursued in the name of an emergent "nation," but in that of an emergent proletariat, understood as a universal community which would eventually include all mankind. As is well known, Stalin, personally, inclined toward the national symbolism, and fell back upon it during the war, when it proved a potent weapon in arousing the will of the Russians to defend the Soviet Union against the German invader.[46] After the war, the Soviet Union sought to revert to the international pattern—a trend which has become more pronounced under the leadership of Khrushchev. But the emergence of a number of communist states, some of them with powerful traditions of national consciousness, obliges the Soviet Union to recognize national idiosyncrasies, that is, the national individuality and modes of expression, political, cultural and social, of these various nations.[47] Whether Khrushchev's Ukrainian background helped him in both com-

[45] Labor Party, 1959, pp. 105–114 (Gaitskell), pp. 522–523 (Foot); 1960, pp. 211–212 (Jenkins); pp. 214–215 (Cousins); pp. 218–221 (Gaitskell).

[46] Friedrich and Brzezinski, 1956, pp. 283ff. The extent to which nationality resentment played a role in feeding the resistance is persuasively described by Fischer, 1952, esp. pp. 62f., 77ff. 90f. and 137f. Cf. also the materials offered in Bloom, 1942, and Barghoorn, 1957.

[47] Brzezinski, 1960, chaps. 3, 9, 12, and *passim.*

prehending and handling this situation may be arguable. But there can be little doubt that the Soviet Union must be forever alert to the divisive forces within its own state, and the dangers which any national diversity in several adjoining communist states engenders. It is undoubtedly true that "the founding of the Cominform was the Soviet response to the challenge presented by the phase of diversity." [48]

Looked at from the viewpoint of the individual Soviet citizen, the nationality problem continues to be a real one. At the same time, two of the ablest and best informed researchers in this field found themselves unable to confirm that "the nationality composition of the Soviet Union is an outstandingly critical feature of its social structure, or that it will play a decisive role in determining the system's long range stability *under normal* conditions." They agree that heavy propaganda might increase nationality feeling, but they believe it is unlikely even then to become "the powder keg" or "tinder box, which so many have asserted them to be." It is a chronic, but not an acute, problem.[49] Are the people of the Soviet Union in the process, then, of becoming a nation? Although great Russian nationalism is on the increase, the answer must be in the negative. Does this mean that the theory which asserts the link between state-building and nation formation ought to be qualified? The question is an open one. The Tsarist state rested upon a nation with a strongly expansionist projection in pan-Slavism; [50] in overthrowing their state, the Bolsheviks managed to substitute the proletariat for the nation as a communal basis of values and beliefs. The Soviet Union has reinforced this basis with a plurality of national selves, and in crisis even by the patriotic notion of a nation-at-large. But the last word has undoubtedly not been spoken.

Nationalities have been the destroyers of states as often as they have been associated with their construction.[51] Time and again, an effort has been made to overcome the resulting difficulties by constructing some kind of federalism. But as shown below (Chapter 32), genuine federalism transcends the classical "state" concept by replacing the "sovereign" with the constituent power which organizes the plural community. It thus seeks to escape the basic difficulty of the crisis of the national state which

[48] Brzezinski, 1960, p. 59. This author has brilliantly analyzed the efforts to overcome national diversity by ideological uniformity, as well as the dangers of "ideological erosion" connected with such efforts. I wonder whether the primary thrust of this diversity is "institutional," however, as he seems to be inclined to think, though he of course recognizes the underlying national selves as expressed in values and beliefs.

[49] Inkeles and Bauer, 1959, chap. XV, at p. 372 (italics mine). The chapter is in part built on Pipes, 1954, and Reshetar, 1952, which see.

[50] See concerning this Kohn, 1953, Mehnert, 1952, and Barghoorn, 1957, as well as the comments in Friedrich and Brzezinski, 1956, pp. 66ff.

[51] Cf. Johannet, 1923; Janowsky, 1945; Hugelmann et al., 1934; Jaszi, 1929. The basic work is, however, Renner, 1907, 1918. Cf. also Znaniecki, 1952.

the rise of nationalities within it heralds. There are those who believe that the end of the national state is at hand [52] because the self-determination of nations (read nationalities?) conflicts with the need for a strong state, needed for economic and other reasons. But while this perspective applies to Europe, it is rendered nugatory by the development of the numerous emergent states and nations, as was stated at the outset. In many cases, even the weakest kind of state is accepted in the search for national self-determination, with federation attempted as the answer to the problem of propping up these hardly viable structures. Wherever we look, nationalities are turning into nations, guided by states of the most diverse internal structure. Even in Europe, the need of unification and federation is accompanied by the reassertion of the continuing importance of the national community as the essential underpinning of such federation. Power is wielded, authority maintained and legitimacy acquired all over the globe in terms of national communities whose values and beliefs are held to be the mainstay of genuine community. Of the several levels of government, the national level is in fact the strongest, even where communism prevails outside the Soviet Union. We would conclude that "not before the vast poverty of Asia and Africa will have been reduced substantially by industrialization, and by gains in living standards and in education—not before then will the age of nationalism and national diversity see the beginning of its end." [53]

[52] W. Friedmann, 1943, esp. pp. 163ff: ". . . the predominant trend of the political, economic and social forces of today lead away from the national state." It is the theme of this able study throughout.

[53] Deutsch, 1953, p. 165.

chapter

31

Empire: Coercive World Order

Empires, since the dawn of civilization,
have been the fruit of an expansive parochial community,
either city-state or nation.
R. Niebuhr

Empires have fallen on evil days and
nations have risen to take their place.
R. Emerson

EVER SINCE CONQUERING HORDES of horsemen brought large territorial realms under their sway, thereby founding large empires by the deployment of coercive power based upon military conquest, the rulers of these vast domains have aspired to make their political order universal.[1] Any communities remaining outside their dominions were looked upon as insignificant and not worth the bother of being included in the civilized order of peace and law which commanded their proper attention. These comprehensive political orders, though now appearing quite antiquated, actually provided effective government for longer periods in man's history than any other type. They are neglected by political theorists except in occasional passing remarks; yet they have been the concern of historians of the different cultures for generations, and the mass of more or less detailed information is impressive. There is no reason at all why the theorist ought not to avail himself of this material on Egypt, China, India, Persia and the Incas, not to speak of Rome, Byzantium and Moscow as well as the Sacrum Imperium of Western Christianity.[2] If for no other reason than to compare and contrast these

[1] A. Weber, 1935, chap. 2.

[2] In a recent book, no less a political philosopher than Reinhold Niebuhr has raised the issue in relation to the "empires" of our time. In 1959, he wrote: "We must examine . . . what is abiding in what seems to be the abandoned structure of the imperial community and power structure," p. 7. His analysis is not satisfactory, because of certain theoretical defects, such as the confounding of power and authority —he says they are "in essence synonymous"—but it suggests the urgency of the task.

structures with the world-wide power systems of the Soviet Union, the United States and the other emergent culture units, such a study should be informative. For it is clear even to the casual observer that there is a profound difference between the totalitarian regimes of our time and these ancient despotisms. Its true range will become discernible only by a comparative evaluation.[3]

The typology of forms of government developed by the Greek philosophers, and their hostility to these empires, as epitomized by that of their Persian enemies, has tended to exclude from political theory the adequate consideration of these orders, especially in the liberal age. Even the judgment in favor of monarchy in medieval and earlier modern times did not include these ancient power structures, since they had been put beyond the pale of Christian government by the general view of history expounded by St. Augustine and retained until well into the seventeenth century. To be sure, there were exceptions, such as Bodin, who included the Turks in his comparative analysis of state and government; also at least the Roman Empire received an increasing amount of attention and even approval as the Renaissance and humanism extolled the virtues of classical culture.[4] But only modern critical historical scholarship has given us the material upon which to base valid generalizations. In so generalizing it is well to take a more cautious approach than is found in the vast and constructivist interpretations of the philosophy of history, valuable as they are in their own dimension of inquiry.[5]

Considering the role of coercive force or violence first, the autocratic regimes of the past and more especially the despotic empires, while lasting over very long periods, experienced considerable ups and downs

[3] Friedrich and Brzezinski, 1956, p. 6.

[4] Bodin, 1584 (1593), e.g., p. 483 (756), where he contrasts the tolerance of the Turks, who will permit many religions, with the intolerance of the Christian empire exterminating the Arians—a view for which he was severaly criticized by many contemporaries; cf. Boccalini, 1630, vol. I, pp. 278ff., where Bodin is tried in the Court of Apollo and condemned to the fire for having advocated *la libertà della coscienza*. Bodin and other writers, especially since Machiavelli, are full of references to the Roman Empire; it was, of course, bitterly condemned by the great Florentine, who composed some of his most passionate pages in execration of Caesar, the destroyer of Roman liberty; cf. *Discorsi*, vol. I, p. 10; this passage is the more noteworthy, as it contradicts what Machiavelli says elsewhere about the founders of states. He contrasts with him "those emperors who merited praise" because they "conformed to the laws like good princes." For another classic treatment along similar lines, cf. Montesquieu's *De la Grandeur*, 1734, chap. XI. For a recent critical appraisal of these issues of Roman history, cf. Syme, 1939.

[5] See below for a few comments on such writers as Spengler, Toynbee, Voegelin, and others noted in the Bibliography. All three and others following them operate, as do the anthropologists, with a concept of "culture" or "spirit" which is inspired by an apolitical, if not an antipolitical, approach which has its roots in Christian theology.

in the degree or intensity of violence employed for their maintenance. Periods of relative order and domestic peace, such as that of the Antonines, alternated with other periods of fierce oppression and tyrannical abuse of power. The first century of the Roman *principatus* saw the benevolent rule of Augustus turn into the absolutism of Tiberius and the criminal license of Nero; comparable contrasts are part of the historical record of every such autocracy.[6] Medieval political thought elaborated the alternative into the dichotomy of monarchy and tyranny, the latter being understood to be the rule of a single man who by the abuse of his power raised serious doubts about his title to rule. The historical record suggests that some sort of cycle is involved in this alternation between intensification and relaxation of autocratic power. To be sure, the adventitious change in rulers who bring a different personality to the task of ruling disrupts the cycle from time to time. Extraneous events, whether natural or man-made, such as plagues, disasters and "barbarian" invasions, may also cause deviations from the natural cycle of gradual intensification of violence which increases until a certain extreme is reached. This is followed by a more or less violent reversal, a return to the original state and the recommencement of the cycle. Even in exceptionally stable ancient Egypt, revolts and usurpations played a significant role throughout.[7] Analysts at present are reluctant to apply this broad historical lesson to the analysis of the Soviet Union, but probably it remains valid. Thus the long rule of Stalin brought a gradual increase in violence which came to a halt at his death; some indeed believe this death to have been a murder committed by persons in his entourage who were in danger of becoming victims of his suspicions. The cycle seems to have recommenced after a period of transition. The process resembles a familiar and repetitive pattern of Russian tsardom. Time and again, the new hope raised by a young emperor that autocracy would end died as the reign matured and the methods of constraint became violent once more.[8] Tsarism arose at the same time as Western absolutism, in the fifteenth and sixteenth centuries, but developed into a much more virulent form of despotism, partly because of the Byzantine heritage, partly because of its struggle against the Tartars and Ottoman Turks. As one leading recent historian has summed up the situation: "While most [Russian] historians give chief weight to

[6] Cf. for a sober descriptive account E. Meyer, vol. I, part 2, for Egypt and Babylonia (Sumer, Akkad, Assyria); for India, cf. B. Prasad, 1928; A. L. Basham, 1954; H. D. Malaviya, 1956; for China, Latourette, 1934, 1942; for Rome, Cary, 1935, 1945, chaps. XI, XXXI, XXXII, XXXVI, XXXVII.

[7] E. Meyer, vol. I, part 2, 1907, 1910, par. 220; for a broad comparative judgment, see vol. I, part 1, par. 28, where Meyer points out that despotism has always been "tempered by assassination." See below, Chap. 33.

[8] Kliuchevski, 1911–1931, *passim;* Sumner, 1943, vol. II, pp. 4 and 5. The quotation below from p. 82.

local causes and Byzantine tradition in the growth of power of the grand-princes of Moscow into Tsarism, other writers ascribe the autocracy of the tsars to imitation, conscious or unconscious, of the Tartar despotism." From Ivan the Great (1462) down to the nineteenth century tsarism as a despotic empire evolved, and the degree of violence varied. But as a system of coercive rule, aspiring to world order, it continued throughout, proudly proclaimed as the Third Rome after the fall of Byzantium by Ivan the Terrible (1547–1584), probably the most violent tsar, yet also one of the greatest.[9] The lesson to be learned from this experience is that autocracy need not be defined in terms of the mode of government of its most violent representatives; neither tsarism nor sovietism nor indeed older forms of autocratic imperial rule are based on pure force.

But empire is top-level rule based predominantly upon coercion, modified in a measure by religious beliefs (Chapter 6, and below). Empire is the method of transcending local and regional power structures, employing one of them for the purpose of subjugating others and welding them into a larger whole. Ultimately, such imperial organizations have tended to seek world domination, that is, to extend their sway to the limits of what was known to them as the politically relevant world. The documentation of the ancient empires is full of rhetoric about world order and peace as the final objective of conquest and submission. Indeed, Toynbee has claimed that each culture as it runs its course eventually arrives at a stage where it becomes united in or under a universal empire;[10] yet Alexander Rüstow, in a less pessimistic mood, has depicted the great empires as the cradles of man's higher culture. He therefore acknowledges their value for man's development, even while decrying their mode of action which he stigmatizes as superimposition (*Überlagerung*).[11] But all such empire-building he sees as ultimately utopian and predestined to be destroyed by its inbuilt weaknesses. They are the weaknesses of all coercive power. It can hardly be denied, however, that these great autocratic structures have shown a rather impressive capacity for survival. Whether legitimized by their achievements in the field of irrigation, as in China, Egypt and Babylon,[12] or by the development of a great bureau-

[9] Sumner, 1943, pp. 91–2 wrote: "All recognize his reign to be of the greatest consequence, both externally and internally, and the latter half to be bloodily seared by his personality; but there agreement ends."

[10] Toynbee, 1957, pp. 1–75. According to him, such universal empires (in his terminology, states) are characterized by three features: (1) they reunite after the breakdown of a civilization, (2) they are a product of dominant minorities who have lost their creative power, and (3) they constitute a rally in the process of disintegration. *Ibid.*, p. 2.

[11] A. Rüstow, 1950, vol. I, esp. pp. 39ff., 118ff., 191ff. Cf. also Friedrich, a1, 1955 and a3, 1955.

[12] Wittfogel, in a brilliant and learned analysis, has stressed this aspect of Oriental despotic empires, calling them "hydraulic" systems; 1957, *passim*.

cratic apparatus for the maintenance of internal peace and prosperity, or by several of these combined,[13] such empires have over long periods provided a nearly universal level of political control and integration. They must be admitted to have been reasonably successful schemes of effective world order. It has been argued that the ancient Middle Eastern empires "symbolized politically organized society as a cosmic analogue," and that "such cosmological symbolization is neither a theory nor an allegory." It is rather "the mythical expression of the participation, experienced as real, of the order of society in the divine being that also orders the cosmos." [14] They are seen and understood as world order, paralleling the order of the universe, whichever of these orders might be assigned the primary role in this interpretation.

Closely associated with such views, if not actually their foundation, is the religious aspect of these "universal" empires. In Egypt as in China, in Persia as in Japan, the emperor is seen as God or godlike (Chapter 6). Such deification of the ruler is not a specific trait of these empires, however. Rather it is the logical extension of the original tribal view which is found in many primitive societies. Thus, as in the Old Testament, so in many other religious documents, the ruler in extending his dominion is merely fighting to secure universal recognition for the power of the particular tribal deities under whose aegis he is operating. It is clear that such identification of the ruler with divine beings and powers greatly enhances his power by providing him with authority of the ultimate kind: an incontestable capacity for reasoned elaboration (Chapter 12). Typically, he speaks through a priesthood which expounds the revealed "truth." In the highest phase of this deification, the ruler becomes the voice of a truly universal religion: Akhnaton in Egypt, Asoka in India. But the subtlety of such challenges to the traditional power structure of a priestly and aristocratic hierarchy undermines the power along with the authority of the ruler. Both these remarkable rulers were followed by breakdown and anarchy, as indeed was their more familiar Roman counterpart, Marcus Aurelius. These rulers, saintly in their aspirations, though not without ruthlessness in their use of violence, embody the "tragedy" of imperial rule which springs from the paradox of power.[15]

Besides the legitimizing of imperial rule, the religious sanction also typically restricted the ruler's arbitrariness by providing a rigid ceremonial. Empires have varied in this as in other respects, but a measure of such ritualistic dependence is from earliest times almost inseparable from the maintenance of this kind of regime. It is one of the great differences

[13] Eisenstadt, a1, 1958, and a2, 1958.

[14] Voegelin, 1956, p. 27. He deals there with the Mesopotamian, Achaemenian and Egyptian empires, contrasting them with the "historical order" of Israel.

[15] For Asoka, cf. the penetrating study by Kern, 1956, esp. pp. 122ff., which clearly brings out the historical parallels referred to. Cf. also A. Rüstow, a, 1961.

between these Oriental despotisms and the totalitarian dictatorships, where a somewhat comparable function is exercised by the official ideology. A great historian, speaking of the Old Empire in Egypt, has written that rebellion apart, it was "indeed the divinity which gives to the ruler his highest dignity and provides a fixed and firm barrier for the kingship: if the ruler were to evade the precise observance of the prescribed regulations, he would cease to be a god; the other gods would not recognize him and men would not obey him." [16] Thus a measure of responsibility is imposed, typically by a priesthood. This priestly control may, at a more advanced stage, take the form of subjection to a faith, a theology, as in ancient Israel and later in the Christian and Moslem empires.[17]

Without entering into the fascinating problems which these religious links of universal empire suggest, we proceed to explore more fully the political aspects of these systems. The Roman and Oriental empires are as we have said the prototypes of these universal states or empires. Such empires aspiring to encompass the entire universe—even when there is a recognition of a vague world beyond the boundaries—have been one of the most important forms of government. Leaving aside the role in culture growth and civilization, these political orders exhibit some quite characteristic traits. Because of their large extent and the as yet rather primitive technology, they develop these traits in the fields of communication and bureaucracy, as well as in those of law and the standardization of currency, weights and measures. There is no reason for describing here in detail what they have done in each of these crucial domains. But it may be well to give some indications. In communications these empires, such as China, Egypt, Babylon and the Incas, have been distinguished by great road systems, fast messenger services and the designing and spreading of a universal language, whether this be the language of the original conquerors (superimposers) or of one of the subject nations; there are examples for both these possibilities. The creation of these universal languages—in China almost by a stroke of the pen, namely, by decree of the founder of the Han dynasty [18]—has been of greatest political consequence, not only in providing the basis for later national development as discussed in the previous chapter, but also for assisting the shaping of appropriate symbols of value and belief.

The problem of bureaucracy having been discussed elsewhere (Chapters 18 and 26 above), it remains to say a word about law and standards. As pointed out earlier, both law (Chapter 15) and measuring rod are basic to the achievement of justice. While a purely situational justice related to very particular events is imaginable, it is not likely to be

[16] E. Meyer, vol. I, part 2, 1913, p. 153.
[17] For Israel, cf. Orlinsky, 1954, esp. chap. VII; and Noth, 1953, *passim.*
[18] Latourette, 1934, 1942.

operationally feasible except under the conditions of the very small and close community. In order to cope with the large number of roughly similar cases, general rules will therefore be extremely helpful in realizing justice (Chapter 14). That being the case, law must be generalized if justice is to prevail in the wider realm of an empire, at least to the extent to which communication and exchange take place among its several parts. Hence empires usually generalize the rules prevalent in a local legal system. The most familiar instance of this procedure is the work of the Roman *praetor peregrinus,* who from year to year sought to resolve the conflict between the Roman law and the laws of the foreigners who traded in Rome.[19] Very often, such a generalized legal system persists even after the empire has perished or receded; the Roman law survived the end of the empire and was eventually revived, and the common law continues in the United States, as well as in the Dominions and India.

As for the weights and measures and more especially the money and coins, not only do the coins provide a symbol for the empire's sway, but the common currency, as well as the uniformity of weights and measures, provides a yardstick by which to determine mutual obligations between the citizens and subjects and to regulate their contributions to the empire. Considering the everyday importance of the activities which all these elements in the social order possess, it is evident that the power and authority of over-all government is deeply embedded in these operations. It is not an accident that empires and federations alike have been dependent upon them for the tensile strength of their political order, while conversely the absence of a common law and of common weights and measures testifies to the as yet incomplete realization of European unification.

In this connection, the census as a basis for effective taxation, the counting of people and their possessions, becomes possible and constitutes a significant instrument of imperial domination. It is encountered wherever imperial rule becomes stabilized.[20] Taxes of every description are thus a concomitant to military rule, and empire always implies that. Tacitus tells of a speech by a Roman official in Gaul who declared that "there can be no peace without troops, no troops without pay, no pay without taxes." [21] It is a valid generalization, supported by universal experience, especially in, but not restricted to, imperial orders.

The imposed peace of imperial dominion makes the military establishment the decisive instrument of rule. Hence armies and their control

[19] Kunkel, 1947, 1952, pp. 44ff. In imperial Rome, the *princeps* became the primary decision-maker.

[20] Cf. E. Meyer, vol. I, part 2, p. 159, for Egypt.

[21] Tacitus, *Histories,* bk. IV, chap. 74.

are at the heart of imperial politics. In the Roman Empire the soldiers eventually achieved supremacy, especially during those periods when all effective authority was lost and legitimacy was at the vanishing point. The brute force of the pretorian guard became the arbiter of effective rule. But the familiar Roman situation has often been paralleled. The problem is always the same: how to maintain "civilian control" over the effective controllers of the means of physical destruction. Organizationally, the answer has been: divide and rule, that is to say, keep the military from forming a cohesive force, by dividing commands, shifting commanders and creating systems of inspection, supervision, and the like. But none of these organizational methods are very reliable, and tend to become corrupted by a variety of means. Hence there is suggested the alternative of influencing the military men themselves by a suitable set of beliefs which surround the imperial office with sacred taboos. The importance of religion for all great empires stems as much from this need to keep order in the imperial establishment and more particularly to control the wielders of physical force as it springs from the need to secure the allegiance of the population at large. Hence the importance of the "imperial idea" providing the spiritual meaning of such systems of rule. The sacred nature of the aspiration to world order, especially in terms of a single god, is linked to a simple view of the world and ignorance as to its real extent.[22]

The colonial empires of recent times hardly ever appeared in this perspective of universal order, after Charles V's endeavor to reconfirm the medieval concept of universal empire had failed.[23] These empires were projections of the European national states; most typically they were "colonies" in the original Greek sense of settlements of Europeans establishing some variant of the European political order; [24] but in India and elsewhere exploitative systems of strictly coercive rule, varying greatly in their detailed patterns and their adaptations to local tradition, were established.[25] These empires typically transcended all regional groupings, even though they more or less extensively recognized them in the patterning of their colonial offices. Such offices were duly differentiated by

[22] A. Rüstow, a, 1961, has stressed this aspect of the matter, esp. p. 541.

[23] Brandi, 1937, 1942, bk. I, chap. 4; also pp. 294ff. Cf. for more detail, Rassow, 1932, esp. chap. V and introd.

[24] Knorr, 1944, chaps. IV, XI and XII, discusses these notions very well, showing how the outlook shifted from an originally predominant merchant interest to an eventual "white man's burden."

[25] The comparative analysis of these "empires" remains to be written; Emerson's interesting recent study, 1960, is actually concerned with the nations emerging from them rather than the empires themselves. See also the concluding chapter by Coleman in Almond and Coleman, 1960, pp. 532ff. Eisenstadt, 1963, offers a comparison of the ancient empires in terms of bureaucracy.

bureaucratic "divisions," as well as colonial "governors" and other officials, routed about from territory to territory and wielding power in a rather abstract and ruthless way. At the outset, they did so in order to enable commercial and later industrial enterprises to collect a rich harvest of exploitation along with a somewhat scantier one of development. This at least was the method in the better administered colonies, as contrasted with the open and undisguised robbery of the Spaniards, for example, in Central America. There was always some of this robbery, but as the more civilized kind of "civilizing mission" proceeded—sometimes aided, sometimes impeded, by the Christianizing mission of the churches—the objectives were transformed into what came to be known as the "white man's burden." The history of this phrase is interesting, as it mirrors the shifting outlook: at first a justification for colonial rule, it eventually became a mockery.

For a while, the technique of "indirect rule"[26] seemed to offer an alternative to the liquidation of these empires. Colonial officials sought to enter into partnership with native rulers who might find it to their interest to make common cause with the colonial power and its citizens in exploiting the native population. Rome had done this very effectively in its day. But such indirect rule proved of short duration, as it was confronted with the challenges of equality: democratization, socialization and communism. Indeed, it served to discredit the native rulers, whom one finds surviving more often in lands where no colonial power gained a foothold, such as Arabia, Iran and Japan, though there are certainly no clear propositions as yet to be formulated in this field.

"Through global conquest the dominant Western powers worked to reshape the world in their own image and thus roused against themselves the forces of nationalism which are both the bitterest enemies of imperialism and perversely, its finest fruit."[27] Thus one of the most competent students of these colonial systems has recently summed up their impact. This imperialism, now pretty universally condemned, lacked as we said a truly imperial idea of world order. It is probably true to say that most of the men associated with its development were sufficiently inspired by the national idea to respect the local cultures as long as they did not interfere in their exploitative enterprise. Veblen in contrasting Englishmen and Germans once put this enterprise into an unforgettable phrase: "The distinguishing mark being that the German usufructuary gentlemen are, in theory at least, gentlemen adventurers of prowess and proud words, whose place in the world's economy it is to glorify God

[26] The classical statement of the most renowned protagonist of such rule is that of Lugard, 1922, on "dual mandate." Cf. also Emerson, 1960, pp. 77ff.

[27] Emerson, 1960, pp. 16–17; whether these nationalisms are the "finest" fruits of the European imperial enterprises, I venture to doubt.

and disturb the peace; whereas their British analogues are gentlemen-investors, of blameless propriety, whose place it is more simply to glorify God and enjoy him forever."[28] Such bitter comment is typical for the growing self-consciousness of Western publics concerning the vacuousness of any "imperial idea." Eventually the West ceased to have any such idea.

In contrast with this lack of an imperial idea, the Soviet Union possesses a clear conception of world dominion. This idea, to be sure, is not stated as that of an empire; indeed it prides itself upon its "antiimperialism." For this imperialist anti-imperialism is directed against the disintegrating colonial empires of the old national states. Lenin and others have devoted some of their best efforts to an analysis of this issue.[29] According to Lenin, a scientifically analyzed imperialism exhibits the following five features: (1) the concentration of production and capital, developed to such a high stage that it has created monopolies . . . , (2) the emergence of "finance capital" and a "financial oligarchy," (3) the export of capital, (4) combines of monopoly capitalists for the exploitation of the world, (5) the division of the world among the capitalist powers. All these characteristics, but more especially the last, lead to strong competition among the advanced capitalist countries. It is obvious that an imperialism thus defined has no application to the Soviet Union; but neither does it comprehend the ancient Oriental empires. Indeed, on our showing, it deals with only one rather marginal form of empire. The more usual features of empire on the other hand are exhibited by the Soviet Union and Red China. Both are coercive structures, dominated by a ruling minority, the controllers of their respective Communist parties, and seeking world dominion in terms of an idea of universal order and peace.[30] This conception was already voiced at the very beginning of the movement in the *Communist Manifesto*'s slogan: "Workers of all the world, unite!" Such an aspiration is deeply embedded in all totalitarian movements, and becomes the basis of imperial enterprises once the movement has crystallized in effective and institutionalized political power.

The design of imperial conquest was more openly admitted and more aggressively practised by fascism. Both the Italian original and its more virulent German mutation gloried not only in such conquest, but in the warlike enterprise which they considered the necessary instrument for its achievement. Such emphasis on war as a desirable form of political

[28] Veblen, 1917, p. 250. Cf. also the comments in Friedrich, 1948, pp. 219ff.; Max Lerner, 1939, pp. 117ff.; Riesman, 1953, *passim.*

[29] Lenin, 1947, vol. I; cf. also Sweezey, 1942, chap. XVII, and A. G. Meyer, 1957, chap. 11. Meyer comments, p. 15, that in his theory of imperialism, Lenin "after much groping, found a way toward real integration of his entire life's work."

[30] Friedrich and Brzezinski, 1956, chap. 6; cf. also Brzezinski, 1960, esp. chap. 16, and 1962, chap. 4.

behavior is one of the distinguishing marks of fascist totalitarianism. It is very common to overlook in this connection the glorification of class war in the communist theory and practice of expansive strategy for world conquest. For since the communists think of the classes as the significant grouping of political communities, as contrasted with the fascist emphasis on the nation, it is only logical for them to employ the war between classes as the spearhead of their thrust.[31] Conquest, whether in the name of class or nation, takes the form of securing power for a minority which is ideologically linked to the minority in the conquering nation. The events leading to the take-over in the so-called satellite (captive) nations bordering on the Soviet Union all conform to this standard procedure. In Rumania, Hungary, Poland, the Baltic states, East Germany and Czechoslovakia it was always the same pattern of utilizing the Soviet Union's military force to install a Communist minority in the key power positions; from these positions the respective Communist parties proceeded to impose a totalitarian regime which was to be subject to central direction by the rulers of the U.S.S.R. The pattern is roughly similar to that employed by the Hitler regime in such countries as the Netherlands, Denmark, Norway and even in a sense France. In light of this record, it is highly misleading to equate the position of America with that of the Soviet Union or Red China, which has followed the same technique in Korea, Vietnam and Tibet and is pushing ahead. At least in terms of nation and empire as here described on the basis of historical experience, to compare the United States and the Soviet Union as empires based on nations is quite erroneous.[32] The United States, in its vigorous support of the United Nations, a loose confederation of most of the world, including the U.S.S.R. (see below), determinedly bypasses the imperial solution to world order. She does so even though the problem of world order is now generally acknowledged to be a vital interest of the United States and though she thereby runs the risk of getting no world order at all. The United States seeks, in other words, to federalize the world, or rather to promote its federalization. The Soviet Union delays and intentionally thwarts such federalization, and has recently put forward reform projects which would transform the United Nations into a part of its imperial enterprise.

[31] The promotion of this class war in other countries takes the form of financing large-scale operations by agents—16,000 in the Federal Republic of Germany alone, according to a recent official report—who infiltrate parties, trade unions and a variety of other organizations, thereby causing a nearly insoluble problem for constitutional democracies in the field of civil liberties.

[32] Niebuhr, 1959, p. 9, has written: "Of these two nations the one tries desperately not to be an empire, while the other claims not to be, but is in fact a secular reincarnation of the classical quasi-universal empire which existed until the dawn of the modern day." His interesting analysis is therein right off to the wrong start.

The existence of such imperial enterprise makes the relations between the Soviet Union and the rest of the world one of constant struggle. The world-revolutionary ideology of Communist Marxism has provided the U.S.S.R. with a potent idea for this empire, in the time-honored terms of order and peace. Not only in eastern Europe, but in the Middle and Far East, these aspirations have become intertwined with ancient Russian imperial propensities, associated as they were with the notion of the Third Rome.[33] The tension which has been developing between the Soviet Union and Red China is a logical consequence of this outlook. For this outlook is matched by a similar secularized imperial view in China, whose rulers traditionally looked upon their country as the center of the world and viewed all other rulers as their vassals. But these differences ought not to be exaggerated. So far, the embracing Communist ideology has definitely outweighed these tensions.[34]

Contrasted with such "unbroken" imperial pretensions as are entertained and openly avowed by the Soviet Union, the "leader of world communism," Western imperialism has become virtually "untenable." Never possessed of a genuine "idea of empire," except possibly in the excusatory slogan of the "white man's burden," as we have noted, colonialist imperialism has no longer any spokesmen whose voice is heard in the world's political market places. Indeed, even the aid to underdeveloped countries offered by the United States and her allies is recurrently under suspicion of representing hidden imperial controls if any restrictions are placed upon it, and the voices are multiplying which demand the surrender of all effective control.[35] The Western world is largely convinced that the colonial empires were without justification even though the historical record shows clearly that at the time of their development there was little doubt entertained concerning their legitimacy. This growing self-consciousness is a striking instance of the disintegration of power under conditions which corrode the legitimacy as well as the authority of the rulers who are to wield it. Empire, although the result of military conquest, that is, force in its crudest form, stands in need of securing both legitimacy and authority in terms of an inclusive "common good," just as much as other forms of political order on whatever level.

It is therefore not surprising that the need for large-scale organization which modern technology has created and is continuing to intensify should have promoted the search for alternative modes of organizing the widening political community. Federation is the response to this

[33] Kohn, 1953; Arendt, 1951, p. 400; Berdiaev, 1947.

[34] Cf. Friedrich and Brzezinski, 1956, p. 67, for further comment. Cf. Zagoria, 1962.

[35] For a striking dramatization of this view, cf. Burdick and Lederer, 1958. The problem is discussed at some length in a number of contributions in *Public Policy*, notably in vols. VI, 1955, X, 1960, and XI, 1961, by Wilhelm, Montgomery and Banfield, respectively.

search, as previously indicated and as will be more fully developed in the next chapter. Such federation may either result from the gradual approach of distinct political orders to each other—sovereign states, to suggest the conventional term—or it may be the outcome of a slow process of relaxing the bonds of empire, of decentralizing rule to the point of effective and legally entrenched local autonomy.

Such a process is actually inherent in large-scale imperial structures. They have all, time and again, struggled with the task of effective decentralization. For there is always the problem of overload at the center to which theorists of modern administration have given considerable attention.[36] The degree of overload is, of course, proportional to the load itself, while being inversely proportional to the state of communications technology. Every ancient empire has therefore as we saw sought to improve its communications in a number of ways, especially by roadbuilding; but the state of the industrial arts being what it was, the primary escape routes from overload were to keep the load down and to decentralize. The former was accomplished by restricting the functions of government to that minimum which defense and exploitation called for; the latter led to a variety of systems all of which have in common an extensive delegation of power to local subrulers.

Such local subrulers—proconsuls, legates, procurators, satraps, governors, and so on—have always caused serious difficulties in imperial systems, especially in conjunction with the military establishment. For, if granted control over the troops in his district, such a local delegate can readily become a center of resistance, defiance and eventually even rebellion. If, on the other hand, he is not granted adequate military support, he is likely to become an ineffectual tool of the military. The Roman Empire struggled with this problem throughout its existence, without ever really solving it. It divided the provinces into senatorial and imperial ones; it divided the power in the imperial ones between a legate and a procurator; but both forms of breakdown occurred time and again.[37]

One writer has dramatically juxtaposed the two tendencies in speaking of "military monarchy" and "military anarchy." The procurator was used time and again as a check upon the legate who was the emperor's plenipotentiary. Even so, rebellions in the provinces were the order of the day in the later empire, while at the same time it was also in the provinces that independent initiative "saved" the empire.[38] To cite one statement for many: "The emperors were jealous of their provincial gov-

[36] H. A. Simon et al., 1947, *passim;* Fesler, 1949, *passim;* Benson, 1941, chaps. II and III. Fesler is editing a series of special studies on decentralization, soon to appear.

[37] Cf. Arnold, 1914, esp. chaps. IV and V; Rostovtzeff, 1926, esp. chaps. IX and X.

[38] Rostovtzeff, 1926, gives many instances of both these events.

ernors, and were casting about for means to diminish their authority. Under the existing system a successful provincial governor was sure some day or other to rebel against his superior. . . ." [39]

It is interesting to note that the empire of the Soviet Union is still beset by similar difficulties, though as yet the reigning ideology is forestalling outright rebellion within the Soviet Union proper, even if not in the satellites. This propensity for an imperial order to break down either as a result of central overload, or because the delegation of coercive power puts men in possession of the instrumentalities for effective resistance places in jeopardy one of the key values of imperial enterprise, namely, the maintenance of peace and order. For the analogue to *pax Romana*, the Roman peace, is typical for all imperial systems in offering to a world torn by parochial or civil strife the pacification for which average men long.[40] It legitimizes a rule which may deprive its subjects of other cherished values, more particularly freedom. In the never ending issue over the ranking priority of values (Chapter 2) empire implies the option for order and peace. To give just two illustrations, the man who was chiefly responsible for organizing the Ch'in Empire (around 200 B.C.) justified the suppression of free speech as follows: "Your majesty possesses a unified empire and has laid down distinctions of right and wrong. . . . Yet there are those who . . . teach what is not according to the laws. When they hear orders promulgated, they criticize them in the light of their own teaching. . . . If such conditions are not prohibited, the imperial power will decline. . . ." [41] Order and peace are preferable to all else, including truth and freedom. The other example is suggested by Herodotus, who tells of a certain Mede, Deioces, who seeking to gain imperial rule achieved it by establishing peace:

As the Medes at that time dwelt in scattered villages without any central power, lawlessness prevailed in the land. . . . Deioces applied himself with great zeal and earnestness to the practice of justice. It was his conviction that justice and injustice are engaged in perpetual war . . . those in the surrounding villages, . . . when they heard of . . . the equity of his decisions, joyfully had recourse to him. . . . Deioces, feeling himself now all-important, announced that he did not intend any longer to hear causes. . . . Hereupon robbery and lawlessness broke out afresh . . . then the Medes assembled . . . and said: "We cannot possibly go on living in this country . . . let us therefore set a king over us so that the land may be well governed, and we ourselves may be able to attend to our own affairs, and not be forced to quit our country on account of anarchy . . ." presently all agreed that Deioces should be king.

[39] Arnold, 1914, p. 172. This statement refers to the second half of the third century, with which chap. X of Rostovtzeff deals.

[40] This is the argument of Syme, 1939, chap. XXIII, esp. p. 477.

[41] Cited by de Bary, in Fairbank (ed.), 1957, p. 179.

Herodotus goes on to tell how Deioces had himself a fortified castle built and ruled the Medes ever after. Thus the leader collected the Medes into a nation (*ethnos*) and ruled over them alone. While this tale is truly the report of the founding of a "national" or monoethnic political order, this order was of the dimensions of an Oriental imperial system, succeeding the Assyrian empire.[42] In any case, it suggests a theoretically important point, namely, the linkage of justice with peace and order (Chapters 14 and 19).

Justice in the sense of a widening sphere of effectively enforced law constitutes another significant value associated with imperial enterprise. The establishment of such justice is one of its historical functions. From the most ancient beginnings, such as the Old Empire in Egypt down to Justinian and the British Empire, the establishment and maintenance of legal order has been central. "A stable legal order with regular procedure and written ordinances and decisions is the characteristic of a civilized state," Eduard Meyer wrote, and claimed it for the Old Empire.[43] Hammurabi has become proverbial for this achievement; he opens his famous code with the comment that he has fixed law and justice, as indeed he did, in a very rigid and unqualified manner.[44]

Intimately linked to the value of justice is that of equality in the arguments advanced for and involved in the building of empires, wherever the distilling of a fixed law becomes a primary concern and function of the ruler and his bureaucracy. It is typically tied in with the liquidation of privileged classes and local potentates, more especially feudal cadres of all sorts.[45] Since feudalism often appears as part of the imperial enterprise, it is evident that equality under the law is not a universal trait of such empires. Yet, that link is so strong and so clearly in response to the laws of politics, that a hypothesis may be advanced in favor of a propensity of imperial, legal and egalitarian operations to be interrelated. In some ways, the greatest issue of the Chinese empire was precisely the struggle between the Confucian feudalists and their legalist opponents, all happily united in their common acceptance of a despotic imperial enterprise.[46]

[42] Cf. Herodotus, bk. I, chaps. 96–101. Herodotus sees it as "winning freedom" for the *ethnos* of the Medes (and others) against the *arche* of the Assyrians, eventually to be replaced by the empire of the Persians. Cf. also E. Meyer, 1928 (vol. II, part 1), pp. 58ff., for a modern account of the reestablishment of the Egyptian empire.

[43] E. Meyer, 1913, vol. I, p. 158. Hammurabi is discussed by the same author in pars. 444ff., esp. (for the law) pp. 638ff. (par. 450). Aron, 1962, chap 23, by contrasting "peace by law" and "peace by empire"—a conventional contrast—overlooks the fact that the extension and maintenance of law is central to empire-building.

[44] Cf. Harper, 1904.

[45] For a comparative study of feudalism, cf. Coulborn (ed.), 1956, esp. chap. I and part III. In the latter, the link between feudalism and empire is discussed and the limits of equality thereby clearly suggested.

[46] Liu (as well as de Bary) in Fairbank (ed.), pp. 105ff. and 163ff.

The imperial enterprise has, by its very nature, caused intercultural contact on a broad front. The superimposition which is its essence brings this about. Such intercultural contact may obviously produce one of three results: (1) the conquering culture absorbs and in the process destroys the subjugated culture; (2) the conquerors adopt the culture of their victims; and (3) an effective process of acculturation produces a composite culture. Students of culture, especially historians and anthropologists, have extensively investigated these processes.[47] It is not our task here to reproduce the results of these extensive investigations. But there is one aspect with which political theory must needs be concerned, and that is the particular political ingredient of cultures-in-contact through imperial conquest. For while the more immediate political activity associated with the imperial enterprise itself is bound to be moulded by the culture of the conquerors, the activities of the subrulers in the far-flung and often distant parts of the empire are likely to adapt to local and regional preferences, values, interests and beliefs. And even at the center such "alien" cultural elements may make their impact. For example, the Roman *princeps* found it increasingly advisable to adopt the posture of a god or godlike being, in accordance with the beliefs of his conquered subjects, especially in Asia, therein following the example of Alexander of Macedon, and like him creating serious problems for himself at home where such a posture appeared to most of his Roman compatriots as preposterous.[48]

Generally speaking, one can say that the "higher" culture conquers the lower one; thus the Chinese absorb their successive alien masters, as did the Romans the Germanic barbarians. But this generalization does not by any means always hold, even if we assume that it is possible to say with certainty which is the higher and which the lower.[49] The process is also affected by the numbers involved: the more numerous tend to absorb the minority, and the more so, the more marked the difference. Political elements of culture, that is to say, generally speaking, those elements which bear upon modes of organizing cooperation in the broadest sense,[50] seem in any case not to follow this general law of the "higher" and of the "more numerous," but to exhibit a common tendency related to the requirements of power under the circumstances of empire (and now of federation).

[47] Kroeber, 1948; Keesing, 1953.

[48] Altheim, 1957, chap. II; for earlier views see Rostovtzeff, 1929, chap. XII and *passim;* J. Burckhardt, 1853, chaps. I and II.

[49] Thus the Germanic peoples were willing to be absorbed into the Roman tradition, while the Arabic peoples were not. Niebuhr, 1959, following Pirenne, 1939, would attribute this difference to religion; while no doubt very important, religion was reinforced by a much greater cultural "gap" in terms of "racial" background.

[50] Almond, 1960, pp. 20–33, has undertaken to combine these elements into the notion of political culture as such; he recognizes fully that the implicit notions have been part of political theory for a long time.

It is theoretically unavoidable, therefore, to analyze somewhat further the intercultural problem involved. In a recent work on contemporary problems, it has been observed that

> It would not be stretching the matter too far to suggest that if anyone now deserves criticism for seeking to overturn established cultures and supplant them with new-fangled inventions, it is the leaders of the underdeveloped peoples and not the ethnocentric spokesmen for the West. To contend at the present time that the underdeveloped countries should remain undisturbed in their own cultures and not make the transition into the modern Western world would be to brand one's self as an old-style colonialist, striving to hold back the peoples who are beginning to come into their own.[51]

That is probably true enough. But what really needs rejection is the conditional alternative. Processes of acculturation have throughout the history of civilization been precipitated by imperial conquest, and the resulting complex patterns of cultural change, affecting fundamentally community and political order, far transcend any personal responsibility. Both native leaders and retreating imperialists are seeking to cope with a situation not of their own making.

There is, as a consequence of the conflicts and emotions attendant upon the liquidation of colonial imperialism, an inclination to overemphasize the differences, to be too solicitous about culturally conditioned diversity, and to forget that in politics human beings have a great deal in common and that the alternatives of political behavior and organization are limited, as far as the basic lines of development are concerned. Just recently, a key African leader rightly stressed this aspect of the matter when he said: "The African concept of democracy is similar to that of the ancient Greeks. . . . To the Greeks, democracy meant simply 'government by discussion among equals.' " Traditional African democracy consists, he thought, in "talking until you agree," and he felt this was a fairly universal concept.[52] Similar statements can be made about many other basic political givens, as the theory of politics here presented has tried to show, and indeed any theory of politics must. In matters of detailed application, on the other hand, specific differences appear—the ultimately unique is not likely to be the ultimately important in politics. This basic hypothesis of all comparative politics and theory is not only the ground upon which empires have always rested in practical operation, but it is also the necessary presupposition of any political order embracing more than one culturally distinctive group, no matter what its range. What has come to be discussed as the "polyethnic state" is possible only because of

[51] Emerson, 1960, p. 13, 14.
[52] Nyerere, a, 1962.

this panhuman foundation of political behavior and activity.[53] The liquidation of empires has brought into being new states a number of which are in turn polyethnic. But since these new political orders typically are not imperial and coercive, but consensual, at least at the outset, federalizing is indicated. The alternatives confronting such polyethnic orders have been described as fourfold: the divergences may be accepted as permanent, and equality granted to the different ethnic groups, or they may be merged by common consent or through gradual processes of assimilation. Or, the different ethnic groups may be subjected to a dominant group. Or finally such groups may be forced into assimilation by violent means. Only the latter two alternatives require imperial dominance, whereas the former are characteristic modes of federal and democratic constitutional orders (see next chapter). It is, however, by no means necessary that an empire be based upon either ethnic domination or assimilation by force. Typically, the great empires have sought to achieve a measure of ethnic equality, often reinforced by religious conformity to a dominant creed. This was the case of the later Roman Empire, as well as of the Chinese and Indian empires over long periods. Thus ethnic heterogeneity was eventually merged into a broadly egalitarian citizenship.[54] The Hapsburg empire tended in the same direction, though German and Hungarian predominance remained marked and contributed to its dissolution.[55] Whenever such ethnic subdivisions are preserved in imperial political orders, the possibility exists for either a division into several national orders or the emergence of a federal system. To the problem of federalism we must now turn.

[53] For panhumanism, cf. Friedrich, 1942, chap. X. The polyethnic state has been the subject of extended discussion in IPSA meetings, more especially at Paris, 1961. Cf. the volume edited by Benjamin Akzin, and more especially his own paper "Political Problems of Poly-ethnic Societies," to be published in 1963.

[54] The problems of the polyethnic societies received a good comparative treatment at the above-mentioned congress by Leslie Lipson. Cf. also the paper by Morgenthau.

[55] Jaszi, 1929, part V, esp. pp. 271–329. At p. 296 we read: ". . . no exaggeration . . . [that] never in the history of the world was the principle of national equality in a great empire and under [sic] so many different nations carried so far as in former Austria." Jaszi believes that the "fiction of the unitary Magyar state" made a further evolution impossible.

chapter

32

Federalism: Consensual World Order

When the conditions exist for the formation of efficient and durable federal unions, the multiplication of them is always a benefit to the world.
John Stuart Mill

On the third level of political order, transcending at times the national state, but at any rate constituting efforts at organizing such order in a wider sphere, a more extended territory, than that of the local and regional community, we saw that one finds, besides empire, federation, both national and supranational. For federation has played a significant role in organizing national "states," or rather communities; even local communities have at times banded together in federations and leagues of cities and tribes, such as the Iroquois and the Creek.[1] Indeed, federation is a very general pattern of political conduct, continually employed by all kinds of organized entities when certain conditions are calling for it. Federations of states and the federal state must be seen as particular applications of a recurrent formula for effective organized cooperation between groups. A federation is a union of group selves, united by one or more common objectives but retaining their distinctive group being for other purposes. Federation is, on the intergroup level, what association is on the interpersonal level. It unites without destroying the selves that are uniting, and is meant to strengthen them in their mutual relations. It organizes cooperation.

[1] Noon, 1949; Swanton, 1928.

If federation, as thus very generally understood, is the alternative to empire, it is because the power wielded in a federation is predominantly consensual, while that of empire is coercive (Chapter 9). That these terms are both relative and correlative, we have shown earlier. In light of that analysis, it is hardly surprising that an empire may be converted into a federation, and a federation into an empire. The British Commonwealth and the Holy Roman Empire provide interesting instances of the first process, the Roman Republic of the second. Either of these structures is exposed to the danger of such transformation. But not to accomplish such transformation may also prove fatal, as it did in the case of the Hapsburg empire.

The most interesting example of a gradual substitution of a federation for an empire is, of course, the transformation of the British Empire into the Commonwealth of Nations. This feat was accomplished over a long stretch of years during which the British were giving "dominion" status to former colonies. A dominion today is a nearly independent state, tied to Britain by bonds of common political tradition as symbolized in a common Crown, though Ireland and India, while associated with the Commonwealth, do not acknowledge this symbol.[2] In this case, we observe the "federalizing" of a once centrally controlled political system to the point of near dissolution.

More common is the occurrence of the federalizing process for the purpose of bringing together hitherto wholly separate and even hostile states. It appears at times as an alternative to unsuccessful attempts to accomplish a common order by the establishment of an empire. Thus in Europe, both the imperial conquests of Napoleon and of Hitler were so completely unacceptable to the developed national subdivisions that their empires collapsed within a few years of their establishment. Indeed Hitler met defeat in the course of the very process of imperial expansion. In lieu of such imperial efforts at unifying Europe, there has now set in a process of accomplishing this objective by building a federal system. While still in its early stages, this process is gaining momentum, having become manifest in the setting up of several "communities" with specific objectives, the Coal and Steel Community, the European Atomic Energy Community and the European Economic Community (Common Market).[3]

A curious blend of empire and federation occurred in the case of Germany, where the unification was accomplished by warlike conquest on the part of Prussia, which transformed Germany into a quasi-federa-

[2] For the complex problems of the Commonwealth, cf. Underhill, 1956, and Mansergh et al., 1958, esp. chap. 1.

[3] Haas, 1958. Aron, 1962, pp. 734ff., also uses this contrast of empire and federation, but his concept of federalism is old-fashioned and legalistic.

tion; the German Empire resulted from this conquest. The federalizing process, set in motion by these partly coercive beginnings, has continued and produced the German Federal Republic, a fully integrated federal system.[4] A parallel endeavor on the part of the Hapsburg monarchy to solve the problems posed by the increasing resistance of subject nationalities to its imperial dominion met with failure.[5] The difference between the two developments is, of course, to a considerable extent due to the centrifugal forces of the culturally divergent nationalities of the Hapsburg lands as contrasted with the centripetal forces provided by a common German "nation" (Chapter 30). But the federalizing process played its part.

India, when confronted with a similar problem, after the disappearance of British imperial control, also sought to solve it by federalizing its political order. This policy was successful, except for the predominantly Mohammedan parts of British India. In this instance, religious as contrasted with national differences proved an unsurmountable obstacle to federal union. As a consequence, two separate states were formed which have been on a rather hostile footing, India proper and Pakistan. But inside both these states the federal pattern was adopted to cope with their further difficulties of linguistic and national differences. It is not possible at the present time to draw any very clear conclusions from these undertakings. More especially in India there has been a steady evolution in the direction of regional differentiation, and prophets of doom predict an eventual breakup of the Indian political order. One need not agree with such counsels of despair to recognize that the last word has not been spoken about the clash of centrifugal and centripetal forces.

All these examples and many more that could be cited suggest that a broader theoretical approach than the customary one is needed. Federalism has to be seen and understood not only as an alternative to empire, which it surely is, but also as the institutional form resulting from a very general process of politics operating on every level of political ordering. This process is on the higher levels intimately linked to constitutionalism because it presupposes the rule of law and the "sanctity" of contracts (Chapter 15).

The concept of federalism is of recent vintage, though the practice of forming federations and leagues is recurrent in history. A review of the history of political thought shows that the concept arose in conjunction with the emerging theory of modern constitutionalism. Federations had been formed by cities in their struggle with the territorial rulers, in Italy, Germany and the Low Countries, as well as Spain. Is is therefore

[4] Heidenheimer, a, 1958; Merkl, a, 1959; Neunreither, a1, 1959, a2, 1959. Cf. also Gablenz, 1960, and Grosser, 1958; English edition, 1960.

[5] Jaszi, 1929; Redlich, 1920, 1926, 1928.

not surprising that effective institutionalization of a federal system is first found in Switzerland and the Netherlands, and that in turn the first theorist of federalism should have drawn upon the experience of these countries in developing his thought. Johannes Althusius built a unique theory of constitutionalism upon a very broadly generalized concept of federal compacts on successive levels of community.[6] He made the bond of union, the *consociatio*, one of the cornerstones of his system. The village was for him a federation of families, as was the guild, while the town was seen as a federation of guilds, the province a federation of villages and towns, the kingdom a federation of provinces and an empire a federation of kingdoms. In its hierarchical structuring, this view of political community bore a close resemblance to medieval realities, but in contrast to much medieval thought, power and authority were said to flow from the base to the top and not from the top down. Hence the term "hierarchy" does not really apply, and the apparent similarities with Thomas Aquinas and Dante are not borne out by closer inspection. Althusius adopted and adapted the Bodinian notion of sovereignty by attributing it to the corporate body politic. On successive levels of community, from the family to the kingdom, he held that those who live together, the *symbiotics*, are united by a pact, express or implied, to share things in pursuit of common interests and utility. The key to this concept of federalism is that on all levels the union is composed of the units of the preceding lower level, so that when we arrive at the top, the members of a political order are neither individual persons nor families, guilds nor other such smaller groupings, but the provinces and free cities. This view puts the Althusian concept of federalism in sharp contrast to the modern view of the "federal state" and identifies him with the notion of confederation. But in the perspective of federalism as a process this difference is not as important as it once seemed to the theorists of federalism.[7]

The next significant contribution to the theory of federalism was Montesquieu's, though the notion of a broad confederation of states had continued to play a role in the various projects for an universal order, from Henry IV's Grand Design to the Abbé Saint Pierre's *Projet* of 1713. These projects were somewhat utopian and decidedly futuristic;

[6] Althusius, 1603. Gierke, 1880, 1939, chap. V, gives a general history of the concept of federalism. For the Althusian doctrine itself, see Friedrich, 1932, introd. For a general, though in spite of its prolixity, incomplete, history see Mogi, 1931.

[7] Grotius, though sharply opposed to Althusius' idea of popular sovereignty, shared this concept of federal union. Writing specifically on the basis of Dutch experience, he saw the political order as a perpetual union of lesser communities, united through *consociatio*, or compact. Cf. Gerbrandy, 1944, for an explicit confrontation.

they certainly did not pretend to describe analytically the actual nature of political relations as Althusius and Grotius had done.[8] That descriptive and analytic approach reappears in Montesquieu when he came to consider the notion of a "federative republic." [9] However, his preoccupation was with the question of how to give defensive strength to several republics. He thus stayed within the limits of what the Greeks had tried to achieve with their several confederations.[10] He described this federative republic as a convention by which several bodies politic consent to become "citizens" of a larger state. He called such a republic a "society of societies." These formulations challenge by their breadth; in spite of a lack of concrete detail it is apparent however that he thought of a very loose federal relationship and did not concern himself with the process by which it may become more close-knit. He developed nonetheless one aspect of federalism which not only became a feature of the American system, but which has since been recognized as an important condition if the federalizing process is to proceed beyond its most elementary stage. That condition is the requirement of homogeneity; Montesquieu thought that a federative republic must be composed of republics—a requirement which reappears in Kant's essay on a world order to be considered presently. But beyond this general norm, Montesquieu did not elaborate the institutional structure of a federative republic.[11] No more than Althusius did he "discover" the American type of federalism.

It is no exaggeration to say that federalism was the most central issue of the Constitutional Convention at Philadelphia in 1787. And what was

[8] Cf. for these projects Friedrich, 1949, chap. VI; for a review of the several plans, with selected texts, see Raumer, 1953.

[9] Montesquieu, 1748, bk. IX, chaps. 1–3. Cf. also bk. II, chap. 4, for the *pouvoirs intermédiaires*.

[10] Ferguson, 1913, pp. 238ff. Sidgwick, 1903, lecture IX, writes, after having reviewed the several types: "And finally the predominance of federalism in the last stages of the history of Greece was chiefly caused by the necessity of having states larger than the old city-states to resist Macedonia. I may add that the necessity of greater strength for defence in war has been the cause of federalism in medieval and modern Europe as well as ancient Greece." (P. 134.) Cf. for this issue the discussion in E. A. Freeman, 1863.

[11] The provision in the American Constitution is art. IV, sec. 4. Similar provisions are found in virtually all federal constitutions. In view of the keen interest of the American Founding Fathers in whatever Montesquieu had to say, the little he did say was carefully considered. Cf. *The Federalist*, no. IX, where Hamilton cites Montesquieu at length to support a federal solution as an alternative to monarchy; curiously enough he speaks of a "confederate republic" when the term "federative" would have suited his propaganda purpose so much better, suggesting that he worked from an inaccurate translation. Cf. also Solberg, 1958, pp. 48ff., who gives the Articles of Confederation of 1781, which much more closely correspond to Montesquieu's notions.

finally adopted constituted an institutional framework which its builders considered a distinct innovation. In the fourteenth chapter of *The Federalist*, James Madison stated this sense of novelty very emphatically. After speaking of the "numerous innovations," he exclaimed: "They [the drafters] accomplished a Revolution which has no parallel in the annals of human society. They reared the fabrics of governments which have no model on the face of the globe. . . ." And he immediately added: "They formed the design of a great confederacy, . . ." showing thereby that he considered the federal structure the most distinctive novelty. Therefore, comments to the effect that the builders of the American system were practical men without a consciousness of their theoretical principles are quite mistaken.[12]

The Federalist is, to a large extent, the theoretical statement of the new concept of federalism which the American Constitution embodied. It is a new design, as Madison insisted, and it is admittedly a design that will evolve. "It is incumbent on their [the drafters'] successors to improve and perpetuate." Here is a hint of the view of federalism as process, but the primary emphasis is on design: how to divide legislative power between the states and the Federal government, how to balance the fields of governmental activity so as to produce a sound equilibrium between states and nation, how to arrange matters so as neither to favor the large nor the small states unduly, and so forth. From these debates there emerged a novel, hitherto unknown, concept of federalism as an integrated system of government, a fully institutionalized "unity in diversity" of interrelated communities, a genuine political order of structured power, and a multicentered authority, democratically legitimized and pluralistically accepting the basic fact that each citizen belongs to two communities, that of his state and that of the nation at large. It is the quintessence of this design that these two levels of community should be clearly distinguished and effectively provided each with its own government, and that in the structuring of the government of the larger community the component states as distinct communities must play a distinctive role.

This new concept of federalism has in the interim been adopted in many countries. Switzerland and Germany, Canada and Australia, India, and a host of other countries have studied the elaborate arguments which *The Federalist* expounded to explain the new concept, have adopted, adapted and developed as well as at times rejected basic features of it. This American concept may be said to embody the discovery of the "federal state," because that was the term which nineteenth-century jurists attached to it when they contrasted it with a confederation of states. Actually, no such dichotomy was ever envisaged by the inventors of the American concept, nor was it employed in its institutional con-

[12] For further details and references, cf. Friedrich, a4, 1960.

cretization.[13] As just mentioned, this concept was the first to recognize that federalism is not a fixed and static pattern, but a process. Hence the founders invented the amending provisions, but in doing so they fully embodied their federal conception in the amending power: both states and nation fully participate in any alteration of the order, and the equal voice of the component units is doubly protected.

In the same period in which the Americans evolved their new conception, federalism had a rebirth in the political philosophies of Rousseau and Kant. Their thought was significantly related to their view on constitutionalism and democracy. It has lately become fashionable to question Rousseau's belief in democracy, even to make him out a crypto-totalitarian.[14] Whatever the kernel of truth in such a view, the genuine penchant of Rousseau's ideas is evident in his well-known recognition that democracy is possible only in small communities, and that a democratic order must therefore be a federal one, thus resuming and continuing the argument of Montesquieu. More especially in his *Considerations on the Government of Poland* he favored the federal elements in Poland's traditional order.[15] But Rousseau had created a formidable obstacle to any genuine federal order, even as static design, by his rejection of representation (Chapter 17). This difficulty is purely theoretical, and derives from his unfortunate doctrine of the "general will." [16] Kant sought to remedy these defects by giving the general will an underpinning in the "categorical imperative," which interprets man's moral conscience as a legislative or rule-making activity of the mind. He also abandoned the radically democratic tendency of Rousseau's general political outlook and returned

[13] The failure to recognize the crucial importance of community pattern, involving values, interests and beliefs, and the participation of citizens, misled Wheare, 1946, chap. I, into preoccupation with the pattern of power as separate, rather than as intertwined. "Does a system of government," he wrote, "embody predominantly a division of powers between general and regional authorities, each of which, in its own sphere, is coordinate with the others and independent of them? If so, that government is federal." (Pp. 33–34.) It produced the very questionable equating of the government of the Weimar Republic and the Soviet Union as "quasi-federal." Actually, the government of the Weimar Republic was involved in an advanced phase of the federalizing process in the direction of unity, while the Soviet Union was and is a "pseudo-federal" government in which the regional entities possess no independent power at all, but only such as the central government wishes to allow them.

[14] Talmon, 1952, pp. 32ff.

[15] Cf. for this, as well as the related ideas of Montesquieu, the interesting essay by Hoffmann, in Maass (ed.), 1959, pp. 113ff. and 120ff. However, it seems to me that Hoffmann overstresses the centralist tendency of Rousseau in terms of the general will, seen as will. For a corrective cf. Derathé, 1948, who shows the rationalism in Rousseau; he does not, however, deal specifically with federal problems.

[16] For this cf. Derathé, 1948, *passim;* Hendel, 1934, pp. 99ff., 157ff., and *passim;* Friedrich, 1948, pp. 171ff.

to Montesquieu's constitutional or "republican" emphasis on a federative republic. But instead of linking the establishment of such a republic to the military needs of defense, he made it the basis of a hope for a worldwide order based on law, relating it to the categorical imperative by claiming as one of its primary substantive rules that "there shall not be war." [17] But the republics composing his federal world order are unitary systems in which corporate entities are instituted by the government and possess no genuine autonomy.

Following these revivals and the major innovations of American practice, writings on federalism multiplied during the nineteenth century. Especially in America and Germany there was a great deal of legal controversy, mostly revolving around the issue of "state" and "sovereignty" and the dichotomy of federal state (*Bundesstaat*) and federation of states (*Staatenbund*)—a theoretically arid controversy of great practical importance as regional units struggled to maintain distinctive institutions related to local values, interests and beliefs, such as slavery.[18] More original and from a theoretical viewpoint more interesting are the views of De Tocqueville and Proudhon. The former's are essentially a commentary on the American innovations.[19] De Tocqueville fully appreciated that they were based on a "novel theory" and considered it "a great invention" in political science. He does not place in the center that aspect which is here considered the crucial one, but he nonetheless clearly recognizes its political implication, namely, that "the subjects of the Union are not States, but private citizens" and that therefore "the national Government levies a tax, not upon the State of Massachusetts, but upon each inhabitant of Massachusetts." Consequently, he recognized the direct legislation by and for the federation as a whole: ". . . the Union rules individuals." In explaining this novel approach, De Tocqueville wisely appreciated what is here considered crucial, namely, that a national community existed along with the regional ones; the several states had long been accustomed to form a portion of one empire, and their regional (De Tocqueville says "national") prejudices had not become pronounced. Most of these thoughts had been stated quite adequately in *The Federalist*, and De Tocqueville merely highlighted them by persuasively contrasting America with earlier federations, such as Germany, Switzerland and the Netherlands. De Tocqueville's remarks derive their charm from the fact

[17] Friedrich, 1948, *passim.*

[18] For the American controversy, see Holcombe, 1950; for the German one, Emerson, 1928, chap. III; for Switzerland, Rappard, 1948, and 1936. Cf. also Friedrich, 1950, chap. XI.

[19] De Tocqueville, 1835 and 1840, chaps. VII and esp. VIII. Cf. also Pierson, 1938, chap. 22, and the interesting comments by Hoffmann as cited above (footnote 15), pp. 124ff. For reasons set forth in the text, I would not be prepared to adopt De Tocqueville as the "saint" of federalism, however, as Hoffmann suggests.

that they assess fifty years of experience which served to confirm the anticipations of *The Federalist*. He could write that "the Union is as happy and as free as a small people, and as glorious and as strong as a great nation"—the terrible ordeal of the War between the States being as yet far away. But De Tocqueville at the same time misjudged the durability of the Union. Thinking of the peoples of the component states as nations, he "refused to believe in the duration of a government which is called upon to hold together forty different peoples." Rightly assuming that the population would reach a hundred million before another hundred years were out, he asserted that "where there are a hundred millions of men, and forty distinct nations, unequally strong, the continuance of the Federal Government can only be a fortunate accident." [20] Had he understood the dynamics of the federalizing process better, he might have avoided this error.

Still, De Tocqueville was writing at a time when Jefferson's doctrine of states' rights was still in its full vigor. The notion of two coordinate governments "each sovereign in its own sphere" had been expressed in the Kentucky Resolutions, which thought of the Union as based on a compact "among parties having no common judge," and hence claiming that "each party has an equal right to judge for itself." Such notions found their culmination in John Calhoun's *Disquisition on Government* (1851),[21] which reverts to the notions of group federalism of an earlier day. The key to his doctrine of such federalism was the idea of "concurrent majorities." By this he meant that a community's "will" can be ascertained only by taking into account the majority preferences in each of its major constituent groups. He speaks of the United States as a democratic federal republic which is a "community of states, and not the government of a single nation." Insisting on the "indivisibility" of sovereignty, he claimed it for the states, thereby trying to undo the innovation of the Philadelphia Convention and its personalist conception of federalism.

This return to the older view had a parallel in the conception of federalism expounded by a great French socialist and anarchist, P. J. Proudhon. The sharp antagonist of Marx's coercive centralism, Proudhon revived the Althusian notion of an all-engulfing federalism. Even his formulations sound at times like translations from Althusius, including the emphasis on contract. Presumably this similarity is due to Proudhon's dependence upon Rousseau.[22] Proudhon speaks of a federal contract and claims that its essence lies in the fact that under such a system the contractants, the heads of families, the communes, the cantons, the provinces

[20] De Tocqueville, 1835 and 1840.

[21] *Works*, 1853, vol. I. See also below, Chap. 34.

[22] Rousseau's indebtedness to Althusius in the matter of contract has been convincingly argued by Derathé, 1950, pp. 92ff., and I have revised my views expressed in 1932.

and eventually the states do "not only oblige themselves bilaterally and mutually toward each other, but they also in forming such a pact reserve for themselves more rights, more freedom, more authority, and more property than they give up." [23] Federalism is characterized by a permanent give-and-take between inclusive community and component communities, and this organic interrelation, cooperation and exchange is a universal principle of political organization. However, Proudhon leans toward a rather loose and imprecise construction which leaves the component units the "last word." In short, the higher level is subordinated to the lower. This is presumably due to his anarchist outlook. The contract of federation has "as its object to guarantee to the component states their sovereignty." He consequently insists that the competence (*attributions*) of the federal government can never exceed in number and substance those of the component units. Apart from the difficulty involved in making the quantitative assessment this argument presupposes, there is no foundation in federal experience for such an assertion. It commits Proudhon also to a static acceptance of a particular phase in the dynamics of the federalizing process.

This review of the major theories of federalism was necessary in order to show that none has given, though occasionally they hinted at, an adequate interpretation of this complex political phenomenon, primarily because of their static approach. Federalism should not be considered a term for a static pattern,[24] designating a particular and precisely fixed division of powers between governmental levels. Instead, "federalism" seems the most suitable term by which to designate the process of federalizing a political community, that is to say the process by which a number of separate political organizations, be they states or any other kind of association, enter into arrangements for working out solutions, adopting joint policies and making joint decisions on joint problems. Conversely, federalism is the process through which a hitherto unitary political community, as it becomes differentiated into a number of separate and distinct political communities, achieves a new organization in which the differentiated communities, now separately organized, become capable of working out separately and on their own those problems they no

[23] For the quotations, see Proudhon, 1863, in the edition by Brun, 1920, pp. 104–105. He universalizes the principle of contract, and more particularly the kind of contract which the *Code Civil* calls *synallagmatique* (bilateral) or *communative* (mutual), as contrasted with unilateral, onerous and gratuitous contracts. Thus it is seen that Proudhon based his federalist thinking on civil-law conceptions of contract, as contrasted with the common-law notions underlying American federalism. He speaks of the reservation noted in the text as "individuelle" for each individual contractant.

[24] The best modern statement of federalism as pattern or design is Wheare, 1946, 1953.

longer have in common. It is not only a matter of decision-making, but of the entire range of power and its exercise (Chapters 3 and 9). The federalizing process accompanies, so to speak, the communal development as its organizational counterpart. If values, interests and beliefs exhibit a stable and structured pattern in which the commonly shared values, interests and beliefs are counterbalanced by values, interests and beliefs that are not shared, though territorially distributed, then a federal development becomes possible. Take for example trade unions, which have formed extensive federations in all industrialized countries, such as the American Federation of Labor and the British Trade Union Congress. Each component unit at first had its own interest, associated with distinctive values and beliefs. But these unions soon discovered that they shared not only values and beliefs, but also broader common interests. Federation then was indicated and was not slow in coming, challenging and eventually eliciting the organizing ability of the leaders of the component units. The same holds true for churches and many other groups. Whenever such groups cannot or rather do not wish to merge, because of their distinctive values and beliefs, their self and identity, yet need to unite for the accomplishment of common objectives, usually springing from common needs, federation is indicated. It is essentially the fact that unity is combined with diversity in such a fashion that there coexist spheres of autonomy for the inclusive and the exclusive community, that there coexist spheres of loyalty for both, and that a distinctive characteristic, whether it be living in a particular territory, belonging to a particular church or practicing a particular trade, can be made the basis of assigning persons to the exclusive as well as the inclusive communities.[25]

The federalizing process may indeed commence in the forming of a league, such as the Council of Europe, the North Atlantic Community, or the Confederation which preceded the forming of the United States of America. Or it may lead to such loose association as that of the British Commonwealth of Nations. But always there is the problem of how to combine local autonomy with comprehensive unity. It is of course the crucial issue in world organization, except for those who are prepared to accept the imperial design of the Soviet Union described above. Autonomy is here taken in its original meaning as signifying the power and authority, as well as the legitimate capacity, to govern oneself in those matters which form the basis of the community. Such autonomy is actually the basis of individual rights and was so interpreted for individuals

[25] I regret the value implication of the words "exclusive" and "inclusive"; they are meant *sine ira et studio*, that is to say, no intrinsic value attaches to either community. A similarly unfortunate implication attaches to Toynbee's "parochial" and "universal" states, though here the association of the parochial states with the "time of troubles" reinforces the prejudice. The so-called "time of troubles" seems in many ways preferable to the universal state.

in the constitutional order by its greatest philosopher.[26] In other words, the autonomy of no entity or being, whether individual or social, is considered as impaired by participation in a wider and more inclusive community, provided the sphere of power of the wider community is instituted, maintained and altered only with the effective participation of the component communities, as likewise the autonomy of the inclusive community is considered unimpaired if its sphere cannot be altered without its effective participation.

Such firm protection of the autonomy of both against the encroachments of either level of the political order obviously cannot be achieved unless embodied in law. That is why this sort of political order can be accomplished only within the context of a constitution, as discussed earlier. In fact, it is precisely such embodiment of the territorial division of power in legal constitutional rules which distinguishes a federal from an imperial order. For empires have often not only permitted but sponsored (as we saw) a large degree of regional autonomy; indeed it may well be questioned by the political theorist, comparing the ancient empires with modern federal structures, whether the regions of such empires as the Ottoman Empire or ancient China or India did not have more substantive autonomy than the component units of federal America or Switzerland. But the difference is that such autonomy might at any time be invaded or indeed wholly obliterated by the whim of the central imperial authorities, while the constitutionally protected autonomy of a unit in a federal system, limited though it may be, is protected against such arbitrary intrusions upon its sphere by suitable constitutional procedures. Soviet federalism is unsatisfactory on this score. It would seem that the autonomy of the several Soviet republics was not and is not adequately protected. In view of the "facade" character of Soviet constitutionalism, the Soviet Union appears to be a unitary, inadequately decentralized political order in which the top leadership, uncontrolled by the cadres, speaks for the Communist Party, which through its hierarchical structure binds the Soviet peoples together and makes them a unitary state.

In short, we have federalism only if a set of political communities coexist and interact as autonomous entities, united in a common order with an autonomy of its own. As the preceding paragraph has implied, such federalism is incompatible with the traditional concept of sovereignty as described before (Chapter 30). No sovereign can be discovered in the federal system; autonomy and sovereignty exclude each other in a political order. At least that is true unless such autonomy is itself designated as "sovereignty," as is in fact done in America, where the states are described in the constitution as "sovereign." That such a usage constitutes a perversion of the classical meaning of sovereignty is evident. The same

[26] Kant, 1785, contains the most persuasive statement.

may be said of all notions that the component units "transfer" part of their sovereignty to the higher level; for such transfer implies divisibility of him who has the last word. The attempt to escape from this difficulty by arguing that the constitutional amending power becomes the sovereign is rather misleading; for this power is intermittent and constitutionally circumscribed in its operation, as are all other uses of power in such an order. The only theoretically clear and admissible way of putting the matter is to admit that instead of being directed by a sovereign power a constitutional system rests upon the constituent power.[27]

A federal system then is a particular kind of constitutional order. The function it is supposed to serve is to restrain the powers wielded by the inclusive community, *as well as* those of the communities included within it. It is as we have just said a kind of division or separation of powers, but applied on a spatial basis.[28] This function of restraint may be and often is hidden by the motivation which leads to the establishment of a federal system. When the need for cooperation is uppermost in the minds of those who establish a federal system, they may think of the restraints purely in terms of concessions to the more reluctant participants. This oversight is less apt to occur in the reverse process of federalizing a preexistent community; here the need for restraining at least the central power is a driving motivation; the federalizing process is set in motion by the desire on the part of the divergent subgroups to take over and govern themselves in all but a few select spheres of joint interests and joint need. In either case, the restraint of power is the crucial objective; in governmental organization, for which territory is of central significance, only territorially delimited communities have been able to achieve such a pattern of mutual restraint and joint operation on a limited scale.[29] The very fact that this pattern of restraints is the organizational manifestation of a peculiarly structured pattern of values, interests and beliefs suggests that spheres of joint interest and joint belief, as well as those of divergent interest and divergent belief, are likely to undergo a steady evolution.

[27] Friedrich, 1950, chap. VIII.

[28] Maass (ed.), 1959, while following the general theory here outlined, has pleaded for using the term "areal" rather than "territorial" or "spatial" division of powers. I remain unconvinced, because in the general theory of government and the state, one speaks of the importance of the territory within the boundaries of which it operates, and the demand for more land has been called the drive for "space" or "territory," not for "area."

[29] The one exception is Esthonia, which after the First World War instituted a nonterritorial system. Here an attempt was made to put to test proposals which Renner, 1918, had advanced for solving the problems of the Hapsburg monarchy, by incorporating each nationality as an electoral body and then federalizing the empire in terms of these ethnic groups constituted by persons without reference to territory and on the basis of personal preference. For Esthonia, see Pallerits, 1931, pp. 39ff., and Uustalu,1952, p. 220 (this work gives the historical background).

This evolution is apt to be both quantitative and qualitative, and the history of every federal system has a distinct tale to tell. In a recent comprehensive review of several federal systems in terms of distinct fields of operation, such as commerce and the like, it was possible to show the variegated pattern of development.[30] Consequently, every federal system evolves in response to such evolving needs, by governmental (administrative, judicial, legislative) interpretation, as well as by formal amendment. Such changes are related to the very basis of the federalizing process itself, and it is therefore important not to confuse the process of federalizing with particular divisions of power which may be characteristic of a federal system under some particular circumstances of time and place.

A great many of the arguments and controversies over whether a particular political order is federal or confederal result from precisely this neglect of process in favor of structure. They have bedeviled the politics of European unification. They are now troubling other federalizing processes, including those in Africa, the Caribbean, and the world at large. The real problem, politically, is whether the federalizing process is in progress and whether the institutional structure as it evolves facilitates the changes required by it. Even the much-argued issue of supranationality, important as it is as a way station in the progress toward federal union, does not compare in importance with the task of setting the federalizing process in motion.

At this point the relation of this federalizing process to the functioning of democracy appears of great importance. If democracy is understood in terms of the absolute and unrestrained rule of the majority of the members of a given political community, as was done by Rousseau and many others (above, Chapter 10), then a stark and unresolvable conflict between federalism and democracy must be acknowledged.[31] Curiously enough, Rousseau does not seem to see it thus, if one considers his position as delineated above. The reason is not difficult to detect: he treats federal arrangements as a static structure of lasting *foedus*, rather than as a process of intercommunal growth; his very hostility to representation prevented a better understanding of the issue. Absolutist democracy is incompatible with federalism, because it does not permit an effective division of power. This aspect probably explains in part the general penchant of radical

[30] E.g., chap. 6 (A. E. Sutherland), chap. 4 (Bowie), chap. 9 (Brinser) and chap. 10 (Friedrich and Mavrinac), concerned with commerce and transportation, defense, agriculture, and labor, respectively in Bowie and Friedrich, 1954, dealing with Australia, Canada, Germany, the United States and Switzerland on a comparative basis.

[31] For a pointed statement of this view, representative of the outlook of many "radical" democrats found among European socialists, cf. Franz L. Neumann, a, in Macmahon, 1955, pp. 44–55.

democrats all over Europe, such as the British Labor Party, to be wary of European federalism. For there can be little doubt that the "sovereign will" of the British electorate might be thwarted if it had to adjust to what other electorates preferred or rejected. More specifically, socialism may become more difficult of achievement if it has to be worked out on a European plane. The weariness toward federalism shown by the British Labor Party may also be due in part to socialist experience in Australia, for there the constitution has been interpreted to prohibit nationalization of any business enterprise operating beyond state boundaries. Hence the Australian Labor Party is committed to abolishing federalism—an impossible undertaking.[32]

The difficulties of federalism can be resolved if a constitutional democracy, instead of an absolutist one, is taken as the basis of theoretical analysis and of practical operation. All that is then required is to recognize that every member of the inclusive political order is part of, that is to say a citizen of, two communities operating on two levels, the regional and the national (federal). A given group of persons, A1, A2, A3 . . . and another group B1, B2, B3 . . . "belong" not only to community *A* or community *B*, but also to community *AB*, which includes them both and is therefore a composite community. The participating decisions of these persons, their "will" in the old-fashioned terminology, shape communal action through effective participation in the communal decisions of *AB* as well as either *A* or *B*. The inclusive community as well as the included community being politically organized, democracy, far from clashing with federalism, now is seen to require it whenever a composite community exhibits more than one level of effective communal existence in terms of distinctive values, interests and beliefs.

From an empirical standpoint, an effectively centralized government, a decentralized government, a federal government, a federation, a confederation or league of governments (states), an alliance, an alignment, a "system" of independent government (states), and, finally, completely unrelated governments—all these could be represented as differences of degree in the relation of governments to the persons subject to their rule and to the territory they occupy. The two extremes are unitary control by one rulership, and complete separateness of control by distinctive rulers, both being marginal cases. Federalism as a process needs to be seen as linking a number of the systems of relationship in the middle section of this series. It constitutes a series of designs of political order suited to situations in which the subject population falls into distinctive territorial groupings of communal diversification, that is, a territorially diversified pattern of values, interests and beliefs which are overarched by joint

[32] See J. D. B. Miller, 1954, 1959, pp. 145–146; for Labor's general attitude see Crisp, pp. 79–82, esp. p. 81.

values, interests and beliefs constituting an inclusive community. It is therefore basically this patterning of values, interests and beliefs which occasions the federalizing of the existing political order in response to an evolving communal diversification or unification, as the case may be.[33]

If it be now asked, in keeping with our general theory, what are the common objectives arising from common interests and needs, as well as the common beliefs and values, the answer is that they are different for different federations. But there appears usually to have been involved the common objective of resisting some outside pressure or threat of a military nature, a potential conquest even, to which all the potential member communities are exposed. Australia is one of the few exceptions.[34] The same holds true conversely: common defense needs will hold a group of differentiating communities together long after other interests have become diversified. If some of the communities entering the federalizing process have formerly been hostile and engaged in a sanguinary conflict, as is not infrequently the case, the elimination of such potential conflict may prove an added inducement in face of a greater threat.[35] It is to be expected, in any case, that there may remain security problems (insecurity feelings) between political communities which formerly were rivals on the international scene. The same kind of problem arises also in the use of other types of organization. A federation of churches may be troubled at times by the continuing effort of each of them to secure new converts, and a federation of industries by the competition between member enterprises or groups of them.

A significant problem impeding the federalizing process may be the fear of weaker members that they will be overpowered and absorbed; in their eyes this process may appear as a kind of peaceful penetration by the stronger units. In a sound federal system, such fears have usually turned out to be unjustified, except for the smallest units. Thus the extended controversies in the Philadelphia Convention over the issue of the large versus the small states proved largely irrelevant in the sequel; the size of states, while of importance in the workings of American federalism, has not become a significant threat to the smaller among them. Likewise in the case of Germany, it is Prussia, the largest state, which has

[33] The foregoing constitutes a restatement of my position as given in a4, found in Macmahon, 1955, and in Friedrich, 1950, chap. XI, esp. p. 190, bringing these earlier statements into line with the general theory of political community.

[34] J. D. B. Miller, 1954, 1959; Crisp, 1949.

[35] Such is the case in Europe today, as it was in Germany, Switzerland and the United States, though in the latter case as a threat rather than an actuality, but a threat made real by some minor skirmishes. See for this point Liska, 1957, pp. 137ff. He wrote rather pointedly: "The enemy is to be 'disarmed' or 'neutralized' either by military destruction, a politico-military encirclement, or a federal embrace," and hence there may be "a very tenuous dividing line between federal integration and war."

disappeared, along with the minute states, such as Lippe-Detmold, rather than even so small a state as Bremen (less than a million inhabitants). Nor was this disappearance of Prussia wholly a result of the Hitler war, though it was decreed by the victorious Allies; it was already being envisaged by the reform of the federal system of the Weimar Republic which was impending at the time of the National Socialist seizure of power.[36] It would therefore seem that the security of the three small states, Belgium, the Netherlands and Luxemburg within the Community of the Six is also reasonably protected by the close balance of the three larger states, France, Italy and Germany's Federal Republic; these three are so nearly equilibrated that the predominance of one among them, though a factor in political oratory from time to time, is not likely to become a major problem, rather, it is the close cooperation of France and Germany. The pressing problem is external defense, as *The Federalist* already argued.[37]

Another major objective resulting from the common interest in prosperity has been in the field of commerce and industry. Indeed, this objective is likely to prove in the long run the lasting underpinning of a structure that might at the outset have been motivated by the needs of common defense. A comparative study of various federal systems, even as loose a one as the United Nations, but certainly the United States, Germany and Switzerland, as well as Canada and Australia, shows that a large market, permitting correspondingly large productive enterprises, eventually became of primary importance. The development of a multitude of common interests associated with such markets and production facilities usually weaves an increasingly dense network of interpersonal relations, from mere verbal communication to *connubium* as the ultimate sign of established community.[38]

The relation of federalism and nationalism is nonetheless an equivocal one. For whereas on the one hand an existing nation has at times been able to overcome the obstacles resulting from its division into several political orders, at other times the existence of nations has slowed down, obstructed or even prevented the federalizing process from taking its course. Again, in the inverse process developing national communities

[36] See for the *Reichsreform* Brecht, 1945, part III, esp. pp. 73–92.

[37] As is well known, the first articles of *The Federalist* are devoted to this problem; see the valuable introduction by B. F. Wright in his fine new edition, as well as the commentary by Cooke in his, both published in 1961.

[38] At this point, the analysis of federalism merges with that of nation formation, as discussed in Chap. 30. The patterns of communication, here as there, provide empirical evidence for the march of the federalizing process. Besides the previously cited work of K. Deutsch mention might be made here of Deutsch et al., 1957, where the early phases of a federalizing process within the framework of an international organization (NATO) are dealt with; note esp. pp. 36ff. and 46ff., and the entire chap. III, which discusses integration as a process.

may help to federalize a formerly unitary structure, or on the contrary a powerful national sentiment may obstruct or prevent such regional differentiation. For the first of these situations, one might cite Germany in the nineteenth century, for the second, Europe at the present time, for the third, the British Commonwealth serves as an illustration, whereas the fourth is in part responsible for France's difficulties in the Saar, Algeria, and elsewhere. Many more examples could be given to show that nationalism and federalism are neither naturally linked nor naturally opposed to each other. It all depends upon the structure of the political communities involved. To the extent that nationalism is the most powerful factor in political community-building, it always affects the federalizing process, by strengthening either the inclusive community or the component ones, and thus operating either to build nations or to transcend them.

At this point, it may be well to add a reflection on the built-in contradiction of nationalism as it is now understood. In contrast to the traditional divisive nationalism of Europe, which is being mirrored in the corresponding divisions of Africa and Latin America, as well as the Middle East, both India and China have been inclined to speak of their very inclusive cultural communities as "nations." They have done so in spite of profound differences in language and other manifestations of culture; for the common written languages of Mandarin and Sanscrit correspond to Latin in medieval Europe; they are literary vehicles of cultural communication beneath which a rich variety of vernaculars provide the means of interpersonal communication. One should therefore perhaps speak rather of culturism than of nationalism in dealing with these comprehensive cultural communities, and the same applies to the emergent European community and other broadly defined areas. It is in these areas where marked diversity is combined with a common framework of culture that political federalism seems to be particularly appropriate as a form of political order. Such vast federal structures may become the eventual building blocks of a viable world order (see final chapter).

There is a typical pattern which such composite federated communities, whether national, supranational or perhaps eventually world-wide develop; it seems the form best suited to the organizing, dividing and restraining of powers. These structural features are intimately bound up with the fact that the federalizing process, when it unites formerly separate communities, or rather organizes their inclusive community, begins with a league or other kind of intergovernmental association. It was so in a number of Western countries, in Switzerland, in the Netherlands, in the United States and in Germany. It is proving the same in Africa, Asia and Europe as a whole at the present time. In view of this circumstance, it is not surprising to find that typically the organizational features of a league are found prevalent in the governmental structure of federated communities.[39] In a sense, it could even be said that the institutional pattern of a league survives in a federal system. It shapes the structure of federation and of a federal "state" in the direction of "organized diversity." Hence the theory of federalism calls for a sketch of the institutional pattern of a league. It is a recurrent pattern and consists of three elements, namely, (1) an assembly of representatives of the constituent communities which after instituting the league, usually by way of a charter or treaty, amends it when necessary; (2) an executive establishment of some sort to carry out the decisions of the assembly; (3) an arbitral or judicial body, interpreting the treaty in its bearing upon the relations between members of the league and between them and the league as a whole, thus seeking to eliminate the recourse to arms.[40]

It is evident that this pattern corresponds to the basic functions of the concrete political order, namely, the settling of disputes, the making of rules, and the taking of measures as analyzed before (Chapters 24–26), while the process of establishing a league by the conclusion of a treaty or the adoption of a charter is composed of those processes which constitute the founding of a political order (Chapter 22). It is therefore hardly surprising that the task of common defense should be a primary function of a league (Chapter 23) and that the development of parties and of traditions should prove as vital to a league as to other kinds of political order (Chapters 27 and 28). There is no need for recapitulating these topics in terms of their particular application to leagues and the federations and federal systems which result from them in the progression of a unifying political process. (In the differentiating progression all the above factors appear on the regional or local level.)

A few comments however on distinctive problems may be appropriate here. Leagues have always been troubled by the issue of equality between the component units. Their assemblies usually are based upon an equal representation of the member communities, each counting for one. The actual difference in power between them is then made up for in the greater weight assumed in the executive establishment, or occasionally an inner group is constituted as a kind of upper house. The rationale for the presumed equality of representation in the assembly is linked with the process of establishing the league: if the smaller communities had not been given equal status, they would either have refused to join or broken away. The records disclose this situation again and again. In the further progress of the federalizing process, when rule-making for the inclusive

[39] Friedrich, 1950, pp. 191ff., gives a more detailed analysis, as well as further literature on the various leagues that have existed in history.

[40] It is evident that this pattern fits both the League of Nations and the United Nations, as well as the Achaean and Aetolian leagues, the North Italian, the Hanseatic, Swabian and Belgian city leagues, the Swiss and Dutch confederations, as well as their American and German counterparts. For further details cf. Friedrich, 1950, as cited.

community becomes important, two representative bodies are developed and combined into one assembly of two houses, one to represent the equality of the component units as communities, the other the equality of the citizens of the inclusive community as persons. This is the situation in Australia, in Canada, in the United States and in Switzerland. In others, such as the German Federal Republic, India and the proposed European Community, the full equality of the member units is somewhat modified, either because the differences are deemed too great in power, and/or democratic belief in the equality of voter-persons is too far advanced.[41]

In many ways the most crucial task to solve if the forming of a league is to initiate a progressive federalizing process, appears to be the establishment of a workable joint executive. It was so understood in the setting up of the European Coal and Steel Community and of the Common Market; its absence has frustrated the Council of Europe. Historical evidence in support of this general proposition is abundant. This is not to say that the creation of such an executive establishment guarantees the forward march of the federalizing process; obstacles to such a development, that is to say, divisive forces, may be too strong for that, in which case such an executive merely ensures the effective operation of the league. The history of the United Nations to date amply corroborates this conclusion.[42] But for all federal systems in their early stages the executive is crucial, because rule-making is restricted to the making of the original treaty and its amendment, except for such interpretative implementation as its application calls forth. The advantages of a developed and responsible bureaucracy (Chapter 18) thus accrue to, and tend to advance, the inclusive community and its federal structure. Naturally, such an executive will be influenced by the nature of its tasks, military, economic or more broadly political. In the selection of the executive, the stage of federalizing will be reflected: the farther developed in the direction of unity it is, the more completely will it be a function of the inclusive community and its representatives. Conversely, the farther developed it is in the direction of diversity, the greater will be the participation of the component communities. Thus, in the United States the President is increasingly the choice of the American people, though originally the electoral college represented the states and even today its division into states plays a vital and at times vitiating role. Proposals for his election by a simple majority of the people have been numerous. In the Federal Republic, the Chancellor is elected by the *Reichstag* representing the German people, not its *Länder,* thus reflecting the more strongly unitary character of that federal system. In the European Coal and Steel and other communities, the several executives, on the other hand, are elected

[41] For the emergent European community, cf. Haas, 1958, chap. 11; Schierwater, 1960, part II, chaps. I and II; Haas, 1960, *passim.*

[42] Claude, 1959, esp. chap. 10.

by the several participating governments representing the component national communities—an arrangement which is typical for all leagues and confederations.[43]

The executive's unifying role is usually greatly aided by some kind of arbitral or judicial body. Such a body can settle disputes concerning the meaning and interpretation of the treaty, charter or constitution which the other federal authorities, especially the executive, are not able to compose. Again typically, the extent of the participation of the component communities in the selection and dismissal of such body and its members is determined by the degree of federal diversity. Both here and in the case of the executive, quantitative studies might throw considerable further light on the extent and degree of proportionality. Such participation may be restricted to participation in the treaty-making or legislation under which the judicial or arbitral body operates, as in the Federal Republic and Switzerland, or it may assign to the component units a substantial share of the appointing. Such share may be indirectly exercised, as in the United States where the Senate representing the states has to "confirm" appointments to high Federal judicial office, or it may be directly exercised, as in the European communities, where the member governments do the appointing themselves; or an intermediary system may be chosen, as in Switzerland, where the highest federal judiciary, the Federal Tribunal, is elected by the federal assembly in one house, in which the component communities, the cantons, are represented *qua* cantons. It is evident that the mode of election of such a body will be a subject of controversy between those persons seeking to accelerate the federalizing process in whichever direction and those seeking to retard it. In a differentiating process, a judicial body may be the last operative bond, as was and is the case with the Privy Council's judicial functions over dominion constitutions.

However constituted, such arbitral or judicial bodies are characteristically an instance of last resort, and whether or not they will forward the federalizing process, in either direction, will often depend upon circumstances of personal predilection or party politics, as the history of federal judiciaries clearly shows. Their operation must be seen in the light of the general propositions which apply to dispute-settling to which they are largely subject, of course (Chapter 24). The prevalence of arbitral as compared with judicial procedures will roughly speaking depend upon the stage of the federalizing process: the more closely knit the federal system, the more formally judicial will these procedures become.[44] No

[43] For further detail, cf. Bowie and Friedrich, 1954, chap. II.

[44] Frankfurter and Landis, 1928, fail to make this point explicit, though it is implicit in their account. McCloskey, 1960, chap. VII, and others, describing the history of such courts, have shown this general trend; cf. Freund in Bowie and Friedrich, 1954, chap. III.

one has attempted effective quantification here, though the materials for some of it are ready at hand.

All federal systems are confronted with the problem of admission of new members and the related one of secession.[45] It is evident that the looser a federal community, the more readily will it admit new members and allow old members to secede. Former theory therefore inclined to make secession the test as to whether a composite political order was federal or confederal. The War between the States as well as the Sonderbund War (Switzerland) were waged to prevent secession of units which had rejected a key policy decision expressive of a broad value preference on the part of the majority (abolition of slavery in the United States, economic liberalism in Switzerland). But in spite of these sanguinary tests, the problems of admission and secession cannot be said to be decisive from either a theoretical or practical viewpoint. At one end of the federalizing process, the ability to secede regardless of the formal right will obviously exist. It will decline and tend to disappear as the inclusive community is extended to ever widening spheres of the common values, interests and beliefs, so that at the other end, neither admission nor secession is likely to occur. Exceptions must be recognized, however, under particular circumstances, such as the admission of formerly dependent colonial territories into a federal union. The cases of Hawaii, Alaska and Puerto Rico come readily to mind. They also illustrate another significant difference. For Puerto Rico's greater cultural separateness, as expressed in her Spanish language preference, has produced a new form of "admission," namely, that of free association.

Free association, as a matter of fact a new dimension of federalism, suggests that there could be an inner and outer group of participating communities, such as is developing in the process of European unification. Free association is also the form in which West Berlin is able to participate in the Federal Republic. It is likewise provided for in the constitution of the Fourth and Fifth Republics of France, but without having been actualized.[46] The idea that an autonomous, self-governing community might be an "associated" member of a federal system is difficult to interpret unless federalism is seen as a process as here described. Once federalism is thus understood, association is comprehensible as an institutional device for organizing a relationship which is close enough for a loose federal tie, but no more. This is the case with Puerto Rico.[47] Or a closer tie may be prevented by outside pressure, as is the situation of West Berlin.[48] Or again, the closer tie may be objected to by allies or confederates, as was the case with Britain's entry into the European Com-

[45] Friedrich, a, chap. 15 in Bowie and Friedrich, 1954.
[46] Bowie and Friedrich, 1954, chap. XIV.
[47] Friedrich, 1959, chap. 2.
[48] Davison, 1958; Speyer, 1961.

munity.[49] Whatever the cause, association constitutes the potential beginning of a federalizing process. The same phenomena that characterize it under more normal conditions are to be observed, and hence there is always the possibility that it will end in actual federal union once the obstructions have been removed or worn down by time.

The specific form of association of Puerto Rico with the United States is rather a close one. It makes the individual citizen of Puerto Rico an American citizen, obliges him to serve in the United States armed forces, commits him to United States foreign policy, subjects him to all those laws which the United States Congress decides to make applicable to Puerto Rico—in consultation with a Puerto Rican representative in Congress, to be sure—but it also makes him, as a citizen of the Commonwealth, more autonomous; for the Commonwealth is more self-governing than the average state, with its own constitution and laws more fully protected.

The feature of this arrangement which calls for somewhat more general comment in connection with federalism is that of common citizenship. Again, we find that the older theory inclined to make such common citizenship the criteria of its dichotomy of the federal and the confederal system, but it was in error in doing so. For the British Commonwealth, which is surely at the most highly differentiated extreme of the federalizing process (or in the old terms, confederal), possesses common citizenship, as it has a common Crown; that is to say, at the very top and the very bottom, there is community.[50] On the other hand, the much closer community of the Six in Europe does not, and presumably will not for some time, have such common citizenship.[51] There are other interesting issues involved here, notably that of acquisition of citizenship when both levels participate. In the United States, citizenship in the states is acquired by residence on the basis of United States citizenship, but subject to detailed legislation. The Swiss and the German Imperial and Weimar constitutions, on the other hand, made federal citizenship a consequence of acquiring citizenship in the component unit though in both cases as well as in the United States some persons could possess federal citizenship

[49] Royal Institute, 1956.

[50] Parry, 1957.

[51] The drafters of the constitution of the European Political Community discussed a rather ingenious compromise: any European who had completed his military service in the European forces or who was born after the Community came into being was to have complete freedom of movement and to enjoy the rights of nationals in all the member states; the question of formal citizenship was left open, while its essential rights were gradually to be extended to a widening circle of persons. The Draft Resolutions of the Study Committee (1952) had proposed that "all the citizens of the Member States shall be citizens of the Community." Cf. Bowie and Friedrich, 1954, p. 819; cf. also therein the comparative study on citizenship by W. J. Schrenk (chap. 12).

without state citizenship. Clearly, the variations are great, and no unequivocal correlation between the pattern of citizenship and the extent of federal integration can be gleaned from a comparative study, except to say that usually a closer union will provide for federal citizenship because federal elections require it.

The theoretical view set forth so far leads to a final point of dispute in connection with federal systems, and that is the provision for amending the formal charter or constitution. If federalism means the process of federalizing, either by building a federated community out of separate communities or by loosening an existing unitary one, then obviously the relative flexibility of any formal constitutional arrangements is of crucial importance. As past federal experience amply demonstrates, the federalizing process presupposes adequate facilities for change. At the same time, such amending of the charter or constitution is bound to be somewhat cumbersome because of the need of providing for adequate participation of the component communities as well as the inclusive one. In a composite community, the constituent power upon which the constitution rests is also composite, and the amending procedure requires adapting to this reality.[52] Without such adaptation, the federal system is likely to break down, as happened in the United States (1861) and Germany (1933). One of the gravest objections to the draft constitution for a European political community was the extreme complexity of its admending provisions, which would have thwarted the federalizing process.[53] A workable amending procedure was one of the great achievements of the men who drafted the American Constitution. It also exists in several of the more recent federal systems.[54] The looser the federation, the more likely it is that the amending procedure will be inadequate, thereby conjuring up the prospect of a breakdown of the federalizing process.

In conclusion, it remains to suggest that federalism holds out the prospect of organizing the world at large as the alternative to imperial domination. The process which has been described in its most general terms in the preceding pages is highly flexible and capable of responding to every variety of need. The "unity in diversity" which it permits can be structured to correspond realistically to the actual distribution of power, and thus can be made legitimate in the view of even so vast and varied a constituency as the present world contains. The Covenant of the League of Nations and the Charter of the United Nations are initial steps in this process. There is need for revising the latter in the light of experience. Unfortunately the procedure for accomplishing this objective is almost unworkable. The intrinsically retrogressive proposals of the Soviet

[52] Cf. Friedrich, 1950, chap. VIII, where the doctrine of the constituent power in its relation to the amending power is elaborated; cf. also above, Chaps. 9 and 10.

[53] Friedrich, a, in Macmahon (ed.), 1955, pp. 526ff.

[54] McWhinney, a, in Bowie and Friedrich, 1954, chap. 16.

Union have this advantage, that they keep the issue open and subject to further exploration. But their specific recommendations, or rather demands, seek to convert this federally conceived political world order into an instrumentality of imperial contest and compromise. If they persist, that is all that will be left of it.

part

VI

Tradition, Revolution and Reform

chapter

33

Tradition and the Role of Education

What from your forebears you inherited,
earn it in order to possess it truly.
Goethe

ANY ANALYSIS OF POLITICAL life which stresses values and beliefs alongside of interests is bound to be concerned with tradition. For such values and beliefs must be transmitted in order to be fully operative. Any strictly temporary belief or value is bound to be of limited impact, except in periods of revolutionary upheaval.[1] There have been numerous occasions in the preceding chapters on which reference has had to be made to tradition, notably in the discussion of ideas, myths, symbols and religion (Chapters 4 to 6), in that of authority and legitimacy (Chapters 12 and 13) and in the earlier chapters of Part IV. The difficulty in the past has been the tendency of political thinkers and theorists either to under- or to overestimate tradition, especially in the great controversies of revolutionary periods. Actually, tradition has been a continuous factor of great importance in politics, but one which has

[1] Accordingly, Max Radin defined tradition as "not a mere fact like an existing custom, nor a story that exhausts its significance in being told; it is an idea which expresses a value judgment. A certain way of acting is regarded as right; a certain order or arrangement is held desirable." ("Tradition" in *ESS.*) Cf. also Friedrich, a, 1953; I there noted, p. 42, that "tradition is essentially a romantic concept," and on p. 46 that "an argument from tradition is an argument from sentiment," and that these "sentiments . . . invest certain past events with a highly positive evaluation."

hindered and hurt as well as helped and supported the political community. Too much tradition ossifies a political order, while too little tradition dissolves it. *Anomie* was coined by the Greeks as a pejorative term to designate the latter situation when there is no *nomos*, no sacred custom and hence no basic law to guide men's actions, while the opposite fault has been castigated by revolutionary writers in terms appropriate to the particular order they were fighting without giving rise to a general term. It might be called *nomocracy*, to describe a state where everything is judged in terms of traditional values and beliefs, where the *nomos* has become the tyrant of the community and forestalls all forward movement. This was the state of affairs in the West at the time of the French and American revolutions; it was more recently the condition of many colonially administered countries. Statesmanship of the highest order will be required to guide them out of this condition into a balanced political order and not to allow them to fall into *anomie*.

In broadest analytical terms, tradition consists of any set of established values and beliefs which have persisted over several generations in a particular political community. It is thus the antithesis of ideology, with which it is often unfortunately confused by those who identify any prevailing system of ideas with ideology (Chapter 4). Traditionalism is a self-conscious and deliberative insistence upon, or more especially a harking back to, such values and beliefs, often embodied in and symbolized by habits, customs, usages, and the like.[2] Thus traditionalism may become itself an ideology of reactionary cast, as has happened in the case of fascism and certain forms of nationalism.[3] This fact has tended to obstruct the recognizing of tradition as an ineluctable element of all community, and more particularly political community. It may cogently be asked whether "it is reasonable to stipulate any traditionless society,"[4] and the question of the role of tradition can thus only be whether a political order is more or less traditional. Indeed rationality itself may

[2] Hoselitz, in his chapter in Braibanti and Spengler, 1961, undertakes systematically to subdivide tradition in terms of habits, usages, norms and ideologies (meaning beliefs), but I doubt the pertinence of this aspect of his otherwise valuable and balanced analysis. For an elaboration of the distinction between tradition and traditionalism, cf. also Shils, a, 1958; this distinction was already used, in a rather similar sense, in *ESS*.

[3] The failure to bring out this dimension mars the otherwise interesting attempt to treat nationalism as a rival ideology in Bowie et al., 1959, esp. pp. 8ff. and 51ff.

[4] Hoselitz, 1961, p. 84. The well-known "reified" alternatives of Weber's typology of authority-legitimacy (see above, Chaps. 12 and 13) and the related notion of Riesman's tradition-directed versus inner- and other-directed (as if tradition were not a factor in both inner- and other-directed conduct) illustrate the widespread propensity to treat tradition pejoratively and to juxtapose it, often by way of a dichotomy, to rational conduct. Hoselitz' paper rightly questions this propensity, as does Polanyi, 1958, pp. 53–54, 374–379, and *passim*. Cf. also Popper, 1957.

well become a tradition, as it has in the modern West, and more particularly in America. One of the obstacles which reactionary attacks against the existing order encounter in the United States is due to this circumstance. An appeal to American traditions and more especially to the Constitution always involves such a plea in a reassertion of the rational values of a constitutional order and its liberties, such as free speech and other forms of self-expression.

A political tradition is more specifically a tradition concerning the political community, its values and beliefs, including the conduct of men as political persons. Political tradition defines how rule is conducted, and how those ruled behave toward the rulers, including their participation in the electing and controlling of them. Such tradition always is embodied in habits, customs, and norms which express the values and beliefs prevalent in a given community.[5] This undoubted context of political tradition has given rise to such notions as that the "agreement on fundamentals" (above p. 237) is essential for any political order, or for some particular type. As we have shown there needs to be a certain measure of agreement and a patterning of values and beliefs, but this fact does not constitute an "agreement" on fundamentals. A measure of consensus there is in any functioning political order, but it may be structured in a highly pluralistic fashion.

But before we enter upon the problems of education and politics, something more needs to be said about tradition and traditionalism.

Tradition, political tradition, poses as we just said very serious problems for effective political change. It has often been remarked that even the most potent revolutionary thrust fails to politically alter highly relevant folkways. These persistent culture traits in the sphere of politics resemble the contour of the land which reemerges largely unchanged after the waters of a great inundation have passed. Even if they become invisible during the revolutionary upheaval, they reappear in the sequel. Striking illustrations are provided by the English and French revolutions, and more recently by the transformations of German political life (Chapter 34). Generally speaking, it can be said on the basis of a great deal of empirical evidence that those political behavior patterns which are closely allied to more intimate forms of conduct are likely to persist. The function of the German representative assemblies has greatly changed as

[5] It is not possible, as Radin would have us do, to exclude all customs from tradition (see above, fn. 1), though it is quite true that not all customs are part of tradition, except in a very general sense. A value or belief must be attached to them. If the particular custom or belief is maintained and based on no other value judgment than that it is a tradition, it becomes traditionalist. Hannah Arendt, 1957, pp. 9ff., in arguing that a particular tradition of political thought began with Plato and ended with Marx, is apt to generate a traditionalist reaction in those who like herself wish to recapture this particular tradition.

the country passed from local monarchies, through empire, Weimar democracy and Hitler regime to the present order; but German deputies have throughout spoken in a distinctive, somewhat academic and rather serious and pompous vein, very different from British, French or Italian colleagues. France has passed through many different forms of government since the great revolution, but local government was conducted in much the same way throughout the period. And not only the over-all traditions, but also the local variations of such subcultures as those of Bavaria and the Rhineland, or Brittany and Gascony, have persisted throughout. The innovator, reformer and even revolutionary has to bear this inertia of political man in mind; political theorists from Aristotle and Machiavelli to the present have commented upon the dangers involved in interfering with deep-rooted values and beliefs.

Reflections upon this persistence of tradition serve to explain, at least in part, why traditionalism appears in politics in certain constellations, more especially in times following upon a revolution or during a period of crisis.[6] Since both crisis and revolution constitute a challenge to established values and beliefs, it is only natural that a conscious reaffirmation should be the response of all those who believe in the existing political order. The most celebrated instance is, of course, the traditionalism which arose in response to the French Revolution. More especially, Edmund Burke sounded the call in his *Reflections on the Revolution in France*. To be sure, it was the term "prescription" rather than "tradition" which he used to argue the case on behalf of the established order of things. All politically organized communities were to him organic wholes, slowly evolving over time and having, if viable and strong, a constitution. This constitution Burke saw as "an elaborate fabric fitted to unite private and public liberty with public force, with order, with peace, with justice, and above all, with the institutions formed for bestowing permanence and stability, through ages, upon this invaluable whole." "It is the result of the thought of many minds, in many ages. It is no simple, no superficial thing. . . ."[7] His many passages in which he celebrated the British constitution as virtually a divine creation, far beyond the comprehension of the rationalizing reformers, all vibrate with the sense of reverence for the past. Society, he insisted, was "a partnership in all science, a partnership in all art, a partnership in every virtue, and in all perfection." Furthermore, this partnership exists "not only for those who are living," but "between those who are living, those who are dead, and those who are yet to be born."[8] Linked with custom and convention on the one hand,

[6] The latter is noted by Hoselitz, 1961, pp. 100ff.

[7] Burke, 1839, vol. III, p. 452. *Ibid.*, p. 179, he says: "If prescription be once shaken, no species of property is secure. . . ." Here and in other passages the link of stability of the political order and security of property is quite plain.

[8] *Ibid.*, p. 120.

with heritage and the like on the other, traditionalism has been a mainstay of conservative thought in Europe ever since the days of Burke. Yet it is a curious, but undeniable, fact that tradition has not been analyzed by those who are most fond of falling back upon it. Men like Moser and Gentz in Germany, De Maistre and Bonald in France, though evidently arguing in terms of tradition, did not try to determine what constitutes the peculiar significance of this concept. Again in our time, conservatives have marshaled tradition against the totalitarians in the face of the fascist glorification of it, while American and European liberals (nowadays a special variety of conservatives) have likewise been inclined to recite the tradition of liberalism against the nationalist traditionalism of the "right."

The term "tradition" has its ecclesiastical roots, as does so much of our political vocabulary. Tradition, in this religious sense, is "the delivering of a precious deposit, whose source is held to be divine, to a specially selected person." [9] But this is only one side of the picture. The other is the pliability of tradition. "In face of traditions become obsolete an appeal was made to other traditions, or to the Bible; where written testimony was uncertain or awanting [sic], recourse was had to tradition; that is, that was declared to be tradition which was not to be justified under another title." [10] The similarity here to be observed is to the process of arguing from precedent in the common law [11] and from ideology in totalitarian systems.[12] In all three cases, the politically crucial question is who possesses the authority to say what is true, that is, what is "tradition" or what is "law" or what is "idea." We are here face to face with a key aspect of authority; reasoning from tradition is considered a genuine elaboration by those who believe in the particular item alleged to be part of the tradition. Such tradition may be embodied in sacred texts, such as Magna Charta, the Constitution or the Declaration of Independence; or it may be found in writings and sayings of founders and fathers. Or it may be derived from the story of act and deed. It always involves authoritative interpretation.

Such authoritative interpretation occurs in all kinds of contexts, but its transmission to subsequent generations is more specifically the task of education. It may even be said that in a measure education, *paideia*, developed in response to this task as much as any other. Eventually, human groups typically crystallize their values in terms of an image of what man ought to be like—an idealized projection of all the relevant aspirations. The Greek *Kalos k'agathos* and the English gentleman embody such aspirational images. All education has, therefore, an eminently political

[9] Radin, in *ESS*, p. 63. His discussion is based upon Harnack, 1885 (English transl. Dover, 1961), vol. III, pp. 207ff., and *passim*.

[10] Harnack, 1961, pp. 207–208.

[11] K. N. Llewellyn, 1960; cf. above, Chap. 15.

[12] Friedrich and Brzezinski, 1956, chaps. 2–4; cf. above, Chap. 4.

function without which it becomes either purely technical or idle play. Education for education's sake is, like art for art's sake, the escapist slogan of a leisure class which has lost a sense of its dependence upon the political order for its survival.[13] Technical utility, as expounded by others, leaves the community without a sense of direction. In the political perspective, then, all education has the function of providing value perspectives through either the transmission of a tradition or the inculcation of an ideological position, or a combination of both. To put it thus is to see it politically as vitally related to cohesion and consensus in a political community. The transmission of a tradition may take place in the family and its intimate associations, as it has for most of mankind until now, or it may become more formally organized in school, church and university. The inculcation of an ideology, seen by traditionalists as the perversion of education into propaganda, typically calls for these more formally organized methods. But whether formal or informal, education is evidently of the highest importance for the maintenance of a community. By supporting the values and beliefs prevalent in a community, education provides the underpinning for an authority and legitimacy which as we have seen depend upon these values and beliefs. For it is in their terms that the reasoned elaboration of authoritative communications has to be cast, and the title to rule has to be argued. It is therefore no wonder that political philosophers and theorists have been interested in education since the days of Plato and Aristotle. Indeed, these thinkers only made explicit what had already become the settled conviction of most Greeks, partly as a result of Sophist teachings. A leading historian of ideas has shown the central position which the notion of *paideia* occupied in all Greek thought and culture,[14] and has traced the interrelationship with politics throughout. But as in so many matters, so in this recognition of the importance of education for politics, the Greeks brought into the full light of consciousness what was practiced and to some extent preached elsewhere. Confucius, for one, certainly had a vivid sense of the importance of education for politics, and his teachings were the cement which held the mighty Chinese community together for thousands of years.[15] Indeed, Chinese Confucianism contains perhaps the most imposing theory and

[13] Cremin, 1960, and below.

[14] Jaeger, 1939–1944, *passim*. The title preserves the Greek term because "education" does not render it accurately. In the German original the title speaks of *Bildung*, which helps because the German *Bildung* more nearly corresponds to the Greek word which lies somewhere between education and culture, in the personal sense. Jaeger himself put it this way: "The ancients were persuaded that education and culture are not a formal art or an abstract theory, distinct from the objective historical structure of a nation's spiritual life. They held them to be embodied in literature. . . ." Vol. II, p. vi. Aristotle discusses this problem when stressing the importance of education for transmitting the ethos of a particular constitution.

[15] Fairbank, 1951, esp. part I.

practice of a political tradition transmitted by education of a fairly formalized sort.[16] It all revolved around the nearly untranslatable concept of *li*, which is *nomos*, mores, custom and manners all rolled into one, yet all focused upon the political order.

The only comparable political achievement is that of Judaism. The Jews succeeded in maintaining a community intact by a similar stress upon education as the mode of transmitting a tradition embodying communal values and beliefs for two millennia. The leader of the community, or rabbi, while also priest and judge, was and is centrally a teacher who by education and example upholds a tradition of faith and law.[17] In keeping with this tradition, Jesus also conceived his function as that of a teacher, and the conception of education thus became doubly rooted in the mind of Western man.

A broad conception of education is also suggested by the study of political order among "primitive," highly traditional societies. Largely informal, education as the process of transmitting a tradition occupies nonetheless a central place in the life of each man and woman. Its importance for the political order is very generally recognized, and anthropological writings are full of illustrations. Education for citizenship may be either formal or informal. Informal education is generally provided by the members of the extended family—parents, grandparents and elder siblings—or by the members of peer groups. Formal education occurs in particular contexts such as initiation ceremonies at puberty, schools, age-grade systems and evening story-telling sessions. Whether formal or informal, education in primitive societies is also intended to ensure the continued existence of the political order by inculcating its norms and values in its future members.[18] The use of these several methods is widely diversified, and by no means all these societies employ formal methods; such methods do, however, occur with sufficient frequency to permit us to consider them perfectly normal.[19] For these processes, the term "socialization" has in recent years been put forward with the intent of avoiding exclusive preoccupation with the formal and rational aspects of education.

[16] Max Weber, 1922–1923, vol. I, pp. 395ff.

[17] *Ibid.*, vol. III. Orlinsky, 1954, chap. 7.

[18] The tribes for which these statements have been checked are: Yahgan, Hausa, Rif, Amhara, Ifaluk, Fanti, Nupe, Tiv, Bemba, Mende, Ganda, Kikuyu, Nuer, Tikopia, Samoa, Alor, Ojibwa, Iroquois. Cf. specifically, Christensen, 1954, pp. 49, 97f.; Evans-Pritchard, 1951, p. 137; Firth, 1936, p. 148; Dubois, 1944, p. 62; Noon, 1949, p. 33; Spiro, 1959, pp. 99, 111; M. Mead, 1928; Messing, 1957, p. 438; Gusinde, 1937, p. 864; Richards, 1956, p. 128; Little, 1951, p. 121; Kenyatta, 1938, pp. 109–110; W. G. Smith, 1955, pp. 99–100; Coon, 1931, pp. 316–317; Nadel, 1942, p. 401; Mair, 1934, p. 66; Hilger, 1939, p. 100.

[19] See E. A. Weber, 1929, for an extended treatment of the practices in connection with initiation of the tribes covered, embedded in a rich comparative treatment.

Thus we read in a recent study that what is meant by socialization is "that all political systems tend to perpetuate their cultures and structures through time, and that they do this mainly by means of the socializing influences of the primary and secondary structures through which the young of the society pass in the process of maturation." "Political socialization is the process of induction into the political culture." [20] What is involved here is a learning process in the course of which the young *discover* what it takes to become a political person in the particular cultural setting which the order structures. Once the process is seen in this perspective, it becomes apparent that the transmission of a culture's values, beliefs and patterns of behavior is a "personalizing" as much as a "socializing" process. More broadly put, it is a "humanizing" process in the course of which the unformed infant becomes a human being. Hence the term "socialization" does not seem desirable, for several reasons related to the foregoing remarks. In the first place, it assumes that there exists a person apart from society who is then "socialized," that is, fitted into society, whereas actually the infant is at the outset begot by the society and in the process of becoming aware of the tradition (and/or ideology) of the society is "personalized," that is to say, put into a position to take his personal, individual place in the political (and social) order. Second, the term has a very different and highly emotive meaning in the political arena, and the inconvenience of one word referring to quite disparate referents should, when possible, be avoided. *Paideia*, in the Greek meaning, would actually be a very good term if it could be effectively popularized, but since this is unlikely, the French-derived term "formation" would seem suitable. Formation suggests that the infant is being formed or shaped by all the different activities and situations which are involved in growing up and that he becomes an effective member of the political (and social) order. Values and beliefs are acquired, but since these are not a rigidly defined constellation of indisputable meaning, but subject to subtle differentiation and variation, the person in growing up chooses within reasonably defined and varying limits his own way of participation. The novel way is not excluded. Innovation, while frowned upon and made difficult by the inertia of tradition referred to above, is possible and keeps occurring as new and unexpected situations are encountered.[21]

Formation of the political person may, as we said, be achieved by having him learn what is needed for effective participation (including

[20] Almond, in Almond and Coleman, 1960, p. 27.

[21] On socialization, cf. Hyman, 1959. Almond and Coleman, 1960, pp. 26ff., adopt and apply the notion to the political. They seek to "combine" the intellectual tendencies, namely, the "rational, voluntarist theory of Enlightenment and liberalism" and the one "stemming from psychoanalytic theory" stressing "the unconscious and latent attitudes." This intent is laudable, but "socialization" is not a good term for fostering the "combination."

conformity to authoritative reasoning and decision). Such learning may be traditional or ideological we said; a modern form is to learn to "think for yourself," to "seek new ways" and to "question authority." These formative processes were the subject of a classic inquiry published under the heading of "making citizens." The editor's own introductory volume in which he undertook to generalize the findings of specific studies on Great Britain, France, Italy, Germany, the Soviet Union and Switzerland, as well as the Duk-Duks, is cast essentially in terms of "civic training," offers an analysis of comparative techniques of civic education, and notes the trend to ever greater formal organization.[22] He would differentiate between learning to value political order as such, cherishing a particular community, such as the United States, and accepting a specific political order.[23] It may be doubted, however, whether these learning processes are ever clearly separated from each other. A young American in the process of growing up learns all three in conjunction and in their interdependence. Actually, Merriam's inclination to view these processes in terms of "civic training" or "the making of citizens" suffers from some of the same shortcomings that attach to the view which sees them as "socialization," namely overemphasis on the collective. To clarify the problem, it is necessary to consider the "future citizen" as a "political person in the making." But whatever may be the particular embodiment of the human values, whether they be rational principles, rituals, felt preferences, or customs and folkways, genuine education–formation–will be concerned with them.[24]

The transmission of tradition is by no means only a matter of values. A great deal of tradition in the broad sense consists of knowledge. The proverbial three R's are tradition, but so is the vast storehouse of science and technology, of learning and the arts. If tradition is, however, restricted along the lines suggested earlier in this chapter, then education–formation–has to be understood as concerned not only with the transmission of tradition and/or ideology, but also with these ranges of knowledge and information. However, in the selection of what to transmit the traditional or ideological values intrude themselves and become the basis for selecting "the more important." That is why in transitional periods controversies inevitably arise as to what should be taught. We hear again and again that the newly emerging nations prize education above all else. Thus we read in a recent comprehensive survey of Africa: "Nobody can travel in tropical Africa without soon being made aware of the importance attached by the African to learning. Ask a hundred literate men what they consider to be the greatest need of their people, and ninety will unhesi-

[22] Merriam, 1931, esp. chaps. iv, v.
[23] Merriam, 1931, pp. 5–7.
[24] Cf. Friedrich, 1942, chap. 9, for a general elaboration.

tatingly reply 'education.' "[25] But what they mean by their reply is an acquisition of certain bodies of information, certain craft skills and technological know-how, rather than formation in deeper value terms. "If education be defined as the whole process by which one generation transmits its culture to the next, then there has been no lack of education in Africa," states the same writer.[26] In the political sphere, such skill and know-how is what is meant by "democracy," although the actual need may be much more for "bureaucracy"—the techniques of modern administration in the West. It is too often forgotten that both administrative and political techniques and behaviors are rooted in the traditional values of the West, and may not be transferable without them.

The same problem arises within a culture when radical transformations in its values and beliefs occur. Modern science rests upon certain values and beliefs without which it makes no coherent sense; scientists are "involved" in these values and beliefs and are personally committed to them.[27] If these values and beliefs are rejected, science is likely to wither on the vine. Though still remote, this possibility cannot be ruled out. The more strictly organizational and political beliefs and practices are even more obviously linked to specific convictions regarding values. If therefore these convictions decline or vanish, the organizational practices become feeble and corrupt (Chapter 33). Hence the inclination of rulers to stem the proclivity to such perversion by educational effort. It may happen, however, that the educational system itself produces the forces which corrode the values upon which the social order rests. A movement for educational "reform" may be profoundly justified by changes in the value pattern of one life sphere, yet may carry lethal implications for another and related one. This difficulty is well illustrated by the movement which became known as "progressive education" in the first half of this century.[28] If we ask, What is the meaning of this "progressivism"? we find it to have been a "many-sided effort to use the schools to improve the lives of individuals." But what did "improvement" here stand for? There was at the start, and there remained, widespread confusion on this vital point. Too often it meant little more than a rejection of prevailing values and beliefs, including more particularly the rejection of such notions as duty, discipline and loyalty. Since each of these notions implied some restriction upon the individual's freedom to "wear his hat as he pleased, inside and out," to use Walt Whitman's vivid phrase, it seemed progressive to be rid of it or at least

[25] Kimble, 1960, chap. 16, p. 93. The author fully realizes that that "is not to say that all Africa is hungering for the white man's learning." *Ibid.*, p. 94.

[26] Kimble, 1960, p. 94.

[27] Polanyi, 1958, esp. pp. 299–324. Cf. above, Introd.

[28] Besides my book of 1942 referred to above, cf. now Cremin, 1961, for an interesting retrospective appraisal.

to reduce its purview.[29] But was such archindividualism really in keeping with the transformations of American society? Or was it rather the piercing shriek of the death agony of American individualism, rugged or other? Did progressive education bear any definite relationship to the dominant trends of American (or indeed Western) society? Or was it rather the expression of an outlook born of leisure-class wants in a monopolistic economy? From the vantage point of the second half of the twentieth century, it would appear that this educational movement was a countertrend, opposed to the rising trend toward large-scale organization in all spheres of activity: government, politics, business and the various professions. The large size of organizations entailed more bureaucracy, stricter hierarchy (Chapter 18), which meant for each person a more rigid system of subordination. Willingness and the ability to take orders and to carry them out faithfully, even when one disagrees, is an outstanding trait of the "well-adjusted" man.[30] Most men have become soldiers in a huge army of workers, though a few manage a measure of "independence" of thought and taste, if not of action. This vast army is nothing new, however. Its conformism is no greater than that found in any reasonably stable political order, including most primitive tribes. There was a curious paradox involved in people who considered themselves progressive organizing a kind of school calculated to hinder rather than help the development of the young to fit into this increasingly conformist society, with consequent nervous disorders and psychic breakdowns.

But the record was by no means all negative, as these criticisms suggest. There was another side to this movement. In so far as it stressed willingness to cooperate and in so far as it organized the practice of "getting along with others," in so far as it was inspired by a realistic insistence upon making the student aware of his social environment, it enhanced the prospects of maturation in terms of a "democratic," that is, a cooperative, order. Here the task of democratic education, of formation of the communal man (not to be mistaken for mass-man—see Chapter 1) was squarely faced, and has left a lasting impression. Autocratic methods in school and home cannot but impede the moulding of a "future citizen." Progressive education was truly progressive here, and helped in the transformation of man to fit into an emergent society.

Another striking instance of the paradoxes in which educational efforts can become involved when related to political thrusts, is provided by

[29] Cremin, 1961, pp. viii–ix, gives what he believes to have been the meaning of this general outlook among progressives, a sort of educational version of the general outlook of progressivism. See pp. 85ff. and 179ff.

[30] Note Peter Viereck's bitter protest in 1956: he proclaimed the unadjusted man the new American hero—as if he had not always been. The instant recognition of the "organization man" and the figure of the "lonely crowd" are other signs; cf. Riesman, 1950, and Whyte, 1956, *passim*.

the occupation experience of America after the Second World War. Policy in both Germany and Japan was inspired by the notion that a democratization of these nations presupposed a "reeducation" which would uproot the ideas which the enemy regimes had implanted. Such reeducation was therefore clearly ideological in orientation. Much effort was spent in urging American devices upon the Germans. In 1948, a subcommittee of a congressional committee reported hereon. "The subcommittee was particularly impressed with the lack of wisdom of an initiative taken in January, 1947, by which German educational authorities were peremptorily requested (a) to expand compulsory schooling to the eighteenth year, (b) to generalize high school education, thereby making it less useful as a preparation for professional study, especially in the universities, (c) to abolish all tuition for high school, . . . (d) to expand social studies. . . ."[31] As the committee observed, these and related proposals were "ill-considered," and the committee therefore said that it "should like to urge greater attention to those reforms which German democratic elements should like to institute" and that American policy should be "inspired by the idea of aiding the Germans to develop their own programs, rather than fashioning and superimposing programs of our own making." In short, the subcommittee felt "that educational policy in Germany had been preoccupied with trying to force upon the Germans the introduction of certain purely organizational features of American education. . . ." It noted that a few of these features were controversial among Americans. Actually, the view of the American Military Governor was rather similar. He wrote soon afterwards: "School reform is still a major objective . . . but such reform obtained by order of the occupation authorities is not likely to be lasting and our hope is that it can be brought about by the German people."[32] Such educational reform was bound to have a different connotation for many Germans who wanted to return to a sounder *tradition* after the bankruptcy of the totalitarian ideology of the defeated regime, as contrasted with the ideological counter-objective of the occupying powers. Such a judgment as that "the intellectual and social limitations of the German idea of 'Bildung' persist,"[33] while quite correct at the time (1947), missed the crucial issue of educational reconstruction much in the same way in which many an ardent advocate of Westernizing education in the new nations fails to appreciate the importance of tradition and its effective transmission for the political order in being. A leading American philosopher put these

[31] U.S. Congress, Final Report on Foreign Aid of the House Select Committee on Foreign Aid, May 1, 1948, p. 136.

[32] Clay, 1950, pp. 298–302, the quote at p. 302. Cf. also the critical estimate by Zink, 1947, chap. 12, and W. Friedmann, 1947, chap. 11.

[33] W. Friedmann, 1947, p. 185.

experiences to account by exploring "what we can learn from teaching Germany."[34] What Americans did learn, here and elsewhere, is that you cannot "force men to be free"; all you can do is to remove those obstacles, including oppressive classes and traditions, which prevent men from becoming free of their own accord (Chapter 20).

These experiences in "democratization" paralleled what happened in various colonial territories. Here the cultural gap often was very much greater, and the reformist tendency was often as much religiously as politically motivated. Mission schools linked the task of conversion to the transmission of much technical knowledge as well as political ideology, ethical tradition and even aesthetic notions. The anomic confusions created by much of this effort are bearing rather macabre fruit in the violent struggles rending many of these lands. In recent studies of these countries, the treatment of education begins with the recurrent statement: "Until the advent of Western influence, education in the Middle East was almost entirely local tradition." Whether it be the Islamic tradition with its emphasis on classical and religious learning or the Buddhist doctrine with its other-worldly stress, or some more primitive cult, the problem remains.[35] These traditional ways were disrupted by the intrusion of Western ways without much thought being given to the ensuing value conflicts. The *anomie* which has since developed in many cases presents a very considerable obstacle to the establishing of a political order; a propensity toward dictatorship and other types of autocracy has been the result. However, not only Western values but also tribal conflicts contribute to these disturbances. Since these are territorially centered, it may prove possible to handle them by some sort of federalism (Chapter 32).

A very interesting instance of the resolution of this problem is provided by Puerto Rico. The difficulties are not as great as elsewhere, because the population is predominantly of Spanish descent and almost entirely Catholic. The issue is therefore one *within* Western culture. There are nonetheless pronounced differences between North American and Latin values, and hence the educational system which the United States developed after Puerto Rico became part of the United States failed to satisfy the Puerto Ricans. This conflict is highlighted by the issue of

[34] Hocking, 1954, *passim.* He comments, p. 18, that "it was also essential to give full credit to the thinking-through and overcoming which the German people themselves were doing; for, after all, this had to be their act and not ours." Cf. also Montgomery, 1957, and Gimbel, 1961.

[35] Cf. the interesting series of studies published by the Human Relations Area Files, notably Harris, 1958; Lipsky, 1959; Lebar and Suddard, 1960; Steinberg, 1959. Each of these books contains a chapter on formal education, as well as material on the transmission of culture. They may be compared with Kimble, 1960.

linguistic training, but has many ramifications related to the values cherished by Puerto Ricans.[36] It is important to realize that the University of Puerto Rico has provided a focal point for self-realization and for the achievement of a goal which might be formulated thus: "Culturally and socially, Puerto Rico would in the course of these years continue to integrate and develop its distinctively Spanish tradition, with the Spanish language continuing as the dominant idiom, but more generally supplemented by English . . . this goal of full and effective bilingualism is in a sense merely the outward sign of an inner achievement, that of effectively blending two cultural ingredients, not in a static, but in a dynamic and growing way, and a highly dynamic task it is. For neither North American nor Latin American culture is going to stand still." [37]

All these situations of cultural conflict and the political compromises which they call for if they are to be superseded by novel and yet viable value systems show the traditional and the ideological component of education in varied combinations. Typically, as in Puerto Rico, two traditions are being transcended and in a measure superseded by a common ideological component: "progressive democracy." In many other lands today, a confused set of ideas associated with industrialization, democratization and rationalization is spoken of as "nationalism." Such nationalism, for example, in Latin America, is politically motivated ideology to the extent to which it seeks to build a nation where there was none before, often out of very disparate elements. It is therefore very different from classical European nationalism, where the nation existed before the nationalist sentiment developed.[38] Such ideological nationalism is stimulated by the movement toward democracy, which presupposes a measure of popular homogeneity, but which has often been misinterpreted as an "agreement on fundamentals." It often overshoots the mark in seeking too much unity. One of the advantages of a democratic political order is that it can manage great divergencies, since democratic ways stimulate a pluralistic social order. Communist totalitarianism, while destructive of much political pluralism, has been tolerant of cultural diversity, at least in the Soviet Union. Its ruling cadres have always taken pride in the relative freedom and diversity of its many nationalities, therein sharply contrasting with fascist totalitarianism. This tolerance is the consequence of the devaluation of cultural values, as contrasted with economic

[36] Cf. the valuable report *The Educational System of Puerto Rico*, 1959, rendered by three European experts, C. Caselman, L. Borghi and M. Bredsdorff. Cf. also Friedrich, 1959, and Padilla, 1958. In addition, compare the very detailed evaluation of educational developments in Puerto Rico in Tumin and Feldman, 1961, chaps. 2–7, but esp. chap. 5, which relates education to political power.

[37] Friedrich, 1959, pp. 62–63.

[38] On the subject of ideology in relation to nationalism see Bowie et al., 1959, esp. chap. 1, and my comments above, Chap. 4.

and political ones. It is the overarching materialist ideology which accounts for the relative indifference about cultural traditions.

Stress on the ideological component of education reaches its pinnacle in totalitarian regimes. Indeed, in certain respects, education becomes indistinguishable from propaganda as it concerns itself with shaping the "new man" whom the revolutionary and postrevolutionary ideology calls for. It becomes "formation" in the most radical sense. Teachers are recruited into the Communist Party, and are primarily concerned with "making Soviet citizens." It might here be argued, and often has been, that the same is true of, for example, American teachers, and that indoctrination in the ways of American democracy is the most vital part of their task. But there appears not only a difference in degree but in kind, as far as the content of the educational message is concerned. Leaving aside for the moment the important distinction between the transmission of tradition and ideology, democratic emphasis upon the need for dissent, upon "thinking for yourself," in short, upon the self and its development, sets the pupil off from the teacher and limits the latter's authority to the range of his transmissible knowledge. In a totalitarian system, on the other hand, the stress is on subordination and the surrender of the self to the collective. The fact that such surrender is also the central objective of many other nondemocratic educational programs, especially in the so-called primitive societies, constitutes one of the main advantages of totalitarian approaches.[39] It is not feasible to counteract this shortcoming by developing a "burning faith" in democracy, as is sometimes advocated; for all such proposals are apt to surrender the quintessence of democratic education.

The nontraditional, metarational premises of a total ideology make it necessary to organize education in strict subordination to the official hierarchy.[40] Not only does it become necessary to force all teachers into the party and its affiliated organizations, but such efforts in the context of formal education will be reinforced by a welter of youth organizations such as Komsomol, Hitler Youth, and Balilla. To quote Stalin: "The Youth is our future, our hope, comrades. The Youth must take our place, the place of the old people. It must carry our banner to final victory. Among the peasants there are not a few old people. . . . Naturally, they are not always able to keep pace with the party, to keep pace with the Soviet government. But that cannot be said of our youth. They are free from the burden of the past, and it is easiest for them to assimilate Lenin's behests." [41] It is these last words which are decisive in what is otherwise

[39] All the works noted in fn. 18 and many others contain some material on this issue.

[40] Friedrich and Brzezinski, 1956, chap. 12, for further detail and references.

[41] Stalin, 1940, p. 451; cf. also chap. 4 of Friedrich and Brzezinski, 1956, for further comparative detail and some statistics.

a rather conventional piece of oratory that could be uttered by any politician in any land. For although Stalin talks of "keeping peace," he actually means the indoctrination with a definite ideology, Leninism, which only the hierarchy and more particularly its chief priest may authoritatively interpret. The imaginations and the energy of youth will by such indoctrination be harnessed to carry on the total reconstruction of society which the ideology calls for. The efforts of all the totalitarians in this field have been very extensive. Over 6 million in Italy, nearly 8 million in Germany and nearly 20 million in the Soviet Union (by the mid-fifties) make it seem credible when the World Federation of Democratic Youth claims 83 million members. In all the affiliated totalitarian regimes the party has assumed responsibility for these organizations and the ideological indoctrination which they provide. Since these organizations also provide the reservoir for the selection of party members, they "form" the youth of such totalitarian systems to an even greater extent than does formal education. Khrushchev is fully alert to the importance of this forming process and has shown considerable skill in balancing the older by the younger generation. The new Party rules explicitly recognize the principle of "rotation in office." Khrushchev spoke at the Twenty-second Party Congress of the importance of opening the way to the promotion of talented young people, as well as generally about the importance of youth.[42]

Education is, however, by no means limited to these doctrinal aspects, and serious errors of judgment have in the past been the result of such overemphasis. The educational transformation outside the valuational sphere which in the older totalitarian societies is beginning to show traces of the mode of transmission of a tradition rather than an ideology, anyhow, is from humanist to realist and indeed to technological concerns. The early ideologues of, for example, the Soviet Union were inclined toward relaxing discipline and stressing humanist values of personal development; they wanted to free the child of all restraints by providing complete freedom in the schools.[43] The same cannot be said of the Fascist and National Socialist regimes, where discipline was stressed from the outset. After a period of experimentation, the Soviet Union also adopted a strongly disciplinary policy. This altered outlook was developed in response to the requirements of industrial civilization as much as to ideological considerations.[44] "In the midst of the First Five Year Plan the leaders of the Soviet Union became acutely aware that the products of their

[42] Fainsod, a, 1961, p. x.

[43] Sidney and Beatrice Webb, themselves partisans of this educational philosophy, have written movingly of these early efforts, 1935, chap. 10 (1), pp. 887ff.

[44] De Witt, 1955; cf. also for the quote, Bauer and Inkeles, 1959, chap. 6, p. 129. For the disciplinary aspect see the instructions quoted in Friedrich and Brzezinski, 1956, pp. 122–123.

lower and middle schools were adequately prepared neither for study in institutions of advanced learning, nor for work in the industrial system that was being rapidly developed." As a consequence, the educational system was after 1931 completely revamped along traditional lines. The results have been remarkable, both in terms of the spread of education and technical and scientific achievements, and of developing loyal, reliable citizens. If a postwar textbook describes Communist education as "the preparation of the younger generation for active participation in the building of communist society, and for the defense of the Soviet government which is building that society,"[45] substantial success in achieving this goal cannot be denied. And since a Soviet citizen can hope to achieve success in life only through such effective participation, the pressure to secure the requisite education is very great. By no means all persons can get the education they desire, and pronounced class differentiation continues to mark the chances of doing so.[46] Many object to the ideological indoctrination, though they most highly approve of the widening opportunities of free education. "The main basis for complaint was the saturation of education with politics" among a group of respondents, while only 10 per cent complained about totalitarian control or the harsh discipline in school.

The major difficulty which has developed in the Soviet Union corresponds to a universal problem: too many of those with primary and secondary education wish to go on to higher education. Khrushchev's proposals for stopping or at least slowing down this pressure by sending every graduate of a high school into factory or farm for several years' manual work have encountered fierce opposition; how rigidly the Soviet Union holds back a large percentage of potential participants is shown by the fact that only 40 out of 1,000 school pupils finish college,[47] a large percentage of them children of the Soviet "upper" and "middle" class.

Higher education and more especially the universities present a special set of problems; for in the university the indoctrination and training aspects of education are linked with the pursuit of learning and the search for truth. Whether one wishes to recognize the founding of the Academy by Plato as the starting point of the university as an institution, or would rather restrict it to the medieval foundations, it is in either case clear that the university is intimately linked to the political order. It is intended to form the men and women who are to participate in the rule over such an order. Plato's and Aristotle's was a distinctively political objective: to achieve the re-form and the re-founding of the ancient order of the

[45] *Pedagogika*, 1948, p. 15, cited after Inkeles and Bauer, 1959, p. 131.

[46] Cf. the interesting supporting data in Inkeles and Bauer, 1959, pp. 135–145. There also support for the next statement.

[47] *Ibid.*, p. 157.

polis;[48] the medieval church's was a similarly distinctive political goal: to reinforce the Christian basis of the medieval order.[49] Nothing shows this more dramatically than Frederick II's challenge to the medieval way: founding the University of Naples without papal sanction "to form intelligent and clever men for the service of the emperor"[50] and acquiring the title of "antichrist" in the bargain. Wittenberg, the university of Luther and the Reformation, was founded also without papal sanction, but this defect was later made up.[51] Thus, the medieval university rested on faith, a faith which was believed to be fixed and in the church's keeping. Humanism, the Renaissance and eventually the Enlightenment "secularized" this university establishment in the name of the "free mind"; philosophy and science became the watchwords epitomized in a new and "open" conception of truth.

For it is truth toward which the university is oriented. It is the one value which even the most fanatic exponents of a value-free science have not been able to eliminate from their thought. Everyone connected with a university is "involved" in truth-seeking. But since the question of Pilate, What is truth? can be answered in a variety of ways, the search for truth may be institutionalized in related forms. We saw earlier (Chapters 14 and 20) that neither justice nor freedom is conceivable except in terms of truth, be it ever so tentative and provisional. Power is likewise dependent upon truth, true knowledge of what it takes to prevail, to rule, whether by persuasion or by coercion. The concern of the rulers with the training of their servants is in frank recognition of the dependence of power upon true knowledge. Modern state and modern university develop together. Hence the clash between "East and West" is dramatically epitomized and only rarely transcended in the rivalry of the universities and academies.[52] But the question arises as to whether the universities in totalitarian regimes have not basically changed their nature.

It is not possible to deny that totalitarian systems also are intensely interested in the search for truth. Not only in the natural sciences but even in the field of the social sciences that search is carried on. What has happened in these systems is that such search for truth is enclosed within

[48] Jaeger, 1933 (English), vol. II, 1943, esp. p. 83, linking the Academy to Plato's passion for politics: "That means that he did not think of politics as the occupation of a few periods in his career; . . . he thought of it as the framework of this entire spiritual life, the principal and comprehensive object of his whole thought." The opposite view is argued by Arendt, a, 1958.

[49] Denifle, 1885, 1956, vol. I.

[50] Kantorowicz, 1927, pp. 124ff. Cf. also Dempf, 1929, pp. 319f., and Hampe, a, 1923.

[51] Friedensburg, 1917; Schöffler, 1936.

[52] Jaspers, 1960, pp. 33–35, maintains that a "university" is not possible in a totalitarian dictatorship, because "nur ein Staat, der selber Freiheit und daher Wahrheit will und auf sie sich gründet, [kann] auch die Universität wollen."

the framework of the truth of the official ideology. That truth cannot be questioned, even though many questions may be put forward as to the precise meaning of the ideology. The same holds true for any theology; it too provides for considerable latitude for arguments about its tenets in terms of "truth." The rather striking similarities have given rise to interpretations of totalitarian ideology in terms of theology.[53]

The basis of such restricted search for truth suggests that the new university rests upon yet another foundation than the revelation and faith of the Middle Ages and the philosophical doubt and scientific inquiry of Enlightenment and liberalism. This new foundation is political conviction. It is most apparent in the universities of totalitarian systems, but it manifests itself strikingly in the many universities springing up in newly established nations. It is also beginning to react upon the life of universities in the older nations of the free world. Perhaps the most telling illustration is the founding of the Free University of Berlin, which occurred in the very midst of the struggle over the blockade of the city. Precipitated by a group of students expelled from the old university in the Soviet sector of the city, the founding was carried through by a joint endeavor of students, faculty and the governmental authorities. Here the older notions of philosophical doubt had yielded place to a political conviction about freedom, which, while akin to the older liberal notions of W. von Humboldt, was yet new in its clearly convictional base.[54] Much of the vigorous discussion about university reform in Germany and elsewhere would gain profile and a sense of direction if this basic shift in the framework of truth-seeking were clearly recognized.[55]

The political function of the university in providing important grounds for a reasoned support of the regime, and hence an underpinning for both authority and legitimacy, must not be allowed to obscure the fact that such truth-seeking raises questions and hence conjures up the specter and ultimate rejection of a political order. Whether it be tradition or ideology that provides the core of education, of the formation of youth, it will be a congeries of propositions about believed-in matters of fact that constitute its content and provide the basis for its meaning. If experience and reflection based upon it raise serious doubts about the tenability of the facts, rival propositions will make their appearance. Universities in totalitarian lands are ineluctably involved in the regime's rule, because the authority of its rulers as well as their legitimacy is tied up with the ideological tenets of the dominant party (Chapters 4, 12, 13). The bitter struggle over such matters as environmentalism in biology and the class basis of language and more recently the "withering away of the

[53] Voegelin, 1938, and many others have expounded such views.
[54] Davison, 1958, pp. 61–62; a fuller treatment is provided in Kotowski, a, 1953.
[55] Friedrich, a, 1962.

state" must perturb the universities and the academies in which the search for truth is carried on. No stress on technology, statistics, and the like will in the long run provide an escape from the fundamental issues.

It is for this reason that universities become one of the important "islands of separateness" in the totalitarian order.[56] The attitude of the rulers of these regimes toward science and the universities is ambivalent; on the one hand, they need the help of science, while on the other the questioning attitude of science constitutes a challenge to the totalitarian order. As a consequence, the preservation of such an island of separateness can even be justified by totalitarian rulers.[57] In such grudging recognition of the role of the independent scholar the totalitarian ambivalence finds poignant expression. This ambivalence has been ably analyzed [58] in terms of five primary premises of scientific endeavor. These are materialism, antiformalism and antisymbolism, verification through practical results, the partisanship of science, and the need of modifying scientific dogma only by action of the political leadership—that is to say, the ideological priesthood. These premises, when considered in the light of parallel Western trends, suggest that (1) there does not appear to be any significant difference between decisions on science and on politics, whether domestic or foreign, and (2) there does prevail a disposition to assert that science can advance only through open and free discussion. The totalitarians do not, and perhaps cannot, fully realize the nature of scientific truth, since they consider truth as given in the regime's ideology, which they assert to be scientific. "They try to make science the anchor of their belief system." [59] But in spite of it they recognize that "a struggle of opinions, professional controversies, and discussions are more and more becoming the norm in our scientific and scholarly groups and this is undoubtedly to the good." But such approval of controversy is not allowed to touch the essentials of the ideological frame. "Discussion of any scientific problem should be based above all on the Leninist principle of the party nature of science and scholarship, and participants in a discussion must approach the solution of all disputes from a position of Marxist-Leninist methodology, the only scientific basis for cognition of the objective world.

[56] Friedrich and Brzezinski, 1956, chap. 24, for a more detailed analysis of the universities and the sciences under totalitarianism. See also Friedrich (ed.), 1956, chap. 1, j, pp. 98ff.

[57] *Ibid.*, 1954, chap. 5. Moore shares the belief that "the Soviet scientist still retains a substantial degree of autonomy . . ." (p. 129).

[58] B. Moore, Jr., 1954, pp. 99ff. Cf. also M. and E. Müller, 1953, *passim.*

[59] B. Moore, Jr., 1954, p. 112. This, Moore believes, "shows that they do not, and perhaps cannot, fully realize the instrumental nature of scientific knowledge." We should rather be inclined to say that they do not fully realize the open-endedness, the incompleteness of scientific knowledge; for even this "open" feature does not make science purely instrumental. Perhaps they even overestimate its instrumental nature!

Fruitful discussion can be based only on the Marxist outlook."[60] This outlook itself can and often does become the subject of scientific inquiry and discussion, however. It implies a continuous "politicizing" of the work of the universities and academies. This politicization has gone hand in hand with an enormous expansion of the establishment of higher education: 1913, nine universities, 1954, thirty-three; 1913, 125,000 students in higher education, 1954, 1,087,000 (plus 654,000 in extension). Notably, while students increased tenfold, universities increased "only" fourfold, a divergence which is partly due to a shift in emphasis toward technical training, but also to a general overcrowding characteristic of all advanced industrial countries. Such expansion would seem to militate against ideological orthodoxy, and it does; but it also invites the regime to redouble its efforts in the direction of effective indoctrination. If, therefore, institutions of higher learning engaged in the search for truth offer some seclusion from the total penetration of life by a totalitarian regime, they also are obliged to fit in, to allow themselves to be coordinated. Attempts to evade the issue by rendering lip-service to the regime, while quite common, have a deleterious effect upon the truth-seeker, since they are fraudulent and hence a violation of his code of truthfulness. The totalitarian ruler is aware of this "separateness." Stalin as well as Hitler gave vent to his resentment. The former once said: "We are confronted by a fortress. The name of this fortress is science with its innumerable branches. We must conquer this fortress. Youth must take this fortress, if it wishes to build the new life, if it wishes to replace the old guard." Whether likened to a fortress or an island, the university is unassimilable, because of its function, a function of profound significance for the political order: the search for truth. Those who are dedicated to it, and to the extent that they are, will of necessity withdraw from the battle cries of the market place into the quiet of laboratory and library, there to reexamine the assumptions upon which the actions of rulers and their helpers are based.

[60] From the journal *Kommunist*, May, 1955, pp. 117–128. The whole article provides a striking instance of the ambivalence which continues to plague the Soviet regime in its relations with science and the universities.

chapter

34

Resistance and Revolution

Revolution . . . brings on the speaking of a new, unheard-of language, . . . another logic . . . a revaluation of all values. . . .
E. Rosenstock-Huessy

THUS FAR, WE HAVE DEALT with the functioning of the political order, giving occasional hints about its malfunctioning. In several connections, notably when discussing creative freedom and innovation (Chapter 21) and the founding and related processes (Chapter 22), we have had occasion to take up revolution. Before considering the possibilities of a new order, revolution as a recurrent political process deserves integral consideration. It had been hoped to put it within the context of a more general consideration of political pathology.[1] This term, suggesting an organic analogy, systematizes such current terms as the "illness" and the "sickness" of a political order, the "cancer," and other such analogical expressions. With due allowance made for the dubious aspects of such organic analogies, the conceptual framework suggested thereby seems more appropriate than the mechanical models implied in terms like "equilibrium" and "disequilibrium"; for like any organic entity, a political community is an "organized disequilibrium" both in the growing and disintegrating phases of its life cycle (see Introduction).

[1] This task has had to be postponed and will be presented in a separate study on political pathology, dealing particularly with corruption, treason, secrecy and propaganda.

While it is doubtful that political orders can simply be equated with organic life cycles, the disturbances are of a comparable kind: processes rather than structures.

Among disturbances, resistance and revolution occupy a particular place: they are explicitly directed toward changing the political order by coercive means. Resistance and revolution belong together, because all revolution starts with resistance, though much resistance does not lead to revolution. Resistance is the micro-, revolution the macrophenomenon.

Resistance occurs where values, interests and beliefs conflict. Not all such conflicts lead to resistance, but resistance presupposes such conflict. Resistance may be organized or spontaneous, continuous or sporadic. It is evident that continuous and organized resistance constitutes a more serious threat to the political order than does spontaneous or sporadic resistance. As a matter of fact, spontaneous and sporadic resistance is found in all political orders; nullification and crime are its familiar modes. Every time a citizen fails to pay the taxes which he knows he owes the government, every time a citizen manages to elude the military service or other civic obligation, every time the police engaged in law enforcement encounter disobedience—to mention only some of the most familiar instances—resistance to the political order is occurring. We ought to know a great deal more than we do about the frequency and the conditions of such occurrence; this would provide significant indices of political disorder (Chapter 19) comparable to Durkheim's index of suicide.[2] But our discussion will leave these phenomena of sporadic and spontaneous resistance aside and concentrate upon the politically more "visible" organized and continuous resistance.

Such resistance occurs in two primary forms, partial and total resistance. Partial resistance often takes the form of nullifying by particular groups or in special regions; such groups or regions typically constitute compact subdivisions of the political community in which values, interests and/or beliefs are different from those in the community at large. Nullification was a significant factor in the antebellum South of the United States, and received its theoretical formulation from John Calhoun.[3] There is only one way, according to him, in which the "organism" of government can be structured so that the abuse of power can be prevented or checked, "by such an organism as will furnish the ruled with the means of *resisting successfully* this tendency on the part of the rulers to oppression and abuse." To this end, Calhoun thought that what he called the principle of the concurrent majority must be applied. What this means is that any distinct subcommunity differentiated from the rest by a sepa-

[2] Durkheim, 1897, part III, and the valuable discussion in Parsons, 1937, pp. 324–338. Strictly speaking, the point in the text refers only to what Durkheim called "anomic suicide."

[3] Calhoun, 1851, in *Works*, 1853, vol. I, pp. 13ff.

rate interest must concur by a distinct vote upon any decision affecting it. "The government of the concurrent majority . . . excludes the possibility of oppression, by giving to each interest, or portion, or order, . . . the means of protecting itself, by its negative, against all measures calculated to advance the peculiar interests of others at its expense."[4] In other words, each well-defined subcommunity must have a veto power, a power to nullify the acts of government. Though this may seem in effect the organization of anarchy, in the style of Poland's *liberum veto,* Calhoun was fully aware that "anarchy" is "the greatest of all evils," and it is precisely this evil which he hoped to combat by the organizing of "concurrent majorities," which indeed he thought he could detect in American federalism (Chapter 32). Calhoun, harking back in some ways to the resistance notions of the feudal order, put into stipulative, normative terms a series of propositions which could be transformed into working hypotheses concerning resistance.

Resistance, organized and continuous, may occur when and if the values, interests and beliefs of a substantial group or region are jeopardized by the political action of a more inclusive community. It will occur regardless of which function the action is related to. It may be legislative, administrative or judicial, and involve a rule, a measure or the settlement of a dispute. This possibility recent experience in the United States with segregation has shown just as clearly as experience in Algeria or the Congo. Calhoun was therefore at least in part justified in claiming that in order to avoid disorder it is important to secure the assent of potent subgroups by "concurrent majority." He was also right in stressing in this connection compromise as the key to what is called "constitutional" government. It would be most valuable to know more precisely at what point such resistance becomes organized and continuous, to what extent the violation of values, interests and beliefs in combination with other factors (such as cultural and other forms of diversity) precipitates such resistance. These phenomena have been imaginatively portrayed by Charles Merriam in terms of the "poverty of power." Here we have a truly descriptive analysis of the role of resistance in political orders. Merriam recognized that the analysis of such resistance is "very difficult, owing to the wide range of situations under which resistance may be made."[5] "There is organized and unorganized resistance, violent, non-violent, and quasi-violent . . . resistance, to special acts or laws or to entire systems and orders of things—racial, religious, economic, political."

Past thought has not so much been concerned with resistance as with the problem of how to prevent it. But a practical solution presupposes

[4] Cf. for this *ibid.*, p. 38. The other quotation is found on p. 12 (italics added).
[5] Merriam, 1934, chap. VI. The quoted passage is found on p. 159.

a much fuller knowledge of the conditions under which resistance occurs than we now have. To some extent such knowledge ought to permit successful quantification. On the other hand, the variety of values, interests and beliefs which can come into play and the possible variations introduced by such variety make it unlikely that it will be easy to formulate universal propositions that would be much more detailed than what we can state now.

In the past, theorizing about resistance has been largely in terms of the "right" of resistance. A large body of doctrine was accumulated during the Middle Ages and in early modern times in connection with the question.[6] Such doctrine was cast in terms of resisting the abuse of power, of overthrowing tyranny. Hence its main bearing was focused upon an analysis of what constitutes a tyrant and how far various persons might go in resisting him. The basic distinction developed was that between the tyrant as usurper (*ab titulo*), and the tyrant as abuser of his rightful powers (*quoad exercitium*). In other words, it was the distinction between a legitimate ruler who becomes tyrannical and an illegitimate ruler. Theorists inclined to allow a more extensive right of resistance against an illegitimate than against a legitimate ruler. Having worked out this aspect of the normative problem, theorists then proceeded to argue about two other ranges of questions, on the one hand the question of who might resist, and on the other how far they might go in resisting. On the latter score the big issue was whether the killing of a tyrant might be permitted. Often, the killing of an illegitimate ruler was held to be permissible, while that of a legitimate one was not—legitimacy in turn usually being defined rather formally as "legality," rather than political legitimacy (Chapter 13). For political legitimacy is lost by the legal ruler who uses his power in such a way as to destroy the belief of the ruled in the rightness of his rule. Hence the two kinds of tyranny are seen as differences in degree rather than kind. For the Middle Ages, prevailing opinion was expressed by Thomas Aquinas, who was most reluctant to concede any right of killing a ruler unless explicit ecclesiastical action had deprived him of his rulership.[7] The argument turns upon Aquinas' careful elaboration of what constitutes the common good, which leads him to the conclusion that "tyrannical government is unjust government because it is directed not to the common good but to the private good of the ruler. . . . Conse-

[6] For a good survey, see Jaszi and Lewis, 1957, part I. It is made in terms of tyrannicide, rather than resistance. Cf. also the more detailed and pointed analysis of Wolzendorff, 1916, which focuses on the natural law aspect, and Pfister (ed.), 1956, who stresses the limits of governmental power. Borch, 1954, has considered the issue specifically in relation to bureaucracy.

[7] *Summa Theologica,* II.II.q.40.art.2, and II.II.q.42.art.2; here is found the first quotation.

quently the disturbing of such a government is not strictly sedition; except perhaps in the case that it is accompanied by such disorder that the community suffers greater harm from the disturbance than from the tyrannical rule. A tyrant is, himself, more seditious. . . ." The argument rests upon the previously argued position that "as soon as a ruler falls under sentence of excommunication for apostasy from the faith, his subjects are by that very fact freed from the rule, and from the oath of fealty which bound them to him."[8] Whether the faithful need to obey a ruler, pagan or infidel, is for the ecclesiastical authorities to decide. What is clear here is that the question turns upon a conflict in values and beliefs; the doctrine is a clear, if cautious, statement in favor of resistance when the believed-in values are at stake. For this view the biblical injunction that a man ought to serve God rather than men is the basic proposition (norm).

As far as the question of who might resist is concerned, both medieval and later thought inclined toward the view that public authorities, rather than private persons, and more especially any body especially constituted for this purpose, such as estates' assemblies, parliaments, and the like were the appropriate resisters. This was the position of Calvin, following Thomas Aquinas and others.[9] The dominant notion was that such bodies had been constituted for the express purpose of seeing to it that the ruler would attend to the common good and not abuse his power for private advantage—a generally recognized danger. At this point, the argument becomes intertwined with that about war and what constitutes a just war (Chapter 14). It depends on the strength of the view that a tyrant is actually an aggressor engaged in war upon the community. In that case the defense of the community becomes a just war.[10] These arguments, which have been revived in connection with the rise of totalitarian dictatorship and the struggle against colonial imperialism, all are preoccupied with the issue of right as contrasted with that of function. Nonetheless, the arguments refer recurrently to the concrete givens by elaborating upon the degree of abuse of power, the prospects of results, the extent of disturbances caused by resistance, and all the rest. These issues are of primary importance in a descriptive analysis of resistance, of course. Under what conditions does it occur and what are its chances of success?

[8] *Summa Theologica,* II.II.q.12.art.2. Cf. also II.II.q.10.art.10.

[9] Cf. Friedrich, 1957, pp. 61ff., for an outline and bibliography of writings. These ideas were interestingly linked to *ratio status.*

[10] *Summa Theologica,* II.II.q.40.art.1, where Aquinas suggests that a just war is a war decreed by authority of the ruler, fought for a just cause, and for the right intent. As for the third of these criteria, he states that those who fight just wars intend to establish peace. Applied to resistance, this would mean that they intend to reestablish peace and public order. Note that many medieval thinkers, for example John of Salisbury, call the tyrant a devil, in contradistinction to the king, who is "like God."

The record of totalitarian dictatorship in this field is instructive, though by no means conclusive. It has been rightly written

Before the advent of modern tyranny, the idea of tyrannicide not only appeared anachronistic to most people in advanced countries but was generally condemned from the viewpoints both of expediency and morality. . . . This argument would be perfectly sound if the individual faced an orderly society in which the public will could be asserted.

The further argument is still concerned with the "justification" of tyrannicide, rather than with the function of resistance, but the politically relevant question is at least adumbrated in asking what is the "function" of tyrannicide. Taking full account of such movements as the German resistance under Hitler, which really faced up to this task of "killing the tyrant," we have three expedient arguments against tyrannicide. First, there is the "danger of individual action," second, there is "the importance of the ruler," that is to say the importance of maintaining public order at all costs, and third, it is claimed that "the assassination of the tyrant will never accomplish the desired ends." [11] It is evident that these arguments, while responding to the functional question, are still cast in the normative mode. This is partly due to focusing on the killing of the dictator, rather than on resisting the rulership in all its ramifications. As we remarked at the outset, resistance is endemic to all political orders; the reason is to be seen in the survival of pockets of divergent value, interest and belief: dissenters whose outlook predisposes them to resist as far as circumstances permit. In the totalitarian systems of our time, the problem is given its poignancy by the dichotomic conjunction of many such dissenters with strong convictions on the one hand, and a regime of very great power instrumentalities on the other hand, determined to destroy any resistance whatsoever.[12]

These dissenters are in part survivals of an earlier and less autocratic regime and, in part, persons whose functions in modern society predispose them to deviance: military men, scientists, scholars, artists, clergymen and technicians of various kinds, including managerial personnel. These persons, especially when assembled into institutional groupings such as a military establishment, an institution of higher learning, a church or a factory, form "islands of separateness," in which resistance may take a variety of forms. To these centers which are predisposed to resist there must be added the family, which for human and emotional rather than

[11] Jaszi and Lewis, 1957, chap. XX; the main quotation is found on p. 233. On the last point, Jaszi misses the most striking argument, which claims (rightly, I believe) that if Hitler had been killed in the summer of 1939, no World War II would have occurred. The attempt was made, but failed, in October, 1939. Cf. Rothfels, 1948.

[12] For the analysis which follows cf. Friedrich and Brzezinski, 1956, chaps. 22–26.

intellectual reasons has a proclivity to set persons apart by providing them with a haven of highly personalized human relationships. All these groupings find it necessary for purposes of survival to resist the total claim of the totalitarian rule which seeks to reduce the persons subject to its rule to isolated "atoms"—the "mass-man" of modern industrialized society—or to keep men in this state whenever they have already reached it. This kind of depersonalized *homunculus*, or manlet, actually appears in the process of industrialization for mass production everywhere and becomes a significant supporter—in the mass—of totalitarian movements. The development is a striking perversion of one of Karl Marx's deepest human concerns: to free man from the "alienation" which modern mass production condemned him to.[13] For communist totalitarianism shows by its procedures how quintessential such alienation is for such a regime.

The resistance which is practiced by special-skill groups might appropriately be designated as "functional resistance." It springs directly from the requirements of the group's special function and as such may actually benefit the dictatorship—a fact which has been noted by at least one observer.[14] For it may provide such an autocracy with better science, better literature and better military performance than would have been possible had no such resistance occurred. In the case of science, the actual behavior patterns of both scientists and rulers are further complicated by the ideological commitment to science which is especially strong in Marxism. Science and the universities play a very special role in modern society. If one takes science in the broad and proper sense of any field of learning which is distinguished by a method or methods upon which a group of scholars are agreed as the most suitable for treating a particular subject (see Introduction), then the very autonomy of such groups of scholars is at variance with the concept of totalitarian rule. The degree of power exercised will determine the extent of the conflict, but it is built into the very situation. Similar reasoning applies to the military. If totalitarian rulers were able to prevail and to destroy all resistance, they would become wholly dependent upon free societies for scientific progress. This in turn would make them dependent militarily and generally in all technical fields of industrial progress. Terror and progress do not coincide. Actually a substantial measure of creative freedom has been allowed (Chapter 21). Functional resistance has been practiced and condoned.

All such functional resistance or at least the very largest part of it, is "passive." The distinction between "active" and "passive" resistance has been important whenever the problem has been discussed. In the

[13] On this key issue, cf. Lederer, 1940, esp. chaps. I and VII; Kojeve, 1947, pp. 173ff.; Löwith, 1939, 1950, pp. 284ff. and 295ff. The trend toward such transformation of men into things has been satirized by Huxley in his negative utopia (see above, Chap. 5). Arendt, 1958, chap. 35.

[14] Note the acute observations of B. Moore, Jr., 1954, chap. 5.

normative argument over the "right" it has been very generally conceded that "conscience," especially when religiously motivated, entitled a man to nonparticipation at least from a moral viewpoint, provided he was willing "to take the consequences." The entire issue of "conscientious objection" to military service, even in fully constitutionalized states, has been developed in this perspective. The vast passive resistance of Gandhi's noncooperation was carried forward on the basis of this belief,[15] as was the passive resistance of Germans to the French invasion of the Ruhr (1923). It has been extensively practiced by religious dissenters throughout the world. Such passive resistance can be a very effective means of undermining the authority as well as the legitimacy of a regime, by dramatizing the divisions in the underlying system of values and beliefs. To the extent that power is affected by the corrosion of authority and legitimacy, such resistance may actually destroy an established rule. In the analysis already referred to, Merriam, after discussing Thoreau, Tolstoy and Gandhi and listing the several forms of protest, concludes that "the range of possibilities in this direction is very great, and has never been thoroughly explored. . . ."[16] These situations urgently call for more detailed analysis. They show the inherent weaknesses of power, and while it may be too much to say that power is "weakest" when it uses violence, and strongest when using the various modes of persuasion, as Merriam does, surely the correlation between degrees of power and resistance is not a simple one. Empirical analysis of power shows (Chapter 9) that the willing consent of those who are "poor" in power is a very real source of power. In any case, it seems clear that passive as well as active resistance, when organized and continuous, is likely to weaken any political order. When the objective of resistance groups becomes that of overthrowing the regime and replacing it with another, sedition, rebellion and revolution are the successive stages of the process. Positive political action replaces negative action. Revolutions are successful rebellions; they are also rebellions on a more comprehensive scale. In fact, in terms of the comparative analysis here pursued, wherein all political processes are seen as occurring in parallel modes on the several levels of the individual person, the group or the comprehensive political order, revolutions are the cataclysmic manifestations of a process that occurs continually on a smaller scale as changes are delayed in personal and group relations. In this perspective one might say that many small revolutions prevent a big one; for as various factors of the social order are "revolutionized" by way of the functioning political process, the tensions which would make the forcible "overthrow" of the political order necessary are alleviated by being "channeled" into constructive operations. That is why

[15] Gandhi, 1948; Gandhi (ed. Jack), 1956; Zacharias, 1933.
[16] Merriam, 1934, p. 175.

some of the most far-reaching social revolutions, notably the industrial revolution, have not necessarily had any political equivalent. To be sure, the great Reform Acts of the thirties of the last century in Great Britain have at times been called a veritable revolution. Such a proposition can be argued if a political revolution is defined (erroneously, we believe) as a radical constitutional change. But the authority of Aristotle notwithstanding, revolution as a political process should be distinguished from evolution by a number of distinctive features, one of which is the employment of physical violence by persons outside the government.

It may be well here to note that when such violence is employed by persons *in* the government or at least associated with its ruling class the process of change is typically what is known as a coup d'état or *Staatsstreich*, that is to say, a stroke at the particular persons wielding power but not at the system or political order as such. The coup d'état displaces the specific ruler or rulers and replaces them by others of the same type. The coup d'état is therefore typical for unstable monocratic systems; it is recurrent in Latin American dictatorship. The coup d'état may of course be the opening phase of a revolution. Napoleon I and III, as well as Mussolini and Hitler, furnish instances of successful coups d'état eventually turned into a revolution.[17]

Trotsky once said that "revolutions are the mad inspirations of history." [18] Such a statement is a poetical way of saying that revolutions occur when a basic change in values, interests and beliefs which has been unable to mould political decisions and institutions "breaks through" into the political realm and serves as the foundation of a new political order (Chapter 22). Revolutions constitute the most decisive form of political pathology; for in their course one political order dies and another takes its place. The difficulty for the analyst arises from the fact that political order is constantly and continuously dying as various of its elements are being replaced and transformed. An understanding of the revolutionary process evidently calls for more than an understanding of the change it signifies. Just as in the organic world we do not consider the life cycle as pathological simply because it involves the death as well as the birth of particular organisms, so in the political world the death of a political order as such is not pathological, but normal. What is pathological is its sudden and violent death. We have already spoken of violence; what of suddenness?

Sudden is something which occurs in a very short time. In the life of bodies politic this may be a matter of days, or weeks or months; but it is characteristic of revolutions that they seem to occur "from one day to the next." This appearance is deceptive. Actually many revolutions have

[17] Malaparte, 1932; Gueli, 1960; Goodspeed, 1962.
[18] Trotsky, 1930, p. 320.

taken many months. Customarily the storming of the Bastille on July 14, 1789, is taken as the beginning of the revolution, the beheading of the king as its culmination. A similar period can be indicated for the English and the Russian revolutions. The naming of these three revolutions brings us face-to-face with an important problem: the range of a revolution. There is evidently a difference between the kind of revolution Aristotle had in mind, and which was typical for the Greek cities, wherein an aristocratic or an oligarchic regime was replaced by a democratic one, or a democratic order by a tyranny, and the "great revolutions" of Western history, notably the English, the French and the Russian. We may call the first type limited, the second unlimited, revolutions. Political science and theory are primarily concerned with the limited revolution–limited, that is, to the political order. But a few observations concerning the unlimited revolution are needed. One philosopher of history has even gone so far as to link these particular revolutions in an evolving sequel to the development of Western culture.[19] According to him, each of the great European revolutions has been made by one of the major nations of Europe which in the course of its revolution has discovered its own style of life, its specific version of Western culture. This interpretation fits the English and French revolutions reasonably well; it is more uncertain in the case of the German revolution, which this author thinks was the Reformation, and even more so in the case of the papal revolution of the thirteenth century through which the Italian people are claimed to have found themselves. The same writer also seeks to show that each of the "total" revolutions has advanced the claim of being a "world revolution" of which the makers expected that its values and beliefs would become the pattern of life for all of the "world," that is to say, all of Europe. This aspect of these great upheavals is least pronounced in the English case, perhaps because of the island position of England; it seems demonstrably true of the others. The bold design of this global interpretation of European history is rounded out by treating the Russian revolution as the last of these "world revolutions," after which Western culture moves "out of revolution." Among the many fascinating details of this theory, it is noteworthy that these revolutions have featured a widening group of active political leaders: one pope, the hundred princes of the Reformation, three to five thousand gentry in England, approximately a hundred thousand bourgeois in France, and finally the one or two million "proletarians" class-consciously supporting the Communist Party of the Soviet Union. This widening of the revolutionary personnel presumably is related to the changing class structure of European society. Hence each of these revolutions was in a way directed against the preceding revolution made by the class whose rule was now to be overthrown. This brilliant synthesis of

[19] Rosenstock-Huessy, 1931, 1938.

Hegelian, Comtian and Marxist elements in terms of an autonomous process of nation-forming is not, of course, primarily a political theory of revolution, although the political element occupies the very center of analysis, as just sketched. But the political change in all its violence and suddenness is merely incidental to the great cultural, that is valuational and convictional, transformation of which it forms a part. It seems important from the standpoint of political theory in the broad sense here developed to distinguish this kind of revolution from the revolution which is "merely" an overthrow of the government and a change of the political order.

In terms of a cross-cultural comparison, such "great" revolutions are a peculiarity of Western culture. They do not seem to have occurred in other cultures, such as China, India or the Moslem-Arab world, to mention only a few. They are also lacking in the Graeco-Roman culture, and in other lands of the Near East, such as Egypt, Babylon and Persia, not to mention the Incas. There was a distinct pattern of change, but the succession of dynasties does not constitute anything resembling the "great" revolutions of the West. Revolutions in the sense of a forcible overthrow of one kind of government and the substitution of another have occurred, however. "Republics" existed in ancient India, and the legalists of ancient China, while not abandoning monarchy, sought to establish a political order very different from the traditional Confucian one. To be sure, there were fewer revolutions in some contexts than others: after the Roman revolution which substituted the principate for the republic there were coups d'état rather than revolutions in the Roman domains for many centuries.

Some contexts seem especially favorable to revolutionary upheavals. One count has it that there were sixty-eight revolutions in Bolivia during the sixty-five years of her existence which had passed by the time the count was made. Many of these were coups d'état (which Aristotle as noted would include within *staseis*, a term denoting any overthrow of the existing ruler). Evidently, Latin America, like Periclean Greece, has provided a political setting highly favorable to revolutionary change, whereas the United States has been singularly free of it, and so has Britain since her seventeenth-century revolutions. We shall see presently what presumably accounts for this phenomenon; it stands in striking if familiar contrast to the experience of France and a number of other European countries, though not of the Scandinavian kingdoms and Switzerland.

In France, a keen feeling for the difference between the Revolution of 1789 and the many revolutions which followed during the nineteenth century has crystallized into the expression *la grande revolution* as an appropriate designation for the "great" revolution. It possessed a universal significance which the others lacked to a greater or lesser degree. This feeling has been generalized in the philosophy described above. A man could be "seized" by its spirit, and become a "new man" thereby. One of the great revolution's most significant voices, Condorcet, became the prophet of universal progress. It is this notion of progress within the context of a cultural whole which has given these great revolutions a decidedly positive accent. To many, they appear in retrospect sound steps forward. Aristotle and a great deal of political theory since has, on the contrary, seen revolution as predominantly negative, has insisted upon the value of stability of the political order. By contrast Western thought has justified the leader of such a great revolution as, at least to an extent, a hero. Glorified in the Hegelian philosophy of history as the "world historical individual," the leader of such a "world historical nation" has been "spiritualized" as an agent of World Spirit, marching forward toward man's final state.[20] The well-known anecdote of Hegel encountering Napoleon, the victor over the Prussian armies, and acclaiming him as the embodiment of the world spirit is the comical reflection of this outlook.

It is rather difficult for the Western political theorist to free himself of this heritage and to consider revolution, not in terms of the grandiose projection of some evolutionary thrust, but as the violent change of government which it usually has been and even was within the context of these shattering affairs. One modern historian has ventured to discover the "anatomy" of revolution by considering these events and abstracting them from their "spiritual" meaning. It may well be questioned whether a process can have an "anatomy"—the stages of development in physiology seem the more appropriate simile.[21] The attempt to abstract the specifically political from the total syndrome is nonetheless worth noting. It turns out that while the deeper impulses remain unfathomable, though the initiated claim to know them, the political pattern of these revolutions seems to be rather uniform. Basing his analysis on the data provided by the English, French, American and Russian revolutions, he formulated some significant inductive generalizations. Such generalizations abstract from the value judgments inherent in the several revolutionary gospels. It is impossible not to have sentiments about them, however, and this needs remembering. So does the inescapable value orientation of any general study, its bearing on what to think of revolution in general (Chapter 2). In formulating generalizations from a restricted Western experience, it is also well to remember that what is being attempted is merely intended to distill the "political" aspect of the peculiar "progressive" revolutions of

[20] Hegel (ed. Friedrich), 1953, pp. 17ff.

[21] Brinton, 1938, *passim*. See below for further detailed comment. The erroneous terminology may be indicative of an approach that is too static, that thinks of revolutions too much in terms of pattern, design and the like, as analyzed in the text. Cf. against this the more penetrating study of Pettee, 1939, discussed below.

the West as a necessary step toward the more general theory, which needs to be based, of course, upon a culturally more diverse and representative sample.

A word, though, first, concerning the American Revolution. The great De Tocqueville thought that America had not had "a democratic revolution," and that this was one of its "great advantages." [22] This assertion was in turn hailed recently as "one of the most fundamental insights." [23] Actually, if the destruction of an established political order by violence and the founding of a new one is the key aspect of a political revolution, the American certainly was one.[24] However, the American Revolution was not a "great" one.[25] That probably accounts for De Tocqueville's judgment, who thought of *la grande revolution* as *the* revolution—the archetype of a revolution, as it were. In truth the American Revolution was rather unusual in more than one respect. In any case, from the standpoint of sampling, it is desirable that the generalization should be based upon a sample which includes at least one revolution that is not "great"; the American Revolution is surely a part of the pattern of progress which distinguishes the European revolutions. As will be seen presently, a number of characteristic features are lacking, and these features may be related to its not being a "great" one.

The signs of an approaching revolution are not very distinctive. There are more and more stresses and strains which are endemic in society, but which eventually lead to a breakdown of the political order. Both legitimacy and authority disintegrate, and such power as is still effectively wielded as rule depends more and more upon coercive means, and is thereby limited. At the same time, hitherto unrecognized elements gain power and influence which eventually crystallize in revolutionary movements, that is to say, in movements which set themselves goals for the

[22] De Tocqueville, 1835–1890, in a famous passage. He argued that from this fact resulted some of her most striking features. What he meant was that she had no "unlimited" revolution. But the difficulty with the whole argument lies in the fact that America represents a new kind of society in which revolutionary changes are continually occurring without a great deal of violence. This "permanent revolution" the Soviet Union has been trying to organize in a different way, and hence it is difficult to fit the Russian revolution into the aforedescribed pattern. The first four stages are clearly discernible, but no "restoration" of the preceding tsarist regime has ever been seriously advocated by any groups with large-scale following, either inside or outside Russia.

[23] Hartz, 1955, p. 35.

[24] If "revolution" is defined in social terms which would include such slow processes as the "industrial revolution," then again America has had a "democratic revolution"—in fact the most thorough revolution of this kind, a democratic revolution in permanence which is still in full swing. The notion of a permanent revolution is Marxist and became popular in the Soviet Union; cf. S. Neumann, 1942, *passim*.

[25] Rosenstock-Huessy, 1931, 1938, pp. 524ff., noted this; the point is elaborated in the English edition, 1938, pp. 662ff.

transformation of the existing society which can only be reached through a destruction of it.

There is a definite succession of stages or phases, a "rhythm," to revolutionary upheavals of the "unlimited" variety. During the first stage, utopian expectations run high, and the revolutionaries engage in massive governmental perfectionism. They set to work to build an "ideal" political order. But this phase does not last very long. The practical tasks of carrying on the government have to be faced, and soon a split develops between the moderates and the radicals.[26] This conflict ends in the failure of the moderates, the rise of the extremists, and the concentration of all power in their hands. This is the second stage. Such concentration then is followed by the "terror," that is to say, by ever increasing deployment of violence for the promotion of the presumed revolutionary goals. The third stage is a desperate attempt to realize these goals at all costs of force and violence. Such over-extension of raw power engenders a reaction. This reaction was called the *Thermidor* in the French case, and it has since been generalized as the "Thermidorean reaction." "All our revolutions had their Thermidors," we learn, and all of them might be called a kind of "convalescence from the fever of revolution." This constitutes the fourth stage. Periods of "convalescence," during which the revolutionary fervor subsides, have led uniformly to "the establishment of a tyrant." [27] The tyrant is really a dictator who is still animated by the revolutionary zeal in this, the fifth stage. But the task of governing and the manipulation of power become paramount and eventually supersede all other goals. The new ruler is preoccupied with the practical problems of how to restore "order" and to organize administration. Old habits of life reappear, though restricted by the dictatorship. The revolutionary symbols, now devoid of psychic appeal, lose their hold on men's minds; as time goes on, the dictatorial power appears increasingly naked, and thus the road is paved for a "restoration"—an attempt to reestablish the old regime. These so-called restorations never truly restore what has been; how could they? The changes brought about by the revolution are too profound, and new institutions are designed to provide for the changed social structure.

[26] Brinton's claim, by the way, that "revolutionaries" are no particular kind of people, that "it takes almost as many kinds of men and women to make a revolution as to make a world," 1938, p. 145, is contradicted by some of his very evidence. Thus he writes, p. 142, that "revolutions are full of men who hold very high standards of human conduct," that "the idealist at last gets a chance." There are many kinds of revolutions, but their assortment of types of people differs, with "idealists" prevailing. The argument cries out for quantitative exploration and firming up. Pettee, 1938, chap. 4, gives a similar analysis.

[27] Brinton, 1938, pp. 245, 247. Brinton suggests that the "tyrant" is of the Greek variety described by Aristotle, but this suggestion seems hardly fair; neither Cromwell nor Napoleon nor yet Stalin nor Khrushchev is in it for "personal gain," as is Aristotle's tyrant. *Politics,* 1311a.

Our historian would, in the thirties, have seen Stalin as the dictator following upon the Thermidorean reaction; this interpretation seems, in retrospect, more than doubtful; Stalin's enterprise was fully in the revolutionary swing toward the third phase: the terror. The terror culminates in his regime. As a matter of fact, as I have argued elsewhere, Hitler was probably the Napoleon of the socialist-communist revolution.[28] Whatever the sound position on the comparison in relation to the revolution and its goals, the regime of Stalin and his successors has one thing in common with the other revolutions, and that is the development of a strong central government.

For, as our historian has noted, and his observation seems correct, the achievement of governmental efficiency is really the most striking uniformity in the political changes wrought by these revolutions. All four countries "emerged from their revolutions with more efficient and more centralized governments." [29]

It is a significant fact that none but the last of these aspects is to be found in the American Revolution. There was neither the victory of the extremists, nor the terror, nor the Thermidor, nor yet the "tyrant" dictator to restore some measure of political order. But a stronger and more efficient government did emerge. We shall presently show that this strengthening of government is a much more universal feature of successful revolutions, closely related to the fact that revolutions are directed against weak governments. But before we elaborate on this point, the explanation of this contrast between the "great" revolutions and ours deserves attention. For other revolutions besides the American are found to exhibit no such sequence of phases as the great European ones have exhibited. The clue may be seen in the distinction between "moderates" and "radicals" in the original division among the revolutionaries. Such a dichotomy can have meaning and significance only if the revolutionaries are believers in an ideology, in the strict technical sense (Chapter 4). For only in that case will there be possible degrees of radicalism. Revolutionaries such as those who merely seek to alter the governmental pattern—the kind that were common in Greece and until recently in Latin America—will simply divide according to their ability to accomplish the goal of overthrowing the government. After such overthrow has been accomplished, nothing remains to be done but to replace the former regime by the desired alternative. The case of the so-called Roman revolution is interesting in this context. Here a disintegrating political order was as-

[28] This interpretation is somewhat daring, and may be merely "clever." It suggests how difficult it is to make historical parallels stick. Perhaps, in another perspective, Khrushchev is the Thermidorean leader, with the Napoleon yet to come. Cf. also the view of Souvarine, 1939, pp. 282ff., on the dubiousness of interpreting the development in Russia under Stalin in such terms; cf. also *ibid.*, pp. 403–404 and later.

[29] Brinton, 1938, p. 274.

saulted by several waves of revolutionaries who would replace the constitutional system of the Republic by an autocratic system of monocratic direction. The key leaders were Sulla, Caesar, Pompey, Antonius and finally Augustus. Not distinguished from each other by being either more or less moderate they were more or less able to accomplish the task. The remarkable achievement of Augustus was to make the revolution "stick" by clothing its autocratic reality in the garb of the bygone constitutional order.[30] By contrast the rather unique feature of the Western revolutions is their distinctly ideological character, by which they are tied into an intellectually definable pattern of progress. It therefore becomes possible, even for the gentle cynic, to discover in them an important fountain for later modes of thinking and feeling.[31] The same cannot be said for revolutions without that ideological character. Here, revolutions appear as "breakdowns," as major instances of the pathology of the body politic. But the revolution itself is, like the fever, not the true illness. That illness precedes the outbreak.

With this observation we are face to face with the problem of the causes of revolutions. A great many analyses of revolution have been cast in terms of such an etiology. Aristotle's celebrated discussion of revolutions (*staseis*) is primarily concerned with what brings on a revolution: disputes about equality on the one hand, about property on the other, seem to him the main *aitiai*, or grounds, leading to revolutionary upheavals and overturns of political regimes. These he analyzes in terms of the feelings and the motives [32] of the persons who make revolutions and the situations which give rise to them. A number of modern writers have resumed the discussion which men like Polybius, Machiavelli and Harrington, to mention only three, had reformulated and sought to refine. Historians, sociologists and political scientists have competed with each other in this search.[33] But no particularly useful purpose is served by listing particular values, such as freedom, security, equality or justice as causes or grounds of revolutionary sentiment. For it is obvious that these

[30] Syme, 1938, esp. chaps. XXI–XXIV and XXXIII. Syme, as is the wont of historians, while admirable on the facts and their realistic interpretation, does not bother to explore the problem of "revolution" as such, in spite of the title.

[31] Brinton, 1938, chap. IX, esp. at pp. 282f.

[32] Aristotle, *Politics,* V. Although usually translated as "causes" of "revolutions," *aitiai* are not merely "efficient causes," which is the prevalent meaning of "cause" today (see above, Introd.), nor is *stasis* strictly speaking merely a revolution, but any kind of overturn. Aristotle's discussion at 1301b would apply to a modern election. He puts the problem in this very broad context in asking: (1) What is the feeling? (2) What are the motives of those who make overturns? and (3) Whence arise political disturbances and quarrels? (1302a. Jowett's transl.). The Greek is more general yet and reads: *pōs échontes kai tinōn heneken.*

[33] Besides the works of Rosenstock-Huessy and Brinton already cited, note Merriman, 1938; Sorokin, 1925; S. Neumann, 1942; Laski, 1943; Pettee, 1938.

very general values motivating all politics, as has been shown, will necessarily enter into any revolutionary enterprise, both as real motivations and as slogans and rationalizations.[34] We have already suggested earlier in this chapter that the development of too many stresses and strains, thwarting various persons and groups and inhibiting their activity—in brief, too great rigidity—is the most general antecedent of revolution. One theorist of revolution has suggested that these stresses and strains be understood as "cramps," because a cramp "implies a maladjustment with accompanying strain, affecting the power situation." [35] He then proceeds to analyze the prerevolutionary situation in terms of economic, ideological, social and political cramps, linked as they are to institutional decay and the decadence of the elite. This discussion serves as a useful detailed account of the several stresses and strains in terms of which the prerevolutionary situation may be described. He rightly insists that only a cumulation of such stresses and strains will add up to a revolutionary outbreak. Out of this congeries of small breakdowns the revolutionaries build the appeals for their movement. Here myth and symbol enter to crystallize positions (Chapter 5) which an ideology embodies (Chapter 4). A clash of loyalties develops which eventually leads to the revolutionary crisis.

All these presumably "value-free" analyses of revolution suffer from the neglect of the objective, or end, of revolutions; this leaves the analysis incomplete. It is not merely a matter of considering what brought on a revolution, in terms of both the situation and the persons becoming operative in the situation, but also a matter of analyzing its thrust. A number of Western revolutions, notably the British, American and French, were directed toward establishing a *constitutional* political order. Others, notably the Russian and Chinese revolutions, were intended to place total power in the hands of social reformers who wished radically to alter the economic system—an objective which had not especially concerned the British and French revolutionaries. Many other revolutions are directed toward nothing but the alteration of the political order, not infrequently in the direction of greater power and authority for the rulers (example

[34] These problems have been explored in earlier chapters; it stands to reason that values which enter into political action generally will enter into that broad range of political actions known as revolutionary. It is not necessary to deprecate such value analysis, as Pettee, 1938, p. 30, unfortunately does, but to see it in its nonspecificity. Pettee later, pp. 161ff., argues in value terms.

[35] Pettee, 1938, p. 33. His able analysis has been unduly neglected. It is partly due to certain contradictions in the analysis. Pettee neglects to develop the distinction between limited and unlimited, or "great," revolutions and fails to restrict his term to "political revolution," although that is clearly what he wishes to discuss. At one point he states that "a great revolution is a reconstitution of the state" (p. 3). It is better to speak of it as violent overthrow of the established political order and the founding of a new one, as shown above.

the Roman, the Gaullist, and a number of revolutions leading to military dictatorship, as in Pakistan, the Sudan and Spain). Realistically, a revolution carried forward by a group which wants to establish a constitutional order (a "constituent group") is a different process from a revolution made by proponents of greater governmental power, especially totally unrestrained power. That is one of the reasons why the Russian revolution differed from the English and French revolutions.

More often than not, constitutional revolutions are "limited." Their focus is on the political order. Such were the negative revolutions of the period following the Second World War in Europe (Chapter 21); such have been some of the revolutions in the formerly colonial world. To the limited constitutional revolution corresponds the even more frequent limited revolution which is not intended to produce a constitutional order. Some of these limited revolutions are hard to distinguish from a coup d'état, for example, the revolutions in the Sudan and Pakistan, which ushered in the establishment of military dictatorship. A well-drawn constitution can anticipate the occurrence of such a limited revolution by so constructing the amending process that developing pressures for change can find expression in suitable constitutional amendments. An amending process may, indeed, provide for the complete revamping of the constitution, as is done in a number of American state constitutions and as happened in Switzerland in 1874. But such overhaulings will be "anticipated" only if the pressures are remaining within the limits of a constitutional outlook. If the demand for change includes the destruction of constitutionalism and not merely the elimination of the particular constitutional order, then no amending process will provide protection for constitutionalism, or "anticipate" the revolution. It is in keeping with the general insight that contemporary constitutions increasingly provide for the outlawry of enemies of the constitutional order. Such provisions, whether in law as in the United States, or in the constitution itself, as in the German Federal Republic,[36] generally fail to draw a distinction between an adversary of the particular constitution and of constitutionalism as such. This failure to distinguish between reformers and subverters of constitutionalism has involved those seeking to enforce such provisions in considerable difficulties when they came to distinguish between allowable criticism of an opposition and "subversive" activities. The problem is aggravated by the role of the communists, who typically have ties with a foreign power and therefore raise the issue of treason in a very serious form.

In this connection, it is important to recognize that Aristotle's theory, while outmoded because of both its presumption in favor of avoiding all change and its consequent failure to recognize the possibility of antici-

[36] For further detail, cf. Friedrich, 1957, chaps. I and VII.

pating revolutionary cataclysm by organizing gradual transformation, still possesses a certain value, because it directs attention to the fourfold aspects of all revolutions (in keeping with his general theory of causation). The material conditions he recognizes in the distribution of wealth and the related class structure, which he sees rather simply as the division between the rich and the poor. The ideational setting is provided by related notions about justice (Chapter 14) which mould party divisions (Chapter 28). The makers of revolutions, the efficient cause, are the leaders of movements which are seeking ascendancy and hence a transformation of the political order. A new or radically altered political order constitutes therefore the end and purpose of a revolution. Aristotle's is thus clearly a theory of limited political revolution, both constitutional and anticonstitutional,[37] based on the recognition that material conditions provide one major cause. Other basic values and beliefs may, however, be associated or even predominant. Typically the colonial revolutions of our time, while surely having an economic aspect, are not primarily economically, but politically and culturally motivated. In periods when religious feelings run high even religious beliefs have been the prime causes or conditions of revolutionary change and overthrow. Aristotle's view was a generalization derived from the particular condition of Greek cities in his time. His theory can be stated more generally by saying that any radical alteration in basic value or belief provides the ground for a revolutionary upheaval. In a more precise application of Aristotle's four "frames of reference" (*aitiai*) it could then be said that the human beings in the revolutionary movement are its "material," the idea of the possibility of a violent alteration its conceptual frame, the leaders the "makers" of the revolution, and the new order its end. But such a reference to four frames does not satisfy modern theory; we do not merely wish to delineate its "design," but also to understand its genesis and to be able to describe its operation in theoretical terms.

Whether the scope of the revolution is limited or unlimited, proconstitutional or anticonstitutional, a revolution will in short invariably have as one of its major objectives the remaking of the political order. In other words, a political revolution is bound to be embedded in every kind of revolution. Certain kinds of major social transformation which are conventionally spoken of as "revolutions," such as the "industrial" revolution or the "scientific" revolution, may be followed by a political revolution, because of the stresses and strains, the "cramps," to which they give rise; such a political revolution would still be said to be embedded in the social transformation without which it would not have occurred. It has

[37] Aristotle's own concept of "constitution" as meaning simply political order does not permit such a distinction, of course. Every revolution is a change of *politeia*. Cf. *Politics*, V.

been one of the major achievements of modern constitutionalism to forestall that kind of development, and thereby to prove that a political revolution is not the necessary consequence of such social revolutions. Constitutional orders have achieved this, as we saw, by an amending process which enables the majority—usually a qualified majority fixed by constitutional rule—to change the constitution in the desired direction.[38] But even the most flexible amending process may not be able to protect a political order against a revolution by those who are opposed to constitutional order as such, who have become persuaded that constitutionalism is a part of liberalism [39] or of capitalism or some other kind of social order and outlook and who are therefore determined to destroy it. The linking of constitutionalism with capitalism is, of course, the mode of thought of conventional Marxism, and has, until fairly recently, complicated the effective cooperation of Marxists in the shaping of constitutional orders through orderly amendment. Britain was spared these difficulties because of the absence of a sharp distinction between constitutional and other kinds of legislation, and the Labor Party has successfully amended the constitution in important respects, even though some of its more radical members, notably Laski, were skeptical about the long-range possibilities.[40] It is therefore noteworthy that the Soviet Union and other communist governments have found it worthwhile to erect a facade of constitutionalism; [41] this fact would seem to prove that a "constitution" has become enough of a symbol of orderly government to contribute to the legitimacy of totalitarian dictatorships today. These "constitutions" are typically amended by ordinary legislative procedure which allows the shifting power relations within the totalitarian hierarchy to express themselves.

One difficulty which confronts the architect of a modern constitution in devising a suitable amending procedure is the conflict between the requirement of flexibility implied in the preceding paragraph and the countervailing consideration that a flexible amending process facilitates a coup d'état and consequent revolution from within by a group wishing

[38] For this process of amendment, cf. Friedrich, 1950, chap. 8. A number of points contained in the analysis of this chapter were anticipations of the present discussion.

[39] Such a view, common in Europe, is untenable in face of the known historical realities of Roman republicanism and medieval political orders far removed from the philosophy of liberalism. Liberalism itself has contributed to the confusion; note the well-known quip that "Thomas Aquinas was the first Whig."

[40] Laski, 1938, esp. pp. 50ff.

[41] Note the constitutions of the Soviet Union of 1919 and 1936, as well as the many constitutions adopted in the satellite states since World War II. To accept these "constitutions" as equivalent to Western constitutions is the great fault of many; it has been the source of grave misunderstandings and policy defects. For a realistic appraisal see such works as Fainsod, 1953; and the literature cited in Friedrich and Brzezinski, 1956.

to destroy the constitution as a system of restraints upon governmental power. This danger was illustrated by the seizure of power by the fascists in Italy and Germany, and the threat of a similar development in France at the time of De Gaulle's resumption of power. It was De Gaulle's personal commitment to constitutionalism ("republicanism") which forestalled the consummation of such a revolutionary transformation of the French political order.[42] These experiences suggest that flexibility in the amending procedure should probably not be carried to the point of allowing ordinary legislation to alter the constitution, though it must be admitted that within the framework of democratic practice and belief there is no possible method of protecting a constitution against revolution once a majority is against the constitutional mode of ordering the political system, no matter what the provisions or what the particular constitution.

There is a further general proposition, derivable from recent experience, and that is the danger of concentrating the amending power in a single legislature, because of the chance it provides for revolutionary minorities to try to coerce such a body into exercising the amending power for the destruction of the constitution. This kind of situation arose in France in 1958, or rather it threatened to do so, but was headed off by De Gaulle's determination just alluded to. It was an important part of Mussolini's strategy. It has been a factor in Latin American politics,[43] and has afflicted several of the newly emergent nations, notably the Sudan, Pakistan and Ghana. Other efforts have, of course, failed, as did for example the famous march on Washington in the Depression,[44] or Hitler's march of 1923 (the Beer Hall putsch, so-called). Whether to tie in amendment procedures with the popular referendum is another question. Experience suggests that in modern mass societies, referendums give too great a scope to "demagogues," that is to say, to irrational, purely emotional appeals; they too have been instruments of totalitarian revolutionary movements, as especially the history of the Weimar Republic tends to show.[45] The only escape from the dangers inherent in all these situations seems to lie in the direction of decentralizing the amending procedure by suitable pluralistic devices, such as are offered by federalism (Chapter 32). Care is suggested by empirical data: if these decentralized

[42] On the German case, see the excellent detailed treatment by Bracher, Sauer and Schultz, 1960; for France, Macridis and Brown, 1960, is most illuminating; also, Williams and Harrison, 1960.

[43] Blanksten, chap. 5 in Almond and Coleman, 1959, esp. at p. 503; also Blanksten, 1951.

[44] Schlesinger, 1957, gives a vivid description on pp. 256–265. The event seems to me to deserve a detailed analysis, supported by quantitative data, in terms of analytical political science.

[45] Bracher, 1957 (transl. Eyck, 1962); Hennis, 1957.

procedures become too cumbersome, they prevent timely adjustments and thus help to produce revolutionary situations.

A curious kind of revolutionary situation is characteristic of much contemporary politics, in both Western and non-Western lands—situations in which there is a lack of positive enthusiasm for the future. These revolutions occur as the result of negating, of rejecting, a past political order because of its failure as well as other defects. In France, Italy and Germany such "negative" revolutions occurred and produced new constitutions which do not possess to any significant extent popular support, loyalty and understanding, let alone affection or enthusiasm. Before the Fourth Republic collapsed, Frenchmen were unanimous only in considering the existing political order more or less unsatisfactory, and in both Germany and Italy the established regimes continue largely because of an absence of viable alternatives and a widespread attitude of resigned skepticism concerning all politics. This atmosphere of general fatigue is typical of postrevolutionary situations, as has been repeatedly noted.[46] It has therefore at times been suggested that the politics of Western Europe resembles the restoration periods following upon the English and French revolutions. However, it is not the Russians, but others, who appear exhausted, and actually the political orders which have been erected are not "restorations," surely, in the Italian and German case, nor are the French really in a restorative mood. The English and French restorations after their great revolutions really believed that the old regime (*ancien régime*) could be revived. The resignation in Western Europe is more basic and extends to the new structures themselves.[47] The sphere within which a measure of enthusiasm prevails, and a sense of urgency to achieve progress motivates those active in it, is that of the European "Community of the Six." Here we are confronted with a quasi-revolutionary situation, and no restoration sentiment at all. It would seem clear from the record to date that the changes will be accomplished by gradual alterations and adaptations and not by revolutionary action in the political field. It is uncertain whether this process will be followed by the founding of a new political order once the growth of community has advanced sufficiently far. (See above, Chapters 22 and 32.)

In conclusion, it might be said that the phenomena of political revolution and resistance are endemic in any political order, and that they are closely related to each other. The effective means of avoiding resistance is to combine enforcement with broad consensus to governmental activities of every kind, and the same holds true for revolution. Every political order is subject to change, and unless means are provided for

[46] Brinton, 1938, pp. 243ff. and pp. 270f.; Pettee, 1938, pp. 141–144.
[47] Friedrich, a, 1949; Montgomery, 1957, chap. 1, p. 14, and chap. 5.

current adaptations of the institutions and processes to evolving values, interests and beliefs, such change will assume forms of violence, either sporadic, as in much resistance, or all-engulfing, as in political revolution. The process of revolution is, in that perspective, simply a marginal instance of the range of processes of political change, and as such it exhibits certain regularities in its successive phases or stages, of which breakdown of the established order is the beginning. Any model order will make allowance for this danger of breakdown and will seek to anticipate and thereby avoid it. Political orders resemble forests and families in that they contain the potentiality of self-renewal, but this potentiality does not exclude the chance of failure and ultimate extinction. Revolution, when successful, signalizes such extinction of a political order. Resistance is its harbinger and potential pathfinder. Both are therefore of primary importance to anyone who would understand the process of politics.

chapter

35

A Model Political Order and the Emergent World

We need not hope in order to act,
nor to succeed in order to persevere.
William of Orange

Don't take me as a road sign but as a map.
It is harder for both of us. But it will lead further.
Besides we don't suffer from a lack of road signs,
but from an excess of them.
Ernst Jünger, SCRAFFITI, 1960

OUR STUDY SO FAR HAS LARGELY been analytical. It has described and analyzed human experience in and with politics: how men in the course of history have built and maintained political orders and have seen them go to rack and ruin. But unless this experience is to be "full of sound and fury, signifying nothing," it should be capable of a synthesis which indicates what a political order ought to be like to be enduring. And when we say enduring, we do not mean unchanging and everlastingly the same, we do not mean an archetype in the Platonic sense, but rather a living whole capable of coping with the tasks which confront us, and that includes the task of adapting itself to new and different tasks to come. There have been hints at such a model order here and there throughout our analysis, but they must now be pulled together and moulded into a coherent whole. All the different component elements of a political order which have been examined in turn will play a part in the synthesis which thus serves as a conclusion of the entire analysis. For if the insistence at the outset upon the interaction of experience and value is taken seriously, all human experience in politics will be projected, or at least be capable of being projected, into the future by providing the ground upon which to argue what is to be preferred because experience has shown it to be more satisfactory in its results.

Thus what ought to be is not deduced from abstract notions but is concluded from concrete observation; it is not final, definitive and eternal, but constellational, tentative and temporal. Yet, it is the *best* for the time being. It is not relative, except in the nondogmatic, presuppositional sense of all science. "On the basis of our present knowledge . . ." is the often unstated, but always assumed, presupposition of every scientific generalization, be it the "law of gravitation," the "theory of relativity," the Mendelian rules of inheritance, or Gresham's law in economics. To take the last one for purposes of illustration: as long as it is true that "bad money drives out good money," the monetary laws, the ought-to-be's of currency legislation, will be guided by it if they are to work well. Also animals will be bred according to our understanding of genetics, bridges will be built according to such insights as the law of gravitation contains, and so throughout the world of human experience. What *ought to be* the model of human effort is derived from what *is* the content of human experience. These reflections, banal as they appear when thus put simply and unadornedly, need repeating at the outset of this synthesis, because a great deal of recent political science has shied away from drawing such synthesizing conclusions from the analysis of experience which is the pride, the justified pride, of its practitioners. Therefore the constitutions which have been made since 1945 and many more that are in the offing call for such synthesis of political knowledge and insight, call for asking plainly and frankly the question: What would be the *best* political order for the political community to be organized?

Yet all these efforts have suffered from the fact that no clearly perceived or scientifically based model provided a definite and distinctive design. On the contrary, whenever someone was suspected of thinking in terms of such a model, he was looked upon as a dreamer and was distrusted as a "theorist." When I first went to Germany to assist American military government authorities in the task of rebuilding German government, the most urgent advice an eminent American colleague had to offer was to tell me to abstain from telling the Germans what would be a good constitution. They must build it themselves, he said, and according to their "traditions." As if they themselves (and the rest of the world) had not had enough of "their" traditions, it was assumed by this American political scientist (and theorist!) that no rational model could conceivably inspire German constitution-making; that if it were not done in terms of German traditions, then necessarily it would be done in terms of American or some other alien tradition. Similarly, when a group of political scientists, Puerto Rican and North American, were engaged upon the task of fashioning a constitution for what has since become the Free and Associated Commonwealth of Puerto Rico, there was received one day a long and agitated telegram from another prominent American political scientist saying that he had heard to his dismay that a British type of system of parliamentary government was being proposed for Puerto Rico and demanding that all such ideas be dropped, lest he exert himself in every possible way to prevent its adoption—a threat which, while a highly arbitrary interference in Puerto Rico's internal affairs, nevertheless had a certain force because of this man's standing in Washington.* Both these instances and many others which occurred in connection with the negative revolutions of Europe's postwar constitution-making (Chapter 34) clearly demonstrate the striking disinclination of the contemporary builders of political orders to face the problem of what is best in structuring a government. This horror of constructive thinking which is the natural consequence of prevailing uncertainties about what is good, because values are seen as arbitrary and unrelated to what is known about the functioning of political institutions (Chapter 2), also manifested itself in the building of the Charter of the United Nations. In this case the difficulties were compounded by the fact that the Soviet Union's outlook had to be compromised with that of the West, which meant that basically nonconstitutional political convictions had to be absorbed into a constitutional structure. The result was highly unsatisfactory and the demands from both sides for the Charter's basic reform have become more and more insistent, each side wishing to make it more nearly conform to its own outlook and general view of politics. Any constructive thought on models of political order cannot avoid facing these problems, because local, national, regional and world order problems are interrelated and linked to each other.

What is best for the world at large can, therefore, not be considered without facing what is best for each part of the world; the world community, though limited in jurisdictional scope, and the parochial communities, whatever their range, form an interacting whole. Conversely, what is best for the more limited communities cannot be stated without facing what is best for the world community at large; the models on the different levels of community need to be fitted to each other if a harmonious and balanced model is to result on any level. These reflections help to resolve a difficulty which confronts all model thinking, and that is the relation of the general model to the particular application of that model. The relation is a dialectical one; a general model can realistically be derived only from particular models providing the empirical basis for the generalization, whereas a particular application can be worked out only by treating it as a reasoned deviation from a general one which serves as

* It was in fact a wholly unfounded fear: the Puerto Ricans were themselves so caught in the conventional notion of "American" government that nothing but a constitution of the typical American state was even considered. Yet all the conditions of the Puerto Rican political community, apart from this belief, argued for another model. It is nonetheless true that the Puerto Ricans have done reasonably well with the traditional pattern they adopted.

matrix and design. What is best for a particular political community is not simply what is best for all political communities, but it cannot be argued at all unless it is seen against the backdrop of a universal design. What is best for Puerto Rico depends, to put it in terms of the over-all perspective of the Puerto Ricans as political persons and their order as an interrelated system of political processes, upon *two* dimensions of the Puerto Ricans: what they have in common with all other human beings as persons, and what differentiates them from all other human beings as persons. Every gardener knows that certain conditions are required for all plants he wishes to grow: soil, moisture, lack of weeds (unwanted competitors), and fertilizer—these are parts of the essential design of a good garden. But he also knows that different kinds of soil, different amounts of moisture, different sorts of fertilizer are called for by different plants, and that only the absence of weeds is a universal requirement calling for no special differentiation. It is a recurrent experience that reality is compounded of the general (universal) and the particular; medicine—a field with many striking analogies to the social sciences and more particularly to the political one—is continuously confronted with the necessity to weigh the requirements of the human body in general as against the requirements of the particular corpus. The neglect of what either recommends would make medicine impossible.

But, it will be said, medicine has the universal lodestar of health to work with. A healthy body is its norm which is accepted by all. But what is the corresponding norm as far as the body politic is concerned? One answer might be simply: a healthy body politic, but such an answer would be begging the question. Another answer could be and has been: the happiness of the members or of their greatest number. But as the work of Aristotle no less than that of Bentham shows, happiness is a highly controversial value. Indeed, as we showed at the outset of our inquiry (Chapter 2), no "highest" value can be convincingly demonstrated as having been universally accepted by human beings, and all attempts at arguing the contrary reveal themselves upon closer scrutiny as tautological: the particular value, such as happiness, is so formally or abstractly conceived as to be virtually identical with value as such. That even happened to Hobbes who, after asserting against Aristotle and the scholastic tradition that no highest value exists, gave "power" such a vague and general connotation as to make it virtually identical with all that human beings desire (Chapter 9). He furthermore posited as the motivating compulsive value man's bodily survival, the loss of which inspired him with such an abiding fear—the fear of violent death—that it overshadowed all other psychic and other considerations. Clearly, then, for Hobbes, man's bodily existence is man's highest value. But it can easily be shown that this assertion is contrary to fact, that time and again human beings have preferred other values to their bodily survival, even if one takes with a grain of salt such celebrated rhetorics as "give me liberty or give me death." In the animal kingdom too the sacrifice of oneself for one's offspring or even, for example, in the case of bees, for the collective, is a common occurrence. The foregoing basic considerations lead one inexorably to the conclusion that no model of a political order can, empirically, be constructed upon man's value preferences at large.

A political order, as we have seen, is an operational whole which enables a group of human beings to arrive at decisions and to evolve policies by way of institutions which provide them with the means of effective cooperation (Chapter 3). If such institutions and processes operate to the satisfaction of a substantial number of the members of a political community, the order will be accepted. The power which is exercised in connection with the operation of such institutions and processes, whether directly (Chapter 9) or indirectly as influence (Chapter 10) will be felt as beneficial, even though it constrains and compels, if those actions which the members of the community believe to be necessary are taken and conversely none or few are taken which are believed to be unnecessary. Under these conditions, the power-holders and wielders are considered to have a right to their power—that is to say, they are legitimate (Chapter 13). Power-wielders are greatly aided in their tasks when they possess the capacity for reasoned elaboration of the grounds of their actions and decisions, when they possess authority (Chapter 12). The satisfaction of members of the political community will obviously be more readily secured when the power which the political order provides is wielded by persons who possess such authority. More specifically, their actions will appear to be just in the sense of being adequate; the adequacy is seen in the fact that the comparative evaluation of the persons involved in the action accords with the values and beliefs of the community (Chapter 14). Law is the congeries of rules expressing the regularities of behavior of the members of a political community, whether actual or potential or normatively required (Chapter 15). These dimensions of power and justice circumscribe fairly well the over-all requirements of a satisfactory political order. An order which corresponds to them may be said to be good; the order which does so better than any other may be said to be best.

With the frame of reference thus laid out, one can proceed to a construction, or rather the discovery, of the model political order which is good. It could be done on any of the several levels of government, local, national, regional or world-wide; for the problems recur on the several levels. But in view of the prevalence of the national political community in the recent past and of its persistence and reassertion in the new political communities now emerging, it may be well to focus attention first upon this level and to discover the best design for a national model, then to proceed to the exploration of its applicability to the supranational and more especially the world-wide community. In short, the question now is: What, if any, is the best political order for a political community of national scope at the present time and in the foreseeable future?

It is indubitably a comprehensive value judgment which we are asking to formulate on the basis of the experience of political life in the past. It is necessary to ask this question, because none of the existing systems or models can be said to be good, in the sense of being able to satisfy the national political community. We noted at the outset (Introduction) that everywhere on earth men are at present more dissatisfied with their government than they apparently were only a short two generations ago, and we asked why this should be so. We then further asked whether this is due to a drift into misgovernment, to an excessive demand and expectation made upon the rulers, or an unmanageable situation? In the course of the analysis, there has been occasion to note instances of all three of these elements. Both nationally and internationally, the technological and organizational developments have created situations which governments are at least at present unable to cope with, yet the peoples, their constituencies, demand that these problems be solved, and more particularly that "freedom from want" and "freedom from fear," that is to say concretely, job security and peace, be provided. The need to pretend that all that is possible is being done in order to legitimize themselves has brought on a universal reliance upon propaganda and opinion manipulation—in older parlance, demagogy—which in turn has served as a cloak for misgovernment. Neither parliamentary government in its various forms, that is, neither the traditional democratic constitutionalism, nor the various forms of dictatorship, notably totalitarian dictatorship (understanding itself as popular democracy) can be said to provide a satisfactory political order. All these tradition-based systems lack authority and legitimacy, that is to say, they fail to provide justice, equality and freedom to an extent which would enable persons living under them to be satisfied with their operation. Defense (Chapter 23) is illusory against the impending nuclear holocaust, disputes (Chapter 24), especially those between management and labor and between racial groups, remain unsettled, rules (Chapter 25) are inadequate in spite of their number and complexity, and many measures (Chapter 26) that need to be taken are not and many others that are not needed engulf the members of industrial communities to an increasing extent, while parties (Chapter 28) either fail to integrate or dominate excessively. Finally, education is proving increasingly inadequate as it confronts a disintegrating tradition without the guidance of creative innovation (Chapter 32). The reformist and revolutionary ardor of bygone days has cooled and universal anarchy as the breakdown of order is the gloomy prospect in ever larger areas of the world (Chapter 33). All these problems and difficulties are most pronounced in newly emergent national communities, but they afflict as well the established communities to an increasing extent.

In face of this mounting chaos we cannot fall back upon formerly satisfactory ways of governing, though we must surely start with them as the springboard of the leap into the unknown. Three tasks emerge as central from the over-all analysis of past experience: how to fashion the political community by a continuous process of renovation, how to plan the various actions which the needs of the political community call for, how to carry out the plans and policies which emerge from such moulding and planning. Totalitarianism is a misguided attempt to remedy the shortcomings of democratic constitutionalism in these three respects; ideology, increased (economic) production and bureaucratic elitism are the three dead-alleys which are supposed to resolve the three functional difficulties. Each is by now recognized as an illusory short-cut to the real solution.

Actually, no existing system is able to fulfill the conditions we have laid down, because ideologically it claims to be an optimal solution—an ideal state, as it were, and in practice it fails even to be a minimal one. The kind of model here sought is, on the other hand, meant to be a statement of minimal requirements of a good political order under the conditions which have prevailed in this century and are likely to prevail for some decades. It is not meant to be best for all times and places, but good at the present time. Such a minimal solution to our problem calls for the following features. First, a government that can act effectively, i.e., take all the measures necessary to cope with the technological requirements of survival, both economically and militarily, including comprehensive planning. Second, some enforceable restraints upon the government's operations which will protect the participant member sufficiently to enable him to become and remain a political person. Third, some operative participation of all adult and sane members in the making of rules, and hence, fourth, general rules expressing the more permanent shared values and beliefs and common interests of the members, and more particularly those rules implied in the first, second and third features. Furthermore, fifth, a judiciary which will interpret the rules and particularly define the terms of settlement for disputes arising under the third. Finally, sixth, several voluntary associations (parties) which will provide the organizational framework for developing decisional alternatives of policy and personnel for the government, of protection for the participant members, of implementation for their operative participation, and of continuous reexamination of and support for the rules. Existing political orders of every type and description exhibit one or more of these features, but none appears to exhibit them all. Hence none of them can be considered good when this model is applied as matrix to them. This judgment applies to local, national and world-wide political order.

We cannot here undertake to show how existing orders, or even the most important ones, such as the United States, the U.S.S.R. and Great Britain, fail to satisfy the model we have suggested on the basis of the preceding analysis. Anyone familiar with particular systems of government and politics will readily be able to supply that kind of specific evaluation. Rather than undertaking such evaluations, we wish to elaborate somewhat further the several features which the model exhibits. Evidently, such an elaboration will be in the nature of a summary of what has been discussed and perhaps to some extent demonstrated in the earlier chapters. But before such an elaboration is undertaken, a reminder is suggested by the last two chapters: the model is neither meant to deny the value and importance of rooted and established political tradition (Chapter 32), nor is it to be read as a clarion call to revolutionary action. Revolution, political revolution, is apt to produce a bad political order at the outset, due to the regularly recurring process of overcommitment we have described; the Soviet leaders in trying to escape this regular result have been able only to vary it in detail. Tradition, on the other hand, is so helpful to any political order because of its contribution to the growth of authority and legitimacy, that political changes are most likely to contribute to the goodness of a political order if they can be made and seen as extensions or meaningful transformations of established tradition. Thus the near-revolutionary transformation in the position of the Negro in the Southern United States in recent years was made and seen as such an extension and meaningful transformation of the existing constitutional order. And some of the radical steps taken by the Soviet Union in recent years, such as decentralization and the introduction of the competitive principle into economic activity, have been undertaken in terms explicitly relating them to established communist tradition. The same may be said of some of the striking changes that have been instituted in Poland and other satellites.

In elaborating our model, it seems best to take up the first and the sixth features conjointly. For the effective operation of a government under contemporary conditions of a complex industrial society presupposes a substantial amount of authority (Chapter 12) and legitimacy (Chapter 13). It cannot, in other words, operate effectively on the basis of power alone. For if power is largely coercive, it fails to bring about the vast multitude of conforming activities; if it becomes consensual, the rulers need to acquire authority and legitimacy (Chapters 9 to 11). It is a stupendous task which confronts contemporary rulers: to acquire the vast power which industrial mass society in the advanced stage of development calls for, and yet to have it remain sufficiently consensual. To possess the required capacity for reasoned elaboration of the grounds upon which the measures are based which economic and military survival calls for, and to maintain the belief that they are entitled to rule, such rulers must organize voluntary support on a large scale, especially as they face also the task of providing for their succession (Chapter 28). This kind of support is typically provided by parties, sometimes called movements to suggest a broader canvas; but if only one such party is allowed, both authority and legitimacy are impaired. The capacity for reasoned elaboration (including its institutionalized variants) then extends only to the community of the party itself. The right to rule is acknowledged only by the members of the party and does not therefore affect the rest of the community. Several parties are necessary; what is not necessary is that these several parties alternate in ruling the country, as was the case of the classical British and American systems. One of the parties may predominate over long periods of time and may be replaced by another which did not in fact play a significant role in the past in opposing the ruling party. Such predominance may be the result of personality, as when one great leader has no significant rival; it may be the consequence of particular circumstances in the constituency; or it may be the response to external threats. A number of the emergent countries strikingly illustrate the first of these ways: Muñoz Marín in Puerto Rico, Bourguiba in Tunisia, and in a different context Nehru in India, and others come readily to mind. Not only the personality of the leader, but the circumstances of the country are, of course, a factor in each case, but the leadership appears to be decisive. Similar is the situation in France; De Gaulle has, especially by his more recent actions, placed himself in a comparable position of predominant party leader. The situation is still further modified in the Federal Republic. Even though Adenauer would have liked to dissolve the competing parties into fragments and thus to insure the indefinite predominance of the Christian Democrats, the rivalry of the Social Democrats for political office has remained real, partly as a result of Germany's federal system under which Social Democrats have governed a number of states. Germany, as well as Austria, is also a case of external threat having an integrating effect.

But not only exceptional circumstances and outstanding leadership, but also other conditions may produce a one-party system. This is the case, for example, in a number of states in the United States, many of them located in the South, but not only there. Vermont and some of the mid-Western states, notably Wisconsin, have seen long periods of virtual one-party rule. In such situations the one party becomes the stage for the decisive political rivalries which may give rise to party-like divisions. It may even split into several parties and thereby return the constituency to a more pluralistic pattern.

If, in light of the foregoing, it be asked why then systems such as prevail in the communist bloc or as those of the fascist era exist, the answer is that without minor parties in active operation, neither the restraints (second feature) nor the operative participation of all citizens (third feature) can be insured. Indeed the insuring of such restraints upon the government, and of such active participation by the citizens, are the primary tasks of rival parties.

For effective restraints upon the government require an active guardian of greater power and resources than the individual whose person may be in jeopardy. That guardian may be a professional group; guilds have in the past at times played this kind of role. But a party is apt to be more broadly conceived and because of its strictly voluntary basis is more likely to be responsive to the view of its members. The need for such restraints is the consequence of the requirements of the freedom of independence and of the freedom of innovation. Their value for political order having been demonstrated (Chapters 20 and 21), at least within definable limits, the operational importance of institutional guarantees is evident.

While the operative participation of all members is likewise required for the sake of freedom, namely, the freedom of participation (Chapter 20), it is also the resultant of the need of political equality (Chapter 16) and of justice (Chapter 14). Nor can authority (Chapter 12) and legitimacy (Chapter 13) be effectively maintained without the periodic tests which a participating citizenry provides for any regime. Representation in its many forms embodies the techniques for making such periodic tests and for thus insuring a sufficient measure of responsibility (Chapter 17). The totalitarian orders provide such participation only for the members of the ruling party. For the occasional "referenda" without alternatives are merely opportunities for acclaiming the political decisions, not for participating in their making. There is a danger that even established democratic regimes permit a gradual substitution of such acclamations for genuine participation as the electorate increases, unless party life is maintained in an active and vigorous state. The participation of only the active party members of the totalitarian order (no matter how it is ideologically justified or veiled) restricts both the authority and the legitimacy of these governments and thus necessitates a larger measure of coercion and force than appears admissible in the over-all context of the model we are seeking to construct. Improvement of these regimes must therefore seek to enlarge such participation.

Effective participation of the common man-citizen presupposes decentralization to the greatest possible extent. The two most generally employed methods for such decentralization are "local self-government" and federalism. Both rest upon the acceptance of a measure of autonomy for the local communities: villages, towns, cities, states, cantons, *Länder*, provinces, and similar subdivisions (Chapters 29 and 32). Such autonomy is explicitly defined in rules of the "constitutional" variety, and they are therefore subject to change in accordance with the rule-making procedures prevailing in the inclusive community. Local self-government typically rests upon ordinary legislation, as in Britain or France, whereas a federal system is more elaborately protected by treaty-like rules which may be formally altered only by agreed-upon modes of qualified majorities, as in the United States, Australia, Switzerland or the Federal Republic. The two modes of local self-government usually appear in combination, and this combination may be considered as part of our model. Under modern conditions and those which the model presupposes, namely, the participation of millions of persons in political decision-making, both local self-government and a federal setup are necessary parts of a model political order; hence the federalizing tendencies in formerly unitary states, such as Russia, Prussia and Italy, as well as the retention of a federal arrangement wherever smaller units are combined into larger wholes, as in Europe, Africa, Arabia, the Caribbean and Malaysia.

It is, however, essential that such decentralizing patterns of the distribution of power be considered as dynamic, rather than static, as continually evolving and oscillating between greater unity and diversity. This continual change is a matter of fact; but unless it is clearly recognized and institutionally provided for, all decentralization of power, but more especially the more rigid arrangements under federalism, are apt to become sources of tension and conflict, as not only the American Civil War but a considerable number of conflicts in all federal states suggest. The resulting arguments against federalism are truly arguments against rigidity in federalism. Their proper remedy is not less but better federalism.

The fourth feature of a good political order is a system of rules, we said, embodying the more permanent shared values and beliefs and common interests of the members. Since these values, beliefs and interests are continually evolving in ways that defy predictive analysis—the noble premise of continual progress having proved untenable—rule-*making* is a crucial process; it must be flexible and organized in such a way as to maximize the operative effectiveness of the government within the limits of regularized restraints and to permit continual participation of all adult and sane members of the political community. Such a system of rules constitutes the core of a system of law, if its thrust is toward the largest possible realization of justice (Chapters 14, 15 and 25). The disagreements over what rules are to be considered just are endemic to any political order and provide the basis for the formation of parties and other voluntary groupings of citizens who seek to realize rival values, beliefs and interests.

But at any one point in the evolution of a political order and its system of rules, disputes require settlement on the basis of the existing rules, and they *are* just for the short run, or rather, they provide the basis for the just political act. Values, interests and beliefs which have not yet crystallized into rules may, however, affect their interpretation; they may also be employed for their implementation wherever persons in authority are called upon to settle disputes. The settling of disputes is the key function in maintaining peace among the members of a community. But a political order can fulfill this function only if it remains alert to the fact that all rules exist only *for the time being*. The settlers of disputes, and more especially judges, will, therefore, in a good political order be disinclined to become partisans of a particular party or grouping espousing a "new" justice, while at the same time cultivating a tolerance and breadth of appreciation for all parties. "With malice towards none, with charity towards all. . . ." In a good political order, judges will be more than lawyers; they will cultivate a broad appreciation of the community's aspirations. They will be "lovers of wisdom," in the classic sense.

It is important to realize that our democracies have no monopoly on a settling of disputes in accordance with such a standard any more than they have on good rules and sound procedures for their making. On the contrary! It is widely felt that the operations of interest groups and the manipulations of party bosses produce on the one hand lopsided decisions which are embodied in rules that are a far cry from the proper balance of values, interests and beliefs prevalent in the community, while on the other these rules provide a conservative judiciary with the needed excuse for settling disputes merely in terms of the short-run justice of the statute book, and without regard to the evolving reorientation of the community. Such criticism, which is very widespread at present, suggests that in a model system the judges and other dispute-settlers ought not to be too closely tied to the rules, as old-fashioned positivism wanted them to be. That positivism rested, as we saw (Chapter 15), upon an assumption of value stability in the liberal age which suited its ruling merchant and industrial elite very well, but did not correspond at all to the facts, as the rapid rise of labor movements clearly testifies.

The difficulty is not, however, easily removed. Obviously, a wise judge should be able to set aside an unjust rule, but what about the unwise judge? The records of various states are full of instances where a new rule achieved by progressive forces after a long struggle has been weakened or even corroded by the sophistries of judicial "interpretation." In the model that has been developed this difficulty disappears; but in adapting existing political orders to the model, it must be given careful consideration. To put it another way, the reform of legislative and judicial methods and procedures ought to go hand in hand; for improvement in one of them may easily be nullified by the lack of it in the other field. In both, it is of primary importance to organize the training and recruitment in such a way as to secure the best available persons. But almost as important is the structuring of the institutions to enable the better performer to become the more powerful. Some of these methods have been indicated earlier (Chapters 24 and 25). But there is no doubt a great deal which needs to be done; it is a field in which the model is incomplete, because inventions are wanted which would enable us to make the innovations which the large number of proposals for new rules call for. Even the employment of the new technology of automation in the legislative and rule-making process is in its infancy. In the discussion of bargaining we hinted at some of the possibilities, but there exist now resources which have barely been tapped for effectively taking into account the variations in values, interests and beliefs among the members of the political community.

The model which has been sketched for a political community is, as it stands, a model for the "closed" community. It would work well, in light of past experience, provided there were no outside disturbances to upset its functioning. Such outside disturbances do, however, exist. Not only are there the links which trade and communications provide, but as the better organized community gains over the less well ordered one, further tensions develop. The attempts at coping with this situation have been reviewed under the heading of defending and expanding the political community (Chapter 23), as well as under that of the contrasting world orders of empire and federation (Chapters 31 and 32). The rival solutions of empire and federation have in the past given rather unsatisfactory results. Wars have continued, have indeed to some extent been increased as a result of these efforts at world order. Yet, it would seem that a model political order presupposes its being "closed," from which it follows that it must be universal.

Basically, the problems of a world order are no different from those of any other concrete political order. War is a problem of government; the elimination or at least the reduction of armed conflict has always been a primary task of government. Indeed, a political order is that structuring of a political community by which strife is reduced and, normatively speaking, eliminated (Chapter 19). Is the model we have been outlining applicable, then, to the world at large? The answer must be in the affirmative. We cannot follow Kant and avoid a world "state" simply because it raises the spectre of a world-wide tyranny. How to avoid tyranny is the obverse of how to avoid anarchy; both are existential threats where an order is in the making.

When we said that the problem of world order is no different from that of any other concrete political order, we meant more specifically that the functions of founding, dispute-settling, rule-making, and measure-taking need to be properly provided for before such an order can be said to exist. Only the function of defending (and obviously that of expanding) the community disappears, or rather, becomes absorbed into the dispute-settling and rule-making function proper. The argument for this proposition is one of compelling logic; it makes no difference how many people are involved in the order which has been outlined, and no particular size was specified. This feature of our model is in contrast to the models which Plato and Aristotle developed. Their ideal order was that of a *polis* or town of quite limited size (cf. Chapter 29), and was not by them held to be usable for larger structures. These they were convinced must be despotic empires. More recent experience has shown that similar political institutions provide a workable order for communities of such different size as Switzerland and India, or Bulgaria and the Soviet Union, so that the difference between the largest of these units and the world is less great than that between the smallest and the largest of the existing units. Any political order that is suitable for 250 million people ought in other words also to be suitable for 2½ billion or 5 billion. If therefore our model suits one of the large units which today constitute "national" states, it presumably also suits the world.

This proposition would not be tenable if our model did not include a federal feature. Only the kind of hierarchical structuring of the decision-making and other political processes which federalism makes possible allows us to speak of our model as one of universal application. What this means is that substantial progress in the direction of our model in the various political orders now existing is a precondition of the establishment of a universal order. This is so because of the requirement of homogeneity; a federalization process cannot work, and is unlikely to be started, unless the component units of the community-in-becoming are reasonably alike in their political orders and in the values, interests and beliefs upon which they are founded (Chapters 8 and 32). The lack of any such homogeneity renders all proposals for a world federation at present utopian in the strict sense (Chapter 5). Proposals for the "reform" of the United Nations which point in the same direction are similarly illusionist. It has been repeatedly pointed out by competent analysis that in the absence of agreement between the major powers (England and France in the case of the League of Nations, the Soviet Union and the United States in the case of the United Nations) any change in the formal arrangements is unlikely to produce effective action where their vital interests are at stake. This observation is not meant to preclude other kinds of reform; as a matter of fact such reforms are urgently needed in the case of the United Nations, because of the change in the number and composition of the states belonging to it. Their present inadequacy is strikingly signalized by the absence of two of the more important states: Communist China and Germany. The reason is, of course, that both happen to be in the center of the contest between the United States and the U.S.S.R. But that inadequacy is also involved in the provisions for membership in the Security Council, in the relation of that Council to the Assembly, in the relation of both to the Secretariat and in many other respects. Since the Charter is a treaty rather than a constitution, it contains very cumbersome provisions for its own amendment and hence change is virtually made impossible. Institutions which obstruct change are a great danger to political order, as has been shown repeatedly.

There is one reason for respecting the world federalist idea, however, and that is its clear recognition of the need of establishing a government if armed conflict is to be prevented. Our analysis has carried this proposition a step further and has shown that a political order approaching our model needs to be established if we are to realize justice and freedom besides peace and order—as the Charter of the United Nations claims to be doing and cannot possibly do. Until the establishment of such an order becomes possible—surely at present a remote prospect—the avoidance of war must remain a task to be achieved by the conventional methods of bargaining (Chapter 27), defending and expanding (Chapter 23). The expansion is included here, for the sake of realism, because the promotion of the model of good government is bound to be associated with the expansion of power of those states which come closest to its realization. But defense and negotiation are the primary techniques. They are greatly aided in the nuclear age by the enormous cost of defense, which precludes powers with limited resources from precipitating major wars, enables the great powers to stop them from spreading, and persuades the latter that such a major war is apt to be suicidal because of the impossibility of winning it without wrecking their own land and people. Hence bargaining becomes a continuous activity, almost an end in itself. "Keep talking," as a counsel of despair is tantamount to "whistling to keep up one's courage," to employ two homely phrases. Such talk, such negotiation, is far preferable to bargaining by threat and counterthreat (Chapter 27).

But bargaining is severely limited by the present international situation. It is bipolar in structure, in contrast to the former European so-called balance of power. The various groupings comprised under that general concept were multipolar and consequently permitted a considerably greater range of possible negotiations. Hence the continuous striving for a "third force" or a "neutral" power or bloc to attenuate the tension between the two poles. No such balance of power actually constitutes a political order; it provides merely a framework for relating such political orders to each other in peace and war. It is rather a "natural" than a political order.

Neither balance of power nor league being a political order in a sufficient degree to prevent armed conflict and the employment of physical force, they nonetheless represent an ordering of sorts. An imperfect order is preferable to no ordering at all, even when the empirical evidence does not support the expectations which men have entertained regarding such an imperfect order. In fact, both have been seen as methods for maintaining peace. There is a probability calculus which justifies the conclusion that these kinds of ordering reduce the probability of war, because of the added opportunity for negotiation which they provide (Chapters 18 and 27). In spite of the fact that there may be occasions when such orderings may even enhance the probability of war, over-all and "in the long run" the evidence seems to point to a reduction.

The balance of power concept is historically analogous to similar concepts in other fields. Balance of trade, balance of affections, and all kinds of other balances in macrocosm and microcosm were in the seventeenth and eighteenth centuries believed to be part of the "beautiful design" which nature exhibited everywhere. Hume, in his *Essay on the Balance of Power*, while by no means the first is perhaps the most felicitous in juxtaposing the balance of power to that of trade. He suggests at the outset that probably only the phrase and not the idea is modern and goes on to recall such balances of power in ancient Asia Minor and among the Greek city-states, as described by Thucydides and Demosthenes, as well as the contrast of universal empire in the days of ancient Rome. "In short," he sums up this historical evidence, "the maxim of preserving the balance of power is founded so much on common sense and obvious reasoning, that it is impossible it could altogether have escaped antiquity." It is therefore not surprising that it should have been noted also by other writers in other cultures, such as Artashastra. In these views, the notion of counterbalancing an emergent universal empire is predominant, rather than that of maintaining peace. We have come a long way from the belief in a natural order by "preestablished harmony," and even the balance of power is increasingly understood as a manipulated affair in which a "balancer" is operative and indeed required. Analysis of the historical experience suggested this insight. But in reality both "balance" and "balancer" are figures of speech only; the former for an existing status quo, the latter for the power or powers interested in maintaining such a status, either through negotiation or by other kinds of bargaining. For the equilibrium of power has never been a material equipoise of forces, resources, and the like. The nature of political power precludes it (Chapter 9). Even if a given situation is assumed to be "in balance," there are continually new factors emerging which alter it. One or more human actors are required to deal with the situation and "reestablish" the balance. In this sense, the "balance of power" is apt to be a rationalization of the status quo. The balancer has often been some person or power placed beyond the immediate range of the power rivalries which it was his "game" to keep under control. The Holy See in Renaissance Italy and England vis-à-vis the Continental powers are a case in point. The "neutrals" aspire to this role in the present world situation between the two "blocs," as does the UN Secretary-General from time to time. For it is important to realize that a league or other kind of loose organization of autonomous powers does not supersede a balance of power, as the Wilsonian utopianism assumed, but provides a slightly more structured "field" for its operation. There is bound to develop a balance of power within such a league as well as around it (if some of the powers remain outside). The two kinds of ordering can therefore not be treated as alternative, but as supplementary, modes of order.

The base model of all balance-of-power situations is that of three powers. Suppose there were only three countries in the world, fairly alike in power and resources, but one of them, *A*, somewhat stronger than each of the other two. In that situation *A* might be tempted to add one of them to its own territory, either in whole or in part, and either by physical force (war) or by other forms of compulsion. If *A* could thus add *C*, in whole or in part, it would then be strong enough to overpower *B* and establish world dominion. Hence, political prudence would suggest to power *B* to support *C* and thereby avert an alteration in the existing balance of power. In this basic model, *B* would operate as the balancer between *A* and *C;* if *A* should thereupon turn against *B*, very probably *C* would act as balancer between *A* and *B*. In such a simple model, the balancer is "inside" the system, and to some extent a balancer always is. But both the Pope and Britain had other concerns than the power system as such; they wished to maintain the existing balance in order to be able to pursue their other goal undisturbed; the same may be said of the "neutrals" or the UN nowadays; they wish to be able to secure peace and prosperity, to put it very simply. If power relations could, in reality, be thus simply manipulated, the model would work perfectly to maintain the balance, and there would never be war. Unfortunately, many factors, including human failings and lack of skill, intervene to convert a certainty into a mere probability, and thus merely to reduce but not to eliminate the chance of war and of its range.

One of the major difficulties arises precisely from the fact that the world is bipolar, and that the potential balancers are not, as in the basic model, equally powerful as the contenders for universal dominion, or nearly so. Indeed, in the case of the UN, the power contenders are themselves entrenched in and form part of the "balancer." Both these circumstances tend to reduce the manipulative potential of the balancer and hence to increase the chance of failure at the crucial moment. The only way out of this difficulty (apart from the utopian notion that the power blocs could be persuaded to enter into and constitute themselves as a genuine political order) is the hope or prospect of transcending the existing bipolarity into a new multipolarity.

The emergent structure of power relations appears to be moving in the direction of a new multipolarity. Through federal unification as well as imperial conquest (disguised as ideological union) the comprehensive cultural wholes seem to be emerging as the component units of this future international system. It will not be inter-national in the old European sense, but rather intercultural, though the term may persist as the term "nation" is broadened to cover such vast cultural complexes as India, Europe or Africa. These units range in the hundreds of millions, considerable variations being observable as indeed always persisted in the European system. And just as there were units which did not fit into the European system, so there will be old-fashioned national states, corresponding to old-fashioned city states and the like in Europe (Venice, Hamburg, etc. until the eighteenth century). Concrete reality never quite fits neatly into logical design. But the emergent multipolarity of these great cultural wholes is nonetheless increasingly apparent. Besides the United States and the Soviet Union, there are now emerging Europe, India, China, Africa, Latin America, Indonesia, Malaysia, Arabia. Much uncertainty surrounds the British Commonwealth, which may itself constitute such a unit or be divided between several of them, with Australia and New Zealand forming a separate entity, perhaps. As this kind of system crystallizes, it may become possible to organize a genuine political order among them, but it is not very likely within this century. The tasks involved in founding and ordering these comprehensive units are so great that they will probably absorb most of the political energy available. But a purposive association may become possible, preoccupied with the task of providing the framework for continuous cooperation and negotiation for the purpose of avoiding military conflict. Instead of a rather inactive Security Council divided from an oratorical Assembly, such an association may be able to provide for genuine representation of the several autonomous political orders. Such a simplified structure might become the starting point for a federalizing process that eventually might culminate in a political order approximating the model we have outlined.

In such a process, the gradual evolution of world law would presumably play a decisive role. Present international law, even as implemented by the Charter of the United Nations, is law only to a limited degree or in a limited sense (Chapter 15). Nonetheless, it is genuine law to the extent that the people who participate in the creation of this law live in constitutionally organized legal communities. This is at present true of more than half of mankind, and as far as the UN is concerned of substantially more than half. It is an imperfect legal community, but it still has meaning and value. In the international sphere, any degree of ordering, even if quite limited, constitutes today a distinct value, because war as an instrument for settling conflict has become of very limited use. Order therefore clearly represents a predominant interest of all participating nations. While it is true that only within the framework of a functioning political order approximating our model it would be possible to integrate the different conceptions of law and justice of the many participating nations, some beginnings are not only possible but are in fact taking place. More rapid progress is, to be sure, being made within regional groupings, but even these evidently reduce the number of disagreements and conflicts. The common search for what in each regional sphere would be right and just is often carried beyond the boundaries of the particular grouping and serves as the basis for broader approaches, and indeed the examples are multiplying. The emergence of the Common Market in Europe is serving as a paradigm of the potentialities that are as yet untapped in this sphere.

"An eventual world law within the framework of a world constitution seems therefore to be quite in line with the progressive realization of the task which law as the approximation to justice presents to mankind. The common concerns of mankind which are growing steadily more numerous as men are brought together can only thus be handled appropriately. The task is an infinitely comprehensive and complex one which will challenge the ingenuity of generations to come."

bibliography

The following bibliography, though extensive, is by no means exhaustive. I have omitted many items given in the bibliographies appended to my other books cited below. It contains primarily those items to which specific reference is made in the footnotes to this work. For each author, the listings are separate for books, articles and joint and edited works, and in each category they are listed according to dates. Where two dates are given, the first usually is meant to refer to the first edition, the second to the edition used and cited; titles are not always given in full, but they ought to suffice to identify the work; lengthy subtitles are frequently omitted. My own selected bibliography is given at the end. I apologize for its length. It embarrasses me, but I finally decided that it was more sensible to be helpful even at the risk of appearing a "m'a tu lu."

ABBOTT, W. L., "The Origin of English Political Parties," *AHR*, 24:578ff., 1918–19.

ABELIN, P. (ed.), *La Fonction publique internationale et l'action internationale d'assistance technique*, 1958.

ACTON, LORD JOHN EMERICH EDWARD DALBERG, *Essays on Freedom and Power* (ed. Gertrude Himmelfarb), 1948.

ADDIO, MARIO D', *L'idea del contratto sociale dai sofisti alla riforma e il "De principatu" di Mario Salamonio*, 1954.

ADLER, MORTIMER J., *Research on Freedom*, vol. I, 1954.

———, *The Idea of Freedom*, vol. I, 1958; vol. II, 1961.

ADORNO, THEODOR W., et al., *The Authoritarian Personality*, 1950.

ALLEMAN, FRITZ RENÉ, *Bonn ist nicht Weimar*, 1956.

ALLEN, C. K., *Law in the Making*, 1927, 1958.

ALLPORT, GORDON W., *Personality: A Psychological Interpretation*, 1937.
———, *Personality and Social Encounter*, 1960.
———, and PHILLIP E. VERNON, *Studies in Expressive Movement*, 1933.
ALMOND, GABRIEL A., and JAMES S. COLEMAN (eds.), *The Politics of the Developing Areas*, 1960.
ALTEKAR, A. S., *A History of Village Communities in Western India*, 1927.
———, *State and Government in Ancient India*, 1949, 1958.
ALTHEIM, FRANZ, *Der unbesiegte Gott: Heidentum und Christentum*, 1957.
ALTHUSIUS, JOHANNES, *Politica Methodice Digesta*, 1603, 1610, 1614 (ed. C. J. Friedrich, 1932).
ALTMANN, RÜDIGER, *Das Erbe Adenauers*, 1960.
American Ethnological Society, *Systems of Political Control and Bureaucracy in Human Societies*, 1958 (*Proceedings*, ed. V. F. Ray).
AQUINAS, ST. THOMAS, *Summa Theologica.*
ARENDT, HANNAH, *The Origins of Totalitarianism*, 1951.
———, *The Human Condition*, 1958.
———, *Die ungarische Revolution und der totalitäre Imperialismus*, 1958.
———, "What Was Authority?" *Nomos I*, pp. 81–112, 1958.
———, *Eichmann in Jerusalem*, 1963.
Arguments, 4. Année, No. 17, is dedicated to bureaucracy; it contains summaries of such writers as Eisenstadt and Merton.
ARISTOTLE, *Nicomachean Ethics.*
———, *Politics.*
———, *Constitution of Athens.*
———, *Rhetoric.*
ARNOLD, THURMAN W., *The Symbols of Government*, 1935.
ARNOULT, P., et al., *La France sous l'occupation*, 1959.
ARON, RAYMOND, *Les Guerres en chaîne*, 1951 (also English).
———, *L'Opium des intellectuels*, 1955.
———, *Paix et guerre entre les nations*, 1962.
ASCOLI, M., *La giustizia*, 1930.
ASHBY, W. ROSS, *An Introduction to Cybernetics*, 1956.
ST. AUGUSTINE, *City of God.*
AUSTIN, JOHN, *The Province of Jurisprudence Determined*, 1832.
BACHOFEN, J. J., "Das Mutterrecht," in *Der Mythos von Orient und Okzident* (ed. M. Schröter), 1926.
BAGEHOT, WALTER, *The English Constitution*, 1867, 1878.
BAILEY, STEPHEN K., and HOWARD D. SAMUEL, *Congress at Work*, 1952.
BAKUNIN, M. A., *Dieu et l'état*, 1871.
BALES, ROBERT F., *Interaction Process Analysis*, 1951.
BALTHASAR, HANS URS VON, *Die Apokalypse der deutschen Seele*, 3 vols., 1939.
———, *Prometheus: Studien zur Geschichte des deutschen Idealismus*, 1947.
BANFIELD, EDWARD C., *Political Influence*, 1961.
———, "American Foreign Aid Doctrine," in *Public Policy*, 11:44–94, 1961.
BARENS, JAN, *Political Science in Western Europe*, 1961.
BARGHORN, FREDRICH, *Soviet Russian Nationalism*, 1951.
BARION, JAKOB, *Recht, Staat und Gesellschaft*, 1949.
BARKER, SIR ERNEST, *Principles of Social and Political Theory*, 1951.

BARNARD, CHESTER I., *The Functions of the Executive*, 1938.
———, "Comments on the Job of the Executive," *Harvard Business Review*, Spring, 1940, pp. 295–308.
BARNET, RICHARD J., "The Protection of Constitutional Rights in Germany," *Virginia Law Review*, 14:1139–1164, 1959.
BARTH, HANS, *Wahrheit und Ideologie*, 1945.
———, *Die Idee der Ordnung-Beiträge zu einer politischen Philosophie*, 1958.
BARY, W. T. DE, "Chinese Despotism and the Confucian Ideal: A Seventeenth Century View," *Chinese Thought and Institutions* (ed. J. K. Fairbank).
BASHAM, A. L., *The Wonder That Was India*, 1954, 1956.
BATTEN, T. R., *Problems of African Development*, 1948, 1960.
BAUER, OTTO, *Die Natioalitätenfrage und die Sozialdemokratie*, 1907.
BAY, CHRISTIAN, *The Structure of Freedom*, 1958.
BEARD, CHARLES A., *An Economic Interpretation of the Constitution of the United States*, 1913.
BEER, SAMUEL H., "Pressure Groups and Parties in Britain," *APSR*, 50:1ff., 1956.
——— and ADAM B. ULAM (eds.), *Patterns of Government*, 1958.
BELL, DAVID, "Allocating Development Resources: Some Observations Based on Pakistan Experience," *Public Policy* (ed. Friedrich and Harris), 9:84–106, 1959.
BELOCH, JULIUS, *Die Bevölkerung der griechisch-römischen Welt*, 1886.
BENDA, JULIEN, *La Trahison des clercs*, 1927; English: *The Treason of the Intellectuals* (transl. R. Aldington), 1928.
BENDIX, REINHARD, *Max Weber: An Intellectual Portrait*, 1954.
BENEDICT, RUTH, *Patterns of Culture*, 1934.
BENÉT, STEPHEN VINCENT, *John Brown's Body*, 1928.
BENN, STANLEY I., and R. S. PETERS, *Social Principles and the Democratic State*, 1959.
BENNIS, W. G., N. BERKOWITZ, M. AFFINITO, and M. MALONE, "Authority, Power and the Ability to Influence," *Human Relations*, 11:143ff., 1958.
BENSON, GEORGE C. S., *The New Centralization*, 1941.
——— (ed.), *Essays in Federalism*, 1961.
BENTHAM, JEREMY, *Works*, (ed. J. Bowring), 11 vols., 1843.
———, *A Fragment on Government*, 1776.
———, *An Introduction to the Principles of Morals and Legislation*. See above, *Works*, vol. I.
BENTLEY, ARTHUR E., *The Process of Government*, 1908, 1935.
BERDIAEV, N., *The Russian Idea*, 1947.
BERGENGRÜN, WERNER, *Der Grosstyrann und das Gericht*, 1949.
BERGER, MONROE, *Equality by Statute: Legal Controls over Group Discrimination*, 1952.
BERLIN, SIR ISAIAH, *Two Concepts of Liberty*, 1958.
BERNAL, J. D., *The Freedom of Necessity*, 1949.
BERNANOS, GEORGES, *The Diary of a Country Priest*, 1937.
BERNERI, MARIE LOUISE, *Journey through Utopia*, 1950.
BERNOULLI, CARL A., *Theologie und Wissenschaft*, 1933.
BERTALANFFY, LUDWIG VON, "Problems of General System Theory," in *General System Theory: A New Approach to Unity of Science*, Symposium of the

American Philosophical Association (December, 1950), paper no. 1, reprinted in *Human Biology*, 23(4):302–312, 1951.

———, "Towards a Physical Theory of Organic Teleology: Feedback and Dynamics," paper no. 6, pp. 346–361, in *ibid.*

BERTHOLET, ALFRED, "Priesthood" and "Religion," *ESS.*

BESSON, W., *Die politische Terminologie des Präsidenten Franklin D. Roosevelt: Eine Studie über den Zusammenhang von Sprache und Politik*, 1955.

BIASCARETTI DI RUFFINO, PAOLO, "Le colettività locali e la costruzione dell'unità Europea: Aspetti giuridico-amministrativi," in *Proceedings of the Conference of Istituto Scienza Amministrazione Publica* (Milano), 1961.

BINDER, LEONARD, *Religion and Politics in Pakistan*, 1961.

———, *Iran: Political Development in a Changing Society*, 1962.

BLACKSTONE, WILLIAM, *Commentaries on the Laws of England*, 4 vols., 1765–1769.

BLANKSTEN, GEORGE I., *Ecuador: Constitutions and Caudillos*, 1951.

BLITZER, CHARLES, *An Immortal Commonwealth: The Political Thought of James Harrington*, 1960.

BLOOM, SOLOMON, *The World of Nations*, 1942.

BLOOMFIELD, LEONARD, *Language*, 1933.

BOBBIO, N., "Giustizia," in *Dizionario di filosofia*, 1957.

———, "La Liberté dans la pensée de Kant," *Annales de la philosophie politique*, vol. IV, 1962.

BOCCALINI, T., *Le ragguagli di Parnaso*, 1630.

BODIN, JEAN, *De la République, 1576; De Republica Libri Lex, 1586;* cf. also Kenneth McRae's edition of Knolles' English translation, 1962.

BOGUE, DONALD J., *The Structure of the Metropolitan Community*, 1949.

BOLINGBROKE, LORD HENRY ST. JOHN, *A Dissertation upon Parties*, 1734.

BOORSTIN, DANIEL J., *America and the Image of Europe: Reflections on American Thought*, 1960.

BOTERO, GIOVANNI, *Delle cause della grandezza delle città, 1588* (English edition 1605).

BOWIE, ROBERT R., and C. J. FRIEDRICH (eds.), *Studies on Federalism*, 1954.

BOWIE, ROBERT R., and Associates, *United States Foreign Policy: Ideology and Foreign Affairs*, 1959.

BRACHER, KARL D., *Die Auflösung der Weimarer Republik*, 1957.

———, WOLFGANG SAUER, and GERHARD SCHULTZ, *Die Nationalsozialistische Machtergreifung: Studien zur Errichtung des totalitären Herrschaftssystems in Deutschland, 1933–1934*, 1960.

BRAIBANTI, RALPH, and JOSEPH J. SPENGLER (eds.), *Tradition, Values and Socio-economic Development*, 1961.

BRANDI, KARL, *Kaiser Karl V*, 2 vols., 1937, 1942.

BRAUBACH, MAX, *Der Westphälische Friede*, 1948.

BRECHT, ARNOLD, *Federalism and Regionalism in Germany*, 1945.

———, *The Political Philosophy of Arnold Brecht* (ed. M. D. Forkosch), 1954.

———, *Political Theory*, 1959.

BREITLING, RUPERT, "Das Geld in der deutschen Parteipolitik," *Politische Vierteljahrsschrift*, pp. 348ff., 1961.

BRINTON, CRANE, The *Anatomy of Revolution*, 1938.

———, *The Jacobins: An Essay in the New History*, 1930.
BRUNER, JEROME S., *Mandate by the People*, 1944.
———, J. J. GOODNOW, and G. A. AUSTIN, *A Study of Thinking*, 1956.
BRUNNER, E., *Die Gerechtigkeit*, 1950.
BRYCE, JAMES, *The American Commonwealth*, 1888, 1924.
BRZEZINSKI, ZBIGNIEW, *The Soviet Bloc: Unity and Conflict*, 1960.
———, *Ideology and Power in Soviet Politics*, 1962.
BUELL, RAYMOND, *The Native Problem in Africa*, 2 vols., 1928.
BULLOCK, ALAN, *Hitler: A Study in Tyranny*, 1952.
Bundeslastenausgleichsbank, *Zehn Jahre Lastenausgleich-Bericht*, Hamburg, 1960.
BURCKHARDT, JAKOB, *Die Zeit Constantins des Grossen, 1853, 1924* (English ed. 1949).
———, *Die Kultur der Renaissance in Italien, 1860* (English eds. 1878, 1921).
———, *Griechische Kulturgeschichte*, 4 vols. (ed. Deri), 1898, 1902, 1930.
BURCKHARDT, WALTHER, *Die Organisation der Rechtsgemeinschaft*, 1927.
BURDICK, EUGENE, and WILLIAM J. LEDERER, *The Ugly American*, 1958.
BURKE, EDMUND, *Works*, 9 vols. (American ed. 1839): vol. I, *Observations on a Late Publication entitled, The Present State of The Nation* (1769); *Thoughts on the Cause of the Present Discontent* (1770); vol. III, *Reflections on the Revolution in France* (1790); vol. V, *Address to the King.*
BURLINGAME, ROGER, *General Billy Mitchell–Champion of Air Defense*, 1952.
BURROWS, E. G., *The People of Ifaluk*, 1949.
BURTON, JOHN W., *Peace Theory: Preconditions of Disarmament*, 1962.
BURY, J. B., *A History of Greece to the Death of Alexander the Great*, 1900, 1913 (Modern Library ed. 1937).
BUSH, VANNEVAR, *Modern Arms and Free Men*, 1949.
BUSIA, K. A., *The Position of the Chief in the Modern Political System of Ashanti: A Study of the Influence of Contemporary Social Changes on Ashanti Political Institutions*, 1951.
CAHN, EDMOND N., *The Sense of Injustice: An Anthropocentric View of Law*, 1949.
CALAMANDREI, PIERO, *Elogio dei giudici scritto da un avvocato*, 1935, 1954 (English ed. 1942).
———, and A. LEVI, *Commentary on the Italian Constitution*, 1950.
CALOGERO, G., "Intorno al concetto di giustizia," *Argomenti*, vol. I, 1941.
CANTRIL, HADLEY, *The Psychology of Social Movements*, 1941.
CARDOZO, BENJAMIN, *The Nature of the Judicial Process*, 1921.
———, *The Growth of the Law*, 1924.
———, *Paradoxes of Legal Science*, 1928.
CARLYLE, SIR R. W., and A. J. CARLYLE, *A History of Medieval Political Theory in the West*, 5 vols.: vol. I, 1903; vol. V, 1928.
CARLYLE, THOMAS, *On Heroes, Hero-Worship and the Heroic in History*, 1841.
———, *Past and Present*, 1843.
CARPENTER, C. R., *A Field Study of the Behavior and Social Relations of Howling Monkeys*, 1934.
———, *A Field Study in Siam of the Behavior and Social Relations of the Gibbon*, 1941.

CARY, M., *A History of Rome down to the Reign of Constantine*, 1935, 1945; 2nd ed., 1954.

CASSINELLI, C. W., *The Politics of Freedom: An Analysis of the Modern Democratic State*, 1961.

CASSIRER, ERNST, *Philosophie der symbolischen Formen*, 3 vols., 1923–1929.

———, *The Question of Jean-Jacques Rousseau* (transl. and ed. P. Gay), 1954.

CATLIN, GEORGE E. G., *The Science and Method of Politics*, 1927.

———, *A Study of the Principles of Politics*, 1930.

———, *A History of the Political Philosophies*, 1950.

———, *On Political Goals*, 1957.

———, *Systematic Politics: Elementa Politica et Sociologica*, 1962.

———, "What Can Philosophy Contribute to the Study of Politics?" Aristotelian Society, *Creativity, Politics and the A Priori*, supplementary vol. XII, pp. 100–117, 1933.

———, "Political Theory: 'What Is It?'" *Political Science Quarterly*, 72:1–29, 1957.

CHABOD, FEDERICO, *Machiavelli and the Renaissance* (transl. D. Moore), 1958.

CHAFEE, ZECHARIAH, JR., *Three Human Rights in the Constitution of 1787*, 1956.

CHAMBERLAIN, NEIL W., *A General Theory of Economic Process*, 1955.

CHARDIN, PIERRE TEILHARD DE, *The Phenomenon of Man*, 1959 (French original 1955).

CHASE, STUART, *The Tyranny of Words*, 1938.

CHEEVER, DANIEL S. and H. FIELD HAVILAND, JR., *Organizing for Peace*, 1954.

CHESTER, D. N., *Central and Local Government: Financial and Administrative Relations*, 1951.

CHILDS, HARWOOD L., *Labor and Capital in National Politics*, 1930.

CHROUST, ANTON-HERMANN, *Socrates: Man and Myth*, 1957.

CHURCHILL, WINSTON S., "Address upon Receiving the Honorary Degree of Doctor of Laws at Harvard University, September 6, 1943," in *The Ceremonies in Honor of the Right Honorable Winston Spencer Churchill*, 1943.

CICERO, *De Republica*.

CLAUDE, INIS L., *Swords into Plowshares*, rev. ed., 1959.

CLAUSEWITZ, KARL VON, *Hinterlassene Werke über Krieg und Kriegführung*, 1832–34 (English *Of War*, 1873, 1908, transl. Graham); 1857 ed. cited in notes.

CLAY, LUCIUS D., *Decision in Germany*, 1950.

CLEVELAND, HARLAN, *The Promise of World Tensions*, 1961.

CLOKIE, HUGH MC D., and J. WILLIAM ROBINSON, *Royal Commissions of Inquiry*, 1937.

COBBAN, ALFRED, *National Self-determination*, 1945.

———, *In Search of Humanity*, 1960.

COHEN, L. JONATHAN, *The Principles of World Citizenship*, 1954.

COHEN, MORRIS R., *Reason and Nature*, 1931.

———, *Law and the Social Order*, 1933.

COKE, SIR EDWARD, *Reports*.

———, *Institutes*.

COKER, FRANCIS W., *Organismic Theories of the State*, 1910.

———, *Recent Political Thought*, 1934.
COLE, KENNETH C., "The Role of the Senate in the Confirmation of Judicial Nominations," *APSR*, 28 (5):875–894, October, 1934.
COLE, R. TAYLOR, *The Canadian Bureaucracy*, 1949.
———, "The West German Federal Constitutional Court: An Evaluation after Six Years," *Journal of Politics*, 20:278ff., 1958.
COLLINGWOOD, R. G., *The Idea of History*, 1946, 1956.
COLSON, ELIZABETH, "The Role of Bureaucratic Norms in African Political Structure," *Proceedings of the American Ethnological Society* (ed. V. F. Ray), pp. 42–50, 1958.
Comité del Gobernador para el Estudio de los Derechos Civiles en Puerto Rico, *Informe al Honorable Gobernador del Estado Libre Associado de Puerto Rico*, 1959.
COMMONS, JOHN R., *The Legal Foundations of Capitalism*, 1924, 1939.
COMTE, AUGUSTE, *Cours de philosophie positive*, 1830–1842.
Conseil d'État, Études et documents, starting 1947.
CONSTANT, BENJAMIN, *Cours de politique constitutionelle*, 1820.
COOKE, JACOB E. (ed.), *The Federalist*, with introd. and notes, 1961.
COON, C. S., *Tribes of the Rif*, 1931.
CORPUZ, O. D., *The Bureaucracy in the Philippines*, 1957.
COSTE, ADOLPHE, *Les principes d'une sociologie objective*, 1899.
COUDENHOVE-KALERGI, COUNT R. N., *Die Europäische Nation*, 1953.
COULANGES: *see* Fustel de.
COULBORN, RUSHTON (ed.), *Feudalism in History*, 1956.
CRAIG, GORDON A., "Delbrück: The Military Historian," in *Makers of Modern Strategy* (ed. E. M. Earle), 1943.
CRANSTON, MAURICE W., *Freedom: A New Analysis*, 1953.
CRISP, L. F., *The Parliamentary Government of the Commonwealth of Australia*, 1949.
CROSSMAN, R. H. S., *Plato Today*, 1937.
DAHL, ROBERT A., *A Preface to Democratic Theory*, 1956.
———, *Who Governs?* 1961.
———, "The Concept of Power," *Behavioral Science*, II:201ff., 1957.
———, "Critique of the Ruling Elite Model," *APSR*, 52(2):463–469, 1958.
———, and C. E. LINDBLOM, *Politics, Economics and Welfare: Planning and Politico-economic Systems Resolved into Basic Social Processes*, 1953.
DAVISON, W. PHILLIPS, *The Berlin Blockade: A Study in Cold War Politics*, 1958.
DAVITT, THOMAS E., *The Elements of Law*, 1959.
DEBRÉ, MICHEL, *La Mort de l'état républicain*, 1947.
———, *La République et ses problèmes*, 1952.
———, *La République et son pouvoir*, 1950.
———, *Les Princes qui nous gouvernent*, 1957.
DE GRAZIA: *see* Grazia.
DE JOUVENEL: *see* Jouvenel.
DELBRÜCK, HANS, *Die Strategie des Perikles erläutert durch die Strategie Friedrichs des Grossen*, 1890.
———, *Geschichte der Kriegskunst im Rahmen der politischen Geschichte*, 7 vols., 1900–1937.

DEMPF, ALOIS, *Sacrum Imperium*, 1929.
DENIFLE, HEINRICH S., *Die Entstehung der Universitäten des Mittelalters bis 1400*, vol. I, 1885, 1956.
DERATHÉ, ROBERT, *Le Rationalisme de Jean-Jacques Rousseau*, 1948.
———, *Jean-Jacques Rousseau et la science politique de son temps*, 1950.
DE TOCQUEVILLE: *see* Tocqueville.
DEUTSCH, KARL, *Nationalism and Social Communication*, 1953.
———, *The Nerves of Government*, 1962.
———, "The Growth of Nations: Some Recurrent Patterns of Political and Social Integration," *World Politics*, 5:168ff., 1953.
——— (ed. and coauthor), *Political Community and the North Atlantic Area: International Organization in the Light of Historical Experience*, 1957.
——— and LEWIS J. EDINGER, *Germany Rejoins the Powers*, 1959.
DEWEY, JOHN, *Experience and Nature*, 1925, 1929.
———, *The Public and Its Problems*, 1927.
———, *The Quest for Certainty*, 1929, 1958.
———, *Theory of Valuation*, 1939.
DE WITT, NICHOLAS, *Soviet Professional Manpower: Its Education, Training and Supply*, 1955.
DICEY, A. V., *Lectures on the Relation between Law and Public Opinion in England during the Nineteenth Century*, 1905.
DIEBOLD, WILLIAM, JR., *The Schuman Plan: A Study in Economic Cooperation, 1950–59*, 1959.
DIESEL, EUGEN, *Germany and the Germans*, 1931.
DIETZE, GOTTFRIED, *The Federalist: A Classic on Federalism and Free Government*, 1960.
———, "America and Europe: Decline and Emergence of Judicial Review," *Virginia Law Review*, 44:1233ff., 1958.
DISTELBARTH, PAUL, *France vivante*, n.d., probably 1936 or 1937.
DJILAS, MILOVAN, *The New Class*, 1957.
DOOB, LEONARD, *Public Opinion and Propaganda*, 1948.
DORN, WALTER L., "The Prussian Bureaucracy in the Eighteenth Century," *Political Science Quarterly*, 46(3):403ff. (part I); 47(1):75–94 (part II); 49(2):259–273 (part III); 1931–1932.
DORPALEN, ANDREAS, *The World of General Haushofer*, 1942.
DREKMEIER, CHARLES, *Kingship and Community in Ancient India*, 1962.
DUBOIS, CORA, *The People of Alor*, 1944.
DÜBLER, ULRICH, *Parteifinanzierung in Deutschland*, 1962.
DUGUIT, LÉON, *L'État: le droit objectif et la loi positive*, 1901.
Duke University, *Commonwealth Perspectives* (ed. N. Mansergh), 1958.
DUNNER, JOSEPH, *The Republic of Israel: Its History and Its Promise*, 1950.
DURKHEIM, ÉMILE, *De la Division du travail social*, 1893, 1932.
———, *Le Suicide*, 1897, 1930.
———, *Les Formes élémentaires de la vie religieuse: Le Système totémique en Australie*, 1912.
DUVERGER, MAURICE, *Les Partis politiques*, 1951 (English ed. 1954).

———, *Méthodes de la science politique*, 1959.

EARLE, EDWARD MEAD (ed.), *Makers of Modern Strategy: Military Thought from Machiavelli to Hitler*, 1943.

EASTON, DAVID, *The Political System: An Inquiry into the State of Political Science*, 1953.

EBBINGHAUS, JULIUS, "Kant's Rechtslehre und die Rechtsphilosophie des Neu-Kantianismus," *Erkenntnis und Verantwortung Festschrift für Theodor Litt*, 1961.

ECKSTEIN, HARRY, "The British Political System," *Patterns of Government* (Beer and Ulam eds.), 1958.

EISELEY, LOREN, *The Immense Journey*, 1946.

EISENSTADT, S. N., *The Political Systems of Empires*, 1963.

———, "Political Struggle in Bureaucratic Societies," *World Politics*, 40(1): 15ff., 1956.

———, "Sociological Aspects of Political Development in Underdeveloped Countries," *Economic Development and Cultural Change*, V:289ff., 1956–57.

———, "Bureaucracy and Bureaucratization," *Current Sociology*, VII(2):99ff., 1958.

———, "Internal Contradictions in Bureaucratic Politics," *Comparative Studies in Society and History*, I(1): 58ff., 1958.

ELIOT, T. S., *Notes toward a Definition of Culture*, 1949.

ELLIOTT, WILLIAM Y., *The Pragmatic Revolt in Politics*, 1928.

———, "The Constitution as the American Social Myth," *The Constitution Reconsidered* (Read and Conyers eds.), 1938.

———, "The Co-organic Concept of Community Applied to Legal Analysis: Constitutional and Totalitarian Systems Compared," *Nomos II*, pp. 50–64, 1959.

ELSBREE, HUGH, "The Political Scientist and the Congress," *Public Policy* 10:332–340, 1960.

EMERSON, RUPERT, *State and Sovereignty in Modern Germany*, 1928.

EMMET, DOROTHY M., *Function, Purpose and Powers*, 1958.

ENGELS, FRIEDRICH, *Die Entwicklung des Sozialismus von der Utopie zur Wissenschaft*, Part III, 1877–1878 (English, *Socialism: Utopian and Scientific*, 1892, reprinted in *Karl Marx: Selected Works* [ed. I. B. Lasker], vol. I, 1946).

———, *Der Ursprung der Familie, des Privateigentums, und des Staats*, 1884; English, *The Origin of the Family, Private Property and the State*, 1948.

ENSOR, R. C. K., *Courts and Judges in France, Germany and England*, 1933.

D'ENTRÈVES, A. P., *Natural Law: An Introduction to Legal Philosophy*, 1951.

———, *La dottrina dello stato*, 1962.

EPICTETUS, *Discourses*, in *The Stoic and Epicurean Philosophers* (ed. W. J. Oates), 1940.

ESCHENBURG, THEODOR, *Staat und Gesellschaft in Deutschland*, 1956.

———, *Ämterpatronage*, 1961.

EVANS-PRITCHARD, E. E., *Social Anthropology*, 1951.

———, *The Divine Kingship among the Shilluk*, 1948.

EYCK, ERICH, *Bismarck und das Deutsche Reich*, 1955.

———, *A History of the Weimar Republic*, 1962.

FAINSOD, MERLE, *How Russia Is Ruled*, 1964.

———, *Smolensk under Soviet Rule*, 1958.

———, *The Twenty-second Party Congress: Problems of Communism*, X, 1961, Special Supplement.

FAIRBANK, JOHN K. (ed.), *Chinese Thought and Institutions*, 1957.

FALLERS, LLOYD A., *Bantu Bureaucracy: A Study of Integration and Conflict in the Political Institutions of an East African People*, 1958.

FAUL, ERWIN, "Soziologie der westdeutschen Wählerschaft," *Wahlen und Wähler*, 1960.

FELD, M. D., "Political Policy and Persuasion: The Role of Communications from Political Leaders," *Conflict Resolution*, II: 78ff., 1958.

FERGUSON, WILLIAM S., *Greek Imperialism*, 1913.

FERRERO, GUGLIELMO, *The Principles of Power*, 1942.

FESLER, JAMES W., *Area and Administration*, 1949.

FIELD, MARK G., *Doctor and Patient in Soviet Russia*, 1957.

FIGGIS, JOHN N., *The Theory of the Divine Right of Kings*, 1896, 1914.

FINER, HERMAN, *The Theory and Practice of Modern Government*, 1932.

FIRTH, R., *We, the Tikopia*, 1936.

FISCHER, GEORGE, *Soviet Opposition to Stalin*, 1952.

FITE, WARNER, *The Platonic Legend*, 1934.

FORD, FRANKLIN L., *Robe and Sword: The Regrouping of French Aristocracy after Louis XIV*, 1953.

FORSTHOFF, ERNST, *Lehrbuch des Verwaltungsrechts*, 1950, 1958.

———, *Zur Problematik der Verfassungsauslegung*, 1961.

FORTES, MEYER, and E. E. EVANS-PRITCHARD (eds.), *African Political Systems*, 1940.

FORTESCUE, SIR JOHN, *The Governance of England: Otherwise Called the Difference Between an Absolute and a Limited Monarchy*, 1476 (ed. Charles Plummer), 1885.

———, *De Laudibus Legum Angliae* (In Praise of Laws of England), 1468–70.

FRAENKEL, OSMOND K., *Our Civil Liberties*, 1944.

FRANK, JEROME, *Law and the Modern Mind*, 1930.

———, *Courts on Trial*, 1949.

FRANKFURTER, FELIX, and JAMES M. LANDIS, *The Business of the Supreme Court: A Study in the Federal Judicial System*, 1928.

FRAZER, J. G., *The New Golden Bough* (ed. T. H. Gaster), 1959.

FREEMAN, EDWARD A., *History of Federal Government from the Foundation of the Achaian League to the Disruption of the United States*, vol. I, 1863.

———, *A History of Federal Government in Greece and Italy* (2nd ed. of the above), 1893.

FREEMAN, HOWARD E., and MORRIS SHOWEL, "Differential Political Influence of Voluntary Association," *Public Opinion Quarterly*, 15: 703ff., 1951.

FREUD, SIGMUND, *Civilization and Its Discontents*, 1930.

———, *The Basic Writings of Sigmund Freud* (ed. A. A. Brill), 1938.

———, *An Outline of Psychoanalysis* (transl. J. Strachey, 1949); originally published in *Internationale Zeitschrift für Psychoanalyse und Imago*, vol. 25, 1940.

FREUND, PAUL A., "Umpiring the Federal System," in *Federalism Mature and Emergent* (ed. Macmahon), 1955.
FRIEDENSBURG, W., *Geschichte der Universität Wittenberg*, 1917.
FRIEDMANN, HERMANN, *Wissenschaft und Symbol*, 1949.
FRIEDMANN, W., *The Crisis of the National State*, 1943.
———, *The Allied Military Government of Germany*, 1947.
FRIEDRICH, PAUL, "Language and Politics in India," *Daedalus*, pp. 543ff., 1962.
FRITZ, KURT VON, and ERNST KAPP (eds.), *Aristotle's Constitution of Athens*, 1950.
FROMM, ERICH, *Escape from Freedom*, 1941.
———, *The Sane Society*, 1955.
FULLER, LON L., *The Law in Quest of Itself*, 1940.
———, "Reason and Fiat in Case Law," *Harvard Law Review*, 59:376ff., 1946.
FURBER, HOLDEN, *Henry Dundas, First Viscount Melville, 1742–1811: Political Manager of Scotland, Statesman, Administrator of British India*, 1931.
FURNISS, EDGAR S., JR., *Weaknesses in French Foreign Policy Making*, 1954.
———, *France, Troubled Ally: De Gaulle's Heritage and Prospects*, 1960.
FUSTEL DE COULANGES, *The Ancient City*, 7th ed., 1889.
GABLENTZ, O. H. VON DER, *Die Versäumte Reform*, 1960.
———, "Autorität und Legitimität im heutigen Staat," *Zeitschrift für Politik*, 5(1):5–27, 1958.
GALBRAITH, JOHN KENNETH, *American Capitalism: The Concept of Countervailing Power*, 1952.
———, "Developed Economic Attitudes and the Underdeveloped Economy," *Public Policy*, 9:73–83, 1959.
GANDHI, M. K., *Gandhi's Autobiography: The Story of my Experiments with Truth*, 1948.
———, *The Gandhi Reader: A Source Book of his Life and Writings* (ed. H. A. Jack), 1956.
GARAUDY, ROGER, *L'Église: Le communisme et les chrétiens*, 1949.
GARCEAU, OLIVER, *The Political Life of the American Medical Association*, 1941.
GARCÍA-GRANADOS, JORGE, *The Birth of Israel*, 1948.
GAULLE, CHARLES DE, *Mémoires de guerre-L'Unité*, 1942–1944, 1956.
GAUS, JOHN M., "A Theory of Organization in Public Administration," in Gaus, White, and Dimock, *The Frontiers of Public Administration*, 1936.
GAUVREAU, ÉMILE, and LESTER COHEN, *Billy Mitchell—Founder of our Airforce and Prophet without Honor*, 1942.
GEHLEN, ARNOLD, *Der Mensch*, 1940 and later.
GELLNER, ERNEST, *Words and Things: A Critical Account of Linguistic Philosophy and a Study in Ideology*, 1959.
General Electric Company, *Report to the Stockholders*, March, 1961.
GENTILE, GIOVANNI, *Che Cosa è il fascismo*, 1925.
GERBRANDY, P. S., *National and International Stability*, 1944.
GERMINO, DANTE L., *The Italian Fascist Party in Power: A Study in Totalitarian Rule*, 1959.
GERTH, HANS H., and C. WRIGHT MILLS, *From Max Weber: Essays in Sociology*, 1946.
GEYL, PIETER, *Napoleon, For and Against*, 1949.

———, *Use and Abuse of History*, 1955.

GIBB, SIR HAMILTON A. R., and HAROLD BOWEN, *Islamic Society and the West*, 2 vols., 1950, 1957.

GIERKE, OTTO VON, *Das Deutsche Genossenschaftsrecht*, 4 vols., 1868–1913.

———, *Johannes Althusius und die Entwicklung der naturrechtlichen Staatstheorien*, 1880; English, *The Development of Political Theory* (transl. B. Freyd), 1939.

GIGON, OLOF A., *Sokrates: Sein Bild in Dichtung und Geschichte*, 1947.

GILBERT, FELIX, *To the Farewell Address: Ideas of Early American Foreign Policy*, 1961.

GIMBEL, JOHN, *A German Community under American Occupation: Marburg, 1945–1952*, 1961.

GLUCKMAN, MAX, "The Kingdom of the Zulu of South Africa," in Fortes and Evans-Pritchard (q.v.), pp. 25ff.

GNEIST, RUDOLF VON, *Der Rechtsstaat und die Verwaltungsgerichte in Deutschland*, 1872, 1879.

GODWIN, WILLIAM, *An Enquiry Concerning Political Justice and Its Influence on General Virtue and Happiness*, 1793, (Repr. and abridged by Preston, 1926).

GOGUEL, FRANÇOIS, "L'Élaboration des institutions de la République dans la Constitution du 4 octobre 1958," *Revue Français de Science Politique*, 9(1):67ff., Mars 1959.

GOLAY, JOHN FORD, *The Founding of the Federal Republic of Germany*, 1958.

GOLDHAMER, HERBERT, and EDWARD A. SHILS, "Types of Power and Status," *American Journal of Sociology*, 45:171ff., 1937.

GOODHART, A. L., *Essays in Jurisprudence and the Common Law*, 1931.

———, *Precedent in English and Continental Law*, 1934.

GOODSPEED, A. L., *The Conspirators: A Study of the Coup d'État*, 1962.

GORCE, M. M., *La France au-dessus des races*, 1934.

GOULD, JOHN, *New England Town Meeting: Safeguard of Democracy*, 1940.

GOULD, WESLEY L., *An Introduction to International Law*, 1957.

GRAZIA, ALFRED DE, *Public and Republic: Political Representation in America*, 1951.

———, "Elements of Social Invention," *The American Behavioral Scientist*, 5:6ff., 1961.

GRAZIA, SEBASTIAN DE, *The Political Community*, 1948.

———, *Errors of Psychotherapy*, 1952.

GREAVES, H. R. G., *The British Constitution*, 1938, 1960.

———, *The Foundations of Political Theory*, 1958.

GREEN, T. H., *Lectures on the Principles of Political Obligation*, 1879–1927.

GREENE, GRAHAM, *The Quiet American*, 1955.

GREENE, WILLIAM C., "Platonism and Its Critics," *Harvard Studies in Classical Philology*, 51:39–71, 1953.

GROB, FRITZ, *The Relativity of War and Peace*, 1949.

GRODZINS, MORTON, "American Political Parties and the American System," *Western Political Quarterly*, 13:974ff., 1960.

GROSSER, ALFRED, *La Démocratie de Bonn*, 1949–1957, 1958.

GROTIUS, HUGO, *De Jure Belli ac Pacis*, 1625.

GUELI, VINCENZO, "Anarchia," *Enciclopedia del diritto*, 1958.
———, "Colpo di Stato," *Enciclopedia del diritto*, 1960.
GULICK, LUTHER H., "Notes on the Theory of Organization," *Papers on the Science of Administration* (ed. Gulick and Urwick), 1937.
GURADZE, HEINZ, *Der Stand der Menschenrechte im Völkerrecht*, 1956.
GUSINDE, MARTIN, *The Yamana*, 1937.
GUTHRIE, WILLIAM K. C., *The Greeks and Their Gods*, 1950, 1955.
HAAS, ERNST B., *The Uniting of Europe: Political, Social and Economic Forces, 1950–1957*, 1958.
———, *Consensus Formation in the Council of Europe*, 1960.
HACKER, ANDREW, *Political Theory: Philosophy, Ideology, Science*, 1961.
———, "Capital and Carbuncles: The Great Books Reappraised," *APSR*, 48:775–786, 1954.
HAINES, CHARLES G., *The Revival of Natural Law Concepts*, 1930.
HAIRE, MASON (ed.), *Modern Organization Theory*, 1959.
HALL, JEROME, *Studies in Jurisprudence and Criminal Theory*, 1958.
HALPERN, BEN, *The Idea of the Jewish State*, vol. I, 1961.
HAMMOND, MASON, *The Augustan Principate in Theory and Practice during the Julio-Claudian Period*, 1933.
HAMON, AUGUSTIN, *Les Maîtres de la France*, 3 vols., 1936–1938.
HAMPE, KARL, in *Abhandlungen der Heidelberger Akademie*, vol. 10, 1923.
HAMPSHIRE, STUART, *Thought and Action*, 1959.
HANSEN, MILLARD, and HENRY WELLS (eds.), "Puerto Rico: A Study in Democratic Development," *Annals of the American Academy of Political and Social Science*, vol. 285, 1953.
HANSON, A. H., "New Thinking on Rates," *Local Government Finance*, 41:5–10, 1957.
HANSON, N. R., *Patterns of Discovery*, 1958.
HARBOLD, WILLIAM H., "The Formulation of Economic Policy in Post-war France," *Public Policy*, 5:125–151, 1954.
HARING, DOUGLAS G., *Personal Character and Cultural Milieu*, 1948.
HARMENING, RUDOLF, *Kommentar zum Lastenausgleichsgesetz*, 1953 and later.
HARNACK, ERNST VON, *Die Praxis der Öffentlichen Verwaltung*, 1936.
HARPER, ROBERT FRANCIS (ed.), *The Code of Hammurabi, King of Babylon*, 1904.
HARRINGTON, JAMES, "A System of Politics," in *Oceana and other Works of James Harrington with an Account of his Life* by John Toland, 1700.
———, *Oceana*, 1656.
HARRISON, MARTIN, "The Constitution of the Fifth Republic: A Commentary," *Political Studies*, 7(1):41ff., 1958.
HARRISON, S. S., *The Most Dangerous Decades: An Introduction to the Comparative Study of Language Policy in Multi-lingual States*, 1957.
HARTLAND, E. S., *Primitive Law*, 1924.
HARTMAN, ROBERT S., "Value, Fact and Science," *Philosophy of Science*, 25:97–108, 1958.
HARTMANN, NICOLAI, *Ethik*, 1926.
HAUSER, RICHARD, *Autorität und Macht*, 1949.
HAYES, CARLTON J. H., *Essays on Nationalism*, 1926.

HEARD, ALEXANDER, *The Costs of Democracy*, 1960, 1962.
HECKSCHER, AUGUST, *A Pattern of Politics*, 1947.
———, *The Public Happiness*, 1962.
HECKSCHER, GUNNAR, *The Study of Comparative Government and Politics*, 1957.
HEGEL, GEORG FRIEDRICH WILHELM, *Wissenschaft der Logik* in *Sämtliche Werke* (ed. Lasson), 1923.
———, *Grundlinien der Philosophie des Rechts*, 1833, 4th ed. (Hoffmeister), 1955.
———, *Die Vernunft in der Geschichte: Einleitung in die Philosophie der Weltgeschichte*, 1822, 1833; new ed. from MS (Georg Lasson), 1920.
———, "Uber die englische Reformbill," in *Berliner Schriften*, 1818–1832 (ed. Hoffmeister, 1956).
———, *The Philosophy of Hegel* (ed. C. J. Friedrich), 1953. (Contains extracts of the above and other writings, in English.)
HEIDEGGER, MARTIN, *Sein und Zeit*, 1927.
———, *Kant und das Problem der Metaphysik*, 1929, 1950.
———, *Holzwege*, 1951. (Note especially the first essay on Hegel's concept of experience.)
HEIDENHEIMER, ARNOLD H., "Federalism and the Party System: The Case of West Germany," *APSR*, vol. 52, 1958.
HEIMANN, EDUARD, *Freedom and Order: Lessons from the War*, 1947.
HEINZE, R., "Auctoritas," *Hermes*, 9(3):348–366, 1925.
HEMPEL, CARL G., "Problems of Concept and Theory Formation in the Social Sciences," I, *Science, Language and Human Rights*, American Philosophical Association, 1952.
———, "Rational Action," *Proceedings and Addresses of the American Philosophical Association*, vol. 35, 1962.
HENDEL, CHARLES W., *Jean-Jacques Rousseau: Moralist*, 1934.
HENNIS, WILHELM, *Meinungsforschung und Repräsentative Demokratie*, 1957.
HERMENS, F. A., *Democracy or Anarchy?* 1941.
———, *Europe Between Democracy and Anarchy*, 1951.
———, *The Representative Republic*, 1958.
HERRING, E. PENDLETON, *Group Representation before Congress*, 1929.
———, *Public Administration and the Public Interest*, 1936.
HERSCH, JEANNE, *Idéologies et réalité*, 1956.
HERTZ, FRIEDRICH, "Werden und Wesen der Nation," *Nation und Nationalität*, 1927.
HEXTER, J. H., *The Reign of King Pym*, 1941.
———, *More's Utopia: The Biography of an Idea*, 1952.
HICKS, GRANVILLE, *Small Town*, 1946.
HICKS, U. K., et al., *Federalism and Economic Growth in Underdeveloped Countries*, 1961.
HIELSCHER, ERWIN, *Der Leidensweg der deutschen Währungsreform*, 1948.
HILGER, I. M., *A Social Study of One Hundred Fifty Chippewa Indian Families*, 1939.
HILL, MARTIN, *Immunities and Privileges of International Officials*, 1947.
HIPPEL, FRITZ VON, *Die Perversion von Rechtsordnungen*, 1955.
HITLER, ADOLF, *Mein Kampf*, 1924 and later.

HOBBES, THOMAS, *Leviathan*, 1651.
———, *De Cive*, 1642.
HOCART, A. M., *Kingship*, 1927.
HOCKING, WILLIAM ERNEST, *Living Religions and a World of Faith*, 1940.
———, *The Coming World Civilization*, 1956.
———, *Strength of Men and Nations*, 1959.
HOEBEL, E. A., *The Political Organization and Law-ways of the Comanche Indians*, 1940.
———, *The Law of Primitive Man*, 1954.
———, "Authority in Primitive Societies," *Nomos I*, pp. 222–234, 1958.
HOFFMANN, STANLEY H., "The French Constitution of 1958," *APSR*, 53(2):332–357, 1959.
——— (ed.), *Contemporary Theory in International Relations*, 1960.
HOHFELD, W. N., *Fundamental Legal Conceptions as Applied in Judicial Reasoning, and other Legal Essays* (ed. W. W. Cook), 1932.
HOLCOMBE, ARTHUR N., *Human Rights in the Modern World*, 1948.
———, *Our More Perfect Union*, 1950.
———, *Organizing Peace in the Nuclear Age*, 1959.
HOLMBERG, ALLAN R., *Nomads of the Long Bow: The Siriono of Eastern Bolivia*, 1950.
HOOKER, RICHARD, *The Laws of Ecclesiastical Polity*, 1594 and later (Modern edition available in Everyman).
HOOTON, EARNEST A., *Why Men Behave Like Apes and Vice Versa*, 1940.
Hoover Institution on *War, Revolution and Peace, France During the German Occupation, 1940–1944*, 3 vols., 1957.
HORN, CARL VICTOR VON, *Beiträge zur Staatslehre St. Augustins*, 1934.
HUGELMANN, KARL GOTTFRIED, *Das Nationalitätenrecht des alten Österreich*, 1934.
HULA, ERICH, "Constitutional and Administrative Readjustments," *Social Research*, 6(2):244–254, 1939.
HUME, DAVID, *A Treatise of Human Nature*, 1739.
———, *Essays Moral, Political and Literary*, 1741.
———, *Essays and Treatises on Several Subjects*, a new edition, 1789.
———, *Hume, Theory of Politics* (ed. Watkins), 1951. A convenient selection from these works.
HUNTER, FLOYD, *Community Power Structure*, 1953.
HUNTER, HOLLAND, *Soviet Transportation Policy*, 1957.
HUNTINGTON, SAMUEL, *The Soldier and the State*, 1957.
———, *The Common Defense: Strategic Programs in National Politics*, 1961.
HUREWITZ, J. C., *The Struggle for Palestine*, 1950.
HUSSERL, EDMUND, *Ideas: General Introduction to Pure Phenomenology*, 1931 (German, 1913).
HUXLEY, ALDOUS, *Brave New World*, 1932.
HYNEMAN, CHARLES S., *The Study of Politics*, 1959.
IKLÉ, CHARLES, and NATHAN LEITES, "Political Negotiation as a Process of Modifying Utilities," *The Journal of Conflict Resolution*, 6:19–28, 1962.
INKELES, ALEX, and R. A. BAUER, *The Soviet Citizen: Daily Life in a Totalitarian Society*, 1959.

JAEGER, WERNER, *Paideia: The Ideals of Greek Culture*, 3 vols. (transl. G. Highet), 1939, 1943, 1944.
———, *Die Theologie der frühen griechischen Denker*, 1958; (English *The Theology of Early Greek Philosophers*, 1947).
JAFFA, HARRY V., "The Case Against Political Theory," *Journal of Politics*, 22:259ff., 1960.
JAMES, WILLIAM, *The Varieties of Religious Experience*, 1902.
JANOWSKY, OSCAR I., *Nationalities and National Minorities*, 1945.
JASPERS, KARL, *Von der Wahrheit*, 1947.
———, *Vom Ursprung und Ziel der Geschichte*, 1949.
———, and KURT ROSSMANN, *Die Idee der Universität*, 1961.
JASZI, O., *The Dissolution of the Hapsburg Monarchy*, 1929.
JAYASWAL, K. P., *Hindu Polity: A Constitutional History of India in Hindu Times*, 1924.
JELLINEK, GEORG, *Allgemeine Staatslehre*, 1st ed., 1900; 3rd ed., 1919.
———, *Die Erklärung der Menschen und Bürgerrechte*, 1895; English *The Declaration of the Rights of Man and Citizen* (transl. Max Farrand), 1901.
JELLINEK, WALTER, *Verwaltungsrecht*, 1928, 1950.
JENNESS, DIAMOND, *The Ojibwa Indians of Parry Island: Their Social and Religious Life*, 1935.
JENNINGS, SIR WILLIAM IVOR, *Parliament*, 1940.
———, *Cabinet Government*, 1936.
JESPERSON, OTTO, *Language: Its Nature, Development and Origin*, 1922.
———, *The Philosophy of Grammar*, 1924.
———, *Mankind: Nation and Individual from a Linguistic Point of View*, 1946.
———, *Language*, 1949.
JOHANNET, R., *Le Principe des nationalités*, new ed., 1927.
JOUVENEL, BERTRAND DE, *Du Pouvoir*, 1945; English *On Power*, 1949.
———, *Du Contrat Social de Jean-Jacques Rousseau*, 1947.
———, *De la Souveraineté*, 1955; English *Sovereignty*, 1957.
———, "Authority: The Efficient Imperative," *Nomos I*, pp. 159–169, 1958.
———, "On the Nature of Political Science," *APSR*, 55:773ff., 1961.
———, "Théorie politique pure," *Revue Française de science politique*, 11:364ff., 1961.
JOUVENEL, ROBERT DE, *La République des camarades*, 1914.
JOYNT, CAREY B., and NICHOLAS RESCHER, "The Problem of Uniqueness in History," *History and Theory*, 1:150ff., 1961.
JUDSON, MARGARET A., *The Crisis of the Constitution*, 1949.
JÜNGER, ERNST, *In Stahlgewittern, ein Kriegstagebuch*, 1926.
———, *An der Zeitmauer*, 1959.
KÄGI, WERNER, *Die Verfassung als rechtliche Grundordnung des Staates*, 1945.
KAFKA, FRANZ, *The Castle*, 1930; Original, 1926.
———, *The Trial*, 1937.
KANT, IMMANUEL, *Kritik der Reinen Vernunft*, 1781; 2nd ed., 1787 (in *Werke*, ed. Cassirer, vol. III).
———, *Kritik der Praktischen Vernunft*, 1788 (*Werke*, vol. V).
———, *Kritik der Urteilskraft*, 1790 (*Werke*, vol. V).

———, *Prolegomena zu einer jeden künftigen Metaphysik*, 1783 (*Werke*, vol. IV).

———, *Grundlegung zur Metaphysik der Sitten*, 1785 (*Werke*, vol. IV, gives 2nd ed. of 1786).

———, *Zum Ewigen Frieden*, 1795 (*Werke*, vol. VII).

———, "Metaphysische Anfangsgründe der Rechtslehre," Part I of *Die Metaphysik der Sitten*, 1797 (*Werke*, vol. VII).

———, *The Philosophy of Kant* (ed. Friedrich), 1949. Contains selections from these and other works.

KANTORWICZ, ERNST, *Kaiser Friedrich II*, 1927.

KAPLAN, MORTON A., *System and Process in International Politics*, 1957.

KARPAT, KEMAL H., *Turkey's Politics: The Transition to a Multiparty System*, 1959.

KATZ, ELIHU, and PAUL F. LAZARSFELD, *Personal Influence: The Part Played by People in the Flow of Mass Communications*, 1955.

KATZENBACH, EDWARD L., JR., "The Horse Cavalry in the Twentieth Century: A Study on Policy Response," *Public Policy*, 8:120–149, 1958.

KAUFMANN, KARLHEINZ, et al., *Kandidaten zum Bundestag*, 1961.

KAUFMANN, WALTER A., *Nietzsche: Philosopher, Psychologist, Anti-Christ*, 1950.

KEESING, FELIX M., *Culture Change: An Analysis and Bibliography to 1952*, 1953.

KEETON, GEORGE W., *The Passing of Parliament*, 1952.

KELSEN, HANS, *General Theory of Law and State*, 1945.

———, *What is Justice? Justice, Law and Politics in the Mirror of Science*, 1957.

KENYATTA, JOMO, *Facing Mount Kenya*, 1938, 1953.

KERN, FRITZ, *Aśoka: Kaiser und Missionar*, 1956.

KESSEL, WOLFGANG, "Auctoritas und potestas als Ordnungsgrundlagen der Demokratie," *Archiv für Rechts- und Sozialphilosophie*, vol. 14, no. 2, 1959.

KEY, V. O., JR., *Southern Politics*, 1949.

———, *Politics, Parties and Pressure Groups*, 4th ed., 1958.

———, *Public Opinion and American Democracy*, 1961.

KEYSERLING, HERMANN, *Das Reisetagebuch eines Philosophen*, 2 vols., 1922.

KIMBLE, GEORGE H. T., *Tropical Africa*, 2 vols., 1960.

KIPNIS, DAVID, "The Effects of Leadership Style and Leadership Power upon the Inducement of an Attitude Change," *Journal of Abnormal and Social Psychology*, 57:173ff., 1958.

KIRCHHEIMER, OTTO, "France from the Fourth to the Fifth Republic," *Social Research*, 25(4):379–414, 1958.

———, *Political Justice*, 1961.

KISSINGER, HENRY A., *A World Restored: Metternich, Castlereagh and the Problem of Peace, 1812–22*, 1957.

———, *Nuclear Weapons and Foreign Policy*, 1957.

———, *The Necessity for Choice: Prospects of American Foreign Policy*, 1961.

KITTREDGE, TRACY BARRETT, *Naval Lessons of the Great War*, 1921.

KLIUCHEVSKI, V. O., *A History of Russia*, 5 vols., 1911–1931 (Russian original 1904–1921).

KLUCKHOHN, CLYDE, *A Mirror for Man*, 1949.

———, "Values and Value-orientations in the Theory of Action: An Exploration in Definition and Classification," *Toward a General Theory of Action* (ed. Parsons and Shils), pp. 388–433, 1951.

KNORR, KLAUS E., *British Colonial Theories, 1570–1850,* 1944.

KÖHLER, WOLFGANG, *The Mentality of Apes* (transl. Ella Winter), 1925, 1927.

KOFFKA, K., *Principles of Gestalt Psychology,* 1935.

KOHN, HANS, *Revolutions and Dictatorships,* 1939.

———, *The Idea of Nationalism,* 1944.

———, *Prophets and Peoples: Studies in Nineteenth-Century Nationalism,* 1946.

———, *Pan-Slavism: Its History and Ideology,* 1953.

———, *Der Schweizerische Nationalgedanke,* 1955.

———, *The Hapsburg Empire, 1804–1918,* 1961.

KOJÈVE, ALEXANDRE, *Introduction à la lecture de Hegel,* 1947.

KOTOWSKI, GEORG, "Der Kampf um die Berliner Universität," *Columbia Festschrift der Freien Universität,* n.d., probably 1958.

KRABBE, H., *Die Lehre der Rechts-Souveränität,* 1906.

———, *The Modern Idea of the State,* 1922 (German original *Die Moderne Staatsidee,* 1919).

KRAINES, OSCAR, *Government and Politics in Israel,* 1961.

KRIGE, E. J. and J. D. KRIGE, *The Realm of a Rain-Queen: A Study of the Pattern of Lovedu Society,* 1943.

KROCKOW, CHRISTIAN, GRAF VON, *Die Entscheidung: Eine Untersuchung über Ernst Jünger, Carl Schmitt, Martin Heidegger,* 1958.

KROEBER, A. L., *Anthropology,* rev. ed., 1948.

———, *Anthropology Today,* 1953.

———, "Caste," *ESS.*

———, "Zuni Kin and Clan," *Anthropological Papers of the American Museum of Natural History,* 18:39–204, 1917.

———, and CLYDE KLUCKHOHN, *Culture: A Critical Review of Concepts and Definitions,* 1952.

KROPOTKIN, P. A., *Paroles d'un révolté,* 1884.

KRÜGER, PAUL, *Geschichte der Quellen und Literatur des Römischen Rechts,* 1888.

KRUSE, F. V., *The Community of the Future,* 1952.

KRUTCH, JOSEPH WOOD, *Human Nature and the Human Condition,* 1959.

KUNKEL, W., *Römische Rechtsgeschichte,* 1947, 1956.

Labor Party (British), *Report of Annual Conference,* 1949, 1959, 1960.

LABROUSSE, ERNEST, *La Société du XVIIIe siécle devant la revolution,* 1953.

LADD, JOHN, "The Concept of Community: A Logical Analysis," *Nomos II,* pp. 269–293, 1959.

LAMB, H., *Hannibal: One Man Against Rome,* 1958.

LANDES, RUTH, *Ojibwa Sociology,* 1937.

LANE, ROBERT, *The Liberties of Wit,* 1962.

LANGER, SUSANNE K., *Philosophy in a New Key,* 1942.

LASKI, HAROLD J., *Studies in the Problem of Sovereignty,* 1917.

———, *The Foundations of Sovereignty, and other Essays,* 1921.

———, *Democracy in Crisis,* 1933.

———, *Parliamentary Government in England*, 1938.
LASLETT, PETER (ed.), *Philosophy, Politics and Society*, 1956.
LASSWELL, HAROLD D., *Psychopathology and Politics*, 1930.
———, *Politics: Who Gets What, When and How*, 1936, 1958.
———, *Power and Personality*, 1948.
———, *National Security and Individual Freedom*, 1950.
———, "Compromise," *ESS.*
———, "Morale," *ESS.*
———, "Current Studies of the Decision Process: Automation versus Creativity," *Western Political Quarterly*, 8:381–399, 1955.
———, R. D. CASEY, and B. L. SMITH, *Propaganda and Promotional Activities*, 1935, 1946.
———, with DOROTHY BLUMENFELD, *World Revolutionary Propaganda*, 1939.
———, NATHAN LEITES, and others, *Language of Politics*, 1949.
———, and A. KAPLAN, *Power and Society*, 1950.
LATHAM, EARL, *Political Theories of Monopoly Power*, 1957.
LATOURETTE, KENNETH SCOTT, *The Chinese: Their History and Culture*, 1934, 1946.
LAVAU, G. E., *Partis politiques et réalités sociales*, 1953.
LEFEBVRE, GEORGES, *Napoléon*, 1935.
LEIBHOLZ, GERHARD, *Das Wesen der Repräsentation unter besonderer Berücksichtigung das Repräsentativsystems*, 1929.
———, *Der Strukturwandel der Modernen Demokratie*, 1952.
———, "Verfassungsrechtliche Sicherung und innere Ordnung der Parteien," *Verhandlungen des 38. deutschen Juristentages*, 1917.
LEIGHTON, ALEXANDER H., *The Governing of Man*, 1945.
LEINHARDT, G., "The Shilluck of the Upper Nile," in *African Worlds* (ed. D. Forde), 1959.
LEITES, NATHAN, *A Study of Bolshevism*, 1953.
LENIN, V. I., *Sochinenya*, 3rd ed., 1935.
———, *What Is To Be Done?* 1902.
———, *Selected Works*, 12 vols., 1943.
LEONI, BRUNO, *Freedom*, 1961.
LERNER, DANIEL, and H. D. LASSWELL (eds.), *The Policy Sciences: Recent Developments in Scope and Method*, 1951.
LERNER, MAX, *Ideas Are Weapons*, 1939.
LÉVI-STRAUSS, CLAUDE, *La Vie familiale et sociale des indiens Nambikuara*, 1948.
LÉVY-BRUHL, LUCIEN, *La Philosophie d'Auguste Comte*, 1900.
LEWIS, GEORGE C., *An Essay on the Influence of Authority*, 1849.
LEWIS, JOHN D., and OSCAR JÁSZI, *Against the Tyrant: The Tradition and Theory of Tyrannicide*, 1957.
LEWIS, OSCAR, *Village Life in Northern India*, 1958.
LINDSAY, A. D., *The Modern Democratic State*, vol. I, 1943.
LINSKY, LEONARD, *Semantics and the Philosophy of Language*, 1952.
LINTON, RALPH, *The Material Culture and Archeology of the Marquesas Islands*, 1925.
———, *The Tree of Culture*, 1955.

———, "Marquesan Culture," in *The Individual and His Society* (ed. A. Kardiner), pp. 138–196, 1939.
LIN YUTANG, *The Wisdom of Confucius*, 1938.
LIPPINCOTT, BENJAMIN E., *Victorian Critics of Democracy*, 1938.
LIPPMANN, WALTER, *Public Opinion*, 1922.
———, *The Public Philosophy*, 1955.
LIPSET, SEYMOUR MARTIN, *Political Man: The Social Bases of Politics*, 1960.
———, *Party Systems and Representation of Social Groups*, 1961.
LIPSON, LESLIE, "The Two-Party System in British Politics," *APSR*, 47:337–358, 1953.
———, "Common Ground and Emerging Conflicts between the British Parties," *Political Quarterly*, 27:182ff., 1956.
———, "Le Système des partis politiques en Suisse," *Revue française de science politique*, 6:813ff., 1956.
———, "Party Systems in the United Kingdom and the Older Commonwealths: Causes, Resemblances and Variations," *Political Studies*, 7:12ff., 1959.
LISKA, JIRI (GEORGE), *International Equilibrium: A Theoretical Essay on the Politics and Organization of Security*, 1957.
LITCHFIELD, EDWARD H. (ed.), "Emergence of German Governments" in *Governing Postwar Germany* (ed. Litchfield), 1953.
LITTLE, K. L., *The Mende of Sierra Leone*, 1951.
LIU, JAMES T. C., "Eleventh-Century Chinese Bureaucrats: Some Historical Classifications and Behavioral Types," *Administrative Science Quarterly*, 4:207ff., 1959.
LIVINGSTON, W. S., "Minor Parties and Minority M.P.'s 1945–1955," *Western Political Quarterly*, 12:1017ff., 1959.
———, "The Decline of Party Politics in Britain," *Texas Quarterly*, 2:78ff., 1959.
LLEWELLYN, KARL N., *The Bramblebush*, 1930, 1951.
———, *Präjudizienrecht und Rechtsprechung im Amerika*, 1933.
———, *The Common Law Tradition*, 1960.
———, *Jurisprudence: Realism in Theory and Practice*, 1962.
———, and E. ADAMSON HOEBEL, *The Cheyenne Way: Conflict and Case Law in Primitive Jurisprudence*, 1941.
LLEWELLYN, RICHARD, *A Man in a Mirror*, 1961.
LOCKE, JOHN, *Essays on the Laws of Nature*, 1660's; (ed. W. von Leyden), 1954.
———, *An Essay concerning Human Understanding*, 1687.
———, *Two Treatises on Government*, 1690. (A critical modern edition with an introduction has been published by Peter Laslett, 1960.)
———, *A Letter Concerning Toleration*, 1690.
LÖWENSTEIN, KARL, *Die Monarchie im Modernen Staat*, 1952.
———, *Political Power and the Governmental Process*, 1957.
———, "Justice," in *Governing Postwar Germany* (ed. Litchfield), 1953.
LÖWITH, KARL, *Von Hegel bis Nietzsche*, 1939, 1950.
———, *Meaning in History*, 1949; German ed., enlarged, 1953.
LONG, NORTON E., *The Polity*, 1962.
LOVEDAY, ALEXANDER, *Reflections on International Administration*, 1956.

LOVEJOY, ARTHUR O., *The Great Chain of Being*, 1936.
LOWIE, R. H., *The Origin of the State*, 1927.
———, *The Crow Indians*, 1935.
LUCE, ROBERT, *Legislative Procedure*, 1922.
LUETHY, HERBERT, *À l'Heure de son clocher: Essai sur la France*, 1955.
LUGARD, SIR FREDERICK D. (later Lord), *The Dual Mandate in British Tropical Africa*, 1922.
LYND, ROBERT S., *Knowledge for What? The Place of Social Sciences in American Culture*, 1939.
———, and HELEN M. LYND, *Middletown: A Study in Contemporary American Culture*, 1929.
———, *Middletown in Transition: A Study in Cultural Conflicts*, 1937.
MAASS, ARTHUR A., *Muddy Waters: The Army Engineers and the Nation's Rivers*, 1951.
———, (ed.), *Area and Power*, 1959.
MABBOTT, J. O., "Moral Rules," *Proceedings of the British Academy*, 39:97ff., 1953.
MACHIAVELLI, NICCOLÒ, *Discorsi*, 1550. (Note also the fine annotated edition in English by Walker, 1950.)
———, *The Prince*.
———, *Libre dell'arte della guerra*, 1521.
MACIVER, ROBERT, *Social Causation*, 1942.
———, *The Web of Government*, 1947.
MACKINDER, HALFORD, *Britain and the British Seas*, 1902; reprint, 1930 from 2nd ed., 1907.
———, *Democratic Ideals and Reality*, 1919.
MACMAHON, ARTHUR W. (ed.), *Federalism: Mature and Emergent*, 1955.
MACRIDIS, ROY, *The De Gaulle Republic: Quest for Unity*, 1960.
MADARIAGA, SALVADOR DE, *Portrait of Europe*, 1950.
MAHAN, ALFRED THAYER, *The Influence of Sea Power upon History, 1660–1783*, 1890.
———, *The Influence of Sea Power upon the French Revolution and Empire, 1793–1812*, 1892.
———, *Sea Power in Its Relation to the War of 1812*, 1905.
MAILER, NORMAN, *The Naked and the Dead*, 1948.
MAINE, SIR HENRY S., *Ancient Law* (introd. T. W. Dwight), 1861, 1873.
MAIR, L. P., *An African People in the Twentieth Century*, 1934.
MAISTRE, COMTE JOSEPH DE, *Considérations sur la France*, 1796, 1845.
———, *Essai sur le principe générateur des constitutions politiques*, 1814.
———, *Du Pape*, 1819, 1843.
MALAPARTE, CURZIO, *Coup d'état: The Technique of Revolution* (transl. Sylvia Saunders), 1932.
MALAVIYA, H. D., *Village Panchayats in India*, 1956.
MALINOWSKI, B., *Argonauts of the Western Pacific*, 1922.
———, *Crime and Custom in Savage Society*, 1926.
———, *Coral Gardens and Their Magic*, 2 vols., 1935.
———, *The Dynamics of Culture Change*, 1945.
———, *A Scientific Theory of Culture*, 1944.

———, "Magic, Science and Religion," in *Science, Religion and Reality* (ed. J. Needham), 1925.

MANGOLDT, H. VON, *Das Bonner Grundgesetz* (2nd ed. by F. Klein, 1955).

MANGONE, GERARD J., *The Idea and Practice of World Government*, 1951.

MANNHEIM, KARL, *Ideology and Utopia*, 1936, 1953. (Contains translation of original German of 1929, chaps. II–IV, an article of 1931, and a new introduction.)

———, *Man and Society in an Age of Reconstruction*, 1940.

———, *Diagnosis of Our Time*, 1943.

MANSERGH, NICHOLAUS (ed.), *Commonwealth Perspectives* (chap. I by Mansergh), 1958.

MANUEL, FRANK E., *The Realities of American-Palestine Relations*, 1949.

———, *The New World of Henri Saint-Simon*, 1956.

MARCH, JAMES G., "An Introduction to the Theory and Measurement of Influence," *APSR*, 49:431ff., 1955.

———, "Influence Measurement in Experimental and Semi-experimental Groups," *Sociometry*, 19:260ff., 1956.

MARSHALL, ALFRED, *Principles of Economics*, 1890; 8th ed., 1922.

MARX, KARL, *Kritik der Hegelschen Rechtsphilosophie*, 1844.

———, *La Misère de la Philosophie*, 1847 (English *The Poverty of Philosophy*, 1936).

———, *Zur Kritik der Politischen Ökonomie*, 1859, preface; (transl. English N. I. Stone), *A Contribution to the Critique of Political Economy*, 1904. There also, Appendix I, "Introduction to the Critique of Political Economy."

———, and FRIEDRICH ENGELS, *Manifest der Kommunistischen Partei*, 1848; English ed. 1888, in *Karl Marx: Selected Works* (ed. I. B. Lasker), vol. I, 1946.

MASTE, ERNST, *Die Republik der Nachbarn: Die Nachbarschaft und der Staatsgedanke Artur Mahrauns*, 1957.

MATTEI, RODOLFO DE, *La politica di Campanella*, 1927.

———, *Studi Campanelliani*, 1934.

MC CLOSKEY, ROBERT G., *The American Supreme Court*, 1960.

MC ILWAIN, CHARLES HOWARD, *Constitutionalism, Ancient and Modern*, 1940.

———, *The Growth of Political Thought in the West: From the Greeks to the End of the Middle Ages*, 1932.

MC KEON, RICHARD, "Aristotle's Conception of Moral and Political Philosophy," *Ethics*, vol. 51, 1941.

———, "The Development and the Significance of the Concept of Responsibility," *Revue internationale de philosophie*, 39:1–30, 1957.

MC RAE, KENNETH DOUGLAS (ed.), *Jean Bodin, The Six Bookes of the Commonweale*, 1962.

MC WHINNEY, EDWARD, *Judicial Review in the English Speaking World*, 1960.

———, *Constitutionalism in Germany and the Federal Constitutional Court*, 1962.

———, *Comparative Federalism: States Rights and National Power*, 1962.

———, "The German Federal Constitutional Court and the Communist Party Decision," *Indiana Law Journal*, 32:295–312, 1957.

———, "The Power Value and Its Public Law Gradations: A Preliminary Excursus," *Journal of Public Law*, 9:43ff., 1960.

MEAD, GEORGE HERBERT, *Mind, Self and Society*, 1934.

MEAD, MARGARET, *Coming of Age in Samoa*, 1928.

———, *The Social Organization of Manua*, 1930.

——— (ed.), *Cooperation and Competition among Primitive Peoples*, 1937.

———, *Male and Female*, 1949.

———, "The Role of the Individual in Samoan Culture," *Journal of the Royal Anthropological Institute*, 58:481ff., 1928.

MEHNERT, KLAUS, *Stalin versus Marx: The Stalinist Historical Doctrine*, 1952.

MEHREN, ARTHUR T. VON, "The Judicial Process in the United States and Germany," *Festschrift für Ernst Rabel*, Band I, 1954.

MEINECKE, FRIEDRICH, *Weltbürgertum und Nationalstaat*, 1908; 7th ed. 1928.

———, *Die Idee der Staatsräson in der neueren Geschichte*, 1924, 1925; English *Machiavellism* (transl. D. Scott), 1957.

MEISEL, JAMES H., *The Myth of the Ruling Class*, 1958.

MELADY, THOMAS PATRICK, *Profiles of African Leaders*, 1961.

MERING, OTTO VON, *A Grammar of Human Values*, 1961.

MERKL, PETER, *The Origin of the West German Republic*, 1963.

MERRIAM, CHARLES E., *The Making of Citizens*, 1931.

———, *Political Power: Its Composition and Incidence*, 1934.

———, *Systematic Politics*, 1945.

MERTON, ROBERT K., *Social Theory and Social Structure*, 1949, 1958.

——— (ed.) et al., *Reader in Bureaucracy*, 1952.

———, L. BROOM, and L. S. COTTRELL (eds.), *Sociology Today: Problems and Prospects*, 1959.

———, "Patterns of Influence: A Study of Interpersonal Influence and of Communications Behavior in a Local Community," *Communications Research*, 1948–49, pp. 180ff.

MESNARD, PIERRE, *L'Essor de la philosophie politique au XVIe siècle*, 1935.

MESSING, E. D., *The Highland Plateau Amara of Ethiopia*, 1957.

MEYER, ALFRED G., *Marxism: The Unity of Theory and Practice*, 1954.

———, *Leninism*, 1957.

MEYER, EDUARD, *Geschichte des Altertums*, 5 vols., 1884–1902; vol. I, 3rd ed. 1910–1913; vols. II–III, 2nd ed. 1928–1937.

MEYNAUD, JEAN, *Introduction à la science politique*, 1959.

MICHELS, ROBERT, *Zur Sociologie des Parteiwesens in der modernen Demokratie*, 1911 (English transl. E. Paul and C. Paul, 1915).

———, *Notes sur les moyens de constater la nationalité*, 1917.

———, *Sozialismus und Fascismus in Italien*, 1925.

———, *Corso di sociologia politica*, 1927; English *First Lectures in Political Sociology* (transl. A. de Grazia), 1949.

———, *Der Patriotismus*, 1929 (English transl. included in previous item).

MIDDLETON, JOHN, and DAVID TAIT (eds.), *Tribes Without Rulers: Studies in African Segmentary Systems*, 1958.

MILL, JAMES A., *Essay on Government*, 1820.

MILL, JOHN STUART, *On Liberty*, 1859.

———, *Considerations on Representative Government*, 1860.
———, *Utilitarianism*, 1863.
MILLER, DELBERT C., "Decision Making Cliques in Community Power Structures: A Comparative Study," *Journal of Sociology*, 44:299–310, 1958–59.
MILLER, J. D. B., *Australian Government and Politics*, 1954, 1959.
———, *The Commonwealth in the World*, 1958.
MILLETT, JOHN D., "Political Science as a Discipline: A Statement, . . ." *APSR*, 56:417ff., 1962.
MILLS, C. WRIGHT, *The Power Elite*, 1956.
MOGI, SOBEI, *The Problem of Federalism: A Study in the History of Political Theory*, 1931.
MOMMSEN, THEODOR, *Römische Geschichte*, 1854–1856.
———, *Römische Forschungen*, 2 vols., 1864–1879.
———, *Römisches Staatsrecht*, 1871–1888.
MOMMSEN, W. G., *Max Weber und die Deutsche Politik*, 1959.
MONTESQUIEU, CHARLES LOUIS DE, *Lettres Persanes*, 1721.
———, *Considérations sur les causes de la grandeur des romains et de leur décadence*, 1734.
———, *De l'esprit des lois*, 1748, in *Oeuvres Complètes*, 1835.
MONTGOMERY, JOHN D., *Forced to Be Free*, 1957.
———, et al., *Cases in Vietnamese Administration*, 1959.
———, "Field Organization, Administrative Relationships and Foreign Aid Policies," *Public Policy*, 10:297–331, 1960.
———, "Public Interest in the Ideologies of National Development," *Nomos V*, pp. 218ff., 1961.
MONYPENNY, WILLIAM F., and G. E. BUCKLE, *The Life of Benjamin Disraeli*, 6 vols., 1910–1920.
MOORE, BARRINGTON, JR., *Terror and Progress USSR: Some Sources of Change and Stability in the Soviet Union*, 1954.
———, *Political Power and Social Theory*, 1958.
MOORE, CLEMENT H., "The National Party: A Tentative Model," *Public Policy*, 10:239ff., 1960.
———, "The Neo-Destour Party of Tunisia: A Structure for Democracy?" *World Politics*, 14:461ff., 1962.
MORGAN, DONALD, *The Responsibility of Congress for Considering Constitutional Questions and the Manner of Its Exercise: The Case of General Bradley*, n.d., probably 1959.
MORGAN, GEORGE ALLEN, JR., *What Nietzsche Means*, 1941.
MORGAN, L. H., *League of the Ho-De-No-Sau-Nee, or Iroquois*, vol. I, 1851, 1901.
MORGENTHAU, HANS J., *Politics Among Nations*, 1948, 1954.
———, *In Defense of the National Interest*, 1951.
MORISON, ELTING E., *Admiral Sims and the Modern American Navy*, 1942.
MORISON, S. E., *History of the United States Navy*, vol. 1, *The Battle of the Atlantic*, 1947. (Introduction by Commander Knox discusses the Billy Mitchell incident.)
MORLEY, JOHN VISCOUNT, *On Compromise*, 1874, 1921.
MORRISON, HERBERT, *Government and Parliament*, 1954, 1956.

MORSTEIN-MARX, FRITZ, *Government in the Third Reich*, 1936.
———, *The Administrative State*, 1957.
MOSCA, GAETANO, *The Ruling Class*, 1939; Italian original *Elementi di scienza politica*, 1896.
MOULIN, LEO, "L'assistance technique sous l'aspect psychologique et humain," *La Fonction publique internationale*, International Civil Service Training Association, 1958.
MÜLLER, MARIANNE, and EGON E. MÜLLER, *Stürmt die Festung Wissenschaft*, 1953.
MULLER, H. J., *The Uses of the Past*, 1952.
———, *Freedom in the Ancient World*, 1961.
———, "Science Under Soviet Totalitarianism," *Totalitarianism* (ed. C. J. Friedrich), 1954.
MUMFORD, LEWIS, *The Story of Utopias*, 1922.
———, *The City in History*, 1961.
———, *The Culture of Cities*, 1938.
MURDOCK, GEORGE PETER, *Africa: Its People and Their Culture History*, 1959.
———, "World Ethnographic Sample," *American Anthropology*, 59:664–687, 1957.
MURPHY, GARDNER (ed.), *Human Nature and Enduring Peace*, 1945.
MUSIL, ALOIS, *The Manners and Customs of the Rwala Beddouins*, 1928.
MUSIL, ROBERT, *Der Mann ohne Eigenschaften*, 1931; final complete ed. 1952.
MUSSOLINI, BENITO, *La dottrina del Fascismo*, 1933.
MYRDAL, GUNNAR, *The Political Element in the Development of Economic Theory*, 1929, 1953.
———, *An American Dilemma*, 1944.
NADEL, S. F., *A Black Byzantium*, 1942, 1961.
NAMIER, LEWIS B., *The Structure of Politics at the Accession of George III*, 1929.
NELSON, BENJAMIN, "Community: Dreams and Realities," *Nomos II*, pp. 135–151, 1959.
NEUHOFF, HANS, "Zehn Jahre Lastenausgleichspolitik: Bericht das Lastenausgleichsausschusses des BVD aus Anlass seiner Zehnjährigen Bestehens," in *Vertriebenen-Korrespondenz*, Band 9, 1958.
NEUMANN, FRANZ L., *The Structure and Practice of National Socialism: Behemoth*, 1942.
———, "Approaches to the Study of Political Power: A Contribution to the Sociology of Leadership," *Political Science Quarterly*, 65:161ff., 1950.
———, "Federalism and Freedom–a Critique," in *Federalism: Mature and Emergent* (ed. Macmahon), 1955.
NEUMANN, SIGMUND, "Toward a Theory of Political Parties," *World Politics*, 6:549ff., 1954.
——— (ed.), *Modern Political Parties*, 1956.
NEUNREITHER, KARLHEINZ, *Der Bundestag zwischen Politik und Verwaltung*, 1959.
———, "Federalism and West German Bureaucracy," *Political Studies*, 6:233–245, 1958.
———, "Politics and Bureaucracy in the West German Bundesrat," *APSR*, 53:713ff., 1959.

NEWMAN, K. J., *Essays on the Constitution of Pakistan*, 1956.
———, "Basic Democracy as an Experiment," *Political Studies*, 10:46ff., 1962.
NICOLSON, HAROLD, *Peacemaking*, 1919, 1933.
NIEBUHR, REINHOLD, *The Structure of Nations and Empires*, 1959.
NIETZSCHE, FRIEDRICH, *Der Wille zur Macht*, 1887.
———, *Also sprach Zarathustra*, 1882.
NILSSON, MARTIN P., *Griechischer Glaube*, 1950.
NOCK, ARTHUR D., *Conversion*, 1933.
Nomos: Yearbook of the American Society for Political and Legal Philosophy: vol. I, "Authority," 1958; vol. II, "Community," 1959; vol. III, "Responsibility," 1960; vol. IV, "Liberty," 1962; vol. V., "The Public Interest," 1962; vol. VI, "Justice," 1963.
NOON, J. A., *Law and Government of the Grand River Iroquois*, 1949.
NORTHROP, F. S. C., *The Meeting of East and West*, 1946.
———, *The Complexity of Legal and Ethical Experience*, 1959.
Northwestern University; *see* Young, R. A. (ed.), 1958.
NOTH, MARTIN, *Die Welt des Alten Testaments*, 2nd ed. 1953.
NOWELL-SMITH, P. H., *Ethics*, 1954, 1959.
———, et al., "Politics, Psychology and Art," *Symposium: Science and Politics, Aristotelian Society*, Supplement, vol. 33, 1949.
NYERERE, JULIUS, "One Party Rule," *Atlas*, 3:185ff., 1962.
OAKESHOTT, MICHAEL, *Experience and Its Modes*, 1933.
———, *The Voice of Poetry in the Conversation of Mankind*, 1959.
———, *Rationalism in Politics and Other Essays*, 1962.
O'CONNELL, D. P., *The Law of State Succession*, 1956.
ODEGARD, PETER H., and ALAN BARTH, "Millions for Defense," *Public Opinion Quarterly*, 5:399ff., 1941.
OGDEN, C. K., and I. A. RICHARDS, *The Meaning of Meaning*, 1923, 1938.
OLIPHANT, HERMAN, "A Return to Stare Decisis," *American Law School Review*, 6:215ff., 1928.
OLIVER, DOUGLAS L., *A Solomon Island Society*, 1955.
OLIVIER-MARTIN, FRANÇOIS JEAN MARIE, *Histoire du droit français des origines à la revolution*, 1948, 1951.
OPPENHEIM, FELIX E., *Dimensions of Freedom*, 1961.
ORLINSKY, HARRY M., *Ancient Israel*, 1954.
ORTEGA Y GASSET, JOSÉ, *The Revolt of the Masses*, 1932.
ORWELL, GEORGE, *1984*, 1949.
OSGOOD, ROBERT E., *Limited War: The Challenge to American Strategy*, 1957.
OSTROGORSKII, MOISEI IAKOVLEVICH, *Democracy and the Organization of Political Parties*, 1902.
OTTO, RUDOLF, *Das Heilige*, 1917, 1929.
OVERACKER, LOUISE, *Money in Elections*, 1932.
———, a series of annual reports on primary elections from 1930 to 1939 in *APSR*, vols. 26, 28, 30, 34.
PAINE, THOMAS, *The Age of Reason*, 1794.
———, *Life and Works*, 10 vols., 1925.
PALADINO, G., *T. Campanella: La città del sole*, 1920.

PARETO, VILFREDO, *The Mind and Society* (transl. Livingston), 4 vols., 1935 (Italian original *Trattato di sociologia generale*, 1923).
PARKINSON, C. NORTHCOTE, *Parkinson's Law*, 1957.
PARRINGTON, VERNON, *Main Currents in American Thought*, 3 vols., 1927–1930.
PARRY, CLIVE, *Nationality and Citizenship Laws of the Commonwealth and of the Republic of Ireland*, 1957.
PARSONS, TALCOTT, *The Structure of Social Action*, 1937.
———, *The Social System*, 1951.
———, *Structure and Process in Modern Societies*, 1960.
———, "The Principal Structures of Community: A Sociological View," *Nomos II*, pp. 152–199, 1959.
———, and EDWARD A. SHILS (eds.), *Toward a General Theory of Action*, 1951.
PASCAL, BLAISE, *Pensées*, 1670 (English ed. with introd. by Saxe Commins, 1941).
PEIRCE, CHARLES S., *Chance, Love and Logic*, 1923.
PELTASON, JOHN, *Fifty-eight Lonely Men*, 1961.
PELZEL, JOHN C., "Notes on the Chinese Bureaucracy," in V. E. Ray (ed.), 1958.
PERELMAN, CHAIM, *De la Justice*, 1945.
———, "La Justice," *Revue internationale de philosophie*, rl:344ff., 1957.
———, and L. OLBRECHTS-TYTECA, *La Nouvelle rhetorique: Traité de l'argumentation*, 1958.
PERRY, RALPH BARTON, *General Theory of Value*, 1926.
PETEGORSKY, DAVID W., *Left-wing Democracy in the English Civil War: A Study of the Social Philosophy of Gerrard Winstanley*, 1940.
PETTEE, GEORGE S., *The Process of Revolution*, 1938.
PFISTER, BERNHARD, and GERHARD HILDEMANN (eds.), *Widerstandsrecht und Grenzen der Staatsgewalt*, 1956.
PIERSON, GEORGE WILSON, *Tocqueville and Beaumont in America*, 1938.
PIPES, RICHARD, *The Formation of the Soviet Union*, 1954.
PIRENNE, HENRI, *Les Villes et les institutions urbaines*, 1925; English *Medieval Cities*, 2nd ed., 1939.
———, *Mahomet et Charlesmagne*, 10th ed. 1937 (transl. B. Miall, 1939).
PLAMENATZ, JOHN, *The English Utilitarians*, 1949.
PLATO, *The Republic*.
———, *Statesman*.
———, *The Laws*.
POLANYI, MICHAEL, *The Logic of Liberty*, 1951.
———, *Personal Knowledge*, 1958.
POLIN, RAYMOND, *La Création des valeurs*, 1944; 2nd ed., 1952.
POPITZ, HEINRICH, *Der entfremdete Mensch*, 1953.
POPPER, KARL, *The Open Society and Its Enemies*, 1945.
———, *The Poverty of Historicism*, 1957.
———, *The Logic of Scientific Discovery*, 1959 (original German 1935, much briefer).
POUND, ROSCOE, *The Spirit of the Common Law*, 1921.
———, Review of Goodhart (q.v.) in *Harvard Law Review*, 48:863ff., 1935.
———, "Codification in Anglo-American Law" in *The Code Napoleon and the Common Law World* (ed. Schwartz), 1956.

PRASAD, BENI, *The State in Ancient India*, 1928.
PRICE, DON K. (ed.), *The Secretary of State*, 1960.
PRICE, HUGH D., "Campaign Finance in Massachusetts in 1952," *Public Policy*, 6:25ff., 1955.
PROTHRO, JAMES W., and CHARLES M. GRIGG, "Fundamental Principles of Democracy: Bases of Agreement and Disagreement," *Journal of Politics*, 22:276ff., 1960.
PROUDHON, P. L., *Idée générale de la révolution au XIXe siècle*, 1851.
———, *Du Principe fédératif*, . . . 1863 (1921, introd. Jean Charles-Brun).
Puerto Rico (Comité del Gobernador), *Report on Civil Liberties*, 1959.
PULLERITZ, ALBERT (ed.), *Estland: Volk, Kultur, Wirtschaft*, 1931.
PYE, LUCIEN, *Politics, Personality and Nation Building: Burma's Search for Identity*, 1962.
RACINE, PIERRE, "La Fonction publique internationale sous l'aspect psychologique et humain," in *La Fonction publique internationale*, 1958.
RADIN, MAX, "Case Law and Stare Decisis: Concerning Präjudizienrecht in Amerika," *Columbia Law Review*, 33:199ff., 1933.
———, "A Restatement of Hohfeld," *Harvard Law Review*, 51:1141–1164, 1938.
RANK, OTTO, *Beyond Psychology*, 1941.
RAPOPORT, ANATOL, *Operational Philosophy*, 1953.
RAPPARD, WILLIAM E., *Uniting Europe*, 1930.
———, *L'individu et l'état dans l'évolution constitutionelle de la Suisse*, 1936.
———, *La Constitution fédérale de la Suisse: 1848–1948*, 1948.
RASSOW, PETER, *Die Kaiser idee Karls V*, 1932.
RATZEL, FRIEDRICH, *Politische Geographie*, 3rd ed. 1923.
RATZENHOFER, GUSTAV, *Wesen und Zweck der Politik: Als Theil der Soziologie und Grundlage der Staatswissenschaften*, 1893.
RAUMER, KURT VON (ed.), *Ewiger Friede, Friedensrufe und Friedenspläne seit der Renaissance*, 1953.
RAVEN, BERTRAM M. H., and JOHN R. P. FRENCH, "Group Support, Legitimate Power and Social Influence," *Journal of Personality*, 26:400ff., 1958.
RAWLS, JOHN, "Two Concepts of Rules," *Philosophical Review*, 64:3ff., 1955.
RAY, VERNE F. (ed.), "Systems of Political Control and Bureaucracy in Human Societies," *Proceedings of the American Ethnological Society*, 1958.
RECASÉNS SICHES, LUIS, et al., *Latin American Legal Philosophy*, 1948.
REDLICH, JOSEF, *Das Recht des englischen Parlamentarismus*, 1906; English *The Procedure of the House of Commons* (transl. A. E. Steinthall), 1908.
———, *Das Österreichische Staats-und Reichsproblem*, 2 vols., 1920, 1926.
———, *Kaiser Franz Joseph von Österreich*, 1928 (transl. 1929).
REIMANN, GUENTER, *The Vampire Economy: Doing Business under Fascism*, 1939.
RENAN, ERNEST, *Qu'est ce qui'une nation?* 1882.
RENNER, KARL, *Der Kampf der österreichischen Nationen um den Staat*, 1907.
———, *Nation und Staat: Das Selbstbestimmungsrecht der Nationen in besonderer Anwendung auf Österreich*, 1918.
RESHETAR, JOHN, *The Ukrainian Revolution, 1917–1920*, 1952.

RICHARDS, A. I., *Chisungu*, 1956.
———, "The Political System of the Bemba Tribe, North East Rhodesia," in Fortes and Evans-Pritchard, q.v., 1940.
——— (ed.), *East African Chiefs: A Study of Political Development in Some Uganda and Tanganyika Tribes*, 1960.
RIESMAN, DAVID, *Thorstein Veblen: A Critical Interpretation*, 1953.
———, *Individualism Reconsidered*, 1954.
———, *The Lonely Crowd*, 1950 (in collaboration with Renel Denney and Nathan Glazer).
———, and NATHAN GLAZER, *Faces in the Crowd*, 1952.
ROBINSON, JAMES A., *Congress and Foreign Policy-making*, 1962.
ROBSON, WILLIAM A., *Justice and Administrative Law*, 1928.
———, *The Government and Misgovernment of London*, 1939, 1948.
———, "The Reform of London Government," *Public Administration*, 39:59ff., 1961.
——— (ed.), *Great Cities of the World: Their Government, Politics and Planning*, 1954. Rev. ed. 1957.
ROCKEFELLER, NELSON, *The Future of Federalism*, 1962.
ROETHLISBERGER, FRITZ J., *Management and Morals*, 1941.
ROMMEN, HEINRICH A., *Die ewige Widerkehr des Naturrechts*, 1936, 1947.
———, *The State in Catholic Thought*, 1945.
RÖPKE, W., "Die Untwickelten Länder als wirtschaftliches, soziales und gesellschaftliches Problem," in A. Hunold, *Entwicklungslaender-Wahn und Wirklichkeit*, 1961.
ROSECRANCE, R. N., *Australian Diplomacy and Japan*, 1945–1951, 1962.
———, *Action and Reaction in World Politics*, 1963.
———, "Categories, Concepts, and Reasoning in the Study of International Relations," *Behavioral Science*, 6:222ff., 1961.
ROSENBERG, HANS W., *Bureaucracy, Aristocracy and Autocracy: The Prussian Experience, 1600–1815*, 1958.
ROSENSTOCK-HUESSY, EUGEN, *Die Europäischen Revolutionen*, 1931, 1951; (English *Out of Revolution*, rev. ed. 1938).
———, *Soziologie*, vol. I, 1956; vol. II, 1958.
ROSSITER, CLINTON, *Constitutional Dictatorship*, 1948.
ROSTOVTSEV, MIKHAIL I., *The Social and Economic History of the Roman Empire*, 1926; German ed. 1929.
ROTH, GOETZ, *Fraktion und Regierungsbildung: Eine monographische Darstellung der Regierungsbildung in Niedersachsen im Jahre 1951*, 1954.
ROTHFELS, HANS, *Carl von Clausewitz: Politik und Krieg*, 1920.
———, *The German Opposition to Hitler: An Appraisal*, 1948.
———, "Clausewitz," *Makers of Modern Strategy* (ed. E. M. Earle), 1943.
ROURKE, FRANCIS E., *Secrecy and Publicity: Dilemmas of Democracy*, 1961.
ROUSSEAU, JEAN-JACQUES, *La Nouvelle Héloise*, 1761.
———, *Émile, ou de l'éducation*, 1762.
———, *Le Contrat social*, 1762.
———, *Les Confessions*, 1782 and later. (I have used the Mussay Pathay ed. of Rousseau's *Oeuvres* of 1827.)
Royal Institute, *Britain in Western Europe*, 1956.

RUDOLPH, LLOYD I., and SUZANNE HOEBER RUDOLPH, "Toward Political Stability in Under-developed Countries: The Case of India," *Public Policy*, 9:149ff., 1959.

RUDOLPH, SUZANNE HOEBER, "Consensus and Conflict in Indian Politics," *World Politics*, 13:385ff., 1961.

RUSSELL, BERTRAND, *Power: A New Social Analysis*, 1938.

RÜSTOW, ALEXANDER, *Ortsbestimmung der Gegenwart*, vol. I, 1950; vol. II, 1952; vol. III, 1957.

———, "Die Staatsautorität im Arbeitskampf," *Europäische Revue*, pp. 588ff., 1929.

———, "Der Idealtypus oder die Gestalt als Norm," *Studium Generale*, 6:54ff., 1953.

———, "Diktatur innerhalb der Grenzen der Demokratie," *Vierteljahrschrift für Zeitzgeschichte*, pp. 87ff., 1959.

———, "Archaisches Weltbild und archaische Weltherrschaft," *Studium Generale*, 14:539ff., 1961.

RUSTOW, DANKWART A., *The Politics of Compromise: A Study of Parties and Cabinet Government in Sweden*, 1955.

———, "The Army and the Founding of the Turkish Republic," *World Politics*, 11:513ff., 1952.

SABINE, GEORGE H., *A History of Political Theory*, 1937, 1950.

———, *The Works of Gerrard Winstanley*, 1941.

SAFRAN, NADAV, *Egypt in Search of Political Community*, . . . 1961.

SAINT SIMON, COMTE CLAUDE H. DE, *Oeuvres*, 47 vols., 1865–1878. (Selections from these works by C. Bouglè, 1925.)

SALIN, EDGAR, *Civitas Dei*, 1926.

SALOMON-DE LATOUR, G., *Politische Soziologie*, 1959.

SALVEMINI, GAETANO, *Under the Axe of Fascism*, 1936.

SALZ, ARTHUR, "Specialization," *ESS*, 1934.

SAMUELSON, PAUL A., *Foundations of Economic Analysis*, 1947.

SANSOM, G. B., *Japan: A Short Cultural History*, 1931, 1943.

SAPIR, EDWARD, "Language," *ESS*, 1933.

———, "Symbolism," *ESS*, 1934.

SARTRE, JEAN-PAUL, *L'Imaginaire: Psychologie phénoménologique de l'imagination*, 1940.

———, *L'Existentialisme est un humanisme*, 1946.

———, *L'Être et le néant*, 1943.

SATOW, ERNEST, *Guide to Diplomatic Practice*, 1917.

SAYRE, W., and HERBERT KAUFMANN, *Governing New York City*, 1960.

SCHAPERA, ISAAC, *The Khoisan Peoples of South Africa*, 1930.

———, *Government and Politics in Tribal Societies*, 1956.

SCHAPIRO, LEONARD B., *The Communist Party of the Soviet Union*, 1958.

SCHATTSCHNEIDER, E. E., *The Struggle for Party Government*, 1948.

SCHELER, MAX, "Der Formalismus in der Ethik und die materiale Wertethik," *Jahrbuch für Philosophie und Phänomenologische Forschung*, 1:405–565, 1913; 2:21–478, 1916; (2nd ed. of this work published as a separate volume 1926).

———, *Vom Ewigen im Menschen*, 1923.

———, *Die Wissensformen und die Gesellschaft*, 1926.
SCHELLING, THOMAS C., *The Strategy of Conflict*, 1960.
———, and MORTON H. HALPERIN, *Strategy and Arms Control*, 1961.
SCHELTING, ALEXANDER VON, *Max Weber's Wissenschaftslehre*, 1934.
———, "Die logische Theorie der Historischen Kulturwissenschaften von Max Weber," *Archif für Sozialwissenschaft und Sozialpolitik*, vol. 49, 1922.
SCHIERWATER, HANS-VICTOR, *Parlament und Hohe Behörde der Montanunion*, 1961.
SCHIFFER, WALTER, *The Legal Community of Mankind*, 1954.
SCHILLER, FRIEDRICH VON, *Wallenstein's Lager*, 1798.
SCHINDLER, DIETRICH, *Die Gleichberechtigung von Individuen als Problem des Völkerrechts*, 1957.
SCHLESINGER, ARTHUR M., *The Age of Roosevelt*, vol. I, *The Crisis of the Old Order*, 1957.
———, *The Age of Roosevelt*, vol. III, *The Politics of Upheaval*, 1960.
SCHMIDT, CARL T., *The Plough and the Sword*, 1938.
SCHMITT, CARL, *Politische Theologie*, 1922.
———, *Verfassungslehre*, 1928.
———, *Der Begriff des Politischen*, 1927, 1932.
———, *Legalität und Legitimität*, 1932.
———, *Der Nomos der Erde im Völkerrecht des jus publicum Europaeum*, 1950.
———, *Gespräch über die Macht und den Zugang zum Machthaber*, 1954.
SCHMOLLER, GUSTAV, *Grundriss der allgemeinen Volkswirtschaftslehre*, 2 vols., 1919–1920.
———, *Deutsches Städtewesen in älterer Zeit*, 1922.
SCHNEIDER, HANS, "Verträge zwischen Gliedstaaten im Bundesstaat," *Veröffentlichungen der Vereinigung der deutschen Staatsrechtslehrer*, 1961.
SCHNEIDER, PETER, *Ausnahmezustand und Norm*, 1957.
SCHOECK, HELMUT, *Was heisst politisch unmöglich?* 1959.
SCHÖFFLER, HERBERT, *Die Reformation*, 1936.
SCHORSKE, CARL E., "The Idea of the City in European Thought: Voltaire to Spengler," in *The City in History* (ed. Handlin and Burchard), to be published, 1963.
SCHUBERT, GLENDON A., *The Public Interest: A Critique of the Theory of a Political Concept*, 1960.
SCHUMPETER, J. A., *The Theory of Economic Development*, 1934 (German original, 1926).
———, *Capitalism, Socialism and Democracy*, 1942.
SCHWARTZ, BENJAMIN, *Chinese Communism and the Rise of Mao*, 1951.
SCOTT, ROBERT E., *Mexican Government in Transition*, 1959.
SEAGLE, WILLIAM, *The Quest for Law*, 1941.
SEELEY, JOHN ROBERT, *Introduction to Political Science*, 1896.
SELZNICK, PHILIP, "Foundations of the Theory of Organization," *American Sociological Review*, 13:25–35, 1948.
SERENO, RENZO, *The Rulers*, 1962.
SHAFER, BOYD, *Nationalism: Myth and Reality*, 1954.
SHAPIRO, MEYER, "Style," *Anthropology Today* (ed. A. L. Kroeber), 1953.

SHARPE, L. J., "The Report of the Royal Commission on Local Government in Greater London," *Public Administration*, 39:73–92, 1961.
SHENTON, HERBERT N., EDWARD SAPIR, and OTTO JESPERSON, *International Communication*, 1931.
SHKLAR, JUDITH N., *After Utopia: The Decline of Political Faith*, 1957.
SIDGWICK, HENRY, *The Development of European Polity*, 1903, 1920.
SIEGFRIED, ANDRÉ, *Tableau politique de la France de l'ouest sous la Troisième République*, 1913.
———, *France: A Study in Nationality*, 1930.
SIEPMANN, CHARLES, *Radio's Second Chance*, 1946.
SIMMEL, GEORG, *Die Religion*, 1912.
SIMON, HERBERT, *Administrative Behavior*, 1947; 2nd ed. 1957.
———, *Models of Man*, 1957.
———, "Notes on the Observation and Measurement of Political Power," *Journal of Politics*, 15:500ff., 1953.
———, DONALD W. SMITHBURG, and VICTOR A. THOMSON, *Public Administration*, 1950.
SIMON, YVES, *Nature and Functions of Authority*, 1940.
SMITH, J. ALLEN, *The Growth and Decadence of Constitutional Government*, 1930.
SMITH, M. G., *Government in Zazzau: 1800–1950*, 1960.
SMITH, SIR THOMAS, *De Republica Anglorum Libri Tres*, 1583.
SMITH, M. G., *The Economy of the Hausa Communities of Zaria*, 1955.
SNOW, SIR CHARLES P., *The Masters*, 1951.
———, *The Two Cultures, and the Scientific Revolution*, 1959.
———, *Science and Government*, 1961.
SNYDER, RICHARD C., H. W. BRUCK, and B. SAPIN, *Decision-making as an Approach to the Study of International Politics*, 1954.
SOHM, RUDOLPH, *Kirchenrecht*, 2 vols., 1892–1923.
SOROKIN, PITIRIM A., *Social and Cultural Dynamics*, 1937.
SPEIER, HANS, *The Soviet Threat to Berlin*, 1961 (German ed. 1961).
———, "The Social Types of War," *American Journal of Sociology*, 41:445ff., 1941.
———, and ALFRED KÄHLER (eds.), *War in Our Time*, 1939.
SPENGLER, OSWALD, *Der Untergang des Abendlandes: Umrisse einer Morphologie der Weltgeschichte*, Band II, *Welthistorische Perspektiven*, 1923.
SPINOZA, BARUCH, *Tractatus Theologico-Politicus*, 1670.
———, *Tractatus Politicus*.
SPIRO, HERBERT J., *Government by Constitution: The Political System of Democracy*, 1959.
———, "Responsibility in Citizenship, Government and Administration," *Public Policy*, 4:116–133, 1953.
SPRANGER, EDUARD, "Wesen und Wert politischer Ideologien," *Vierteljahrshefte für Zeitgeschichte*, 2:118–130, 1954.
SPROUT, MARGARET TUTTLE, "Mahan: Evangelist of Sea Power," in *Makers of Modern Strategy* (ed. Earle), 1943.
SPYKMAN, NICHOLAS J., *American Strategy in World Politics*, 1942.
STALIN, J., *Problems of Leninism*, 1940.

STAMP, SIR JOSIAH, "The Administrator in a Planned Society," Inaugural address as President of the Institution of Public Administration, London, October 29, 1937; *see The Times*, October 30, 1937, p. 9.

STECCHINI, LIVIO C., "Prospects in Retrospect: Inventiveness," *The American Behavioral Scientist*, 5:3–5, 1961.

STEIN, HAROLD (ed.), *Public Administration and Policy Development: A Case Book*, 1952.

STEIN, LORENZ VON, *Geschichte der Sozialen Bewegung in Frankreich von 1789 bis auf unsere Tage*, 1849, 1921.

STERN, FREDERICK MARTIN, *The Citizen Army: Key to Defense in the Atomic Age*, 1957.

STERN, WILLIAM, *Ableitung und Grundlehre des Kritischen Personalismus*, vol. I of *Person und Sache*, 2nd ed. 1923.

STERNBERGER, DOLF, *Lebende Verfassung: Studien über Koalition und Opposition*, 1956.

———, *Authorität, Freiheit und Befehlsgewalt*, 1959.

———, *Grund und Abgrund der Macht*, 1962.

STEVENS, CARL M., "On the Theory of Negotiation," *Quarterly Journal of Economics*, 72:77–97, 1958.

STEVENSON, CHARLES L., *Ethics and Language*, 1944.

STORING, HERBERT J. (ed.), *Essays on the Scientific Study of Politics*, 1962.

STOUFFER, SAMUEL A., et al., *The American Soldier*, 2 vols., 1949.

STRAUSS, LEO, *Thoughts on Machiavelli*, 1958.

———, *The Political Philosophy of Hobbes: Its Basis and Its Genesis*, 1936.

———, *What is Political Philosophy? and Other Studies*, 1959.

STRAUSZ-HUPÉ, ROBERT, *Geopolitics: The Struggle for Space and Power*, 1942.

STRAYER, JOSEPH R., and DANA C. MUNRO, *The Middle Ages: 395–1500*, 4th ed. 1959.

STUBBS, WILLIAM, *Select Charters and Other Illustrations of English Constitutional History*, 9th ed. (rev. H. W. C. Davis), 1921.

SUMNER, B. H., *A Short History of Russia*, 1943.

SUTTON, FRANCIS X., *Contemporary Studies in Society and History*, 1959.

SWANTON, J. R., *Social Organization and Social Usages of the Indians of the Creek Confederacy*, 1928.

SWAYZE, HAROLD, *Political Control of Literature in the U.S.S.R., 1946–1959*, 1962.

SWEEZEY, PAUL M., *The Theory of Capitalist Development*, 1942.

SWISHER, CARL BRENT, *American Constitutional Development*, 1943.

SYME, SIR RONALD, *The Roman Revolution*, 1939, 1960.

SZASZ, THOMAS S., "Psychiatry, Psychotherapy and Psychology," *A.M.A. Archives of General Psychiatry*, 1:455–463, 1959.

———, *The Myth of Mental Illness*, 1961.

TACITUS, *Historiae* (Loeb Classic).

———, *Germania* (Loeb Classic).

TAFT, PHILIP, *The Structure and Government of Labor Unions*, 1954.

TALMON, J. L., *The Rise of Totalitarian Democracy*, 1952.

TAWNEY, R. H., *Equality*, 1931.

TAYLOR, A. E., *Socrates*, 1933.

TAYLOR, OVERTON H., *A History of Economic Thought,* 1960.
TAYLOR, PAUL W., "When Is Uttering 'an Ought' Sentence an Act of Prescribing?" abstract in *Journal of Philosophy,* 56:953f., 1959.
TAYLOR, TELFORD, *Final Report to the Secretary of the Army on the Nürnberg War Crimes Trials under Control Council of Law No. 10,* 1949.
TEILHARD: *see* Chardin.
THIBAUDET, ALBERT, *La République des professeurs,* 1927.
THOMAS, ELIZABETH MARSHALL, *The Harmless People,* 1959.
THOREAU, HENRY DAVID, *Resistance to Civil Government,* 1849.
THRUPP, SYLVIA L., "The City as the Idea of Social Order," in *The City in History* (ed. Handlin and Burchard), to be published 1963.
THUCYDIDES, *The Peloponnesian War.*
TILLION, GERMAINE, *Algeria and the Realities,* 1958.
TOCQUEVILLE, ALEXIS DE, *De la démocratie en Amérique,* 1835–1840; English (ed. P. Bradley) 1948.
TOMPKINS, DOROTHY C., *Wire Tapping: A Selected Bibliography,* 1955.
TORRANCE, E. PAUL, "An Experimental Evaluation of 'No Pressure' Influence," *Journal of Applied Psychology,* 43:109ff., 1959.
TOULMIN, S. E., *An Examination of the Place of Reason in Ethics,* 1950.
TOUT, THOMAS R., *Chapters on the Administrative History of Mediaeval England,* 6 vols., 1920–1933.
———, *The English Civil Service in the Fourteenth Century,* 1916, in *Collected Papers,* vol. III, 1934.
TOYNBEE, ARNOLD J., *A Study of History,* 10 vols., 1933 and later.
TREITSCHKE, HEINRICH VON, *Politik,* 1879–1898, 2 vols., (English ed. 1916).
TREVELYAN, G. M., *The Two-party System in English Political History,* 1926.
TREVES, PAOLO, *La filosofia politica di Tomaso Campanella,* 1930.
TREVES, RENATO (ed.), *Le Elites politiche, atti del IV congreso mondiale di sociologia,* 1961.
TRISKA, JAN F. (ed.), *Soviet Communism: Programs and Rules,* 1962.
TRUMAN, DAVID B., *The Governmental Process,* 1951.
TUCKER, ROBERT C., *Philosophy and Myth in Karl Marx,* 1961.
———, "Towards a Comparative Politics of Movement—Regimes," *APSR,* 55:281ff., 1961.
TUGWELL, REXFORD G., *The Stricken Land: The Story of Puerto Rico,* 1947.
TUMIN, MELVIN M., and ARNOLD FELDMAN, *Social Class and Social Change in Puerto Rico,* 1961.
TUSSMAN, JOSEPH, *Obligation and the Body Politic,* 1960.
TYLOR, EDWARD B., *Primitive Culture: Researches into the Development of Mythology, Philosophy, Religion, Language, Art and Custom,* 2 vols., 1871.
UNDERHILL, FRANK H., *The British Commonwealth: An Experiment in Cooperation among Nations,* 1956.
United States Congress, "Limitations of Appellate Jurisdiction of the U.S. Supreme Court," *Hearings of the Senate Judiciary Committee on S.2646,* 85th Congress, 1st and 2nd Sessions, 1957–1958.
———, "The Government of Metropolitan Washington," Staff Study for Joint Committee, 85th Congress, 2nd Session, 1958.

United States Strategic Bombing Survey, *The Effects of the Strategic Bombing on German Morale,* 2 vols., 1947.

United States Supreme Court, *Okanogan Indians v. United States* (Pocket Veto Case), 279 U.S. 655 (1928).

UUSTALU, EVALD, *The History of the Esthonian People,* 1952.

VALENTINE, D. G., *The Court of Justice of the European Coal and Steel Community,* 1955.

VARRO, M. T., *Antiquitates rerum humanarum et divinarum.*

VAUGHAN, C. E., *The Political Writings of Rousseau,* 1915.

VEBLEN, THORSTEIN, *The Theory of Business Enterprise,* 1904, 1919.

———, *An Inquiry into the Nature of Peace and the Terms of Its Perpetuation,* 1917.

VECCHIO, GIORGIO DEL, *La Giustizia,* 5th ed. 1951.

VENDRYES, JOSEPH, *Le language: Introduction linguistique à l'historie,* 1921; English ed. (transl. Paul Radin), 1925.

VERHAEREN, ÉMILE, *Les Villes tentaculaires,* 4th ed. 1908.

VERNADSKY, G., *A History of Russia,* 2nd ed. 1930.

VERNON, RAYMOND, *Metropolis 1985,* 1960.

VIERECK, PETER R., *Metapolitics: From the Romantics to Hitler,* 1941.

———, *The Unadjusted Man—A New Hero for Americans: Reflections on the Distinction between Conforming and Conserving,* 1956.

VLASTOS, G., "Justice, le sens du terme et son évolution . . . anglaise et américaine," *Revue internationale de philosophie,* 39:324ff., 1957.

VÖGELIN, ERICH, *Die politischen Religionen,* 1938.

VOEGELIN, ERIC, *Order and History,* vol. I, 1956; vol. II, 1957; vol. III, 1957.

VOSSLER, K., *Geist und Kultur in der Sprache,* 1925; English *The Spirit of Language in Civilization,* 1932.

WAHL, NICHOLAS, "Aux origines de la nouvelle constitution," *Revue française de science politique,* 9:30–66, 1959.

WALINE, MARCEL, *Le pouvoir discrétionnaire de l'administration et la limitation par le contrôle jurisdictionel,* 1930, 1949.

———, *Droit administratif,* 1944.

WALLACE, ERNEST, and E. ADAMSON HOEBEL, *The Comanches: Lords of the South Plains,* 1952.

WALTZ, KENNETH N., *Man, the State and War: A Theoretical Analysis,* 1959.

WARD, BARBARA (Lady Jackson), "Development and Dependence in Emergent Africa," *Public Policy,* 9:341–352, 1959.

WARNER, W. L., *A Black Civilization,* 1937, 1958.

WARREN, ROBERT PENN, *All the King's Men,* 1946.

WARSOFF, LOUIS A., *Equality and the Law,* 1938.

WATKINS, FREDERICK M., *The State as a Concept of Political Science,* 1934.

———, *The Political Tradition of the West,* 1948.

———, "The Problem of Constitutional Dictatorship," *Public Policy,* 1:324–379, 1940.

WEBB, SIDNEY, and BEATRICE WEBB, *Industrial Democracy,* 1897, rev. ed. 1902.

——— and ———, *Soviet Communism: A New Civilization?* 1936.

WEBER, ALFRED, *Kulturgeschichte als Kultursoziologie,* 1935.

———, *Der dritte oder der vierte Mensch,* 1953.

WEBER, ELIZABETH ANN, *The Duk-Duks: Primitive and Historic Types of Citizenship*, 1929.

WEBER, MAX, *Parlament und Regierung im neugeordneten Deutschland*, 1918.

———, *Gesammelte Aufsätze zur Wissenschaftslehre*, 1922; English *Max Weber on Law in Economy and Society* (transl. M. Rheinstein and E. Shils), 1954. See also *From Max Weber: Essays in Sociology* (transl. and ed. H. H. Gerth and C. W. Mills), 1946.

———, *Gesammelte Aufsätze zur Religionssoziologie*, 3 vols., 1922–1923; English (in part) *Protestant Ethic and the Spirit of Capitalism* (transl. Talcott Parsons), 1930.

———, *Wirtschaft und Gesellschaft*, 2nd ed. 1925; English *Max Weber: The Theory of Social and Economic Organization* (transl. A. M. Henderson and Talcott Parsons), 1947.

WEIL, SIMONE, *L'Enracinement*, 1949; English *The Need for Roots*, 1952.

———, *Oppression et liberté*, 5th ed. 1955.

WEINREICH, URIEL, *Languages in Contact*, 1953.

WEISS, PAUL, *The Nature of Systems*, 1930.

WEIZMANN, CHAIM, *Trial and Error*, 1949.

———, *Reden und Aufsätze* (ed. Krojanker), 1937.

WELDON, THOMAS D., *The Vocabulary of Politics*, 1953.

WELLS, ROGER H., "Local Government" and "State Government," chaps. III and IV, in *Governing Postwar Germany* (ed. Litchfield), 1953.

WELSH, PAUL, "Means and Ends in Dewey's Ethical Theory," abstract in *Journal of Philosophy*, 56:960f., 1959.

WELZEL, HANS, *Naturrect und Materiale Gerechtigkeit*, 1951.

WERNER, MORRIS R. (ed.), *Stalin's Kampf: Joseph Stalin's Credo, Written by Himself*, 1940.

WESTEN, KLAUS, *Die rechtstheoretischen und rechtspolitischen Ansichten Josef Stalins*, 1959.

WESTERFIELD, H. BRADFORD, *Foreign Policy and Party Politics*, 1955.

WESTIN, ALAN F., "The Wire-tapping Problem: An Analysis and a Legislative Proposal," *Columbia Law Review*, 52:165–208, 1952.

WETTER, J. GILLIS, *The Styles of Appellate Judicial Opinions: A Case Study in Comparative Law*, 1960.

WHEARE, K. C., *Federal Government*, 1946, 1953.

WHITE, LEONARD D., *Introduction to the Study of Public Administration*, 1926. Rev. ed. 1942.

———, *The Federalists: A Study in Administrative History*, 1948.

WHITE, LLEWELLYN, *The American Radio*, 1947.

WHITE, MORTON, *The Age of Analysis*, 1955.

———, "The Analytic and the Synthetic: An Untenable Dualism," in *Semantics and the Philosophy of Language* (ed. Leonard Linsky), 1952.

WHITEHEAD, A. N., *Religion in the Making*, 1926.

———, *Symbolism, Its Meaning and Effect*, 1927.

———, *Process and Reality*, 1929.

———, *Adventures of Ideas*, 1933.

WHITTLESEY, DERWENT S., *The Earth and the State*, 1939.

———, "Haushofer: The Geopoliticians," *Makers of Modern Strategy* (ed. E. M. Earle), 1943.

WHYTE, WILLIAM H., JR., *The Organization Man*, 1956.
WIENER, NORBERT, *Human Use of Human Beings: Cybernetics and Society*, 1950.
WILD, JOHN, *Plato's Modern Enemies and the Theory of Natural Law*, 1953.
WILDENMANN, RUDOLF, *Partei und Fraktion*, 1954.
WILHELM, DONALD, JR., "The Place of Public Administration in the Overseas Technical Assistance Programs," *Public Policy*, 6:182–208, 1955.
WILLIAMS, PHILIP M., and MARTIN HARRISON, *De Gaulle's Republic*, 1960.
WILSON, E. BRIGHT, JR., *An Introduction to Scientific Research*, 1952.
WINSPEAR, A. D., *The Genesis of Plato's Thought*, 1940.
WISSLER, CLARK, *Man and Culture*, 1923.
WITTFOGEL, KARL, *Oriental Despotism*, 1957.
WOLF, ERIK, *Das Problem der Naturrechtslehre: Versuch einer Orientierung*, 1955.
WOLF, WILLIAM J., *The Almost Chosen People: A Study of the Religion of Abraham Lincoln*, 1959.
WOLFF, BERTRAM D., *Three Who Made a Revolution*, 1948.
WOLFF, HANS J., *Organschaft und juristische Person*, vol. II, *Theorie der Vertretung*, 1934.
WOLIN, SHELDON S. (with V. V. ALMENDINGER), *Politics and Vision: Continuity and Innovation in Western Political Thought*, 1960.
WOOD, ROBERT C., *1400 Governments: The Political Economy of the New York Metropolitan Region*, 1961.
WOODBURY, COLEMAN, *Urban Studies: Some Questions of Outlook and Selection*, 1960.
WOOLNER, ALFRED C., *Language in History and Politics*, 1938.
WRIGHT, BENJAMIN F. (ed.), *The Federalist*, 1961.
WRIGHT, QUINCY et al., *A Study of War*, 2 vols., 1942.
——— (ed.), *The World Community*, 1948.
WYLIE, LAWRENCE W., *Village in the Vaucluse*, 1957.
YERKES, ROBERT M., and ADA W. YERKES, "Social Behavior of Infrahuman Primates," in *A Handbook of Social Psychology* (ed. Carl Murchison), 1935.
YOUNG, ROLAND A., *The American Congress*, 1934, 1943, 1958.
———, *The British Parliament*, 1962.
——— (ed.), *Approaches to the Study of Politics*, 1958.
———, and JAMES A. ROBINSON, "Parliamentary Decision-Making in Great Britain: The Case of the Common Market," paper delivered at American Political Science Association meeting, 1962.
ZACHARIAS, H. C. E., *Renascent India*, 1933.
ZAIDLER, KARL, "Gedanken zum Fernsehurteil," *Archiv für Öffentliches Recht*, 86:361ff., 1961.
ZIEGLER, DONALD J., *Prelude to Democracy: A Study of Proportional Representation and the Heritage of Weimar Germany*, 1871–1920, 1958.
ZIEGLER, HEINZ O., *Die moderne Nation: Ein Beitrag zur politischen Soziologie*, 1931.
ZILLIACUS, K., *Why I Was Expelled*, 1949.
ZIMMER, HEINRICH, *Mythen und Symbole indischer Kunst and Kultur*, 1951.
ZINK, HAROLD W., *American Military Government in Germany*, 1947.

ZNANIECKI, FLORIAN, *Modern Nationalities: A Sociological Study*, 1952.
ZUCKERMAN, SOLLY, *The Social Life of Monkeys and Apes*, 1932.
———, *Functional Affinities of Man, Monkeys and Apes*, 1933.

Bibliography of Carl J. Friedrich

Politica Methodice Digesta of Johannes Althusius (Althaus), 1932.
Constitutional Government and Politics, 1937.
Foreign Policy in the Making: The Search for a New Balance of Power, 1938.
Constitutional Government and Democracy, 1941, 1946, 1950.
The New Belief in the Common Man, 1942; rev. *The New Image of the Common Man*, 1950.
Inevitable Peace, 1948.
The Age of the Baroque, 1952, 1958, 1962.
Cours d'histoire des idees politiques: Évolution de la liberté constitutionelle en Angleterre à travers les deux révolutions, Les Cours de Droit, 1956.
Constitutional Reason of State, 1957.
The Philosophy of Law in Historical Perspective, 1958 (German, 1956).
Puerto Rico: Middle Road to Freedom—Fuero Fundamental, 1959.
Die politische Wissenschaft, 1961.
with TAYLOR COLE, *Responsible Bureaucracy: A Study of the Swiss Civil Service*, 1932.
with JEANNETTE SAYRE, *The Development of the Control of Advertising on the Air*, 1940.
with CHARLES BLITZER, *Age of Power*, 1954.
with Z. K. BRZEZINSKI, *Totalitarian Dictatorship and Autocracy*, 1965.

Edited:

Public Policy, 1940 to present.
The Philosophy of Kant, 1949.
The Philosophy of Hegel, 1953.
Totalitarianism, 1954.
The Soviet Zone of Germany, 1956 (Human Relations Area Files).
Nomos, 1956 to present.
with ROBERT G. MCCLOSKEY, *From the Declaration of Independence to the Constitution*, 1954.

Articles:

"Remarks on Llewellyn's View of Law, Official Behavior and Political Science," *Political Science Quarterly*, pp. 419–431, 1935.
"The Peasant as Evil Genius of Dictatorship," *Yale Review*, 26:724ff., 1937.
"The Agricultural Basis of Emotional Nationalism," *Public Opinion Quarterly*, 1:50–61, 1937.
"Public Policy and the Nature of Administrative Responsibility," *Public Policy*, 1:3–24, 1940.
"Rights, Liberties, Freedoms," *University of Pennsylvania Law Review*, 91: 312ff., 1942.
"Congress and the Control of Radio Broadcasting" (with E. STERNBERG), *APSR*, part I, 37:797–818, 1943; part II, 37:1014–1026, 1943.

"Planning for the Greater Boston Metropolitan Area" (with associates), *Public Administration Review*, 5:113ff., 1945.
"*The Road to Serfdom* by Friedrich A. Hayek," *APSR*, 39:575–579, 1945.
"Political Science in the United States in War Time," *APSR*, 41:978–989, 1947.
"Rebuilding the German Constitution," *APSR*, 43:704–720, 1949.
"The Israeli Covenant," *Jewish Frontier*, 16:24ff., 1949.
"The Political Theory of the New Democratic Constitutions," *Constitutions and Constitutional Trends Since World War II* (ed. Arnold J. Zurcher), 1951, 1955.
"Some Observations on Weber's Analysis of Bureaucracy," *Reader in Bureaucracy* (ed. Merton et al.), 1952.
"The Constitution of the German Federal Republic" (with HERBERT J. SPIRO), *Governing Postwar Germany* (ed. Litchfield), 1953.
"Policy: A Science?" *Public Policy*, 4:269–281, 1953.
"Israel and the End of History," *Israel: Its Role in Civilization* (ed. M. Davis), 1954.
"The Political Thought of Neo-Liberalism," *APSR*, vol. 49, 1955.
"Style as the Principle of Historical Interpretation," *Journal of Aesthetics*, 14:143–151, 1955.
"Federal Constitutional Theory and Emergent Proposals," in *Federalism, Mature and Emergent* (ed. Macmahon), 1955.
"Die Philosophie der Geschichte als Form der Überlagerung," in *Wirtschaft und Kultursystem* (ed. G. Eisermann), 1955.
"The Ideological and Philosophical Background," in *The Code Napoleon and the Common-Law World* (ed. Schwartz), 1956.
"Authority, Reason and Discretion," *Nomos I*, pp. 28–48, 1958.
"Political Philosophy and the Science of Politics," in *Approaches to the Study of Politics* (ed. Roland Young), 1958.
"The New French Constitution in Political and Historical Perspective," *Harvard Law Review*, 72:801ff., 1959.
"Hans Barth, Die Idee der Ordnung," *Kyklos*, 12:227ff., 1959.
"Freiheit und Verantwortung," *Festausgabe des Hamburger Jahrbuchs für Wirtschafts–und Gesellschaftspolitik*, 1959.
"Demokratie," in *Handwërterbuch der Sozialwissenschaften*, new ed. 1959.
"Filosofia politica, ideologia e impossibilidad," *Revista de estudios politicos*, pp. 183ff., 1960.
"Organization Theory and Political Style," *Public Policy*, 10:44–61, 1960.
"The Dilemma of Administrative Responsibility," *Nomos III*, 1960.
"Origin and Development of the Concept of Federalism in the United States," *Jahrbuch des öffentlichen Rechts*, pp. 29ff., 1960.
"Die Legitimität in politischer Perspektive," *Politische Vierteljahrschrift*, 1:119ff., 1960.
"Political Leadership and the Problem of the Charismatic Power," *The Journal of Politics*, 23:3ff., 1961.
"Politische Herrschaftssysteme," in *Staatslexikon*, 6th ed. 1961.

A more complete bibliography is included in *Zur Theorie und Politik der Verfassungsordnung*, 1963.

additional bibliography

BURDEAU, GEORGES, *Traité de la Science Politique, 1949, 7 vols., esp. I and V.*
CREMIN, LAWRENCE, *The Transformation of the School; Progressivism in American Education 1876–1957*, 1961.
EMERSON, RUPERT, *From Empire to Nation*, 1960.
HARTZ, LOUIS, *The Liberal Tradition in America*, 1955.
KELSON, HANS, *Law and Peace in International Relations*, 1942.
MAIR, LUCY, *Primitive Government*, 1961.
SAITERPACHT, SIR HERSH, *International Law and Human Rights*, 1950.
LEISERSON, A., *Parties and Politics*, 1958.
PLESSNER, HELMUTH, *Conditio Humana*, 1963.
PRELÔT, MARCEL, *Histoire des idées politiques*, 2d ed., 1960.
PRICE, DON K. and K. H. STONE, *City Manager Government in Nine Cities*, 1940.
SARTORI, GIOVANNI, *Democratic Theory*, 1962.
STONE, JULIUS, *The Province and Function of Law*, 1946.

index

This index is selective and refers the reader only to significant points in the text concerning a topic. Names in footnotes and Bibliography are not included.